Practically Identical Bibles: The Geneva Bible, the KJV, and the NKJV?

By Rick Norris

Statesville, NC

Practically Identical Bibles: the Geneva Bible, the KJV, and the NKJV?

Introduction

According to the Scriptures, God is the source and determiner of all truth (Deut. 32:4, 1 John 5:20, John 14:6, John 16:13).   God is not only the source of truth; He is very truth itself. As the God of truth, God is rational.   If God has spoken, (and He has), He has spoken truthfully and logically for the God of the Scriptures is not insane, irrational, or illogical.   Since God is the God of truth and since God cannot lie or contradict Himself (2 Cor. 1:18, Titus 1:2, Heb. 6:18), it can be concluded that God would not violate the chief rule of reason or logic [the law of non-contradiction].   Because reason or logic came from God, God can communicate and reason with man whom He created (Isa. 1:18).   As the Sovereign Creator, God is the supreme authority over all.   He is the God of knowledge (1 Sam. 2:3).   Man needs revelation from God.   The Lord God has revealed Himself to man through His Word--the Bible.   The Scriptures reveal the mind or thoughts of God to the extent that God in His wisdom chose to reveal Himself.   Only God can reveal God.   The Scriptures in the original languages were given by inspiration of God to the prophets and apostles.

The original-language Scriptures given by inspiration of God have been translated into other languages.   This translation of the Scriptures into various languages has a long history.   The subject of Bible translation has great importance since most people cannot read the original language Scriptures.   This subject is one that is worthy of serious, careful study and consideration.   The subject of Bible translation can involve several complex matters or concepts, which can be oversimplified and misunderstood.   David Cloud acknowledged: "The subject of Bible texts and versions is complicated" (*Bible Version Question/Answer*, p. 120).   In the past and also in the present day, many believers have been divided over this subject of Bible translation and their claimed accuracy and trustworthiness.   R. B. Ouellette acknowledged that "many Bible-believing Christians disagree on the Bible issue" (*A More Sure Word*, p. 27). Sometimes the divisions concerning this subject may have been based on sound reasoning, but other times it may have been based on insufficient or inaccurate information and on inconsistent or faulty reasoning.   A failure to know and understand logic and logical fallacies would contribute to incorrect reasoning.   More importantly, the divisions can also involve the understanding or misunderstanding of scriptural truths.   Sound interpretation of the Scriptures and rightly dividing them is key to correct understanding concerning Bible translations.   Sometimes a contributing factor to division concerning this subject may be linked to a failure to define clearly and precisely important terms that relate to it.   Considering and understanding the meaning of key terms would be essential to understanding this subject.   Another possible contributing factor may be that some people simply accept and repeat what they have been told or what they have read without checking out objectively the facts and evidence for themselves.   People may believe what they see or feel without realizing that their sight or feelings may not be clear and objective because of subjective experience, bias, or blinders.   What a person has been taught and already believes would tend to make it easier for him to see and accept what agrees with his beliefs and to reject whatever conflicts with them.   It is also possible for people to jump to wrong conclusions based on insufficient, misrepresented, or faulty information.   It is even possible for people to draw wrong conclusions from accurate information or reliable evidence if they look at it based on one-sided, biased, unwarranted, or incorrect assumptions.   If a proposition, assertion, or argument is true, it will remain true regardless of whether it is believed or not.   If a proposition, assertion, or argument is not true, it will remain not true regardless of how many may believe or claim that it is true.   Along with the problem of accepting unproven premises or assumptions, subjective feelings or emotions can also interfere with objectively or logically considering the facts in the light of consistent truth.

Since words would have no meaning in a Bible translation or concerning the subject of Bible translations without logic, words or language would presuppose logic, which came from God.   To learn and understand anything about God and His truth, God's truth and logic are needed.   God encouraged people to reason together with Him (Isa. 1:18). The rules of thought or words such as the law of contradiction or non-contradiction indicate that a word must mean one thing and not its contradiction. Without logic, all words would be no more than the chattering of monkeys. Logic is not an axiom prior to or independent of God because all true reason depends on God's thinking and His revelation to man. God does not come from logic, but sound logic must come from God. Greg Bahnsen stated: "Logical laws are elaborations upon the fact that God does not contradict himself" (*Always Ready*, p. 149). John Frame noted: "That God is logical is implied by the scriptural teachings that he is wise, just, faithful, and true--attributes which would be meaningless if God were free to contradict himself" (*Apologetics to the Glory of God*, p. 158). Gordon Clark observed: "Scripture throughout assumes the law of contradiction, *viz.*, a truth cannot be false" (*Lord God of Truth*, p. 40). Gordon Clark asserted: "The chief law of logic is the law of contradiction, and it is this law that maintains the distinction between truth and falsity" (*God's Hammer*, p. 77). G. D. B. Pepper stated: "Whatever is condemned by truth is condemned by the God of truth" (Jenkens, *Baptist Doctrines*, p. 462). In his commentary on Galatians, Merrill Tenney noted: "Since the Bible is the Word of God to man, its truth is expressed in human language in order to make it understandable; for an incomprehensible revelation would be of no value at all" (p. 135). In his manuscript entitled *On the Truth of Holy Scripture*, John Wycliffe is translated as writing: "The logic of Scripture, however, stands eternally, because it has been established by the indestructible truth" (Levy, *John Wyclif*, p. 71). Ian Levy noted that "it is taken for granted that logic is an important tool to be put to use in the interpretation of the sacred text, which itself is understood to contain logical propositions" (p. 11).

People must use logic in order to communicate truth to others; otherwise, their words would be mere nonsense in an attempted discussion of any subject. All thoughts must be shared or communicated by the medium of rational language. Without common and logical agreement on the meaning of most words, communication would cease. Whatever is logically true must also be really true. The only way for man to avoid logic is to stop thinking. People cannot question or oppose logic without presupposing it. Wilhelmus a Brakel observed: "If a man must cease to deliberate and think, he would have to dehumanize himself" (*The Christian's Reasonable Service*, I, p. 49). All statements or concepts of truth would involve logic. Truth cannot be discredited by truth. Truth cannot be self-contradictory. Truth is not contrary or contradictory to sound, true doctrine. The truth seeks and forms no alliance with error, fallacy, and falsehood. On the other hand, human logic, reasoning, and arguments are not infallible. If men start with incorrect premises, inconsistent assumptions, and hasty generalizations and use unjust measures, their conclusions based on them would not be trustworthy, sound, or true. The starting premises first would have to be true before the deductions, inferences, or conclusions drawn from them can possibly be true.

Some English-speaking believers may consider multiple varying English Bibles to be practically identical or basically the same while others may consider only one English Bible to be good, acceptable, or even perfect. Would accepting all English Bible translations or only one English Bible translation be the only two choices that can be made by believers? Some believers may consider one English translation to be superior based on good reasons or based on poor reasons. Likewise, some believers may accept several English Bibles based on good reasons or based on poor reasons. Is there a sound way to determine which view is better? While God's Word does not actually name or identify which specific Bible translation believers should read and trust, it does teach many important truths which would directly relate to this subject. In order to make correct, righteous judgments concerning this subject of Bible translations, scriptural truths must be rightly understood, accepted, and applied justly.

The term Translation considered

In order to discuss and understand properly and soundly the subject of Bible translation, important key terms such as **translation** need to be clearly defined, explained, and considered.

Understanding key terms is an important step in any serious effort to understand correctly this subject. Herb Evans asserted: "Any error in definition can mean a more serious error in concept" (*Bible Believers' Bulletin*, March, 1981, pp. 1, 3; *Flaming Torch*, July/August/September, 1996, p. 5). J. C. Settlemoir wrote: "Without properly defining terms, a writer invites misunderstanding and misapprehension even though unintentional. He clouds his propositions and makes it unlikely the reader will understand his meaning" (*Landmarkism Under Fire*, p. 25). Edward Carnell asserted: "Terms may be used in one of three ways: with but one meaning (univocally), with different meanings (equivocally), and with a proportional meaning—partly the same, partly different (analogically)" (*Introduction to Christian Apologetics*, p. 144). Failure to define terms clearly and failure to understand in which way the term is used can lead to serious misunderstandings in concept concerning this important subject. Unclearness, inconsistency, and ambiguity in use of important terms may lead to misunderstanding. Some people may incorrectly assume that terms can only be used two ways (univocally and equivocally) when they can actually be used three ways. Would using the term translation univocally (with one meaning) for most Bible translations while attempting to use it equivocally (with a different meaning) concerning the KJV cause misunderstanding and lead to error in concept?

The very word **translation** by definition, when used to refer to something that is translated from one language into another language, would require its need of a source or sources from which to be translated and on which it is therefore dependent. By reason of its proper, exact definition concerning what constitutes its being a translation, it is unequivocally or univocally termed a "translation." Of what is it a translation? A translation is univocally a translation as a necessary consequence of its being translated from an original language source into a different language. What is more essential to the being, state, or constitution of a translation than having source or sources from which it was translated and derived? A Bible translation cannot be something other than what it is. By definition and by the laws of causality and of non-contradiction, a Bible translation would be in a different state, classification, category, or order of thing or being than untranslated original language texts of Scripture. A proper definition of a term would include the whole category or class of things which it seeks to define and would exclude what does not properly come under that term or name. Edward Carnell asserted: "For it is impossible to relate two different orders of being by the same terms with exactly the same meaning to each" (*Introduction to Christian Apologetics*, p. 145). It should be clear that a Bible translation does not belong in the same category or classification as untranslated original language texts of Scriptures. A correct analytic statement would be true by virtue of the accurate meanings of its terms alone. A translation remains what it actually or truly is. Whatever is essential to its constitution as a translation is essential to it. By definition, a translation would not be the translation of nothing. By definition, a Bible translation is not the source or cause of itself. A translation cannot create itself. There could not be a translation without a source or sources from which it is translated, to which it is related, and to which it may be compared and evaluated for accuracy. A translation without any underlying texts or sources to which it is related by being translated from them would not by definition be a translation. Likewise, a translation cannot be an exact or identical duplicate of its source or sources; otherwise, by definition it would not be a translation but would instead be an identical copy or duplicate.

A translation is not free from all causes and independent of all sources and authorities. By definition, a translation is of necessity translated from and based on something in another language or languages. Translation would be a relative term since it is connected with another object. The source of a translation would be one of its essential causes since it would be necessary for the source to exist before a translation into another language could be made from it. Therefore, the correct use and true sense of the term translation indicate that a translation is an effect or consequence that presupposes a cause or causes on which it is dependent. Since a translation is an effect, it cannot be the rule or authority greater than its sources or causes. Can an effect surpass the authority of its cause? Reasoning that would attempt to reverse cause and effect would be erroneous.   Can the antecedent be denied and the consequent affirmed? According to the laws of causality, of good and necessary consequence, and of non-contradiction, the original language texts of Scripture cannot be and not be the authority, cause, source, and foundation for a translation at the same time and in the same respect.   In his commentary on Matthew, Charles Spurgeon observed: "There is no possibility of the effect being higher and better than the cause" (p. 44).   Reformer Francis Turretin asserted: "That which has a fallible foundation cannot be infallible because the effect cannot be greater in every respect than its cause" (*Institutes*, I, p. 39).   According to the law of causality, a translation that has a beginning has a cause.   A cause would need to be first in time, order, and authority over its effect.   The necessity of a translation being dependent or being an effect or consequence indicates that it derives or acquires its authority from a greater authority than itself [its textual sources].   A translation that is not direct revelation from God or is not directly given by inspiration of God is not independent and underived since that translation depends on the greater authority of its antecedent underlying texts for its derived or secondary authority.

By definition, the term **translation** would maintain that there is both a difference and a relationship between the translation and its source or sources that can be compared and evaluated.   A translation can be evaluated or tested for its accuracy in presenting the in-context meaning of the original language words from which it is translated.   A translation can be and will be either accurate or inaccurate since it is in a dependent, proportional relationship to its source or sources from which it is translated.   In any places where a translation is inaccurate in relationship to its underlying texts or sources, it can be and should be corrected.   It is possible to overgeneralize in adjectives used to describe a translation.   A translation can still be considered overall accurate when it has a few individual inaccurate renderings.   What may be true of a few individual renderings may not be true of the whole overall translation just as what may be considered true overall of the whole translation may not be true of each individual rendering. Henry Virkler noted: "The fallacy of composition occurs when someone assumes that what is true of the individual members of a class is true of the entire class" (*Christian's Guide to Critical Thinking*, p. 202).   Henry Virkler observed: "A person commits the fallacy of division when he or she says that what is true of a group is also true of the individual members of a group" (p. 204). Use of an adjective to describe the whole text of a translation can involve use of the fallacy of composition when or if it is assumed that what is true of a few individual renderings or even of many individual renderings is true of all the renderings in that translation.

According to a sound definition and explanation of the term **translation**, a translation could be understood to act as a borrower.   "The borrower is servant to the lender" (Prov. 22:7).   One clear way in which a Bible translation could properly be considered to act as a servant would be in how it borrows, derives, or acquires its own text and its authority from its master or source original-language Scripture text or texts from which it is made (Prov. 22:7).   By definition, a translation would be a borrower from its original language texts.   As a borrower, a translation would act as servant to the lender or lenders [its original language texts] according to what is stated at Proverbs 22:17.   Should what the Scriptures directly state about a borrower be denied or rejected?   The specific words of the master original language texts of Scripture should determine which different words in another language should be in a Bible translation.   The original meaning of the words as used in context in the master original language texts should give rise to which words should be used in a translation of those texts.   The different words of a translation are under the authority of the original language words from which they are translated. The exact original-language words that proceeded directly from God set the standard and are the proper authority for what the words of a translation should say (John 12:49, Matt. 4:4). Therefore, it is sound and scriptural to conclude that the preserved original-language words of Scripture have greater authority than the translated words that borrow or derive authority from their underlying source or sources.

Principles or truths derived from an application of the meaning of other scripture verses would also support this truth that a translation acts as a borrower or servant. Since a borrower is clearly described as being a servant, scriptural truths that apply to a servant could soundly apply to a borrower. "The disciple is not above his master, nor the servant above his lord" (Matt. 10:24). In like manner, can it be inferred or deduced that a translation, which acts as a borrower, would not be above the master underlying texts from which it is translated? "The servant is not greater than his lord; neither he that is sent greater than he that sent him" (John 13:16). Likewise, a translation is not greater in authority than the original language source or sources [the master text] from which it was made and translated and that gave it its proper derived authority. The lord or master gives authority to his servants (Mark 13:34). The servants do not give authority to the master nor do they have greater authority than the one who delegates authority to them. The person or servant who is sent is not greater than the one who sent him (John 13:16b). In like manner, a translation is not greater than the underlying texts from which it was made. A translation acts as a servant ambassador or messenger that attempts to present faithfully or accurately the meaning of the original language words of its underlying texts in the words of the receptor language. By its definition and in its clear role as a borrower, a Bible translation can be properly considered servant to the master original-language Scripture texts from which it was made and translated.

According to the definition of the term translation, it should be clear that a translator/interpreter does not stand in the same place as the author or authors of a work or text. Kevin Vanhoozer noted: "The author, as the one who originates and guarantees authenticity, also commands and controls meaning. Authorship implies ownership" (*Is There a Meaning in this Text*, p. 46). Kevin Vanhoozer observed: "The author is responsible both for the existence of the text (*that* it is) and for its specific nature (*what* it is)" (p. 228). Vanhoozer asserted: "The original meaning alone is the *authentic* meaning, the author's actual, authoritative meaning" (p. 46). A translator/interpreter does not even stand in the same place as a prophet or an apostle who received revelation or scripture supernaturally and directly from God. Translators/interpreters do not give authority to the prophets and apostles who were directly given the Scriptures by the miracle of inspiration of God. Translators do not give authority to the original-language words of Scripture given by inspiration of God, and they do not determine the actual, original, authentic, authoritative meaning of those inspired words. Translators are men under the authority of God and under the authority of the Scriptures which God gave to the prophets and apostles (Matt. 8:9, Luke 7:8, Matt. 10:24, Mark 13:34, John 13:16). Translators are accountable to something prior to themselves [the texts which they translate]. Kevin Vanhoozer asserted: "The prime directive for the interpreter [or translator] is in fact a commandment: 'Thou shalt not bear false witness'" (*Is There a Meaning in this Text*, p. 5). The work of translators is clearly secondary, derivative, and dependent. Clearly a translator should not be transformed into an usurper who is granted the power, authority, and rights of the author.

In examining this subject of Bible translations, the term **authority** needs to be discussed. Peter Ruckman asserted: "The issue is FINAL AUTHORITY" (*Bible Believers' Bulletin*, October, 1978, p. 1; *Alexandrian Cult*, Part One, p. 16). The matter of translation does involve the issue of authority, but it has not been demonstrated that a translation should be assumed to be the final authority. By definition, the final or ultimate authority is independent of and above all other authorities. By definition, the final authority is the first and foremost authority, before and above all others and beyond which there is no other. The final authority has primacy, pre-eminence, predominance, and power over all other authorities. The final authority for the Scriptures would have to have existed before 1611. The final authority is not dependent on anything else for its text and authority. The true ramifications of a proper definition of final authority and a proper definition of a translation would conflict with the modern KJV-only claim that a translation in 1611 can supposedly be considered the final authority. Since the final authority for the Scriptures on earth existed before 1611, what was that authority in pure, perfect, inerrant, tangible form that could be used for the making of secondary or lesser authorities such as translations? A Bible translation cannot give power, authority, credence, or inspiration to its underlying sources or texts. The derived nature of a Bible translation does not permit it to be an independent, final authority, superior to its sources. A Bible translation does not have independent, absolute, final authority without any limits. The inherent nature and qualities of a translation after A. D. 100 cannot be greater than the inherent nature of the texts from which it was translated or the earlier translations of which it was a revision. If an inherent quality is supposedly absent from the underlying original language texts, how can it be present in a translation of those same texts? The underlying texts or sources must have greater authority than the translation since that translation is derived from those texts and acquires its authority from them. A translation must be built on its foundation [the texts from which it was translated] and should not be separated from it. A translation rests on the foundation of its underlying texts, and not the underlying texts on the translation. The words of a translation built on and made from the preserved Scriptures in the original languages is not more fixed and solid than their underlying foundation. A translation may be and should accurately attempt to be representative of its underlying texts, but it cannot have greater authority than them or be superior to them. By virtue of its origin as a translation by men that were not directly inspired of God and that did not receive direct revelation or Scriptures by direct inspiration, it is clear that such a translation cannot be correctly regarded to be the final authority beyond which there is no other. By the proper standard of the greater authority of the original-language words of Scripture, the derived authority of a translation will be justified. From the laws of causality, of good and necessary consequence, and of non-contradiction and from the correct and true definition of the terms "translation" and "final authority," it can be correctly deduced and understood that a translation is not the final authority beyond which there is no other. It would be logically and scripturally impossible for a translation by men who were not given their translation decisions directly by God to be the ultimate authority beyond which there is no other. Translations of something must all alike be compared to that something from which they were translated.

God is the God of order, and He established the order or primacy [the state of being first or foremost] with the preserved Scriptures in the original languages serving as the one foundation and authority on which Bible translations would need to be based or built. The Scriptures in the original languages obviously preceded any translations. No other foundation for Bible translations can be laid than the one God laid when He gave the Scriptures in the original languages by the miracle of inspiration to the prophets and apostles (Eph. 2:20, 2 Tim. 3:16, 2 Pet. 1:21, Eph. 3:5, 1 Cor. 2:13, Ps. 11:3). Puritan William Whitaker wrote: "The church is said (Eph. 2:20) to be built upon the foundation of the prophets and apostles, that is, upon the prophetic and apostolic doctrine; therefore the prophetic and apostolic doctrine, that is, the whole scripture, and the approbation of the same, preceded the church" (*Disputation*, pp. 347-348). William Whitaker added: "The foundation of the prophets and apostles in this place actually does denote the scripture" (p. 348). Whitaker also observed that "Ambrose says that by the foundation in this place is understood the old and new Testaments" (p. 349). Again concerning Ephesians 2:20, William Whitaker asserted: "this foundation denotes the doctrine of the scriptures, promulgated by the prophets and apostles" (p. 50). Reformer Francis Turretin noted that the word of God is "the foundation upon which we are built (Eph. 2:20)" (*Institutes*, I, p. 55). Francis Turretin maintained that "the church is built upon the Scripture (Eph. 2:20) and borrows all authority from it" (I, p. 88). In 1684, David Dickson wrote: "The Scriptures are the foundation, upon which the church is built (Eph. 2:20) (*Truth's Victory over Error*, p. 3). Concerning Ephesians 2:20 in his commentary, John MacArthur asserted: "The foundation of the apostles and prophets refers to the divine revelation that they taught, which in its written form is the New Testament" (p. 82). Concerning this same verse, *the Henry Morris Study Bible* noted: "The 'foundation of the apostles and prophets,' upon which the great house must be built, clearly refers to the Scriptures which they wrote under divine inspiration. The New Testament was given 'by revelation' (3:3), 'revealed unto his holy apostles and prophets by the Spirit' (3:5)" (p. 1809). Vishal Mangalwadi wrote: "The church was 'built on the foundation of the apostles and the prophets,' that is, on the New and Old Testaments" (*Book that Made Your World*, p. 397). Scriptural truth concerning the foundation established by God would conflict with any attempt to make a translation the final authority.

The term KJV-only defined and explained

In a serious discussion of the subject of English Bible translations that includes the KJV, it becomes necessary to consider a present view known as **KJV-only**.   In 2005, David Cloud claimed: "The term 'King James Only' was invented by those who oppose the defense of the King James Bible" (*Bible Version Question/Answer*, p. 7), but he provided no documented evidence for his claim.   This writer does not know who may have first invented the term KJV-only, but he first saw this term in the writings of KJV defenders themselves back as early as the 1970's or 1980's.   The more important matter would not be who first used the term, but whether the term can be used as an accurate one for describing a certain position.   Since the KJV is an English Bible translation, the term KJV-only would be used soundly and correctly to describe a certain viewpoint concerning English Bible translations, not concerning Bible translations in other languages.   The accurate term **KJV-only** is used to define and describe any view that accepts or makes some type of exclusive, only claims for one English Bible translation—the KJV.   Holders of a KJV-only view would in effect attempt to suggest, assume, or claim that the KJV is the word of God in English in some different sense than any other English translation is the word of God in English.   While perhaps admitting the fact that the KJV is a translation, holders of a KJV-only view attempt in effect to treat the KJV as though it is in a different category than all other English translations or as though it is not a translation in the same sense (univocally) as other English Bibles.   It is not reading only the KJV that would be considered to constitute a KJV-only view.   It is not using only the KJV in teaching or preaching that would be considered to constitute a KJV-only view.   A KJV-only view would concern a person's beliefs, opinions, and claims concerning the KJV, not his reading only it or using only it in teaching or preaching.   Someone can accept the Hebrew Masoretic text and the Textus Receptus and still be KJV-only if they make any exclusive, only claims for the KJV.   Any view that suggests or implies perfection, inerrancy, or inspiration for the KJV and any view that supposes or assumes that its translating is the word of God in a different sense (equivocally) than any other English Bible would be KJV-only.   The subjective opinion or unproven assumption that the KJV alone is a perfect English translation or that the KJV is the final authority would be a KJV-only view.   The subjective opinion that the KJV is the only faithful and true English translation would also qualify as being a KJV-only view.   The accurate term KJV-only does not suggest that every person who makes KJV-only claims holds and accepts all the same ideas

Some KJV defenders strongly object to being identified as KJV-only even though they clearly have made exclusive claims for the KJV.   For one example, D. A. Waite has clearly made some exclusive "only" claims for the KJV that would provide valid, sound, convincing evidence for considering his position to be a form of "KJV-only" view.   D. A. Waite claimed: "There are no good translations except the King James Bible" (*Central Seminary Refuted,* p. 129).   Waite asserted: "The King James Bible is the only accurate English translation in existence today" (p. 47).   He declared: "If you use any other version than the King James Bible you are tampering with the Words of God" (p. 136).   Waite claimed: "The King James Bible is always superior to all others in the English language" (p. 80).   Waite declared: "I believe that the King James Bible is the only one that English speaking Christians ought to use" (p. 5).   Waite wrote: "The only valid Bible is the King James Bible" (p. 131).   Waite asserted: "I believe that one translation should be set up as a standard.   The translation of the King James Bible is a standard" (p. 23).   Waite claimed: "Loyalty to Christ and His Words are measured by what version you use" (p. 133).   In another book, Waite stated: "I am one of the Christians who contend that only the King James Bible gives us the **Words** of God in English" (*Fundamental Deception*, p. 33).   Waite maintained that the KJV "is the only acceptable translation from the preserved Hebrew and Greek texts" and "is the only true Bible in the English language" (*Fuzzy Facts,* pp. 8-9).   Waite asserted that the KJV "is the only accurate translation" or "the only accurate, faithful, and true translation" (*Critical Answer to James Price's,* pp. 5, 41, 131).   Waite asserted: "I do not say that the King

James Bible is 'fallible' or 'errant.'   I don't believe that there are any translation errors in the King James Bible" (*Fuzzy Facts,* p. 44).   When Waite contended that the KJV "is 'God's Word kept intact'" and that that means "nothing harms or defiles it," he would seem to be in effect claiming or implying perfection for the KJV (*Defending the KJB,* p. 1).   Waite alleged that KJV-only is "a slanderous smear term" (*Critical Answer to Michael Sproul's,* p. 13), but he failed to prove his allegation to be true.   Waite's very own stated exclusive, only claims for the KJV would indicate that the term as soundly defined and explained in this book can be properly and accurately applied to his own stated claims.   According to his own statements, it should be clear that Waite does use "only" in the literal sense of "solely and exclusively" concerning English Bible translations.   Does Waite try to ignore and avoid a definition of KJV as being an English Bible translation when he gives his partial definition of the term KJV-only?   His definition may define "only", but it does not soundly and accurately define KJV-only reasoning and what constitutes it.   Does Waite in effect try to have it both ways by making exclusive only claims for the KJV while trying to deny holding any form of a KJV-only view?

Waite seemed to try to suggest that the term KJV-only would apply only to Peter Ruckman and his followers.   Waite claimed: "The Ruckman position's 'only' is 'only' in English (no Spanish, no Italian, no French" (*Central Seminary Refuted,* p. 20), but that incorrect claim would misrepresent and distort what Ruckman has actually written.   According to a just application of Waite's definition, Peter Ruckman would not be KJV-only since Ruckman does not claim that the word of God is only in the English KJV and that all Bible translations in other languages are not the word of God.   Peter Ruckman asserted: "There is nothing wrong with a missionary using the *Diodati* translation in Italy instead of the *Authorized Version.*   There is nothing wrong with a missionary using the *Olivetan* version in France instead of the *Authorized Version,* and there is nothing wrong with a missionary in Germany using Luther's version instead of the Authorized Version" (*Bible Babel,* p. 2).   Peter Ruckman recommended "Valera's Spanish version" and "Martin Luther's German version" (*Scholarship Only Controversy,* p. 1).   In his commentary on the book of Revelation, Peter Ruckman wrote: "Martin Luther's German Bible is the same text as the King James, 1611" (p. 80).   Ruckman wrote: "Martin's *German Bible* is the German *King James Bible.*   It is the equivalent of the 'King's English,' and so all affirm" (*Biblical Scholarship,* p. 146).   Ruckman wrote: "God produced a *German Textus Receptus* for the Continent" (p. 230).   Ruckman asserted: "Never hesitate to correct any Greek text with the text of the 'Reichstext'" (*Monarch of the Books,* p. 19).

Many KJV-only claims, opinions, assumptions, and allegations are considered in this discussion to see whether or not they are actually in agreement with all the relevant facts and with a just application of scriptural truth.   In order to focus on facts, a person has to consider and determine which claims are actually factual and which are not.   What may be assumed or claimed to be factual or true may not be actually factual or true.   Believers are commanded to "prove all things" and to "hold fast that which is good" (1 Thess. 5:21).   Believers should prove "what is acceptable unto the Lord" (Eph. 5:10).   Believers are instructed to speak the truth and to judge righteous judgment or true judgment (John 7:24, Zech. 7:9, Zech. 8:16, Eph. 4:25, Eph. 4:15).   Would blindly accepting the subjective opinions or unproven assumptions of men without proving them be sound and right?   Assuming something to be true by use of fallacies [false arguments] would not be proving all things, would not be holding fast to what is good, would not be making a righteous or true judgment, and could lead to being deceived by vain words. Instead of offering subjective or biased opinions or vain words, believers should be willing to give clear, true answers and sound reasons concerning their hopes and assertions relating to Bible translations.

Many actual claims and statements made by KJV defenders or KJV-only advocates will be quoted so that they may be considered in the light of the relevant facts and in the light of scriptural truths.   When different individuals are quoted in the same paragraph, it is not at all being suggested that they would agree in all their individual claims concerning the textually-varying editions of the Textus Receptus or concerning the varying editions of the KJV. Their own assertions are given in each one's own words so that each is permitted to speak for himself or herself. There is more than one group or camp of believers who defend the KJV to the point of holding or making claims for it that can properly and soundly be considered to be KJV-only, and each distinct group may have its differences with others and may even criticize the other camps. Quoting more than one person sometimes results in repetition of the same basic claim, but it will demonstrate that the claim of each individual is not being misrepresented as holding the position of another KJV-only group. The different KJV-only groups may at times make claims that contradict those of another group. Even an individual KJV-only advocate may make claims that would in effect contradict other of his own claims when followed to their logical conclusions. An individual KJV defender may deny being KJV-only while at the same time making some exclusive claims or assertions concerning the KJV that would qualify as being KJV-only or that display KJV-only reasoning according to an accurate definition of that term. Thus, some individuals may in effect attempt to be KJV-only and not KJV-only at the same time.

David Cloud suggested that "all of these varied positions on the TR and the KJV are based upon the same promises of Scripture and the same basic theological position" (*For Love of the Bible*, p. 9). Is David Cloud saying that the same basic position underlies the views of all the different KJV-only groups? Has this basic theological position, which is claimed to underlie the varying forms of a KJV-only view, been demonstrated to be consistent, logical, sound, true, and scriptural? In available KJV-only writings, it has not been soundly demonstrated from the Scriptures that the promises in it and that its teachings concerning inspiration and preservation of the Scriptures must lead to a KJV-only view. A KJV-only view has not been proven to be the only conclusion that must follow from a sound understanding of the scriptural doctrines of the inspiration and preservation of the Scriptures.

KJV-only claims concerning copyright

This particular discussion of issues relating to English Bible translations seeks to focus primarily on facts concerning three English Bible translations--the Geneva Bible, the KJV, and the NKJV. One way that KJV-only advocates attempt to distinguish the KJV from other English Bibles is in their claims concerning copyright. William Grady asserted: "The basic difference between the King James Bible and all modern facsimiles can be determined by the presence (or absence) of that little c meaning copyright" (*Final Authority*, p. 284). Bruce Cummons declared: "I believe the KJV is the Word of God because of its lack of copyright" (*Foundation and Authority of the Word of God*, p. 51). Jim Ellis asserted: "One of the most obvious arguments in favor of the King James Bible is that it is the only one that is not copyrighted" (*Only Two Bibles*, p. 17). Barry Burton claimed: "Is the King James copyrighted? No! Why? You cannot copyright God's Word" (*Let's Weigh the Evidence*, p. 79). Gail A. Riplinger declared: "The KJV is the only version not bound by a copyright" (*New Age Bible Versions*, p. 171). Randy Starr claimed: "The KJV has no publisher or copyright" (*Why We Use only the KJB of the Bible*, p. 18). Charles Turner wrote: "The King James Version is the only text of the Bible that has no copyright" (*Why the KJV*, p. 2). Jack Hyles claimed: "The King James Bible is not copyrighted" (*Need for an Every-Word Bible*, p. 150). William Bradley stated: "The King James Bible is not, nor has it ever been, copyrighted" (*To All Generations*, p. 69). Michael O'Neal wrote: "The text of your King James Bible, beloved, is not copyrighted" (*Do We Have*, p. 19). Ansel Metz claimed: "The Authorized King James Bible is not copyrighted. It is public domain and always has been" (*The Informer*, August, 1996, "Analysis of the KJ-21", part II, p. 10). Len Smith wrote: "The text of the King James is neither owned nor controlled by man" (*Age of Reason*, D22, p. 17). Peter Ruckman incorrectly claimed that the KJV "is the only bible in the world that anyone can reproduce, print, or copy without consulting anyone but God" (*Bible Babel*, p. 22). Jeff Fugate commented: "You look in your Bible, and if it's a King James (if it's not, you may as well just throw it away, because it's not an inspired book any more than the song book is), but if you'll look at the King James Bible you will not find a copyright in it" (*Revival Fires*, July, 1996, p. 13). Dennis Corle asserted: "The King James Bible is not copyrighted. God holds the copyright to it" (*God's Inspired Book*, p. 51). M. H. Tabb wrote: "The King James Bible has no copyright;

nobody owns it" (*Inspiration*, p. 65).   Are these KJV-only claims factual?

Do KJV-only advocates ever discuss whether or not the Geneva Bible has a copyright? The actual fact is that the KJV had what amounted to the copyright of that day.   The copyright of that day existed more for the government and for the benefit of printers than for the authors or translators.   John Tebbel wrote: "There had been a copyright of sorts in England from 1518" (*History of Book Publishing*, p. 46).   James Paterson pointed out: "The Crown and the patentees of the Crown have sometimes set up rights more or less amounting to a perpetual copyright, and sometimes resembling a monopoly" (*Liberty of the Press*, p. 282).   Robert Sargent, a KJV-only advocate, noted that Robert Barker paid 3,500 pounds for the copyright of the KJV and that Barker's firm held the rights to print the KJV until 1709 (*English Bible: Manuscript Evidence*, p. 226).   *The Oxford Dictionary of the Christian Church* also pointed out that Robert Barker bought the final manuscript of the KJV (now lost) for 3,500 pounds, "which included the copyright" (p. 135).   Donald Brake asserted: "In 1610 Barker had paid 3,500 pounds for exclusive printing rights for the King James Version" (*Visual History of KJB*, p. 163). W. H. T. Wrede noted that Cantrell Legge, printer at Cambridge, attempted to print the 1611 KJV in 1614, but Robert Baker "claimed the sole right of Bible printing under his Patent" and prevented him from printing it (*Short History*, pp. 5-6).   Christopher Anderson quoted William Ball as writing in 1651 the following: "I conceive the sole printing of the Bible and Testament with power of restraint in others, to be of right the propriety of one Matthew Barker, citizen and stationer of London, in regard that his father paid for the amended or corrected Translation of the Bible 3500 [pounds]:   by reason whereof the translated copy did of right belong to him and his assignees" (*Annals*, II, p. 384).   Theodore Letis, wrote: "This Bible [the KJV] had the *Cum Privilegio* ("with privilege") printed on it which meant that the Crown of England, as the official head of the state church, held the copyright to this Bible, giving permission only to those printers which the Crown had chosen" (*Revival of the Ecclesiastical Text and the Claims of the Anabaptists*, p. 29).   This "*Cum pivilegio*" is found on the title page for the New Testament in the 1611 edition, but it is found on the title page for the whole Bible in later KJV editions printed in 1613, 1614, 1615, 1617, 1618, 1619, etc.   David Cloud maintained that "the King James Bible was produced under the direct authority of the British Crown and is owned and 'copyrighted' by the crown of England" (*Faith*, p. 584).

Some KJV defenders have in effect suggested that the NKJV made many changes to KJV renderings just in order to be able to obtain a copyright.   Doug Stauffer claimed: "The only way to qualify for a new copyright is to make a sufficient number of changes to an existing text" (*One Book Stands Alone*, p. 121).   Doug Stauffer also asserted: "In order to qualify for a new copyright, the revisers know that they must change a significant amount of the text" (p. 97). Mickey Carter alleged: "Some publishers change just enough of the Bible to obtain a copyright on it" (*Things That Are Different*, p. 140).   D. A. Waite claimed: "There is a certain number of words which must be changed in order to obtain a copyright" (*Central Seminary*, p. 116).   James Rasbeary asserted: "The new versions, in order to meet copyright laws, have to replace the simpler KJV words with complex, multi-syllable words" (*What's Wrong with the Old Black Book* p. 120).   Gail Riplinger asserted: "To establish their copyrights, each new version editor must find different words, which have not yet been copywritten by other new version editors" (*In Awe of Thy Word*, p. 108).

Is the KJV a derivative work just as is claimed for the NKJV and are the same claims applied to it?   Did the KJV make a sufficient number of changes in the earlier English Bibles of which it was a revision to merit a separate copyright?   When the 1611 KJV is placed side by side to one of the pre-1611 English Bibles such as the Geneva Bible or Bishops' Bible, can it easily be seen that the KJV owes them as being its source of many renderings?   Should it be assumed that the exact same copyright rules apply to the translating of old texts as may apply to the revision of an author's own earlier copyrighted work?   While all English translations of other language sources may be properly considered derivative works, are all English translations always properly considered to be a derivative work of a previous English translation?   When there may be a limited number of ways to translate accurately a certain original language word into English, does each new translator have to use a different rendering than each previous translator according to actual copyright law? The fact that the 1994 21st Century KJV and the 1998 Third Millennium Bible that are almost identical in text both have copyrights would seem to conflict with the KJV-only claims about copyright of English translations. According to actual copyright law, are Bible translators or revisers required to replace factual or accurate renderings of original-language words in earlier English Bibles with different words? Richard Stim maintained: "Under copyright law, factual works receive less protection than works of fiction because the underlying facts are legally considered to be in the public domain" (*Patent, Copyright & Trademark*, p. 239). Lloyd Jassin and Steven Schechter wrote: "Because copyright does not protect ideas and facts, copying alone is not enough to prove copyright infringement" (*Copyright Permission*, p. 20). Jassin and Schechter added: "Where fact and expression merge, such as in the portrayal of factual truths, copyright protection is said to be extremely 'thin'" (Ibid.). Jassin and Schechter maintained: "Extracting pure facts from a copyrighted work is not copyright infringement" (p. 55). Jassin and Schechter asserted: "Unfortunately, no simple rule exists for distinguishing uncopyrightable facts from their copyrightable expression" (Ibid.).

KJV-only view's good tree, line, or stream of Bibles arguments

A good number of those who read the KJV including many that hold a KJV-only view would profess a high regard for the pre-1611 English Bibles of which the KJV was a revision. Do KJV-only advocates consider each of those pre-1611 English Bibles to be a translation of the Scriptures in the same sense (univocally) or in the same way that the 1611 KJV is a translation? Do KJV defenders consider each or any of the pre-1611 English Bibles to be Scripture in the same sense (univocally) that they may claim for the KJV? Would acceptance and even praise for any of the pre-1611 English Bibles provide sound support for a KJV-only view or could such praise be a problem for it? KJV defenders or KJV-only advocates may especially attempt to link the 1611 KJV to the popular, accepted, and loved 1560 Geneva Bible. Some KJV defenders and KJV-only authors have suggested or even have directly asserted that the Geneva Bible is based on the same original language texts as the KJV and that it is practically identical or is basically the same as the KJV in its translating. Perhaps connected to this high regard for pre-1611 English Bibles including the Geneva Bible would be the KJV-only view's good-tree-of-Bibles or pure-stream-of-Bibles argument, which is one of its main or essential arguments. The KJV-only view's good tree, good line, or pure stream of Bibles includes the 1560 Geneva Bible. Since it includes the Geneva Bible, should it also include the NKJV according to a consistent application of their very own argument and assertions?

One of the ways in which some believers have attempted to claim scriptural support for their KJV-only view is through their use of a tree analogy or metaphor. The use of an analogy or a metaphor is one way to attempt to explain an abstract or complex subject by use of a comparison. God made use of comparisons in the Scriptures. In an analogy or with use of a metaphor, there is not complete agreement between the things compared, and there is also not complete disagreement. Kevin Vanhoozer declared: "Thanks to metaphor, we can set the unfamiliar in the context of the familiar in order to understand it in new ways" (*Is There a Meaning in this Text*, p. 129). Edward Carnell asserted: "The success of *any* analogy turns upon the strength of the univocal element in it" (*Introduction to Christian Apologetics*, p. 147). Edward Carnell observed: "Without fear of confutation we may say that the basis for any analogy is non-analogical, *i. e.*, univocal" (Ibid.). Henry Virkler maintained that a writer can use an analogy fallaciously if he "may believe that an analogy proves something to be true," and he asserted: "An analogy never proves anything. Its purpose is to illuminate something that people do not understand by comparing it with something they do" (*Christian's Guide to Critical Thinking*, p. 207). On the tree charts in several KJV-only books, Bible translations are listed or pictured as branches of a tree. At the bottom of one of his two tree charts, J. J. Ray proclaimed: "The tree is known by his fruit (Matthew 12:33)" (*God Wrote Only one Bible*, p. 71). At the bottom of his good-tree-of-Bibles chart, Peter Ruckman asserted: "Good fruit comes from a good tree (Matt. 12:33)" (*Bible Babel*, p. 82). Ruckman declared: "An incorrupt tree cannot bring forth corrupt fruit" (*Alexandrian Cult*, Part Seven, p. 26). Paul Fadena seems to have copied Ruckman's tree in his booklet (*We Have It in Writing*, p. 16). Mickey Carter's good tree (*Things That Are Different*, p. 112) seems to be the same chart as the one in Ray's book. Doug Stauffer declared: "Pure fruit can come only from a pure tree (Matthew 7:15-20)" (*One Book Stands Alone*, p. 5). Concerning "how to judge a Bible," Ed DeVries said: "Go to the source" as he appealed to Matthew 7:16-18 (*Divinely Inspired*, p. 25). Jack McElroy also cited and appealed to Matthew 7:17 and Luke 6:44, which refer to a good tree and its good fruit (*Which Bible Would Jesus Use*, p. 308). Alan O'Reilly claimed: "Vindication of the AV1611 as the pure word of God rightly begins with a study of its roots" (*O Biblios*, p. 4). After citing Matthew 7:17-18, Ed Moore declared: "When this principle is applied to translating the Bible, we can know that the good manuscripts when faithfully adhered to, will produce a faithful translation in any language" (*Final Authority*, p. 15).

Would the whole tree with all its branches and their fruit have to be good since the good tree is known by its good fruit (Matt. 12:33, Matt. 7:17-18, Luke 6:43-44, Rom. 11:16)? A good tree would have many good branches with good fruit. The tree and its roots have to be good before it can bring forth good fruit on its branches. Can any natural branch bring forth fruit that is contrary to the qualities of the fruit of the other natural branches of this same good tree? All the natural branches of the same tree derive their qualities from the same identical source. No tree can give to its natural branches what it itself does not possess. If the root is holy, all the branches are also holy (Rom. 11:16). The holiness and other qualities of one branch is of no other nature than that of all the other branches of the same tree. The innate, inherent, ingrained qualities or essential constitution of all the natural branches of one tree are the same. Thus, truth derived from God's Word would indicate that whatever is affirmed of one natural branch of a tree must be affirmed concerning all its branches. Would it be unscriptural and contradictory to try to claim that one branch is holy and inspired but the other branches of the same tree are not? Is one branch superior and greater in authority than another branch? Two branches or even all the branches of the same tree that are claimed to have the same qualities as this tree are equal to each other.

The branches of a tree (individual translations according to this KJV-only argument) have no life of their own and cannot produce fruit if they are separated from the trunk or tree of the preserved Scriptures in the original languages. Therefore, the tree or trunk (the preserved Scriptures in the original languages) would need to be the standard for judging or evaluating all the branches. A branch is not of the same importance as the trunk of the tree. A branch cannot outrank the trunk or the root. A branch cannot bear fruit of itself (John 15:4). A branch does not bear, produce, or support the trunk or the root (Rom. 11:18). Any branch cut off from the trunk cannot live by itself. How could one branch (the KJV) be claimed to be the final standard beyond which there is no other for evaluating all other branches? It cannot be correctly said that one branch outranks another branch of the same tree. If one branch [one translation] must be inspired, inerrant, perfect, incorruptible, preserved, living, or self-authenticating, all the branches must have these same qualities or attributes. If the attribute or quality was not already present in the family tree, it could not have been passed on to the branch. If the qualities were not already present in the trunk and tree [the preserved Scriptures in the original languages], how did they supposedly get into one natural branch of that tree? If the qualities were supposedly somewhat lacking in the other branches (the pre-1611 English Bibles of which the KJV is a revision), how were they transferred to or reproduced in a later branch (the KJV)? Any attribute of one natural branch must be present in the trunk and in all the other natural branches of the same tree. Otherwise, it is being illogically claimed that contradictory and opposite qualities are part of the same tree. Otherwise, it is being claimed or implied that one natural branch belongs to a completely different species than the other natural branches of the same tree. No one branch (translation) can possibly be superior in authority to the tree itself. What sort of a good tree would supposedly have only one good or one "perfect" branch? Can one branch of a tree that is still part of that tree be claimed to be alive if the trunk, roots, and other branches of that same tree are implied to be dead? Do KJV-only advocates apply their own incorrupt, good-tree argument consistently and justly to both branches--the Geneva Bible and the KJV? This major argument for a KJV-only view has not been lightly passed over since it has been carefully examined and discussed.

Why would KJV-only advocates include the pre-1611 English Bibles on their good tree of Bibles if they did not have the correct words and were not the word of God in English? Lloyd Streeter asserted: "Most KJV advocates believe that there were English Bibles before 1611 which were the Word of God" (*Seventy-five Problems*, p. 43). Lloyd Streeter claimed: "Most KJV-only people believe that the Traditional Text of the Word of God when translated into English results in an inspired Bible when it is translated accurately" (Ibid.). On the other hand, Dennis Corle declared: "Since all Bibles don't agree, one of them has to be the Word of God and all the rest of them have to be counterfeits" (*God's Inspired Book*, p. 86). The pre-1611 English Bibles are as much sources of the KJV as its underlying original-language texts if not more so since the KJV is actually more of a revision than it is a completely new translation. If these pre-1611 Bibles were the word of God in English as the KJV translators themselves suggested in their preface to the 1611, did they supposedly cease to be the word of God after other men revised or updated them in a later translation? Did the first authorized English Bible [the Great Bible] expire or cease to be the word of God at some point? Did the Geneva Bible [the authorized English Bible in Scotland] cease to be the word of God at a certain date? Did the Bishops' Bible [the second authorized Bible in England] cease to be the word of God in English at some point? If these pre-1611 English Bibles were not the word of God in English and were counterfeits, what would that suggest about the KJV which is truly a revision of them? Was the KJV a revision of earlier English Bibles that were not profitable for doctrine, for reproof, for correction, and for instruction in righteousness? Was the KJV a revision of earlier English Bibles that were not "holy," "accurate," "correct," "good," "valid," "acceptable," "legitimate," "pure," or "true" Bibles according to a consistent application of KJV-only reasoning? Were all the words of the pre-1611 English Bibles fixed, solid, and pure? According to the law of non-contradiction, can the KJV have qualities which are not in common with the earlier English Bibles of which it was a revision? Can the pre-1611 English Bibles of which the KJV was a revision produce, reproduce, or transfer qualities that were not present in them? How could a pre-1611 English Bible give the KJV something that it does not have itself? According to a consistent application of some KJV-only reasoning, would not common sense dictate that for the descendant [the KJV] to retain inspiration its ancestors [the pre-1611 English Bibles] would have first had to have inspiration? Could the KJV supposedly inherit inspiration from pre-1611 English Bibles that were not directly given by inspiration of God? Can the KJV inherit perfection, purity, or incorruption from pre-1611 English Bibles that had some imperfections, impure renderings, or other faults according to a consistent application of KJV-only reasoning? Without a direct miracle of God, can any imperfection, impurity, or corruption in the pre-1611 English Bibles lead to perfection, purity, or incorruption? There is way too much diversity or too many variations in the pre-1611 English Bibles for any attempt to draw a sweeping KJV-only generalization. The many actual differences between the pre-1611 English Bibles (of which the KJV is a revision) and the 1611 KJV are not infrequent, are not all incidental, and are not all minor. While KJV-only advocates may appear to want English-speaking believers to go back to 1611, many of them in effect imply that you cannot go back before 1611 and have a perfect English Bible.

How can KJV-only advocates tolerate or in effect accept renderings in the pre-1611 English Bibles or in the margins of the 1611 KJV that they would condemn as wrong, corrupt, or heretical in later English translations? How can they identify translations on their own tree or line as being good when these translations have any readings that they would consider to be departures from the traditional Hebrew or Greek texts of Scripture or any renderings that they consider to be errors? If the words added by Erasmus from the Latin Vulgate must be kept, what about the words from the Latin Vulgate added by Miles Coverdale in his English translations? Should the additional words in the old Wycliffe's Bible from the Latin Vulgate be kept? If the pre-1611 English translations may be the word of God and profitable for doctrine though less than 100%

perfect and inerrant, then the same could also be true of the 1611 KJV. If the various English translations before 1611 and Luther's German Bible with many differences from the KJV were and are the word of God, then translations after 1611 with differences can also be the word of God. There are hundreds and even thousands of actual differences, including some significant or major ones, which can be found between the Bibles on the KJV-only view's good tree/line/stream. In at least some places, one of the pre-1611 English Bibles has a rendering that is more accurate than the one in the KJV when compared to the preserved Scriptures in the original languages. H. C. Conant noted that in the KJV "passages are mistranslated, which Tyndale and Coverdale and the Genevan--some or all of them--had translated right" (*The English Bible,* p. 441). Blackford Condit asserted that "the revisers of King James' Bible sometimes passed over correct readings of earlier versions, or placed them in the margin when it would have been better to have put them in the text" (*History of the English Bible,* p. 346). Glenn Conjurske, who defends the KJV as the best overall English translation, acknowledged that in a few places the KJV is inferior to the Geneva and Bishops' Bibles (*Olde Paths,* March, 1996, p. 57). Gerald Hammond claimed: "It is clear that where the Authorized Version departs from Tyndale it is not usually for the better" (*Making of the English Bible,* p. 64). In his introduction to his 1858 commentary on Mark, J. A. Alexander noted: "While the common version [KJV], though to some extent influenced by all the others, is founded mainly upon Tyndale's, with occasional changes for the worse and for the better, but a frequent adherence to him even when in error" (p. xv). The clear and serious inconsistencies in KJV-only claims and assumptions are a sure sign of error in the KJV-only view. The truth is consistent. Actual facts from the Bibles placed on the KJV-only view's own good tree/stream/line of Bibles will reveal that some important assumptions and logical implications of KJV-only reasoning do not hold up as being sound, true, or scriptural.

Perhaps one way by which KJV defenders attempt to get around the problems with the KJV-only view's good-tree-of-Bibles analogy or argument is with what amounts to a process of purification argument. In this form or variation of the argument from a tree, stream, or line of good Bibles, William Byers claimed that the KJV is the seventh translation in the English language from the pure text and is thus "purified seven times" (*The History of the KJB*, pp. 9, 23, 97-98). William Byers wrote that the Geneva Bible was the "sixth translation" (p. 9), but later he wrote that "Geneva is five" (p. 97). Although beginning his list with Wycliffe's Bible, Timothy Morton made a similar claim to that of Byers when he wrote: "Each of these Bibles was (and still is) a valuable translation, but the King James of 1611 is the purest--the seventh and final purification" (*Which Translation Should You Trust,* p. 9). Doug Stauffer maintained that "the King James Bible became the seventh purification of the English translation in fulfillment of this prophecy" [Ps. 12:6] (*One Book Stands,* p. 282). David H. Sorenson claimed that "the KJV was the seventh refinement of God's Word in English from Tyndale" (*God's Perfect Book*, p. 137). David Sorenson declared that the KJV "has been purified at least seven times as it were in a furnace of earth" (p. 116). John W. Sawyer declared that the Geneva Bible was "the fifth refining of the Word of God in English" and that the Bishops' Bible was "the sixth refining" (*Legacy of our English Bible,* pp. 8, 9).

William Bradley stated: "The King James Bible was the seventh major English translation of the Scriptures" (*To All Generations,* p. 29). Bradley also began his list with Wycliffe's Bible and included Tyndale's, Coverdale's, Matthew's, Great, and Geneva Bibles, but he omitted the important Bishops' Bible of which the KJV was officially a revision. In his later book, Bradley actually listed a total of eight English translations in two consecutive paragraphs [Wycliffe's, Tyndale's, Coverdale's, Matthew's, Great, Geneva, Bishops', KJV], which actually made the KJV the eighth translation (*Purified Seven Times,* p. 116). Nevertheless, Bradley claimed: "When the seventh major English translation of the Bible was published, the Word of God in English was complete; it was perfect" (Ibid., p. 131). Ed DeVries also asserted that the KJV is "the seventh major translation of the Bible in the English language" (*Divinely Inspired,* p. 28). In his list, Ed DeVries listed Wycliffe's, Tyndale's, Matthew's, Great, Geneva, Bishops', and KJV, but he omitted the important 1535 Coverdale's Bible. After citing Psalm 12:6, William P. Grady claimed that the

KJV is "the *seventh* major English translation," *purified seven times* (*Given by Inspiration*, pp. 105-106). Phil Stringer also proposed: "It took several decades and seven major translations (Tyndale, Coverdale, Matthew's, Great Bible, Bishops, Geneva, King James) in order to get the pure Word of God in English" (Carter, *Elephant*, p. 47). Ben Pierce claimed that "the printing and publication of the King James 1611 would be the 7th and final completed English translation" (*Valiant for the Truth*, p. 106). Joey Faust listed the KJV as the seventh English translation, and he asserted: "The Authorized Version (i. e. KJV) is the final purification. This is a fulfillment of God's promise to preserve His pure words" (*The Word*, p. 45). T. S. Luchon also used this argument, listing the KJV as the claimed seventh English Bible (*From the Mind of God*, p. 66).

Gail Riplinger also adopted a variation of this same KJV-only argument. Gail Riplinger contended that "the English Bible was 'purified seven times' and that "the KJV is its seventh and final purification" (*In Awe of Thy Word*, p. 131). In her book, Riplinger maintained that "the English Bible's seven purifications are covered, including, the Gothic, the Anglo-Saxon, the pre-Wycliffe, the Wycliffe, the Tyndale/Coverdale/Great/Geneva, the Bishops, and the King James Bible (p. 33) [see also pp. 131, 843, 852]. She proposed that "the KJV was the seventh polishing of the English Bible" (p. 137). This seems to be one of the main themes of her KJV-only book. Would it be acceptable KJV-only math and reasoning for four translations to be counted as one?

David Cloud listed the KJV as number 9 on his list of the "unmatched heritage" of the KJV (*Faith*, p. 433). David Norris asserted that "between 1526 and 1611, nine English translations of Scripture of significance were made" (*Big Picture*, p. 333). David Daniell observed: "There were ten new English versions of the Bible or New Testament between Tyndale's first New Testament in 1526 and the famous King James or Authorised Version of 1611, and all were influential" (*Bible in English*, p. 126). D. A. Waite listed the KJV as being number 17 on his chronological list of complete English Bibles (*Defending the KJB*, p. 203). Pre-1611 English Bibles would include the following: Wycliffe's Bible (1388), Tyndale's New Testament (1526, 1534), Tyndale's Pentateuch (1530), George Joyce's New Testament (1533), Coverdale's Bible (1535), Matthew's Bible (1537), Coverdale's Latin-English New Testament (1538), Taverner's Bible (1539), the Great Bible (1539), Coverdale's revision of Tyndale's (1549), Bishop Becke's Bible (1551), Richard Jugge's New Testament (1552), Whittingham's New Testament (1557), Geneva Bible (1560), Bishops' Bible (1568), Lawrence Tomson's New Testament (1576), and Rheims New Testament (1582). In addition, there was more than one edition of many of these Bibles with some changes and revisions in them. The 1526 edition of Tyndale's New Testament differs from his 1534 edition in many places. The 1539 edition of the Great Bible has several differences with the 1540 edition of the Great Bible or with its 1541 edition. The Geneva Bible editions with the 1560 edition's New Testament have a good number of differences when compared to the Geneva Bible editions with the 1576 Tomson's New Testament. The 1568 edition of the Bishops' Bible has some differences when compared to the 1569 edition or to the 1572 edition.

There are also some significant textual differences found in the pre-1611 English Bibles that comprise the heritage of the KJV. Some pre-1611 English Bibles such as Tyndale's New Testament and Matthews Bible did not have three whole verses (Mark 11:26, Luke 17:36, Revelation 21:26) because those verses were not in the editions of the Greek text of Erasmus. The 1535 Coverdale's Bible has three whole verses in Psalm 14, which are not found in the KJV. From the varying Textus Receptus editions, some other significant textual differences, which involve clauses, phrases, or words, could also be noted.

Since each new English Bible was not always an improvement at every verse over the one before it, the next one was not more purified and more accurate than the prior one. Was the rendering "penance" found in the 1535 Coverdale's Bible at Matthew 3:8, 12:41, Luke 10:13, 11:32, 15:7, 10, 16:30, Acts 3:19 and 26:20 more purified or more accurate than Tyndale's?

Even those translations that may have been overall better than the previous one usually had at least a few renderings that were poorer or less accurate than those in the earlier Bible. The 1539 Great Bible is not overall more pure in all its renderings than the 1537 Matthew's Bible. Sometimes the next Bible in the line made some changes by adding words from the Latin Vulgate as in the case of the Great Bible. In several additions from the Latin Vulgate including three whole verses in Psalm 14, the Great Bible has over one hundred words in the book of Psalms that are not in the KJV. Because of additions from the Latin Vulgate, the Great Bible also has over one hundred words in one New Testament book (Acts) which are not found in the KJV (check Acts 4:25, 4:27, 5:15, 13:30, 14:7, 15:34c, 15:41c, 18:4, 23:24c, 24:17). Were the significant textual additions from the Latin Vulgate in the Great Bible changes towards more purity or changes for the worse? The 1568 Bishops' Bible was considered by many to be overall a poorer translation than the 1560 Geneva Bible. The Bishops' Bible has a number of added explanatory words and phrases (likely over 200 words) with many of them not kept in the KJV. Many actual facts from the pre-1611 English Bibles would demonstrate that each later English Bible was not more purified than the prior one, which would contradict a claimed purification process.

What consistent sound criteria was used to determine objectively and justly which English translations to include? It seems that KJV-only authors cannot agree on which Bibles to include on their lists and on which Bibles to leave off. Did they start with the assumption that the KJV has to be the seventh one and then subjectively pick out six others to make their count work? If believers were to accept the unproven claim that men can purify God's word in a series of translations, on whose authority do we base this claim that the KJV is the seventh and final purification? Are William Byers and some other KJV-only authors in effect also suggesting that all people have to have seven Bible translations into their language before they can have a reliable and accurate one? Do they think that it takes God seven attempts before the Holy Spirit can guide translators to produce an acceptable, good translation? Would they suggest that the KJV improves on the Hebrew and Greek? Would they imply or suggest that the preserved Scriptures in the original languages can be made more pure through a process of revision and corrections in Bible translations? These questions are based on a consistent application of the logical implications of some actual KJV-only claims or reasoning.

The truth that is stated in Psalm 12:6 is the fact that "the words of the LORD are pure words" meaning 100% absolutely and wholly pure. Pure used in the particular context of describing the quality of the words of the LORD given to the prophets and apostles would clearly be asserting 100% absolute, complete purity or perfection with no mixture of any impurities at all. After the assertion of fact, then an illustration, simile, or comparison is given [as] to confirm that truth, not to contradict it by suggesting that there were some impurities in the pure words given to the prophets and apostles. Thus, the phrase "purified seven times" (Ps. 12:6) actually stated clearly concerning silver on earth is used to illustrate and affirm that the words of the LORD are 100% wholly, absolutely, completely, and perfectly pure when given by God. This phrase about the refining or purification of silver obviously and clearly does not contradict the earlier assertion or statement of fact. That phrase does not indicate or assert that the words of the LORD are mostly pure or almost pure with a few impurities, defects, faults, corruptions, errors, or contaminants mixed in so that they needed to go through a gradual improvement or refining process of seven purifications in seven English translations or in seven purifications of the various editions of the KJV. Words of the LORD asserted to be wholly and completely pure in the positive or absolute degree could not be made more pure. Thus, the quality of being completely pure and completely free from all impurities that is asserted concerning the words of the LORD could not be increased. Nothing can be asserted to be more pure than what is already 100% absolutely pure according to the meaning of pure used in the context. Pure in the positive degree simply make an assertion about what is described as being pure, and it does not compare it to other things. Pure is clearly not used in a comparative degree concerning the 100% absolutely and completely pure and perfect words of the LORD. The word of the LORD is perfect (Ps. 19:7). Pure words of the LORD have the very same absolute, complete purity as very pure words (Ps. 119:140). The use of "very" would emphasize the fact of the absolute purity, but it could not increase the purity of words that are already 100% wholly and absolutely pure.

KJV-only subjective, private interpretations or misinterpretations suggesting a purification process based on Psalm 12:6 could be considered an example of eisegesis, reading into a verse ideas that were not actually stated in it. KJV defender Thomas Corkish agreed: "Some have mistakenly said that the Bible has need to be 'tried' ('refined') seven times in order for it to be given as 'pure.' Actually, it was as 'refined' silver from the beginning" (Brandenburg, *Thou Shalt Keep Them,* pp. 143-144). He added: "The Bible is not a pure Word because of any derivation, development, revision, recovery, or improvement" (p. 149). KJV-only author Gary Miller wrote: "Purifying something seven times makes it *almost* perfect. But God's words *are* perfect" (*Why the KJB,* p. 16). H. D. Williams acknowledged: "God's Words are in no need of being 'cleansed' or 'purified'" (*Pure Words,* p. 53).

The accepted and loved pre-1611 English Bible—the Geneva Bible

Do all the Bibles that make up the KJV-only view's good stream of Bibles have the exact same water with no foreign matter? KJV defender D. A. Waite maintained that "the Traditional Text (the Textus Receptus) is like a river, wherever you take a sample, it is virtually the same text" (*Fundamentalist Mis-Information on Bible Versions,* p. 81). Waite asserted: "It must be recognized that the English translations that preceded the King James Bible were almost unanimously taken from the same Hebrew and Greek texts as were used in its translation—that is, the Hebrew Masoretic Text and the Greek Textus Receptus" (p. 85). David Sorenson maintained that the Geneva Bible "used the Traditional Text" (*Neither Oldest Nor Best,* p. 30). Joe Gresham asserted that "the Geneva Bible (1557-1560) used the Received Text" (*Dealing with the Devil's Deception,* p. 34). Bob Steward acknowledged that the Geneva Bible "is the product of the Received Text" (*God's Invisible Hand,* p. 11). Robert Barnett noted: "These Bibles [the Tyndale, the Coverdale, the Matthews, the Great Bible, the Geneva Bible, and the Bishops' Bible] were all following the majority or traditional Greek texts" (*Word of God on Trial,* p. 25). Dick Cimino maintained that the pre-1611 English Bibles such as the Geneva Bible "come from the SAME TYPE OF GREEK TEXT" as the KJV (*The Book,* 14). In a similar manner, David Cloud asserted: "All of the translations of the Protestant Reformation were based on the same Greek text" (*Faith vs. the Modern Bible Versions,* p. 64). David Cloud declared: "Any sound translation from the Masoretic Hebrew and the Greek Received texts is the preserved Word of God in that language" (*Bible Version Question/Answer Database,* p. 109). According to a consistent application of David Cloud's own statement, can the 1560 Geneva Bible be considered the preserved word of God in English since it is a sound translation from the Hebrew Masoretic and Greek Received texts? Is the Geneva Bible considered to be the Scriptures in English in the same sense (univocally) as the KJV? Does the Geneva Bible have the exact same water with no foreign matter as the KJV?

William Bradley asserted that "the Geneva Bible translators used all the previous English translations" and that "the translators changed virtually nothing from William Tyndale's New Testament in the New Testament of the Geneva Bible" (*Purified Seven Times,* p. 87). Bradley maintained that "the italics in the Geneva Bible" ... "represent the translators' honesty and integrity" (p. 86). Bradley observed: "The Geneva Bible represents the first combined effort of a committee of godly men, determined to give the people a Bible they could love and call their own" (p. 84). Mickey Carter asserted that the Geneva "differs from the King James Version only in differing English renderings of the same Greek texts" (*Things That Are Different,* p. 48). Pastor Carter placed the 1560 Geneva Bible on his "good tree [of Bibles]—produced from pure and strong stock" (p. 112). Carter maintained that the Geneva Bible "came from the same source, the same text" as the KJV and that it is "trustworthy" (p. 121). Carter noted that the Geneva Bible was "taken from the Textus Receptus," and he indicated that "there were no doctrinal differences" between the Geneva and the KJV (p. 125). Mickey Carter asserted that the Geneva Bible "is from the same manuscripts as the King James" (*Revival Fires,* Sept., 1996, p. 17). J. J. Ray listed the Geneva Bible on his good tree of Bibles (*God Wrote Only One Bible,* 109). Chester Murray, another KJV-only advocate, claimed: "There is not one difference suggested in the Geneva and the KJ Bible" (*Authorized KJB Defended*, p. 160). Ray McBerry asserted that the KJV "exhibited very few differences from the Geneva Bible, even down to the word-for-word rendering" (*Clash of Swords*, p. 113). J. W. Sawyer claimed that "the Geneva New Testament of 1557 is within five percent of being the A. V. of 1611" (*Legacy of our English Bible*, p. 11).

H. D. Williams identified the Geneva Bible as being an "excellent translation" that is "based on the Received Texts of the original languages of the Bible" (*Word-for-Word Translating,* p. 238). H. D. Williams maintained that "the KJB translators chose many of the same English words that Tyndale and the Geneva Bible used for translation because of using the same underlying texts and the providential care of God in translation of His 'pure' Words" (*Pure Words of God*, p. 53). In his book edited by D. A. Waite, H. D. Williams referred to the Geneva Bible as one of the "previous literal verbal plenary translations" (*Word-for-Word Translating*, p. 121). Ben Pierce maintained that the Geneva Bible was "translated using the Textus Receptus" (*Valiant for the Truth*, p. 58). Thomas Holland listed the Geneva Bible as one of the early English translation that was "based on the Traditional Text" (*Crowned with Glory*, p. 77). D. A. Waite asserted that "the Geneva Bible (1557-60) used the Received Text" (*Defending the KJB,* p. 48). D. A. Waite maintained that "the Geneva Bible was based on the Traditional Text/Textus Receptus" (*Foes of the KJB Refuted*, p. 38). Doug Stauffer placed the Geneva Bible on his "original text line preserved" (*One Book One Authority*, p. 16). William R. Byers listed the Geneva Bible as one of "those English translations that came of the pure text" (*History of the KJB*, p. 97). Ben Carter maintained that "the early English translations were based upon this family of manuscripts [the Received Text] including the Geneva Bible and the Bishops' Bible" (*Bible and How It Came to Us*, p. 134). Edward F. Hills suggested that "the early Protestant versions, such as Luther's, Tyndale's, the Geneva, and the King James, were actually varieties of the Textus Receptus" (*KJV Defended*, p. 114). W. MacLean asserted that "the English versions of Tyndale, Coverdale, Matthews (or Rogers), the Great Bible, the Geneva Bible, the Bishops' Bible, and the Authorised Version were all based upon this little company of Greek documents, in which was preserved the Greek Text generally received throughout the Greek Church since the Apostolic ages" (*Providential Preservation*, p. 10).

David Cloud maintained that the predecessors of the KJV were "the same basic Bibles" (*For Love of the Bible*, p. 48). Cloud added: "They were based upon the same Greek text and employed the same type of translation methodology" and were "formal equivalencies" (p. 48). David Cloud suggested that the earlier English versions such as the Geneva Bible "differed only slightly from the King James Bible" (*Bible Version Question/Answer,* p. 92). David Cloud maintained that "all of these English Bibles from 1526 until 1611 were based on the Greek Received Text" (Ibid.). David Cloud noted that the Geneva Bible was "a product of persecution and spiritual revival, having been produced by men who were in exile for their faith" (*Glorious History of the KJB*, pp. 132-133). Cloud pointed out: "The Geneva Bible was a milestone in many important ways" (p. 122).

James Rasbeary likewise maintained that the pre-1611 English Bibles and the KJV were "basically the same" and that "all came from the same text--the Received Text,' and that "they translated word for word" (*What's Wrong with the Old Black Book*, p. 91). James Rasbeary asserted that "the Geneva translators used Tyndale's Bible as well as several other Bibles in the *Textus Receptus* line, including the French Bible, which was the Bible of the Waldensian Baptists" (p. 90). David Loughran wrote: "The Geneva Bible is a true 'version' having been translated from the original Hebrew and Greek throughout" (*Bible Versions,* p. 11; Woods, *King's Bible*, p. 34). David W. Daniels wrote: "English speaking people after him [William Tyndale] continued the effort to translate and perfect a Bible that matched the ancient scriptures. One of the best of these is the Geneva Bible" (*Answers to your Bible Version Questions*, p. 13). David Daniels listed the Geneva Bible as one of the "Antiochian Bibles" (p. 18). Concerning the Geneva, David L. Brown maintained that "the revision was made from a careful collation of Hebrew and Greek originals, with the use of Latin versions, especially Beza's, and the standard French and German versions" (*Indestructible Book*, p. 323). Robert Sargent referred to it as "a very good translation" (*English Bible*, p. 197). William Grady noted that the Geneva Bible was "the first English Bible translated entirely out of the original languages" (*Final Authority*, p. 140). Michael Bates affirmed that "this Geneva Bible was the first complete English version translated entirely from the original languages" (*Inspiration, Preservation*, and the KJV, p. 290). Tim Fellure also maintained that the Geneva Bible "was the first complete English Bible translated entirely out of the original languages" (*Neither jot nor tittle*, p. 160). Timothy Morton suggested that the pre-1611 English Bibles such as the Geneva Bible "were all valuable translations and God's word in their time" (*From the Original Texts to the English Bible*, p. 8). E. W. Whitten maintained that the Geneva Bible was "the translated Majority Text" (*Truth According to Scripture*, p. 105). Troy Clark described the Geneva Bible as the "first complete Majority Text English Bible formally translated from the original Hebrew and Greek languages" (*Perfect Bible*, p. 158). Troy Clark suggested that each of the pre-1611 English Bibles "ALWAYS contained the same Majority Text Scripture" (p. 133). Troy Clark asserted: "Different names never means different Bibles in the succession of Majority Text Holy Scriptures" (pp. 133-134).

Gail Riplinger maintained that the earlier English Bibles such as Tyndale's and the Geneva are "practically identical to the KJV" (*Language of the KJB*, p. 5). Riplinger also wrote: "The Geneva text is almost identical to the KJV" (*In Awe of thy Word*, p. 566). Riplinger asserted that "generally speaking, the early English Bibles are the same" (p. 130; *Hidden History*, p. 37). Riplinger asserted that "the words that differ in the early English Bibles are pure synonyms" (*In Awe of Thy Word*, p. 859). Riplinger maintained that "both the Bishops' and the KJV are literal, word-for-word renderings of the Greek text and show *all* words, even if they seem repetitive" (p. 288). Riplinger even indicated that those previous early English Bibles "were no less perfect, pure, and true than the KJB" (*Hidden History of the English Scriptures*, p. 59). Riplinger asserted that the Geneva "follows the traditional text underlying the King James Version" (*Which Bible Is God's Word*, p. 51). Riplinger described the English translation in the 1599 Nuremberg Polyglot [which was an edition of the Geneva Bible] as "pure" and as "the Bible before the KJV of 1611" (*In Awe of Thy Word*, pp. 41, 1048, 1052-1108). Riplinger claimed: "According to the rules of translation, the [KJV] translators' final authority was early English Bibles, particularly the Bishops'" (*Hidden History*, p. 41).

Peter Ruckman included the Geneva Bible on his good tree that is described at the bottom of the page as "the one, true, infallible, God-breathed Bible" (*Bible Babel*, p. 82). Ruckman wrote: "I recommend ... the Geneva Bible" (*Scholarship Only Controversy*, p. 1). Ruckman asserted that "we will not condemn them" [referring to pre-1611 English Bibles including the Geneva Bible] (*Bible Babel*, p. 2). Ruckman maintained that the pre-1611 English Bibles such as the Geneva "have substantially the same Greek and Hebrew texts as the King James Bible" (Ibid.). Ruckman described the Geneva Bible as "a revision of Tyndale" and "the most anti-Catholic translation to date" (*Biblical Scholarship*, pp. 158, 157). Ruckman maintained that John Roger's work in the Matthew's Bible "is the basis for the *Geneva Bible* of the Puritans" (p. 155).

David Cloud referred to the Geneva Bible as "an edition of the Tyndale" and to the KJV as "another edition of Tyndale" (*Rome and the Bible*, p. 106; *Faith*, p. 510; *Glorious History of the KJB*, p. 102). Cloud also referred to the KJV as "a revision of the Tyndale Bible" (*Faith*, p. 577). Cloud also noted: "Our Authorized English Bible is a direct descendant of Tyndale's faithful Version" (*O Timothy*, Vol. 14, Issue 5, 1997, p. 10). Cloud asserted: "In fact, the King James Bible is a revision of that line of Received Text English Bibles stretching back to Tyndale in 1524" (*For Love of the Bible*, p. 8). Robert Sargent referred to the Geneva Bible as the "third revision of Tyndale's Bible" and to the Bishops' Bible as the "fourth revision of Tyndale's Bible" (*English Bible*, pp. 197, 198). All these documented statements made by KJV defenders and KJV-only advocates should clearly demonstrate their own stated high regard and praise for the 1560 Geneva Bible. They have been granted the opportunity to be witnesses for themselves as to their own stated view of the Geneva Bible.

Other authors and Bible scholars also speak highly of the Geneva Bible. J. Paterson Smyth described the Geneva Bible as "a careful translation" (*How We Got Our Bible*, p. 126). Donald Brake observed that "modern scholars have no problem admitting that it was one of the finest translations ever made" (*Visual History of the English Bible*, p. 149). Benson Bobrick maintained that the Geneva Bible "paid meticulous attention to the Greek and Hebrew originals, and made use of the best of the most recent translations into Latin and French" (*Wide as the Waters,* p. 175). Bobrick concluded: "It was unquestionably the most scholarly, well-annotated, and accurate English Bible yet to appear" (<u>Ibid</u>.). David Daniell noted that "the Geneva translators' aim, successfully achieved, was to reproduce what the original says from Genesis to Malachi" (*The Bible in English*, p. 297). In his introduction to a modern-spelling edition of Tyndale's New Testament, David Daniell maintained that the Geneva Bible "set a new standard in Greek and Hebrew scholarship, particularly important in the Old Testament books that Tyndale had not reached" (pp. xi-xii). Daniell described it as "a triumph of textual, theological, and linguistic excellencies, universally admired" (p. xii). Charles Butterworth noted: "The Geneva Bible is above all anxious to be accurate; it is clean-cut, honest, and straightforward: it is both scholarly and pious" (*Literary Lineage*, p. 236).

Donald Brake pointed out that "the Geneva Bible was an excellent translation" (*Visual History of the KJB*, p. 67). Concerning the Geneva Bible, Glenn Conjurske asserted: "Accuracy was its main concern and its main characteristic" (*Olde Paths,* April, 1993, p. 86). John C. Mincy maintained that the Geneva Bible "was an accurate translation" (Williams, *From the Mind of God*, p. 129). Likewise, Vishal Mangalwadi observed that the Geneva Bible "excelled as an accurate translation" (*Book That Made Your World*, p. 154). David Daiches claimed: "On the whole, the Geneva translators sacrificed style to accuracy" (*Critical History of English Literature*, Vol. 2, p. 470). John Greider described the Geneva Bible as "a very good translation" (*English Bible Translations*, p. 277). Ward Allen and Edward Jacobs referred to the Geneva Bible as "the Puritan translation whose accuracy and readability made it a vast favorite with the people" (*Coming of King James Gospels*, p. 3). Andrew Hadfield maintained that the Geneva Bible "became the edition preferred by Elizabethans seeking an accurate English translation" (O'Sullivan, *The Bible as Book*, p. 152). Irving Jenson wrote: "The Geneva Bible excelled in accuracy and was very popular" (*Jensen's Survey of the N. T.*, p. 33). Ken Connolly suggested that the Geneva Bible translators "painstakingly worked over minute details of the text, giving a faithful translation and achieving agreement between all the collaborators" (*Indestructible Book,* p. 155). Ismar Peritz asserted: "No version since Tyndale's has so much claim in regard on account of its scholarship and accuracy as the Geneva. It was throughout based upon the original languages and made by competent and conscientious scholars" (*The Christian Advocate*, April 13, 1911, p. 486).

Thomas Timpson noted that the Geneva Bible was "esteemed as a faithful version of the Holy Scriptures" (*Bible Triumphs*, p. 100). Henry Morley asserted that the Geneva Bible "was as faithful as its translators could make it" (*English Writers*, Vol. 8, p. 206). Concerning the Geneva, George Henry Nettleton wrote: "The dominant note of the translation was faithful accuracy to the original texts" (*English Bible*, p. xxxix). Kenneth Latourette wrote: "Embodying thorough scholarship, it also had an English style which delighted the rank and file of readers, was printed in Roman rather than black letters and in convenient style, and enjoyed a wide circulation" (*History of Christianity,* II, p. 817). David Lawton asserted: "The Geneva Bible is a superb production in the tradition of Tyndale" (*Faith*, p. 64). Derek Wilson described it as "a most scrupulous piece of translation" (*People's Bible*, p. 65). David Allen asserted: "The Geneva text showed a scholarly expertise throughout" (*Jewel in the King's Crown*, p. 59). Walter Scott wrote: "The Geneva Bible was the first complete translation into the English from the originals throughout" (*Story of our English Bible,* p. 153). John Kerr wrote: "With the Geneva we have a true 'people's Bible'--written in vigorous English, exhibiting careful scholarship without sounding pedantic, and widely available" (*Ancient Texts,* p. 93).   Frank Gaebelein observed: "Whittingham and his co-workers produced a translation of notable scholarship and beauty" (*Story,* p. 40).   P. W. Raidabaugh asserted that "the men who prepared it were scholars acquainted with the original; and, though they derived assistance from other versions, did not follow any of them with servility" (*History of the English Bible,* p. 45).   Blackford Condit maintained that "the language of the Geneva version is remarkable for its Saxon simplicity" (*History,* p. 252).   Arthur Peake contended that the Geneva Bible "was an admirable translation, both learned and accurate" (*Bible: Its Origin,* p. 54).   John Eadie noted: "The vitality of the Genevan Bible was wonderful" (*English Bible,* II, p. 51).   Concerning the Geneva Bible, Spencer Cone and William Wyckoff asserted: "This was another instance of translation without royal and episcopal authority, and displayed the advantages of this freedom in the earnestness of the translators to give as fully as possible the plain English meaning of the original Greek" (*Primitive Church Magazine,* Vol. IX, June, 1852, p. 169).

Irena Backus asserted that "their main Greek text for the New Testament was the 1550 text of Stephanus" (*Reformed Roots of the English New Testament,* p. 13).   The Geneva Bible translators could only consult the 1556-1557 Latin New Testament of Beza since the second edition that included a Greek text had not yet been printed [1565].   Jan Krans maintained that Beza's Latin New Testament influenced the 1560 Geneva Bible "both in the translation and in the marginal notes" (*Beyond What Is Written,* p. 197).   Charles Butterworth pointed out: "Broadly defined, the Geneva Bible was a sweeping revision of the text of the Great Bible in the Old Testament and a careful revision of the edition of 1557 in the New Testament" (*Literary Lineage,* p. 165).   It was influenced by Olivetan's French Bible.   Backus maintained that "there is no doubt about the strong influence which the French Geneva Bible had on the text of the English Geneva" (*Reformed Roots,* p. 13).

In an appendix entitled "When and how we get our Bible," a Sunday School Scholars' Edition of the KJV stated that the Geneva Bible "is pre-eminently the Protestant Bible" (p. 6). Donald Brake maintained that "the Geneva Bible became the cornerstone of the Reformation" (*Visual History of the English Bible,* p. 150).   Brad Taliaferro asserted that the Geneva Bible "became the Bible of the reformation" (*Bible Version Encyclopedia,* p. 66).   An article in *Unpublished Word* suggested that "the Geneva Bible was the Bible that gave momentum to the Protestant Reformation" (Spring, 2009, p. 11).   Concerning the Geneva Bible, Leland Ryken asserted: "This is the Bible of the Reformers" (*Word of God in English,* p. 49).   David Daniell reported: "It was a masterpiece of Renaissance scholarship and printing, and Reformation Bible thoroughness" (*Bible in English,* p. 291).   Larry Stone observed: "The Geneva Bible became part of England's Protestant national identity" (*Story of the Bible,* p. 73).   Andrew Hadfield suggested that the Geneva Bible "with its extensive commentary helped impose a Protestant outlook on wide sections of the population" (O'Sullivan, *Bible as Book,* pp. 152-153).   Reader's Digest's book *ABC's of the Bible* maintained that the Geneva Bible "helped shape the course of English history" and was "influencing English and American religious thought over several generations" (pp. 303-304).

David Norton cited Sir John Harington (1560-1612) as calling the Geneva Bible "the best translation read in our church" (*History of the English Bible as Literature,* p. 40).   In 1772, David Durell (Hebrew scholar and friend of Benjamin Blayney) maintained that "it [the KJV] does not exhibit in many places the sense of the text so exactly as the version of 1599 [the Geneva]" (*Critical Remarks on the Books,* p. vi).   In 1799, John Rowe claimed: "It is the opinion of some good judges, that where our present version has departed from them [the preceding translations], the change has frequently been for the worse rather than for the better; so that it does not appear that it is much superior in purity and accuracy, to the Geneva Bible" (*A Discourse,* p. 33).   In 1827, Baptist Samuel Green asserted that "some learned men speak highly of this copy [the Geneva] of the English Scriptures, and do not hesitate to declare, that it is at least equal to that of King James's translators" (*Miscellanies,* p. 256).   In an article "Some account of Miles

Coverdale" in a book entitled *Writings of John Fox, Bale, and Coverdale* that was printed in 1831, this is written: "This version [referring to the Geneva Bible] is in some respects superior to our present translation [the KJV]" (p. 4; see also *The Scottish Journal of Topography, Antiquities, Tradition*, Vol, II, 1848, p. 87). In 1835, B. B. Edwards claimed that "on further examination of the Geneva Bible, it appeared that many of the obsolete words and errors in grammar and syntax, found in James's version, are not in the Geneva" (*Biblical Repository*, Vol. 6, p. 478). Edwards maintained that though the Geneva was "sometimes improved in the last translation [the KJV]" that the Geneva Bible "contained many preferable translations" (Ibid.). In 1845, Christopher Anderson referred to the Geneva version being "in several passage preferable to our own, and especially in translating '*love*,' not '*charity*'" (*Annals of the English Bible*, Vol. II, p. 546). In 1845, F. H. A. Scrivener asserted: "King James's revisers sometimes retain the renderings of the Bishops' Bible, where they are decidedly inferior to that of the Geneva New Testament" (*Supplement of the Authorized English Version*, Vol. I, p. 94).

The 1560 Geneva Bible is the source of many of the better and more accurate renderings in the KJV. Much of the translating work involved in the making of the Geneva Bible was kept in the KJV. Blackford Condit asserted that the Geneva Bible "makes the Authorized version what it is now" (*History,* p. 265). David Daniell maintained that the KJV translators "took over a great deal of Geneva's text verbatim" (Introduction to *Tyndale's New Testament*, p. xiii). David Daniell suggested that the Geneva Bible's "text, with only minor changes in 1576, remained constant, and was the main stream which carried Tyndale forward to King James's translators" (*The Bible in English*, p. 301). James D. G. Dunn maintained that "more than eighty percent of the language of the most popular Geneva Bible was drawn from Tyndale" (Burke, *KJV at 400*, p. 255). Ronald Cammenga observed: "In spite of the king's antipathy towards the Geneva Bible, it was given a prominent place as the translators went about their work" (*Protestant Reformed Theological Journal*, November, 2011, p. 58). Gerald Hammond maintained that "the Geneva Bible, not the Bishops' Bible, became the foundation of the Authorized Version" (*Making of the English Bible,* p. 144). Cleland Boyd McAfee contended that "the Genevan version was most influential" in the making of the KJV (*Greatest English Classic,* p. 62). W. F. Moulton asserted that "though the Bishops' Bible nominally furnished the basis for the new translation [the KJV], it is clear that the Geneva exercised a much more powerful influence" (*History of the English Bible*, p. 201). David Norton affirmed: "Though not the draft the KJB translators were directed to base their work on, it [the Geneva Bible] was the immediate predecessor that had most influence on the KJB" (*KJB: a Short History*, p. 19). Steven Voth wrote: "Recognizing the fact that the Bishops' Bible was used as the basic text, it is generally agreed that the changes incorporated into the KJV were most influenced by the Geneva Bible" (Youngblood, *Challenge of Bible Translation*, p. 332). Leland Ryken maintained that the Geneva Bible "contributed more than any other version to the King James Bible of 1611" (*Worldly Saints,* p. 138). John Greider observed: "The Geneva Bible was the most influential Bible in the preparation of the Authorized Version of 1611; its form, style, and content served, more than that of any other English Bible, as the model for the translators of the Bible of 1611" (*English Bible Translations*, p. 278). James Stobaugh asserted that "examination of the 1611 King James Bible shows clearly that its translators were influenced much more by the Geneva Bible than any other source" (*Studies in World History*, Vol. 2, p. 119). Charles Butterworth wrote: "In the lineage of the King James Bible this volume [the Geneva Bible] is by all means the most important single volume" (*Literary Lineage of the KJB,* p. 163). David Allen wrote: "The heavy dependence of the King James Bible upon the Geneva Bible demonstrates its superior excellence by providing the King James's men with more material than any other single source" (*Jewel in the King's Crown*, p. 59). Marvin Vincent maintained that the Geneva Bible "exercised the most marked influence of all the early translations upon the Authorized Version of 1611" (*History of the Textual Criticism*, p. 59). *The Cambridge History of the Bible* observed that the "Geneva contributed clarity and precision" to the KJV (Vol. 3, p. 167). H. Wheeler Robinson maintained that in the KJV "sometimes the Geneva text and the Geneva margin is taken over intact, sometimes the text becomes the margin and the margin the text" (*Bible in its Ancient and English Versions*, p. 206).

KJV-only author Jack Moorman noted that "many of its [the Geneva Bible's] improvements, in phrase or in interpretation, were adopted in the Authorised Version" (*Forever Settled,* pp. 180-181). KJV defender Kirk DiVietrio claimed: "Although King James told them to use the Bishops' Bible as their source, it was in fact the Geneva Bible which was used as the base of the King James Bible" (*Cleaning-Up Hazardous Materials*, p. 221). Kirk DiVietro declared that "the King James Bible came in large part directly from the Geneva Bible" (p. 219). Peter Ruckman noted that "the AV translators did not use the Geneva Bible for every reading" (*Bible Babel*, p. 64), which would suggest that he recognized that they did adopt many renderings from it.

The 1560 Geneva Bible was the word of God in English before the KJV ever existed. The Geneva Bible was also "able-to-make-thee-wise-unto-salvation" Scripture translated into English (2 Tim. 3:15) and "profitable-for-doctrine" Scripture (2 Tim. 3:16) before the KJV was ever translated and printed. Many English speakers read the engrafted word which is able to save their souls (James 1:21) in the Geneva Bible. English-speaking believers could read, study, learn, memorize, preach, and live by the Geneva Bible, and they did. In their comments to the brethren of England, Scotland, Ireland, etc. in the 1560 edition, the Geneva Bible translators wrote: "Seeing the great opportunity and occasions, which God presented unto us in this church, by reason of so many godly and learned men and such diversities of translations in divers tongues, we undertook this great and wonderful work (with all reverence, as in the presence of God, as intreating the words of God, whereunto we think ourselves insufficient) which now God according to his divine providence and mercy hath directed to a most prosperous end. And this we may with good conscience protest, we have in every point and word, according to the measure of that knowledge which it pleased almighty God to give us, faithfully rendered the text, and in all hard places most sincerely expounded the same. For God is our witness that we have, by all means endeavored to set forth the purity of the word and right sense of the Holy Ghost for the edifying of the brethren in faith and charity."

Who were the translators and Bible revisers that produced the Geneva Bible? There is no official complete list or record that presents all the men that may have been involved in the translating of this good English Bible. David Norton maintained that the Geneva Bible "was the work of a dozen or so Protestant scholars living in exile from an England that had returned to Catholicism under Queen Mary" (*KJB: a Short History*, p. 19). David Daniell noted that "a manuscript *Life* of Whittingham in the Bodleian Library in Oxford tells of a group of 'learned men' in Geneva meeting to 'peruse' the existing English versions of the New Testament" (*Bible in English*, p. 278). Daniell pointed out that those mentioned as being part of this group include Miles Coverdale, Christopher Goodman, Anthony Gilbey, Thomas Sampson, William Cole, and William Whittingham, and that "they were possibly joined in committee by John Knox, and certainly later for the whole Bible by William Kette (or Kethe), John Baron, John Pullain, John Bodley, and W. Williams" (Ibid.). Diarmaid MacCulloch suggested that "English admirers of Calvin produced" the Geneva Bible (*The Reformation*, p. 240). In his 1730 book, Anthony Johnson referred to a group of men in Geneva who "employed themselves, in translating the Holy Bible into English, intending to do it with more exactness than hitherto had been done, having the opportunity of consulting with Calvin and Beza in order thereunto" (*Historical Account of the Several English Translations*, p. 66). In his 1739 book, John Lewis listed the translators as Miles Coverdale, Christopher Goodman, Anthony Gilby, William Whittingham, Thomas Sampson, and William Cole, and noted that some add John Knox, John Bodleigh, and John Pullain to that list (*Complete History of the Several Translations,* p. 206). At its entry for the Geneva Bible, the *New Cambridge Bibliography of English Literature* also numbered the same above first six names as among its translators (p. 1835). Olga Opfell enumerated its translators as Whittingham, Gilby, Sampson, and "possibly William Kethe, William Cole, John Baron, and William Williams" (*KJB Translators,* p. 22). David Bannerman maintained that William Keith was "one of the translators of the Geneva Bible" (*Worship of the Presbyterian Church*, p. 36). *The Dictionary of National Biography* also claimed that William Kethe (?-1608) "acted as one of the translators of the Geneva Bible" (XI, p. 74). This same reference work noted that Cole (?-1600) joined with

Coverdale, Whittingham, Gilby, Sampson, and others in producing the Geneva Bible (IV, p. 731). Benjamin Brook maintained that the translators of the Geneva Bible "were Coverdale, Goodman, Gilby, Whittingham, Sampson, Cole, Knox, Bodleigh, and Pullain, all celebrated puritans" (*Lives of the Puritans,* I, p. 125). KJV-only author David Cloud noted that "it is even possible that John Knox assisted in the project" (*Faith,* p. 521). John Strype asserted that John Knox was one of the Geneva translators (*Life of Matthew Parker,* I, p. 409). Williston Walker also claimed that John Knox "laboured on the Genevan version" (*History of the Christian Church,* pp. 369-370). In his introduction to a facsimile reprint of the 1560 Geneva Bible, Lloyd Berry noted that "a letter from Miles Coverdale to William Cole in Geneva, dated February 22, 1560, indicates that Gilby, Cole, Kethe, Baron, and Williams had remained with Whittingham to finish the work on the Bible and to see it through the press" (p. 8). All the available information and evidence together suggests that there was likely a larger group who began the preparation and translating work with a smaller group finishing it. Perhaps one possible reason some of those that may have been involved in the translating may not be known is that the accession of Queen Elizabeth in England permitted some of them to return to England in 1559. John Knox and Christopher Goodman had been chosen or elected as pastors of the congregation of English exiles at Geneva. Miles Coverdale, who was godfather to John Knox's son, became an elder of this congregation. Ken Connolly maintained that Whittingham succeeded Knox as pastor of the English congregation in Geneva in 1559 (*Indestructible Book,* p. 154).

Alan Macgregor asserted that "Knox's congregation bore the cost of the translation" (*400 Years On,* p. 284). David Daniell also noted that "the costs of the making were borne by the English congregation generally" (*Bible in English,* p. 294). F. F. Bruce maintained that "the expense of publishing the first edition of the Geneva Bible appears to have been borne by the English-speaking colony in Geneva" (*History of the Bible in English,* p. 91). John Eadie observed: "The cost of the first edition had been defrayed by the English congregation at Geneva" (*English Bible,* Vol. II, p. 32). Was the Geneva Bible the only early English Bible translation that may have been the work of the members of a local congregation in cooperation with its pastors? Kenneth Bradstreet maintained that the Geneva Bible translators "were among the Reformation's spiritual giants" (*KJV in History,* p. 111).

Along with indicating acceptance of its underlying text and its translating, KJV-only authors also acknowledge the popularity and wide use of the Geneva Bible. William Bradley wrote: "The Geneva Bible was the Bible of the people, the Bible of the persecuted Christians and martyrs of the faith, the Bible of choice among English-speaking people for over one hundred years, from its initial printing in 1560, fifty years before the King James Bible, until the 1660's" (*Purified Seven Times,* p. 87). Steven White asserted: "When the Geneva Bible was first printed, it quickly became the 'Bible of choice' by conservative scholars, preachers, evangelists, and pastors" (*White's Dictionary,* Vol. 2, p. 19). White added: "Overall, the Geneva Bible is a fine English Bible that was used by many great old preachers and churches alike" (p. 20). Robert Sargent and Laurence Vance both confirmed that the Geneva Bible "became the Bible of the people" (*English Bible,* p. 197; *Brief History,* p. 19). Michael Bates also maintained that "the Geneva Bible became the Bible of the people, dearly beloved by all" (*Inspiration, Preservation, and the KJV,* p. 291). Phil Stringer referred to the Geneva as "the people's Book" and as "the Bible of the common man" (*History of the English Bible,* p. 13). William Bradley commented: "The Geneva Bible was the most widespread English Bible for a period of about one hundred years, from the 1560's to the 1660's" (*To All Generations,* p. 64). David L. Brown wrote: "The Geneva Version quickly became very popular in England" (*Indestructible Book,* p. 324). Michael Bates claimed: "The Geneva Bible retained its dominance even after the publication of the KJV. It would be more than a hundred years before the Geneva Bible would finally give way to the KJV" (*Inspiration, Preservation, and the KJV,* p. 291). James Kahler wrote: "Much of England would use the Geneva Bible until the middle of the 1600's" (*Charted History of the Bible,* p. 16). J. W. Sawyer maintained that the Geneva "was the most read Bible in Great Britain, even years after the Authorized Version was published in 1611" (*Legacy of our English Bible,* pp. 8-9). David Cloud asserted: "The Geneva quickly became the most popular English Bible and wielded a powerful influence for almost 100 years" (*Rome and the Bible,* p. 108, *Glorious History,*

p. 123).

Likewise, other authors also point out the fact of the wide acceptance and popularity of the Geneva Bible. Robert Girdlestone asserted that the Geneva Bible "from 1560 to 1640 was practically the authorized version of the English people" (*How to Study the English Bible*, p. 11). Leland Ryken maintained that "the Geneva Bible was 'the King James Bible' of its day" (*Legacy of the KJB*, ebook without page numbers). Benson Bobrick claimed that "the Geneva enjoyed de facto official status, and some of its bindings in folio even had 'Queen Elizabeth Bible' stamped on their bindings" (*Wide as the Waters*, p. 215). Ronald Cammenga wrote: "Without question, the Bible that was of greatest influence among English-speaking people prior to the King James Bible was the Geneva Bible" (*Protestant Reformed Theological Journal*, November, 2011, p. 48). David Norton maintained that the Geneva Bible "was by far the most successful English Bible for at least eighty years, going through about 140 editions up to 1644" (*KJB: A Short History*, p. 19).

John Kerr maintained that "the Geneva translators strove for a version that everyone could read" (*Ancient Texts*, p. 91). John Kerr asserted: "With the Geneva Bible we have a true 'people's Bible'—written in vigorous English, exhibiting careful scholarship without sounding pedantic, and widely available" (p. 93). Leland Ryken observed that "this Bible quickly became the household Bible of English-speaking Protestants" (*Word of God in English*, p. 49). Gustavus Paine noted that "the household Bible of the English people was the one which was produced at Geneva" (*Men Behind the KJV,* p. 9). Alan Macgregor observed: "The book of the people was undoubtedly the Geneva Bible" (*400 Years On*, p. 286). Ira Price asserted that "the Geneva Bible immediately sprang into full-grown popularity" (*Ancestory of our English Bible,* p. 265). In an introductory article to a 2006 modern-spelling edition of a 1599 edition of the Geneva Bible, Marshall Foster asserted: "The Geneva Bible was an instant success that captures the hearts of the people with its powerful, uncompromising prose" (p. xxiv). Marshall Foster maintained that "for generations after its first printing, the Geneva Bible remained the Bible of personal study in England, Scotland, and then in America" (p. xxiv). Ismar Peritz wrote: "The success of the Geneva Bible was unprecedented. It was hailed with delight by the common people" (*The Christian Advocate*, April 13, 1911, p. 486). *The Dictionary of National Biography* pointed out that the Geneva Bible "was the Bible on which most Englishmen in Elizabethan England were brought up" (Vol. XXI, p. 152). Vishal Mangalwadi asserted: "For more than a hundred years, the Geneva Bible dominated the English-speaking world" (*Book That Made Your World*, p. 155). Alison Jack wrote: "During the Elizabethan and much of the Jacobite era, it was the Geneva Bible that was the most widely read Bible in the English-speaking world" (*Bible and Literature*, p. 2). Jacobus Naude asserted that "the Puritan's Geneva Version (in print 1560-1644) enjoyed broad popularity as the most widely read Bible of the Elizabethan era and subsequently of the Jacobean era" (Burke, *KJV at 400*, p. 160). Derek Wilson noted: "During the Queen's reign alone it went through forty impressions, and for at least two generations thereafter it was to be the most popular Bible for family reading and private devotional use" (*People's Bible*, p. 68). *The Oxford Illustrated History of the Bible* indicated that the Geneva Bible "enjoyed great popularity among English Protestants for the rest of the century and to the end of the next" (p. 117). Paul Olson referred to the Geneva Bible as "the most widely used Bible in England and the Bible that Shakespeare used most often" (*Beyond a Common Joy*, p. 126). In an introductory essay in a reprint of the 1602 edition of the Geneva New Testament, Gerald Sheppard observed: "The Geneva Bible became the most popular Bible in England and America and remained so until about 1640" (p. 1). Ed Hindson acknowledged that the Geneva Bible "was the most popular Bible of its day" (*Popular Encyclopedia of Church History*, p. 156). Gerald Bray confirmed that "the Geneva Bible became and remained the popular text, read and studied by all classes of the population" (*Documents of the English Reformation,* p. 355). Diarmaid MacCulloch maintained that the Geneva Bible "proved a best-seller in the English-speaking world" (*The Reformation*, p. 240). James Stobaugh wrote: "The Geneva Bible became English-speaking Christians' Bible of choice for over 100 years" (*Studies in World History*, Vol. 2, p. 119). Concerning the Geneva, H. D. M. Spence wrote: "It became the most popular of all versions, and was largely read in England" (*The Church of England: A History*, Vol. III, p. 370).

John Brown wrote: "For nearly a hundred years the Genevan Bible was the favourite version of the common people" (*History of the English Bible*, p. 81). H. Rondel Rumburg acknowledged that "the small Geneva Bibles had found their ways into the homes and hearts of the common people" (*William Bridge*, p. 16). Basil Hall asserted that the Geneva Bible "was for almost a century the most popular Bible version in English" (Backus, *Reformed Roots*, p. xii). J. Patterson Smyth maintained that "The Genevan was the favorite of the people in general" (*How We Got Our Bible*, p. 123). John C. Mincy asserted that the Geneva Bible "was the common people's Bible of Scotland and England from its publication in 1560 until 1660" (Williams, *From the Mind of God*, p. 129). Samuel Newth noted that the Geneva Bible "was the form of the Bible most largely circulated in this country [Great Britain]" "for nearly a century onward" (*Lectures*, p. 26). Christopher Anderson maintained that "the readers of the Geneva Bible, as a body, cannot be distinguished by any opprobrious party epithet of the day, for that version was to be found in all the families of England where the Scriptures were read at all" (*Annals*, II, p. 355). Blackford Condit asserted that the Geneva Bible "very soon became the Bible of the household, and for more than a century and a half it maintained its place as the Bible of the people" (*History*, p. 245). Blackford Condit also observed: "So universally was this Bible accepted, that it was read from the pulpit, quoted in sermons, cited by authors, and adopted in the family" (p. 250). Benson Bobrick wrote: "Within England its recognized superiority to all other versions, and its wide distribution and use, made it a powerful instrument of religious reform" (*Wide as the Waters*, p. 175). *The Oxford Companion to English Literature* noted that the Geneva Bible "became the most popular English Bible for a century" (p. 125).

Neil Lightfoot maintained that the Geneva Bible "continued its popular acceptance even after the appearance of the King James Version" (*How We Got Our Bible*, p. 181). Edwin W. Rice asserted: "For more than twenty years after the issue of the King James Version the Genevan Version was widely, if not generally, used in private and public worship" (*Our Sixty-six Sacred Books*, p. 14). Jacobus Naude claimed that "it took decades for the KJV to displace the Geneva Version in popular acceptance" (Burke, *KJV at 400*, p. 162). Concerning the Geneva Bible, Boyd Winchester wrote: "Its advantages were so many and so great that it at once secured and--even after the appearance of King James's Bible--continued to retain a firm hold upon the bulk of the English nation" (*The Swiss Republic*, p. 275). Alister McGrath asserted: "The irrefutable evidence is that, far from rushing out to buy or make use of this new translation [the KJV], people preferred to use an English translation from fifty years earlier--the Geneva Bible" (*In the Beginning*, pp. 277-278). Derek Wilson wrote: "As for the Geneva Bible it remained the most popular version of Scripture for at least a generation after 1611" (*People's Bible*, p, 120). Samuel Fisk acknowledged that "the influence of the Geneva Bible continued for a considerable time even after publication of the King James Version in 1611" (*Calvinistic Paths*, p. 74). Andrew E. Hill maintained that "it would take fifty years for the KJB to overtake the popularity of the Geneva Bible" (Burke, *KJV at 400*, p. 348). Andrew Edgar noted that "long after 1611 the Geneva version continued to be the household Bible of a large portion of the English people" (*Bibles of England*, p. 326). John Kerr claimed: "In fact, the Geneva Bible continued to be the most popular version of the Bible for a generation after the King James Version came out in 1611" (*Ancient Texts*, p. 92). John Kerr also commented: "The public clung to their love for the Geneva Bible and it took a generation for the KJV to replace it in popular affection" (p. 130). Norman Landis wrote: "The Geneva in fact, remained more popular than the King James Version until decades after its original release in 1611" (*Do You Know Your Bible*, p. 34). After referring to the publication of the 1611, Richard Lovett asserted that "for twenty-five years the Geneva Bible continued in use in many churches" (*Printed English Bible*, p. 150). Harold Bloom claimed: "The Geneva Bible prevailed for a hundred years, blocking out the KJB for its first fifty years or so" (*Shadow of a Great Rock*, p. 19). Charles Pastoor maintained that "only after the Restoration [1660] did the King James Bible replace the Geneva in popular esteem" (*A to Z of the Puritans*, p. 133). Adam Nicolson asserted: "Geneva Bibles continued to be printed until 1644, and only the Restoration in 1660 did the King James Bible . . . come to take its place as the Bible itself, the national text" (*God's Secretaries*, p. 229). Eugene Chen Eoyang claimed: "Actually, it was two generations before the KJV assumed its place as the supreme English translation of the

Bible. The Geneva Bible, and not the King James Version (or Authorized Version), was the most popular for at least a generation after the appearance of the KJV" (*Borrowed Plumage: Polemical Essays on Translation*, p. 105). Charles Boyce observed that "the Geneva Bible was so powerful a literary text that the Bishops' Bible actually relied on it to some extent, as, later did the creators of the King James Version" (*Shakespeare A to Z*, p. 63).

In his introduction to his modern-spelling edition of Tyndale's 1534 New Testament, David Daniell pointed out: "This, the Geneva Bible, was made for readers at all levels, and it was for nearly a century the Bible of the English people, used by all wings of the English church" (p. xi). Diarmaid MacCulloch indicated that a "half a million copies of the Geneva Bible" were printed and that the surviving copies indicate that they "have usually been read to bits" (*Reformation,* p. 569). Dale S. Kuehne maintained that the Geneva Bible "continued to be the Bible of Calvinists in both England and America into the 1700's" (Kries, *Piety and Humanity*, p. 214). L. C. Vass noted that "like a Scotchman, he [George Durant] brought his Geneva Bible with him" to North Carolina in 1662 (*History of the Presbyterian Church in New Bern*, p. 11). David Norton cited where Thomas Ward in 1688 indicated that Bibles printed in 1562, 1577, and 1579 [editions of the Geneva Bible] were still "in many men's hands" (*History of the English Bible as Literature*, p. 39). In a footnote, Norton pointed out that "sixteenth-century Geneva Bibles with eighteenth-century inscriptions are quite common" (p. 39, footnote 3). He gave the example of one Geneva Bible in a New Zealand library that "contains signatures, comments and records that date from 1696 to 1877." Alec Gilmore observed that there is some evidence that a 1610 edition of the Geneva Bible "was still being used in Aberdeenshire as late as 1674" (*Dictionary,* p. 84). John Brown noted that "as late as the close of the 18th century a Genevan Bible was still in use in the church of Crail in Fifeshire" (*History of the English Bible,* p. 84).

It should also be noted that some editions of the Geneva Bible had been printed after 1644. David Daniell noted that the Geneva-Tomson-Junius edition was reprinted in 1776 with Matthew Parker's preface to the Bishops' and that the Geneva Bible without the Apocrypha was again reprinted in 1778 (*Bible in English,* p. 621). T. H. Darlow and H. F. Moule listed a 1776 "reprint of the Geneva Bible, with Tomson's revised New Testament and Junius' Revelation" and referred to "a similar reprint of 1778" (*Historical Catalogue of the Printed Editions*, I, p. 301). Donald Brake affirmed that editions of the Geneva Bible were printed in 1776 and 1778 (*Visual History of the English Bible,* p. 160). In 1841, Samuel Bagster reprinted the 1557 Geneva or Whittingham's New Testament in *The English Hexapla*. In 1842, a facsimile reprint of the 1557 Genevan New Testament was printed for Samuel Bagster. The 1962 *New Testament Octapla* included the N. T. text of the 1560 Geneva Bible. A facsimile reprint of the 1560 Geneva Bible was printed by the University of Wisconsin Press in 1969. A 1602 edition of the Geneva New Testament was reprinted in 1989 by the Pilgrim Press. A modern-spelling edition of the 1557 Geneva or Whittingham's New Testament as edited by John Wesley Sawyer was printed in 1990. A facsimile reprint of a 1599 edition of the Geneva Bible was printed in 1991 by the Geneva Publishing Company. A facsimile of a 1591 Cambridge edition of the Geneva Bible was printed in 1993 by Cambridge University Press. The text of a 1587 edition of the Geneva Bible was available as a reprint from the Bible Reader's Museum. The Bible Museum in Arizona had a facsimile edition of the 1560 Geneva Bible printed in 2006. A modern-spelling edition of the 1599 Geneva Bible was published by Tolle Lege Press in 2006. The 1969 facsimile edition of the 1560 Geneva Bible was reprinted by Hendrickson Publishers in 2007. Thus, the Geneva Bible is a presently available English translation.

Perhaps one of the reasons for the popularity of the Geneva Bible was its generally informative and helpful marginal notes. The value of the notes in this Bible was pointed out by Gerald Hammond in the following statement: "What the Geneva translators had done, in effect, was to give every reader the tools to be his own Bible scholar" (*Making of the English Bible*, p. 95). In his introduction to the facsimile edition, Lloyd Berry maintained that in the Geneva Bible "the English people had a Bible, scholarly in translation, but also designed for use by the laity;

and it is quite evident that the 'aids' the translators provided accounted for its extraordinary popularity among the people" (p. 13). William Bradley asserted that the Geneva Bible "was designed to be a 'self-help' study Bible, in case the Christians remained in exile indefinitely" (*Purified Seven Times,* p. 85). Bradley noted that "the notes were placed there to aid in Bible study and to assist the exiled believers in proper Biblical interpretation and in 'rightly dividing the word of truth'" (Ibid.). Doug Stauffer maintained that the Geneva Bible "included thousands of explanatory notes which promoted study and understanding of the text" (*One Book Stands Alone,* p. 283). David Cloud observed: "The Geneva Bible contained many notes, explaining the text, teaching Protestant doctrine, and in some cases, condemning Roman Catholicism" (*Glorious History of the KJB,* p. 121). Gerald Hammond wrote: "The Geneva Bible gave the English people not only a verse-divided, thoughtfully annotated, easily acquired, and portable version of the Scriptures, but one whose translation itself was equal in scholarship of anything that had appeared on the continent, and one whose style was, in more than its basics, the style of the Authorized Version" (*Making of the English Bible,* pp. 135-136). Bernard Levinson and Joshua Berman concluded: "The usefulness of the marginal notes made the Geneva Bible very popular among the general population" (*KJB at 400,* p. 4). David Daniell maintained: "The notes work most of the time to increase the reader's understanding of the text" (*Bible in English,* p. 307). Daniell asserted: "The point of the Geneva Bibles is to help understanding and faith" (p. 375). Daniell observed: "In the Geneva Old Testament there are more notes in the poetic and prophetic books than in the narrative histories and laws" (p. 298). Daniell claimed that "the sheer strangeness of Hebrew poetry needs interpretative help if it is to mean anything in English" (Ibid.). Daniell contended: "Stripping away Geneva's marginal notes to the Prophets can produce in a reader of KJV a nearly total lack of understanding, something often close to gibberish" (p. 315). Hannibal Hamlin wrote: "The Geneva Bible was the first 'Study Bible' geared to the average, inexpert reader" (*KJB after 400 Years,* p. 214). Hannibal Hamlin noted: "These copious notes made this Bible popular with everyone, however, since most of them were not polemical but interpretative. Such notes were designed for private reading" (*Bible in Shakespeare,* p. 11). As a personal teaching Bible, David Norton observed that the Geneva Bible places "the emphasis very strongly on private ownership, close study and doctrinal correctness" (*History of the English Bible,* p. 81). Concerning the Geneva, Lori Ferrell wrote: "This multitude of 'helps,' along with its compact size, made it the first Bible designed to assist the common English readers, which in turn made it popular on an unprecedented scale" (*The Bible and the People,* p. 83). *The Cambridge History of the Bible* observed that "the notes of the original 1560 Geneva Bible are as a whole generally Protestant in intention rather than specifically Calvinist" (Vol. 3, p. 158). After mentioning that the marginal notes in the KJV were "an educational aid," David Norton noted that "the Geneva notes provided much more substantial aid, and those were what the people missed most in the KJV" (Burke, *KJV at 400,* p. 19). Benson Bobrick asserted that "legions of readers had also come to depend on the Geneva notes, professing that without 'such spectacles' they could not understand the text" (*Wide as the Waters,* pp. 253-254). In his article in a modern-spelling edition of the 1599 Geneva Bible, Marshall Foster wrote: "When the Geneva Bible disappeared, there were widespread complaints that people 'could not see into the sense of Scripture for lack of the spectacles of those Genevan annotations'" (p. xxiv).

The Geneva Bible had a very important influence on America and its founding. Jack P. Lewis maintained that "the Mayflower Compact was signed on the Geneva Bible, and the Geneva played an important role in the history of early America" (*The English Bible from KJV to NIV,* p. 26). Robert McCrum asserted that "the first New England settlements always championed the use of the Geneva Bible" (*Globish: How the English Language,* p. 90). David Daniell noted: "The Geneva Bible was at the heart of the founding of those colonies, as will be seen, in a greater way than even [the] KJV" (*Bible in English,* p. 221). Daniell contended: "This evidence of the regular use of the Geneva Bible can be supported by many documents from the colonies" (p. 425). Cotton Mather (1663-1729) in his history of Harvard referred to "the notes in the Geneva Bible (which were considered authoritative)" (Hall, *Genevan Reformation and the American*

Founding, p. 313). David Cloud maintained that "the Bible brought to America by its first settlers in the early 1600's was the Geneva Bible" (*Rome and the Bible*, p. 106). Steve Green and Todd Hillard asserted: "Throughout the 1600's as people fled the religious persecution of England by crossing the Atlantic, they brought with them their precious Geneva Bibles rather than the 'King's Bible.' The Geneva Bible was more popular than the King James Version for several decades" (*The Bible in America*, p. 33). G. S. Wegener maintained that the Geneva Bible "was to become equally popular in America, where it accompanied many who exiled themselves from Britain for conscience's sake" (*6000 Years*, p. 237). Jack Lewis also confirmed that "the Geneva played an important role in the history of early America" (*English Bible*, p. 26). James P. Stobaugh asserted: "American was founded upon the Geneva Bible, not the King James Bible" (*Studies in World History*, Vol. 2, p. 120). J. Paul Foster wrote: "It can truthfully be said that this version shaped America. For it was the Geneva Bible that the Pilgrims brought over with them to America, and, as all their laws and institutions were founded on that Book, and their Bible was the Geneva version, was not America's childhood shaped by that version?" (*The Christian Nation*, Vol. 54, June 7, 1911, p. 5). David Hall asserted: "Primary documents confirm the thesis we have been documenting: the Declaration of Independence, acts of the Continental Congress between 1776 and 1787, and the United States Constitution all bear the impress of two centuries of Calvinistic thinking" (*Genevan Reformation*, p, 420). Hall wrote: "Other transporters of Calvinism to the West were the Geneva Bible and Beza's *New Testament Annotations*" (p. 286).

Many KJV-only advocates seem to be unaware of the fact that most (if not all) of the same types of differences can be found between earlier pre-1611 English Bibles such as the Geneva Bible and the KJV as can be found when the KJV is compared to later English Bibles such as the NKJV. If any of them are aware of this fact, they evidently try to avoid it or at least minimize it. Regardless of their praise for the overall textual basis and translating in the Geneva Bible, KJV-only advocates may acknowledge that they disagree with a few of its individual renderings which differ from those in the KJV. The few Geneva Bible renderings that KJV-only authors have criticized may indicate that they assume that the number of differences would be few and mostly minor in nature.

For example concerning Hebrews 10:12, KJV-only author David Daniels asserted: "So the King James rightly said Jesus' one sacrifice for sins was forever. The Geneva instead says that Jesus offered one sacrifice for sins, then set down forever. But anyone can see this is false, when we compare it to Stephen's visions of heaven, as being stoned to death in Acts 7:55-56" (*Can You Trust Just One Bible*, ebook without page numbers). The placement of the comma in Hebrews 10:12 would change the understanding or interpretation of the verse. Evidently David Daniels is unaware of the fact that beginning with the 1638 Cambridge standard edition of the KJV until a London edition printed by George Eyre and Andrew Spottiswoode in 1838, most KJV editions had the comma after "sins" and before "forever sat down." For two hundred years, the presentation or punctuation that David Daniels condemned as false was standard in most KJV editions. The standard 1762 Cambridge KJV edition and the standard 1769 Oxford KJV edition still had the comma after "sins" and before "forever sat down."

Sometimes the KJV has more words than the 1560 Geneva Bible or 1568 Bishops' Bible, and sometimes it has fewer words. At times the makers of the KJV sometimes changed one part of speech or one grammatical form in one or more of the earlier pre-1611 English translations into another one. Many actual differences between the Geneva Bible and the KJV can be found in number of words, in meaning of words, in whether a noun or pronoun is used, in number or person of pronouns, in whether a phrase, clause, adjective, or adverb is used, in shifting of the position of words, phrases, or clauses in a sentence, in use of italics, etc. Several of the many differences between the 1560 Geneva Bible and the 1611 KJV can be considered significant, and at least a few of the differences were textual.

Many times the makers of the KJV changed the part of speech or grammatical form of the original language words, sometimes translated an original language word by more than one English word, and sometimes did not give a literal word-for-word rendering of original language words. David Cloud acknowledged: "We understand that the translation of the Scriptures requires certain changes in words and sentence structures because of the nature of human language" (*Faith vs. the Modern Bible Versions*, p. 371; *Bible Version Question/Answer*, p. 32). David Cloud asserted: "We know that the translation will not have exactly the same number and order of words as the original" (<u>Ibid</u>.). On the other hand, David Cloud also claimed: "The omission even of single words is frequently a significant doctrinal issue" (*Bible Version Question/Answer*, p. 29). Doug Stauffer admitted: "One cannot translate from one language into another without introducing some variation, since certain words must be added in order to complete the sense of the new language" (*One Book Stands Alone,* p. 240). Concerning Greek verbs, Gail Riplinger claimed: "No translation translates them uniformly. It is virtually impossible" (*Hazardous Materials*, p. 390). Gail Riplinger admitted: "Greek verb tenses do not match English verb tenses" (p. 457). Peter Ruckman asserted: "No translator ever translated all the articles from any text" (*Bible Believers' Bulletin*, June, 1980, p. 7). H. D. Williams acknowledged that "changing a word in a translation cannot be compared to changing the original received Words" (*Pure Words*, p. 75). Some KJV-only advocates will sometimes make claims that in effect contradict Williams' assertion since they do seem to assert that changing any words in the KJV is comparable to changing original received words.

<u>KJV-only allegations concerning the NKJV considered</u>

While ignoring or avoiding many relevant facts concerning the actual existence of these same types of differences between the Geneva Bible and the KJV, some KJV-only advocates will inconsistently and unjustly assert that any of these same differences between the KJV and the NKJV are to be in effect considered comparable to changing preserved original language words and are to be considered dynamic equivalencies, serious defects, or errors in the NKJV. For example, these same types of differences between the KJV and the NKJV are labeled by D. A. Waite as "not faithfulness in translation," not accuracy in translation," "not reliability in translation," but as "diabolical dynamic equivalency" (*NKJV compared to KJV*, pp. xi-xiii). D. A. Waite had claimed: "These three things, subtracting, changing, and adding to the Word of God, are the essence and heart of dynamic equivalency in its approach to translation" (*Defending the KJB*, p. 93). Waite alleged: "There's nothing more Satanic than altering or changing the Words of God" (<u>Ibid</u>., p. 107). Waite maintained that the dynamic equivalency technique "is devilish" (*Central Seminary Refuted,* p. 15). Waite asserted: "When you use the technique of dynamic equivalency you do not preserve truth" (*Foes*, p. 121). He also alleged: "The King James Bible translators did not use dynamic equivalency" (<u>Ibid.</u>, p. 62). Waite claimed that "the 'Christian faith' is also 'threatened' by the sloppy and inaccurate translation technique of these paraphrased so-called 'translations' in their use of 'dynamic equivalency'" (*Fundamentalist Deception,* p. 19). Waite contended: "This whole idea of dynamic equivalence, either modified, or complete, is still adding, subtracting, or changing in some way the Words of God. It is not proper translation and it is sin" (p. 100). Would KJV-only advocates be correct and just in their apparent attempts to apply inconsistently the scriptural teachings concerning the specific, exact original language words given by inspiration of God to the prophets and apostles to the work of revision and translation in post-1611 English Bibles but not to the same work of revision and translation in the pre-1611 English Bibles and in the 1611 KJV?

In complete contrast to their very positive comments and praise for the 1560 Geneva Bible and other pre-1611 English Bibles, documented evidence will reveal that many KJV defenders and KJV-only authors are often unedifying, intemperate, presumptuous, extremely critical, very negative, unfair, derogatory, or harsh toward the NKJV. Broad-sweeping generalizations and serious accusations have been made concerning the NKJV that have not actually proven to be factually true and that have not demonstrated to be based on use of consistent, sound, just measures or standards. Some of the KJV-only accusations are extreme and outrageous, and they may often be based on use of fallacies and double standards. Many actual allegations against the NKJV made by KJV-only advocates and quoted in their own words will clearly demonstrate that the adjectives above used to describe those KJV-only allegations are fair and accurate.

On her cassette entitled "Detailed Update," Gail Riplinger claimed the following about the NKJV: "Every time they change from the King James to something different they follow the New World Translation of Jehovah Witnesses." In a taped interview with Texe Marrs, Gail Riplinger asserted that "the KJV always has easier words than the NKJV." Riplinger asked: "Why does the NKJV use harder words than the KJV?" (*Language of the KJB,* p. 152). Riplinger alleged: "Gross deviations from the world's ancient and pure Bible are seen in the NIV, TNIV, HCSB, NCV, ESV, NLT, NASB, and NKJV, which are shown to yoke their unsuspecting readers with the fringe Jehovah Witness sect and the sin-tinged Roman Catholic system" (*In Awe of Thy Word,* p. 41). Riplinger contended that "the resident evil and heresy in the New King James Version (NKJV) . . . lies in their editor's use of lexicons, all of which are corrupt" (*Hazardous Materials,* p. 29). Riplinger claimed that "all lexicons and Bible study 'helps' should be buried to prevent the spread of their deadly hazards" (p. 70). Riplinger even alleged that "the words seen today in the NKJV . . . were spawned in a cesspool of Satanic unbelief" (Ibid., p. 14).

William Bradley wrote: "Every word change in the text of the New King James Version was taken directly from the text that produced the Revised Standard Version, the New International Version, and all the other so-called bibles, the minority text of Westcott and Hort" (*Purified Seven Times,* pp. 121-122). Troy Clark claimed: "Anytime a word change is made away from the King James Bible, the NKJV new word matches identically the *New World Translation*--the Jehovah Witness Bible" (*Perfect Bible,* p. 233). Mickey Carter asserted: 'Even the slightest changes in the King James Version, including the *New King James Version,* came from the polluted 'stream'" (*Things that are Different,* p. 171). David Daniels contended that the NKJV "has instead copied the perverted NIV, NASV, or RSV" (*Answers,* p. 171). David Daniels alleged that "the Greek and Hebrew behind the NKJV are the same as for the modern perversions" (p. 178). Doug Stauffer claimed "that when the NKJV varies from the King James Bible reading, it follows the perverted readings of the NIV, NASV, RSV, etc." (*One Book One Authority,* p. 159). Doug Stauffer contended: "Even the *New King James Version* follows these corrupted readings when it differs from the *Textus Receptus*" (p. 591). Doug Stauffer even maintained that "The NWT, NIV, and NKJV are three peas in a pod" (*One Book Stands Alone,* p. 180). Stauffer alleged that the NKJV is "one of the most insidious bibles ever to hit the market" (p. 167). Michael D. O'Neal accused the NKJV of being one of "the devil's more crafty handiworks" (*Do We Have the Word of God,* p. 29). Malcolm Watts claimed that "in the actual text of the NKJV New Testament there are a great many departures from the Received Text when Critical Text readings have been apparently preferred and followed" although he only cited six supposed examples for his allegation (*NKJV: a Critique,* p. 8). Bruce A. Borders claimed that "the corrupted manuscripts of Alexandria were the predominate source for the translation [the NKJV]" (*The Only Bible,* p. 68). Bruce Borders contended that the NKJV "resembles the *New International Version* much more than it does the *King James Version*" (p. 69). Norman Hopkins asserted that the NKJV "is straight from hell" (*Right Bible,* p. 4). Jack Hyles accused the NKJV of being "of the Devil" or "satanically inspired" (*Need for an Every-Word Bible,* pp. 104, 97). Hyles alleged that "those rascals who edited and published the *New King James Bible* are false teachers" (p. 87).

Al Lacy argued that modern translations including even the NKJV "are corrupt because they came from Satan's preserved Alexandrian manuscripts" (*Can I Trust My Bible,* p. 18). David Sorenson alleged that "in reality, the NKJV is thoroughly adulterated with critical readings in both the Old and New Testaments" (*Neither Oldest Nor Best,* p. 35). D. A. Waite asserted that the NKJV has "more similarity to the English Revised Version (ERV) of 1881, the American Standard Version (ASV) of 1901, the New American Standard Version (NASV) of 1968, or the New International Version (NIV) of 1978, than to the KJV of 1611" (*NKJV Compared to KJV,* p. viii; *Defects in the NKJV,* p. 9). Waite's *Defined KJB* listed the NKJV on a corrupt tree of Bibles with

English Bibles made from the Critical Text (p. 1695). Waite claimed that "the New King James Version is the most dangerous Bible version on the market today" (*Defects in the NKJV*, p. 8). Waite contended that "the New King James Version Old Testament text is based on a different Hebrew text than the KJV" (p. 10). James Rasbeary also alleged that the NKJV "used a different Hebrew text than which was used to produce the King James Bible" (*What's Wrong with the RSV*, p. 48). Rasbeary claimed that "the NKJV is really just another piece of corrupt fruit from the Origen-Westcott-Hort family tree" and "is an Alexandrian version in disguise" (p. 46). David Cloud asserted that "the New King James Version (NKJV) is a deception" (*Answering the Myths*, p. 201). Bob Steward claimed that "the New King James Version is not a word for word translation" (*Why not the NKJV*, p. 5). William Grady contended that the NKJV "represents Satan's ultimate deception to oppose God's remnant" (*Final Authority*, p. 303). Grady claimed that the NKJV was "literally laced with 'old' readings from the Revised Standard and New American Standard Versions" and implied that these readings were a "revival of Alexandrian readings" (p. 305). The likely source of Grady's claim may have been Peter Ruckman. Ruckman asserted that "when the 'New' *KJV* came out, it was discovered that it had altered the *King James* text in more than five hundred places to bring it back in line with the RSV" (*How To Teach the 'Original' Greek,* p. 102). Charles Kriessman's book has the same corrupt tree chart from Waite's *DKJB* that listed the NKJV on its claimed corrupt tree (*Modern Version Failures*, p. 130). Do these extreme unproven allegations against the NKJV match up with some other assertions which have been made by KJV-only authors?

For example, KJV-only advocates assert that they consider fairly all the relevant evidence and deal with it objectively. D. A. Waite asserted: "It was Dean John William Burgon's method to take ALL of the evidence. This is what we ought to do" (*Fundamentalist Mis-Information*, p. 82). John William Burgon as edited by Edward Miller wrote: "My leading principle is to build solely upon facts, --upon real, not fancied facts, --not upon a few favourite facts, but upon all that are connected with the question under consideration" (*Traditional Text of the Holy Gospels*, p. 89). John William Burgon as edited by Edward Miller noted: "We are nothing, if we are not grounded in facts; our appeal is to facts, our test lies in facts, so far as we can we build testimonies upon testimonies and pile facts upon facts" (p. 238). KJV defender Edward Hills noted that believers need "to deal faithfully and conscientiously with all the pertinent facts" (*Unholy Hands*, Vol. 1, p. xxxvi). Doug Stauffer asserted: "When truth and error are examined side by side, the facts become clear" (*One Book Stands Alone*, p. 316). Peter Ruckman claimed: "At Pensacola Bible Institute, we give the students all the FACTS" (*How to Teach the Original Greek*, p. 99). David Cloud asserted: "It is my desire to give all the relevant facts in the Bible text-version debate" (*Faith vs the Modern Bible Versions*, p. 13). R. B. Ouellette maintained that "we have attempted to show facts that can be documented or qualified" (*A More Sure Word*, p. 21). Jeff McArdle observed: "A man who won't face facts will have to go against the truth and violate his own conscience" (*Bible Believer's Guide to Elephant Hunting*, p. 12). Roy Branson asked: "Why should we fear facts? Why should we fear the arguments of the opposition? If we can be proven wrong, should we not be grateful?" (*KJV 1611: Perfect*, p. 89). Marty Braemer noted: "Always weigh the evidence before determining your position in an argument" (*This Little Light,* p. 10). Thomas Corkish asserted: "There is no certainty, credibility, nor confidence without substantiality, foundation, evidence, data, verification, or documentation" (Brandenburg, *Thou Shalt Keep Them*, p. 139). Peter Ruckman acknowledged: "To 'say,' or to 'affirm' something is entirely different from proving it" (*Bible Babel*, p. 60). Ruckman suggested: "You can misrepresent a fact by omitting other facts" (*Problem Texts,* p. 357). Ruckman admitted that "with double standards you can prove anything" (*Biblical Scholarship*, p. 324), but he ignored the use of double standards evident in much KJV-only reasoning and in KJV-only allegations concerning the NKJV.

Do KJV defenders consistently practice what they preach or assert? Have KJV-only advocates actually taken all the evidence, evaluated it using consistent, just standards or measures, faced all the pertinent facts, and then proven their serious allegations against the NKJV? Do KJV-only advocates omit, overlook, or avoid many pertinent facts from and concerning the Geneva Bible, the KJV, and the NKJV, which could involve use of the fallacy of concealed evidence? Wilbur Pickering observed: "The truth is best served by the facts, the evidence. And the evidence should be presented in a straightforward fashion, without undue appeal to emotion" (*God Has Preserved His Text*, p. 243). David Cloud in effect acknowledged the problem with some inconsistent, unproven, extreme KJV-only allegations when he stated: "When our speaking and writing is filled with error of fact and is characterized by shoddy research and indefensible extremism, we discredit our entire position" (*O Timothy*, Issue 8, 1994, p. 12). David Cloud admitted: "It is true that the writings of some King James defenders contain an inordinate number of mistakes" (*Bible Version Question/Answer*, p. 120). Wilbur Pickering asserted: "The basic deficiency, both fundamental and serious, of any characterization based upon subjective criteria is that the result is only opinion; it is not objectively verifiable" (*Identity of NT Text II*, p. 52; *Identity of NT Text IV*, p. 84). Do KJV-only advocates make or repeat dogmatic, extreme allegations against the NKJV without checking their accuracy or without proving them to be true with use of just measures or standards? Do they make hasty overgeneralizations concerning the NKJV before they provide sufficient factual evidence to warrant them? Are the often broad-sweeping KJV-only generalizations and misleading, extreme accusations concerning the NKJV factually true when compared to all the valid, sound, pertinent evidence considered in the light of consistent just standards or measures? Do KJV defenders in effect seek to discredit the NKJV in a seemingly dishonest manner? Have KJV defenders justly and soundly divided that which is right from that which is wrong in their allegations against the NKJV? Is the KJV-only characterization of the NKJV based on consistent, objective criteria or on subjective criteria and use of fallacies? Do KJV-only authors typically present an objective, accurate, straightforward, balanced, just caricature of the NKJV and its translators, or do they present a subjective, inaccurate, unbalanced, unjust, biased, emotionally-charged one? Would many of the extreme KJV-only allegations against the NKJV involve the use of the fallacy of composition as the entire text of the NKJV is seemingly condemned based on a relatively small number of individual renderings? Would a consistent, just application of actual KJV-only allegations against the NKJV also to the KJV harm it?

Any fair, objective, consistent, sound analysis, test, and evaluation of several typical KJV-only assertions, conclusions, and accusations concerning the NKJV compared to their own positive assertions concerning the pre-1611 English Bibles such as the Geneva Bible could lead to the sound deduction or conclusion that they must be based on different measures, standards, or weights. In comparing the two sets of assertions and facing the pertinent facts, it is very obvious and clear that KJV defenders would have to be using one weight or measure for the pre-1611 English Bibles such as the Geneva Bible while using a different one for the NKJV. This evident use of different measures indicates a very serious problem concerning the accuracy of their assertions or accusations concerning the NKJV since the use of divers weights, divers measures, unjust balances, or double standards is wrong according to the Scriptures (Prov. 16:11, 10:10, 11:1, 20:23, Deut. 25:13-16, Ezek. 45:10, Lev. 19:35-36, Micah 6:11). Unrighteous divers weights, uneven or unjust balances, or unrighteous, untrue judgments are not of the LORD (Ps. 19:9). It should not be difficult for believers to see the clear inconsistency, hypocrisy, and duplicity in the use of unjust measures or double standards in allegations against the NKJV. A failure to use consistent, "altogether just" measures, standards, or principles (Deut. 16:20, Prov. 16:11, Ezek. 45:10, Deut. 25:15, Rom. 2:1-3) in comparing Bible translations would condemn the unfair, uneven, unreliable, and unjust judgments and accusations that would result. Would the use of inconsistent, unjust measures or standards in KJV-only allegations discredit their position concerning the NKJV and be disobedience to plain scriptural teachings?

The Reformers and early English Bible translators' view of the Scriptures

According to the early English translators including the KJV translators, Bible translations should be tried, evaluated, and compared to the preserved original language texts of Scripture. The title page and preface of the 1611 KJV maintained that it was translated from the Scriptures in the original languages. The separate title page for the New Testament in the 1611 edition asserted that it was "newly translated out of the original Greek." The first rule for the translating referred to "the truth of the original." The sixth and fifteen rule referred to "Hebrew" and "Greek."

Lancelot Andrewes, a leading KJV translator, wrote: "Look to the original, as, for the New Testament, the Greek text; for the Old, the Hebrew" (*Pattern of Catechistical Doctrine*, p. 59). In a sermon on Romans 1:16, Miles Smith referred to "the fountain of the prophets and apostles, which are the only authentic pen-men, and registers of the Holy Ghost" (*Sermons*, p. 75). In the preface to the 1611 KJV entitled "The Translators to the Reader," Miles Smith (representing all the translators) favorably quoted Jerome as writing "that as the credit of the old books (he meaneth the Old Testament) is to be tried by the Hebrew volumes, so the New by the Greek tongue, he meaneth the original Greek." Then Miles Smith presented the view of the KJV translators themselves as follows: "If truth be to be tried by these tongues [Hebrew and Greek], then whence should a translation be made, but out of them? These tongues therefore, we should say the Scriptures, in those tongues, we set before us to translate, being the tongues in which God was pleased to speak to his church by his prophets and apostles." In this same preface, Smith also noted: "If you ask what they had before them, truly it was the Hebrew text of the Old Testament, the Greek of the New." Earlier on the third page of the preface, Smith referred to "the original" as "being from heaven." Laurence Vance cited the report of the British delegates (including KJV translator Samuel Ward) to the 1618 Synod of Dort that included a reference to "the truth of the original text" (*King James, His Bible*, p. 47). In the dedication to King James in the 1611, Thomas Bilson also acknowledged that the KJV was a translation made "out of the original sacred tongues." John Eadie noted that the account of the Hampton Court conference written by Patrick Galloway, the king's Scottish chaplain, ["an account revised by the king himself"] stated "that a translation be made of the whole Bible, as consonant as can be to the original Hebrew and Greek" (*English Bible*, Vol. II, p. 179).

William Tyndale (1494-1536) noted: "The Scripture is nothing else but that which the Spirit of God hath spoken by the prophets and apostles" (*Doctrinal Treatises*, p. 88). In his preface to his 1534 New Testament, William Tyndale wrote: "I had taken in hand to look over the New Testament again and to compare it with the <u>Greek</u>, and to mend whatsoever I could find amiss." Tyndale clearly regarded the Greek New Testament as superior to his translation and as the proper standard for revising or correcting it. The preface of the folio edition of the Geneva Bible printed in 1578 stated: "The holy Scriptures, faithfully and plainly translated according to the languages wherein they were first written by the Holy Ghost" (Richmond, *Fathers*, VIII, p. 173). In response to the question (What do you call 'the Word of God'), Theodore Beza (1519-1605) stated: "That which the prophets and apostles recorded in writings, having received it from the Spirit of God, which book we call the Old and New Testaments" (*Book of Christian Questions and Responses*, p. 5). At John 15:26, the 1560 Geneva Bible and an edition of the KJV printed in 1672 have the following note: "the holy Ghost speaketh no otherwise, than he spake by the mouth of the Apostles." The Geneva Bible and a KJV edition printed in 1672 have the following note at 1 Corinthians 14:32: "The doctrine which the prophets bring, which are inspired with God's Spirit." Tyndale's, Matthew's, Great, Whittingham's, and Bishops' Bibles rendered Mark 12:36 as follows: "for David himself inspired with the Holy Ghost." In their preface to the 1611, the KJV translators wrote: "For whatever was perfect under the sun, where apostles or apostolike men, that is, men endued with an extraordinary measure of God's Spirit, and privileged with the privilege of infallibility, had not their hand."

In his 1583 book that defended the typical Reformation view or Protestant view of Bible translation, Puritan William Fulke (1538-1589) stated: "We say indeed, that by the Greek text of the New Testament all translations of the New Testament must be tried; but we mean not by every corruption that is in any Greek copy of the New Testament" (*A Defence of the Sincere and True Translations*, p. 44). Puritan William Whitaker (1547-1595) asserted: "That scripture only, which the prophets, apostles, and evangelists wrote by inspiration of God, is in every way credible on its own account and authentic" (*Disputation on Holy Scripture*, p. 138). William Whitaker asserted that our churches determine "that the Hebrew of the old Testament, and the Greek of the new, is the sincere and authentic scripture of God; and that, consequently, all questions are to determined by these originals, and versions only so far approved as they agree with these originals" (p. 111). Whitaker maintained that "the authentic originals of the scripture of the old Testament are extant in Hebrew, of the new in Greek" (p. 138). Whitaker observed:

"The papists contend that their Latin text is authentic of itself, and ought not to be tried by the text of the originals. Now in this sense no translation ever was, or could be, authentic. For translations of scripture are always to be brought back to the originals of scripture, received if they agree with those originals, and corrected if they do not. That scripture only, which the prophets, apostles, and evangelists wrote by inspiration of God, is in every way credible on its own account and authentic" (p. 138). Whitaker asserted: "That is called authentic, which is sufficient to itself, which commends, sustains, proves itself, and hath credit and authority from itself" (p. 332). John Diodati (1576-1649), translator of the 1607 Italian Bible, is translated as writing: "The authentic text of Scripture, and that which is truly God-breathed, consists only of the Hebrew originals in the Old Testament and Greek originals in the New Testament" (Ferrari, *Diodati's Doctrine of Holy Scripture*, p. 47). A bill for revising the English translation of the Scriptures in the 1650's passed by Parliament affirmed this view held in that day. John Stoughton cited this bill as stating: "it is our duty to endeavour to have the Bible translated in all places as accurately and as perfectly agreeing with the original Hebrew and Greek as we can attain unto" (*Ecclesiastical History of England,* II, p. 545). In his 1659 book, Brian Walton, editor of the London Polyglot, wrote: "That neither the Hebrew nor Greek texts of the Old or New Testament are corrupted by heretics or others, but that they remain pure and entire; and that they always were, and still are, the authentic rule in all matters of faith and religion, and that by them all translations are to be tried and examined" (Todd, *Memoirs,* II, p. 51). In his 1654 book, Edward Leigh wrote: "We hold that the Hebrew for the Old Testament and the Greek for the New is the sincere and authentical writing of God; therefore that all things are to be determined by them; and that the other versions are so far to be approved of, as they agree with these fountains" (*System or Body of Divinity,* p. 59).

The view of the Reformation Bible translators including the KJV translators may be regarded as sound and scripturally-based. The Scriptures are the specific revealed, written words of God given by the miracle of inspiration to the prophets and apostles. According to the Scriptures, God revealed His Word to the prophets and apostles by the Holy Spirit (Eph. 3:5, 2 Pet. 1:21, 2 Pet. 3:1-2, Rom. 15:4, 1 Cor. 2:10-13, Rom. 16:25-26, Heb. 1:1-2, Acts 1:2, Eph. 2:20, Acts 3:21, John 16:13, John 17:8, 14, John 3:34, 2 Sam. 23:2, Luke 24:25, 27, 44). The word of the LORD came to the prophets and apostles (1 Sam. 15:10, 2 Kings 20:4, Isa. 38:4, Jer. 1:4, Jer. 29:30, Ezek. 6:1, Dan. 9:2, Jonah 1:1, Zech. 7:8, Acts 3:21). A true prophet spoke from the mouth of the LORD (2 Chron. 36:12, Luke 1:70, Jer. 1:9, Acts 3:21, 2 Sam. 23:2, Deut. 18:22). The actual specific words that proceeded out of the mouth of God or that God breathed out are those original language words given by inspiration to the prophets and apostles (Matt. 4:4, Deut. 8:3). God's Word is "the Scriptures of the prophets" (Rom. 16:26, Matt. 26:56). God gave His words or spoke by the mouth of the prophets (Luke 1:70, Jer. 1:9, Acts 1:16, Acts 3:21, Ps. 68:11, 2 Chron. 36:12). All Scripture was given by inspiration of God to those prophets and apostles (2 Tim. 3:16, 2 Pet. 1:21, 2 Pet. 3:1-2, Eph. 3:5, Eph. 2:20, Jude 1:3). While 2 Timothy 3:16 may not directly mention the prophets and apostles, the parallel verse concerning inspiration (2 Pet. 1:21) clearly connected the miracle of inspiration to them when considered with other related verses. Comparing scripture with scripture, the holy men of God moved or borne along by the Holy Spirit in the miracle of inspiration were clearly the prophets and apostles (2 Pet. 1:21, Eph. 3:5, Eph. 2:20, 2 Pet. 3:1-2, Rom. 16:26, Luke 1:70, Matt. 26:56). The exact same words that the psalmist wrote in Psalm 95 the Holy Spirit spoke or said (compare Ps. 95:7 with Hebrews 3:7). What Moses said to Pharaoh as the LORD told him (Exod. 9:13), the Scripture said (Rom. 9:17, Exod. 9:16). The overall teaching of the Scriptures would indicate that there can be no new inspired works without living apostles or prophets (2 Peter 1:21, Eph. 3:3-5, Heb. 1:1-2, Luke 1:70, 24:27, 44-45, Acts 1:16, 3:21, 26:27, Matt. 2:5, Rom. 1:2, Rom. 16:25-26, Jer. 29:19, 2 Chron. 36:12, Dan. 9:10, Amos 3:7).

Since the entire Old Testament was designated by God with names such as "Moses and the prophets," "the law and the prophets," "all the prophets and the law," and "the scriptures of the prophets," this could be understood to indicate that all the O. T. writers were prophets (Luke 16:29, 16:31, 24:27; Matt. 5:17, 7:12, 11:13, 22:40, 26:56; Luke 16:16; John 6:45, Acts 24:14,

26:22, 28:23; Rom. 1:2, 3:21, 16:26).   The writer of Hebrews could be understood to describe the entire Old Testament as what God spoke by the prophets (Heb. 1:1).   At Luke 16:29, the writer (Moses) is put for his writings.   Moses was a prophet (Deut. 34:16).   Since the Psalms is sometimes included in the designation "the prophets," it would suggest that the writers of the individual psalms could have been considered prophets.   In addition, individual writers of the Psalms were referred to as prophets (Matt. 13:35, Acts 2:30).   The writers who received the revelation concerning Christ that would be recorded in the New Testament also seem to be regarded as being prophets or apostles or both (Eph. 3:3-5, 2:20).   The N. T. prophets given to the church may refer especially to those prophets that were given revelation that would be written as part of the New Testament (1 Cor. 12:28, Eph. 4:11, Eph. 3:3-5, Eph. 2:20).   Along with the Old Testament, New Testament writings are also called Scripture (2 Pet. 3:15-16, 1 Tim. 5:18). The apostle Peter asserted that the commandment of the apostles are connected with the words revealed and spoken by the prophets (2 Pet. 3:1-2).   The apostle Paul noted that his writing or epistle was "the commandments of the Lord" (1 Cor. 14:37).

The inspiration of the Scriptures considered in relationship to Bible translations

The sixteenth verse in 2 Timothy in the KJV stated "all Scripture is given by inspiration of God," but the verse does not actually say or assert that it would be later translated by inspiration. There is no mention of the process of translating in the verse.   Do some try to assume by the fallacy of begging the question that somehow the process of translating is found in the verse? Do some try to use a weak argument from silence and try to find something in the verse that is not directly stated?   Would the Holy Spirit of truth guide believers to assume opinions by fallacies?   Would trying to suggest that 2 Timothy 3:16 teaches something it does not state be evidence of sound spiritual discernment?

According to the Scriptures themselves, it could be soundly concluded that inspiration would be a term for the way, method, or process by which God directly gave the Scriptures to the prophets and apostles or for the way that the words proceeded from the mouth of God to the prophets and apostles (2 Tim 3:16, 2 Pet. 1:21, Matt. 4:4, Eph. 3:5).   Jim Taylor defined the term **inspiration** as follows: "A process by which God breathed out his very words through holy men in order that his very words could be recorded'" (*In Defense of the TR*, p. 328).   Jim Taylor affirmed: "As a theological definition, inspiration is a process" (p. 33).   Jim Taylor asserted: "Inspiration is a process which was completed when the last New Testament writer wrote the last word" (p. 34).   David Cloud maintained that 2 Timothy 3:16 "describes the original process of the giving of Scripture," and he noted that "the same process is described in 2 Peter 1:19-21" (*Glorious History of the KJB*, p. 213).   David Cloud observed: "Inspiration does not refer to the process of transcribing or translating the Bible, but to the process of God giving the words to the men who wrote the Bible" (*O Timothy*, Vol. 11, Issue 11, 1994, p. 4).   D. A. Waite asserted: "The process of inspiration does apply to the original manuscripts (known as the autographs). This **process** was never repeated" (*Fundamentalist Mis-Information*, p. 106).   Charles Kriessman wrote: "Inspiration is a process by which God breathed out His Words from Genesis to Revelation" (*Modern Version Failures*, p. 46).   Kriessman quoted Thomas Strouse as stating: "Inspiration is a process whereby the Holy Spirit led the writers of Scripture to record accurately His very Words; the product of this process was the inspired originals" (p. 47).   Irving Jensen noted: "We cannot explain the supernatural process of inspiration, which brought about the original writings of the Bible.   Paul refers to the process as *God-breathing*" (*Jensen's Survey of the OT*, p. 19).   Gregory Tyree asserted: "This process of inspiration will never again be repeated because the canon has been closed" (*Does It Really Matter*, p. 32).

This verse in the third chapter of 2 Timothy does not actually assert nor infer that there is a giving or re-giving of the Scriptures by inspiration of God each time it was copied or each time it was translated into a different language.   This verse does not assert nor teach that the process or method for the making of Bible translations is by inspiration.   It has not been soundly demonstrated from the Scriptures that inspiration would be a correct term for the way, method, or process by which the original-language Scriptures are copied or are translated into other languages including into English. Do KJV-only authors clearly demonstrate that they merely let the Scriptures themselves define inspiration, and do they present that definition? Perhaps it has never occurred to some KJV-only advocates that their definition, understanding, and interpretation of inspiration may not be sound or perfect. What is their clear, precise, sound definition and understanding of inspiration that can be applied consistently, soundly, and justly in the same sense (univocally) including both before and after 1611?

The term Scripture would refer to words of God that are written, but the process of writing would not be its definition. According its usage and meaning in the Scriptures, the noun Scripture does not include all words that ever have been written. Words can be written without them being Scripture. Words can even be written in or added to a copy of the Scriptures without them being Scripture. Marginal notes or commentary can be added to a copy of the Scriptures without the added words being Scripture. According to truths suggested in several verses of Scripture (Deut. 4:2, Deut. 12:32, Prov. 30:6, Rev. 22:18-19, would words added by men in a copy of the Scriptures become Scripture? Would any errors written by imperfect men in a copy of the Scriptures become Scripture according to a correct definition of it? Would any errors introduced by printers in a printed edition of Scripture become Scripture according to its correct definition? The term Scripture refers to actual words given by inspiration of God, but this process of the giving by inspiration is not actually stated to be its definition.

Should a Greek adjective at 2 Timothy 3:16 be considered the definition for the Greek noun translated "Scripture"? While an adjective can describe a certain noun, that adjective would not be the total definition of that noun. For example, while all Scripture is profitable for doctrine, being "profitable" is not the definition for the term Scripture. Something can be "profitable" even "profitable for doctrine" without it being Scripture. While the words of Scripture are pure (Ps. 19:8, Prov. 30:5, Ps. 12:6), being "pure" is not the definition of the term Scripture. Something can be pure without it being Scripture. The word of the LORD is tried (Ps. 18:30), but that does not mean that being "tried" would be the correct definition for the term Scripture. Something can be tried without it being Scripture. Being "perfect" is not the definition of scripture even though the word of God is perfect (Ps. 19:7). The words of Scripture are true (Ps. 19:9, John 17:17, John 119:160), but the adjective "true" is not actually the definition of the term "Scripture." Something can be true without it being Scripture. The words or commandments of the LORD are sure (Ps. 111:7, Ps. 92:5, Ps. 19:7, 2 Pet. 1:19), but the adjective "sure" is not their definition. Something can be sure without it being Scripture. The Scriptures are described by the adjective "holy" (2 Tim. 3:15), but that does not mean that this adjective is its definition. The prophets and the apostles were also described by the adjective holy (Rev. 22:6, Eph. 3:5, Rev. 18:30) so would that make them the Scriptures if holy is claimed to be its definition? While all Scripture is God-inspired or God-breathed, being "inspired" has not been demonstrated to be the actual definition of the term Scripture.

The use of an English noun inspiration as part of the rendering for an adjective in Greek is not providing a form-equivalent rendering [adjective for an adjective]. Concerning 2 Timothy 3:16, Lloyd Perry and Robert Culver suggested that the words "is given by" are "an interpolated interpretation--intended to help translate, but joined with 'inspiration,' really being a rather inept carry-over from the Latin Vulgate." Perry and Culver added: "The situation is thus: The first clause of verse 16 in Greek is *pasa* (all) *graphe* (scripture) *theopneustos* (God-breathed). The clause requires the supply of 'is' between 'scripture' and 'God-breathed' for translation into English. Hence we should read, 'All scripture (is) God-breathed'" (*How to Search the Scriptures*, pp. 59-60). The Latin Vulgate as found in Coverdale's 1538 Latin-English New Testament began 2 Timothy 3:16 as follows: "*Omnis scriptura divinitus inspirata*," and the Latin Vulgate also has "*inspirati*" in its rendering at 2 Peter 1:21. Stephen Westcott's modern-spelling edition of the 1388 Wycliffe New Testament has the following rendering of 2 Peter 1:21: "for prophecy was not brought at any time by man's will, but the holy men of God, inspired with the Holy Ghost, spoke it." Miles Coverdale's rendering of the Latin Vulgate in his 1538 English New Testament at 2 Peter 1:21 is the following: "For the prophecy was never brought by the will of man, but the holy men of God spake as they were inspired by the holy Ghost." In 1642, John Davenport noted that "all Scripture is by divine inspiration, or inbreathing of God" (*Profession of the Faith*, p. 2). Edward Young wrote: "Now the term *inspiration* is, in the humble opinion of the present writer, not a happy one. The word inspiration means that which is breathed in. It come to us from the Latin, and in the Latin translation of the Bible, commonly known as the Vulgate, is used as a rendering of the Greek *theopneustos* (God-breathed). We are not satisfied with this translation, for the English word inspiration as has just been remarked, means a 'breathing in,' and, as we have seen, that is not at all what Paul intends to say." Edward Young added: "The Scriptures, Paul vigorously asserts, are writings which came into being because they were breathed out by God Himself" (*Thy Word is Truth*, pp. 21-22). Benjamin Warfield claimed: "There is, we may well admit, nothing in the word *theopneustos* to warrant the in- of the Vulgate rendering: this word speaks not of an 'in*spiration'* by God, but of a 'spiration' by God" (*Inspiration*, p. 277). In his 1828 Dictionary, Noah Webster indicated that the English word **inspire** came from the "Latin *inspiro*; *in* and *spiro*, to breathe." Gordon Clark noted: "The Greek word does not mean *breathed into*, it means *breathed out*. God breathed out the Scriptures" (*God's Hammer*, p. 4).

KJV-only author William Grady referred to "'all Scripture' (i.e. *autographs, copies,* and *translations*)" (*Given by Inspiration*, p. 98). Peter Ruckman claimed: "The word '**scripture**' in the Bible is ALWAYS used of copies or translations" (*Biblical Scholarship*, p. 354). Ruckman contended: "If it is SCRIPTURE, God gave it; if God gave it, the method He used was by inspiration" (p. 355). Gail Riplinger asserted: "'All scripture is given by inspiration of God...'— every word, every *true* copy and translation (2 Tim. 3:16)" (*In Awe of Thy Word*, p. 550). Riplinger suggested that the context in 2 Timothy 3:16 "includes copies and translations" (Ibid.). Riplinger claimed: "Bible inspiration, preservation, and translation are one" (p. 547). Riplinger claimed that "the verse—'All scripture is given by inspiration of God'—is stating that the originals, the copies, and the vernacular translations are 'given by inspiration of God'" (*Hazardous Materials*, p. 1162). David Cloud wrote: "We have seen that Paul's doctrine of inspiration in 2 Timothy chapter 3 allows for copies and translations to be viewed as the inspired Word of God" (*Way of Life Encyclopedia*, p. 311). Do KJV-only advocates demonstrate that 2 Timothy 3:16 is actually teaching that Bible translations are made by the process of inspiration of God? Do KJV-only advocates soundly prove that any reference to Scripture in the New Testament was a direct, clear reference to the KJV or that the readers of the Greek New Testament would have recognized any of its references to Scripture as referring to the KJV?

Concerning 2 Timothy 3:15, KJV defender Thomas Strouse observed: "The words 'holy scriptures' translate *hiera grammata*, literally 'sacred' or 'temple writings'" (*The Lord God*, p. 42). Concerning 2 Timothy 3:16, Thomas Strouse noted: "But the word 'scripture' translates *graphe*, which means 'scripture' and refers to the *autographa*." Strouse added: "Paul obviously used a different word to differentiate between the *apographa* [copies] and the *autographa* [original autographs], especially with regard to the scope of inspiration" (Ibid.).

Jim Taylor asserted: "The word 'scripture' merely describes the source of a writing as being divine without any intended comment on inspiration, preservation, or translation" (*In Defense of the TR*, p. 109). Could the term Scripture possibly and properly be used for the Geneva Bible, the KJV, or the NKJV analogically (with a proportional meaning)? The same name or term can be properly given with some difference in its meaning to something different. The same name or term may be used in three ways, not just in one way or two ways. The Geneva Bible, the KJV, or the NKJV could be called Scripture because they are translations of the preserved Scriptures in the original languages. The assumption (likely involving the use of the fallacy of begging the question) that the KJV has to be directly given by a miracle of inspiration of God in order to be called scripture is not actually stated in 2 Timothy 3:16. It could also become an example of use of a false analogy if it is assumed that because two distinct things are alike in some ways or qualities that they must be alike in all ways or qualities. The key term translation (in reference to a Bible translation) was defined and discussed earlier. A sound definition of the term Bible translation would have a bearing on how the term Scripture could or should be used for one. A Bible translation can have proper derived authority from the greater authority of its underlying original-language Scripture texts. It is very possible and even likely that there could be some degree of difference in meaning in the use of the term Scripture when used for a Bible translation such as the Geneva Bible, the KJV, or the NKJV as compared when used for copies of the original-language Scriptures. Are translations a different category or classification that should be distinguished somewhat from untranslated original-language texts of Scripture? A Bible translation may be substantially or mostly the same as its underlying original-language Scripture text, but there are still differences between the two. A Bible translation with its different words in a different language can be compared to its underlying original-language texts, but it does not have the exact same, identical, specific original-language words given by inspiration of God to the prophets and apostles. Mickey Carter asserted: "Things that are different are not the same. Bibles that are different are not the same" (*Things That Are Different*, p. 77). Do some KJV-only advocates attempt to ignore the truth that a Bible translation has different words than the original-language words given by inspiration of God? Would they in effect contradict their own claim and assert that different words are not different? There would be some greater differences between the original-language words and the English words in the KJV than the differences between the KJV's English words and the NKJV's English words.

When it is speculated, assumed, or claimed that the term **Scripture** in 2 Timothy 3:16 must refer to copies and especially even to translations, a consistent, just, and logical application of this speculative reasoning would in effect be asserting that it must include **all** that belong in the same sense (univocally) to those two classifications: copies and translations. Including all copies of the preserved original-language Scriptures would in effect make inspiration include any errors introduced by imperfect men in their copying of Scripture. Including all printed translations of Scripture would make inspiration include any errors made by translators or printers and include the conflicting and even contradictory renderings in varying Bible translations in different languages. Thus, consistency and just measures in applying the word "all" to Bible translations would be a serious problem for exclusive KJV-only reasoning concerning only one English translation. If the term Scripture in a univocal sense at 2 Timothy 3:16 is assumed to include Bible translations, KJV-only advocates have not demonstrated from the Scriptures that it should apply only to the KJV and not also to the pre-1611 English Bibles such as the Geneva Bible and to post-1611 English Bibles such as the NKJV. Could some KJV-only advocates attempt to read into or to draw from 2 Timothy 3:16 a specific conclusion about translating that has not clearly and legitimately been shown to be actually stated or taught by the verse? Do KJV-only advocates attempt to go beyond what 2 Timothy 3:16 actually states to try to make it say something additional to which it does not directly and clearly refer? The sixteenth verse of 2 Timothy did not actually directly assert that God gave all Bible translations or one English Bible translation by the process or method of inspiration. Do KJV-only advocates use the term inspiration with one meaning (univocally) when they attempt to apply it to Bible translations? Do they use the term Bible translation with one meaning (univocally) if they attempt selectively to try to call one translation Scripture while denying the same for other English Bible translations? Do they attempt to read their own subjective, modern KJV-only opinions that were not in the mind of Paul into this verse? Did the earlier KJV-only opinions shape the later KJV-only interpretation of 2 Timothy 3:16? Is the modern KJV-only interpretation of 2 Timothy 3:16 possibly an example of eisegesis? Is this KJV-only interpretive result already found in the unproven KJV-only premise or premises with which the KJV-only reader began? Is every man teaching that 2 Timothy 3:16 is a reference to the KJV advocating a non-scriptural opinion of men? Could KJV-only advocates confuse what the text actually says and means with their way of reading it or into it? Are some KJV-only advocates setting up their own reason and private interpretation as the final canon of truth? Are some KJV-only advocates seeking to manufacture support in the Scriptures for certain non-scriptural, human dogma or tradition which they may have merely presumed or assumed by use of fallacies such as begging the question and have accepted without proper, consistent, sound scriptural support? KJV-only advocates do not prove that their KJV-only doctrine is found and taught in any Greek New Testament manuscript. KJV-only advocates do not demonstrate that they soundly believe the Book when they merely read their own subjective KJV-only opinions into verses that do not actually directly state what they allege.

Some KJV-only advocates attempt to stress the point of the KJV's added English verb "is" or "is given" being in the present tense at 2 Timothy 3:16. For example, Gail Riplinger claimed: "In English, 'is given' is a present tense verb; it is not time sensitive" (*Hazardous Materials*, p. 1146). Doug Stauffer asserted: "Notice the scriptural use of the present tense verb--**is**" (*One Book One Authority*, p. 431). William Grady contended that 2 Timothy 3:16 uses "the word 'give' in the present tense" (*Given by Inspiration*, p. 98). Yet even KJV-only author William Grady admitted that "past action may sometimes be described with present tense usage" (p. 68), but he ignored how that admission would be a problem for the new KJV-only private interpretation concerning 2 Timothy 3:16. *Webster's New Twentieth Century Dictionary* identified **given** as the "past participle of *give*." KJV defender Kirk DiVietro asserted: "The English verb of the sentence 'is given' is composed of the auxiliary verb *is* and the past participle of *give* which forms the English perfect tense.   This tense indicates a past punctiliar event with continuing effect. The words exist today because they were given in the past.   It does not mean they are constantly being given" (*Cleaning-Up*, pp. 272-273).   DiVietro is correct in asserting that "given" is the past participle of "give," but he is incorrect in saying that "is given" forms the perfect tense since the perfect tense uses forms of the helping verb "have."   A particle can function as part of a verb phrase or as a modifier.   A past particle can express previous action in time past.   For example, the past particle "written" in the clause "it is written" (Matt. 2:5, Matt. 4:4) can refer to what was written in the past [previous action].   Likewise, the past particle "given" can refer to what was given in the past even when used with a present tense be verb.   Even a present particle could refer to previous action in time past.   KJV-only advocates fail to show that the use of the present tense verb "is" at 2 Timothy 3:16 proves what they allege or assume.   It does not follow that because God directly gave the original-language Scriptures by inspiration to the prophets and apostles that a Bible translation has to be given by inspiration.

At least two or three KJV-only authors seem to try to find another way to try to support their new interpretation of 2 Timothy 3:16.   William Grady asserted that "the *first* and most critical usage [of the word inspiration] is found in Job 32:8" (*Given By Inspiration*, p. 90).   William Grady contended: "As Job is the oldest book in the Bible, we marvel that the *first* writer of Scripture 'just happens' to record the definitive statement on inspiration" (p. 90).   Are Grady's declarations proven to be sound, true, and correct?   Peter Ruckman asserted that "the verse in the Old Testament (Job 32:8) is usually ignored by those who write about 'verbal, plenary inspired, original autographs'" (*Biblical Scholarship*, p. 337).   In his note at Job 32:8 in his *Ruckman Reference Bible*, Peter Ruckman claimed: "The verse is a direct cross reference to 2 Timothy 3:16" (p. 759).   Concerning 2 Timothy 3:16 and Job 32:8, Jack McElroy also claimed: "Comparing the two helps you understand how the Bible defines the word [*inspiration*]" (*Which Bible Would Jesus Use*, p. 241).   After citing Job 32:8, Jack McElroy asserted: "According to the Bible, *inspiration* not only applies to the original autographs but it's also an ongoing ministry of the Holy Spirit whereby he gives men (including you) *understanding* of the words of God" (p. 233).

Do these two verses (2 Timothy 3:16 and Job 32:8) use the same original-language word in the same exact sense concerning the same exact subject that would indicate that they should be considered parallel passages?   Does the use of the same English word "inspiration" to translate two different words in two different verses in different contexts prove that these two verses are actually both about the same subject--the giving of the Scriptures by inspiration to the prophets and apostles? Is it clearly demonstrated that the assertion (Job 32:8) made by Elihu is about the same subject of the Scriptures as the verse in 2 Timothy 3:16 is? Does Elihu actually define the meaning of inspiration at 2 Timothy 3:16? Would a possibly more obscure or less clear use of an English word be properly considered the key to understanding a clearer use of that same word? Has it been soundly demonstrated that the Hebrew word used in Job 32:8 has the exact, same meaning as the Greek adjective used in 2 Timothy 3:16? The Greek adjective at 2 Timothy 3:16 is actually translated in the KJV by five words ["given by inspiration of God"], not by one word [inspiration]. Do these KJV-only authors ignore or avoid any consideration of how the same Hebrew word translated "inspiration" at Job 32:8 is translated in over twenty other verses in the KJV's Old Testament? Could any of the other verses where the same Hebrew word is used contribute to understanding its use at Job 32:8? Would presenting one result of "the inspiration of the Almighty" ["giveth them understanding"] actually provide Elihu's clear definition of it? According to the doctrine of Bible inspiration, are all the words stated by Job's three friends and Elihu true and directly from God or are all their words recorded by inspiration of God as they had stated them regardless of whether they were right or wrong in some of them? Is Job 32:8 proven soundly to be the key to understanding 2 Timothy 3:16 as these KJV-only authors alleged? Do KJV-only authors truly prove that Job 32:8 presents the "definitive statement on inspiration" of the Scriptures? Is this appeal to Job 32:8 an effort to avoid an actual verse that does relate or is parallel to 2 Timothy 3:16—2 Peter 1:21? Milton Terry observed: "The obscure or doubtful passages are to be explained by what is plain and simple" (*Biblical Hermeneutics*, p. 186). Phil Stringer wrote: "The proper meaning is determined by 'context'-- the way the words are used in a given situation" (Williams, *Word-for-Word Translating*, p. 149).

Evidently KJV defenders disagree among themselves in their interpretation of 2 Timothy 3:16. According to their own writings, a good number of KJV defenders would reject the new KJV-only interpretation of this verse suggested by a few modern KJV-only authors. Even Peter Ruckman himself had evidently understood and interpreted this verse differently in the past than he later did. In a letter written to Robert Sumner in 1971, Peter Ruckman himself had asserted: "Verbal inspiration has to do with 2 Timothy 3:16 and deals with the original autographs, as we all know" (photocopy of letter, p. 2). In 1988, Peter Ruckman wrote: "Although we cannot claim direct inspiration **in the original Biblical sense** for the King James text, we could claim that the King James text presents an infallible text, preserved without proven error in the language in which God intended for us to have it" [bold type added] (*Theological Studies,* Book 15, p. 15). Peter Ruckman asserted: "So our position is this: **The King James Bible may not claim for itself the original inspiration of God**, breathing through the men who spoke when they were copied down by a writer at the time they spoke. However, it can be claimed to be preserved without proven error in the universal language of the world" [bold type added] (p. 23). In his commentary on the Pastoral Epistles, Peter Ruckman wrote: "We do not refer to the AV as the 'verbally inspired, inerrant Word of God'" (p. 270). Ruckman claimed: "I've never said that the *King James Bible* was inspired, although I've broadly intimated it sometimes" (*Why I Believe the KJV,* p. 8). In his note at Job 32:8, Peter Ruckman wrote: "When we say the KJV is '**the holy scriptures'** in English (Rom. 1:2), or '**given by inspiration**' (2 Tim. 3:16), we mean that the Holy Spirit of God guided its translators in their work and then breathed on that Book when they got through with it" (*Ruckman Reference Bible*, p. 759). Do some of Ruckman's own statements conflict with other of his statements?

In the preface of the book *Cleaning-Up Hazardous Materials* by Kirk DiVietro, H. D. Williams wrote: "The false application of 'is given,' to translations throughout the centuries must stop. Inspiration of translations is a false doctrine concocted by men to justify a position when they were caught proclaiming a doctrine that cannot be substantiated by the Scripture; by the grammar of passages in question, or by history" (p. v). Phil Stringer asserted: "The verse does not say that the words that God gave are preserved, transmitted, or translated by 'inspiration'" (Brown, *Indestructible Book*, p. 394). D. A. Waite contended: "There is no scriptural proof that any translation of God's Words is inspired of God" (*A Warning on Gail Riplinger's*, p. 32). D. A.

Waite observed: "The accurate view of Bible inspiration is found in 2 Timothy 3:16. That verse refers to the way that the original Hebrew, Aramaic, and Greek Words were produced by God's true plenary verbal inspiration" (p. 20). Charles L. Surrett wrote: "There is no theological reason (no statement from God) to believe that a translation into any language would be inspired in the same way that the original writings in Hebrew and Greek were. No translation has been 'God-breathed,' as 2 Timothy 3:16 says of the originals" (*Certainty of the Words*, p. 75).

D. A. Waite wrote: "God never once caused any human writers or translators to operate any more under his DIVINE INSPIRATION of the words in any translation or version throughout human history thus far (nor will He in the future) in the same or even in a similar sense as He did when He originally gave His Word under DIVINE INSPIRATION" (*Dean Burgon News,* August, 1980, p. 1). H. D. Williams wrote: "Inspiration refers solely to the original and preserved God-breathed Words, which were recorded by the prophets and Apostles" (*Pure Words,* p. 20). H. D. Williams asserted: "The Greek word, *graphe*, in 2 Timothy 3:16 refers to the autographs" (*Hearing the Voice of God*, p. 193). In the preface of Kirk DiVietro's book *Cleaning-Up Hazardous Materials*, H. D. Williams quoted D. A. Waite concerning the three Greek words that make up the first part of 2 Timothy 3:16. Waite noted that "these three Words refer exclusively to God's miraculous action of His original breathing out of His Hebrew, Aramaic, and Greek Words of the Old and New Testaments" (p. iv, also p. 2). Waite added: "These Words do not refer to any Bible translation in any language of the world" (Ibid.).

H. D. Williams quoted D. A. Waite as noting: "*Theopneustos* is a compound adjective which comes from two Greek words, *theos* (God) and *pneustos* (an adjective meaning 'breathed'). *Pneustos* comes from the verb, *peno* 'to breathe.' It does not come from nor is it synonymous with the noun, *pneuma*. It comes clearly from the verb, *pneo* (to breathe)" (*Cleaning-Up*, p. iv). Ralph Earle asserted that the Greek word "literally means 'God breathed'--*theos*, 'God,' and *pneo*, 'breathe'" (*Word Meanings*, p. 409). Marvin Vincent also maintained that this word comes from the Greek noun for God and the Greek verb 'to breathe' and meant "God-breathed" (*Word Studies*, IV, p. 317). E. W. Bullinger defined the Greek word as "God-breathed, God-inspired" (*Lexicon*, p. 414). Waite asserted: "Gail Riplinger and others are totally in error to claim that an adjective (*pneustos*) could be taken as a noun (*pneuma*). This is contrary to all Greek grammar, whether classical or Koine. It is clearly false teaching and false doctrine" (DiVietro, *Cleaning-Up*, p. iv).

KJV defender Ian Paisley noted: "And let me emphasize that inspiration has only to do with the writing of the original Scripture and is divinely limited to that. Inspiration has not to do with the translation of the Bible into English or any other language" (*Fundamentalist Digest*, January/February, 1995, p. 15). Charles Kriessman asserted: "The proper interpretation of 2 Timothy 3:16 is that it refers solely to the Hebrew, Aramaic, and Greek Words that were originally given by God" (*Modern Version Failures*, p. 48). Thomas Strouse wrote: "The word behind 'is given by inspiration of God' is *theopneustos*, meaning literally 'is God-breathed.' Paul's claim then, is that only, and all, of the *autographa* [original autographs] is inspired by God, or is God breathed. The process of inspiration extends to *only* the *autographa*, and to *all* of the *autographa*" (*The Lord God,* pp. 42-43). Solomon Caesar Malan wrote: "Strictly speaking, 'verbal inspiration' as it is called, can apply only to the inspired autographs of the holy men who wrote the canon of Scripture" (*Gospel,* p. xiii). Homer Massey wrote: "No passage of Scripture tells us that God ever performed or planned to perform the operation of inspiration on any copier or translator. Again: Bible proof nowhere extends inspiration, the inerrant work of the Holy Spirit, to acts of copying the Greek manuscripts or to tasks of translating Scripture into other languages" (*Fundamental Baptist Crusader*, October, 1980, p. 2). Homer Massey added: "Strictly speaking, the inspiration (as it has been discussed) only took place when God moved upon the human writers of Scripture in their original writings. No claim should be made for that which cannot be clearly proved by Scripture" (Ibid.). Robert Sargent noted: "The inspiration of the Scriptures was miraculous" (*English Bible*, p. 231).

David Cloud indicated that *inspiration* concerned "the divinely-guided writing of the original manuscripts (2 Tim. 3:16; 2 Pet. 1:21) (*Way of Life Encyclopedia,* p. 45). William Byers asserted that "the process of inspiration is spoken of in 2 Timothy 3:16" and that "in 2 Peter 1:21, you see the personnel of inspiration" (*History of the KJB,* p. 7). Concerning 2 Timothy 3:14-17, David Cloud wrote: "The term 'given by inspiration' applies directly only to the original process of the giving of Scripture. The same process is described in 2 Peter 1:19-21" (*Faith,* p. 54). Cloud added: "No translation can lay claim to this process. No translation is 'given by inspiration'" (pp. 55, 593). Evangelist Harold Boyd, a KJV-only advocate, asserted: "If you want a good definition for inspiration, I believe you will find this in 2 Peter 1:21" (*Flaming Torch,* August, 1981, p. 3). D. A. Waite wrote: "By the term 'inspiration' we must understand primarily the process by which God caused His original words to be penned down by the 'Holy Men of God' (2 Peter 1:20-21) whom He assigned to that task" (*Dean Burgon News,* June, 1980, p. 3). H. D. Williams wrote: "Other verses refer to inspiration without using the word, inspiration, but teach that men were '*moved by the Holy Spirit*' to record the Words in the autographs, the original manuscripts" (*Hearing the Voice of God,* p. 194). Concerning 2 Peter 1:21, Tim Fellure asserted: "Though the apostle Peter did not use the word, he did define the process of inspiration" (*Neither jot nor tittle,* p. 23). Homer Massey wrote: "The primary Scripture passage describing how inspiration was accomplished is found in 2 Peter 1:21" (*Fundamental Baptist Crusader,* Oct., 1980, p. 2). R. B. Ouellette wrote: "There is a second passage used as a parallel to 2 Timothy 3:16--2 Peter 1:21" (*More Sure Word,* p. 30). R. B. Ouellette then cited 2 Peter 1:21 for "the *method* of inspiration" (p. 32). R. B. Ouellette also acknowledged that "inspiration was completed in the past" (p. 34). Jeff Farnham wrote: "The Timothy and Peter portions are New Testament declarations of inspiration" (*God's Forever Word,* p. 145). Referring to 2 Timothy 3:16 and 2 Peter 1:21, Gail Riplinger wrote: "The two verses most often used in a discussion of the Bible's inspiration are parallel" (*Hazardous Materials,* p. 1184). In his note on 2 Timothy 3:16, Peter Ruckman asserted: "The process of '**inspiration**' is the Holy Spirit breathing His words through somebody's mouth (2 Pet. 1:21) and these words then being written down" (*Ruckman Reference Bible,* p. 1591).

David Sorenson wrote: "The simple truth is that God inspired the words of Scripture once when He spoke to or through holy men of old" (*God's Perfect Book,* p. 44). Sorenson noted: "Inspiration took place when holy men of old penned the very words of Scripture, whether Moses, Ezra, David, Peter, or Paul. Inspiration did not take place again in the 17th century" (p. 45). Sorenson asserted: "Inspiration was a one-time act of God for each respective section of the Bible" (p. 93). D. A. Waite wrote: "The only proper 'inspiration' of Scripture was a one-time miracle, never to be repeated, when God Himself caused to be written down the Word of the Bible in Hebrew, a little Aramaic, and Greek" (*A Warning on Gail Riplinger's,* p. 38). H. D. Williams wrote: "*Inspiration* refers solely to the original and Preserved God-breathed Words 'once delivered,' which were recorded by the prophets and apostles" (*Miracle of Biblical Inspiration,* p. 115). H. D. Williams wrote: "The Words of God were given by inspiration only '*once*' in the original tongues to the penman of the Scriptures at various times over the centuries (Jude 1:3)" (*Word-for-Word,* p. 78). Charles Kriessman asserted: "The proper interpretation of 2 Timothy 3:16 is that it refers solely to the Hebrew, Aramaic, and Greek Words that were originally given by God" (*Modern Version Failures,* p. 48). Michael Bates wrote: "God has given His word by inspiration one time" (*Inspiration,* p. 37). What the Scripture stated and taught at 2 Peter 1:20-21 and Jude 1:3 would would seem to conflict with any new KJV-only private interpretation of 2 Timothy 3:16. Would the once giving or delivery of the Scriptures in old time or in time past to the prophets and apostles support any new KJV-only private interpretation that would imply or suggest a second or seventh giving by inspiration in 1611 or 1769? Evidently those KJV-only advocates who appeal to 2 Timothy 3:16 to support their KJV-only view did not clearly and soundly define words such as "inspiration," "scripture," and "all' from the Scriptures and did not present a strong-enough scriptural case so that other KJV defenders would accept their attempt to apply this verse exclusively to one English translation as sound or true.

A number of KJV defenders or KJV-only advocates will assert that they are not claiming any second inspiration when they use the term for the KJV.   Some may refer to a "derived inspiration."   Charles Kriessman observed: "Derivative inspiration is a belief that translated Bible's Words derive inspiration from the underlying original Words" (*Modern Version Failures*, p. 53).   David Cloud maintained that he believes that the KJV "has DERIVED its inspiration from the text upon which it was based" (*O Timothy*, Vol. 11, Issue 11, 1994, p. 3).   Lloyd Streeter asserted: "The King James Bible does have a derived inspiration" (*Seventy-five Problems*, p. 45).   If some KJV-only advocates in effect indicate that they are not using the term inspiration with but one meaning (univocally) for the process of the giving of the Scriptures to the prophets and apostles and for the process of the making of the KJV, would they be suggesting that they may use the term inspiration analogically or with a proportional meaning (partly the same, partly different)?   At least a couple KJV-only authors suggest that the term inspiration cannot be used analogically.   Lloyd Streeter claimed: "Inspiration is not in degrees, nor is it a higher or a lower level" (*Seventy-five Problems*, p. 47).   Streeter declared: "There is no lesser inspiration or lower degree of inspiration" (p. 45).   Lloyd Streeter contended that saying that the KJV "is not inspired 'IN THE SAME SENSE' as the original text is to downplay the inspiration of the Bible" (p. 46).   In contrast, H. D. Williams asserted: "There is no such thing as re-inspiration, double inspiration, derivative inspiration, or advanced revelation for any translation to allow reinscripturation" (*Word-for-Word Translating*, p. 83).   D. A. Waite declared: "I do not believe there is such a thing as 'derivative inspiration'" (*Fundamentalist Deception*, p. 116).   Waite asserted: "There is no such thing as derivative when you tak about God-breathing (inspiration) of His words" (*Central Seminary Refuted*, p. 137).   H. D. Williams claimed: "Every person holding the view that the King James Bible is inspired, derivatively inspired, derivatively pure, or derivatively perfect is not only linguistically and historically incorrect, he is theologically incorrect" (*Pure Words,* p. 21).   H. D. Williams asserted: "If we attribute purity and inspiration to the translated Words of God in any language, we are in reality claiming double inspiration, double purity, and double Apostolic and prophet-like men who chose them and who wrote them" (p. 63).   H. D. Williams contended: "Since the Words of God are unchanging in their original pure, perfect, inspired *'jots and tittles,'* **no** derivative can be formed" (*Pure Words*, p. 17).   Arthur Pink maintained that "2 Timothy 3:16 preclude[s] different degrees of inspiration" (*Studies in the Scriptures*, December, 1949, p. 16).   Jim Taylor argued against the idea of derived inspiration, and he noted that "inspiration is not an attribute.   It is a process" (*In Defense of the TR*, p. 39, footnote 33).   Jim Taylor maintained that "inspiration does not extend to a translation" (p. 39).   Taylor concluded: "Since inspiration is not an ongoing process, nor a quality, 'derivative inspiration' is not possible" (p. 327).   David Cloud asserted: "Inspiration was the supernatural process by which the Holy Spirit gave chosen words to holy men of old so that what they wrote was the inerrant Word of God.   No translation can lay claim to this process.   No translation is 'given by inspiration'" (*Glorious History of the KJB*, p. 214).

<u>The preservation of the Scriptures including in relation to Bible translations</u>

Those KJV defenders who do not attempt to use the term inspiration with one meaning (univocally) to try to justify their KJV-only reasoning may appeal instead to the term **preservation**.   According to the typical KJV-only reasoning of some, it is suggested that since God gave perfect, inerrant Scriptures in the original manuscripts that He must preserve them without error in one English translation—the KJV.   David Cloud asserted: "The King James Bible is a product of preservation, not inspiration" (*Bible Version Question/Answer*, p. 8).   David Sorenson commented: "Though the King James Version *as a translation* is not inspired, verbal preservation has carried the *results* of inspiration through to this hour in the King James Version.   Those results are inerrancy and infallibility" (*God's Perfect Book*, p. 211).   Do some KJV-only advocates clearly define what they mean univocally by preservation and then do they use that term consistently, soundly, and justly when they attempt to apply it to one English Bible translation in 1611?   In his *Concise KJB Dictionary*, David Cloud defined **preserve** as "to maintain, to protect, to keep" (p. 70). In the book entitled *Thou Shalt Keep Them* edited by Kent Brandenburg, the following definition is given for **preservation**: "complete, inerrant protection and general accessibility of every writing (vowels and consonants, words, and orders of letters and words) of the Bible, the sixty-six books of the Old and New Testaments, for every generation of believers" (p. 13). Ken Brandenburg asserted: "The position taken by the men writing this book is that scripture teaches God has preserved every and all of His Words to the very letter, and these Words are available to every generation. This is verbal, plenary preservation. These Words are preserved in the Hebrew and Aramaic Old Testament and the Greek New Testament" (p. 23). The *Encarta World English Dictionary* gave as its second definition of the word **preservation**: "A keeping of something unchanged" while its first definition was "protection from harm" (p. 1422). Would not a consistent, sound view of Bible preservation be true both before and after 1611?

Lloyd Streeter asserted: "The doctrine of verbal-plenary inspiration necessitates the doctrine of perfect preservation of the text" (*Seventy-five Problems*, p. 126). Charles Nichols claimed: "Perfect inspiration without perfect preservation would leave inspiration a worthless Biblical doctrine" (Brandenburg, *Thou Shalt Keep Them*, p. 68). Nichols asked: "What value is an inspired Scripture for extended generations of human beings if it is not preserved in that inspired form?" (p. 66). Nichols maintained: ""The necessity of Scripture for the perfect preparation of the man of God also demands the preservation of every Word of God for every man of God in every generation" (p. 68). In the same book, Thomas Corkish wrote: "Without the guarantee of the pure preservation of Scripture, the inspiration of the originals would be of little value" (p. 151). Barry Burton asked: "Did God preserve His Word perfect for us today, or was it only perfect 'in the original autographs?" (*Let's Weigh*, p. 7). Samuel Gipp asked: "Why did God inspire a perfect original if He didn't plan on preserving it?" (*Answer Book*, p. 85). David Cloud wrote: "If Bible preservation is not miraculous, the doctrine of miraculous inspiration is meaningless" (*Myths*, p. 101). William Grady asserted: "Without infallible preservation, we are forced to conclude that God's breath evaporated with the deterioration of His originals" (*Final Authority*, p. 17). Grady asked: "If God's breath rested on the very originals He intended to preserve, wouldn't common sense dictate that the final ancestor would also have to retain inspiration?" (p. 22). R. B. Ouellette wrote: "Verbal inspiration demands verbal preservation" (*More Sure Word*, p. 138). Arlin Horton asked: "What good to us today is the doctrine of divine inspiration if God has not providentially preserved His Word for us?" (*PCC Update*, Fall, 2001, p. 9). David Norris asked: "Why would God take such care in giving the Scriptures by verbal inspiration in the first place only for them to be later lost to us?" (*Big Picture*, p. 61). Michael O'Neal asked: "What good is it if the inspired scriptures were not preserved?" (*Do We Have*, p. 12). Robert Sargent asked: "Why would God give us the Bible, taking meticulous care with the very words of Scripture, then allow their distortion or loss to occur over time" (*English Bible*, p. 82).

R. B. Ouellette asserted: "What is the *practical* difference between a 'divinely inspired Word of God' and a "divinely preserved Word of God'? None. If God both inspired and preserved His Word, then we can have the confidence that the preserved Word is equal to the inspired Word for all practical purposes today--they are one in the same" (*More Sure Word*, p. 156). Concerning "preservation and inspiration," D. A. Waite wrote: "There is no problem with asserting these things on an equal footing" (*Critical Answer to Michael*, p. 29). Did Waite's own statement in effect equate preservation and inspiration? Wendell Runion claimed: "The truth of the matter is, inspiration and preservation are like Siamese twins who are conjoined at birth, with one heart between them" (*Northwest News*, Summer, 2009, p. 7).

Do all KJV defenders and many of the holders of a KJV-only view clearly and adequately distinguish between these two different terms preservation and inspiration? While the doctrine of preservation is tied or linked to the doctrine of inspiration and is dependent upon it, it does not mean that there are no clear or significant distinctions between the two. If KJV defenders need to be allowed to redefine Bible words or need to be allowed to use inconsistently these terms, does that suggest that their KJV-only view or KJV-only reasoning is sound, true, and scriptural? Do KJV defenders attempt to make other believers play by their rules and accept their unpresented definitions, imperfect definitions, and unproven assumptions? Do KJV-only advocates adequately and clearly distinguish between the inspiration of the Scriptures given to the prophets and apostles and the later preservation or transmission of them in copies? Do KJV-only advocates adequately distinguish between preservation of the actual, exact, specific words that God gave by inspiration to the prophets and apostles and the later translation of them into different words in other languages? Would they separate or distinguish between inspiration and preservation in the pre-1611 English Bibles such as the 1537 Matthew's Bible or the 1560 Geneva Bible? If they [or the KJV translators] could in effect and in practice distinguish between inspiration and preservation before 1611 in the pre-1611 English Bibles, why can the same thing not be done in and after 1611 or 1769? If some KJV defenders or holders of a KJV-only view according to their own statements make the word "preserved" mean practically or essentially the same thing as "inspired," do they practically hold the same basic view as Peter Ruckman? They may deny that they claim that the KJV is inspired and may claim that they reject Ruckman's view. But if they will at the same time claim that the KJV is the preserved word of God while making preservation in effect equal in meaning to inspiration, what is the clear, essential difference between their view and Ruckman's?

Consider these statements by one KJV defender that were all made in the same book. D. A. Waite asserted: "To have any kind of genuine Bible preservation, you must have the verbal plenary preservation of God's Hebrew, Aramaic, and Greek Words, not through 'translations'" (*Fundamentalist Deception on Bible Preservation,* p. 98). Waite claimed: "Bible 'preservation' that is not 'perfect' is not 'preservation'" (p. 117). Waite also stated: "I believe that in the King James Bible we have God's Words preserved in English" (p. 110). He also wrote: "I do not use the phrase 'perfectly preserved Word of God when I am talking about the King James Bible" (p. 113). Are all these statements by Waite about preservation consistent, clear, reliable, and true? Were the words relating to preservation used in the exact same sense or with the exact same meaning (univocally) in all of these statements? Do these statements adequately distinguish between the preservation of the Scriptures in the original languages and "God's Words preserved in English?" D. A. Waite admitted in one place in his book: "There are two senses in which I use 'preservation. The capital 'P' sense of Preservation as at the Hebrew, Aramaic and Greek level'" (p. 75). Waite added: "The small 'p' sense of preservation is what I say about the King James Bible. It preserved all of the Hebrew, Aramaic, and Greek Words of the Bible by means of an accurate English translation of those **Words**" (p. 75). Waite claimed: "In our King James Bible we have God's Words kept intact in English because of its accurate translation into English of the verbal plenary preserved Hebrew, Aramaic, and Greek **Words** that underlie it" (p. 130). Would other holders of a KJV-only view accept all of Waite's statements as being true? How is every individual preserved original-language word of Scripture actually kept intact and unchanged in the KJV when the 1611 KJV changed them to different words and even gave no English word for some of them according to what the KJV translators themselves stated in their marginal notes? Every jot and tittle of the inspired original-language words of Scripture and all the actual, specific original-language words are not directly preserved in a Bible translation such as the KJV.

In his book criticizing some fundamentalists, D. A. Waite alleged: "In order for them to say that 'God has preserved His Word,' they must redefine Biblical Preservation to a meaningless sense of only the 'message' or 'thought' or 'idea' or 'concept' being 'preserved,' but not the WORDS? They must say only God's Word (in the sense of 'message' or 'thought' or 'idea' or 'concept' has been preserved" (*Fundamentalist Distortions on Bible Version,* p. 44). Considering those actual places where the KJV does not have literal, word-for-word equivalents for the preserved original language words of Scripture, would those KJV-only advocates who use the word preserved concerning the KJV be in effect changing or redefining Biblical preservation to a sense of "message," "meaning," "thought," or "dynamic-equivalent" preservation? Are some

KJV-only advocates possibly guilty of redefining the term preservation or are they using it analogically or equivocally in some of their own stated claims for the KJV?

KJV defenders themselves are unable to agree in their own claims concerning preservation and concerning the KJV. Contradicting other KJV defenders, Peter Ruckman claimed: "To teach that word for word inspiration has to be word for word preservation because of word for word 'originals' is HERESY" (*Alexandrian Cult*, Part Seven, p. 10). Dennis Corle accused other KJV defenders or KJV-only advocates of "theological double-talk" if they accept what he claimed is "the false idea that the King James Bible is preserved but it is not inspired" (*God's Inspired Book*, p. 11). Dennis Corle asked: "If we begin with something inspired, and we preserve it, how do we lose inspiration in the process of preservation" and "if we preserve what is inspired, how can we possibly lose inspiration in the process of preservation?" (pp. 11, 20). Dennis Corle failed to prove his own personal KJV-only assumptions and opinions to be true, sound, and scriptural so perhaps he assumes or advocates a non-scriptural or even a false idea. Assuming a non-scriptural claim would not be believing scriptural truth. The different process of Bible translating is not same as the process of preserving and sustaining the actual, specific, exact original-language words given by inspiration of God to the prophets and apostles. A Bible translation does not take the actual original-language words that were given by inspiration and preserve them. The inspired, preserved original-language words are changed to different words in a translation. Jim Taylor asserted: "In a strict biblical sense, preservation only applies to what God has given by inspiration, and not what has been accomplished by translation" (*In Defense of the TR*, p. 57). Bible translation into English before 1611 and in 1611 did not prevent the original-language words of Scripture from changing during translating since the process of translation actually changes most of them into different English words, provides no English words for some original-language words of Scripture, and adds many words for which there was no original-language word of Scripture. Every exact inspired original-language word of Scripture and every jot and tittle of every original-language word is not actually preserved exactly or identically in Bible translations.

The exact, specific words spoken by Paul and other apostles by means of the Holy Spirit and later written referred to those words that were written in the original languages (1 Cor. 2:13, 2 Pet. 1:21, 2 Pet. 3:16, 2 Pet. 3:2, John 17:8, Luke 18:31, Heb. 1:1-2). The Lord Jesus Christ directly referred to "the things that are **written by the prophets**" (Luke 18:31), and the actual words directly written by the prophets themselves would have been in the original language in which God gave them by inspiration to the prophets. The oracles of God [the Old Testament Scriptures] given to the prophets were committed unto the Jews in the Jews' language (Rom. 3:2, Matt. 5:17-18, Luke 16:17). The specific features "jot" and "tittle" at Matthew 5:18 and the "tittle" at Luke 16:17 would indicate the particular original language words of the Scriptures given by inspiration of God to the prophets. The actual, specific, exact words which the LORD of hosts sent in His Spirit by the prophets would be in the original language in which God gave them (Zech. 7:12). Would not the actual words written by the prophet be in the same language in which he originally wrote them (Matt. 2:5, Luke 18:31)? Would not the words spoken by the LORD by the prophets be in the language in which God gave them (2 Kings 21:10, 2 Kings 24:2)? It would be sound to conclude that the actual words of the prophets themselves would be in the original language in which they were given (Acts 15:15). The scriptures of the prophets (Rom. 15:26) would be in the language in which they were given to them. A writing from Elijah would be written in the language in which Elijah wrote it (2 Chron. 21:12). The actual words of Haggai the prophet would be in the language in which he spoke or wrote them (Haggai 1:12). The apostle John referred to his own actual words he himself was writing in the language in which he wrote them (1 John 2:12-14). "Moses wrote all the words of the LORD" (Exod. 24:4). The Lord Jesus Christ stated: "For had ye believed Moses, ye would have believed me: for he wrote of me. But if ye believe not **his writings**, how shall ye believe my words?" (John 5:46-47). In another apparent reference to the writings of Moses, Jesus asked the Pharisees concerning whether they had not read them (Matt. 19:4, 7-8). The actual writings of Moses referred to by Jesus would have to be in the original language in which Moses directly wrote them. When later

Jewish scribes made a copy of the writings of Moses, they copied his same words in the same language in which Moses had originally wrote them. Do the Scriptures teach or at least clearly infer that the doctrine of preservation would concern the actual specific original-language words given by inspiration of God to the prophets and apostles?

A sound understanding of some additional Bible truths would affirm or demonstrate that Bible preservation would have to concern the Scriptures in the original languages. The scriptural truths (Deut. 4:2, Deut. 12:32, Prov. 30:6, Rev. 22:18-19) that warn against adding to and taking away from the Scriptures would clearly and directly relate to the doctrine of preservation and to the making of copies of the original-language Scriptures. Concerning which specific words did God directly state these warnings and instructions? These commands and instructions must embrace the Scriptures in the original languages since the very nature of translation requires that words may have to be added or omitted to make it understandable in another language. Thus, these verses were important instructions and warnings given particularly and directly concerning the Scriptures in the original languages. These verses could also be understood to suggest that God gave to men an important role or responsibility in preservation of the Scriptures on earth. These commands or instructions would indicate the need and responsibility for the making of exact, accurate copies of the Scriptures in the original languages. These commands or instructions also demonstrate that the source being copied was the standard and authority for evaluating the copy made from it. These commands would also suggest that the copies of Scripture were not given or made by the means or process of a miracle of inspiration. For when a king [or whoever] copied them, he would have needed to make an accurate, exact, and complete copy of them to be able to "keep all the words" (Deut. 17:18-19).

A copy of Scripture should have the exact, same words as the source from which it was copied, and it could be tested or evaluated by its source (Exod. 34:1, Deut. 10:2, 4, Deut. 17:18, Deut. 27:8, Jer. 36:28, John 17:8, Jer. 23:28). Greg Bahnsen noted: "God provided for the rewriting of the words of the original tablets (Exod. 34:1, 27-28), and Scripture makes the point that these second tablets were written 'according to the first writing' (Deut. 10:2, 4). Here is a significant model for all later copying of the biblical autographs; they should reproduce the words that were on the first tablet or page" (Geisler, *Inerrancy*, p. 165). KJV-only author H. D. Williams asserted: "The model for preservation of inspired Words is also included in the Bible. **God made the first copy of His inspired Words** as the model. He copied the exact same Words that were on the first tablet containing the Ten Commandments (Exod. 34:1). He commanded Jeremiah to make a copy of the **exact** Words He gave him to record in the scroll that King Jehoiakim cut-up and destroyed with a penknife and by burning the manuscript (Jer. 36ff)" (*Hearing the Voice of God*, pp. 194-195; *Miracle of Biblical Inspiration*, pp. 44-45). Jesus gave the exact same words to the apostles or disciples that God the Father gave to Him (John 17:8, John 14:24, John 12:50).

A logical and sound deduction or necessary consequence from these instructions in several verses of Scripture (Deut. 4:2, Deut. 12:32, Prov. 30:6, Rev. 22:18-19) would indicate and affirm that copies would need to be carefully examined, searched, tried, or evaluated to make sure that no additions were made, that nothing was omitted, that no words were changed, and that the meaning of words according to their context was not diminished. The truth stated in these verses could be properly understood to indicate that whatever adds to, takes away, or diminishes (whether intentional or unintentional) would not be the word of God. These scriptural instructions and truths provide sound guidance concerning how to know the words which the LORD has or has not spoken (Deut. 18:21, Jer. 23:16, Jer. 23:35, Ezek. 22:28). Would words that go beyond those words that God actually gave to the prophets and apostles be considered the actual pure words of God (Num. 22:18)? There is such a thing as the possible adding of words in copies or in Bible translations. It can be properly concluded from the Scriptures that God has not directly spoken words added by men and that any words omitted by copiers should be restored (Deut. 4:2, Deut. 12:32, Prov. 30:6, Rev. 22:18). According to scriptural truth, words added by men cannot soundly be considered as being words given by inspiration of God. Since the law or word of the LORD is perfect (Ps. 19:7, James 1:25) and since perfection by definition would exclude the presence of even one imperfection, would imperfect renderings made by men or any errors introduced by men be identical to the perfect words of God given to the prophets and apostles? Since the statues or words of the LORD are right (Ps. 19:8, Ps. 33:4) and since the words of God are true (Ps. 19:9, John 17:17, Ps. 119:160, Dan. 10:21), it can be soundly and scripturally concluded that any wrong words or errors introduced by imperfect men would not be the absolutely pure words of God. It can be also properly concluded that any errors introduced by men in copying, in printing, or in translating are not words spoken or given by God. Any error introduced by a copier, printer, or whomever in copies and in Bible translations can be and should be corrected. It could also be soundly concluded that any words perverted, diminished, or mistranslated by men are not actual words spoken by God (Jer. 23:36, Deut. 4:2, Jer. 23:28, Deut. 12:32, 2 Cor. 2:17, Jer. 23:16, Jer. 26:2).

Just as the source definitely had to be the correct standard, proper authority, and just measure or balance for evaluating the copy; likewise, the words in the preserved original language sources would have to be the proper standard and greater authority for evaluating the different words in a translation made from them (Rom. 11:18, Prov. 16:11, Deut. 16:20, Job 14:4, Deut. 25:13-15, Lev. 19:35-36, Ezek. 45:10, Matt. 7:17, Prov. 11:1, Micah 6:11). Do the Scriptures themselves provide examples that would show that original-language words would be the authority, source, and standard for translated words that translate, interpret, or give the meaning in another language (Matt. 1:23, Mark 5:41, Mark 15:22, Mark 15:34, John 1:41, Acts 4:36)? Appeals to what was written by a prophet or by the prophets would be an acknowledgement of the authority and standard of the original-language words of Scripture (Matt. 2:5, Luke 18:31, John 5:47). Unless the preserved Scriptures in the original languages are the authority, norm, and standard for Bible translations, there would be no sound, true criteria for distinguishing between a good, accurate translation and a poor, inaccurate translation. Would not the original-language Scriptures given by inspiration of God and preserved by God be profitable for correction of any errors made or introduced by imperfect men in translating and in printing?

Jim Taylor maintained that preservation is not "an attribute" but that it "is a process" (*In Defense of the TR*, p. 40). Taylor asserted that "translations are not preserved because preservation is not an attribute" (Ibid.). Taylor noted: "Add to this the fact that God preserved what he gave. God gave us his words in Greek and Hebrew and thus, he preserves his words in those languages" (Ibid.). Tim Fellure observed: "Obviously, it's not required that preservation extends to a translation if the Word of God has been preserved in the Greek and Hebrew text" (*Neither jot nor tittle*, p. 71). Thomas Corkish acknowledged that "it is true that He [God] has not promised to preserve versions" (Brandenburg, *Thou Shalt Keep Them*, p. 210). Raymond Blanton claimed: "God has not preserved His Words mingled with the words of men" (*Flaming Torch*, May, 1988, p. 8).

The scriptural truths concerning righteous judgments and just measures also provide sound guidance in determining how to know which words the LORD has or has not spoken or given as part of Scripture. The use of any unrighteous divers weights, unequal or false balances, inconsistent divers measures, unfair or untrue judgments, or double standards in evaluating, judging, trying, or comparing original language manuscript copies of Scripture [likewise printed original language texts and translations] would be wrong according to a consistent, sound application of scriptural truths and principles (Prov. 16:11, 20:10, 11:1, 20:23, Deut. 25:13-15, Ezek. 45:10, Lev. 19:35-36, Amos 8:5, Ps. 82:2, Lev. 19:15, Luke 16:10, Matt. 7:2, John 7:24, Lev. 10:10, Ps. 58:1, Deut. 16:18-20, Ps. 19:7-9). The scriptural principles of using just measures and not using unjust measures would be timeless and edifying, and they would not be limited to a specific situation or time period. Use of these scriptural principles would aid in proving all things, in proving what is acceptable to God, and in holding fast that which is good (1

Thess. 5:21, Eph. 5:10, Rom. 12:9). These instructions to use just measures and not use unjust measures are not in conflict with other scriptural teaching, but instead they are in agreement with other scriptural teaching. Applying scriptural truths justly would agree with and become sound doctrine (Titus 2:1, 2 Tim. 4:3). The use of inconsistent, unjust measures or double standards could be soundly connected to being double-minded (James 1:8).

Like physical measurements, mental and spiritual judgments or measures also should be good, true, upright, and just or righteous (John 7:24, Lev. 19:35, Lev. 19:15, Ps. 19:9, Ps. 119:39, Zech. 7:9, Prov. 12:17, Ps. 119:66, 1 Thess. 5:21, Ps. 119:137, Prov. 31:9, Deut. 1:16, Phil. 4:8, Eph. 4:25, 2 Cor. 4:2). Believers are instructed and commanded to think on things that are honest, just, and pure (Phil. 4:8) and to speak the truth (Eph. 4:25). According to what the Scriptures state and teach, it would be clear that the holy, just God would oppose the wicked perverting or wresting of righteous judgment by use of unjust measures (Job 34:12, Job 8:3, Exodus 23:7, Exodus 23:2, Rev. 15:3). Have KJV-only advocates actually demonstrated that they choose the way of truth and the mind of Christ if they choose to use inconsistent, unjust measures or double standards (Ps, 119:30, Prov. 12:17, Prov. 16:11)? Every false or evil way including that of the making of inconsistent, unrighteous judgments and the use of unjust measures should be hated or abhorred by believers (Ps. 119:104, 128, Rom. 12:9, Ps. 97:10). Should not believers denounce the hidden things of dishonesty and unjustness (2 Cor. 4:2)? Would unrighteous judgments or use of unjust measures be things that exalt themselves against the knowledge, wisdom, and truth of God (2 Cor. 10:5)? What fellowship has righteousness with unrighteousness (2 Cor. 6:14)? What fellowship has truth with fallacies or false claims? Righteous judgments based on just measures and in line with the wisdom that is from God above would be without partiality and without hypocrisy (James 3:17, Deut. 1:16-17). Showing partiality or respect of persons to one group of Bible translators would not be agreement with the wisdom from above and with righteous judgment. The making of sound, true, righteous judgments would be properly considered a weightier matter (Matt. 23:23). A failure to use consistent, "altogether just" measures, standards, criteria, or principles (Deut. 16:20, Prov. 16:11, Ezek. 45:10, Deut. 25:15, Ps. 19:9) in comparing or trying manuscript copies or translations of Scripture would condemn the inconsistent, unfair, uneven, and unjust judgments that would result. According to scriptural truth, should anyone who would use unjust measures or would be unjust concerning textual differences that are considered least be trusted in greater textual differences (Luke 16:10)? In order to be faithful, true, and just in that which is least, one would need to use consistent, just measures/standards. That the preserved copies of the Scriptures in the original languages as collated, searched, evaluated, and discerned by use of consistent, just measures should be the proper standard, measure, and authority for trying or evaluating translations of the Scriptures would be a valid and sound implication or deduction drawn from what several verses of Scripture state, teach, or infer.

Testing KJV-only allegations concerning the NKJV

In addition to the primary comparison to the proper standard of the preserved Scriptures in the original languages, one interesting secondary way to test, measure, and check many of the KJV-only accusations against the NKJV is by a comparison to the 1560 Geneva Bible, which is praised by KJV-only advocates, which is one of the pre-1611 English Bibles of which the KJV was a revision, which is inseparably connected with the KJV, and which was the accepted and loved translation of English-speaking believers before 1611 and for a time afterwards. With this measure or test, it can be clearly and fairly determined whether the exact same measures or standards were and are used in comparing the pre-1611 English Bibles and the KJV as in comparing the KJV and the NKJV. Should Bible believers not conclude that the use of any unrighteous divers weights, unjust or false balances, divers measures, untrue judgments, or double standards in evaluating, judging, trying, or comparing translations would be wrong according to what the Scriptures teach in several verses (Prov. 16:11, 20:10, 11:1, 20:23, Deut. 25:13-15, Ezek. 45:10, Lev. 19:35-36, Amos 8:5, Ps. 82:2, Lev. 19:15, Luke 16:10, Lev. 10:10)?

Gail Riplinger asserted: "Many enjoy the comfort zone of generalities and cannot function in the realm of particulars" (*Hazardous Materials*, pp. 24-25). Riplinger declared: "God is a God of particulars" (Ibid.). In her book *In Awe of Thy Word*, Gail Riplinger referred to her "word-for-word collation of earlier English Bibles with the KJV" and her "word-for-word analysis of the English Bibles before the KJV" (pp. 17, 18). According to her very own assertions of what she claimed to have done, it would be reasonable to think or conclude that Riplinger should have been aware of the particulars or evidence found in the comparisons that will be presented here. Did she ignore or skip over many actual particulars in the Geneva Bible that would have contradicted or refuted her over-generalized, misleading, or incorrect accusations against the NKJV? It cannot be validly or reasonably assumed, claimed, or implied by KJV defenders that any renderings in the NKJV that were already in the good **1560** Geneva Bible or other pre-1611 English Bibles could only come from 1800's or modern editions of the Hebrew and Greek texts, from modern translations, or from 1800's or modern lexicons. Since the wording in the Geneva Bible was acceptable enough to be used by God and loved by English-speaking believers in 1560 and for around one hundred years, why would God not accept the same wording or wording with the same meaning when found in the NKJV? Since Gail Riplinger could assert that the Geneva Bible was "practically identical" to the KJV, would she in effect contradict herself if she claims that the same or very similar renderings in the NKJV are not also "practically identical"? If the pre-1611 English Bibles and the KJV are basically the same Bibles as KJV-only authors have claimed, is not the same true of the KJV and the NKJV according to consistent application of the same reasoning or the same measures? Does the NKJV differ only slightly from the KJV according to a consistent application of actual KJV-only assertions concerning the Geneva Bible? Can the NKJV properly be said to be a revision or an edition of the KJV according to a consistent, just application of the KJV-only claims that the KJV is a revision or an edition of Tyndale's, the Geneva, or another pre-1611 English Bible? If it would be wrong to suggest that the KJV was a revision of counterfeit Bibles or false Bibles if the pre-1611 English Bibles were not every-word Bibles, is it also not wrong to make the same accusation against the NKJV? According to the sound use of consistent, just measures, should the NKJV be considered part of the very same stream of Bibles as the Geneva Bible and the KJV?

As in this test and examination of KJV-only accusations against the NKJV by a comparison with the Geneva Bible, it can be seen that stated KJV-only reasoning may be borrowed and applied to the Geneva Bible in order to see if it is valid, sound, or true. Some thought-provoking questions that attempt to apply KJV-only claims, KJV-only questions, and KJV-only reasoning consistently and justly may help to test, try, and evaluate it. If KJV-only advocates really believe that the Geneva Bible was the inspired or pure Word of God in English in 1560 and believe their own claims concerning the word of God, should they have been unwilling to have one word or even one syllable of it changed? Do Ruckman and other KJV-only advocates take the English translation "given by inspiration" at 2 Timothy 3:16 in the 1560 Geneva Bible "to be the truth" and to mean that the Geneva Bible was given by inspiration of God [for example, see Ruckman's *Biblical Scholarship*, p. 355]? Do KJV-only advocates maintain that the Geneva Bible, which was the translation received, accepted, believed, and used by English-speaking believers before 1611, was "given by inspiration" or "divinely inspired" by definition of Scripture or the word of God? Should English-speaking believers in 1560 have accepted the Geneva Bible as their providentially-appointed final authority according to a consistent, just application of KJV-only reasoning? Should believers have assumed that God so protected His word in the Geneva Bible so that nothing could have been lost in the translating and so that there could be no errors in it to mislead its readers? Were English-speaking believers in 1560 and for the next fifty years supposed to accept and believe every word of their received English Bible that God had provided them as pure, inspired, and perfect? Were those saved under witnessing, teaching, or preaching from the Geneva Bible born of corruptible seed or incorruptible seed? Since the Geneva Bible was sufficient for English-speaking believers for at least fifty years and perhaps one hundred years, did it supposedly become insufficient in 1611 or in 1660? Which English Bible did Jesus or the Holy Spirit use from 1560 until 1610? Since the Lord Jesus Christ used the Geneva Bible for at least fifty years, would He change and use a different one according to a consistent application of KJV-only reasoning? If Jesus had brought a KJV to church with Him in 1611, would it supposedly undermine the historical integrity of His words in English the previous fifty years? Had our English Scriptures been wrong for over 50 years until a new group of translators finally got them right in 1611? If the 1560 Geneva Bible did not contain all the words of the LORD without error, is it being suggested that God made an error in permitting it to be made, published, and received in the first place? If English-speaking believers did not have in the 1560 Geneva Bible a translation containing all of God's words and only God's words with not one word added and not one word taken away, would KJV-only reasoning suggest that God gave them a defective foundation and authority? Would KJV-only reasoning suggest that God preserved error instead of truth in the 1560 Geneva Bible? If the pre-1611 English Bible such as the Geneva Bible was not perfect, do KJV-only advocates claim that God didn't preserve His word? What kind of God does KJV-only reasoning suggest that we have to give the generation in 1560 a worse Bible than today? Do KJV-only advocates imply that God revoked inspiration at some point in time before 1611 [such as in 1560] and only reinstated it in 1611? Did the making of a new English translation in 1611 call into question the accuracy of the pre-1611 English Bible? Why did the English Bible need changing in 1611? When readers of the 1611 KJV saw that some words and phrases found in the Geneva Bible were missing in the KJV, when they saw that the KJV added words, phrases, clauses, or a verse not found in the Geneva Bible, and when they saw the hundreds and thousands of differences between the two, were they supposed to assume that the doctrines of Bible inspiration, preservation, and inerrancy were destroyed?

Since God was the same in 1560 as in 1611, according to what scriptural truths can it be implied that the guiding of the Holy Spirit for the Geneva Bible translators was different than the guiding for the KJV translators? Did some of the textual or translation decisions of the Geneva Bible translators slip by God? What makes the translation of the multiversionists who made the KJV better or more accurate than the translation chosen by the Geneva Bible translators under the guiding of the Holy Spirit? The Geneva Bible translators were guided by the same overseeing preserver of Scripture, the Holy Spirit, as may be inconsistently and unjustly claimed by some to be only for the KJV translators. Does a consistent application of KJV-only claims suggest or assert that God helped produce an incomplete or fragmented English Bible in 1560? Would KJV-only reasoning suggest that the LORD God was incompetent and powerless in His guiding and involvement in the making of the Geneva Bible? Would a consistent application of KJV-only reasoning suggest that if the Geneva Bible had any errors that it would mean that God somehow lost control of His Word at some point in history? If the Geneva Bible was wrong in all the places where the makers of the KJV changed it, is it being suggested that God was wrong to bless its usage as the accepted English Bible for many years? Since God was just as faithful in 1560 as in 1611, would God bless and use the Geneva Bible for fifty years, possibly for around 100 years, or even for one year if any of its renderings were unacceptable or incorrect words of man and if it was missing any words of God according to a consistent application of KJV-only assertions? If God had a controversy with the Geneva Bible, would God have blessed and used it for fifty years and would God have permitted it to be one of the primary English sources of the KJV? According to a consistent application of KJV-only reasoning, could God use both the 1560 Geneva Bible and the 1611 KJV when they say and mean differing or conflicting things in some places? If the LORD supposedly replaced the Geneva Bible with the KJV, would He in effect be undermining the integrity of the "brand" that He had established fifty years earlier? Were the 1560 Geneva Bible and the 1611 KJV dual or competing authorities for twenty or more years? Did God call English-speaking believers before 1611 to preach an inspired Bible on which they could not put their hands?

According to the consistent application of some KJV-only reasoning, the KJV-only view in effect permits an exclusive group of Church of England scholars/critics in 1611 to sit in judgment on the received Protestant Reformation Text and the pre-1611 Holy Bible in English [the Geneva Bible] and to alter it and introduce many changes to it. The actual evidence will show that the makers of the KJV made both some textual and many translational changes to the Geneva Bible. Were any of the changes that the KJV translators made to the Geneva Bible simply for the sake of variety? Were any of the many changes that the KJV translators made to the English text of the Geneva Bible the result of doctrinal bias or the result of an effort to promote or favor Episcopal church government or the divine-right-of-kings view of King James I? According to a consistent application of some KJV-only reasoning, did those Church of England scholars usurp the authority of the received Book of the English-speaking believers in their day [the Geneva Bible] in order to assert their own authority [for example, see p. 34 in Ruckman's *Biblical Scholarship*]? Do KJV-only advocates in effect set up the KJV translators as an authority over the pre-1611 Bible in the original languages and over the pre-1611 English Bible? Does KJV-only reasoning in effect place the KJV translators as being in the position of having to sit in judgment on the pre-1611 English Bible—the 1560 Geneva Bible? Was it a serious indictment for the makers of the KJV to change and tamper with the pre-1611 word of God in English [see p. 101 in *Hyles' Need for an Every-Word Bible*]? Should Bible believers have any trouble in providing clear direct answers to these questions based on a consistent application of KJV-only reasoning and its logical implications? Peter Ruckman asserted that "our practice will match our profession" (p. 64), but do the facts support that assertion? KJV-only advocates clearly do not practice what they preach as it would relate to the English Bible before 1611, and they may not want their evident use of inconsistent, unjust measures judged by the Book.

A consistent application of Gail Riplinger's very broad-sweeping, generalized accusation that **all** lexicons and all Hebrew and Greek study tools "are corrupt" would also seem to include or apply to the actual Hebrew and Greek lexicons used by the KJV translators (*Hazardous Materials*, pp. 29, 37, 38). Could the Church of England translators of the KJV have been blinded by "Catholic-touched Latin-Greek lexicons" (p. 216)? It is known that the Hebrew-Latin lexicons and Greek-Latin lexicons available to and used by the KJV translators sometimes or even often had Latin definitions for Hebrew words or for Greek words that were borrowed from the Latin Vulgate of Jerome, which would be classified a corrupt translation according to typical KJV-only reasoning or according to the KJV-only two-streams-of-Bibles argument. Other Latin definitions in those Hebrew-Latin and Greek-Latin lexicons would have likely come from commentaries by unsaved Jews and from commentaries by Roman Catholic church fathers. In 1847, *The Churchman's Monthly Review* maintained that "the Thesauraus of Santes Pagninus [1470-1541] was one of the earliest Hebrew Latin lexicons" (p. 129). This source noted that Pagninus was "a Jesuit" and that his lexicon "contains the Latin Vulgate translation of every word in the Hebrew Bible" (Ibid.). It also indicated that this lexicon by Pagninus was used by Protestants as well as by Roman Catholics. Bishop Grindal is said to have had a copy of an edition of the Lexicon of Pagninus printed in 1577 that he left to the library at Queen's College at Oxford. David Norton observed that KJV translator Edward Lively had a copy of "Pagninus's *Thesaurus Lingue Sanctae*" (*KJB: Short History*, p. 69). Jones, Moore, and Reid noted that KJV translator "Henry Savile himself gave to the library a copy of Pagninus's *Thesaurus Linguae Sanctae*" (Moore, *Manifold Greatness*, p. 96). The author of *Principles and Problems of Biblical Translation* asserted that Reuchlin in his Hebrew-Latin dictionary or lexicon "gives the equivalent Latin expression, generally more than one, for every Hebrew word and then adduces examples for each meaning. These examples are naturally taken from the Old Testament; they are not quoted in Hebrew but in the Latin of the Vulgate" (pp. 76-77). David H. Price maintained that Johannes Reuchlin's Hebrew-Latin lexicon in his *Rudiments of Hebrew* "rejected Jerome's text in several hundred places" (*Johannes Reuchlin,* p. 61), which would suggest that it gave Jerome's Latin renderings as definitions of Hebrew words in the thousands of other cases. R. Cunningham Didham contended that the "Hebrew lexicons of those days rather perpetuated the errors of the Vulgate than the sense of the Hebrew" (*New Translation of the Psalms,* p. 7). Didham added: "Even the Lexicon of the celebrated Sebastian Munster was no more than that, as Wolf assures us, the Latin words of the Vulgate" (Ibid.). Herbert Marsh noted: "When Sebastian Munster composed his *Dictionarium Hebraicum*, he added to each Hebrew word the sense in Latin. And whence did he derive those Latin senses? From the Vulgate" (*Lectures,* p. 521). Munster also compiled a Latin-Greek-Hebrew dictionary. Henry Kiddle and Alexander Schem maintained that until the 1800's "the Greek language was studied through the medium of the Latin, and there were no Greek-English, but only Greek-Latin lexicons" (*Cyclopaedia,* p. 224). Paul Botley wrote: "Many scholars learnt Greek through the Vulgate, and compiled their elementary Greek-Latin lexica from a collation of the Vulgate Bible with its Greek equivalents.

Consequently, the equations of the Vulgate often formed the basis of the lexica" (*Latin Translation in the Renaissance*, p. 96). Gail Riplinger admitted: "The few lexicons the KJB translators did use were generally in Latin, not English" (*Hazardous Materials,* p. 1187). Would a consistent application of the reasoning in Riplinger's book suggest that the KJV translators were wrong to use any lexicons that borrowed any definitions from a Bible translation [the Latin Vulgate of Jerome] placed on the KJV-only view's line of corrupt Bibles and any from secular pagan authors, unbelieving Jews, or Roman Catholic Church fathers? Is Riplinger in effect implying that use of any lexicon with definitions from a corrupt translation such as the Roman Catholic Latin Vulgate of Jerome would have contaminated the KJV? Would tracing any KJV readings or renderings back to the Latin Vulgate by means of Hebrew-Latin or Greek-Latin lexicons prove them to be correct or incorrect? Riplinger's apparent use of fallacies to attempt to smear all lexicons and modern translations is misleading and wrong, and a consistent application of her inconsistent, faulty reasoning would even condemn the actual lexicons and original language texts used by the early English translators including the KJV translators.

Along with indirect influence on the KJV through use of Hebrew-Latin and Greek-Latin lexicons, an edition of the Latin Vulgate of Jerome was one of the varying sources directly consulted by the KJV translators. In addition, the 1582 Rheims New Testament translated from an edition of the Latin Vulgate of Jerome was also consulted and used in the making of the KJV. Charles Butterworth noted: "There are instances where the Rheims New Testament reads differently from all the preceding versions and yet has been followed later by similar readings in the King James Bible, indicating that the translators of 1611 by no means ignored the work that was done in 1582" (*Literary Lineage of the KJV*, p. 195). T. H. Darlow and H. F. Moule wrote: "This Rheims New Testament exerted a very considerable influence on the version of 1611, transmitting to it not only an extensive vocabulary, but also numerous distinctive phrases and turns of expression" (*Historical Catalogue of the Printed Editions*, p. 96). Darlow and Moule noted that "the Rheims New Testament, though not mentioned, contributed appreciably to the changes introduced" (p. 134). David Daniell wrote: "Another, more serious, push toward Latinity came from the influence on the [KJV] panels of the extremely Latinate Roman Catholic translation from Rheims" (*Tyndale's N. T.,* p. xiii). David Norton asserted that "Rheims's prime contribution to the KJB was an added sprinkle of latinate vocabulary in the NT" (*KJB: a Short History*, p. 32). John R. Kohlenberger III observed: "Although Bancroft did not list the Catholic Rheims (1582) translation of the New Testament as a resource to be used, and although Miles Smith does not cite it by name, the translators occasionally followed its readings" (Burke, *Translation That Openeth the Window*, p. 47).

J. R. Dore wrote: "A very considerable number of the Rhemish renderings, which they introduced for the first time, were adopted by the revisers of King James's Bible of 1611" (*Old Bibles*, p. 303). Charles Butterworth observed that the Rheims version "recalled the thought of the [KJV] translators to the Latin structure of the sentences, which they sometimes preferred to the Greek for clarity's sake, thus reverting to the pattern of Wycliffe or the Coverdale Latin-English Testaments, and forsaking the foundation laid by Tyndale" (*Literary Lineage of the KJV,* p. 237). In an introductory article on "The English Bible" in *The Interpeter's Bible,* Allen Wikgren also noted that the Rheims "exerted a considerable influence upon the King James revision, in which many of its Latinisms were adopted" (Vol. I, p. 93). Herbert May confirmed that "some of its [the Rheims] phrases were used by the King James Version translators" (*Our English Bible in the Making,* p. 47). In his 1808 answer to the reprinting of Ward's 1688 book *Errata of the Protestant Bible*, Edward Ryan referred to the KJV translators "adopting the Romish Version in very many instances" and to their making corrections "agreeably to the popish construction" (*Analysis,* pp. 5-6). Benson Bobrick also observed; "From the Rheims New Testament, the translators saw fit to borrow a number of Latinate words" (*Wide as the Waters*, p. 244). Samuel Fisk also acknowledged that the Rheims had "an influence upon the King James Version" (*Calvinistic Paths,* p. 74). James Carleton noted: "One cannot but be struck by the large number of words which have come into the Authorized Version from the Vulgate through the medium of the Rhemish New Testament" (*Part of Rheims in the Making of the English Bible*, p. 32).   In his book, Carleton gave charts or comparisons in which he gave the rendering of the early Bibles and then the different rendering of the Rheims and KJV.

It is most likely that the KJV translators obtained their knowledge of the Rheims New Testament from a book by William Fulke which compared the Rheims N. T. side by side with the Bishops' N. T.   In his introduction to a 1911 facsimile reprint of the 1611, A. W. Pollard maintained that "probably every reviser of the New Testament for the edition of 1611" possessed a copy of Fulke's book that "was regarded as a standard work on the Protestant side" (p. 23). John Greider observed that "This work [by Fulke] was studied by the translators of the 1611 Bible" (*English Bible Translations*, p. 316).   Peter Thuesen pointed out: "William Fulke's popular 1589 annotated edition of the Rheims New Testament, though intended as an antidote to popery, in reality had served as the vehicle by which some of the Rhemists' Latinisms entered the vocabulary of the King James Bible" (*In Discordance*, p. 62).   David Norton noted that KJV translator William Branthwaite had a copy of "Fulke's parallel edition of the Rheims and Bishops" in his personal library (*KJB: Short History*, p. 64).   Norton also pointed out that the Bodleian Library in 1605 had a copy of Fulke's edition of the Rheims and Bishops' New Testaments (Ibid.). Even Gail Riplinger confirmed that the KJV translators had Fulke's book with these verse comparisons, but she in effect ignored the evidence that they followed some of the renderings of the Rheims (*In Awe*, p. 536).   Instead, she implied that the translators of the KJV avoided "multi-syllable Latin root-words" (p. 535).

W. F. Moulton stated: "The Rhemish Testament was not even named in the instructions furnished to the translators, but it has left its mark on every page of their work" (*History of the English Bible*, p. 207).   Diarmaid MacCulloch and Elizabeth Solopova asserted that in the KJV "it was possible to see some of the readings of the Doua-Rheims version amid all the work of Tyndale, Coverdale and the Geneva translators" (Moore, *Manifold Greatness*, p. 38).   Ward Allen maintained that "the Rheims New Testament furnished to the Synoptic Gospels and Epistles in the A. V. as many revised readings as any other version" (*Translating the N. T. Epistles*, p. xxv).   Allen and Jacobs claimed that the KJV translators "in revising the text of the synoptic Gospels in the Bishops' Bible, owe about one-fourth of their revisions, each, to the Genevan and Rheims New Testaments" (*Coming of the King James Gospels,* p. 29).   About 1 Peter 1:20, Ward Allen noted: "The A. V. shows most markedly here the influence of the Rheims Bible, from which it adopts the verb in composition, the reference of the adverbial modifier to the predicate, the verb *manifest*, and the prepositional phrase *for you*" (*Translating for King James*, p. 18).   Concerning 1 Peter 4:9, Allen suggested that "this translation in the A. V. joins the first part of the sentence from the Rheims Bible to the final phrase of the Protestant translations" (p. 30). Allen also observed: "At Col. 2:18, he [KJV translator John Bois] explains that the [KJV] translators were relying upon the example of the Rheims Bible" (pp. 10, 62-63).   The note of John Bois cited a rendering from the 1582 Rheims ["willing in humility"] and then cited the margin of the Rheims ["willfull, or selfwilled in voluntary religion"] (p. 63).   Was the KJV's rendering "voluntary" borrowed from the margin of the 1582 Rheims?   The first-hand testimony of a KJV translator clearly acknowledged or confirmed the fact that the KJV was directly influenced by the 1582 Rheims.   KJV defender Laurence Vance admitted that the 1582 "Rheims supplies the first half of the reading" in the KJV at Galatians 3:1 and that the "Rheims supplies the last half of the reading" at Galatians 3:16 (*Making of the KJV NT*, p. 263).

KJV-only author Doug Stauffer referred to the Douay-Rheims as "the Jesuit English Roman Catholic Bible" (*One Book Stands Alone*, p. 204).   Diarmaid MacCulloch noted that the Roman Catholic English translation "was not for ordinary folks to read, but for priests to use as a polemical weapon—the explicit purpose that the 1582 title-page and preface of the Rheims New Testament proclaimed" (*The Reformation*, p. 566).   In the introductory articles in Hendrickson's reprint of the 1611, Alfred Pollard maintained that "the exiled Jesuit, Gregory Martin, must be recognized as one of the builders of the [1611] version of the Bible" (p. 28).   David Norton affirmed that the words borrowed from the Rheims "make Martin a drafter of the KJB" (*KJB: a Short History*, p. 32). Norton added: "Since most of them are transliterations of Jerome's Latin, they also make Jerome an author of the KJB" (Ibid.). Norton pointed out that "the Roman Catholic John Hingham (fl. 1639) was to claim that the KJB in fact supported Roman Catholic, not Protestant views" (*History of the English Bible*, p. 54). Robert R. Dearden, Jr. observed that "it must be conceded that his [Gregory Martin's] translations exerted a pronounced influence on the King James Version of 1611, transmitting to it distinctive phrases and style of expression" (*Guiding Light*, p. 219).

The sound evidence of the direct influence of the Roman Catholic Rheims New Testament on the KJV is a serious problem for a KJV-only view and its claims. In his book edited by D. A. Waite, H. D. Williams asserted the following as one of his criteria for translating: "Under no circumstances should a version which is not based upon the Received Texts be used as an example" (*Word-for-Word Translating*, p. 230). Troy Clark claimed that the Douay-Rheims "was translated strictly from the Critical Text Latin Vulgate bible of Rome," and he listed it in his "Critical text" stream of Bibles (*Perfect Bible*, pp. 267, 296). Mickey Carter listed the 1582 on his "corrupted tree" of Bibles (*Things That Are Different*, p. 104). H. D. Williams maintained that "the Douay-Rheims Bible is based upon Jerome's Latin Vulgate" (*Word-for-Word*, p. 42). Peter Ruckman acknowledged that "the textual basis of the *Douay-Rheims* is Jerome's *Latin Vulgate*," but he also claimed in his endnotes that "the Greek *text* of the *Rheims* Jesuit bible was the Westcott and Hort Greek text" (*Biblical Scholarship*, pp. 162, 517). Ruckman referred to "Satan's interest in reinstituting the Dark Age Jesuit Rheims Bible of 1582" (*Alexandrian Cult*, Part Eight, p. 2). Jim Taylor asserted that "Jerome's Latin Vulgate generally agrees with the Westcott and Hort Text" (*In Defense of the TR*, p. 204). Were the KJV translators wrong to consult and make use of any edition of Jerome's Latin Vulgate and of the 1582 Rheims New Testament that were not based on the Received Texts as an example or as a source for some renderings? Should the KJV translators have changed, revised, or corrected the Geneva Bible by borrowing renderings from the 1582 Rheims? Would not the fact that the makers of the KJV followed or borrowed renderings from Bibles on the KJV-only view's corrupt stream/line of Bibles be a problem for KJV-only reasoning? Does a consistent application of KJV-only reasoning suggest that the makers of the KJV borrowed renderings from a corrupted source when they borrowed from the 1582 Rheims? Would KJV-only advocates suggest that Satan's interest was involved in the KJV's borrowing of renderings from the 1582 Rheims? Is a Pandora's box opened when professed Bible believers accept any renderings from the Latin Vulgate or the 1582 Rheims being inserted into their claimed pure stream of Bibles? Would a consistent application of KJV-only reasoning suggest that a little leaven from the 1582 Rheims would leaven the whole KJV? Considering the fact of the multiple textually-varying sources used in the making of the KJV and the borrowed renderings from the 1582 Rheims, would it be accurate to suggest that the KJV emerges solely from the Received Text? Do renderings from the 1582 Rheims make the KJV a hybrid Bible? Could the KJV's borrowing from the Latin Vulgate or 1582 Rheims serve as a bridge to the modern versions? Is it now very clear that Williams and other KJV-only advocates do not apply their own measures, criteria, or requirements concerning translating to the pre-1611 English Bibles and the KJV even though they may inconsistently use them to criticize later English Bibles?

Considering the sound, credible evidence of readings added by Erasmus (a Roman Catholic) to the Greek New Testament from an edition of the Latin Vulgate of Jerome and of several renderings from the 1582 Roman Catholic Rheims found in the KJV, it seems very inconsistent and even hypocritical for KJV-only advocates to attempt to condemn all modern translations as supposedly being Roman Catholic Bibles. For example, Peter Ruckman asserted that "all the New Bibles are the Roman Catholic Vulgate of Jerome restored via Westcott and Hort" (*Handbook of Manuscript Evidence*, p. 155). Peter Ruckman contended that "every Bible translated since 1880 is a Roman Catholic Bible, or a Communist Bible" (p. 156). Ruckman suggested that all other English versions besides the KJV "are Roman Catholic Bibles from the Jesuit Rheims Bible of 1582" (*Bible Believers' Bulletin*, March, 1981, p. 4). Ruckman claimed that "every Bible translated since 1880 contained the Jesuit readings of 1582" (*Differences in the KJV Editions*, p. 4). In a booklet, Ruckman referred to "the Jesuit Text of Vaticanus (1582)" and "the Dark Age Bible of 1582," claiming that it is being published in present English Bibles (*Alexandrian Cult*, Part Seven, p. 12). Ruckman referred to a line of Bibles "that match the Jesuit Rheim's Bible of 1582, published by the Vatican State" (*Monarch of the Books*, p. 19). Both W. Bruce Musselman and R. A. Seely claimed that "correcting the authorized King James Bible reinstates the Roman Catholic Bible" (*Bible Believers' Bulletin*, December, 1979, p. 4 and July, 1981, p. 4). Would a consistent application of Ruckman's own allegations in effect condemn or harm the KJV? Would Ruckman condemn the KJV translators for their use of the 1582 Rheims as a model or source for some renderings introduced in the 1611 KJV? How do KJV-only advocates explain any changes or alterations made in the KJV to the good pre-1611 English Bibles that would have pleased Roman Catholics and were in agreement with the 1582 Rheims, which they have placed on their line of corrupt Bibles? Would KJV-only advocates suggest that revising or correcting the pre-1611 English Bibles with renderings from the 1582 Rheims was partially reinstating the Roman Catholic Bible? If KJV-only advocates in effect permit the KJV translators the latitude to adopt a reading or a rendering from non-received text sources, on what consistent, just basis can they condemn another translation for supposedly doing the same thing? Evidently, KJV-only allegations are not based on the use of consistent, just measures or standards.

Will actual particulars or facts from the 1560 Geneva Bible support or refute KJV-only accusations against the NKJV? In the following comparisons of renderings in the Geneva Bible, the KJV, and the NKJV, spelling in those from the 1560 edition of the Geneva Bible was updated to be like that in present KJV editions. In a few places the verse divisions or numbering in the Geneva Bible differs from the KJV, and in any such cases, the Geneva rendering is listed according to the verse numbering in the KJV. Renderings in the 1599 edition of the Geneva Bible that has the New Testament as revised by Laurence Tomson in 1576 would differ in some cases from those in the 1560 edition. Renderings in different editions of the KJV also may vary in some of the examples from the rendering in the Oxford KJV edition in the Scofield Reference Bible. There may be some possible differences in editions of the NKJV. In some places, the NKJV may vary from both the Geneva Bible and the KJV just as in other places where the KJV and NKJV agree, the Geneva Bible may be the one that varies. These type differences and this amount of variation can be expected to be found in translations from the same original-language texts of Scripture. In the first group of particulars or facts, a large number of places where the 1560 Geneva Bible differs from both the KJV and the NKJV are listed. Sometimes the different English renderings may have the same basic meaning. In other cases, the makers of the KJV improved on the renderings in the Geneva Bible, and the NKJV basically follows or keeps the KJV's renderings, sometimes merely updating the spelling or English. One important example in the Old Testament of where the makers of the KJV improve on the Geneva Bible is in the fact that the KJV indicates for readers a distinction between which Hebrew name is used for God by having "LORD" or "GOD" for the Hebrew name which was also translated Jehovah eight times in the KJV while the Geneva Bible does not. This one case would involve over 5,000 places where the KJV could be considered to have improved on renderings in the Geneva Bible. The NKJV also has these over 5,000 improvements to the Geneva Bible's Old Testament. If the NKJV is an improvement over the Geneva Bible in a large number of places, what does that suggest about the positive praise for the Geneva Bible on the part of KJV-only advocates when compared to their extremely negative attacks on the NKJV? Did Gail Riplinger miss or skip over all the many places where the Geneva Bible differs from both the KJV and NKJV in her word-for-word collation and analysis of the pre-1611 English Bibles? Will actual evidence and particulars soundly demonstrate the KJV-only use of a different measure or criteria for the Geneva Bible than for the NKJV? If the NKJV translators kept or followed many of the improvements made to the Geneva Bible by the KJV translators, could it suggest that the NKJV could be considered more practically identical to the KJV than the Geneva Bible is?

Examples of places where the Geneva Bible differs from both the KJV and the NKJV

Gen. 1:4 God separated (Geneva) God divided (KJV, NKJV)
Gen. 1:7 parted the waters (Geneva) divided the waters (KJV, NKJV)
Gen. 1:18 separate (Geneva) divide (KJV, NKJV)
Gen. 1:22 Then God (Geneva) And God (KJV, NKJV)
Gen. 1:27 Thus God (Geneva) So God (KJV, NKJV)
Gen. 1:28 rule (Geneva) have dominion (KJV, NKJV)
Gen. 2:7 The Lord God also (Geneva) And the LORD God (KJV, NKJV)
Gen. 2:8 And the Lord God (Geneva) And the LORD God (KJV) The LORD God (NKJV)
Gen. 2:9 the Lord God (Geneva) the LORD God (KJV, NKJV)
Gen. 2:15 the Lord God (Geneva) the LORD God (KJV, NKJV)
Gen. 2:16 the Lord God (Geneva) the LORD God (KJV, NKJV)
Gen. 2:17 as touching (Geneva) of (KJV, NKJV)
Gen. 2:18 the Lord God (Geneva) the LORD God (KJV, NKJV)
Gen. 2:19 the Lord God (Geneva) the LORD God (KJV, NKJV)
Gen. 2:20 The man (Geneva) Adam (KJV, NKJV)
Gen. 2:21 the Lord God (Geneva) the LORD God (KJV, NKJV)
Gen. 2:21 the man (Geneva) Adam (KJV, NKJV)
Gen. 3:1 the Lord God (Geneva) the LORD God (KJV, NKJV)
Gen. 3:2 we eat (Geneva) we may eat (KJV, NKJV)
Gen. 3:4 not die at all (Geneva) not surely die (KJV, NKJV)
Gen. 3:7 breeches (Geneva) aprons (KJV) coverings (NKJV)
Gen. 3:8 the Lord God (Geneva) the LORD God (KJV, NKJV)
Gen. 3:9 the Lord God (Geneva) the LORD God (KJV, NKJV)
Gen. 3:13 the Lord God (Geneva) the LORD God (KJV, NKJV)
Gen. 3:14 the Lord God (Geneva) the LORD God (KJV, NKJV)
Gen. 3:20 And the man (Geneva) And Adam (KJV, NKJV)
Gen. 3:20 Hevah (Geneva) Eve (KJV, NKJV)
Gen. 3:21 the Lord God (Geneva) the LORD God (KJV, NKJV)
Gen. 3:22 the Lord God (Geneva) the LORD God (KJV, NKJV)
Gen. 3:23 the Lord God (Geneva) the LORD God (KJV, NKJV)
Gen. 3:24 Thus he cast out (Geneva) So he drove out (KJV) So He drove out (NKJV)
Gen. 3:24 the blade of a sword shaken (Geneva) a flaming sword which turned every way (KJV, NKJV)
Gen. 4:1 Afterward the man (Geneva) And Adam (KJV) Now Adam (NKJV)
Gen. 4:1 Hevah (Geneva) Eve (KJV, NKJV)
Gen. 4:1 by the Lord (Geneva) from the LORD (KJV, NKJV)
Gen. 4:2 Habel (Geneva) Abel (KJV, NKJV)
Gen. 4:4 the Lord (Geneva) the LORD (KJV, NKJV)
Gen. 4:9 the Lord (Geneva) the LORD (KJV, NKJV)
Gen. 4:13 the Lord (Geneva) the LORD (KJV, NKJV)
Gen. 4:15 the Lord (Geneva) the LORD (KJV, NKJV)
Gen. 4:16 the Lord (Geneva) the LORD (KJV, NKJV)
Gen. 4:17 Kain also (Geneva) And Cain (KJV, NKJV)
Gen. 4:17 Henoch (Geneva) Enoch (KJV, NKJV)
Gen. 4:25 Sheth (Geneva) Seth (KJV, NKJV)
Gen. 4:26 the Lord (Geneva) the LORD (KJV, NKJV)
Gen. 5:1 God created Adam (Geneva) God created man (KJV, NKJV)
Gen. 5:10 Kenan (Geneva) Cainan (KJV, NKJV)
Gen. 6:3 the Lord (Geneva) the LORD (KJV, NKJV)
Gen. 6:6 the Lord (Geneva) the LORD (KJV, NKJV)
Gen. 6:7 the Lord (Geneva) the LORD (KJV, NKJV)
Gen. 6:8 the Lord (Geneva) the LORD (KJV, NKJV)
Gen. 6:9 upright (Geneva) perfect (KJV, NKJV)
Gen. 7:1 the Lord (Geneva) the LORD (KJV, NKJV)

Gen. 7:3 upon the whole earth (Geneva) upon the face of all the earth (KJV) on the face of all the earth (NKJV)

Gen. 7:16 the Lord (Geneva) the LORD (KJV, NKJV)

Gen. 8:20 the Lord (Geneva) the LORD (KJV, NKJV)

Gen. 8:21 the Lord (Geneva) the LORD (KJV, NKJV)

Gen. 9:12 Then God (Geneva) And God (KJV, NKJV)

Gen. 9:26 the Lord God (Geneva) the LORD God (KJV, NKJV)

Gen. 10:9 the Lord (Geneva) the LORD (KJV, NKJV)

Gen. 11:5 the Lord (Geneva) the LORD (KJV, NKJV)

Gen. 11:6 the Lord (Geneva) the LORD (KJV, NKJV)

Gen. 11:8 the Lord (Geneva) the LORD (KJV, NKJV)

Gen. 11:9 the Lord (Geneva) the LORD (KJV, NKJV)

Gen. 12:1 the Lord (Geneva) the LORD (KJV, NKJV)

Gen. 12:4 the Lord (Geneva) the LORD (KJV, NKJV)

Gen. 12:7 the Lord (Geneva) the LORD (KJV, NKJV)

Gen. 12:8 the Lord (Geneva) the LORD (KJV, NKJV)

Gen. 12:17 the Lord (Geneva) the LORD (KJV, NKJV)

Gen. 13:4 the Lord (Geneva) the LORD (KJV, NKJV)

Gen. 13:7 a debate (Geneva) a strife (KJV, NKJV)

Gen. 13:8 mine herdsmen (Geneva) my herdsmen (KJV, NKJV)

Gen. 13:10 the Lord (Geneva) the LORD (KJV, NKJV)

Gen. 13:13 the Lord (Geneva) the LORD (KJV, NKJV)

Gen. 13:14 the Lord (Geneva) the LORD (KJV, NKJV)

Gen. 13:18 dwelled (Geneva) dwelt (KJV, NKJV)

Gen. 13:18 builded (Geneva) built (KJV, NKJV)

Gen. 14:1 And in the days (Geneva) And it came to pass in the days (Geneva)

Gen. 14:22 the Lord (Geneva) the LORD (KJV, NKJV)

Gen. 15:1 the Lord (Geneva) the LORD (KJV, NKJV)

Gen. 15:2 Lord God (Geneva) Lord GOD (KJV, NKJV)

Gen. 15:4 the Lord (Geneva) the LORD (KJV, NKJV)

Gen. 15:6 the Lord (Geneva) the LORD (KJV, NKJV)

Gen. 15:7 the Lord (Geneva) the LORD (KJV, NKJV)

Gen. 15:8 O Lord God (Geneva) Lord GOD (KJV, NKJV)

Gen. 15:18 the Lord (Geneva) the LORD (KJV, NKJV)

Gen. 16:2 the Lord (Geneva) the LORD (KJV, NKJV)

Gen. 16:4 her dame (Geneva) her mistress (KJV, NKJV)

Gen. 16:5 Thou doest me wrong (Geneva) My wrong be upon thee (KJV) My wrong be upon you (NKJV)

Gen. 16:8 my dame (Geneva) my mistress (KJV, NKJV)

Gen. 16:9 the Lord (Geneva) the LORD (KJV, NKJV)

Gen. 16:9 thy dame (Geneva) thy mistress (KJV) your mistress (NKJV)

Gen. 16:10 the Lord (Geneva) the LORD (KJV, NKJV)

Gen. 16:10 will so greatly increase (Geneva) will multiple (KJV, NKJV)

Gen. 16:11 Angel of the Lord (Geneva) angel of the LORD (KJV) Angel of the LORD (NKJV)

Gen. 16:11 for the Lord (Geneva) because the LORD (KJV) Because the LORD (NKJV)

Gen. 16:13 the Lord (Geneva) the LORD (KJV, NKJV)

Gen. 17:1 the Lord (Geneva) the LORD (KJV, NKJV)

Gen. 17:1 God all sufficient (Geneva) the Almighty God (KJV) Almighty God (NKJV)

Gen. 17:7 Moreover (Geneva) And (KJV, NKJV)

Gen. 17:9 Again God (Geneva) And God (KJV, NKJV)

Gen. 17:20 And as concerning (Geneva) And as for (KJV, NKJV)

Gen. 17:21 Izhak (Geneva) Isaac (KJV, NKJV)

Gen. 18:1 the Lord (Geneva) the LORD (KJV, NKJV)

Gen. 18:7 the beasts (Geneva) the herd (KJV, NKJV)

Gen. 18:10 come again (Geneva) return (KJV, NKJV)

Gen. 18:13 the Lord (Geneva) the LORD (KJV, NKJV)

Gen. 18:17 the Lord (Geneva) the LORD (KJV, NKJV)
Gen. 18:19 way of the Lord (Geneva) way of the LORD (KJV, NKJV)
Gen. 18:19 that the Lord (Geneva) that the LORD (KJV, NKJV)
Gen. 18:20 Then the Lord (Geneva) And the LORD (KJV, NKJV)
Gen. 18:22 the Lord (Geneva) the LORD (KJV, NKJV)
Gen. 18:26 the Lord (Geneva) the LORD (KJV, NKJV)
Gen. 19:9 Away hence (Geneva) Stand back (KJV, NKJV)
Gen. 19:13 before the Lord (Geneva) before the face of the LORD (KJV, NKJV)
Gen. 19:13 and the Lord (Geneva) and the LORD (KJV, NKJV)
Gen. 19:14 for the Lord (Geneva) for the LORD (KJV, NKJV)
Gen. 19:16 the Lord (Geneva) the LORD (KJV, NKJV)
Gen. 19:24 the Lord (Geneva) the LORD (KJV, NKJV)
Gen. 19:29 God thought upon (Geneva) God remembered (KJV, NKJV)
Gen. 20:4 Notwithstanding Abimelech (Geneva) But Abimelech (KJV, NKJV)
Gen. 20:6 even with an upright mind (Geneva) in the integrity of thy heart (KJV) in the integrity of your heart (NKJV)
Gen. 20:13 Now when God (Geneva) And it came to pass, when God (KJV, NKJV)
Gen. 20:18 the Lord (Geneva) the LORD (KJV, NKJV)
Gen. 21:1 Now the Lord (Geneva) And the LORD (KJV, NKJV)
Gen. 21:1 and did unto her (Geneva) and the LORD did unto Sarah (KJV) and the LORD did for Sarah (NKJV)
Gen. 21:1 had promised (Geneva) had spoken (KJV, NKJV)
Gen. 21:3 Izhak (Geneva) Isaac (KJV, NKJV)
Gen. 21:18 the child (Geneva) the lad (KJV, NKJV)
Gen. 21:20 the child (Geneva) the lad (KJV, NKJV)
Gen. 21:22 And at the same time (Geneva) And it came to the pass at that time (KJV, NKJV)
Gen. 22:1 And after these things (Geneva) And it came to pass after these things (KJV) Now it came to pass after these things (NKJV)
Gen. 22:5 And said (Geneva) And Abraham said (KJV, NKJV)
Gen. 22:5 servants (Geneva) young men (KJV, NKJV)
Gen. 22:5 the child (Geneva) the lad (KJV, NKJV)
Gen. 22:8 Then Abraham answered (Geneva) And Abraham said (KJV, NKJV)
Gen. 22:9 builded (Geneva) built (KJV, NKJV)
Gen. 22:9 couched (Geneva) laid (KJV) placed (NKJV)
Gen. 22:12 the child (Geneva) the lad (KJV, NKJV)
Gen. 22:15 Angel of the Lord (Geneva) angel of the LORD (KJV) Angel of the LORD (NKJV)
Gen. 22:16 the Lord (Geneva) the LORD (KJV, NKJV)
Gen. 22:19 servants (Geneva) young men (KJV, NKJV)
Gen. 22:20 after these things (Geneva) it came to pass after these things (KJV, NKJV)
Gen. 22:21 *To wit*, Uz his eldest son (Geneva) Huz his firstborn (KJV, NKJV)
Gen. 23:6 a prince of God (Geneva) a mighty prince (KJV, NKJV)
Gen. 23:16 the Hittites (Geneva) the sons of Heth (KJV, NKJV)
Gen. 23:17 & over against Mamre (Geneva) which was before Mamre (KJV, NKJV)
Gen. 23:19 over against Mamre (Geneva) before Mamre (KJV, NKJV)
Gen. 23:20 by the Hittites (Geneva) by the sons of Heth (KJV, NKJV)
Gen. 24:1 the Lord (Geneva) the LORD (KJV, NKJV)
Gen. 24:3 by the Lord God of the heaven (Geneva) by the LORD, the God of heaven (KJV, NKJV)
Gen. 24:7 The Lord God (Geneva) The LORD God (KJV, NKJV)
Gen. 24:12 O Lord God (Geneva) O LORD God (KJV, NKJV)
Gen. 24:18 Drink sir (Geneva) Drink, my lord (KJV, NKJV)
Gen. 24:26 the Lord (Geneva) the LORD (KJV, NKJV)
Gen. 24:27 the Lord God (Geneva) the LORD God (KJV, NKJV)
Gen. 24:42 O Lord, the God (Geneva) O LORD God (KJV, NKJV)
Gen. 24:48 the Lord God (Geneva) the LORD God (KJV, NKJV)
Gen. 24:49 deal mercifully (Geneva) deal kindly (KJV, NKJV)

Gen. 24:67 Izhak (Geneva) Isaac (KJV, NKJV)

Gen. 25:1 wife called Keturah (Geneva) wife, and her name was Keturah (KJV, NKJV)

Gen. 25:2 Which bare him (Geneva) And she bare him (KJV, NKJV)

Gen. 25:4 Also the sons (Geneva) And the sons (KJV, NKJV)

Gen. 25:20 the Aramite (Geneva) the Syrian (KJV, NKJV)

Gen. 25:21 the Lord (Geneva) the LORD (KJV, NKJV)

Gen. 25:23 And the Lord (Geneva) And the LORD (KJV, NKJV)

Gen. 25:25 as a rough garment (Geneva) like an hairy garment (KJV) like a hairy garment (NKJV)

Gen. 25:34 Esau contemned (Geneva) Esau despised (KJV, NKJV)

Gen. 26:2 the Lord (Geneva) the LORD (KJV, NKJV)

Gen. 26:12 Afterward Izhak (Geneva) Then Isaac (KJV, NKJV)

Gen. 26:24 And the Lord (Geneva) And the LORD (KJV, NKJV)

Gen. 26:28 the Lord (Geneva) the LORD (KJV, NKJV)

Gen. 26:19 the Lord (Geneva) the LORD (KJV, NKJV)

Gen. 27:7 before the Lord, afore my death (Geneva) before the LORD before my death (KJV, NKJV)

Gen. 27:9 Get thee now (Geneva) Go now (KJV, NKJV)

Gen. 27:27 the Lord (Geneva) the LORD (KJV, NKJV)

Gen. 27:46 what availeth it me to live (Geneva) what good shall my life do me (KJV) what good will my life be to me (NKJV)

Gen. 28:1 Izhak (Geneva) Isaac (KJV, NKJV)

Gen. 28:3 God all sufficient (Geneva) God Almighty (KJV, NKJV)

Gen. 28:5 Izhak (Geneva) Isaac (KJV, NKJV)

Gen. 28:5 the Aramite (Geneva) the Syrian (KJV, NKJV)

Gen. 28:6 Izhak (Geneva) Isaac (KJV, NKJV)

Gen. 28:10 went to Haran (Geneva) went toward Haran (KJV, NKJV)

Gen. 28:13 the Lord (Geneva) the LORD (KJV, NKJV)

Gen. 28:13 the Lord God (Geneva) the LORD God (KJV, NKJV)

Gen. 28:13 God of Izhak (Geneva) God of Isaac (KJV, NKJV)

Gen. 28:21 the Lord (Geneva) the LORD (KJV, NKJV)

Gen. 29:1 Jaakob lift up his feet (Geneva) Jacob went on his journey (KJV, NKJV)

Gen. 29:11 Jaakob (Geneva) Jacob (KJV, NKJV)

Gen. 29:28 Jaakob (Geneva) Jacob (KJV, NKJV)

Gen. 29:28 Rahel (Geneva) Rachel (KJV, NKJV)

Gen. 29:31 the Lord (Geneva) the LORD (KJV, NKJV)

Gen. 29:32 the Lord (Geneva) the LORD (KJV, NKJV)

Gen. 29:33 the Lord (Geneva) the LORD (KJV, NKJV)

Gen. 29:35 Moreover she (Geneva) And she (KJV, NKJV)

Gen. 29:35 the Lord (Geneva) the LORD (KJV, NKJV)

Gen. 30:1 Jaakob (Geneva) Jacob (KJV, NKJV)

Gen. 30:2 Then Jaakob's (Geneva) And Jacob's (KJV, NKJV)

Gen. 30:2 which hath withholden (Geneva) who hath withheld (KJV) who has withheld (NKJV)

Gen. 30:6 God hath given sentence on my side (Geneva) God hath judged me (KJV) God has judged my case (NKJV)

Gen. 30:6 the second son (Geneva) a second son (KJV, NKJV)

Gen. 30:13 daughters will bless me (Geneva) daughters will call me blessed (KJV, NKJV)

Gen. 30:16 Jaakob (Geneva) Jacob (KJV, NKJV)

Gen. 30:17 Jaakob (Geneva) Jacob (KJV, NKJV)

Gen. 30:20 mine husband (Geneva) my husband (KJV, NKJV)

Gen. 30:23 my rebuke (Geneva) my reproach (KJV, NKJV)

Gen. 30:35 she goats with little and great spots (Geneva) she goats that were speckled and spotted (KJV) female goats that were speckled and spotted (NKJV)

Gen. 30:36 Jaakob (Geneva) Jacob (KJV, NKJV)

Gen. 30:39 sheep were in heat (Geneva) flocks conceived (KJV, NKJV)

Gen. 31:2 Also Jaakob (Geneva) And Jacob (KJV, NKJV)

Gen. 31:3 the Lord (Geneva) the LORD (KJV, NKJV)

Gen. 31:4 Rahel (Geneva) Rachel (KJV, NKJV)
Gen. 31:5 Then said he (Geneva) And said (KJV, NKJV)
Gen. 31:20 the Aramite (Geneva) the Syrian (KJV, NKJV)
Gen. 31:24 the Aramite (Geneva) the Syrian (KJV, NKJV)
Gen. 31:35 Then said she (Geneva) And she said (KJV, NKJV)
Gen. 32:7 sheep, and the beeves (Geneva) flocks, and the herds (KJV, NKJV)
Gen. 32:13 tarried (Geneva) lodged (KJV, NKJV)
Gen. 32:29 Jaakob demanded (Geneva) Jacob asked (KJV, NKJV)
Gen. 33:13 the ewes and kine (Geneva) the flocks and herds (KJV, NKJV)
Gen. 33:17 Jaakob went forward toward (Geneva) Jacob journeyed to (KJV, NKJV)
Gen. 33:20 The mighty God of Israel (Geneva) El-elohe-Israel (KJV) El Elohe Israel (NKJV)
Gen. 34:12 Ask of me abundantly (Geneva) Ask me never so much (KJV) Ask me ever so much (NKJV)
Gen. 34:25 on the third day (Geneva) it came to pass on the third day (KJV, NKJV)
Gen. 35:5 Then they went on their journey (Geneva) And they journeyed (KJV, NKJV)
Gen. 35:6 So came Jaakob (Geneva) So Jacob came (KJV, NKJV)
Gen. 35:7 The God of Bethel (Geneva) El-beth-el (KJV) El Bethel (NKJV)
Gen. 35:11 God all sufficient (Geneva) God Almighty (KJV, NKJV)
Gen. 35:18 as she was about to yield up the ghost (Geneva) as her soul was departing (KJV, NKJV)
Gen. 35:23 Jaakob's eldest son (Geneva) Jacob's firstborn (KJV, NKJV)
Gen. 35:24 Rahel (Geneva) Rachel (KJV, NKJV)
Gen. 36:1 which is Edom (Geneva) who is Edom (KJV, NKJV)
Gen. 36:6 all the souls (Geneva) all the persons (KJV, NKJV)
Gen. 36:19 the children of Esau (Geneva) the sons of Esau (KJV, NKJV)
Gen. 38:20 his neighbor (Geneva) his friend (KJV, NKJV)
Gen. 38:22 no whore (Geneva) no harlot (KJV, NKJV)
Gen. 38:24 after three months (Geneva) it came to pass about three months after (KJV, NKJV)
Gen. 38:24 she is great with child (Geneva) she is with child (KJV, NKJV)
Gen. 39:1 Eunuch (Geneva) officer (KJV, NKJV)
Gen. 39:2 the Lord (Geneva) the LORD (KJV) The LORD (NKJV)
Gen. 39:3 the Lord (Geneva) the LORD (KJV, NKJV)
Gen. 39:14 for to have slept with me (Geneva) to lie with me (KJV, NKJV)
Gen. 39:18 I lift (Geneva) I lifted (KJV, NKJV)
Gen. 39:21 But the Lord (Geneva) But the LORD (KJV, NKJV)
Gen. 39:21 got him favour (Geneva) gave him favour (KJV) gave him favor (NKJV)
Gen. 39:21 master of the prison (Geneva) keeper of the prison (KJV, NKJV)
Gen. 39:23 the Lord (Geneva) the LORD (KJV, NKJV)
Gen. 40:4 the chief steward (Geneva) the captain of the guard (KJV, NKJV)
Gen. 40:10 of grapes waxed ripe (Geneva) brought forth ripe grapes (KJV, NKJV)
Gen. 40:11 mine hand (Geneva) my hand (KJV, NKJV)
Gen. 40:15 Ebrews (Geneva) Hebrews (KJV, NKJV)
Gen. 41:1 two years after (Geneva) it came to pass at the end of two full years (KJV, NKJV)
Gen. 41:43 best charet (Geneva) second chariot (KJV, NKJV)
Gen. 42:9 weakness of the land (Geneva) nakedness of the land (KJV, NKJV)
Gen. 43:14 in the sight of the man (Geneva) before the man (KJV, NKJV)
Gen. 43:33 the eldest (Geneva) the firstborn (KJV, NKJV)
Gen. 44:1 commanded his steward (Geneva) commanded the steward of his house (KJV, NKJV)
Gen. 44:16 the wickedness (Geneva) the iniquity (KJV, NKJV)
Gen. 45:2 wept and cried (Geneva) wept aloud (KJV, NKJV)
Gen. 45:10 sheep & thy beasts (Geneva) flocks, and thy herds (KJV) flocks and your herds (NKJV)
Gen. 45:11 perish through poverty (Geneva) come *to* poverty (KJV) come to poverty (NKJV)
Gen. 46:2 in a vision by night (Geneva) in the visions of the night (KJV, NKJV)
Gen. 47:31 Israel worshipped (Geneva) Israel bowed himself (KJV, NKJV)
Gen. 48:18 eldest (Geneva) firstborn (KJV, NKJV)

Gen. 49:3 mine eldest son (Geneva) my firstborn (KJV, NKJV)
Gen. 49:4 *Thou wast* light as water (Geneva) Unstable as water (KJV, NKJV)
Gen. 50:26 chest (Geneva) coffin (KJV, NKJV)
Exod. 1:5 Jaakob (Geneva) Jacob (KJV, NKJV)
Exod. 1:6 that whole generation (Geneva) all that generation (KJV, NKJV)
Exod. 1:7 encreased in abundance (Geneva) increased abundantly (KJV, NKJV)
Exod. 1:12 vexed (Geneva) afflicted (KJV, NKJV)
Exod. 1:13 by cruelty caused the children of Israel to serve (Geneva) made the children of Israel to serve with rigour (KJV) made the children of Israel serve with rigor (NKJV)
Exod. 1:14 by sore labour (Geneva) with hard bondage (KJV, NKJV)
Exod. 1:16 the women of the Ebrewes (Geneva) the Hebrew women (KJV, NKJV)
Exod. 1:17 preserved (Geneva) saved (KJV, NKJV)
Exod. 1:20 prospered (Geneva) dealt well (KJV, NKJV)
Exod. 1:22 man child (Geneva) son (KJV, NKJV)
Exod. 2:3 ark *made* of reed (Geneva) ark of bulrushes (KJV, NKJV)
Exod. 2:3 among the bulrushes (Geneva) in the flags (KJV) in the reeds (NKJV)
Exod. 2:5 among the bulrushes (Geneva) among the flags (KJV) among the reeds (NKJV)
Exod. 2:11 And in those days (Geneva) And it came to pass in those days (KJV) Now it came to pass in those days (NKJV)
Exod. 2:14 a man of authority (Geneva) a prince (KJV, NKJV)
Exod. 2:16 for to water (Geneva) to water (KJV, NKJV)
Exod. 2:19 the sheep (Geneva) the flock (KJV, NKJV)
Exod. 2:24 Izhak (Geneva) Isaac (KJV, NKJV)
Exod. 3:1 drove the flock (Geneva) led the flock (KJV, NKJV)
Exod. 3:4 the Lord (Geneva) the LORD (KJV, NKJV)
Exod. 3:6 God of Izhak (Geneva) God of Isaac (KJV, NKJV)
Exod. 3:19 by strong hand (Geneva) by a mighty hand (KJV, NKJV)
Exod. 4:5 Izhak (Geneva) Isaac (KJV, NKJV)
Exod. 4:17 do miracles (Geneva) do signs (KJV) do the signs (NKJV)
Exod. 4:31 they bowed down (Geneva) they bowed their heads (KJV, NKJV)
Exod. 5:1 celebrate a feast (Geneva) hold a feast (KJV, NKJV)
Exod. 5:3 We worship the God of the Ebrews (Geneva) The God of the Hebrews hath met with us (KJV) The God of the Hebrews has met with us (NKJV)
Exod. 6:3 Izhak (Geneva) Isaac (KJV, NKJV)
Exod. 6:15 Zoar (Geneva) Zohar (KJV, NKJV)
Exod. 6:25 the principal fathers (Geneva) the heads of the fathers (KJV, NKJV)
Exod. 6:28 And at that time (Geneva) And it came to pass on the day (KJV) And it came to pass, on the day (NKJV)
Exod. 7:11 charmers (Geneva) magicians (KJV, NKJV)
Exod. 7:12 devoured their rods (Geneva) swallowed up their rods (KJV, NKJV)
Exod. 7:14 obstinate (Geneva) hardened (KJV) hard (NKJV)
Exod. 7:16 The Lord God of the Ebrews (Geneva) The LORD God of the Hebrews (KJV, NKJV)
Exod. 7:18 it shall grieve the Egyptians (Geneva) the Egyptians shall lothe (KJV) the Egyptians will loathe (NKJV)
Exod. 7:22 enchanters (Geneva) magicians (KJV, NKJV)
Exod. 8:4 frogs shall climb (Geneva) frogs shall come (KJV, NKJV)
Exod. 8:7 sorcerers (Geneva) magicians (KJV, NKJV)
Exod. 8:8 Pray ye unto the Lord (Geneva) Intreat the LORD (KJV) Entreat the LORD (NKJV)
Exod. 8:18 enchanters (Geneva) magicians (KJV, NKJV)
Exod. 8:19 enchanters (Geneva) magicians (KJV, NKJV)
Exod. 8:23 miracle (Geneva) sign (KJV, NKJV)
Exod. 8:24 the earth (Geneva) the land (KJV, NKJV)
Exod. 8:27 desert (Geneva) wilderness (KJV, NKJV)
Exod. 9:1 Lord God of the Ebrews (Geneva) LORD God of the Hebrews (KJV, NKJV)
Exod. 9:7 was obstinate (Geneva) was hardened (KJV) became hard (NKJV)
Exod. 9:11 And the sorcerers (Geneva) And the magicians (KJV, NKJV)

Exod. 9:15 mine hand (Geneva) my hand (KJV) My hand (NKJV)
Exod. 9:23 lightening (Geneva) fire (KJV, NKJV)
Exod. 10:1 miracles (Geneva) signs (KJV, NKJV)
Exod. 10:2 miracles (Geneva) signs (KJV, NKJV)
Exod. 10:4 grasshoppers (Geneva) locusts (KJV, NKJV)
Exod. 10:12 grasshoppers (Geneva) locusts (KJV, NKJV)
Exod. 10:14 So the grasshoppers (Geneva) And the locusts (KJV, NKJV)
Exod. 10:18 *Moses* then went (Geneva) And he went (KJV) So he went (NKJV)
Exod. 10:22 black darkness (Geneva) thick darkness (KJV, NKJV)
Exod. 11:2 require (Geneva) borrow (KJV) ask (NKJV)
Exod. 11:10 suffered not (Geneva) would not let (KJV) did not let (NKJV)
Exod. 12:9 feet (Geneva) legs (KJV, NKJV)
Exod. 12:29 Now at midnight (Geneva) And it came to pass, that at midnight (KJV) And it came to pass at midnight (NKJV)
Exod. 12:41 And when the (Geneva) And it came to pass at the end of the (KJV, NKJV)
Exod. 12:45 A stranger (Geneva) A foreigner (KJV) A sojourner (NKJV)
Exod. 14:9 his host (Geneva) his army (KJV, NKJV)
Exod. 14:12 Let us be in rest (Geneva) Let us alone (KJV, NKJV)
Exod. 15:2 and praise (Geneva) and song (KJV, NKJV)
Exod. 15:3 his Name is Jehovah (Geneva) the LORD is his name (KJV) The LORD is His name (NKJV)
Exod. 15:6 bruised the enemy (Geneva) dashed in pieces the enemy (KJV) dashed the enemy in pieces (NKJV)
Exod. 15:7 in thy great glory (Geneva) in the greatness of thine excellency (KJV) in the greatness of Your excellency (NKJV)
Exod. 15:15 shall wax faint hearted (Geneva) shall melt away (KJV) will melt away (NKJV)
Exod. 16:4 will cause bread to rain (Geneva) will rain bread (KJV, NKJV)
Exod. 16:5 But the sixt day (Geneva) And it shall come to pass, that on the sixth day (KJV) And it shall be on the sixth day (NKJV)
Exod. 16:5 they shall bring *home* (Geneva) they bring in (KJV, NKJV)
Exod. 16:8 even (Geneva) evening (KJV, NKJV)
Exod. 16:9 Draw near (Geneva) Come near (KJV, NKJV)
Exod. 16:10 Now as Aaron (Geneva) And it came to pass, as Aaron (KJV) Now it came to pass, as Aaron (NKJV)
Exod. 16:14 on the earth (Geneva) on the ground (KJV, NKJV)
Exod. 16:31 MAN (Geneva) Manna (KJV, NKJV)
Exod. 16:33 MAN (Geneva) manna (KJV, NKJV)
Exod. 16:35 did eat MAN (Geneva) did eat manna (KJV, NKJV)
Exod. 17:5 answered (Geneva) said (KJV, NKJV)
Exod. 17:7 or no (Geneva) or not (KJV, NKJV)
Exod. 17:14 a remembrance (Geneva) a memorial (KJV, NKJV)
Exod. 17:16 he will have war (Geneva) the LORD *will have* war (KJV, NKJV)
Exod. 18:15 to seek God (Geneva) to enquire of God (KJV) to inquire of God (NKJV)
Exod. 18:16 ordinances (Geneva) statutes (KJV, NKJV)
Exod. 18:19 report (Geneva) bring (KJV, NKJV)
Exod. 18:20 admonish them (Geneva) teach them (KJV, NKJV)
Exod. 18:21 men of courage, fearing God (Geneva) able men, such as fear God (KJV, NKJV)
Exod. 18:25 men of courage (Geneva) able men (KJV, NKJV)
Exod. 19:7 all these things (Geneva) all these words (KJV, NKJV)
Exod. 19:8 commanded (Geneva) spoken (KJV, NKJV)
Exod. 19:12 marks (Geneva) bounds (KJV, NKJV)
Exod. 19:18 trembled exceedingly (Geneva) quaked greatly (KJV, NKJV)
Exod. 20:3 none other gods (Geneva) no other gods (KJV, NKJV)
Exod. 20:5 Lord thy God (Geneva) LORD thy God (KJV) LORD your God (NKJV)
Exod. 20:12 be prolonged (Geneva) be long (KJV, NKJV)
Exod. 20:26 filthiness (Geneva) nakedness (KJV, NKJV)

Exod. 21:1 laws (Geneva) judgments (KJV, NKJV)
Exod. 21:12 shall die the death (Geneva) shall be surely put to death (KJV) shall surely be put to death (NKJV)
Exod. 21:15 shall die the death (Geneva) shall be surely put to death (KJV) shall surely be put to death (NKJV)
Exod. 21:17 shall die the death (Geneva) shall surely be put to death (KJV, NKJV)
Exod. 21:23 if death follow (Geneva) if *any* mischief follow (KJV) if *any* harm follows (NKJV)
Exod. 21:33 open a well (Geneva) open a pit (KJV, NKJV)
Exod. 22:22 trouble (Geneva) afflict (KJV, NKJV)
Exod. 23:17 the Lord Jehovah (Geneva) the Lord GOD (KJV, NKJV)
Exod. 23:21 and hear (Geneva) and obey (KJV, NKJV)
Exod. 23:31 coasts (Geneva) bounds (KJV, NKJV)
Exod. 24:2 Moses himself alone (Geneva) Moses alone (KJV, NKJV)
Exod. 25:24 cover it (Geneva) overlay it (KJV, NKJV)
Exod. 26:5 Fifty strings (Geneva) Fifty loops (KJV, NKJV)
Exod. 26:10 fifty strings (Geneva) fifty loops (KJV, NKJV)
Exod. 28:8 garde (Geneva) girdle (KJV) band (NKJV)
Exod. 28:42 privities (Geneva) nakedness (KJV, NKJV)
Exod. 29:11 the calf (Geneva) the bullock (KJV) the bull (NKJV)
Exod. 32:2 Pluck off (Geneva) Break off (KJV, NKJV)
Exod. 32:13 Izhak (Geneva) Isaac (KJV, NKJV)
Exod. 32:14 Lord changed his mind (Geneva) LORD repented (KJV, NKJV)
Exod. 32:15 returned (Geneva) turned (KJV, NKJV)
Exod. 33:1 Izhak (Geneva) Isaac (KJV, NKJV)
Exod. 33:4 they sorrowed (Geneva) they mourned (KJV, NKJV)
Exod. 33:6 *after Moses came down* from the mount Horeb (Geneva) by the mount Horeb (KJV) by Mount Horeb (NKJV)
Exod. 34:3 sheep nor cattle (Geneva) flocks nor herds (KJV, NKJV)
Exod. 34:6 The Lord, the Lord (Geneva) The LORD, The LORD God (KJV) The LORD, the LORD God (NKJV)
Exod. 34:7 Reserving mercy (Geneva) Keeping mercy (KJV, NKJV)
Exod. 34:13 overthrow (Geneva) destroy (KJV, NKJV)
Exod. 34:15 a compact (Geneva) a covenant (KJV, NKJV)
Exod. 34:23 the Lord Jehovah God (Geneva) the Lord GOD, the God (KJV, NKJV)
Exod. 34:25 speak with *God* (Geneva) speak with him (KJV) speak with Him (NKJV)
Exod. 36:4 all the holy work (Geneva) all the work of the sanctuary (KJV, NKJV)
Exod. 36:11 strings (Geneva) loops (KJV, NKJV)
Exod. 36:19 pavillion (Geneva) tent (KJV, NKJV)
Exod. 38:3 besoms (Geneva) shovels (KJV, NKJV)
Exod. 39:5 garde (Geneva) girdle (KJV) band (NKJV)
Exod. 39:24 skirts (Geneva) hems (KJV) hem (NKJV)
Lev. 3:1 drove (Geneva) herd (KJV, NKJV)
Lev. 3:6 obation (Geneva) offering (KJV, NKJV)
Lev. 4:20 And *the Priest* shall do (Geneva) And he shall do (KJV, NKJV)
Lev. 5:2 if one (Geneva) if a soul (KJV) if a person (NKJV)
Lev. 6:2 deny unto his neighbour (Geneva) lie unto his neighbour (KJV) lying to his neighbor (NKJV)
Lev. 6:3 denieth it (Geneva) lieth concerning it (KJV) lies concerning it (NKJV)
Lev. 6:6 bring for his trespass (Geneva) bring his trespass offering (KJV, NKJV)
Lev. 7:6 All the males (Geneva) Every male (KJV, NKJV)
Lev. 8:5 the company (Geneva) the congregation (KJV, NKJV)
Lev. 11:18 redshake (Geneva) swan (KJV) the white owl (NKJV)
Lev. 11:22 grasshopper (Geneva) locust (KJV, NKJV)
Lev. 11:22 hagab after his kind (Geneva) grasshopper after his kind (KJV, NKJV)
Lev. 11:30 the rat (Geneva) the ferret (KJV) the gecko (NKJV)
Lev. 13:1 and to Aaron (Geneva) and Aaron (KJV, NKJV)

Lev. 13:24 or pale (Geneva) or white (KJV, NKJV)
Lev. 14:24 shall shake (Geneva) shall wave (KJV, NKJV)
Lev. 16:26 into the host (Geneva) into the camp (KJV, NKJV)
Lev. 18:6 shame (Geneva) nakedness (KJV, NKJV)
Lev. 18:7 shame of thy father (Geneva) nakedness of thy father (KJV) nakedness of your father (NKJV)
Lev. 18:7 shame of thy mother (Geneva) nakedness of thy mother (KJV) nakedness of your mother (NKJV)
Lev. 18:7 discover (Geneva) uncover (KJV, NKJV)
Lev. 18:8 discover (Geneva) uncover (KJV, NKJV)
Lev. 18:9 discover (Geneva) uncover (KJV, NKJV)
Lev. 18:10 The shame (Geneva) The nakedness (KJV, NKJV)
Lev. 18:10 discover (Geneva) uncover (KJV, NKJV)
Lev. 18:11 The shame (Geneva) The nakedness (KJV, NKJV)
Lev. 18:12 the shame (Geneva) the nakedness (KJV, NKJV)
Lev. 18:13 discover (Geneva) uncover (KJV, NKJV)
Lev. 18:13 the shame (Geneva) the nakedness (KJV, NKJV)
Lev. 18:15 discover (Geneva) uncover (KJV, NKJV)
Lev. 18:16 discover (Geneva) uncover (KJV, NKJV)
Lev. 18:16 shame (Geneva) nakedness (KJV, NKJV)
Lev. 18:17 discover (Geneva) uncover (KJV, NKJV)
Lev. 18:17 shame (Geneva) nakedness (KJV, NKJV)
Lev. 18:18 shame (Geneva) nakedness (KJV, NKJV)
Lev. 18:19 shame (Geneva) nakedness (KJV, NKJV)
Lev. 19:12 defile the Name (Geneva) profane the name (KJV, NKJV)
Lev. 19:20 lieth and meddleth (Geneva) lieth carnally (KJV) lies carnally (NKJV)
Lev. 19:23 for meat (Geneva) for food (KJV, NKJV)
Lev. 19:25 I am the Lord your God (Geneva) I *am* the LORD your God (KJV, NKJV)
Lev. 19:32 dread thy God (Geneva) fear thy God (KJV) fear your God (NKJV)
Lev. 20:1 die the death (Geneva) surely be put to death (KJV, NKJV)
Lev. 20:3 pollute (Geneva) profane (KJV, NKJV)
Lev. 20:10 shall die the death (Geneva) shall surely be put to death (KJV, NKJV)
Lev. 20:11 shame (Geneva) nakedness (KJV, NKJV)
Lev. 20:15 shall die the death (Geneva) shall surely be put to death (KJV, NKJV)
Lev. 20:17 it is vilannie (Geneva) it *is* a wicked thing (KJV, NKJV)
Lev. 21:3 his sister a maid (Geneva) his sister a virgin (KJV) his virgin sister (NKJV)
Lev. 21:4 lament (Geneva) defile (KJV, NKJV)
Lev. 21:6 pollute (Geneva) profane (KJV, NKJV)
Lev. 21:6 the sacrifices (Geneva) the offerings (KJV, NKJV)
Lev. 21:9 she polluteth (Geneva) she profaneth (KJV) she profanes (NKJV)
Lev. 21:12 the holy place of his God (Geneva) the sanctuary of his God (KJV, NKJV)
Lev. 21:13 a maid unto his wife (Geneva) a wife in her virginity (KJV, NKJV)
Lev. 21:23 pollute (Geneva) profane (KJV, NKJV)
Lev. 22:23 a sheep (Geneva) a lamb (KJV, NKJV)
Lev. 22:32 pollute (Geneva) profane (KJV, NKJV)
Lev. 23:2 holy assemblies (Geneva) holy convocations (KJV, NKJV)
Lev. 23:11 shake the sheaf (Geneva) wave the sheaf (KJV, NKJV)
Lev. 23:12 shake (Geneva) wave (KJV, NKJV)
Lev. 23:20 shake them to and fro (Geneva) wave them (KJV, NKJV)
Lev. 23:43 posterity (Geneva) generations (KJV, NKJV)
Lev. 24:9 And the *bread* (Geneva) And it (KJV, NKJV)
Lev. 24:10 in the host (Geneva) in the camp (KJV, NKJV)
Lev. 24:18 shall restore it (Geneva) shall make it good (KJV, NKJV)
Lev. 25:43 cruelly (Geneva) with rigour (KJV) with rigor (NKJV)
Lev. 25:46 cruelty (Geneva) rigour (KJV) rigor (NKJV)
Lev. 25:53 cruelly (Geneva) with rigour (KJV) with rigor (NKJV)

Lev. 26:11 lothe (Geneva) abhor (KJV, NKJV)
Lev. 26:23 walk stubbornly (Geneva) walk contrary (KJV, NKJV)
Lev. 26:41 will walk stubbornly (Geneva) have walked contrary (KJV, NKJV)
Lev. 26:45 covenant of old (Geneva) covenant of their ancestors (KJV, NKJV)
Num. 1:18 they called (Geneva) they assembled (KJV, NKJV)
Num. 1:20 the sons of Reuben (Geneva) the children of Reuben (KJV, NKJV)
Num. 1:22 the sons of Simeon (Geneva) the children of Simeon (KJV, NKJV)
Num. 1:23 The sum of them, *I say,* of the tribe (Geneva) Those that were numbered of them, *even* of the tribe (KJV) those who were numbered of the tribe (NKJV)
Num. 1:24 the sons of Gad (Geneva) the children of Gad (KJV, NKJV)
Num. 1:26 the sons of Judah (Geneva) the children of Judah (KJV, NKJV)
Num. 2:5 sons of Issachar (Geneva) children of Issachar (KJV, NKJV)
Num. 2:20 sons of Manasseh (Geneva) children of Manasseh (KJV, NKJV)
Num. 2:27 sons of Asher (Geneva) children of Asher (KJV, NKJV)
Num. 3:3 whom *Moses* (Geneva) whom he (KJV, NKJV)
Num. 5:30 when a man is moved with a jealous mind (Geneva) when the spirit of jealousy cometh upon him (KJV) when the spirit of jealousy comes upon a man (NKJV)
Num. 6:4 As long as his abstinence endureth (Geneva) All the days of his separation (KJV, NKJV)
Num. 6:5 While he is separate by his vow (Geneva) All the days of the vow of his separation (KJV, NKJV)
Num. 7:6 chariots (Geneva) wagons (KJV) carts (NKJV)
Num. 9:2 celebrate (Geneva) keep (KJV, NKJV)
Num. 9:4 celebrate (Geneva) keep (KJV, NKJV)
Num. 10:23 tribe of the sons of Manasseh (Geneva) tribe of the children of Manasseh (KJV, NKJV)
Num. 10:24 sons of Benjamin (Geneva) children of Benjamin (KJV, NKJV)
Num. 11:6 this MAN (Geneva) this manna (KJV, NKJV)
Num. 11:7 The MAN also (Geneva) And the manna (KJV) Now the manna (NKJV)
Num. 12:4 by and by (Geneva) suddenly (KJV, NKJV)
Num. 13:19 walled towns (Geneva) strongholds (KJV, NKJV)
Num. 13:24 the river Eschol (Geneva) the brook Eschol (KJV) the Valley of Eschol (NKJV)
Num. 14:37 vile slander (Geneva) evil report (KJV, NKJV)
Num. 14:44 presumed obstinately to go up (Geneva) presumed to go up (KJV, NKJV)
Num. 15:35 shall die the death (Geneva) shall be surely put to death (KJV, NKJV)
Num. 17:4 before *the Ark* of the Testimony (Geneva) before the testimony (KJV) before the Testimony (NKJV)
Num. 19:2 red cow (Geneva) red heifer (KJV, NKJV)
Num. 19:3 the host (Geneva) the camp (KJV, NKJV)
Num. 19:5 cow (Geneva) heifer (KJV, NKJV)
Num. 19:7 into the host (Geneva) in the camp (KJV, NKJV)
Num. 20:15 handled us evil (Geneva) vexed us (KJV) afflicted us (NKJV)
Num. 20:21 denied (Geneva) refused (KJV, NKJV)
Num. 21:1 toward the South (Geneva) in the south (KJV) in the South (NKJV)
Num. 21:1 took of them (Geneva) took *some* of them (KJV, NKJV)
Num. 21:2 mine hand (Geneva) my hand (KJV, NKJV)
Num. 21:4 and the people were sore grieved (Geneva) and the soul of the people was much discouraged (KJV) and the soul of the people became very discouraged (NKJV)
Num. 21:8 set it up for a sign (Geneva) set it upon a pole (KJV) set it on a pole (NKJV)
Num. 21:11 departed (Geneva) journeyed (KJV, NKJV)
Num. 21:14 rivers of Arnon (Geneva) brooks of Arnon (KJV) brooks of the Arnon (NKJV)
Num. 21:23 gave Israel no licence (Geneva) would not suffer Israel (KJV) would not allow Israel (NKJV)
Num. 21:24 conquered (Geneva) possessed (KJV) took possession (NKJV)
Num. 21:35 conquered (Geneva) possessed (KJV) took possession (NKJV)
Num. 22:19 I may wit (Geneva) I may know (KJV, NKJV)

Num. 22:39 city of Huzoth (Geneva) Kirjath-huzoth (KJV) Kirjath Huzoth (NKJV)
Num. 23:4 and *Balaam* said (Geneva) and he said (KJV, NKJV)
Num. 23:5 an answer (Geneva) a word (KJV, NKJV)
Num. 23:10 can tell the dust (Geneva) can count the cost (KJV, NKJV)
Num. 23:14 Sede-Sophim (Geneva) field of Zophim (KJV, NKJV)
Num. 24:5 Jaakob (Geneva) Jacob (KJV, NKJV)
Num. 24:8 bruise (Geneva) break (KJV, NKJV)
Num. 25:3 coupled (Geneva) joined (KJV, NKJV)
Num. 26:11 sons of Korah (Geneva) children of Korah (KJV, NKJV)
Num. 26:65 shall die (Geneva) shall surely die (KJV, NKJV)
Num. 27:2 And stood (Geneva) And they stood (KJV, NKJV)
Num. 27:3 among the assembly (Geneva) in the company (KJV, NKJV)
Num. 27:14 ye were disobedient (Geneva) ye rebelled (KJV) you rebelled (NKJV)
Num. 27:16 the Lord God (Geneva) the LORD, the God (KJV, NKJV)
Num. 31:3 Harass (Geneva) Arm (KJV, NKJV)
Num. 31:7 against Midian (Geneva) against the Midianites (KJV, NKJV)
Num. 31:17 by carnal copulation (Geneva) by lying with him (KJV) intimately (NKJV)
Num. 32:21 in harass (Geneva) armed (KJV, NKJV)
Num. 32:27 for to fight (Geneva) to battle (KJV, NKJV)
Num. 34:9 coast (Geneva) border (KJV, NKJV)
Num. 35:31 no recompense (Geneva) no satisfaction (KJV) no ransom (NKJV)
Deut. 1:7 and depart (Geneva) and take your journey (KJV, NKJV)
Deut. 1:7 Perath (Geneva) Euphrates (KJV, NKJV)
Deut. 1:8 Izhak (Geneva) Isaac (KJV, NKJV)
Deut. 1:10 in number (Geneva) for multitude (KJV) in multitude (NKJV)
Deut. 1:39 Moreover, your children (Geneva) Moreover your little ones (KJV, NKJV)
Deut. 2:4 And warn (Geneva) And command (KJV, NKJV)
Deut. 2:6 procure water (Geneva) buy water (KJV, NKJV)
Deut. 2:8 departed from (Geneva) passed by from (KJV) passed beyond (NKJV)
Deut. 2:16 So when all (Geneva) So it came to pass, when all (KJV) So it was, when all (NKJV)
Deut. 2:20 a fore time (Geneva) in old time (KJV) formerly (NKJV)
Deut. 2:24 Rise up *therefore, said the Lord* (Geneva) Rise ye up (KJV) Rise (NKJV)
Deut. 2:24 and provoke him to battle (Geneva) and contend with him in battle (KJV) and engage him in battle (NKJV)
Deut. 2:25 upon all people (Geneva) upon all nations (KJV, NKJV)
Deut. 3:4 country of Argob (Geneva) region of Argob (KJV, NKJV)
Deut. 3:6 overthrew them (Geneva) utterly destroyed them (KJV, NKJV)
Deut. 3:13 country of Argob (Geneva) region of Argob (KJV, NKJV)
Deut. 3:28 bolden him (Geneva) strengthen him (KJV, NKJV)
Deut. 4:1 ordinances (Geneva) statutes (KJV, NKJV)
Deut. 4:2 shall put nothing (Geneva) shall not add (KJV, NKJV)
Deut. 4:5 ordinances (Geneva) statutes (KJV, NKJV)
Deut. 4:6 ordinances (Geneva) statutes (KJV, NKJV)
Deut. 4:8 ordinances (Geneva) statutes (KJV, NKJV)
Deut. 4:11 darkness, clouds and mist (Geneva) darkness, clouds, and thick darkness (KJV) darkness, cloud, and thick darkness (NKJV)
Deut. 4:14 ordinances and laws (Geneva) statutes and judgments (KJV, NKJV)
Deut. 4:17 any feathered (Geneva) any winged (KJV, NKJV)
Deut. 4:21 And the Lord (Geneva) Furthermore the LORD (KJV, NKJV)
Deut. 4:26 to record (Geneva) to witness (KJV, NKJV)
Deut. 4:40 ordinances (Geneva) statutes (KJV, NKJV)
Deut. 4:45 the witnesses (Geneva) the testimonies (KJV, NKJV)
Deut. 5:7 before my face (Geneva) before me (KJV) before Me (NKJV)
Deut. 5:30 say unto them (Geneva) say to them (KJV, NKJV)
Deut. 6:1 ordinances (Geneva) statutes (KJV, NKJV)
Deut. 6:1 and laws (Geneva) and the judgments (KJV) and judgments (NKJV)

Deut. 6:2 ordinances (Geneva) statutes (KJV, NKJV)
Deut. 6:7 rehearse them continually (Geneva) teach them diligently (KJV, NKJV)
Deut. 6:14 walk after (Geneva) go after (KJV, NKJV)
Deut. 6:15 wrath of the Lord thy God (Geneva) anger of the LORD thy God (KJV) anger of the LORD your God (NKJV)
Deut. 6:17 ordinances (Geneva) statutes (KJV, NKJV)
Deut. 7:15 all infirmities (Geneva) all sickness (KJV, NKJV)
Deut. 7:21 a God mighty & dreadful (Geneva) a mighty God and terrible (KJV) the great and awesome God (NKJV)
Deut. 7:23 they be brought to nought (Geneva) they be destroyed (KJV) they are destroyed (NKJV)
Deut. 8:2 for to humble (Geneva) to humble (KJV, NKJV)
Deut. 8:3 with MAN (Geneva) with manna (KJV, NKJV)
Deut. 8:7 rivers of water (Geneva) brooks of water (KJV, NKJV)
Deut. 8:13 beasts (Geneva) herds (KJV, NKJV)
Deut. 8:13 sheep (Geneva) flocks (KJV, NKJV)
Deut. 8:15 was thy guide (Geneva) led thee (KJV) led you (NKJV)
Deut. 8:16 with MAN (Geneva) with manna (KJV, NKJV)
Deut. 8:17 strength (Geneva) might (KJV, NKJV)
Deut. 9:5 Izhak (Geneva) Isaac (KJV, NKJV)
Deut. 9:7 to anger (Geneva) to wrath (KJV, NKJV)
Deut. 9:8 to anger (Geneva) to wrath (KJV, NKJV)
Deut. 9:19 wrath (Geneva) anger (KJV, NKJV)
Deut. 9:21 your sin, *I mean* the calf (Geneva) your sin the calf (KJV, NKJV)
Deut. 9:21 burnt him (Geneva) burnt it (KJV) burned it (NKJV)
Deut. 9:21 ground him small (Geneva) ground *it* very small (KJV, NKJV)
Deut. 9:22 to anger (Geneva) to wrath (KJV, NKJV)
Deut. 9:27 Izhak (Geneva) Isaac (KJV, NKJV)
Deut. 10:1 In the same time (Geneva) At that time (KJV, NKJV)
Deut. 10:5 departed (Geneva) turned (KJV, NKJV)
Deut. 10:8 The same time (Geneva) At that time (KJV, NKJV)
Deut. 10:10 I tarried (Geneva) I stayed (KJV, NKJV)
Deut. 10:16 harden your necks no more (Geneva) be no more stiff-necked (KJV) be stiff-necked no longer (NKJV)
Deut. 11:4 host of the Egyptians (Geneva) army of Egypt (KJV, NKJV)
Deut. 11:24 Perath (Geneva) Euphrates (KJV, NKJV)
Deut. 11:32 commandments (Geneva) statutes (KJV, NKJV)
Deut. 11:32 and the laws (Geneva) and judgments (KJV, NKJV)
Deut. 12:1 ordinances (Geneva) statues (KJV, NKJV)
Deut. 12:19 Beware (Geneva) Take heed (KJV, NKJV)
Deut. 12:21 bullocks (Geneva) herd (KJV, NKJV)
Deut. 12:21 sheep (Geneva) flocks (KJV, NKJV)
Deut. 12:28 Take heed (Geneva) Observe (KJV, NKJV)
Deut. 12:29 shall destroy (Geneva) shall cut off (KJV) cuts off (NKJV)
Deut. 14:4 the beef (Geneva) the ox (KJV, NKJV)
Deut. 14:5 unicorn (Geneva) pygarg (KJV) mountain goat (NKJV)
Deut. 14:16 redshank (Geneva) swan (KJV) white owl (NKJV)
Deut. 15:2 freedom (Geneva) release (KJV, NKJV)
Deut. 15:3 stranger (Geneva) foreigner (KJV, NKJV)
Deut. 15:12 Ebrew (Geneva) Hebrew man (KJV, NKJV)
Deut. 15:12 Ebrewess (Geneva) Hebrew woman (KJV, NKJV)
Deut. 16:19 the reward (Geneva) a gift (KJV) a bribe (NKJV)
Deut. 17:7 take him many wives (Geneva) multiply wives (KJV, NKJV)
Deut. 18:7 remain (Geneva) stand (KJV, NKJV)
Deut. 18:10 a marker of the flying of souls (Geneva) enchanter (KJV) one who interprets omens (NKJV)

Deut. 21:3 take away *the cry* of innocent blood (Geneva) put away *the guilt* of innocent blood (KJV, NKJV)

Deut. 21:20 riotour (Geneva) glutton (KJV, NKJV)

Deut. 24:5 go a warfare (Geneva) go out to war (KJV, NKJV)

Deut. 27:17 mark (Geneva) landmark (KJV, NKJV)

Deut. 27:19 hindereth (Geneva) perverteth (KJV) perverts (NKJV)

Deut. 28:20 shame (Geneva) rebuke (KJV, NKJV)

Deut. 31:6 dread not (Geneva) fear not (KJV) do not fear (NKJV)

Deut. 31:23 And *God* (Geneva) And he (KJV) Then He (NKJV)

Deut. 32:3 glory (Geneva) greatness (KJV, NKJV)

Deut. 32:4 the mighty God (Geneva) the Rock (KJV, NKJV)

Deut. 32:15 the strong God (Geneva) the Rock (KJV, NKJV)

Deut. 32:18 the mighty God (Geneva) the Rock (KJV, NKJV)

Deut. 32:30 their strong God (Geneva) their Rock (KJV, NKJV)

Deut. 32:31 For their god (Geneva) For their rock (KJV, NKJV)

Deut. 32:31 our God (Geneva) our Rock (KJV, NKJV)

Deut. 32:33 cruel gall (Geneva) cruel venom (KJV, NKJV)

Josh. 1:1 the Lord spake (Geneva) it came to pass, that the LORD spake (KJV) it came to pass that the LORD spoke (NKJV)

Josh. 1:4 Perath (Geneva) Euphrates (KJV, NKJV)

Josh. 1:7 and of a most valiant courage (Geneva) and very courageous (KJV, NKJV)

Josh. 1:14 your children (Geneva) your little ones (KJV, NKJV)

Josh. 2:2 Then report was made (Geneva) And it was told (KJV, NKJV)

Josh. 2:3 all the land (Geneva) all the country (KJV, NKJV)

Josh. 2:11 And we had heard it (Geneva) And as soon as we had heard *these things* (KJV, NKJV)

Josh. 2:12 mercy (Geneva) kindness (KJV, NKJV)

Josh. 2:14 mercifully (Geneva) kindly (KJV, NKJV)

Josh. 3:11 all the world (Geneva) all the earth (KJV, NKJV)

Josh. 4:18 And when the Priests (Geneva) And it came to pass, when the priests (KJV, NKJV)

Josh. 4:24 the world (Geneva) the earth (KJV, NKJV)

Josh. 5:12 the MAN (Geneva) the manna (KJV, NKJV)

Josh. 5:13 And when Joshua (Geneva) And it came to pass, when Joshua (KJV, NKJV)

Josh. 6:2 strong men of war (Geneva) mighty men of valour (KJV) mighty men of valor (NKJV)

Josh. 6:9 And the men of arms (Geneva) And the armed men (KJV) The armed men (NKJV)

Josh. 6:18 execrable thing (Geneva) accursed thing (KJV) accursed things (NKJV)

Josh. 6:27 all the world (Geneva) all the country (KJV, NKJV)

Josh. 7:1 the excommunicate thing (Geneva) accursed thing (KJV) accursed things (NKJV)

Josh. 7:3 And returned (Geneva) And they returned (KJV, NKJV)

Josh. 7:15 excommunicate thing (Geneva) accursed thing (KJV, NKJV)

Josh. 8:28 wilderness (Geneva) desolation (KJV, NKJV)

Josh. 9:1 And when (Geneva) And it came to pass, when (KJV) And it came to pass when (NKJV)

Josh. 9:2 fight against Joshua (Geneva) fight with Joshua (KJV, NKJV)

Josh. 9:17 took their journey (Geneva) journeyed (KJV, NKJV)

Josh. 10:1 Now when (Geneva) Now it came to pass, when (KJV) Now it came to pass when (NKJV)

Josh. 10:7 of might (Geneva) of valour (KJV) of valor (NKJV)

Josh. 10:13 sun abode (Geneva) sun stood still (KJV, NKJV)

Josh. 10:30 gave (Geneva) delivered (KJV, NKJV)

Josh. 11:1 And when (Geneva) And it came to pass, when (KJV, NKJV)

Josh. 11:2 unto the Kings (Geneva) to the kings (KJV, NKJV)

Josh. 15:9 the mountain (Geneva) the hill (KJV, NKJV)

Josh. 15:14 sons of Anak (Geneva) children of Anak (KJV, NKJV)

Josh. 17:2 sons of Manasseh (Geneva) children of Manasseh (KJV, NKJV)

Josh. 17:2 sons of Helek (Geneva) children of Helek (KJV, NKJV)

Josh. 17:12 could not destroy (Geneva) could not drive out (KJV, NKJV)
Josh. 18:2 divided their inheritance (Geneva) received their inheritance (KJV, NKJV)
Josh. 18:9 men departed (Geneva) men went (KJV, NKJV)
Josh. 18:12 coast (Geneva) border (KJV, NKJV)
Josh. 21:12 land of the city (Geneva) fields of the city (KJV, NKJV)
Jud. 1:1 After that Joshua was dead (Geneva) Now after the death of Joshua (KJV, NKJV)
Jud. 1:6 the thumbs of his hands and of his feet (Geneva) his thumbs and his great toes (KJV) his thumbs and big toes (NKJV)
Jud. 1:7 the thumbs of their hands and of their feet (Geneva) their thumbs and their great toes (KJV) their thumbs and big toes (NKJV)
Jud. 1:9 Afterward also (Geneva) And afterward (KJV, NKJV)
Jud. 1:18 Azzah (Geneva) Gaza (KJV, NKJV)
Jud. 1:23 caused to view (Geneva) sent to descry (KJV) sent men to spy out (NKJV)
Jud. 1:28 Nevertheless when Israel was strong (Geneva) And it came to pass, when Israel was strong (KJV, NKJV)
Jud. 2:11 wickedly in the sight of the Lord (Geneva) evil in the sight of the LORD (KJV, NKJV)
Jud. 2:12 And forsook the Lord God (Geneva) And they forsook the LORD God (KJV, NKJV)
Jud. 2:14 And the wrath of the Lord (Geneva) And the anger of the LORD (KJV, NKJV)
Jud. 2:15 he punished them sore (Geneva) they were greatly distressed (KJV, NKJV)
Jud. 2:19 worship (Geneva) bow down (KJV, NKJV)
Jud. 4:1 began again to do wickedly (Geneva) again did evil (KJV, NKJV)
Jud. 4:5 And this Deborah (Geneva) And she (KJV, NKJV)
Jud. 5:3 Hearken (Geneva) Give ear (KJV, NKJV)
Jud. 5:9 Mine heart (Geneva) My heart (KJV, NKJV)
Jud. 5:28 so long a coming (Geneva) so long in coming (KJV, NKJV)
Jud. 6:1 the children of Israel committed wickedness in the sight of the Lord (Geneva) the children of Israel did evil in the sight of the LORD (KJV, NKJV)
Jud. 6:12 valiant man (Geneva) mighty man of valour (KJV) mighty man of valor (NKJV)
Jud. 6:25 the same night (Geneva) it came to pass the same night (KJV, NKJV)
Jud. 6:32 Let Baal plead for himself (Geneva) Let Baal plead against him (KJV, NKJV)
Jud. 7:15 When Gideon heard (Geneva) And it was so, when Gideon heard (KJV) And so it was, when Gideon heard (NKJV)
Jud. 7:18 say, For the Lord (Geneva) say, *The sword* of the LORD (KJV, NKJV)
Jud. 8:3 their spirits abated toward him (Geneva) their anger was abated toward him (KJV) their anger toward him subsided (NKJV)
Jud. 8:5 morsels of bread (Geneva) loaves of bread (KJV, NKJV)
Jud. 8:11 in tabernacles (Geneva) in tents (KJV, NKJV)
Jud. 8:11 was careless (Geneva) was secure (KJV) felt secure (NKJV)
Jud. 8:14 a servant (Geneva) a young man (KJV, NKJV)
Jud. 8:19 my mother's children (Geneva) the sons of my mother (KJV, NKJV)
Jud. 8:23 the Lord shall reign (Geneva) the LORD shall rule (KJV, NKJV)
Jud. 8:27 was the destruction (Geneva) became a snare (KJV, NKJV)
Jud. 8:35 mercy (Geneva) kindness (KJV, NKJV)
Jud. 9:15 in deed (Geneva) in truth (KJV, NKJV)
Jud. 9:23 brake their promises (Geneva) dealt treacherously (KJV, NKJV)
Jud. 9:30 wrath (Geneva) anger (KJV, NKJV)
Jud. 9:54 his page that bare his harness (Geneva) the young man his armourbearer (KJV) the young man his armorbearer (NKJV)
Jud. 10:6 wrought wickedness (Geneva) did evil (KJV, NKJV)
Jud. 10:7 wrath of the Lord (Geneva) anger of the LORD (KJV, NKJV)
Jud. 10:8 beyond Jordan (Geneva) on the other side Jordan (KJV) on the other side of the Jordan (NKJV)
Jud. 10:9 tormented (Geneva) distressed (KJV, NKJV)
Jud. 11:2 woman's children were come to age (Geneva) wife's sons grew up (KJV, NKJV)
Jud. 11:5 fought with Israel (Geneva) made war against Israel (KJV, NKJV)
Jud. 11:13 quietly (Geneva) peaceably (KJV, NKJV)

Jud. 11:27 offended thee (Geneva) sinned against thee (KJV) sinned against you (NKJV)
Jud. 11:35 And when he saw (Geneva) And it came to pass, when he saw (KJV, NKJV)
Jud. 11:37 suffer me two months (Geneva) let me alone two months (KJV) let me alone for two months (NKJV)
Jud. 12:2 Iphtah (Geneva) Jephthah (KJV, NKJV)
Jud. 12:3 mine hands (Geneva) my hands (KJV, NKJV)
Jud. 12:3 into mine hands (Geneva) into my hand (KJV, NKJV)
Jud. 12:4 runagates (Geneva) fugitives (KJV, NKJV)
Jud. 13:5 to save (Geneva) to deliver (KJV, NKJV)
Jud. 13:6 the wife (Geneva) the woman (KJV, NKJV)
Jud. 13:6 the fashion (Geneva) the countenance (KJV, NKJV)
Jud. 13:10 the wife (Geneva) the woman (KJV, NKJV)
Jud. 13:24 the wife (Geneva) the woman (KJV, NKJV)
Jud. 14:5 upon him (Geneva) against him (KJV, NKJV)
Jud. 14:7 woman which was beautiful in the eyes of Samson (Geneva) woman; and she pleased Samson well (KJV, NKJV)
Jud. 14:8 body of the lion (Geneva) carcase of the lion (KJV) carcass of the lion (NKJV)
Jud. 15:5 riekes (Geneva) shocks (KJV, NKJV)
Jud. 15:8 with a mighty plague (Geneva) with a great slaughter (KJV, NKJV)
Jud. 16:1 Azzah (Geneva) Gaza (KJV, NKJV)
Jud. 16:26 the servant (Geneva) the lad (KJV, NKJV)
Jud. 17:2 in mine hearing (Geneva) in mine ears (KJV) in my ears (NKJV)
Jud. 17:3 of mine hand (Geneva) from my hand (KJV, NKJV)
Jud. 17:5 who was (Geneva) who became (KJV, NKJV)
Jud. 17:6 good (Geneva) right (KJV, NKJV)
Jud. 18:10 a careless people (Geneva) a people secure (KJV) a secure people (NKJV)
Jud. 18:22 pursued after (Geneva) overtook (KJV, NKJV)
Jud. 18:27 and without mistrust (Geneva) and secure (KJV, NKJV)
Jud. 18:28 none to help (Geneva) no deliverer (KJV, NKJV)
Jud. 19:1 Also in those days (Geneva) And it came to pass in those days (KJV, NKJV)
Jud. 19:2 and there continued the space of four months (Geneva) and was there four whole months (KJV, NKJV)
Jud. 19:9 to thy tent (Geneva) home (KJV, NKJV)
Jud. 19:11 sore spent (Geneva) far spent (KJV, NKJV)
Jud. 19:15 when he came (Geneva) when he went in (KJV, NKJV)
Jud. 19:16 children of Iemini (Geneva) Benjamites (KJV, NKJV)
Jud. 19:19 boy (Geneva) young man (KJV, NKJV)
Jud. 19:29 laid hand (Geneva) laid hold (KJV, NKJV)
Jud. 21:25 good in his eyes (Geneva) right in his own eyes (KJV, NKJV)
Ruth 1:1 In the time that the judges ruled (Geneva) Now it came to pass in the days when the judges ruled (KJV, NKJV)
Ruth 1:4 wives of the Moabites (Geneva) wives of the women of Moab (KJV, NKJV)
Ruth 1:15 And *Naomi* said (Geneva) And she said (KJV, NKJV)
Ruth 1:21 the Almighty has brought me unto adversity (Geneva) the Almighty hath afflicted me (KJV) the Almighty has afflicted me (NKJV)
Ruth 2:9 the servants (Geneva) the young men (KJV, NKJV)
Ruth 4:11 Rahel (Geneva) Rachel (KJV, NKJV)
Ruth 4:22 Ishai (Geneva) Jesse (KJV, NKJV)
1 Sam. 1:10 troubled in her mind (Geneva) in bitterness of soul (KJV, NKJV)
1 Sam. 1:27 my desire (Geneva) my petition (KJV, NKJV)
1 Sam. 2:2 no God like our God (Geneva) any rock like our God (KJV, NKJV)
1 Sam. 2:3 enterprises are established (Geneva) actions are weighed (KJV, NKJV)
1 Sam. 2:8 seat of glory (Geneva) throne of glory (KJV, NKJV)
1 Sam. 2:10 The Lord's adversaries shall be destroyed (Geneva) The adversaries of the LORD shall be broken in pieces (KJV, NKJV)
1 Sam. 2:15 boy (Geneva) servant (KJV, NKJV)

1 Sam. 2:26 child Samuel profited and grew (Geneva) child Samuel grew on (KJV) child Samuel grew in stature (NKJV)

1 Sam. 3:13 his sons ran into a slander (Geneva) his sons made themselves vile (KJV, NKJV)

1 Sam. 4:1 And Samuel spake unto all Israel (Geneva) And the word of Samuel came to all Israel (KJV, NKJV)

1 Sam. 6:5 similitudes (Geneva) images (KJV, NKJV)

1 Sam. 8:2 eldest son (Geneva) firstborn (KJV, NKJV)

1 Sam. 8:15 Eunuches (Geneva) officers (KJV, NKJV)

1 Sam. 11:1 besieged (Geneva) encamped against (KJV, NKJV)

1 Sam. 12:14 not disobey the word of the Lord (Geneva) not rebel against the commandment of the LORD (KJV, NKJV)

1 Sam. 12:15 disobey the Lord's mouth (Geneva) rebel against the commandment of the LORD (KJV, NKJV)

1 Sam. 14:15 a fear (Geneva) trembling (KJV, NKJV)

1 Sam. 14:15 it was *stricken* with fear by God (Geneva) it was a very great trembling (KJV, NKJV)

1 Sam. 15:4 assembled (Geneva) gathered (KJV, NKJV)

1 Sam. 15:5 and set watch at the river (Geneva) and laid wait in the valley (KJV) and lay in wait in the valley (NKJV)

1 Sam. 15:9 the better sheep (Geneva) the best of the sheep (KJV, NKJV)

1 Sam. 15:13 I have fulfilled (Geneva) I have performed (KJV, NKJV)

1 Sam. 15:23 cast away the word of the Lord (Geneva) rejected the word of the LORD (KJV, NKJV)

1 Sam. 16:3 Ishai (Geneva) Jesse (KJV, NKJV)

1 Sam. 16:11 Ishai (Geneva) Jesse (KJV, NKJV)

1 Sam. 17:1 Philistims (Geneva) Philistines (KJV, NKJV)

1 Sam. 17:17 And Ishai said (Geneva) And Jesse said (KJV, NKJV)

1 Sam. 17:49 the stone sticked (Geneva) the stone sunk (KJV) the stone sank (NKJV)

1 Sam. 17:58 Ishai (Geneva) Jesse (KJV, NKJV)

1 Sam. 20:9 God keep that from thee (Geneva) Far be it from thee (KJV) Far be it from you (NKJV)

1 Sam. 20:27 Ishai (Geneva) Jesse (KJV, NKJV)

1 Sam. 21:15 mine house (Geneva) my house (KJV, NKJV)

1 Sam. 22:9 Ishai (Geneva) Jesse (KJV, NKJV)

1 Sam. 22:10 asked counsel of the Lord (Geneva) enquired of the LORD (KJV) inquired of the LORD (NKJV)

1 Sam. 23:4 asked counsel (Geneva) enquired (KJV) inquired (NKJV)

1 Sam. 25:10 Ishai (Geneva) Jesse (KJV, NKJV)

1 Sam. 25:18 frailes of raisins (Geneva) clusters of raisins (KJV, NKJV)

1 Sam. 26:15 one of the folk (Geneva) one of the people (KJV, NKJV)

1 Sam. 26:18 persecute (Geneva) pursue (KJV, NKJV)

1 Sam. 28:6 asked counsel (Geneva) enquired (KJV) inquired (NKJV)

1 Sam. 28:8 changed himself (Geneva) disguised himself (KJV, NKJV)

1 Sam. 28:14 lapped in a mantel (Geneva) covered with a mantle (KJV, NKJV)

1 Sam. 29:2 princes of the Philistims (Geneva) lords of the Philistines (KJV, NKJV)

1 Sam. 30:14 We roved (Geneva) We made an invasion (KJV, NKJV)

1 Sam. 31:2 Philistims pressed sore (Geneva) Philistines followed hard (KJV, NKJV)

2 Sam. 1:1 After the death (Geneva) Now it came to pass after the death (KJV, NKJV)

2 Sam. 1:2 host (Geneva) camp (KJV, NKJV)

2 Sam. 1:7 looked back (Geneva) looked behind him (KJV, NKJV)

2 Sam. 1:17 mourned (Geneva) lamented (KJV, NKJV)

2 Sam. 1:26 Wo is me for thee (Geneva) I am distressed for thee (KJV) I am distressed for you (NKJV)

2 Sam. 2:6 mercy (Geneva) kindness (KJV, NKJV)

2 Sam. 2:21 his weapons (Geneva) his armour (KJV) his armor (NKJV)

2 Sam. 3:1 David waxed stronger (Geneva) David waxed stronger and stronger (KJV) David grew stronger and stronger (NKJV)

2 Sam. 3:2 children (Geneva) sons (KJV) Sons (NKJV)

2 Sam. 3:32 beside the sepulcher (Geneva) at the grave (KJV, NKJV)

2 Sam 5:19 asked counsel (Geneva) enquired (KJV) inquired (NKJV)

2 Sam. 7:18 mine house (Geneva) my house (KJV, NKJV)

2 Sam. 8:1 took the bride of bondage (Geneva) took Metheg-ammah (KJV) took Metheg Ammah (NKJV)

2 Sam. 8:6 Aram (Geneva) Syria (KJV, NKJV)

2 Sam. 8:6 saved David (Geneva) preserved David (KJV, NKJV)

2 Sam. 10:6 the Aramites (Geneva) the Syrians (KJV, NKJV)

2 Sam. 10:11 succour (Geneva) help (KJV, NKJV)

2 Sam. 10:12 Be strong (Geneva) Be of good courage (KJV, NKJV)

2 Sam. 11:8 the Kings palace (Geneva) the king's house (KJV, NKJV)

2 Sam. 11:15 of the strength of the battle (Geneva) of the hottest battle (KJV, NKJV)

2 Sam. 12:2 many sheep and oxen (Geneva) many flocks and herds (KJV, NKJV)

2 Sam. 12:3 one little sheep (Geneva) one little ewe lamb (KJV, NKJV)

2 Sam. 12:4 stranger (Geneva) traveller (KJV) traveler (NKJV)

2 Sam. 12:25 For *the Lord* had sent (Geneva) And he sent (KJV) and He sent (NKJV)

2 Sam. 12:26 the city of the kingdom (Geneva) the royal city (KJV, NKJV)

2 Sam. 13:39 pacified (Geneva) comforted (KJV, NKJV)

2 Sam. 14:2 subtile woman (Geneva) wise woman (KJV, NKJV)

2 Sam. 14:17 in hearing of good and bad (Geneva) to discern good and bad (KJV) in discerning good and bad (NKJV)

2 Sam. 15:12 treason (Geneva) conspiracy (KJV, NKJV)

2 Sam. 16:1 two hundredth *cakes* (Geneva) two hundred *loaves* (KJV, NKJV)

2 Sam. 16:1 dried figs (Geneva) summer fruits (KJV, NKJV)

2 Sam. 16:2 dried figs (Geneva) summer fruit (KJV, NKJV)

2 Sam. 16:7 murtherer (Geneva) bloody man (KJV) bloodthirsty man (NKJV)

2 Sam. 16:8 murtherer (Geneva) bloody man (KJV) bloodthirsty man (NKJV)

2 Sam. 16:11 son of Iemini (Geneva) Benjamite (KJV, NKJV)

2 Sam. 16:12 and do me good (Geneva) and that the LORD will requite me (KJV) that the LORD will repay me (NKJV)

2 Sam. 17:8 valiant warriar (Geneva) man of war (KJV, NKJV)

2 Sam. 17:10 shrink and faint (Geneva) utterly melt (KJV) melt completely (NKJV)

2 Sam. 17:18 a young man (Geneva) a lad (KJV, NKJV)

2 Sam. 17:19 the wife (Geneva) the woman (KJV, NKJV)

2 Sam. 17:21 as soon as they were departed (Geneva) it came to pass, after they were departed (KJV) it came to pass, after they had departed (NKJV)

2 Sam. 18:8 over all the country (Geneva) over the face of all the country (KJV) over the face of the whole countryside (NKJV)

2 Sam. 18:14 through Absalom (Geneva) through the heart of Absalom (KJV) through the Absalom's heart (NKJV)

2 Sam. 18:15 ten servants (Geneva) ten young men (KJV, NKJV)

2 Sam. 18:19 delivered him (Geneva) avenged him (KJV, NKJV)

2 Sam. 18:23 overwent (Geneva) overran (KJV) outran (NKJV)

2 Sam. 18:28 Peace *be with thee* (Geneva) All is well (KJV, NKJV)

2 Sam. 19:4 hid his face (Geneva) covered his face (KJV, NKJV)

2 Sam. 19:16 son of Iemini (Geneva) Benjamite (KJV, NKJV)

2 Sam. 19:20 I have done amiss (Geneva) I have sinned (KJV, NKJV)

2 Sam. 19:24 washed his feet (Geneva) dressed his feet (KJV) cared for his feet (NKJV)

2 Sam. 19:24 dressed (Geneva) trimmed (KJV, NKJV)

2 Sam. 20:1 Ishai (Geneva) Jesse (KJV, NKJV)

2 Sam. 20:3 enclosed (Geneva) shut up (KJV, NKJV)

2 Sam. 20:20 God forbid, God forbid it me (Geneva) Far be it, far be it from me (KJV, NKJV)

2 Sam. 21:1 asked counsel (Geneva) enquired (KJV) inquired (NKJV)

2 Sam. 21:7 had compassion (Geneva) spared (KJV, NKJV)

2 Sam. 21:16 sons of Haraphah (Geneva) sons of the giant (KJV, NKJV)

2 Sam. 21:18 sons of Haraphah (Geneva) sons of the giant (KJV, NKJV)

2 Sam. 21:19 slew Goliath (Geneva) slew *the brother* of Goliath (KJV) killed *the brother* of Goliath (NKJV)

2 Sam. 21:20 son of Haraphah (Geneva) born to the giant (KJV, NKJV)

2 Sam. 21:21 reviled (Geneva) defiled (KJV, NKJV)

2 Sam. 22:5 pangs of death (Geneva) waves of death (KJV, NKJV)

2 Sam. 22:23 laws (Geneva) judgments (KJV, NKJV)

2 Sam. 22:31 uncorrupt (Geneva) perfect (KJV, NKJV)

2 Sam. 22:47 my strength (Geneva) my rock (KJV) my Rock (NKJV)

2 Sam. 23:3 strength of Israel (Geneva) Rock of Israel (KJV, NKJV)

2 Sam. 23:20 strong men (Geneva) lionlike men (KJV) lion-like heroes (NKJV)

2 Sam. 24:9 delivered the number *and* sum (Geneva) gave up the sum of the number (KJV) gave the sum of the number (NKJV)

1 Kings 1:6 would not displease him from his childhood (Geneva) had not displeased him at any time (KJV) had not rebuked him at any time (NKJV)

1 Kings 1:7 took counsel of Joab (Geneva) conferred with Joab (KJV, NKJV)

1 Kings 1:31 God save my lord King David for ever (Geneva) Let my lord king David live for ever (KJV) Let my lord King David live forever (NKJV)

1 Kings 1:36 So be it (Geneva) Amen (KJV, NKJV)

1 Kings 2:37 For that day (Geneva) For it shall be, *that* on the day (KJV) For it shall be, on the day (NKJV)

1 Kings 2:37 the river of Kidron (Geneva) the brook Kidron (KJV) the Brook Kidron (NKJV)

1 Kings 2:38 The thing is good (Geneva) The saying is good (KJV, NKJV)

1 Kings 3:3 the ordinances (Geneva) the statues (KJV, NKJV)

1 Kings 3:7 young child (Geneva) little child (KJV, NKJV)

1 Kings 3:8 be told (Geneva) be numbered (KJV, NKJV)

1 Kings 3:10 And this pleased the Lord well (Geneva) And the speech pleased the LORD (KJV) The speech pleased the LORD (NKJV)

1 Kings 3:10 desired (Geneva) asked (KJV, NKJV)

1 Kings 3:14 ordinances (Geneva) statues (KJV, NKJV)

1 Kings 3:14 prolong (Geneva) lengthen (KJV, NKJV)

1 Kings 3:16 came two harlots (Geneva) came there two women, *that were* harlots (KJV) two women *who were* harlots came (NKJV)

1 Kings 4:22 victuals (Geneva) provision (KJV, NKJV)

1 Kings 4:24 he ruled (Geneva) he had dominion (KJV, NKJV)

1 Kings 4:25 dwelt without fear (Geneva) dwelt safely (KJV, NKJV)

1 Kings 8:41 touching (Geneva) concerning (KJV, NKJV)

1 Kings 8:45 judge (Geneva) maintain (KJV, NKJV)

1 Kings 9:1 When Salomon (Geneva) And it came to pass, when Solomon (KJV, NKJV)

1 Kings 9:5 will I stablish (Geneva) I will establish (KJV, NKJV)

1 Kings 10:2 sweet odors (Geneva) spices (KJV, NKJV)

1 Kings 10:2 gold exceeding much (Geneva) very much gold (KJV, NKJV)

1 Kings 10:5 his drinking vessels (Geneva) his cupbearers (KJV, NKJV)

1 Kings 10:5 she was greatly astonied (Geneva) there was no more spirit in her (KJV, NKJV)

1 Kings 10:9 which loved (Geneva) which delighted (KJV) who delighted (NKJV)

1 Kings 10:10 six score (Geneva) an hundred and twenty (KJV) one hundred and twenty (NKJV)

1 Kings 10:13 she returned (Geneva) she turned (KJV, NKJV)

1 Kings 10:15 princes (Geneva) governors (KJV, NKJV)

1 Kings 10:17 house of the wood (Geneva) house of the forest (KJV) House of the Forest (NKJV)

1 Kings 10:24 all the world (Geneva) all the earth (KJV, NKJV)

1 Kings 10:25 sweet odors (Geneva) spices (KJV, NKJV)

1 Kings 10:27 wild fig trees (Geneva) sycomore trees (KJV) sycamores (NKJV)

1 Kings 11:1 outlandish women (Geneva) strange women (KJV) foreign women (NKJV)

1 Kings 11:5 the god (Geneva) the goddess (KJV, NKJV)

1 Kings 11:6 wrought wickedness (Geneva) did evil (KJV, NKJV)

1 Kings 11:7 the mountain that is over against (Geneva) the hill that is before (KJV) the hill that is

east of (NKJV)

1 Kings 11:8 outlandish wives (Geneva) strange wives (KJV) foreign wives (NKJV)

1 Kings 11:18 and took men (Geneva) and they took men (KJV, NKJV)

1 Kings 11:28 man of strength (Geneva) mighty man (KJV, NKJV)

1 Kings 11:29 And at that time (Geneva) And it came to pass at that time (KJV) Now it happened at that time (NKJV)

1 Kings 11:33 the god of the Zidonians (Geneva) the goddess of the Zidonians (KJV, NKJV)

1 Kings 12:4 his sore yoke (Geneva) his heavy yoke (KJV, NKJV)

1 Kings 12:6 took counsel (Geneva) consulted (KJV, NKJV)

1 Kings 12:14 with rods (Geneva) with whips (KJV, NKJV)

1 Kings 12:16 Ishai (Geneva) Jesse (KJV, NKJV)

1 Kings 12:30 this thing turned to sin (Geneva) this thing became a sin (KJV, NKJV)

1 Kings 12:32 made a feast (Geneva) ordained a feast (KJV, NKJV)

1 Kings 13:1 commandment of the Lord (Geneva) word of the LORD (KJV, NKJV)

1 Kings 13:4 And when (Geneva) And it came to pass, when (KJV) So it came to pass when (NKJV)

1 Kings 14:17 the young man died (Geneva) the child died (KJV, NKJV)

1 Kings 14:30 continually (Geneva) all *their* days (KJV, NKJV)

1 Kings 15:6 as long as he lived (Geneva) all the days of his life (KJV, NKJV)

1 Kings 15:13 from her estate (Geneva) from *being* queen (KJV, NKJV)

1 Kings 15:18 Aram (Geneva) Syria (KJV, NKJV)

1 Kings 16:3 thine house (Geneva) thy house (KJV) your house (NKJV)

1 Kings 16:16 people of the host (Geneva) people *that were* encamped (KJV) people *who were* encamped (NKJV)

1 Kings 16:23 In the one and thirty year (Geneva) In the thirty and first year (KJV) In the thirty-first year (NKJV)

1 Kings 16:24 the mountain (Geneva) the hill (KJV, NKJV)

1 Kings 17:4 the river (Geneva) the brook (KJV, NKJV)

1 Kings 17:6 the river (Geneva) the brook (KJV, NKJV)

1 Kings 17:7 the river dried up (Geneva) the brook dried up (KJV, NKJV)

1 Kings 17:16 by the hand of Eliah (Geneva) by Elijah (KJV, NKJV)

1 Kings 17:17 son of the wife of the house (Geneva) son of the woman, the mistress of the house (KJV) son of the woman who owned the house (NKJV)

1 Kings 18:1 After many days (Geneva) And it came to pass *after* many days (KJV, NKJV)

1 Kings 18:6 And so they (Geneva) So they (KJV, NKJV)

1 Kings 18:12 And when I am gone from thee (Geneva) And it shall come to pass, *as soon as* I am gone from thee (KJV, NKJV)

1 Kings 18:23 let them chuse the one (Geneva) let them choose one bullock for themselves (KJV) let them choose one bull for themselves (NKJV)

1 Kings 18:24 your god (Geneva) your gods (KJV, NKJV)

1 Kings 18:28 loud (Geneva) aloud (KJV, NKJV)

1 Kings 18:35 ditch (Geneva) trench (KJV, NKJV)

1 Kings 18:44 at the seventh time (Geneva) it came to pass at the seventh time (KJV) it came to pass the seventh *time* (NKJV)

1 Kings 19:13 covered his face (Geneva) wrapped his face (KJV, NKJV)

1 Kings 19:15 over Aram (Geneva) over Syria (KJV, NKJV)

1 Kings 19:20 Go, return (Geneva) Go back again (KJV, NKJV)

1 Kings 20:19 the host (Geneva) the army (KJV, NKJV)

1 Kings 20:20 Aramites (Geneva) Syrians (KJV, NKJV)

1 Kings 20:23 King of Aram (Geneva) king of Syria (KJV, NKJV)

1 Kings 20:28 God of the mountains (Geneva) God of the hills (KJV, NKJV)

1 Kings 20:39 if he be lost and want (Geneva) if by any means he be missing (KJV) if by any means he is missing (NKJV)

1 Kings 21:1 After these things (Geneva) And it came to pass after these things (KJV, NKJV)

1 Kings 22:53 unto wrath (Geneva) to anger (KJV, NKJV)

2 Kings 1:5 to whom he said (Geneva) he said unto them (KJV) he said to them (NKJV)

2 Kings 1:6 they answered (Geneva) they said (KJV, NKJV)
2 Kings 1:6 shalt die the death (Geneva) shalt surely die (KJV) shall surely die (NKJV)
2 Kings 1:8 they said (Geneva) they answered (KJV, NKJV)
2 Kings 1:14 devoured (Geneva) burnt up (KJV) burned up (NKJV)
2 Kings 2:1 And when the Lord (Geneva) And it came to pass, when the LORD (KJV, NKJV)
2 Kings 2:3 children of the Prophets (Geneva) sons of the prophets (KJV, NKJV)
2 Kings 2:5 children of the Prophets (Geneva) sons of the prophets (KJV, NKJV)
2 Kings 2:13 the cloke (Geneva) the mantle (KJV, NKJV)
2 Kings 2:15 children of the Prophets (Geneva) sons of the prophets (KJV, NKJV)
2 Kings 3:21 able to put on harness (Geneva) able to put on armour (KJV) able to bear arms (NKJV)
2 Kings 4:6 when the vessels (Geneva) it came to pass, when the vessels (KJV, NKJV)
2 Kings 5:2 the Aramites (Geneva) the Syrians (KJV, NKJV)
2 Kings 5:5 King of Aram (Geneva) king of Syria (KJV, NKJV)
2 Kings 6:1 children of the Prophets (Geneva) sons of the prophets (KJV, NKJV)
2 Kings 6:9 Aramites (Geneva) Syrians (KJV, NKJV)
2 Kings 6:29 we sod (Geneva) we boiled (KJV, NKJV)
2 Kings 7:4 Aramites (Geneva) Syrians (KJV, NKJV)
2 Kings 8:6 an Eunuch (Geneva) a certain officer (KJV, NKJV)
2 Kings 8:9 in his hand (Geneva) with him (KJV, NKJV)
2 Kings 8:9 Aram (Geneva) Syria (KJV, NKJV)
2 Kings 8:18 in the ways (Geneva) in the way (KJV, NKJV)
2 Kings 9:1 Then Elisha (Geneva) And Elisha (KJV, NKJV)
2 Kings 9:4 gat (Geneva) went (KJV, NKJV)
2 Kings 9:16 gat up (Geneva) rode (KJV, NKJV)
2 Kings 9:21 either of them (Geneva) each (KJV, NKJV)
2 Kings 9:22 yet in great number (Geneva) *so* many (KJV, NKJV)
2 Kings 9:33 Cast her down (Geneva) Throw her down (KJV, NKJV)
2 Kings 10:13 He met (Geneva) Jehu met (KJV, NKJV)
2 Kings 11:6 keep watch in the house of Massah (Geneva) keep the watch of the house, that it be not broken down (KJV) keep the watch over the king's house, lest it be broken down (NKJV)
2 Kings 11:8 as he goeth out and in (Geneva) as he goeth out and as he cometh in (KJV) as he goes out and as he comes in (NKJV)
2 Kings 11:13 noise of the running of the people (Geneva) noise of the guard *and* of the people (KJV) noise of the escorts *and* the people (NKJV)
2 Kings 12:2 good (Geneva) right (KJV, NKJV)
2 Kings 12:3 offered yet (Geneva) still sacrificed (KJV, NKJV)
2 Kings 12:4 All the silver (Geneva) All the money (KJV, NKJV)
2 Kings 12:10 Kings secretary (Geneva) king's scribe (KJV, NKJV)
2 Kings 12:11 undertook the work (Geneva) did the work (KJV, NKJV)
2 Kings 12:13 instruments of music (Geneva) snuffers (KJV) trimmers (NKJV)
2 Kings 12:20 wrought treason (Geneva) made a conspiracy (KJV) formed a conspiracy (NKJV)
2 Kings 13:4 trouble of Israel (Geneva) oppression of Israel (KJV, NKJV)
2 Kings 13:4 Aram (Geneva) Syria (KJV, NKJV)
2 Kings 13:5 Aramites (Geneva) Syrians (KJV, NKJV)
2 Kings 13:8 Concerning the rest (Geneva) Now the rest (KJV, NKJV)
2 Kings 13:23 had mercy (Geneva) was gracious (KJV, NKJV)
2 Kings 13:24 Aram (Geneva) Syria (KJV, NKJV)
2 Kings 14:19 wrought treason (Geneva) made a conspiracy (KJV) formed a conspiracy (NKJV)
2 Kings 14:28 Concerning the rest (Geneva) Now the rest (KJV, NKJV)
2 Kings 15:19 Asshur (Geneva) Assyria (KJV, NKJV)
2 Kings 15:19 gave Phul (Geneva) gave Pul (KJV, NKJV)
2 Kings 15:30 wrought treason (Geneva) made a conspiracy (KJV) led a conspiracy (NKJV)
2 Kings 16:3 after the abominations (Geneva) according to the abominations (KJV, NKJV)
2 Kings 16:4 offered (Geneva) sacrificed (KJV, NKJV)
2 Kings 16:6 At the same time (Geneva) At that time (KJV, NKJV)

2 Kings 16:6 of Aram (Geneva) of Syria (KJV, NKJV)
2 Kings 16:11 altar in all points like that (Geneva) altar according to all that (KJV, NKJV)
2 Kings 16:17 took the caldrons (Geneva) removed the laver (KJV) removed the lavers (NKJV)
2 Kings 16:19 Concerning the rest (Geneva) Now the rest (KJV, NKJV)
2 Kings 17:4 treason (Geneva) conspiracy (KJV, NKJV)
2 Kings 17:5 Asshur (Geneva) Assyria (KJV, NKJV)
2 Kings 17:13 testified to Israel (Geneva) testified against Israel (KJV, NKJV)
2 Kings 17:14 would not obey (Geneva) would not hear (KJV, NKJV)
2 Kings 17:15 refused (Geneva) rejected (KJV, NKJV)
2 Kings 17:17 they made (Geneva) they caused (KJV, NKJV)
2 Kings 17:18 was exceeding wroth (Geneva) was very angry (KJV, NKJV)
2 Kings 17:20 the Lord cast off (Geneva) the LORD rejected (KJV, NKJV)
2 Kings 17:23 Lord put Israel away (Geneva) LORD removed Israel (KJV, NKJV)
2 Kings 17:24 Babel (Geneva) Babylon (KJV, NKJV)
2 Kings 17:27 of the country (Geneva) of the land (KJV, NKJV)
2 Kings 17:30 Babel (Geneva) Babylon (KJV, NKJV)
2 Kings 17:31 Avims (Geneva) Avites (KJV, NKJV)
2 Kings 17:31 Sepharuims (Geneva) Sepharvites (KJV, NKJV)
2 Kings 18:4 took away (Geneva) removed (KJV, NKJV)
2 Kings 18:8 Azzah (Geneva) Gaza (KJV, NKJV)
2 Kings 18:10 And after three years (Geneva) And at the end of three years (KJV, NKJV)
2 Kings 18:16 At the same season (Geneva) At that time (KJV, NKJV)
2 Kings 18:18 chanceller (Geneva) scribe (KJV, NKJV)
2 Kings 18:23 give hostages (Geneva) give pledges (KJV) give a pledge (NKJV)
2 Kings 18:25 without the lord (Geneva) without the LORD (KJV, NKJV)
2 Kings 18:32 land of wheat (Geneva) land of corn (KJV) land of grain (NKJV)
2 Kings 18:34 the god (Geneva) the gods (KJV, NKJV)
2 Kings 18:37 chanceller (Geneva) scribe (KJV, NKJV)
2 Kings 19:2 chanceller (Geneva) scribe (KJV, NKJV)
2 Kings 19:3 day of tribulation (Geneva) day of trouble (KJV, NKJV)
2 Kings 19:7 hear a noise (Geneva) hear a rumour (KJV) hear a rumor (NKJV)
2 Kings 19:10 Asshur (Geneva) Assyria (KJV, NKJV)
2 Kings 19:12 gods of the heathen (Geneva) gods of the nations (KJV, NKJV)
2 Kings 19:24 the plant of my feet (Geneva) the sole of my feet (KJV) the soles of my feet (NKJV)
2 Kings 20:12 The same season (Geneva) At that time (KJV, NKJV)
2 Kings 20:14 from Babel (Geneva) from Babylon (KJV, NKJV)
2 Kings 21:6 caused his sons (Geneva) made his son (KJV, NKJV)
2 Kings 21:16 replenished (Geneva) had filled (KJV, NKJV)
2 Kings 21:16 from corner to corner (Geneva) from one end to another (KJV, NKJV)
2 Kings 21:17 Concerning the rest (Geneva) Now the rest (KJV, NKJV)
2 Kings 21:25 Concerning the rest (Geneva) Now the rest (KJV, NKJV)
2 Kings 22:8 chanceller (Geneva) scribe (KJV, NKJV)
2 Kings 22:9 chanceller (Geneva) scribe (KJV, NKJV)
2 Kings 22:10 chanceller (Geneva) scribe (KJV, NKJV)
2 Kings 22:12 chanceller (Geneva) scribe (KJV, NKJV)
2 Kings 23:5 Chererim (Geneva) idolatrous priests (KJV, NKJV)
2 Kings 24:2 Aramites (Geneva) Syrians (KJV, NKJV)
2 Kings 24:5 Concerning the rest (Geneva) Now the rest (KJV, NKJV)
2 Kings 24:7 Babel (Geneva) Babylon (KJV, NKJV)
2 Kings 24:11 Babel (Geneva) Babylon (KJV, NKJV)
2 Kings 24:12 eunuches (Geneva) officers (KJV, NKJV)
2 Kings 24:13 brake (Geneva) cut in pieces (KJV, NKJV)
2 Kings 24:15 into Babel (Geneva) to Babylon (KJV, NKJV)
2 Kings 24:15 eunuches (Geneva) officers (KJV, NKJV)
2 Kings 25:10 chief steward (Geneva) captain of the guard (KJV, NKJV)
2 Kings 25:12 chief steward (Geneva) captain of the guard (KJV, NKJV)

2 Kings 25:14 besomes (Geneva) shovels (KJV, NKJV)
2 Kings 25:18 chief steward (Geneva) captain of the guard (KJV, NKJV)
2 Kings 25:21 Babel (Geneva) Babylon (KJV, NKJV)
2 Kings 25:23 host (Geneva) armies (KJV, NKJV)
1 Chron. 1:10 in the earth (Geneva) upon the earth (KJV) on the earth (NKJV)
1 Chron. 1:28 Izhak (Geneva) Isaac (KJV, NKJV)
1 Chron. 2:12 Ishai (Geneva) Jesse (KJV, NKJV)
1 Chron. 2:13 Ishai (Geneva) Jesse (KJV, NKJV)
1 Chron. 2:23 All these were the sons (Geneva) All these *belonged to* the sons (KJV, NKJV)
1 Chron. 3:1 eldest (Geneva) firstborn (KJV, NKJV)
1 Chron. 4:10 cause me t*o be delivered* from evil (Geneva) keep *me* from evil (KJV, NKJV)
1 Chron. 5:1 eldest son of Israel (Geneva) firstborn of Israel (KJV, NKJV)
1 Chron. 5:3 eldest son (Geneva) firstborn (KJV, NKJV)
1 Chron. 5:6 Asshur (Geneva) Assyria (KJV, NKJV)
1 Chron. 5:12 chiefest (Geneva) chief (KJV, NKJV)
1 Chron. 5:12 the second (Geneva) the next (KJV, NKJV)
1 Chron. 5:20 holpen (Geneva) helped (KJV, NKJV)
1 Chron. 5:26 Asshur (Geneva) Assyria (KJV, NKJV)
1 Chron. 6:49 burnt incense (Geneva) offered (KJV, NKJV)
1 Chron. 7:29 places (Geneva) borders (KJV, NKJV)
1 Chron. 9:2 chief inhabitants (Geneva) first inhabitants (KJV, NKJV)
1 Chron. 9:13 the chief (Geneva) heads (KJV, NKJV)
1 Chron. 9:30 of sweet odours (Geneva) of the spices (KJV, NKJV)
1 Chron. 10:2 pursed (Geneva) followed hard (KJV, NKJV)
1 Chron. 10:14 Ishai (Geneva) Jesse (KJV, NKJV)
1 Chron. 11:3 by the hand of Samuel (Geneva) by Samuel (KJV, NKJV)
1 Chron. 12:2 weaponed with bows (Geneva) armed with bows (KJV, NKJV)
1 Chron. 13:1 counseled (Geneva) consulted (KJV, NKJV)
1 Chron. 13:7 guided the cart (Geneva) drave the cart (KJV) drove the cart (NKJV)
1 Chron. 13:10 wrath (Geneva) anger (KJV, NKJV)
1 Chron. 15:2 bear the Ark of the Lord and (Geneva) carry the ark of God and (KJV, NKJV)
1 Chron. 15:4 the sons of Aaron (Geneva) the children of Aaron (KJV, NKJV)
1 Chron. 15:15 And the sons (Geneva) And the children (KJV, NKJV)
1 Chron. 15:23 porters (Geneva) doorkeepers (KJV, NKJV)
1 Chron. 15:24 porters (Geneva) doorkeepers (KJV, NKJV)
1 Chron. 16:3 cake of bread (Geneva) loaf of bread (KJV, NKJV)
1 Chron. 16:8 Praise the Lord (Geneva) Give thanks unto the LORD (KJV) Oh, give thanks to the
LORD (NKJV)
1 Chron. 16:29 the glorious Sanctuary (Geneva) the beauty of holiness (KJV, NKJV)
1 Chron. 16:36 So be it (Geneva) Amen (KJV, NKJV)
1 Chron. 17:7 a prince (Geneva) ruler (KJV, NKJV)
1 Chron. 17:8 have destroyed (Geneva) have cut off (KJV, NKJV)
1 Chron. 18:6 Aramites (Geneva) Syrians (KJV, NKJV)
1 Chron. 19:10 Aramites (Geneva) Syrians (KJV, NKJV)
1 Chron. 19:12 Aram (Geneva) Syrians (KJV, NKJV)
1 Chron. 19:13 Be strong (Geneva) Be of good courage (KJV, NKJV)
1 Chron. 19:18 Aramites (Geneva) Syrians (KJV, NKJV)
1 Chron. 20:4 of Haraphah (Geneva) of the giant (KJV, NKJV)
1 Chron. 20:6 Haraphah (Geneva) the giant (KJV, NKJV)
1 Chron. 20:7 reviled (Geneva) defied (KJV, NKJV)
1 Chron. 20:8 Haraohah (Geneva) the giant (KJV, NKJV)
1 Chron. 22:4 without number (Geneva) in abundance (KJV, NKJV)
1 Chron. 23:30 for to stand (Geneva) to stand (KJV, NKJV)
1 Chron. 24:5 distributed them by lot (Geneva) divided by lot (KJV, NKJV)
1 Chron. 27:3 sons of Perez (Geneva) children of Perez (KJV, NKJV)
1 Chron. 27:29 the oxen (Geneva) the herds (KJV, NKJV)

1 Chron. 27:34 captain (Geneva) general (KJV, NKJV)

1 Chron. 28:18 Cherubs (Geneva) cherubims (KJV) cherubim (NKJV)

1 Chron. 29:3 the house of the Sanctuary (Geneva) the holy house (KJV, NKJV)

1 Chron. 29:26 Ishai (Geneva) Jesse (KJV, NKJV)

2 Chron. 1:11 treasures (Geneva) wealth (KJV, NKJV)

2 Chron. 1:12 treasures (Geneva) wealth (KJV, NKJV)

2 Chron. 4:11 besomes (Geneva) shovels (KJV, NKJV)

2 Chron. 4:15 twelve bulls (Geneva) twelve oxen (KJV, NKJV)

2 Chron. 4:16 besomes (Geneva) shovels (KJV, NKJV)

2 Chron. 6:28 grasshopper (Geneva) locusts (KJV, NKJV)

2 Chron. 6:30 be merciful (Geneva) forgive (KJV, NKJV)

2 Chron. 7:3 to the earth (Geneva) to the ground (KJV, NKJV)

2 Chron. 7:6 David praised *God* by them (Geneva) David praised by their ministry (KJV) David offered praise by their ministry (NKJV)

2 Chron. 7:8 made a feast (Geneva) kept the feast (KJV, NKJV)

2 Chron. 7:13 the grasshopper (Geneva) the locusts (KJV, NKJV)

2 Chron. 7:14 seek my presence (Geneva) seek my face (KJV) seek My face (NKJV)

2 Chron. 7:14 hear in heaven (Geneva) hear from heaven (KJV, NKJV)

2 Chron. 7:14 be merciful to their sin (Geneva) will forgive their sin (KJV, NKJV)

2 Chron. 7:18 not want (Geneva) not fail (KJV, NKJV)

2 Chron. 7:20 a commune talk (Geneva) a byword (KJV, NKJV)

2 Chron. 8:1 And after (Geneva) And it came to pass at the end of (KJV) It came to pass at the end of (NKJV)

2 Chron. 8:15 declined not (Geneva) departed not (KJV) did not depart (NKJV)

2 Chron. 8:15 touching all things (Geneva) concerning any matter (KJV, NKJV)

2 Chron. 9:1 sweet odours (Geneva) spices (KJV, NKJV)

2 Chron. 9:1 much gold (Geneva) gold in abundance (KJV, NKJV)

2 Chron. 9:6 of thy great wisdom (Geneva) of the greatness of thy wisdom (KJV) of the greatness of your wisdom (NKJV)

2 Chron. 9:7 stand before thee all way (Geneva) stand continually before thee (KJV) stand continually before you (NKJV)

2 Chron. 9:8 loved thee (Geneva) delighted in thee (KJV) delighted in you (NKJV)

2 Chron. 9:9 six score talents (Geneva) an hundred and twenty talents (KJV) one hundred and twenty talents (NKJV)

2 Chron. 9:9 of sweet odours exceeding much (Geneva) of spices great abundance (KJV) spices in great abundance (NKJV)

2 Chron. 9:16 house of the wood (Geneva) house of the forest (KJV) House of the Forest (NKJV)

2 Chron. 9:20 house of the wood (Geneva) house of the forest (KJV) House of the Forest (NKJV)

2 Chron. 9:22 excelled (Geneva) passed (KJV) surpassed (NKJV)

2 Chron. 9:29 Ieedo the Seer (Geneva) Iddo the seer (KJV, NKJV)

2 Chron. 10:15 had spoken by Ahijah (Geneva) spake by the hand of Ahijah (KJV) had spoken by the hand of Ahijah (NKJV)

2 Chron. 11:5 strong cities (Geneva) cities for defence (KJV) cities for defense (NKJV)

2 Chron. 11:11 repaired (Geneva) fortified (KJV, NKJV)

2 Chron. 11:18 Ishai (Geneva) Jesse (KJV, NKJV)

2 Chron. 11:19 sons (Geneva) children (KJV, NKJV)

2 Chron. 12:1 And when (Geneva) And it came to pass, when (KJV) Now it came to pass, when (NKJV)

2 Chron. 13:7 resist (Geneva) withstand (KJV, NKJV)

2 Chron. 13:9 driven away (Geneva) cast out (KJV, NKJV)

2 Chron. 13:20 the Lord plagued him (Geneva) the LORD struck him (KJV, NKJV)

2 Chron. 16:7 Aram (Geneva) Syria (KJV, NKJV)

2 Chron. 16:14 burnt him with an exceeding great fire (Geneva) made a very great burning for him (KJV, NKJV)

2 Chron. 18:8 an eunuch (Geneva) one *of his* officers (KJV, NKJV)

2 Chron. 18:29 I will change myself (Geneva) I will disguise myself (KJV, NKJV)

2 Chron. 18:30 Aram (Geneva) Syria (KJV, NKJV)

2 Chron. 19:6 in the cause *and* judgment (Geneva) in the judgment (KJV, NKJV)

2 Chron. 20:18 to the earth (Geneva) to the ground (KJV, NKJV)

2 Chron. 20:21 praise *him that is* in the beautiful Sanctuary (Geneva) praise the beauty of holiness (KJV, NKJV)

2 Chron. 20:22 began to shout (Geneva) began to sing (KJV, NKJV)

2 Chron. 23:1 Jehoiada waxed bold (Geneva) Jehoiada strengthened himself (KJV, NKJV)

2 Chron. 23:18 by the appointment of David (Geneva) by David (KJV, NKJV)

2 Chron. 24:7 For wicked Athaliah & her children (Geneva) For the sons of Athaliah, that wicked woman (KJV, NKJV)

2 Chron. 24:11 silver in abundance (Geneva) money in abundance (KJV, NKJV)

2 Chron. 24:19 *God* sent Prophets (Geneva) he sent prophets (KJV) He sent prophets (NKJV)

2 Chron. 24:24 army of Aram (Geneva) army of the Syrians (KJV, NKJV)

2 Chron. 25:1 five and twenty year old (Geneva) twenty and five years old (KJV)

2 Chron. 25:5 assembled (Geneva) gathered (KJV, NKJV)

2 Chron. 25:11 was encouraged (Geneva) strengthened himself (KJV, NKJV)

2 Chron. 25:13 men of the army (Geneva) soldiers of the army (KJV, NKJV)

2 Chron. 26:10 cisterns (Geneva) wells (KJV, NKJV)

2 Chron. 26:14 stones to sling (Geneva) slings *to cast* stones (KJV, NKJV)

2 Chron. 26:15 because *God* did help him marvelously (Geneva) for he was marvellously helped (KJV) for he was marvelously helped (NKJV)

2 Chron. 27:3 wall of the castle (Geneva) wall of Ophel (KJV, NKJV)

2 Chron. 27:5 King of the children of Ammon (Geneva) king of the Ammonites (KJV, NKJV)

2 Chron. 27:6 directed his way (Geneva) prepared his ways (KJV, NKJV)

2 Chron. 28:3 burnt his sons (Geneva) burnt his children (KJV, NKJV)

2 Chron. 28:6 six score thousand (Geneva) an hundred and twenty thousand (KJV) one hundred and twenty thousand (NKJV)

2 Chron. 28:13 fierce wrath *of God* against Israel (Geneva) fierce wrath against Israel (KJV, NKJV)

2 Chron. 28:19 had humbled Judah (Geneva) brought Judah low (KJV, NKJV)

2 Chron. 28:21 King of Asshur (Geneva) king of Assyria (KJV, NKJV)

2 Chron. 29:7 in the Sanctuary (Geneva) in the holy *place* (KJV, NKJV)

2 Chron. 29:25 by the hand of the Prophets (Geneva) by his prophets (KJV, NKJV)

2 Chron. 29:30 praised with joy (Geneva) sang praises with gladness (KJV, NKJV)

2 Chron. 30:9 convert unto him (Geneva) return unto him (KJV) return to Him (NKJV)

2 Chron. 31:6 the holy tithes (Geneva) the tithe of holy things (KJV, NKJV)

2 Chron. 31:15 And at his hand (Geneva) And next him (KJV) And under him (NKJV)

2 Chron. 32:5 took courage (Geneva) strengthened himself (KJV, NKJV)

2 Chron. 32:11 entice you (Geneva) persuade you (KJV, NKJV)

2 Chron. 32:15 seduce (Geneva) persuade (KJV, NKJV)

2 Chron. 32:17 he gat him treasures (Geneva) he made himself treasuries (KJV, NKJV)

2 Chron. 33:11 Babel (Geneva) Babylon (KJV, NKJV)

2 Chron. 34:4 in his sight (Geneva) in his presence (KJV, NKJV)

2 Chron. 34:9 residue (Geneva) remnant (KJV, NKJV)

2 Chron. 34:27 heart did melt (Geneva) heart was tender (KJV, NKJV)

2 Chron. 35:5 in the Sanctuary (Geneva) in the holy *place* (KJV, NKJV)

2 Chron. 35:23 I am very sick (Geneva) I am sore wounded (KJV) I am severely wounded (NKJV)

2 Chron. 36:6 to Babel (Geneva) to Babylon (KJV, NKJV)

2 Chron. 36:13 against Nebuchadnezzar (Geneva) against king Nebuchadnezzar (KJV) against King Nebuchadnezzar (NKJV)

Ezra 4:10 rest of the people (Geneva) rest of the nations (KJV, NKJV)

Ezra 6:22 Asshur (Geneva) Assyria (KJV, NKJV)

Ezra 7:6 from Babel (Geneva) from Babylon (KJV, NKJV)

Ezra 7:17 with this silver (Geneva) with this money (KJV, NKJV)

Ezra 7:25 judges & arbiters (Geneva) magistrates and judges (KJV, NKJV)

Ezra 8:28 Ye are consecrate (Geneva) Ye are holy (KJV) You are holy (NKJV)

Ezra 9:1 from corner to corner (Geneva) from one end to another (KJV, NKJV)
Ezra 10:11 give praise (Geneva) make confession (KJV, NKJV)
Neh. 1:6 be attent (Geneva) be attentive (KJV, NKJV)
Neh. 1:8 among the people (Geneva) among the nations (KJV, NKJV)
Neh. 1:11 butler (Geneva) cupbearer (KJV, NKJV)
Neh. 2:1 Now in the month Nisan (Geneva) And it came to pass in the month Nisan (KJV, NKJV)
Neh. 2:3 God save the King (Geneva) Let the king live (KJV) May the king live (NKJV)
Neh. 2:7 the captains (Geneva) the governors (KJV, NKJV)
Neh. 2:9 to the captains (Geneva) to the governors (KJV, NKJV)
Neh. 2:10 wealth (Geneva) welfare (KJV) well-being (NKJV)
Neh. 2:13 ports (Geneva) gates (KJV, NKJV)
Neh. 2:17 misery (Geneva) distress (KJV, NKJV)
Neh. 3:3 fish port (Geneva) fish gate (KJV) Fish Gate (NKJV)
Neh. 3:7 fortified (Geneva) repaired (KJV, NKJV)
Neh. 3:24 fortified (Geneva) repaired (KJV, NKJV)
Neh. 4:4 shame (Geneva) reproach (KJV, NKJV)
Neh. 4:16 young men (Geneva) servants (KJV, NKJV)
Neh. 9:10 tokens (Geneva) signs (KJV, NKJV)
Neh. 9:30 by the hand of thy Prophets (Geneva) in thy prophets (KJV) in Your prophets (NKJV)
Neh. 11:2 thanked (Geneva) blessed (KJV, NKJV)
Neh. 13:25 reproved them (Geneva) contended with them (KJV, NKJV)
Esther 1:1 In the days (Geneva) Now it came to pass in the days (KJV, NKJV)
Esther 1:2 sat on his throne (Geneva) sat on the throne of his kingdom (KJV, NKJV)
Esther 1:3 the captains and governours (Geneva) the nobles and princes (KJV) the nobles, and the princes (NKJV)
Esther 1:4 riches & glory of his kingdom (Geneva) riches of his glorious kingdom (KJV, NKJV)
Esther 1:7 and changed vessel after vessel (Geneva) the vessels being diverse one from another (KJV) each vessel being different from the other (NKJV)
Esther 1:9 Ahashuerosh (Geneva) Ahasuerus (KJV, NKJV)
Esther 1:15 Ahashuerosh (Geneva) Ahasuerus (KJV, NKJV)
Esther 1:18 princesses (Geneva) ladies (KJV) *noble* ladies (NKJV)
Esther 1:18 despitefulness (Geneva) contempt (KJV, NKJV)
Esther 1:20 kingdom (Geneva) empire (KJV, NKJV)
Esther 2:4 the maid (Geneva) the maiden (KJV) the young woman (NKJV)
Esther 2:4 let her reign in the stead (Geneva) be queen instead (KJV, NKJV)
Esther 2:5 a man of Iemini (Geneva) a Benjamite (KJV, NKJV)
Esther 2:6 Babel (Geneva) Babylon (KJV, NKJV)
Esther 2:7 nourished (Geneva) brought up (KJV, NKJV)
Esther 2:9 maid (Geneva) maiden (KJV) young woman (NKJV)
Esther 2:12 Ahashuerosh (Geneva) Ahasuerus (KJV, NKJV)
Esther 2:17 found grace (Geneva) obtained grace (KJV, NKJV)
Esther 2:20 was nourished (Geneva) was brought up (KJV, NKJV)
Esther 3:1 exalted (Geneva) advanced (KJV, NKJV)
Esther 3:12 Ahashuerosh (Geneva) Ahasuerus (KJV, NKJV)
Esther 4:12 certified (Geneva) told to (KJV) told (NKJV)
Esther 4:14 comfort and deliverance (Geneva) enlargement and deliverance (KJV) relief and deliverance (NKJV)
Esther 5:12 bidden (Geneva) invited (KJV, NKJV)
Esther 5:14 a tree (Geneva) a gallows (KJV, NKJV)
Esther 6:2 Ahashuerosh (Geneva) Ahasuerus (KJV, NKJV)
Esther 6:4 on the tree (Geneva) on the gallows (KJV, NKJV)
Esther 7:5 Ahashuerosh (Geneva) Ahasuerus (KJV, NKJV)
Esther 7:10 on the tree (Geneva) on the gallows (KJV, NKJV)
Esther 9:3 exalted the Jews (Geneva) helped the Jews (KJV, NKJV)
Esther 10:1 Ahashuerosh (Geneva) Ahasuerus (KJV, NKJV)
Job 1:6 children of God (Geneva) sons of God (KJV, NKJV)

Job 1:18 And whiles he (Geneva) While he (KJV, NKJV)
Job 2:1 children of God (Geneva) sons of God (KJV, NKJV)
Job 2:17 tyranny (Geneva) troubling (KJV, NKJV)
Job 4:15 the wind (Geneva) a spirit (KJV, NKJV)
Job 5:4 salvation (Geneva) safety (KJV, NKJV)
Job 5:22 dearth (Geneva) famine (KJV, NKJV)
Job 6:23 tyrants (Geneva) mighty (KJV) oppressor (NKJV)
Job 8:4 children (Geneva) sons (KJV, NKJV)
Job 13:3 dispute with God (Geneva) reason with God (KJV, NKJV)
Job 15:20 tyrant (Geneva) oppressor (KJV, NKJV)
Job 19:23 written (Geneva) printed (KJV) inscribed (NKJV)
Job 20:16 gall (Geneva) poison (KJV, NKJV)
Job 21:5 abashed (Geneva) astonished (KJV, NKJV)
Job 21:7 wax old (Geneva) become old (KJV, NKJV)
Job 23:3 Would God *yet* I knew (Geneva) Oh that I knew (KJV, NKJV)
Job 25:2 Power (Geneva) Dominion (KJV, NKJV)
Job 26:6 The grave (Geneva) Hell (KJV) Sheol (NKJV)
Job 27:13 tyrants (Geneva) oppressors (KJV, NKJV)
Job 28:2 out of the dust (Geneva) out of the earth (KJV) from the earth (NKJV)
Job 29:3 mine head (Geneva) my head (KJV, NKJV)
Job 29:14 justice (Geneva) righteousness (KJV, NKJV)
Job 30:6 clefts of rivers (Geneva) cliffs of the valleys (KJV) clefts of the valleys (NKJV)
Job 30:11 Because that *God* (Geneva) Because he (KJV) Because He (NKJV)
Job 31:13 contemn (Geneva) despise (KJV) despised (NKJV)
Job 36:14 Their soul (Geneva) They (KJV, NKJV)
Job 36:20 Be not careful in the night (Geneva) Desire not the night (KJV) Do not desire the night (NKJV)
Job 36:26 God *is* excellent (Geneva) God *is* great (KJV, NKJV)
Job 37:1 mine heart is atonied (Geneva) my heart trembleth (KJV) my heart trembles (NKJV)
Job 38:7 children of God (Geneva) sons of God (KJV, NKJV)
Job 38:13 corners (Geneva) ends (KJV, NKJV)
Job 41:28 The archer (Geneva) The arrow (KJV, NKJV)
Ps. 2:2 his Christ (Geneva) his anointed (KJV) His Anointed (NKJV)
Ps. 2:6 mine holy mountain (Geneva) my holy hill (KJV) My holy hill (NKJV)
Ps. 2:9 crush them with a scepter of iron (Geneva) break them with a rod of iron (KJV, NKJV)
Ps. 2:10 be learned (Geneva) be instructed (KJV, NKJV)
Ps. 3:3 buckler (Geneva) shield (KJV, NKJV)
Ps. 3:4 holy mountain (Geneva) holy hill (KJV, NKJV)
Ps. 4:7 joy of heart (Geneva) gladness in my heart (KJV, NKJV)
Ps. 5:1 understand (Geneva) consider (KJV, NKJV)
Ps. 5:9 constancy (Geneva) faithfulness (KJV, NKJV)
Ps. 5:10 from their counsel (Geneva) by their own counsels (KJV, NKJV)
Ps. 6:6 I fainted (Geneva) I am weary (KJV, NKJV)
Ps. 6:6 mourning (Geneva) groaning (KJV, NKJV)
Ps. 7:3 mine hands (Geneva) my hands (KJV, NKJV)
Ps. 7:8 innocency (Geneva) integrity (KJV, NKJV)
Ps. 8:5 than God (Geneva) than the angels (KJV, NKJV)
Ps. 8:9 world (Geneva) earth (KJV, NKJV)
Ps. 9:12 complaint of the poor (Geneva) cry of the humble (KJV, NKJV)
Ps. 9:19 Up, Lord (Geneva) Arise, O LORD (KJV, NKJV)
Ps. 10:2 with pride (Geneva) in *his* pride (KJV, NKJV)
Ps. 12:7 preserve him (Geneva) preserve them (KJV, NKJV)
Ps. 16:9 mine heart (Geneva) my heart (KJV, NKJV)
Ps. 19:10 And more to be desired (Geneva) More to be desired (KJV, NKJV)
Ps. 25:17 mine heart (Geneva) my heart (KJV, NKJV)
Ps. 26:11 innocency (Geneva) integrity (KJV, NKJV)

Ps. 29:4 is glorious (Geneva) is full of majesty (KJV, NKJV)
Ps. 41:8 mischief (Geneva) evil disease (KJV, NKJV)
Ps. 54:3 tyrants (Geneva) oppressors (KJV, NKJV)
Ps. 58:2 imagine mischief (Geneva) work wickedness (KJV, NKJV)
Ps. 60:2 land (Geneva) earth (KJV, NKJV)
Ps. 60:11 against trouble (Geneva) from trouble (KJV, NKJV)
Ps. 61:6 many ages (Geneva) many generations (KJV, NKJV)
Ps. 61:7 faithfulness (Geneva) truth (KJV, NKJV)
Ps. 62:2 strength (Geneva) rock (KJV, NKJV)
Ps. 63:7 mine helper (Geneva) my help (KJV, NKJV)
Ps. 67:4 the people (Geneva) the nations (KJV, NKJV)
Ps. 68:9 gracious rain (Geneva) plentiful rain (KJV, NKJV)
Ps. 69:2 I stick fast (Geneva) I sink (KJV, NKJV)
Ps. 69:5 faults (Geneva) sins (KJV, NKJV)
Ps. 70:5 mine helper (Geneva) my help (KJV, NKJV)
Ps. 71:21 mine honour (Geneva) my greatness (KJV, NKJV)
Ps. 72:20 son of Ishai (Geneva) son of Jesse (KJV, NKJV)
Ps. 73:21 mine heart (Geneva) my heart (KJV, NKJV)
Ps. 76:4 puissant (Geneva) excellent (KJV, NKJV)
Ps. 76:6 Jaakob (Geneva) Jacob (KJV, NKJV)
Ps. 78:16 floods (Geneva) streams (KJV, NKJV)
Ps. 78:24 MAN (Geneva) manna (KJV, NKJV)
Ps. 78:36 dissembled (Geneva) lied (KJV, NKJV)
Ps. 78:46 grasshopper (Geneva) locust (KJV, NKJV)
Ps. 78:47 with the hailstone (Geneva) with frost (KJV, NKJV)
Ps. 79:7 Jaakob (Geneva) Jacob (KJV, NKJV)
Ps. 81:16 *God* would have fed (Geneva) He should have fed (KJV) He would have fed (NKJV)
Ps. 84:6 vale of Baca (Geneva) valley of Baca (KJV) Valley of Baca (NKJV)
Ps. 86:15 a pitiful God (Geneva) a God full of compassion (KJV, NKJV)
Ps. 87:4 Babel (Geneva) Babylon (KJV, NKJV)
Ps. 89:7 God is very terrible (Geneva) God is greatly to be feared (KJV, NKJV)
Ps. 89:35 mine holiness (Geneva) my holiness (KJV) My holiness (NKJV)
Ps. 89:44 dignity (Geneva) glory (KJV, NKJV)
Ps. 89:51 So be it, even so be it (Geneva) Amen and Amen (KJV, NKJV)
Ps. 90:3 sons of Adam (Geneva) children of men (KJV, NKJV)
Ps. 91:1 in the shadow (Geneva) under the shadow (KJV, NKJV)
Ps. 91:2 say unto the Lord (Geneva) say of the LORD (KJV, NKJV)
Ps. 91:2 mine hope (Geneva) my refuge (KJV, NKJV)
Ps. 91:3 hunter (Geneva) fowler (KJV, NKJV)
Ps. 91:5 fear of the night (Geneva) terror by night (KJV, NKJV)
Ps. 91:9 mine hope (Geneva) my refuge (KJV, NKJV)
Ps. 92:1 to praise (Geneva) to give thanks (KJV, NKJV)
Ps. 92:1 to sing unto (Geneva) to sing praises unto (KJV) to sing praises to (NKJV)
Ps. 92:2 truth (Geneva) faithfulness (KJV, NKJV)
Ps. 92:4 rejoice (Geneva) triumph (KJV, NKJV)
Ps. 92:5 how glorious (Geneva) how great (KJV, NKJV)
Ps. 92:15 none iniquity (Geneva) no unrighteousness (KJV, NKJV)
Ps. 94:1 O Lord God the advenger (Geneva) O LORD God, to whom vengeance belongeth (KJV)
O LORD God, to whom vengeance belongs (NKJV)
Ps. 94:7 Jaakob (Geneva) Jacob (KJV, NKJV)
Ps. 94:14 will not fail (Geneva) will not cast off (KJV, NKJV)
Ps. 94:15 to justice (Geneva) unto righteousness (KJV) to righteousness (NKJV)
Ps. 94:16 the wicked (Geneva) the evildoers (KJV, NKJV)
Ps. 95:1 let us rejoice (Geneva) let us sing (KJV, NKJV)
Ps. 95:2 before his face (Geneva) before his presence (KJV) before His presence (NKJV)
Ps. 95:10 have I contended (Geneva) was I grieved (KJV) I was grieved (NKJV)

Ps. 96:6 Strength and glory (Geneva) Honour and majesty (KJV) Honor and majesty (NKJV)
Ps. 98:2 The Lord declared (Geneva) The LORD hath made known (KJV) The LORD has made known (NKJV)
Ps. 99:4 power (Geneva) strength (KJV, NKJV)
Ps. 99:4 justice (Geneva) righteousness (KJV, NKJV)
Ps. 99:6 heard them (Geneva) answered them (KJV, NKJV)
Ps. 100:5 generation to generation (Geneva) all generations (KJV, NKJV)
Ps. 101:8 Betimes (Geneva) early (KJV) Early (NKJV)
Ps. 102:4 Mine heart (Geneva) My heart (KJV, NKJV)
Ps. 102:12 generation to generation (Geneva) all generations (KJV, NKJV)
Ps. 103:22 Praise the Lord (Geneva) Bless the LORD (KJV, NKJV)
Ps. 104:4 messengers (Geneva) angels (KJV, NKJV)
Ps. 104:16 The high trees (Geneva) The trees of the LORD (KJV, NKJV)
Ps. 104:21 meat at God (Geneva) meat from God (KJV, NKJV)
Ps. 105:2 sing praise (Geneva) sing psalms (KJV, NKJV)
Ps. 105:34 grasshoppers (Geneva) locusts (KJV, NKJV)
Ps. 105:41 flowed out (Geneva) gushed out (KJV, NKJV)
Ps. 106:5 felicity (Geneva) good (KJV) benefit (NKJV)
Ps. 106:24 contemned (Geneva) despised (KJV, NKJV)
Ps. 107:1 Praise the Lord, because he is good (Geneva) O give thanks unto the LORD, for *he is* good (KJV) Oh, give thanks to the LORD, for *He is* good (NKJV)
Ps. 107:2 the oppressor (Geneva) the enemy (KJV, NKJV)
Ps. 107:8 lovingkindness (Geneva) goodness (KJV, NKJV)
Ps. 107:8 sons of men (Geneva) children of men (KJV, NKJV)
Ps. 107:9 thirsty soul (Geneva) longing soul (KJV, NKJV)
Ps. 107:22 offer sacrifices of praise (Geneva) sacrifice the sacrifices of thanksgiving (KJV, NKJV)
Ps. 107:23 occupy (Geneva) do business (KJV, NKJV)
Ps. 107:33 floods (Geneva) rivers (KJV, NKJV)
Ps. 108:12 against trouble (Geneva) from trouble (KJV, NKJV)
Ps. 109:21 O Lord my God (Geneva) O GOD the Lord (KJV, NKJV)
Ps. 109:25 a rebuke (Geneva) a reproach (KJV, NKJV)
Ps. 111:3 beautiful (Geneva) honourable (KJV) honorable (NKJV)
Ps. 112:3 Riches and treasures (Geneva) Wealth and riches (KJV, NKJV)
Ps. 115:5 a mouth (Geneva) mouths (KJV, NKJV)
Ps. 116:5 The Lord is merciful (Geneva) Gracious is the LORD (KJV, NKJV)
Ps. 116:11 in my fear (Geneva) in my haste (KJV, NKJV)
Ps. 118:27 The Lord is mighty (Geneva) God is the LORD (KJV, NKJV)
Ps. 119:20 My heart (Geneva) My soul (KJV, NKJV)
Ps. 119:22 shame (Geneva) reproach (KJV, NKJV)
Ps. 119:90 truth (Geneva) faithfulness (KJV, NKJV)
Ps. 121:5 shadow (Geneva) shade (KJV, NKJV)
Ps. 140:7 O Lord God (Geneva) O GOD the Lord (KJV, NKJV)
Prov. 1:1 parables of Salomon (Geneva) proverbs of Solomon (KJV, NKJV)
Prov. 1:6 a parable (Geneva) a proverb (KJV, NKJV)
Prov. 1:17 without cause (Geneva) in vain (KJV, NKJV)
Prov. 1:22 foolish (Geneva) simple ones (KJV, NKJV)
Prov. 1:32 the foolish (Geneva) the simple (KJV, NKJV)
Prov. 4:7 the beginning (Geneva) the principal thing (KJV, NKJV)
Prov. 5:2 counsel (Geneva) discretion (KJV, NKJV)
Prov. 6:1 neighbour (Geneva) friend (KJV, NKJV)
Prov. 6:6 pismire (Geneva) ant (KJV, NKJV)
Prov. 6:15 destruction (Geneva) calamity (KJV, NKJV)
Prov. 6:17 haughty eyes (Geneva) proud look (KJV, NKJV)
Prov. 6:23 lantern (Geneva) lamp (KJV, NKJV)
Prov. 7:20 silver (Geneva) money (KJV, NKJV)
Prov. 8:5 foolish men (Geneva) simple (KJV) simple ones (NKJV)

Prov. 9:5 my meat (Geneva) my bread (KJV, NKJV)
Prov. 9:13 troublesome (Geneva) clamorous (KJV, NKJV)
Prov. 10:7 memorial (Geneva) memory (KJV, NKJV)
Prov. 10:18 dissembleth hatred (Geneva) hideth hatred (KJV, NKJV)
Prov. 11:25 person (Geneva) soul (KJV, NKJV)
Prov. 12:7 *God* overthroweth the wicked (Geneva) The wicked are overthrown (KJV, NKJV)
Prov. 12:27 The deceitful man (Geneva) The slothful *man* (KJV) The lazy *man* (NKJV)
Prov. 13:9 candle (Geneva) lamp (KJV, NKJV)
Prov. 13:14 instruction (Geneva) law (KJV, NKJV)
Prov. 14:15 The foolish (Geneva) The simple (KJV, NKJV)
Prov. 14:18 The foolish (Geneva) The simple (KJV, NKJV)
Prov. 14:34 Justice (Geneva) Righteousness (KJV, NKJV)
Prov. 15:15 a good conscience (Geneva) he that is of a merry heart (KJV) he who is of a merry heart (NKJV)
Prov. 16:27 A wicked man (Geneva) An ungodly man (KJV, NKJV)
Prov. 17:11 A sedicious person (Geneva) An evil *man* (KJV, NKJV)
Prov. 18:15 A wise heart (Geneva) The heart of the prudent (KJV, NKJV)
Prov. 20:29 beauty of young men (Geneva) glory of young men (KJV, NKJV)
/Prov. 20:29 glory of the aged (Geneva) beauty of old men (KJV) splendor of old men (NKJV)
Prov. 21:4 light of the wicked (Geneva) plowing of the wicked (KJV, NKJV)
Prov. 21:11 the foolish (Geneva) the simple (KJV, NKJV)
Prov. 21:12 teacheth (Geneva) considereth (KJV) considers (NKJV)
Prov. 22:3 seeth the plague (Geneva) forseeth the evil (KJV) foresees evil (NKJV)
Prov. 22:6 in the trade of his way (Geneva) in the way he should go (KJV, NKJV)
Prov. 22:25 destruction (Geneva) a snare (KJV, NKJV)
Prov. 25:1 parables (Geneva) proverbs (KJV, NKJV)
Prov. 26:10 The excellent (Geneva) The great *God* (KJV, NKJV)
Prov. 27:6 wounds of a lover (Geneva) wounds of a friend (KJV, NKJV)
Prov. 27:20 The grave (Geneva) Hell (KJV, NKJV)
Prov. 31:10 the pearls (Geneva) rubies (KJV, NKJV)
Eccl. 1:11 no memory (Geneva) no remembrance (KJV, NKJV)
Eccl. 1:13 mine heart (Geneva) my heart (KJV, NKJV)
Eccl. 1:14 I have considered (Geneva) I have seen (KJV, NKJV)
Eccl. 1:17 mine heart (Geneva) my heart (KJV, NKJV)
Eccl. 1:17 madness and foolishness (Geneva) madness and folly (KJV, NKJV)
Eccl. 1:18 in multitude of wisdom (Geneva) in much wisdom (KJV, NKJV)
Eccl. 2:1 with joy (Geneva) with mirth (KJV, NKJV)
Eccl. 4:1 I turned (Geneva) I returned (KJV, NKJV)
Eccl. 5:2 God *is* in the heavens (Geneva) God *is* in heaven (KJV, NKJV)
Eccl. 5:8 be not astonied (Geneva) marvel not (KJV) do not marvel (NKJV)
Eccl. 5:9 abundance (Geneva) profit (KJV, NKJV)
Eccl. 5:12 him that travaileth (Geneva) labouring man (KJV) laboring man (NKJV)
Eccl. 5:15 belly (Geneva) womb (KJV, NKJV)
Eccl. 7:3 Anger (Geneva) Sorrow (KJV, NKJV)
Eccl. 7:6 noise of the thorns (Geneva) crackling of thorns (KJV, NKJV)
Eccl. 7:14 day of wealth (Geneva) day of prosperity (KJV, NKJV)
Eccl. 7:15 in his justice (Geneva) in his righteousness (KJV, NKJV)
Eccl. 7:15 in his malice (Geneva) in his wickedness (KJV, NKJV)
Eccl. 8:11 children of men (Geneva) sons of men (KJV, NKJV)
Eccl. 8:12 *God* prolongeth *his days* (Geneva) his *days* be prolonged (KJV) his *days* are prolonged (NKJV)
Eccl. 9:9 Rejoice (Geneva) Live joyfully (KJV, NKJV)
Eccl. 9:14 compassed it about (Geneva) besieged it (KJV, NKJV)
Eccl. 10:6 excellency (Geneva) dignity (KJV, NKJV)
Eccl. 10:19 They prepare bread for laughter (Geneva) A feast is made for laughter (KJV, NKJV)
Eccl. 10:20 fowl of the heaven (Geneva) bird of the air (KJV, NKJV)

Eccl. 11:10 take away grief (Geneva) remove sorrow (KJV, NKJV)
Eccl. 12:10 pleasant words (Geneva) acceptable words (KJV, NKJV)
Eccl. 12:11 one pastor (Geneva) one shepherd (KJV) one Shepherd (NKJV)
Eccl. 12:12 much reading (Geneva) much study (KJV, NKJV)
Eccl. 12:13 the end of all (Geneva) the conclusion of the whole matter (KJV, NKJV)
Isa. 1:5 fall away (Geneva) will revolt (KJV, NKJV)
Isa. 1:5 whole heart is heavy (Geneva) whole heart faint (KJV) whole heart faints (NKJV)
Isa. 1:19 consent and obey (Geneva) be willing and obedient (KJV) are willing and obedient (NKJV)
Isa. 1:24 Lord God of hosts (Geneva) the Lord, the LORD of hosts (KJV, NKJV)
Isa. 3:1 the Lord God of hosts (Geneva) the Lord, the LORD of hosts (KJV, NKJV)
Isa. 7:1 in the days (Geneva) it came to pass in the days (KJV, NKJV)
Isa. 7:5 Aram (Geneva) Syria (KJV, NKJV)
Isa. 7:18 in that day (Geneva) it shall come to pass in that day (KJV, NKJV)
Isa. 8:7 Asshur (Geneva) Assyria (KJV, NKJV)
Isa. 9:12 Aram before (Geneva) The Syrians before (KJV, NKJV)
Isa. 10:1 wicked decrees (Geneva) unrighteous decrees (KJV, NKJV)
Isa. 10:33 the Lord God of hosts (Geneva) the Lord, the LORD of hosts (KJV, NKJV)
Isa. 11:1 stock of Ishai, and a grass (Geneva) stem of Jesse, and a Branch (KJV, NKJV)
Isa. 11:10 Ishai (Geneva) Jesse (KJV, NKJV)
Isa. 13:11 tyrants (Geneva) terrible (KJV, NKJV)
Isa. 13:18 children (Geneva) young men (KJV, NKJV)
Isa. 13:21 Ziim (Geneva) wild beasts of the desert (KJV, NKJV)
Isa. 14:4 Babel (Geneva) Babylon (KJV, NKJV)
Isa. 16:4 face of the destroyer (Geneva) face of the spoiler (KJV, NKJV)
Isa. 17:3 The munition (Geneva) The fortress (KJV, NKJV)
Isa. 17:10 God of thy strength (Geneva) rock of thy strength (KJV) Rock of your stronghold (NKJV)
Isa. 19:23 path (Geneva) highway (KJV, NKJV)
Isa. 19:24 Asshur (Geneva) Assyria (KJV, NKJV)
Isa. 20:2 by the hand of Isaiah (Geneva) by Isaiah (KJV, NKJV)
Isa. 21:5 Prepare thou the table (Geneva) Prepare the table (KJV, NKJV)
Isa. 23:8 chapmen (Geneva) traffickers (KJV) traders (NKJV)
Isa. 24:4 proud people (Geneva) haughty people (KJV, NKJV)
Isa. 24:21 in that day (Geneva) it shall come to pass in that day (KJV, NKJV)
Isa. 25:1 a stable truth (Geneva) faithfulness and truth (KJV, NKJV)
Isa. 25:3 mighty people (Geneva) strong people (KJV, NKJV)
Isa. 25:3 strong nations (Geneva) terrible nations (KJV, NKJV)
Isa. 25:4 trouble (Geneva) distress (KJV, NKJV)
Isa. 25:8 destroy death (Geneva) swallow up death (KJV, NKJV)
Isa. 25:10 in Madmenah (Geneva) for the dunghill (KJV) for the refuse heap (NKJV)
Isa. 25:11 stretch (Geneva) spread (KJV, NKJV)
Isa. 25:12 defense (Geneva) fortress (KJV, NKJV)
Isa. 26:3 By an assured purpose (Geneva) whose mind is stayed on thee (KJV) Whose mind is stayed on You (NKJV)
Isa. 26:4 strength for evermore (Geneva) everlasting strength (KJV, NKJV)
Isa. 26:5 high city (Geneva) lofty city (KJV, NKJV)
Isa. 26:7 make equal (Geneva) weigh (KJV, NKJV)
Isa. 26:13 We have conceived (Geneva) We have been with child (KJV, NKJV)
Isa. 27:1 visit (Geneva) punish (KJV, NKJV)
Isa. 27:4 Anger (Geneva) Fury (KJV, NKJV)
Isa. 27:12 in that day (Geneva) it shall come to pass in that day (KJV, NKJV)
Isa. 28:2 mighty and strong host (Geneva) mighty and strong one (KJV, NKJV)
Isa. 28:4 afore summer (Geneva) before the summer (KJV, NKJV)
Isa. 28:7 they fail in vision (Geneva) they err in vision (KJV, NKJV)
Isa. 28:10 line unto line (Geneva) line upon line (KJV, NKJV)

Isa. 28:11 a stammering tongue (Geneva) stammering lips (KJV, NKJV)
Isa. 28:13 line unto line (Geneva) line upon line (KJV, NKJV)
Isa. 28:15 under vanity (Geneva) under falsehood (KJV, NKJV)
Isa. 28:17 vain confidence (Geneva) refuge of lies (KJV, NKJV)
Isa. 28:22 increase (Geneva) be made strong (KJV, NKJV)
Isa. 29:2 the altar (Geneva) Ariel (KJV, NKJV)
Isa. 29:7 the altar (Geneva) Ariel (KJV, NKJV)
Isa. 29:10 spirit of slumber (Geneva) spirit of deep sleep (KJV, NKJV)
Isa. 29:22 Jaakob (Geneva) Jacob (KJV, NKJV)
Isa. 30:1 lay sin upon sin (Geneva) add sin to sin (KJV, NKJV)
Isa. 30:4 unto Hanes (Geneva) to Hanes (KJV, NKJV)
Isa. 30:8 for the last day (Geneva) for the time to come (KJV) for time to come (NKJV)
Isa. 30:10 flattering things (Geneva) smooth things (KJV, NKJV)
Isa. 30:12 have cast off this word (Geneva) despise this word (KJV, NKJV)
Isa. 30:22 pollute (Geneva) defile (KJV, NKJV)
Isa. 30:28 river (Geneva) stream (KJV, NKJV)
Isa. 30:31 Asshur (Geneva) Assyria (KJV, NKJV)
Isa. 31:1 unto Egypt (Geneva) to Egypt (KJV, NKJV)
Isa. 32:1 in justice (Geneva) in righteousness (KJV, NKJV)
Isa. 32:11 be astonied (Geneva) be troubled (KJV, NKJV)
Isa. 33:2 have mercy (Geneva) be gracious (KJV, NKJV)
Isa. 33:4 grasshoppers (Geneva) locusts (KJV, NKJV)
Isa. 33:7 messengers (Geneva) valiant ones (KJV, NKJV)
Isa. 33:15 in justice (Geneva) righteously (KJV, NKJV)
Isa. 34:4 folden like a book (Geneva) rolled together as a scroll (KJV) rolled up like a scroll (NKJV)
Isa. 34:5 be drunken (Geneva) be bathed (KJV, NKJV)
Isa. 34:9 rivers (Geneva) streams (KJV, NKJV)
Isa. 35:2 florish (Geneva) blossom (KJV, NKJV)
Isa. 35:7 dry ground (Geneva) parched ground (KJV, NKJV)
Isa. 35:9 noisome beasts (Geneva) ravenous beast (KJV, NKJV)
Isa. 36:1 in the fourteenth year (Geneva) it came to pass in the fourteenth year (KJV, NKJV)
Isa. 36:2 Asshur (Geneva) Assyria (KJV, NKJV)
Isa. 36:2 great host (Geneva) great army (KJV, NKJV)
Isa. 36:3 chanceller (Geneva) scribe (KJV, NKJV)
Isa. 36:4 Asshur (Geneva) Assyria (KJV, NKJV)
Isa. 36:19 mine hand (Geneva) my hand (KJV, NKJV)
Isa. 36:21 kept silence (Geneva) held their peace (KJV, NKJV)
Isa. 36:22 chanceller (Geneva) scribe (KJV, NKJV)
Isa. 37:2 chanceller (Geneva) scribe (KJV, NKJV)
Isa. 37:6 Asshur (Geneva) Assyria (KJV, NKJV)
Isa. 40:19 silver plates (Geneva) silver chains (KJV, NKJV)
Isa. 47:1 daughter Babel (Geneva) daughter of Babylon (KJV, NKJV)
Isa. 50:3 a sack their covering (Geneva) sackcloth their covering (KJV, NKJV)
Isa. 55:2 laid out silver (Geneva) spend money (KJV, NKJV)
Isa. 56:10 Their watchmen (Geneva) His watchmen (KJV, NKJV)
Isa. 57:3 witches children (Geneva) sons of the sorceress (KJV, NKJV)
Isa. 57:5 sacrificing the children (Geneva) slaying the children (KJV, NKJV)
Isa. 57:17 his wicked covetousness (Geneva) iniquity of his covetousness (KJV, NKJV)
Isa. 59:17 habergeon (Geneva) breastplate (KJV, NKJV)
Isa. 63:7 mercies of the Lord (Geneva) lovingkindnesses of the LORD (KJV, NKJV)
Isa. 66:15 with wrath (Geneva) with fury (KJV, NKJV)
Jer. 1:10 pluck up (Geneva) root out (KJV, NKJV)
Jer. 2:3 thing hallowed (Geneva) holiness (KJV, NKJV)
Jer. 2:18 Asshur (Geneva) Assyria (KJV, NKJV)
Jer. 2:25 from bareness (Geneva) from being unshod (KJV, NKJV)

Jer. 2:34 wings (Geneva) skirts (KJV, NKJV)
Jer. 3:12 disobedient Israel (Geneva) backsliding Israel (KJV, NKJV)
Jer. 3:14 disobedient children (Geneva) backsliding children (KJV, NKJV)
Jer. 3:19 armies of the heathen (Geneva) hosts of nations (KJV, NKJV)
Jer. 3:22 rebellions (Geneva) backslidings (KJV, NKJV)
Jer. 4:7 from his den (Geneva) from his thicket (KJV, NKJV)
Jer. 4:16 heathen (Geneva) nations (KJV, NKJV)
Jer. 5:26 wicked persons (Geneva) wicked *men* (KJV, NKJV)
Jer. 6:3 pastors (Geneva) shepherds (KJV, NKJV)
Jer. 6:7 cruelty (Geneva) violence (KJV, NKJV)
Jer. 6:18 Gentiles (Geneva) nations (KJV, NKJV)
Jer. 8:7 in the air (Geneva) in the heaven (KJV) in the heavens (NKJV)
Jer. 9:5 friend (Geneva) neighbour (KJV) neighbor (NKJV)
Jer. 9:24 shew mercy (Geneva) exercise lovingkindness (KJV) exercising lovingkindness (NKJV)
Jer. 10:10 the God of truth (Geneva) the true God (KJV, NKJV)
Jer. 11:18 taught (Geneva) given me knowledge (KJV) gave me knowledge (NKJV)
Jer. 13:5 Perath (Geneva) Euphrates (KJV, NKJV)
Jer. 13:24 black Moor (Geneva) Ethiopian (KJV, NKJV)
Jer. 15:1 mine affection (Geneva) my mind (KJV) My mind (NKJV)
Jer. 15:18 my plague desperate (Geneva) my wound incurable (KJV, NKJV)
Jer. 17:21 your souls (Geneva) yourselves (KJV, NKJV)
Jer. 18:4 was broken (Geneva) was marred (KJV, NKJV)
Jer. 18:13 very filthily (Geneva) a very horrible thing (KJV, NKJV)
Jer. 18:16 perpetual derision (Geneva) perpetual hissing (KJV, NKJV)
Jer. 18:17 destruction (Geneva) calamity (KJV, NKJV)
Jer. 18:18 imagine (Geneva) devise (KJV, NKJV)
Jer. 18:21 robbed (Geneva) bereaved (KJV, NKJV)
Jer. 18:22 a host (Geneva) a troop (KJV, NKJV)
Jer. 20:13 of the wicked (Geneva) of evildoers (KJV, NKJV)
Jer. 23:11 do wickedly (Geneva) are profane (KJV, NKJV)
Jer. 23:13 foolishness (Geneva) folly (KJV, NKJV)
Jer. 23:19 the tempest (Geneva) a whirlwind (KJV, NKJV)
Jer. 24:8 naughty figs (Geneva) evil figs (KJV) bad figs (NKJV)
Jer. 28:3 Within two years space (Geneva) Within two full years (KJV, NKJV)
Jer. 29:7 the prosperity of the city (Geneva) the peace of the city (KJV, NKJV)
Jer. 30:5 terrible voice (Geneva) voice of trembling (KJV, NKJV)
Jer. 31:7 Rejoice with gladness (Geneva) Sing with gladness (KJV, NKJV)
Jer. 36:9 in the fifth year (Geneva) it came to pass in the fifth year (KJV, NKJV)
Jer. 37:2 by the ministry of the Prophet Jeremiah (Geneva) by the prophet Jeremiah (KJV, NKJV)
Jer. 37:5 host (Geneva) army (KJV, NKJV)
Jer. 37:7 the Lord God of Israel (Geneva) the LORD, the God of Israel (KJV, NKJV)
Jer. 37:7 host (Geneva) army (KJV, NKJV)
Jer. 37:10 host (Geneva) army (KJV, NKJV)
Jer. 37:11 host (Geneva) army (KJV, NKJV)
Jer. 38:4 wealth (Geneva) welfare (KJV, NKJV)
Jer. 38:12 the black Moor (Geneva) the Ethiopian (KJV, NKJV)
Jer. 39:5 host (Geneva) army (KJV, NKJV)
Jer. 40:2 chief steward (Geneva) captain of the guard (KJV, NKJV)
Jer. 46:9 the black Moors (Geneva) the Ethiopians (KJV, NKJV)
Jer. 48:10 negligently (Geneva) deceitfully (KJV, NKJV)
Jer. 48:38 mourning (Geneva) lamentation (KJV, NKJV)
Jer. 48:41 The cities are taken (Geneva) Kerioth is taken (KJV, NKJV)
Jer. 49:1 the children of Ammon (Geneva) the Ammonites (KJV, NKJV)
Jer. 49:25 glorious city (Geneva) city of praise (KJV, NKJV)
Jer. 50:1 concerning Babel (Geneva) against Babylon (KJV, NKJV)
Jer. 50:21 land of rebels (Geneva) land of Merathaim (KJV, NKJV)

Jer. 50:39 Ziims (Geneva) wild beasts of the desert (KJV) wild desert beasts (NKJV)
Jer. 51:20 hammer (Geneva) battle ax (KJV) battle-ax (NKJV)
Jer. 52:24 chief steward (Geneva) captain of the guard (KJV, NKJV)
Lam. 1:2 continually (Geneva) sore (KJV) bitterly (NKJV)
Lam. 1:2 unfaithfully (Geneva) treacherously (KJV, NKJV)
Lam. 1:4 because no man (Geneva) because none (KJV) Because no one (NKJV)
Lam. 1:4 discomfited (Geneva) afflicted (KJV, NKJV)
Lam. 1:8 she is in derision (Geneva) she is removed (KJV) she has become vile (NKJV)
Lam. 1:9 mine affliction (Geneva) my affliction (KJV, NKJV)
Lam. 1:10 The enemy (Geneva) The adversary (KJV, NKJV)
Lam. 1:22 mine heart (Geneva) my heart (KJV, NKJV)
Lam. 2:1 darkened (Geneva) covered (KJV) has covered (NKJV)
Lam. 2:2 destroyed (Geneva) swallowed up (KJV, NKJV)
Lam. 2:4 wrath (Geneva) fury (KJV, NKJV)
Lam. 3:4 caused to wax old (Geneva) made old (KJV) aged (NKJV)
Lam. 3:11 stopped (Geneva) turned aside (KJV, NKJV)
Lam. 3:21 mine heart (Geneva) my mind (KJV, NKJV)
Lam. 3:25 trust in him (Geneva) wait for him (KJV) wait for Him (NKJV)
Lam. 3:31 forsake (Geneva) cast off (KJV, NKJV)
Lam. 3:32 send affliction (Geneva) cause grief (KJV) causes grief (NKJV)
Lam. 3:33 punish (Geneva) afflict (KJV, NKJV)
Lam. 3:58 maintained (Geneva) pleaded (KJV, NKJV)
Lam. 4:2 The noble men of Zion (Geneva) The precious sons of Zion (KJV, NKJV)
Lam. 4:11 indignation (Geneva) fury (KJV, NKJV)
Lam. 4:21 be drunken and vomit (Geneva) be drunken, and shall make thyself naked (KJV)
become drunk and make yourself naked (NKJV)
Lam. 5:5 we are weary (Geneva) we labour (KJV) we labor (NKJV)
Lam. 5:6 Asshur (Geneva) Assyria (KJV, NKJV)
Lam. 5:11 They defiled (Geneva) They ravished (KJV, NKJV)
Lam. 5:17 heart is heavy (Geneva) heart is faint (KJV, NKJV)
Ezek. 1:13 similitude (Geneva) likeness (KJV, NKJV)
Ezek. 1:14 the beasts (Geneva) the living creatures (KJV, NKJV)
Ezek. 1:15 the beasts (Geneva) the living creatures (KJV, NKJV)
Ezek. 1:16 fashions (Geneva) appearance (KJV, NKJV)
Ezek. 1:19 beasts (Geneva) living creatures (KJV, NKJV)
Ezek. 1:21 When the *beasts* went (Geneva) When those went (KJV, NKJV)
Ezek. 1:28 likeness (Geneva) appearance (KJV, NKJV)
Ezek. 7:11 Cruelty (Geneva) Violence (KJV, NKJV)
Ezek. 8:1 in the sixth year (Geneva) it came to pass in the sixth year (KJV, NKJV)
Ezek. 8:3 Divine vision (Geneva) visions of God (KJV, NKJV)
Ezek. 8:9 caused me to enter at the gate (Geneva) brought me to the door (KJV, NKJV)
Ezek. 10:12 their rings (Geneva) their backs (KJV) their back (NKJV)
Eek. 10:20 beast (Geneva) living creature (KJV, NKJV)
Ezek. 12:12 chiefest (Geneva) prince (KJV, NKJV)
Ezek. 14:8 example (Geneva) sign (KJV, NKJV)
Ezek. 14:23 enterprises (Geneva) doings (KJV, NKJV)
Ezek. 18:30 return (Geneva) Repent (KJV, NKJV)
Ezek. 19:12 in wrath (Geneva) in fury (KJV, NKJV)
Ezek. 20:1 in the seventh year (Geneva) it came to pass in the seventh year (KJV, NKJV)
Ezek. 20:46 Temin (Geneva) the south (KJV, NKJV)
Ezek. 21:15 fear (Geneva) point (KJV, NKJV)
Ezek. 21:19 Babel (Geneva) Babylon (KJV, NKJV)
Ezek. 21:28 children of Ammon (Geneva) Ammonites (KJV, NKJV)
Ezek. 22:4 come unto thy term (Geneva) come *even* unto thy years (KJV) come to *the end of
your
years* (NKJV)

Ezek. 22:5 vile in name (Geneva) infamous (KJV, NKJV)
Ezek. 22:7 despised (Geneva) set light by (KJV) made light of (NKJV)
Ezek. 22:8 polluted (Geneva) profaned (KJV, NKJV)
Ezek. 22:9 commit abomination (Geneva) commit lewdness (KJV, NKJV)
Ezek. 22:11 wickedly (Geneva) lewdly (KJV, NKJV)
Ezek. 22:13 thy covetousness (Geneva) thy dishonest gain (KJV) the dishonest profit (NKJV)
Ezek. 22:22 wrath (Geneva) fury (KJV, NKJV)
Ezek. 22:24 wrath (Geneva) indignation (KJV, NKJV)
Ezek. 22:25 riches (Geneva) treasure (KJV, NKJV)
Ezek. 22:26 broken (Geneva) violated (KJV, NKJV)
Ezek. 22:26 defiled (Geneva) profaned (KJV, NKJV)
Ezek. 22:29 against right (Geneva) wrongfully (KJV, NKJV)
Ezek. 22:31 rendered (Geneva) recompensed (KJV, NKJV)
Ezek. 23:7 Asshur (Geneva) Assyria (KJV, NKJV)
Ezek. 23:10 shame (Geneva) nakedness (KJV, NKJV)
Ezek. 23:12 and princes (Geneva) and rulers (KJV, NKJV)
Ezek. 23:12 clothed with divers suits (Geneva) clothed most gorgeously (KJV, NKJV)
Ezek. 23:14 painted (Geneva) pourtrayed (KJV) portrayed (NKJV)
Ezek. 23:16 As soon, I say, as she saw them (Geneva) And as soon as she saw them with her eyes (KJV) As soon as her eyes saw them (NKJV)
Ezek. 23:18 shame (Geneva) nakedness (KJV, NKJV)
Ezek. 23:19 encreased (Geneva) multiplied (KJV, NKJV)
Ezek. 23:20 servants (Geneva) paramours (KJV, NKJV)
Ezek. 23:20 the members (Geneva) the flesh (KJV, NKJV)
Ezek. 23:23 and princes (Geneva) and rulers (KJV, NKJV)
Ezek. 23:24 multitude of people (Geneva) assembly of people (KJV) horde of people (NKJV)
Ezek. 23:25 indignation (Geneva) jealousy (KJV, NKJV)
Ezek. 23:27 wickedness (Geneva) lewdness (KJV, NKJV)
Ezek. 23:29 dispitefully (Geneva) hatefully (KJV, NKJV)
Ezek. 23:29 shame (Geneva) nakedness (KJV, NKJV)
Ezek. 23:35 wickedness (Geneva) lewdness (KJV, NKJV)
Ezek. 23:41 costly (Geneva) stately (KJV, NKJV)
Ezek. 23:44 wicked women (Geneva) lewd women (KJV, NKJV)
Ezek. 23:45 manner of harlots (Geneva) manner of adulteresses (KJV, NKJV)
Ezek. 23:45 manner of murtherers (Geneva) manner of women that shed blood (KJV) manner of women who shed blood (NKJV)
Ezek. 23:48 wickedness (Geneva) lewdness (KJV, NKJV)
Ezek. 24:2 Babel (Geneva) Babylon (KJV, NKJV)
Ezek. 24:5 one of the best sheep (Geneva) choice of the flock (KJV, NKJV)
Ezek. 24:7 upon an high rock (Geneva) upon the top of a rock (KJV, NKJV)
Ezek. 24:21 pollute (Geneva) profane (KJV, NKJV)
Ezek. 25:5 a dwelling place (Geneva) a stable (KJV, NKJV)
Ezek. 25:17 with rebukes of mine indignation (Geneva) with furious rebukes (KJV, NKJV)
Ezek. 26:1 in the eleventh year (Geneva) it came to pass in the eleventh year (KJV, NKJV)
Ezek. 26:9 weapons (Geneva) axes (KJV, NKJV)
Ezek. 26:18 be astonished (Geneva) tremble (KJV, NKJV)
Ezek. 26:21 I will bring thee to nothing (Geneva) I will make thee a terror (KJV) I will make you a terror (NKJV)
Ezek. 27:12 They of Tarshish *were* (Geneva) Tarshish *was* (KJV, NKJV)
Ezek. 27:16 They of Aram *were* (Geneva) Syria *was* (KJV, NKJV)
Ezek. 28:13 garment (Geneva) covering (KJV, NKJV)
Ezek. 28:13 ruby (Geneva) sardius (KJV, NKJV)
Ezek. 28:13 chrysolite (Geneva) beryl (KJV, NKJV)
Ezek. 28:24 thorn (Geneva) brier (KJV, NKJV)
Ezek. 29:10 upon thy rivers (Geneva) against thy rivers (KJV) against your rivers (NKJV)
Ezek. 30:5 Phut (Geneva) Libya (KJV, NKJV)

Ezek. 31:1 in the eleventh year (Geneva) it came to pass in the eleventh year (KJV, NKJV)
Ezek. 31:32 fear (Geneva) terror (KJV, NKJV)
Ezek. 38:5 Cush, and Phut (Geneva) Ethiopia, and Libya (KJV, NKJV)
Ezek. 38:18 At the same time (Geneva) And it shall come to pass at the same time (KJV, NKJV)
Ezek. 39:18 the weathers (Geneva) rams (KJV, NKJV)
Ezek. 39:20 valiant men (Geneva) mighty men (KJV, NKJV)
Ezek. 39:25 compassion (Geneva) mercy (KJV, NKJV)
Ezek. 40:2 a divine vision (Geneva) the visions of God (KJV, NKJV)
Ezek. 40:3 similitude (Geneva) appearance (KJV, NKJV)
Ezek. 44:8 ordinances (Geneva) charge (KJV, NKJV)
Ezek. 45:9 cruelty (Geneva) violence (KJV, NKJV)
Daniel 1:2 into his gods treasury (Geneva) into the treasure house of his god (KJV, NKJV)
Daniel 1:8 But he had determined (Geneva) But he purposed (KJV, NKJV)
Daniel 2:12 Babel (Geneva) Babylon (KJV, NKJV)
Daniel 2:13 sentence (Geneva) the decree (KJV, NKJV)
Daniel 2:14 the King's chief steward (Geneva) captain of the king's guard (KJV, NKJV)
Daniel 2:16 give him leasure (Geneva) give him time (KJV, NKJV)
Daniel 2:22 He discovereth (Geneva) He revealeth (KJV) He reveals (NKJV)
Daniel 2:27 enchanters (Geneva) magicians (KJV, NKJV)
Daniel 2:48 governour (Geneva) ruler (KJV, NKJV)
Daniel 3:2 the receivers (Geneva) the treasurers (KJV, NKJV)
Daniel 3:3 the receivers (Geneva) the treasurers (KJV, NKJV)
Daniel 3:5 trumpet (Geneva) flute (KJV, NKJV)
Daniel 3:7 trumpet (Geneva) flute (KJV NKJV)
Daniel 3:15 trumpet (Geneva) flute (KJV, NKJV)
Daniel 3:22 was strait (Geneva) was urgent (KJV, NKJV)
Daniel 3:28 save their own God (Geneva) except their own God (KJV, NKJV)
Daniel 4:5 mine head (Geneva) my head (KJV, NKJV)
Daniel 4:6 Babel (Geneva) Babylon (KJV, NKJV)
Daniel 4:7 enchanters (Geneva) magicians (KJV, NKJV)
Daniel 4:9 enchanters (Geneva) magicians (KJV, NKJV)
Daniel 4:12 boughs (Geneva) leaves (KJV, NKJV)
Daniel 4:36 mine understanding (Geneva) my reason (KJV, NKJV)
Daniel 4:36 my glory was augmented toward me (Geneva) excellent majesty was added unto me (KJV) excellent majesty was added to me (NKJV)
Daniel 5:20 heart was pust up (Geneva) heart was lifted up (KJV, NKJV)
Daniel 6:12 sealed the decree (Geneva) signed a decree (KJV, NKJV)
Daniel 7:7 the visions by night (Geneva) the night visions (KJV, NKJV)
Daniel 7:15 mine head (Geneva) my head (KJV, NKJV)
Daniel 8:4 pushing against the West (Geneva) pushing westward (KJV, NKJV)
Daniel 8:15 similitude of a man (Geneva) appearance of a man (KJV, NKJV)
Daniel 9:10 by the ministry of his servants the Prophets (Geneva) by his servants the prophets (KJV) by His servants the prophets (NKJV)
Daniel 10:1 the word *was* true (Geneva) the thing *was* true (KJV) The message *was* true (NKJV)
Daniel 10:2 three weeks of days (Geneva) three full weeks (KJV, NKJV)
Daniel 10:6 the Chrysolite (Geneva) the beryl (KJV) beryl (NKJV)
Daniel 11:13 then a fore (Geneva) than the former (KJV, NKJV)
Daniel 11:27 talk of disceit (Geneva) speak lies (KJV, NKJV)
Daniel 11:32 cause to sin (Geneva) corrupt (KJV, NKJV)
Daniel 11:38 god Mauzzim (Geneva) God of forces (KJV) god of fortresses (NKJV)
Hosea 1:6 She conceived yet again (Geneva) And she conceived again (KJV, NKJV)
Hosea 1:6 pity (Geneva) mercy (KJV, NKJV)
Hosea 1:10 told (Geneva) numbered (KJV, NKJV)
Hosea 2:4 pity (Geneva) mercy (KJV, NKJV)
Hosea 2:6 stop thy way (Geneva) hedge up thy way (KJV) hedge up your way (NKJV)
Hosea 2:8 bestowed upon Baal (Geneva) prepared for Baal (KJV, NKJV)

Hosea 2:9 shame (Geneva) nakedness (KJV, NKJV)
Hosea 2:10 no man (Geneva) none (KJV) no one (NKJV)
Hosea 2:12 wild beasts (Geneva) beasts of the field (KJV, NKJV)
Hosea 2:13 she followed (Geneva) she went after (KJV, NKJV)
Hosea 2:18 the wild beasts (Geneva) the beasts of the field (KJV, NKJV)
Hosea 2:18 to sleep safely (Geneva) to lie down safely (KJV, NKJV)
Hosea 2:19 in mercy and in compassion (Geneva) in lovingkindness, and in mercies (KJV)
in lovingkindness and mercy (NKJV)
Hosea 2:20 marry (Geneva) betroth (KJV, NKJV)
Hosea 2:23 that was not pitied (Geneva) that had not obtained mercy (KJV) *who* had not obtained
mercy (NKJV)
Hosea 3:1 of *her* husband (Geneva) of *her* friend (KJV) by a lover (NKJV)
Hosea 3:5 convert (Geneva) return (KJV, NKJV)
Hosea 4:2 and whoring (Geneva) and committing adultery (KJV, NKJV)
Hosea 4:6 refused knowledge (Geneva) rejected knowledge (KJV, NKJV)
Hosea 5:4 give their minds (Geneva) frame their doings (KJV) direct their deeds (NKJV)
Hosea 5:6 their sheep (Geneva) their flocks (KJV, NKJV)
Hosea 5:7 transgressed (Geneva) dealt treacherously (KJV, NKJV)
Hosea 5:8 shaume in Ramah (Geneva) trumpet in Ramah (KJV, NKJV)
Hosea 5:14 lions whelp (Geneva) young lion (KJV, NKJV)
Hosea 6:9 work mischief (Geneva) commit lewdness (KJV, NKJV)
Hosea 7:8 cake on the hearth not turned (Geneva) cake not turned (KJV) cake unturned (NKJV)
Hosea 7:11 like a dove deceived (Geneva) like a silly dove (KJV, NKJV)
Hosea 8:4 a King (Geneva) kings (KJV, NKJV)
Hosea 8:8 is devoured (Geneva) is swallowed up (KJV, NKJV)
Hosea 8:9 Asshur (Geneva) Assyria (KJV, NKJV)
Hosea 8:14 increased (Geneva) multiplied (KJV, NKJV)
Hosea 9:4 offer wine (Geneva) offer wine *offerings* (KJV, NKJV)
Hosea 9:12 deprive them (Geneva) bereave them (KJV, NKJV)
Hosea 9:13 in a cottage (Geneva) in a pleasant place (KJV, NKJV)
Hosea 10:4 wormwood (Geneva) hemlock (KJV, NKJV)
Hosea 10:5 Chermarims (Geneva) priests (KJV, NKJV)
Hosea 11:11 sparrow (Geneva) bird (KJV, NKJV)
Hosea 12:6 hope still in thy God (Geneva) wait on thy God continually (KJV) wait on your God
continually (NKJV)
Hosea 12:12 Aram (Geneva) Syria (KJV, NKJV)
Hosea 12:13 reserved (Geneva) preserved (KJV, NKJV)
Hosea 13:3 morning dew (Geneva) early dew (KJV, NKJV)
Hosea 13:7 leopard in the way of Asshur (Geneva) leopard by the way will I observe them (KJV)
leopard by the road I will lurk (NKJV)
Hosea 14:4 rebellion (Geneva) backsliding (KJV, NKJV)
Joel 1:4 grasshopper (Geneva) locust (KJV) swarming locust (NKJV)
Joel 1:5 pulled (Geneva) cut off (KJV, NKJV)
Joel 1:18 mourn (Geneva) groan (KJV, NKJV)
Joel 2:1 shout (Geneva) sound an alarm (KJV, NKJV)
Joel 2:2 blackness (Geneva) gloominess (KJV, NKJV)
Joel 2:2 obscurity (Geneva) thick darkness (KJV, NKJV)
Joel 2:4 sight of horses (Geneva) appearance of horses (KJV, NKJV)
Joel 2:10 shall tremble (Geneva) shall quake (KJV) quakes (NKJV)
Joel 2:10 heavens shall shake (Geneva) heavens shall tremble (KJV) heavens tremble (NKJV)
Joel 2:16 assemble the children (Geneva) gather the children (KJV, NKJV)
Joel 2:18 spare (Geneva) pity (KJV, NKJV)
Joel 2:25 grasshopper (Geneva) locust (KJV) swarming locust (NKJV)
Joel 3:9 Publish (Geneva) Proclaim (KJV, NKJV)
Joel 3:10 Break (Geneva) Beat (KJV, NKJV)
Joel 3:11 mighty men (Geneva) mighty ones (KJV, NKJV)

Joel 3:14 valley of threshing (Geneva) valley of decision (KJV, NKJV)

Joel 3:19 waste (Geneva) a desolation (KJV, NKJV)

Amos 1:1 saw upon Israel (Geneva) saw concerning Israel (KJV, NKJV)

Amos 1:3 I will not turn to it (Geneva) I will not turn away *the punishment* thereof (KJV) I will not turn away its *punishment* (NKJV)

Amos 1:5 Aram (Geneva) Syria (KJV, NKJV)

Amos 1:6 Azzah (Geneva) Gaza (KJV, NKJV)

Amos 1:6 to shut them up in Edom (Geneva) to deliver *them* up to Edom (KJV, NKJV)

Amos 1:7 walls of Azzah (Geneva) wall of Gaza (KJV, NKJV)

Amos 1:9 I will not turn to it (Geneva) I will not turn away *the punishment* thereof (KJV) I will not turn away its *punishment* (NKJV)

Amos 1:10 walls (Geneva) wall (KJV, NKJV)

Amos 1:11 I will not turn to it (Geneva) I will not turn away *the punishment* thereof (KJV) I will not turn away its *punishment* (NKJV)

Amos 1:11 spoiled him evermore (Geneva) did tear perpetually (KJV) tore perpetually (NKJV)

Amos 1:11 his wrath watched him always (Geneva) he kept his wrath for ever (KJV) he kept his wrath forever (NKJV)

Amos 1:13 I will not turn to it (Geneva) I will not turn away *the punishment* thereof (KJV) I will not turn away its *punishment* (NKJV)

Amos 2:4 I will not turn to it (Geneva) I will not turn away *the punishment* thereof (KJV) I will not turn away its *punishment* (NKJV)

Amos 2:4 cast away (Geneva) despised (KJV, NKJV)

Amos 2:6 I will not turn to it (Geneva) I will not turn away *the punishment* thereof (KJV) I will not turn away its *punishment* (NKJV)

Amos 2:7 gape (Geneva) pant (KJV, NKJV)

Amos 2:14 save his life (Geneva) deliver himself (KJV, NKJV)

Amos 2:15 save his life (Geneva) deliver himself (KJV, NKJV)

Amos 3:4 lions whelp (Geneva) young lion (KJV, NKJV)

Amos 3:14 shall be broken off (Geneva) shall be cut off (KJV, NKJV)

Amos 4:1 destroy the needy (Geneva) crush the needy (KJV, NKJV)

Amos 4:2 away with thorns (Geneva) away with hooks (KJV) away with fishhooks (NKJV)

Amos 4:3 ye shall cast your selves (Geneva) ye shall cast *them* (KJV) you will be cast (NKJV)

Amos 4:10 your tents (Geneva) your camps (KJV, NKJV)

Amos 5:15 be merciful (Geneva) be gracious (KJV, NKJV)

Amos 5:16 to lamentation (Geneva) to mourning (KJV, NKJV)

Amos 5:17 lamentation (Geneva) wailing (KJV, NKJV)

Amos 5:20 no light (Geneva) no brightness (KJV, NKJV)

Amos 5:23 multitude (Geneva) noise (KJV, NKJV)

Amos 5:24 mighty river (Geneva) mighty stream (KJV, NKJV)

Amos 6:3 seat of iniquity (Geneva) seat of violence (KJV, NKJV)

Amos 7:9 temples (Geneva) sanctuaries (KJV, NKJV)

Amos 7:9 shall be destroyed (Geneva) shall be laid waste (KJV, NKJV)

Amos 9:6 laid the foundation of his globe of elements in the earth (Geneva) founded his troop in the earth (KJV) founded His strata in the earth (NKJV)

Amos 9:6 upon the open earth (Geneva) upon the face of the earth (KJV) on the face of the earth (NKJV)

Amos 9:13 shall touch the mower (Geneva) shall overtake the reaper (KJV, NKJV)

Micah 1:5 wickedness of Jaakob (Geneva) transgression of Jacob (KJV, NKJV)

Micah 1:9 her plagues (Geneva) her wound (KJV) her wounds (NKJV)

Micah 2:1 imagine (Geneva) devise (KJV, NKJV)

Micah 3:7 soothsayers (Geneva) diviners (KJV, NKJV)

Micah 3:11 prophesy for money (Geneva) divine for money (KJV, NKJV)

Micah 4:10 Sorrow and mourn (Geneva) Be in pain, and labour to bring fourth (KJV) Be in pain, and labor to bring forth (NKJV)

Micah 4:12 in the barn (Geneva) into the floor (KJV) to the threshing floor (NKJV)

Micah 4:13 substance unto the ruler of the whole world (Geneva) substance unto the LORD of the whole earth (KJV) substance to the Lord of the whole earth (NKJV)

Micah 5:1 O daughter of garrisons (Geneva) O daughter of troops (KJV, NKJV)

Micah 5:5 Asshur (Geneva) the Assyrian (KJV, NKJV)

Micah 5:6 destroy (Geneva) waste (KJV, NKJV)

Micah 5:7 sons of Adam (Geneva) sons of men (KJV, NKJV)

Micah 6:8 to humble thyself, to walk with thy God (Geneva) to walk humbly with thy God (KJV) to walk humbly with your God (NKJV)

Micah 6:11 Shall I justify (Geneva) Shall I count *them* pure (KJV) Shall I count pure *those* (NKJV)

Micah 6:12 full of cruelty (Geneva) full of violence (KJV, NKJV)

Micah 7:3 speaketh out the corruption of his soul (Geneva) uttereth his mischievous desire (KJV) utters his evil desire (NKJV)

Micah 7:4 confusion (Geneva) perplexity (KJV, NKJV)

Micah 7:7 for God may Saviour (Geneva) for the God of my salvation (KJV, NKJV)

Micah 7:9 wrath (Geneva) indignation (KJV, NKJV)

Micah 7:17 like worms (Geneva) like worms of the earth (KJV) like snakes of the earth (NKJV)

Nahum 1:3 but *he is* great in power (Geneva) and great in power (KJV, NKJV)

Nahum 1:5 tremble for him (Geneva) quake at him (KJV) quake before Him (NKJV)

Nahum 1:6 wrath (Geneva) indignation (KJV, NKJV)

Nahum 1:6 rocks are broken (Geneva) rocks are thrown down (KJV, NKJV)

Nahum 1:15 that declareth & publisheth peace (Geneva) that bringeth good tidings, that publisheth peace (KJV) who brings good tidings, Who proclaims peace (NKJV)

Nahum 2:1 The destroyer (Geneva) He that dasheth in pieces (KJV) He who scatters (NKJV)

Nahum 2:1 strength (Geneva) power (KJV, NKJV)

Nahum 2:2 glory of Jaakob (Geneva) excellency of Jacob (KJV) excellence of Jacob (NKJV)

Nahum 2:2 glory of Israel (Geneva) excellency of Israel (KJV) excellence of Israel (NKJV)

Nahum 2:4 like lamps (Geneva) like torches (KJV, NKJV)

Nahum 2:10 sorrow (Geneva) much pain (KJV, NKJV)

Nahum 2:11 pasture of the lions whelps (Geneva) feedingplace of the young lions (KJV) feeding place of the young lions (NKJV)

Nahum 2:13 Behold, I *come* unto thee (Geneva) Behold, I *am* against thee (KJV) Behold, I *am* against you (NKJV)

Nahum 3:1 O bloody city (Geneva) Woe to the bloody city (KJV, NKJV)

Nahum 3:4 selleth the people (Geneva) selleth nations (KJV) sells nations (NKJV)

Nahum 3:4 the nations (Geneva) families (KJV, NKJV)

Nahum 3:5 I *come* upon thee (Geneva) I *am* against thee (KJV) I *am* against you (NKJV)

Nahum 3:5 filthiness (Geneva) nakedness (KJV, NKJV)

Nahum 3:6 cast filth (Geneva) cast abominable filth (KJV, NKJV)

Nahum 3:7 Nineveh is destroyed (Geneva) Nineveh is laid waste (KJV, NKJV)

Nahum 3:7 will have pity upon her (Geneva) will bemoan her (KJV, NKJV)

Nahum 3:8 ditch (Geneva) rampart (KJV, NKJV)

Nahum 3:14 temper the morter (Geneva) tread the morter (KJV) tread the mortar (NKJV)

Nahum 3:18 strong men lie down (Geneva) nobles shall dwell *in the dust* (KJV) nobles rest *in the dust* (NKJV)

Nahum 3:19 malice (Geneva) wickedness (KJV, NKJV)

Zechariah 1:10 through the world (Geneva) through the earth (KJV, NKJV)

Zechariah 1:11 gone through the world (Geneva) walked to and fro through the earth (KJV) sent to wak to and fro throughout the earth (NKJV)

Zechariah 1:12 be unmerciful to Jerusalem (Geneva) not have mercy on Jerusalem (KJV, NKJV)

Zechariah 1:16 mine house (Geneva) my house (KJV) My house (NKJV)

Zechariah 1:17 with plenty (Geneva) through prosperity (KJV, NKJV)

Zechariah 2:7 Babel (Geneva) Babylon (KJV, NKJV)

Zechariah 2:10 Rejoice and be glad (Geneva) Sing and rejoice (KJV, NKJV)

Zechariah 2:13 Let all flesh be still (Geneva) Be silent, O all flesh (KJV) Be silent, all flesh (NKJV)

Zechariah 3:1 Jehoshua (Geneva) Joshua (KJV, NKJV)

Zechariah 3:2 The Lord reprove (Geneva) The LORD rebuke (KJV, NKJV)

Zechariah 3:3 Jehoshua (Geneva) Joshua (KJV, NKJV)

Zechariah 3:6 Jehoshua (Geneva) Joshua (KJV, NKJV)
Zechariah 3:7 mine House (Geneva) my house (KJV) My house (NKJV)
Zechariah 3:8 O Jehoshua (Geneva) O Joshua (KJV, NKJV)
Zechariah 4:6 Neither by army nor strength (Geneva) Not by might, nor by power (KJV, NKJV)
Zechariah 4:14 ruler of the whole earth (Geneva) Lord of the whole earth (KJV, NKJV)
Zechariah 5:2 flying book (Geneva) flying roll (KJV) flying scroll (NKJV)
Zechariah 5:6 the sight of them (Geneva) their resemblance (KJV, NKJV)
Zechariah 6:6 the land of the North (Geneva) the north country (KJV, NKJV)
Zechariah 6:8 have pacified (Geneva) have quieted (KJV) have given rest (NKJV)
Zechariah 6:11 Jehoshua (Geneva) Joshua (KJV, NKJV)
Zechariah 7:7 by the ministry of the former Prophets (Geneva) by the former prophets (KJV) through the former prophets (NKJV)
Zechariah 7:14 waste (Geneva) desolate (KJV, NKJV)
Zechariah 8:6 unpossible in the eyes (Geneva) marvelous in the eyes (KJV, NKJV)
Zechariah 8:6 unpossible in my sight (Geneva) marvelous in mine eyes (KJV) marvelous in My eyes (NKJV)
Zechariah 8:9 be builded (Geneva) be built (KJV, NKJV)
Zechariah 8:20 great cities (Geneva) many cities (KJV, NKJV)
Zechariah 8:22 great people (Geneva) many people (KJV) many peoples (NKJV)
Zechariah 9:16 deliver (Geneva) save (KJV, NKJV)
Zechariah 10:2 soothsayers (Geneva) diviners (KJV, NKJV)
Zechariah 10:3 wrath (Geneva) anger (KJV, NKJV)
Zechariah 10:6 preserve (Geneva) save (KJV, NKJV)
Zechariah 10:7 giant (Geneva) mighty *man* (KJV) mighty man (NKJV)
Zechariah 10:10 Asshur (Geneva) Assyria (KJV, NKJV)
Zechariah 11:4 sheep (Geneva) flock (KJV, NKJV)
Zechariah 11:7 sheep of slaughter (Geneva) flock of slaughter (KJV, NKJV)
Zechariah 11:10 might disannul (Geneva) might break (KJV, NKJV)
Malachi 1:1 by ministry of Malachi (Geneva) by Malachi (KJV, NKJV)
Malachi 1:4 is angry (Geneva) hath indignation (KJV) will have indignation (NKJV)
Malachi 1:7 unclean bread (Geneva) polluted bread (KJV) defiled bread (NKJV)
Malachi 1:7 is not to be regarded (Geneva) is contemptible (KJV, NKJV)
Malachi 1:8 prince (Geneva) governor (KJV, NKJV)
Malachi 1:12 is not to be regarded (Geneva) is contemptible (KJV, NKJV)
Malachi 2:7 preserve knowledge (Geneva) keep knowledge (KJV, NKJV)
Malachi 2:8 fall by the Law (Geneva) stumble at the law (KJV, NKJV)
Malachi 2:11 defiled (Geneva) profaned (KJV, NKJV)
Malachi 3:2 endure (Geneva) stand (KJV, NKJV)
Malachi 3:3 fine the sons (Geneva) purify the sons (KJV, NKJV)
Malachi 3:3 purify them (Geneva) purge them (KJV, NKJV)
Malachi 3:4 be acceptable (Geneva) be pleasant (KJV, NKJV)
Malachi 3:5 soothsayers (Geneva) sorcerers (KJV, NKJV)
Malachi 3:8 spoil *his* gods (Geneva) rob God (KJV, NKJV)
Malachi 3:8 spoiled me (Geneva) robbed me (KJV) robbed Me (NKJV)
Malachi 3:9 spoiled (Geneva) robbed (KJV, NKJV)
Malachi 4:5 fearful day (Geneva) dreadful (KJV, NKJV)
Malachi 4:6 with cursing (Geneva) with a curse (KJV, NKJV)

Matt. 2:23 Nazarite (Geneva) Nazarene (KJV, NKJV)
Matt. 3:11 to amendment of life (Geneva) unto repentance (KJV, NKJV)
Matt. 4:17 Amend your lives (Geneva) Repent (KJV, NKJV)
Matt. 5:47 be friendly (Geneva) salute (KJV) greet (NKJV)
Matt. 6:2 make a trumpet to be blown (Geneva) do not sound a trumpet (KJV, NKJV)
Matt. 6:24 God and riches (Geneva) God and mammon (KJV, NKJV)
Matt. 8:23 into the ship (Geneva) into a ship (KJV) into a boat (NKJV)
Matt. 8:25 Master (Geneva) Lord (KJV, NKJV)

Matt. 9:4 Jesus saw their thoughts (Geneva) Jesus knowing their thoughts (KJV, NKJV)
Matt. 10:16 innocent as doves (Geneva) harmless as doves (KJV, NKJV)
Matt. 11:11 John Baptist (Geneva) John the Baptist (KJV, NKJV)
Matt. 11:12 John Baptist (Geneva) John the Baptist (KJV, NKJV)
Matt. 11:19 a drinker of wine (Geneva) a winebibber (KJV, NKJV)
Matt. 11:20 great works (Geneva) mighty works (KJV, NKJV)
Matt. 11:21 great works (Geneva) mighty works (KJV, NKJV)
Matt. 11:22 be easier (Geneva) be more tolerable (KJV, NKJV)
Matt. 11:23 great works (Geneva) mighty works (KJV, NKJV)
Matt. 11:24 easier (Geneva) more tolerable (KJV, NKJV)
Matt. 11:28 ease you (Geneva) give you rest (KJV, NKJV)
Matt. 12:5 break the Sabbath (Geneva) profane the Sabbath (KJV, NKJV)
Matt. 12:7 the innocents (Geneva) the guiltless (KJV, NKJV)
Matt. 12:25 brought to naught (Geneva) brought to desolation (KJV, NKJV)
Matt. 13:2 resorted (Geneva) were gathered together (KJV, NKJV)
Matt. 13:5 And some fell (Geneva) Some fell (KJV, NKJV)
Matt. 13:6 were parched (Geneva) were scorched (KJV, NKJV)
Matt. 13:11 And he answered (Geneva) He answered (KJV, NKJV)
Matt. 13:55 Marie (Geneva) Mary (KJV, NKJV)
Matt. 13:58 great works (Geneva) mighty works (KJV, NKJV)
Matt. 14:2 John Baptist (Geneva) John the Baptist (KJV, NKJV)
Matt. 14:2 risen again from the dead (Geneva) risen from the dead (KJV, NKJV)
Matt. 15:6 of no authority (Geneva) of none effect (KJV) of no effect (NKJV)
Matt. 15:9 mens precepts (Geneva) commandments of men (KJV, NKJV)
Matt. 15:19 sclanders (Geneva) blasphemies (KJV, NKJV)
Matt. 15:22 a woman, a Cananite (Geneva) a woman of Canaan (KJV, NKJV)
Matt. 15:31 halt (Geneva) lame (KJV, NKJV)
Matt. 15:37 sufficed (Geneva) filled (KJV, NKJV)
Matt. 15:38 and little children (Geneva) and children (KJV, NKJV)
Matt. 16:5 to take bread *with them* (Geneva) to take bread (KJV, NKJV)
Matt. 16:14 John Baptist (Geneva) John the Baptist (KJV, NKJV)
Matt. 16:22 Master, pity thyself (Geneva) Be it far from thee, Lord (KJV, NKJV)
Matt. 16:24 forsake (Geneva) deny (KJV, NKJV)
Matt. 16:26 should win (Geneva) shall gain (KJV) gains (NKJV)
Matt. 17:15 Master (Geneva) Lord (KJV, NKJV)
Matt. 17:15 have pity (Geneva) have mercy (KJV, NKJV)
Matt. 18:21 Master (Geneva) Lord (KJV, NKJV)
Matt. 18:24 oght (Geneva) owed (KJV, NKJV)
Matt. 18:28 oght (Geneva) owed (KJV, NKJV)
Matt. 18:29 Appease thine anger towards me (Geneva) Have patience with me (KJV, NKJV)
Matt. 18:33 had pity (Geneva) had compassion (KJV, NKJV)
Matt. 22:7 warriors (Geneva) armies (KJV, NKJV)
Matt. 27:61 Marie Magdalene (Geneva) Mary Magdalene (KJV, NKJV)
Mark 1:7 stronger then I (Geneva) mightier than I (KJV, NKJV)
Mark 1:9 Nazaret *a city* of Galile (Geneva) Nazareth of Galilee (KJV, NKJV)
Mark 1:10 *John* saw the heavens cloven in twain (Geneva) he saw the heaven opened (KJV) He saw the heavens parting (NKJV)
Mark 1:20 anon (Geneva) straightway (KJV) immediately (NKJV)
Mark 1:22 astonied (Geneva) astonished (KJV, NKJV)
Mark 1:24 Saying, Ah (Geneva) Saying, Let us alone (KJV, NKJV)
Mark 1:27 they demanded one of another (Geneva) they questioned among themselves (KJV, NKJV)
Mark 1:27 foul spirits (Geneva) unclean spirits (KJV, NKJV)
Mark 1:30 mother in law (Geneva) mother (KJV, NKJV)
Mark 1:31 by and by (Geneva) immediately (KJV, NKJV)
Mark 2:2 anon (Geneva) straightway (KJV) immediately (NKJV)

Mark 2:10 authority (Geneva) power (KJV, NKJV)
Mark 2:12 by and by (Geneva) immediately (KJV, NKJV)
Mark 2:14 as Jesus passed by (Geneva) as he passed by (KJV) As He passed by (NKJV)
Mark 3:5 mourning (Geneva) being grieved (KJV, NKJV)
Mark 3:7 Jesus avoided (Geneva) Jesus withdrew (KJV, NKJV)
Mark 3:12 they should not utter him (Geneva) they should not make him known (KJV) they should not make Him known (NKJV)
Mark 3:34 sat in compass about him (Geneva) sat about him (KJV) sat about Him (NKJV)
Mark 4:5 by and by (Geneva) immediately (KJV, NKJV)
Mark 4:6 it caught heat (Geneva) it was scorched (KJV, NKJV)
Mark 4:33 preached (Geneva) spake (KJV) spoke (NKJV)
Mark 4:37 waves dashed (Geneva) waves beat (KJV, NKJV)
Mark 5:2 incontinently (Geneva) immediately (KJV, NKJV)
Mark 5:5 in the graves (Geneva) in the tombs (KJV, NKJV)
Mark 5:35 diseasest (Geneva) troublest (KJV) trouble (NKJV)
Mark 6:2 astonied (Geneva) astonished (KJV, NKJV)
Mark 6:12 should amend their lives (Geneva) should repent (KJV, NKJV)
Mark 6:14 John Baptist (Geneva) John the Baptist (KJV, NKJV)
Mark 7:8 observe the tradition (Geneva) hold the tradition (KJV, NKJV)
Mark 7:13 none authority (Geneva) none effect (KJV) no effect (NKJV)
Mark 8:10 anon (Geneva) straightway (KJV) immediately (NKJV)
Mark 8:28 *Some say* John Baptist (Geneva) John the Baptist (KJV, NKJV)
Mark 8:37 for recompense (Geneva) in exchange (KJV, NKJV)
Mark 9:10 demanded (Geneva) questioning (KJV, NKJV)
Mark 10:9 coupled (Geneva) joined (KJV, NKJV)
Mark 10:24 astonied (Geneva) astonished (KJV, NKJV)
Mark 10:33 high Priests (Geneva) chief priests (KJV, NKJV)
Mark 10:41 to disdain at James and John (Geneva) to be much displeased with James and John (KJV) to be greatly displeased with James and John (NKJV)
Mark 10:52 thy faith hath saved thee (Geneva) thy faith hath made thee whole (KJV) your faith has made you well (NKJV)
Mark 11:18 astonied (Geneva) astonished (KJV, NKJV)
Mark 11:32 a very prophet (Geneva) a prophet indeed (KJV, NKJV)
Mark 12:1 a strange country (Geneva) a far country (KJV, NKJV)
Mark 12:4 brake his head (Geneva) wounded *him* in the head (KJV, NKJV)
Mark 12:20 no issue (Geneva) no seed (KJV) no offspring (NKJV)
Mark 12:28 disputing together (Geneva) reasoning together (KJV, NKJV)
Mark 12:40 a colour (Geneva) a pretence (KJV) pretense (NKJV)
Mark 12:44 superfluity (Geneva) abundance (KJV, NKJV)
Mark 13:3 secretly (Geneva) privately (KJV, NKJV)
Mark 13:24 shall wax dark (Geneva) shall be darkened (KJV) will be darkened (NKJV)
Mark 13:37 And these things that I say (Geneva) And what I say (KJV, NKJV)
Mark 14:5 they grudged (Geneva) they murmured (KJV) they criticized (NKJV)
Mark 14:26 a psalm (Geneva) a hymn (KJV, NKJV)
Mark 14:62 of the power *of God* (Geneva) of power (KJV) of the Power (NKJV)
Mark 14:70 anon after (Geneva) a little after (KJV) a little later (NKJV)
Mark 15:1 anon (Geneva) straightway (KJV) immediately (NKJV)
Mark 15:10 high Priests (Geneva) chief priests (KJV, NKJV)
Mark 16:18 take away serpents (Geneva) take up serpents (KJV, NKJV)
Luke 1:27 Marie (Geneva) Mary (KJV, NKJV)
Luke 1:28 freely beloved (Geneva) highly favoured (KJV) highly favored (NKJV)
Luke 1:35 most High (Geneva) Highest (KJV, NKJV)
Luke 1:37 unpossible (Geneva) impossible (KJV, NKJV)
Luke 2:5 Marie (Geneva) Mary (KJV, NKJV)
Luke 2:7 first begotten son (Geneva) firstborn son (KJV) firstborn Son (NKJV)
Luke 2:12 cratch (Geneva) manger (KJV, NKJV)

Luke 2:13 heavenly soldiers (Geneva) heavenly host (KJV, NKJV)
Luke 2:14 in the high *heavens* (Geneva) in the highest (KJV, NKJV)
Luke 2:16 Marie (Geneva) Mary (KJV, NKJV)
Luke 2:16 cratch (Geneva) manger (KJV, NKJV)
Luke 2:24 oblation (Geneva) sacrifice (KJV, NKJV)
Luke 3:8 worthy amendment of life (Geneva) worthy of repentance (KJV, NKJV)
Luke 4:5 in the twinkling of an eye (Geneva) in a moment of time (KJV, NKJV)
Luke 4:36 foul spirits (Geneva) unclean spirits (KJV, NKJV)
Luke 5:9 utterly atonied (Geneva) astonished (KJV, NKJV)
Luke 6:46 Master, Master (Geneva) Lord, Lord (KJV, NKJV)
Luke 9:10 what great things they had done (Geneva) all that they had done (KJV, NKJV)
Luke 9:14 Cause them (Geneva) Make them (KJV, NKJV)
Luke 9:15 caused (Geneva) made (KJV, NKJV)
Luke 9:17 satisfied (Geneva) filled (KJV, NKJV)
Luke 9:19 John Baptist (Geneva) John the Baptist (KJV, NKJV)
Luke 9:28 words (Geneva) sayings (KJV, NKJV)
Luke 9:31 departing (Geneva) decease (KJV, NKJV)
Luke 9:41 crooked (Geneva) perverse (KJV, NKJV)
Luke 9:42 rent him (Geneva) threw him down (KJV, NKJV)
Luke 9:44 for it shall come to pass, that the Son (Geneva) for the Son (KJV, NKJV)
Luke 9:51 settled himself fully (Geneva) stedfastly set his face (KJV) steadfastly set His face (NKJV)
Luke 9:52 town (Geneva) village (KJV, NKJV)
Luke 9:53 behaviour (Geneva) face (KJV, NKJV)
Luke 9:55 But Jesus (Geneva) But he (KJV) But He (NKJV)
Luke 9:58 birds of the heaven (Geneva) birds of the air (KJV, NKJV)
Luke 9:59 the same said (Geneva) he said (KJV, NKJV)
Luke 9:61 mine house (Geneva) my house (KJV, NKJV)
Luke 10:1 before him (Geneva) before his face (KJV) before His face (NKJV)
Luke 10:13 miracles (Geneva) mighty works (KJV, NKJV)
Luke 10:14 easier (Geneva) more tolerable (KJV, NKJV)
Luke 10:19 nothing shall hurt you (Geneva) nothing shall by any means hurt you (KJV, NKJV)
Luke 10:20 subdued (Geneva) subject (KJV, NKJV)
Luke 10:21 I confess (Geneva) I thank (KJV, NKJV)
Luke 10:22 given me (Geneva) delivered to me (KJV) delivered to Me (NKJV)
Luke 10:25 expounder of the Law (Geneva) lawyer (KJV, NKJV)
Luke 10:39 Marie (Geneva) Mary (KJV, NKJV)
Luke 10:42 Marie (Geneva) Mary (KJV, NKJV)
Luke 11:1 Master (Geneva) Lord (KJV, NKJV)
Luke 11:21 the things he possessed (Geneva) his goods (KJV, NKJV)
Luke 11:26 worse (Geneva) more wicked (KJV, NKJV)
Luke 11:31 rise in judgment (Geneva) rise up in the judgment (KJV, NKJV)
Luke 11:32 rise in judgment (Geneva) rise up in the judgment (KJV, NKJV)
Luke 11:45 expounders of the Law (Geneva) lawyers (KJV, NKJV)
Luke 11:46 interpreters of the Law (Geneva) lawyers (KJV, NKJV)
Luke 11:52 interpreters of the Law (Geneva) lawyers (KJV, NKJV)
Luke 12:11 rulers (Geneva) magistrates (KJV, NKJV)
Luke 12:19 take thy pastime (Geneva) be merry (KJV, NKJV)
Luke 12:21 gathereth riches (Geneva) layeth up treasure (KJV) lays up treasure (NKJV)
Luke 12:27 royalty (Geneva) glory (KJV, NKJV)
Luke 12:31 ministered (Geneva) added (KJV, NKJV)
Luke 12:41 Master (Geneva) Lord (KJV, NKJV)
Luke 12:56 the face of the earth, and of the sky (Geneva) the face of the sky and of the earth (KJV, NKJV)
Luke 13:3 amend your lives (Geneva) repent (KJV, NKJV)
Luke 13:5 amend your lives (Geneva) repent (KJV, NKJV)

Luke 15:14 dearth (Geneva) famine (KJV, NKJV)
Luke 15:23 fat calf (Geneva) fatted calf (KJV, NKJV)
Luke 15:25 heard melody (Geneva) heard musick (KJV) heard music (NKJV)
Luke 15:26 one of his servants (Geneva) one of the servants (KJV, NKJV)
Luke 16:30 amend their lives (Geneva) repent (KJV, NKJV)
Luke 21:4 superfluity (Geneva) abundance (KJV, NKJV)
Luke 24:4 shining vestures (Geneva) shining garments (KJV, NKJV)
John 1:1 that Word was God (Geneva) the Word was God (KJV, NKJV)
John 1:46 Then Nathanael (Geneva) And Nathanael (KJV, NKJV)
John 2:3 the wine failed (Geneva) they wanted wine (KJV) they ran out of wine (NKJV)
John 2:11 Cana *a town* of Galilee (Geneva) Cana of Galilee (KJV, NKJV)
John 3:36 obeyeth not (Geneva) believeth not (KJV) does not believe (NKJV)
John 4:10 water of life (Geneva) living water (KJV, NKJV)
John 4:19 I see (Geneva) I perceive (KJV, NKJV)
John 4:22 we worship that which we know (Geneva) we know what we worship (KJV, NKJV)
John 4:31 the disciples (Geneva) his disciples (KJV) His disciples (NKJV)
John 4:35 the regions (Geneva) the fields (KJV, NKJV)
John 4:46 Cana *a town* of Galilee (Geneva) Cana of Galilee (KJV, NKJV)
John 4:49 ruler (Geneva) nobleman (KJV, NKJV)
John 6:11 the bread (Geneva) the loaves (KJV, NKJV)
John 6:12 the broken meat (Geneva) the fragments (KJV, NKJV)
John 7:4 be famous (Geneva) be known openly (KJV, NKJV)
John 7:38 water of life (Geneva) living water (KJV, NKJV)
John 8:50 praise (Geneva) glory (KJV, NKJV)
John 10:19 dissention (Geneva) division (KJV, NKJV)
John 11:1 Marie (Geneva) Mary (KJV, NKJV)
John 11:12 shall be safe (Geneva) shall do well (KJV) will get well (NKJV)
John 11:18 Bethania (Geneva) Bethany (KJV, NKJV)
John 11:31 Marie (Geneva) Mary (KJV, NKJV)
John 11:35 *And* Jesus wept (Geneva) Jesus wept (KJV, NKJV)
John 11:47 high Priests (Geneva) chief priests (KJV, NKJV)
John 12:48 refuseth me (Geneva) rejecteth me (KJV) rejects Me (NKJV)
John 14:2 dwelling places (Geneva) mansions (KJV, NKJV)
John 14:27 nor fear (Geneva) neither let it be afraid (KJV, NKJV)
John 16:2 excommunicate you (Geneva) put you out of the synagogues (KJV, NKJV)
John 18:3 high Priests (Geneva) chief priests (KJV, NKJV)
John 18:40 murtherer (Geneva) robber (KJV, NKJV)
John 19:3 rods (Geneva) hands (KJV, NKJV)
John 19:25 Marie Magdalene (Geneva) Mary Magdalene (KJV, NKJV)
John 20:25 mine hand (Geneva) my hand (KJV, NKJV)
John 20:27 mine hands (Geneva) my hands (KJV) My hands (NKJV)
John 21:5 Sirs (Geneva) Children (KJV, NKJV)
John 21:10 fishes (Geneva) fish (KJV, NKJV)
Acts 1:21 was conversant (Geneva) went in and out (KJV, NKJV)
Acts 2:5 men that feared God (Geneva) devout men (KJV, NKJV)
Acts 2:27 grave (Geneva) hell (KJV) hades (NKJV)
Acts 2:31 grave (Geneva) hell (KJV) hades (NKJV)
Acts 2:38 Amend your lives (Geneva) Repent (KJV, NKJV)
Acts 2:47 from day to day (Geneva) daily (KJV, NKJV)
Acts 3:2 creple (Geneva) lame (KJV, NKJV)
Acts 3:3 desired to receive an alms (Geneva) asked an alms (KJV) asked for alms (NKJV)
Acts 3:15 Lord of life (Geneva) Prince of life (KJV, NKJV)
Acts 3:19 Amend your lives (Geneva) Repent (KJV, NKJV)
Acts 5:3 Then said Peter (Geneva) But Peter said (KJV, NKJV)
Acts 5:8 Peter said (Geneva) Peter answered (KJV, NKJV)
Acts 5:24 high priests (Geneva) chief priests (KJV, NKJV)

Acts 5:31 lift up (Geneva) exalted (KJV, NKJV)

Acts 5:39 destroy (Geneva) overthrow (KJV, NKJV)

Acts 6:14 Nazaret (Geneva) Nazareth (KJV, NKJV)

Acts 7:16 *son* of Sychem (Geneva) *father* of Sychem (KJV, NKJV)

Acts 8:2 *certain* men fearing God (Geneva) devout men (KJV, NKJV)

Acts 8:13 the signs and great miracles (Geneva) the miracles and signs (KJV, NKJV)

Acts 8:19 lay the hands (Geneva) lay hands (KJV, NKJV)

Acts 8:20 Then said Peter (Geneva) But Peter said (KJV, NKJV)

Acts 8:20 obtained (Geneva) purchased (KJV, NKJV)

Acts 8:21 this business (Geneva) this matter (KJV, NKJV)

Acts 8:25 towns (Geneva) villages (KJV, NKJV)

Acts 8:26 waste (Geneva) desert (KJV, NKJV)

Acts 8:33 humility (Geneva) humiliation (KJV, NKJV)

Acts 8:36 doeth let me (Geneva) doth hinder me (KJV) hinders (NKJV)

Acts 9:7 stood amazed (Geneva) stood speechless (KJV, NKJV)

Acts 9:14 of the high Priests (Geneva) from the chief priests (KJV, NKJV)

Acts 9:28 conversant (Geneva) coming in and going out (KJV, NKJV)

Acts 9:41 restored her (Geneva) presented her (KJV, NKJV)

Acts 10:7 soldier that feared God (Geneva) devout soldier (KJV, NKJV)

Acts 10:10 waxed he an hungred (Geneva) he became very hungry (KJV, NKJV)

Acts 10:12 of the heaven (Geneva) of the air (KJV, NKJV)

Acts 10:14 polluted (Geneva) common (KJV, NKJV)

Acts 10:22 captain (Geneva) centurion (KJV, NKJV)

Acts 10:45 astonied (Geneva) astonished (KJV, NKJV)

Acts 11:2 contended against him (Geneva) contended with him (KJV, NKJV)

Acts 11:8 God forbid, Lord (Geneva) Not so, Lord (KJV, NKJV)

Acts 11:8 nothing polluted (Geneva) nothing common (KJV, NKJV)

Acts 11:17 could let God (Geneva) could withstand God (KJV, NKJV)

Acts 11:29 purposed to send succor (Geneva) determined to send relief (KJV, NKJV)

Acts 12:9 So *Peter* came out (Geneva) And he went out (KJV) So he went out (NKJV)

Acts 12:19 be led to be punished (Geneva) be put to death (KJV, NKJV)

Acts 13:14 Antiochia *a city* of Pisidia (Geneva) Antioch in Pisidia (KJV, NKJV)

Acts 13:15 the lecture (Geneva) the reading (KJV, NKJV)

Acts 14:13 bulls (Geneva) oxen (KJV, NKJV)

Acts 14:21 preached to that city (Geneva) preached the gospel to that city (KJV, NKJV)

Acts 14:22 disciples' hearts (Geneva) souls of the disciples (KJV, NKJV)

Acts 15:2 ordained that Paul (Geneva) determined that Paul (KJV, NKJV)

Acts 15:37 counseled (Geneva) determined (KJV, NKJV)

Acts 16:20 governors (Geneva) magistrates (KJV, NKJV)

Acts 16:21 preach ordinances (Geneva) teach customs (KJV, NKJV)

Acts 16:26 by and by (Geneva) immediately (KJV, NKJV)

Acts 17:6 subverted the state of the world (Geneva) turned the world upside down (KJV, NKJV)

Acts 17:14 by and by (Geneva) immediately (KJV, NKJV)

Acts 17:19 Mars street (Geneva) Aropagus (KJV, NKJV)

Acts 18:4 disputed (Geneva) reasoned (KJV, NKJV)

Acts 19:9 disobeyed (Geneva) believed not (KJV) did not believe (NKJV)

Acts 19:32 assembly was out of order (Geneva) assembly was confused (KJV, NKJV)

Acts 21:8 the seven *Deacons* (Geneva) the seven (KJV, NKJV)

Acts 21:15 we trussed up our fardels (Geneva) we took up our carriages (KJV) we packed (NKJV)

Acts 21:35 grieces (Geneva) stairs (KJV, NKJV)

Acts 24:3 We acknowledge it wholly (Geneva) We accept *it* always (KJV, NKJV)

Acts 26:20 do works worthy amendment of life (Geneva) works meet for repentance (KJV) works befitting repentance (NKJV)

Rom. 1:4 sanctification (Geneva) holiness (KJV, NKJV)

Rom. 2:17 gloriest in God (Geneva) makest thy boast of God (KJV) makes your boast in God

(NKJV)
Rom. 2:20 teacher of the unlearned (Geneva) teacher of babes (KJV, NKJV)
Rom. 2:23 gloriest (Geneva) makest thy boast (KJV) make your boast (NKJV)
Rom. 3:1 preference (Geneva) advantage (KJV, NKJV)
Rom. 3:7 verity (Geneva) truth (KJV, NKJV)
Rom. 3:23 derived (Geneva) come short (KJV) fall short (NKJV)
Rom. 6:13 weapons (Geneva) instruments (KJV, NKJV)
Rom. 7:2 which is in subjection to a man (Geneva) which hath an husband (KJV) who has a husband (NKJV)
Rom. 7:2 law of the man (Geneva) law of *her* husband (KJV, NKJV)
Rom. 7:3 the man liveth (Geneva) *her* husband liveth (KJV) *her* husband lives (NKJV)
Rom. 9:22 suffer with long patience (Geneva) endured with much longsuffering (KJV, NKJV)
Rom. 10:18 But I demand (Geneva) But I say (KJV, NKJV)
Rom. 11:1 I demand (Geneva) I say (KJV, NKJV)
Rom. 12:1 serving of God (Geneva) service (KJV, NKJV)
Rom. 12:7 Or an office (Geneva) Or ministry (KJV, NKJV)
Rom. 13:3 For princes (Geneva) For rulers (KJV, NKJV)
Rom. 14:16 commodity (Geneva) good (KJV, NKJV)
Rom. 15:22 let (Geneva) hindered (KJV, NKJV)
Rom. 15:31 are disobedient (Geneva) do not believe (KJV, NKJV)
1 Cor. 1:24 *we preach* Christ (Geneva) Christ (KJV, NKJV)
1 Cor. 1:28 vile things of the world (Geneva) base things of the world (KJV, NKJV)
1 Cor. 2:2 I esteemed (Geneva) I determined (KJV, NKJV)
1 Cor. 2:4 plain evidence (Geneva) demonstration (KJV, NKJV)
1 Cor. 2:14 perceiveth (Geneva) receiveth (KJV) does not receive (NKJV)
1 Cor. 4:1 disposers of the secrets (Geneva) stewards of the mysteries (KJV, NKJV)
1 Cor. 4:2 disposers (Geneva) stewards (KJV, NKJV)
1 Cor. 4:7 separateth thee (Geneva) maketh thee to differ (KJV) makes you differ (NKJV)
1 Cor. 6:9 buggerers (Geneva) abusers of themselves with mankind (KJV) sodomites (NKJV)
1 Cor. 7:40 is more blessed (Geneva) is happier (KJV, NKJV)
1 Cor. 10:6 ensamples (Geneva) examples (KJV, NKJV)
1 Cor. 10:15 them which have understanding (Geneva) wise men (KJV, NKJV)
1 Cor. 11:16 lust to be (Geneva) seem to be (KJV, NKJV)
1 Cor. 12:3 execrable (Geneva) accursed (KJV, NKJV)
1 Cor. 12:10 operations of great works (Geneva) working of miracles (KJV, NKJV)
1 Cor. 13:2 knew all secrets (Geneva) understand all mysteries (KJV, NKJV)
1 Cor. 13:4 is bountiful (Geneva) is kind (KJV, NKJV)
1 Cor. 16:1 gathering (Geneva) collection (KJV, NKJV)
1 Cor. 16:17 the want of you (Geneva) that which was lacking on your part (KJV) what was lacking on your part (NKJV)
1 Cor. 16:22 be had in execration (Geneva) be Anathema (KJV) be accursed (NKJV)
2 Cor. 1:1 Timotheus (Geneva) Timothy (KJV, NKJV)
2 Cor. 1:8 affliction (Geneva) trouble (KJV, NKJV)
2 Cor. 1:12 godly pureness (Geneva) godly sincerity (KJV, NKJV)
2 Cor. 2:4 For in great affliction (Geneva) For out of much affliction (KJV, NKJV)
2 Cor. 2:7 heaviness (Geneva) sorrow (KJV, NKJV)
2 Cor. 2:11 his enterprises (Geneva) his devices (KJV, NKJV)
2 Cor. 3:1 praise (Geneva) commend (KJV, NKJV)
2 Cor. 3:1 epistles of recommendation (Geneva) epistles of commendation (KJV, NKJV)
2 Cor. 3:10 in this point (Geneva) in this respect (KJV, NKJV)
2 Cor. 3:12 such trust (Geneva) such hope (KJV, NKJV)
2 Cor. 3:14 minds are hardened (Geneva) minds were blinded (KJV, NKJV)
2 Cor. 4:2 cast from us the clokes (Geneva) renounced the hidden things (KJV, NKJV)
2 Cor. 4:2 declaration of the truth (Geneva) manifestation of the truth (KJV, NKJV)
2 Cor. 4:4 *that is*, of the infidels (Geneva) which believe not (KJV) who do not believe (NKJV)
2 Cor. 4:8 in poverty, but not overcome of poverty (Geneva) we *are* perplexed, but not in despair

(KJV, NKJV)
2 Cor. 4:9 but we perish not (Geneva) but not destroyed (KJV, NKJV)
2 Cor. 4:15 praise of God (Geneva) glory of God (KJV, NKJV)
2 Cor. 4:17 far most excellent (Geneva) far more exceeding (KJV, NKJV)
2 Cor. 5:6 alway bold (Geneva) always confident (KJV, NKJV)
2 Cor. 5:8 bold (Geneva) confident (KJV, NKJV)
2 Cor. 5:9 both dwelling at home, and removing from home (Geneva) whether present or absent (KJV, NKJV)
2 Cor. 5:10 every man (Geneva) every one (KJV) each one (NKJV)
2 Cor. 5:10 or evil (Geneva) or bad (KJV, NKJV)
2 Cor. 5:12 praise (Geneva) commend (KJV, NKJV)
2 Cor. 5:12 in the face (Geneva) in appearance (KJV, NKJV)
2 Cor. 5:13 be out of our wit (Geneva) be beside ourselves (KJV, NKJV)
2 Cor. 5:19 sins (Geneva) trespasses (KJV, NKJV)
2 Cor. 6:3 should not be reprehended (Geneva) be not blamed (KJV) may not be blamed (NKJV)
2 Cor. 6:14 with the infidels (Geneva) with unbelievers (KJV, NKJV)
2 Cor. 7:1 grow up unto full holiness (Geneva) perfecting holiness (KJV, NKJV)
2 Cor. 7:2 consumed (Geneva) corrupted (KJV, NKJV)
2 Cor. 7:6 the abject (Geneva) those that are cast down (KJV) the downcast (NKJV)
2 Cor. 7:7 to meward (Geneva) toward me (KJV) for me (NKJV)
2 Cor. 7:10 worldly sorrow (Geneva) sorrow of the world (KJV, NKJV)
2 Cor. 8:2 their joy abounded (Geneva) the abundance of their joy (KJV, NKJV)
2 Cor. 8:2 their most extreme poverty (Geneva) their deep poverty (KJV, NKJV)
2 Cor. 8:8 naturalness of your love (Geneva) sincerity of your love (KJV, NKJV)
2 Cor. 8:10 I shew *my* mind (Geneva) I give *my* advice (KJV) I give advice (NKJV)
2 Cor. 8:13 grieved (Geneva) burdened (KJV, NKJV)
2 Cor. 8:14 upon like condition (Geneva) by an equality (KJV, NKJV)
2 Cor. 8:16 the same care (Geneva) the same earnest care (KJV, NKJV)
2 Cor. 8:19 prompt mind (Geneva) ready mind (KJV, NKJV)
2 Cor. 8:21 but also before men (Geneva) but also in the sight of men (KJV, NKJV)
2 Cor. 8:23 to youward (Geneva) concerning you (KJV, NKJV)
2 Cor. 9:3 rejoicing over you (Geneva) boasting of you (KJV, NKJV)
2 Cor. 9:6 liberally (Geneva) bountifully (KJV, NKJV)
2 Cor. 9:7 wisheth (Geneva) purposeth (KJV) purposes (NKJV)
2 Cor. 9:9 sparsed (Geneva) dispersed (KJV, NKJV)
2 Cor. 9:10 fruits of your benevolence (Geneva) fruits of your righteousness (KJV, NKJV)
2 Cor. 9:12 ministration (Geneva) administration (KJV, NKJV)
2 Cor. 10:10 sore and strong (Geneva) weighty and powerful (KJV, NKJV)
2 Cor. 10:10 speech is of no value (Geneva) speech contemptible (KJV, NKJV)
2 Cor. 10:13 rejoice (Geneva) boast (KJV, NKJV)
2 Cor. 10:18 allowed (Geneva) approved (KJV, NKJV)
2 Cor. 11:1 suffer me (Geneva) bear with me (KJV, NKJV)
2 Cor. 11:2 pure virgin (Geneva) chaste virgin (KJV, NKJV)
2 Cor. 11:17 in this my great boasting (Geneva) in this confidence of boasting (KJV, NKJV)
2 Cor. 11:30 I will rejoice (Geneva) I will glory (KJV, NKJV)
2 Cor. 12:12 great works (Geneva) mighty deeds (KJV, NKJV)
2 Cor. 12:13 have not been slothful to your hindrance (Geneva) was not burdensome to you (KJV, NKJV)
2 Cor. 12:14 the fathers (Geneva) the parents (KJV, NKJV)
2 Cor. 12:15 most gladly bestow (Geneva) very gladly spend (KJV, NKJV)
2 Cor. 12:16 I charged you not (Geneva) I did not burden you (KJV, NKJV)
2 Cor. 12:17 pill you (Geneva) make a gain of you (KJV) take advantage of you (NKJV)
2 Cor. 13:3 experience of Christ (Geneva) proof of Christ (KJV, NKJV)
2 Cor. 13:5 Prove yourselves (Geneva) Examine yourselves (KJV, NKJV)
2 Cor. 13:11 fare ye well (Geneva) farewell (KJV, NKJV)
Gal. 1:7 is not another *Gospel* (Geneva) is not another (KJV, NKJV)

Gal. 1:10 For now preach I mans *doctrine* (Geneva) For do I now persuade men (KJV, NKJV)
Gal. 1:21 coasts of Syria (Geneva) regions of Syria (KJV, NKJV)
Gal. 2:17 made righteous by Christ (Geneva) justified by Christ (KJV, NKJV)
Gal. 2:18 trespasser (Geneva) transgressor (KJV, NKJV)
Gal. 2:21 abrogate (Geneva) frustrate (KJV) set aside (NKJV)
Gal. 3:15 doth abrogate (Geneva) disannulleth (KJV) annuls (NKJV)
Gal. 3:24 made righteous by faith (Geneva) justified by faith (KJV, NKJV)
Gal. 3:28 Grecian (Geneva) Greek (KJV, NKJV)
Gal. 4:3 rudiments of the world (Geneva) elements of the world (KJV, NKJV)
Gal. 4:22 by a servant (Geneva) by a bondmaid (KJV) by a bondwoman (NKJV)
Gal. 4:31 the servant (Geneva) the bondwoman (KJV, NKJV)
Gal. 5:7 did let you (Geneva) did hinder you (KJV) hindered you (NKJV)
Gal. 5:10 trust in you (Geneva) confidence in you (KJV, NKJV)
Gal. 5:10 condemnation (Geneva) judgment (KJV, NKJV)
Gal. 5:11 slander of the cross (Geneva) offence of the cross (KJV) offense of the cross (NKJV)
Gal. 5:12 Would to God (Geneva) I would (KJV) I could wish (NKJV)
Gal. 5:20 debate (Geneva) variance (KJV) contentions (NKJV)
Gal. 5:21 gluttony (Geneva) revelings (KJV) revelries (NKJV)
Gal. 6:17 put me to business (Geneva) trouble me (KJV, NKJV)
Eph. 1:3 God even the Father (Geneva) the God and Father (KJV, NKJV)
Eph. 1:3 in heavenly things (Geneva) in heavenly *places* (KJV) in the heavenly *places* (NKJV)
Eph. 1:5 to be adopted (Geneva) unto the adoption of children (KJV) to adoption as sons (NKJV)
Eph. 1:7 according to his rich grace (Geneva) according to the riches of his grace (KJV) according to the riches of His grace (NKJV)
Eph. 1:8 wisdom and understanding (Geneva) wisdom and prudence (KJV, NKJV)
Eph. 1:9 And hath opened (Geneva) Having made known (KJV, NKJV)
Eph. 1:11 we are chosen (Geneva) we have obtained an inheritance (KJV, NKJV)
Eph. 1:14 possession purchased (Geneva) purchased possession (KJV, NKJV)
Eph. 1:18 his glorious inheritance (Geneva) the glory of his inheritance (KJV) the glory of His inheritance (NKJV)
Eph. 1:22 made all things subject (Geneva) put all things (KJV, NKJV)
Eph. 2:2 after the prince that ruleth in the air (Geneva) according to the prince of the power of the air (KJV, NKJV)
Eph. 2:3 the will of the flesh (Geneva) the desires of the flesh (KJV, NKJV)
Eph. 2:9 should boast himself (Geneva) should boast (KJV, NKJV)
Eph. 2:15 In abrogating (Geneva) having abolished (KJV, NKJV)
Eph. 2:15 the hatred (Geneva) the enmity (KJV, NKJV)
Eph. 2:16 hatred (Geneva) enmity (KJV, NKJV)
Eph. 2:18 an entrance (Geneva) access (KJV, NKJV)
Eph. 3:5 was not opened (Geneva) was not made known (KJV, NKJV)
Eph. 3:9 make clear unto all men (Geneva) make all *men* see (KJV) make all see (NKJV)
Eph. 3:12 entrance (Geneva) access (KJV, NKJV)
Eph. 4:2 humbleness of mind (Geneva) lowliness (KJV, NKJV)
Eph. 4:2 supporting one another through love (Geneva) forbearing one another in love (KJV) bearing with one another in love (NKJV)
Eph. 4:4 vocation (Geneva) calling (KJV, NKJV)
Eph. 4:6 which is above (Geneva) who is above (KJV, NKJV)
Eph. 4:12 gathering together of the saints (Geneva) perfecting of the saints (KJV) equipping of the saints (NKJV)
Eph. 4:15 let us follow the truth in love (Geneva) speaking the truth in love (KJV, NKJV)
Eph. 4:16 every joint, for the furniture *thereof* (Geneva) every joint supplieth (KJV) every joint supplies (NKJV)
Eph. 4:18 cogitation (Geneva) understanding (KJV, NKJV)
Eph. 4:18 being strangers (Geneva) being alienated (KJV, NKJV)
Eph. 4:18 hardness (Geneva) blindness (KJV, NKJV)
Eph. 4:22 deceiveable lusts (Geneva) deceitful lusts (KJV, NKJV)

Eph. 4:31 crying (Geneva) and clamour (KJV) clamor (NKJV)
Eph. 4:32 courteous (Geneva) kind (KJV, NKJV)
Eph. 5:7 companions (Geneva) partakers (KJV, NKJV)
Eph. 5:10 pleasing (Geneva) acceptable (KJV, NKJV)
Eph. 5:18 fulfilled with the Spirit (Geneva) filled with the Spirit (KJV, NKJV)
Eph. 5:27 without blame (Geneva) without blemish (KJV, NKJV)
Eph. 5:32 great secret (Geneva) great mystery (KJV, NKJV)
Eph. 5:33 fear (Geneva) reverence (KJV) respects (NKJV)
Eph. 6:4 information of the Lord (Geneva) admonition of the Lord (KJV, NKJV)
Eph. 6:7 serving the Lord (Geneva) doing service, as to the Lord (KJV, NKJV)
Eph. 6:11 assaults of the devil (Geneva) wiles of the devil (KJV, NKJV)
Eph. 6:13 able to resist (Geneva) able to withstand (KJV, NKJV)
Eph. 6:14 verity (Geneva) truth (KJV, NKJV)
Eph. 6:18 will all manner prayer (Geneva) with all prayer (KJV, NKJV)
Eph. 6:19 secret of the Gospel (Geneva) mystery of the gospel (KJV, NKJV)
Eph. 6:21 mine affairs (Geneva) my affairs (KJV, NKJV)
Eph. 6:22 mine affairs (Geneva) our affairs (KJV, NKJV)
Eph. 6:24 to *their* immortality (Geneva) in sincerity (KJV, NKJV)
Phil. 1:3 *having* you in perfect memory (Geneva) upon every remembrance of you (KJV, NKJV)
Phil. 1:4 gladness (Geneva) joy (KJV, NKJV)
Phil. 1:6 And I am persuaded (Geneva) Being confident (KJV, NKJV)
Phil. 1:7 you in remembrance (Geneva) you in my heart (KJV, NKJV)
Phil. 1:8 from the very heart root (Geneva) in the bowels (KJV) with the affection (NKJV)
Phil. 1:10 discern things that differ *one from another* (Geneva) approve things that are excellent (KJV) approve the things that are excellent (NKJV)
Phil. 1:10 pure (Geneva) sincere (KJV, NKJV)
Phil. 1:14 dare more frankly speak the word (Geneva) are much more bold to speak the word without fear (KJV, NKJV)
Phil. 1:16 not purely (Geneva) not sincerely (KJV, NKJV)
Phil. 1:18 or sincerely (Geneva) or in truth (KJV, NKJV)
Phil. 1:19 help (Geneva) supply (KJV, NKJV)
Phil. 1:20 As I heartly look for (Geneva) According to my earnest expectation (KJV, NKJV)
Phil. 1:21 advantage (Geneva) gain (KJV, NKJV)
Phil. 1:27 fighting together (Geneva) striving together (KJV, NKJV)
Phil. 1:30 same fight (Geneva) same conflict (KJV, NKJV)
Phil. 2:2 of one judgement (Geneva) of one mind (KJV, NKJV)
Phil. 2:12 make an end of your own salvation (Geneva) work out your own salvation (KJV, NKJV)
Phil. 2:14 reasonings (Geneva) disputings (KJV) disputing (NKJV)
Phil. 2:15 and pure (Geneva) and harmless (KJV, NKJV)
Phil. 2:15 naughty and crooked nation (Geneva) crooked and perverse nation (KJV, NKJV)
Phil. 3:1 it is a sure thing (Geneva) *it is* safe (KJV, NKJV)
Phil. 3:5 kindred of Israel (Geneva) stock of Israel (KJV, NKJV)
Phil. 3:7 vantage (Geneva) gain (KJV, NKJV)
Phil. 3:10 vertue (Geneva) power (KJV, NKJV)
Phil. 3:10 fellowship of his afflictions (Geneva) fellowship of his sufferings (KJV, NKJV)
Phil. 3:14 follow hard toward (Geneva) press toward (KJV, NKJV)
Phil. 3:16 proceed (Geneva) walk (KJV, NKJV)
Phil. 3:19 damnation (Geneva) destruction (KJV, NKJV)
Phil. 4:2 of one accord (Geneva) of the same mind (KJV, NKJV)
Phil. 4:19 fulfil all your necessities (Geneva) supply all your need (KJV, NKJV)
Col. 1:3 always praying (Geneva) praying always (KJV, NKJV)
Col. 1:6 truly (Geneva) in truth (KJV, NKJV)
Col. 1:22 make you holy (Geneva) present you holy (KJV, NKJV)
Col. 1:24 fulfill (Geneva) fill up (KJV, NKJV)
Col. 1:28 admonishing (Geneva) warning (KJV, NKJV)
Col. 2:1 great fighting (Geneva) great conflict (KJV, NKJV)

Col. 2:13 And ye (Geneva) And you (KJV, NKJV)
Col. 2:16 condemn you (Geneva) judge you (KJV, NKJV)
Col. 2:18 advancing himself in those things (Geneva) intruding into those things (KJV, NKJV)
Col. 2:18 rashly (Geneva) vainly (KJV, NKJV)
Col. 2:20 are ye burdened with traditions (Geneva) are ye subject to ordinances (KJV) do you subject yourselves in regulations (NKJV)
Col. 2:23 not sparing the body (Geneva) neglecting the body (KJV) neglect of the body (NKJV)
Col. 3:8 maliciousness (Geneva) malice (KJV, NKJV)
Col. 3:8 cursed speaking (Geneva) blasphemy (KJV, NKJV)
Col. 3:9 his works (Geneva) his deeds (KJV, NKJV)
Col. 3:11 Grecian (Geneva) Greek (KJV, NKJV)
Col. 3:15 amiable (Geneva) thankful (KJV, NKJV)
Col. 3:18 comely (Geneva) fit (KJV) fitting (NKJV)
Col. 4:1 do (Geneva) give (KJV, NKJV)
Col. 4:4 I may utter it (Geneva) I may make it manifest (KJV, NKJV)
Col. 4:5 Walk wisely (Geneva) Walk in wisdom (KJV, NKJV)
Col. 4:6 powdered with salt (Geneva) seasoned with salt (KJV, NKJV)
Col. 4:10 my prison fellow (Geneva) my fellowprisoner (KJV) my fellow prisoner (NKJV)
Col. 4:12 and full (Geneva) and complete (KJV, NKJV)
Col. 4:17 epistle *written* from Laodicea (Geneva) epistle from Laodicea (KJV, NKJV)
1 Thess. 1:3 effectual faith (Geneva) work of faith (KJV, NKJV)
1 Thess. 1:3 diligent love (Geneva) labour of love (KJV) labor of love (NKJV)
1 Thess. 1:4 that ye are elect of God (Geneva) your election of God (KJV) your election by God (NKJV)
1 Thess. 2:5 God *is* record (Geneva) God *is* witness (KJV, NKJV)
1 Thess. 2:16 to preach (Geneva) to speak (KJV, NKJV)
1 Thess. 2:16 to fulfil (Geneva) to fill up (KJV, NKJV)
1 Thess. 2:16 the wrath of God (Geneva) the wrath (KJV) wrath (NKJV)
1 Thess. 2:17 enforced (Geneva) endeavoured (KJV) endeavored (NKJV)
1 Thess. 3:7 necessity (Geneva) distress (KJV, NKJV)
1 Thess. 3:9 recompense (Geneva) render (KJV, NKJV)
1 Thess. 4:4 holiness (Geneva) sanctification (KJV, NKJV)
1 Thess. 5:11 exhort (Geneva) comfort (KJV, NKJV)
1 Thess. 5:27 all the brethren the saints (Geneva) all the holy brethren (KJV, NKJV)
2 Thess. 1:3 We ought to thank God (Geneva) We are bound to thank God (KJV, NKJV)
2 Thess. 1:4 suffer (Geneva) endure (KJV, NKJV)
2 Thess. 1:8 rendering vengeance unto (Geneva) taking vengeance on (KJV, NKJV)
2 Thess. 1:9 everlasting perdition (Geneva) everlasting destruction (KJV, NKJV)
2 Thess. 2:2 suddenly moved (Geneva) soon shaken (KJV, NKJV)
2 Thess. 2:3 disclosed (Geneva) revealed (KJV, NKJV)
2 Thess. 2:4 Which is an adversary (Geneva) Who opposeth (KJV) Who opposes (NKJV)
2 Thess. 2:8 abolish (Geneva) destroy (KJV, NKJV)
2 Thess. 2:13 we ought (Geneva) we are bound (KJV, NKJV)
2 Thess. 2:13 the faith of truth (Geneva) belief of the truth (KJV) belief in the truth (NKJV)
2 Thess. 2:15 instructions (Geneva) traditions (KJV, NKJV)
2 Thess. 3:1 Furthermore (Geneva) Finally (KJV, NKJV)
2 Thess. 3:4 we are persuaded (Geneva) we have confidence (KJV, NKJV)
2 Thess. 3:5 guide (Geneva) direct (KJV, NKJV)
2 Thess. 3:6 inordinately (Geneva) disorderly (KJV, NKJV)
2 Thess. 3:6 instruction (Geneva) tradition (KJV, NKJV)
2 Thess. 3:7 inordinately (Geneva) disorderly (KJV, NKJV)
2 Thess. 3:11 inordinately (Geneva) disorderly (KJV) in a disorderly manner (NKJV)
2 Thess. 3:14 our sayings (Geneva) our word (KJV, NKJV)
1 Tim. 1:2 Timotheus (Geneva) Timothy (KJV, NKJV)
1 Tim. 1:2 *my* natural son (Geneva) *my* own son (KJV) a true son (NKJV)
1 Tim. 1:3 I departed (Geneva) I went (KJV, NKJV)

1 Tim. 1:3 command (Geneva) charge (KJV, NKJV)
1 Tim. 1:7 doctours of the Law (Geneva) teachers of the law (KJV, NKJV)
1 Tim. 1:9 given unto (Geneva) made for (KJV, NKJV)
1 Tim. 1:9 to sinners (Geneva) for sinners (KJV, NKJV)
1 Tim. 1:10 to buggerers (Geneva) for them that defile themselves with mankind (KJV) for sodomites (NKJV)
1 Tim. 1:10 wholsome doctrine (Geneva) sound doctrine (KJV, NKJV)
1 Tim. 1:11 committed unto me (Geneva) committed to my trust (KJV, NKJV)
1 Tim. 1:12 which hath made me strong (Geneva) who hath enabled me (KJV) who has enabled me (NKJV)
1 Tim. 1:12 in *his* service (Geneva) into the ministry (KJV, NKJV)
1 Tim. 1:13 was received to mercy (Geneva) obtained mercy (KJV, NKJV)
1 Tim. 1:13 through unbelief (Geneva) in unbelief (KJV, NKJV)
1 Tim. 1:15 true saying (Geneva) faithful saying (KJV, NKJV)
1 Tim. 1:15 by all means worthy to be received (Geneva) worthy of all acceptation (KJV) worthy of all acceptance (NKJV)
1 Tim. 1:16 was I received to mercy (Geneva) I obtained mercy (KJV, NKJV)
1 Tim. 1:16 ensample (Geneva) pattern (KJV, NKJV)
1 Tim. 1:18 This commandment (Geneva) This charge (KJV, NKJV)
1 Tim. 1:18 Timotheus (Geneva) Timothy (KJV, NKJV)
1 Tim. 1:18 good fight (Geneva) good warfare (KJV, NKJV)
1 Tim. 2:9 comely apparel (Geneva) modest apparel (KJV, NKJV)
1 Tim. 3:1 unreprovable (Geneva) blameless (KJV, NKJV)
1 Tim. 3:2 harberous (Geneva) given to hospitality (KJV) hospitable (NKJV)
1 Tim. 3:6 He may not be a young scholar (Geneva) Not a novice (KJV, NKJV)
1 Tim. 3:11 not evil speakers (Geneva) not slanderers (KJV, NKJV)
1 Tim. 3:13 great liberty (Geneva) great boldness (KJV, NKJV)
1 Tim. 4:1 evidently (Geneva) expressly (KJV, NKJV)
1 Tim. 4:2 burned (Geneva) seared (KJV, NKJV)
1 Tim. 4:9 true saying (Geneva) faithful saying (KJV, NKJV)
1 Tim. 4:10 are rebuked (Geneva) suffer reproach (KJV, NKJV)
1 Tim. 4:12 ensample (Geneva) example (KJV, NKJV)
1 Tim. 4:12 pureness (Geneva) purity (KJV, NKJV)
1 Tim. 4:15 These things exercise (Geneva) Mediate upon these things (KJV) Mediate on these things (NKJV)
1 Tim. 4:16 learning (Geneva) doctrine (KJV, NKJV)
1 Tim. 5:2 pureness (Geneva) purity (KJV, NKJV)
1 Tim. 5:9 wife of one husband (Geneva) wife of one man (KJV, NKJV)
1 Tim. 5:10 if she have ministred unto them which were in adversity (Geneva) if she have relieved the afflicted (KJV) if she has relieved the afflicted (NKJV)
1 Tim. 5:14 govern the house (Geneva) guide the house (KJV) manage the house (NKJV)
1 Tim. 6:9 perdition and destruction (Geneva) destruction and perdition (KJV, NKJV)
1 Tim. 6:10 desire of money (Geneva) love of money (KJV, NKJV)
1 Tim. 6:15 prince only (Geneva) only Potentate (KJV, NKJV)
1 Tim. 6:20 Timotheus (Geneva) Timothy (KJV, NKJV)
2 Tim. 1:2 Timotheus (Geneva) Timothy (KJV, NKJV)
2 Tim. 1:5 assured (Geneva) persuaded (KJV, NKJV)
2 Tim. 2:3 suffer affliction (Geneva) endure hardness (KJV, NKJV)
2 Tim. 2:10 I suffer (Geneva) I endure (KJV, NKJV)
2 Tim. 2:11 true saying (Geneva) faithful saying (KJV, NKJV)
2 Tim. 2:14 protest before the Lord (Geneva) charging *them* before the Lord (KJV, NKJV)
2 Tim. 2:16 Stay prophane (Geneva) But shun profane (KJV, NKJV)
2 Tim. 2:22 lusts of youth (Geneva) youthful lusts (KJV, NKJV)
2 Tim. 2:26 come to amendment (Geneva) recover themselves (KJV) come to their senses (NKJV)
2 Tim. 3:2 cursed speakers (Geneva) blasphemers (KJV, NKJV)

2 Tim. 3:5 shew of godliness (Geneva) a form of godliness (KJV, NKJV)
2 Tim. 3:7 *Which women are* ever learning (Geneva) Ever learning (KJV) always learning (NKJV)
2 Tim. 3:9 evident (Geneva) manifest (KJV, NKJV)
2 Tim. 3:11 I suffered (Geneva) I endured (KJV, NKJV)
2 Tim. 3:15 through the faith (Geneva) through faith (KJV, NKJV)
2 Tim. 3:16 For the whole scripture (Geneva) All scripture (KJV) All Scripture (NKJV)
2 Tim. 3:16 to improve (Geneva) for reproof (KJV, NKJV)
2 Tim. 3:17 be absolute (Geneva) be perfect (KJV) be complete (NKJV)
2 Tim. 4:2 improve (Geneva) reprove (KJV) Convince (NKJV)
2 Tim. 4:3 wholsome doctrine (Geneva) sound doctrine (KJV, NKJV)
2 Tim. 4:5 suffer adversity (Geneva) endure afflictions (KJV, NKJV)
2 Tim. 4:9 Make speed (Geneva) Do thy diligence (KJV) Be diligent (NKJV)
2 Tim. 4:10 embraced (Geneva) loved (KJV, NKJV)
2 Tim. 4:15 our preaching (Geneva) our words (KJV, NKJV)
2 Tim. 4:16 assisted me (Geneva) stood with me (KJV, NKJV)
2 Tim. 4:17 assisted me (Geneva) stood with me (KJV, NKJV)
2 Tim. 4:21 Make speed (Geneva) Do thy diligence (KJV) Do your utmost (NKJV)
Titus 1:7 not forward (Geneva) not selfwilled (KJV) not self-willed (NKJV)
Titus 1:8 harberous (Geneva) lover of hospitality (KJV) hospitable (NKJV)
Titus 1:8 wise (Geneva) sober (KJV) sober-minded (NKJV)
Titus 2:1 wholsome doctrine (Geneva) sound doctrine (KJV, NKJV)
Titus 2:2 sound in the faith (Geneva) sound in faith (KJV, NKJV)
Titus 2:5 subject unto their husbands (Geneva) obedient to their own husbands (KJV, NKJV)
Titus 2:7 Above all things (Geneva) In all things (KJV) in all things (NKJV)
Titus 2:7 ensample (Geneva) pattern (KJV, NKJV)
Titus 2:8 *And* with the wholesome word (Geneva) Sound speech (KJV) sound speech (NKJV)
Titus 2:10 good faithfulness (Geneva) good fidelity (KJV, NKJV)
Titus 3:4 bountifulness (Geneva) kindness (KJV, NKJV)
Titus 3:8 true saying (Geneva) faithful saying (KJV, NKJV)
Titus 3:9 stay foolish (Geneva) avoid foolish (KJV, NKJV)
Titus 3:13 expounder of the law (Geneva) lawyer (KJV, NKJV)
Philemon 1:2 to *our* dear *sister* Apphia (Geneva) to *our* beloved Apphia (KJV) to the beloved Apphia (NKJV)
Philemon 1:4 I give thanks to my God (Geneva) I thank my God (KJV, NKJV)
Philemon 1:17 count our things common (Geneva) count me therefore a partner (KJV) count me as a partner (NKJV)
Philemon 1:18 hurt thee (Geneva) wronged thee (KJV) wronged you (NKJV)
Philemon 1:21 Trusting (Geneva) Having confidence (KJV, NKJV)
Heb. 1:1 old time (Geneva) time past (KJV, NKJV)
Heb. 1:3 ingraved form (Geneva) express image (KJV, NKJV)
Heb. 1:3 bearing up all things (Geneva) upholding all things (KJV, NKJV)
Heb. 1:3 by his mighty word (Geneva) by the word of his power (KJV) by the word of His power (NKJV)
Heb. 1:3 sitteth at the right hand (Geneva) sat down on the right hand (KJV) sat down at the right hand (NKJV)
Heb. 1:3 in the highest places (Geneva) on high (KJV, NKJV)
Heb. 1:4 much more excellent (Geneva) much better (KJV, NKJV)
Heb. 1:6 *his* first begotten Son (Geneva) the first begotten (KJV) the firstborn (NKJV)
Heb. 1:10 established the earth (Geneva) laid the foundation of the earth (KJV, NKJV)
Heb. 2:1 diligently to give heed (Geneva) give the more earnest need (KJV, NKJV)
Heb. 2:3 preached (Geneva) spoken (KJV, NKJV)
Heb. 2:6 witnessed (Geneva) testified (KJV, NKJV)
Heb. 2:7 a little inferior (Geneva) a little lower (KJV, NKJV)
Heb. 2:8 subdued unto him (Geneva) put under him (KJV, NKJV)
Heb. 2:9 a little inferior (Geneva) a little lower (KJV, NKJV)
Heb. 2:10 consecrate the Prince of their salvation (Geneva) make the captain of their salvation

(KJV, NKJV)

Heb. 2:10 afflictions (Geneva) sufferings (KJV, NKJV)

Heb. 3:1 vocation (Geneva) calling (KJV, NKJV)

Heb. 3:2 *was* in all his house (Geneva) *was faithful* in all his house (KJV) *was faithful* in all His house (NKJV)

Heb. 3:5 a witness (Geneva) a testimony (KJV, NKJV)

Heb. 3:9 forty years long (Geneva) forty years (KJV, NKJV)

Heb. 3:12 evil heart and unfaithful (Geneva) evil heart of unbelief (KJV, NKJV)

Heb. 4:2 to be deprived (Geneva) to come short of it (KJV, NKJV)

Heb. 4:12 mighty in operation (Geneva) powerful (KJV, NKJV)

Heb. 4:16 receive mercy (Geneva) obtain mercy (KJV, NKJV)

Heb. 5:5 took not to himself this honour (Geneva) glorifed not himself (KJV) did not glorify Himself (NKJV)

Heb. 5:9 being consecrate (Geneva) being made perfect (KJV) having been perfected (NKJV)

Heb. 5:12 the word of God (Geneva) oracles of God (KJV, NKJV)

Heb. 6:6 a mock of him (Geneva) to an open shame (KJV, NKJV)

Heb. 6:8 reproved (Geneva) rejected (KJV, NKJV)

Heb. 6:14 I will abundantly bless (Geneva) blessing I will bless (KJV, NKJV)

Heb. 6:14 multiply thee marvelously (Geneva) multiplying I will multiply thee (KJV) multiplying I will multiply you (NKJV)

Heb. 6:15 tarried patiently (Geneva) patiently endured (KJV, NKJV)

Heb. 7:7 blessed of the greater (Geneva) blessed of the better (KJV) blessed by the better (NKJV)

Heb. 7:10 of his father *Abraham* (Geneva) of his father (KJV, NKJV)

Heb. 7:24 everlasting Priesthood (Geneva) unchangeable priesthood (KJV, NKJV)

Heb. 8:5 pattern (Geneva) example (KJV) copy (NKJV)

Heb. 8:7 first *Testament* (Geneva) first *covenant* (KJV, NKJV)

Heb. 8:9 Not like the Testament (Geneva) Not according to the covenant (KJV, NKJV)

Heb. 8:10 For this is the Testament (Geneva) For this is the covenant (KJV, NKJV)

Heb. 8:13 a new *Testament* (Geneva) A new *covenant* (KJV, NKJV)

Heb. 9:5 glorious Cherubims (Geneva) cherubims of glory (KJV) cherubim of glory (NKJV)

Heb. 9:7 the ignorances of the people (Geneva) the errors of the people (KJV) the people's sins *committed* in ignorance (NKJV)

Heb. 9:10 rites (Geneva) ordinances (KJV, NKJV)

Heb. 9:15 through death (Geneva) by means of death (KJV, NKJV)

Heb. 9:16 of him that made the testament (Geneva) of the testator (KJV, NKJV)

Heb. 9:19 purple wool (Geneva) scarlet wool (KJV, NKJV)

Heb. 9:21 all the ministring vessels (Geneva) all the vessels of the ministry (KJV, NKJV)

Heb. 10:2 offerers (Geneva) worshippers (KJV) worshipers (NKJV)

Heb. 10:4 unpossible (Geneva) not possible (KJV, NKJV)

Heb. 10:10 once *made* (Geneva) once *for all* (KJV, NKJV)

Heb. 10:14 with one offering (Geneva) by one offering (KJV, NKJV)

Heb. 10:14 consecrated (Geneva) perfected (KJV, NKJV)

Heb. 10:16 Testament (Geneva) covenant (KJV, NKJV)

Heb. 10:19 the Holy place (Geneva) the holiest (KJV) the Holiest (NKJV)

Heb. 10:25 the fellowship (Geneva) the assembling (KJV, NKJV)

Heb. 10:39 conservation of the soul (Geneva) saving of the soul (KJV, NKJV)

Heb. 11:1 ground (Geneva) substance (KJV, NKJV)

Heb. 11:3 world was ordained (Geneva) worlds were framed (KJV, NKJV)

Heb. 11:4 greater sacrifice (Geneva) more excellent sacrifice (KJV, NKJV)

Heb. 11:6 unpossible (Geneva) impossible (KJV, NKJV)

Heb. 11:25 adversary (Geneva) affliction (KJV, NKJV)

Heb. 11:26 rebuke of Christ (Geneva) reproach of Christ (KJV, NKJV)

Heb. 11:28 ordained the Passover (Geneva) kept the passover (KJV) kept the Passover (NKJV)

Heb. 11:31 peaceably (Geneva) with peace (KJV, NKJV)

Heb. 11:37 hewn (Geneva) sawn (KJV, NKJV)

Heb. 11:38 wildernesses (Geneva) deserts (KJV, NKJV)
Heb. 12:1 every thing that presseth down (Geneva) every weight (KJV, NKJV)
Heb. 12:5 consolation (Geneva) exhortation (KJV, NKJV)
Heb. 12:7 God offereth himself unto you (Geneva) God dealeth with you (KJV) God deals with you (NKJV)
Heb. 12:8 correction (Geneva) chastisement (KJV) chastening (NKJV)
Heb. 12:13 straight steps (Geneva) straight paths (KJV, NKJV)
Heb. 12:15 fall away from (Geneva) fail of (KJV) fall short of (NKJV)
Heb. 12:20 were not able to abide (Geneva) could not endure (KJV, NKJV)
Heb. 12:23 And to the congregation of the first born (Geneva) To the general assembly and church of the firstborn (KJV, NKJV)
Heb. 12:24 new Testament (Geneva) new covenant (KJV, NKJV)
Heb. 13:2 lodge (Geneva) entertain (KJV, NKJV)
Heb. 13:2 received Angels (Geneva) entertained angels (KJV, NKJV)
Heb. 13:5 I will not fail thee (Geneva) I will never leave thee (KJV) I will never leave you (NKJV)
Heb. 13:6 mine helper (Geneva) my helper (KJV, NKJV)
Heb. 13:7 have the oversight (Geneva) have the rule (KJV) rule (NKJV)
Heb. 13:9 stablished (Geneva) established (KJV, NKJV)
Heb. 13:16 distribute (Geneva) communicate (KJV) share (NKJV)
Heb. 13:17 have the oversight (Geneva) have the rule (KJV) rule (NKJV)
Heb. 13:23 Timotheus (Geneva) Timothy (KJV, NKJV)
Heb. 13:24 have the oversight (Geneva) have the rule (KJV) rule (NKJV)
James 1:14 concupiscence (Geneva) lusts (KJV) desires (NKJV)
James 2:1 faith of our glorious Lord Jesus Christ (Geneva) faith of our Lord Jesus Christ, *the Lord of glory* (KJV, NKJV)
James 2:2 company (Geneva) assembly (KJV, NKJV)
James 2:7 named (Geneva) called (KJV, NKJV)
James 2:13 merciless (Geneva) without mercy (KJV, NKJV)
James 2:14 What availeth it (Geneva) What *doth it* profit (KJV) What *does it* profit (NKJV)
James 2:16 and fill your bellies (Geneva) and filled (KJV, NKJV)
James 2:16 what helpeth it (Geneva) what *doth it* profit (KJV) what *does it* profit (NKJV)
James 2:21 through works (Geneva) by works (KJV, NKJV)
James 2:22 through the works (Geneva) by works (KJV, NKJV)
James 3:6 wickedness (Geneva) iniquity (KJV, NKJV)
James 3:7 whole nature of beasts (Geneva) every kind of beasts (KJV) every kind of beast (NKJV)
James 3:16 sedition (Geneva) confusion (KJV, NKJV)
James 3:17 without judging (Geneva) without partiality (KJV, NKJV)
James 4:1 contentions (Geneva) fightings (KJV) fights (NKJV)
James 4:2 ye envy (Geneva) ye kill (KJV) You murder (NKJV)
James 4:2 have indignation (Geneva) desire to have (KJV) covet (NKJV)
James 4:4 amity of the world (Geneva) friendship of the world (KJV, NKJV)
James 4:6 But *the Scripture* offereth more grace (Geneva) But he giveth more grace (KJV) But He gives more grace (NKJV)
James 4:10 Cast down yourselves (Geneva) Humble yourselves (KJV, NKJV)
James 5:10 ensample (Geneva) example (KJV, NKJV)
James 5:16 Acknowledge (Geneva) Confess (KJV, NKJV)
1 Pet. 1:4 immortal (Geneva) incorruptible (KJV, NKJV)
1 Pet. 1:8 glorious (Geneva) full of glory (KJV, NKJV)
1 Pet. 1:11 Spirit which testified before of Christ which was in them should declare (Geneva) Spirit of Christ which was in them did signify, when it testified beforehand (KJV) Spirit of Christ who was in them was indicating when He testified beforehand (NKJV)
1 Pet. 1:23 born a new (Geneva) born again (KJV, NKJV)
1 Pet. 1:23 mortal seed (Geneva) corruptible seed (KJV, NKJV)
1 Pet. 2:1 dissimulation (Geneva) hypocrisies (KJV) hypocrisy (NKJV)
1 Pet. 2:13 superior (Geneva) supreme (KJV, NKJV)

1 Pet. 2:18 courteous (Geneva) gentle (KJV, NKJV)
1 Pet. 2:21 ensample (Geneva) example (KJV, NKJV)
1 Pet. 3:3 apparelling (Geneva) adorning (KJV) adornment (NKJV)
1 Pet. 3:4 the hid (Geneva) the hidden (KJV, NKJV)
1 Pet. 3:5 tier themselves (Geneva) adorned themselves (KJV, NKJV)
1 Pet. 3:6 sir (Geneva) lord (KJV, NKJV)
1 Pet. 3:7 interrupted (Geneva) hindered (KJV, NKJV)
1 Pet. 3:8 one suffer with another (Geneva) having compassion one of another (KJV) having compassion for one another (NKJV)
1 Pet. 3:14 upon them that do evil (Geneva) against them that do evil (KJV) against those who do evil (NKJV)
1 Pet. 4:3 in gluttony (Geneva) revellings (KJV) revelries (NKJV)
1 Pet. 4:9 Be ye herberous (Geneva) Use hospitality (KJV) Be hospitable (NKJV)
1 Pet. 4:10 good disposers (Geneva) good stewards (KJV, NKJV)
1 Pet. 5:8 Be sober and watch (Geneva) Be sober, be vigilant (KJV, NKJV)
2 Pet. 1:3 godly power (Geneva) divine power (KJV, NKJV)
2 Pet. 1:4 most great (Geneva) exceeding great (KJV, NKJV)
2 Pet. 1:4 godly nature (Geneva) divine nature (KJV, NKJV)
2 Pet. 1:4 in that ye flee (Geneva) having escaped (KJV, NKJV)
2 Pet. 1:8 idle (Geneva) barren (KJV, NKJV)
2 Pet. 1:12 stablished (Geneva) established (KJV, NKJV)
2 Pet. 1:14 the time is at hand (Geneva) shortly (KJV, NKJV)
2 Pet. 1:14 lay down (Geneva) put off (KJV, NKJV)
2 Pet. 1:16 deceivable fables (Geneva) cunningly devised fables (KJV, NKJV)
2 Pet. 1:20 private motion (Geneva) private interpretation (KJV, NKJV)
2 Pet. 2:5 Noe (Geneva) Noah (KJV, NKJV)
2 Pet. 2:7 uncleanly (Geneva) filthy (KJV, NKJV)
2 Pet. 2:11 railing judgment (Geneva) railing accusation (KJV, NKJV)
2 Pet. 2:16 foolishness (Geneva) madness (KJV, NKJV)
2 Pet. 2:18 beguile with wantonness (Geneva) allure through the lusts of the flesh (KJV, NKJV)
2 Pet. 2:18 wrapped in error (Geneva) live in error (KJV, NKJV)
2 Pet. 2:20 filthiness of the world (Geneva) pollutions of the world (KJV, NKJV)
2 Pet. 3:7 destruction (Geneva) perdition (KJV, NKJV)
2 Pet. 3:18 for ever more (Geneva) for ever (KJV) forever (NKJV)
1 John 1:2 life appeared (Geneva) life was manifested (KJV, NKJV)
1 John 1:9 we acknowledge (Geneva) we confess (KJV, NKJV)
1 John 2:1 My babes (Geneva) My little children (KJV, NKJV)
1 John 2:2 reconciliation (Geneva) propitiation (KJV, NKJV)
1 John 2:6 he remaineth (Geneva) he abideth (KJV) he abides (NKJV)
1 John 2:18 Babes (Geneva) Little children (KJV, NKJV)
1 John 3:1 what love (Geneva) what manner of love (KJV, NKJV)
1 John 3:2 Dearly beloved (Geneva) Beloved (KJV, NKJV)
1 John 3:12 of the wicked (Geneva) of that wicked one (KJV) of the wicked one (NKJV)
1 John 3:14 are translated (Geneva) have passed (KJV, NKJV)
1 John 4:10 reconciliation (Geneva) propitiation (KJV, NKJV)
1 John 5:14 assurance (Geneva) confidence (KJV, NKJV)
1 John 5:21 Babes (Geneva) Little children (KJV, NKJV)
Jude 1:3 once given (Geneva) once delivered (KJV) once for all delivered (NKJV)
Jude 1:3 earnestly contend for *the maintenance* of the faith (Geneva) earnestly contend for the faith (KJV) contend earnestly for the faith (NKJV)
Jude 1:4 God the only Lord (Geneva) the only Lord God (KJV, NKJV)
Jude 1:5 delivered (Geneva) saved (KJV, NKJV)
Jude 1:5 out of Egypt (Geneva) out of the land of Egypt (KJV, NKJV)
Jude 1:7 ensample (Geneva) example (KJV, NKJV)
Jude 1:9 cursed speaking (Geneva) railing accusation (KJV) reviling accusation (NKJV)
Jude 1:10 as beasts which are without reason (Geneva) as brute beasts (KJV) like brute beasts

(NKJV)
Jude 1:15 To give judgement against all men (Geneva) To execute judgment upon all (KJV) to execute judgment on all (NKJV)
Jude 1:19 fleshly (Geneva) sensual (KJV, NKJV)
Jude 1:20 edify yourselves (Geneva) building up yourselves (KJV) building yourselves up (NKJV)
Rev. 1:10 I was *ravished* in spirit (Geneva) I was in the Spirit (KJV, NKJV)
Rev. 3:1 Sardi (Geneva) Sardis (KJV, NKJV)
Rev. 3:2 Be awake (Geneva) Be watchful (KJV, NKJV)
Rev. 3:9 call themselves Jews (Geneva) say they are Jews (KJV, NKJV)
Rev. 3:19 and amend (Geneva) and repent (KJV, NKJV)
Rev. 5:2 which preached (Geneva) proclaiming (KJV, NKJV)
Rev. 5:12 and praise (Geneva) and blessing (KJV, NKJV)
Rev. 6:2 that he might overcome (Geneva) and to conquer (KJV, NKJV)
Rev. 8:6 to blow the trumpets (Geneva) to sound (KJV, NKJV)
Rev. 9:1 blew the trumpet (Geneva) sounded (KJV, NKJV)
Rev. 9:9 habergeons (Geneva) breastplates (KJV, NKJV)
Rev. 9:13 blew the trumpet (Geneva) sounded (KJV, NKJV)
Rev. 9:16 number of horsemen of war (Geneva) number of the army of the horsemen (KJV, NKJV)
Rev. 9:17 fiery habergeons (Geneva) breastplates of fire (KJV, NKJV)
Rev. 9:20 remnant (Geneva) rest (KJV, NKJV)
Rev. 9:20 nor go (Geneva) nor walk (KJV, NKJV)
Rev. 10:6 for evermore (Geneva) for ever and ever (KJV) forever and ever (NKJV)
Rev. 11:8 corpses (Geneva) dead bodies (KJV, NKJV)
Rev. 11:14 anon (Geneva) quickly (KJV, NKJV)
Rev. 11:15 blew the trumpet (Geneva) sounded (KJV, NKJV)
Rev. 11:18 Gentiles (Geneva) nations (KJV, NKJV)
Rev. 12:7 a battle (Geneva) war (KJV, NKJV)
Rev. 16:9 boiled (Geneva) were scorched (KJV, NKJV)
Rev. 18:14 apples (Geneva) fruits (KJV) fruit (NKJV)
Rev. 19:3 for evermore (Geneva) for ever and ever (KJV) forever and ever (NKJV)
Rev. 20:4 seats (Geneva) thrones (KJV, NKJV)
Rev. 21:2 bride trimmed (Geneva) bride adorned (KJV, NKJV)
Rev. 21:24 people (Geneva) nations (KJV, NKJV)
Rev. 22:12 shortly (Geneva) quickly (KJV, NKJV)
Rev. 22:15 enchanters (Geneva) sorcerers (KJV, NKJV)
Rev. 22:18 I protest (Geneva) I testify (KJV, NKJV)

In the second large group of particulars, many examples of places where the 1560 Geneva Bible and the NKJV differ from the KJV are given. In many of them the Geneva Bible and the NKJV are basically in agreement while it is the KJV that differs more. Did the NKJV translators update, revise, and improve any renderings in the KJV with renderings basically in agreement with those already in the earlier 1560 Geneva Bible? In any of these examples, did the NKJV translators bring the English translation back more accurately in line with the preserved original-language texts of Scripture? In some cases, it would be difficult and perhaps impossible for KJV-only advocates to demonstrate that the KJV's rendering is better, more accurate, or purer than the rendering in the earlier 1560 Geneva Bible. While some archaic language in the Geneva Bible was updated in the KJV, would the KJV itself be in less need of updating today if it had followed some of these renderings in the 1560 Geneva Bible instead of some of the more archaic renderings in the 1568 or 1602 edition of the Bishops' Bible? Did the makers of the KJV make any unnecessary changes to the good Geneva Bible?

Many places where the KJV differs from both the Geneva Bible and the NKJV

Gen. 1:3 Then God (Geneva, NKJV) And God (KJV)
Gen. 1:5 So the evening (Geneva, NKJV) And the evening (KJV)

Gen. 1:9 into one place (Geneva, NKJV) unto one place (KJV)
Gen. 1:11 Then God (Geneva, NKJV) And God (KJV)
Gen. 1:14 Then God (Geneva, NKJV) And God (KJV)
Gen. 1:19 So the evening (Geneva, NKJV) And the evening (KJV)
Gen. 1:21 according to their kind (Geneva, NKJV) after their kind (KJV)
Gen. 1:24 according to (Geneva, NKJV) after (KJV)
Gen. 1:28 said to them (Geneva, NKJV) said unto them (KJV)
Gen. 1:28 fill the earth (Geneva, NKJV) replenish the earth (KJV)
Gen. 1:31 So the evening (Geneva, NKJV) And the evening (KJV)
Gen. 2:3 God had created (Geneva, NKJV) God created (KJV)
Gen. 2:6 a mist went up (Geneva, NKJV) there went up a mist (KJV)
Gen. 2:13 Cush (Geneva, NKJV) Ethiopia (KJV)
Gen. 2:15 Then (Geneva, NKJV) And (KJV)
Gen. 2:22 to the man (Geneva, NKJV) unto the man (KJV)
Gen. 2:24 to his wife (Geneva, NKJV) unto his wife (KJV)
Gen. 3:1 to the woman (Geneva, NKJV) unto the woman (KJV)
Gen. 3:1 God indeed said (Geneva, NKJV) God said (KJV)
Gen. 3:4 Then the (Geneva, NKJV) And the (KJV)
Gen. 3:4 to the woman (Geneva, NKJV) unto the woman (KJV)
Gen. 3:7 Then the eyes (Geneva, NKJV) And the eyes (KJV)
Gen. 3:8 among (Geneva, NKJV) amongst (KJV)
Gen. 3:9 called to (Geneva, NKJV) called unto (KJV)
Gen. 3:12 Then the man (Geneva, NKJV) And the man (KJV)
Gen. 3:13 to the woman (Geneva, NKJV) unto the woman (KJV)
Gen. 3:14 said to (Geneva, NKJV) said unto (KJV)
Gen. 3:15 He shall bruise (Geneva, NKJV) it shall bruise (KJV)
Gen. 3:17 to Adam (Geneva, NKJV) unto Adam (KJV)
Gen. 4:7 do well (Geneva, NKJV) doest well (KJV)
Gen. 4:9 Then the (Geneva, NKJV) And the (KJV)
Gen. 4:13 said to the (Geneva, NKJV) said unto the (KJV)
Gen. 4:16 Then (Geneva, NKJV) And (KJV)
Gen. 4:17 built a city (Geneva, NKJV) builded a city (KJV)
Gen. 4:21 play on the harp (Geneva) handle the harp (KJV) play the harp (NKJV)
Gen. 4:23 Then Lamech (Geneva, NKJV) And Lamech (KJV)
Gen. 5:5 So all (Geneva, NKJV) And all (KJV)
Gen. 5:6 Enosh (Geneva, NKJV) Enos (KJV)
Gen. 5:8 So all (Geneva, NKJV) And all (KJV)
Gen. 5:9 Enosh (Geneva, NKJV) Enos (KJV)
Gen. 5:11 So all (Geneva, NKJV) And all (KJV)
Gen. 5:23 So all the (Geneva, NKJV) And all the (KJV)
Gen. 5:27 So all the (Geneva, NKJV) And all the (KJV)
Gen. 5:31 So all the (Geneva, NKJV) And all the (KJV)
Gen. 6:5 the Lord (Geneva) GOD (KJV) the LORD (NKJV)
Gen. 7:7 So Noah (Geneva, NKJV) And Noah (KJV)
Gen. 7:14 all cattle (Geneva, NKJV) all the cattle (KJV)
Gen. 7:15 to Noah (Geneva, NKJV) unto Noah (KJV)
Gen. 7:18 ark went upon the waters (Geneva) ark went upon the face of the waters (KJV) ark moved about on the surface of the waters (NKJV)
Gen. 7:19 The waters prevailed (Geneva, NKJV) And the waters prevailed (KJV)
Gen. 7:22 the spirit of life did breathe (Geneva) *was* the breath of life (KJV) *was* the breath of the spirit of life (NKJV)
Gen. 7:23 So he destroyed every thing (Geneva) And every living substance was destroyed (KJV) So He destroyed all living things (NKJV)
Gen. 8:11 came to him (Geneva, NKJV) came in to him (KJV)
Gen. 8:12 he waited (Geneva, NKJV) he stayed (KJV)
Gen. 8:15 Then God (Geneva, NKJV) And God (KJV)

Gen. 8:18 So Noah (Geneva, NKJV) And Noah (KJV)
Gen. 8:20 Then Noah built (Geneva, NKJV) And Noah builded (KJV)
Gen. 8:20 altar to (Geneva, NKJV) altar unto (KJV)
Gen. 9:1 said to them (Geneva, NKJV) said unto them (KJV)
Gen. 9:8 to Noah (Geneva, NKJV) unto Noah (KJV)
Gen. 9:13 sign (Geneva, NKJV) token (KJV)
Gen. 9:17 to Noah (Geneva, NKJV) unto Noah (KJV)
Gen. 9:17 sign (Geneva, NKJV) token (KJV)
Gen. 9:18 Now the sons (Geneva, NKJV) And the sons (KJV)
Gen. 9:29 So all (Geneva, NKJV) And all (KJV)
Gen. 10:6 Put (Geneva, NKJV) Phut (KJV)
Gen. 10:20 according to (Geneva, NKJV) after (KJV)
Gen. 10:22 The sons (Geneva, NKJV) The children (KJV)
Gen. 10:23 sons of Aram (Geneva, NKJV) children of Aram (KJV)
Gen. 10:31 according to their families (Geneva, NKJV) after their families (KJV)
Gen. 11:1 and one speech (Geneva, NKJV) and of one speech (KJV)
Gen. 11:3 Come (Geneva, NKJV) Go to (KJV)
Gen. 11:5 But the (Geneva, NKJV) And the (KJV)
Gen. 11:7 Come on (Geneva) Go to (KJV) Come (NKJV)
Gen. 11:31 to Haran (Geneva, NKJV) unto Haran (KJV)
Gen. 11:32 So the days (Geneva, NKJV) And the days (KJV)
Gen. 12:5 Then Abram (Geneva, NKJV) And Abram (KJV)
Gen. 12:5 and they departed (Geneva, NKJV) and they went forth (KJV)
Gen. 12:6 Shechem (Geneva, NKJV) Sichem (KJV)
Gen. 12:8 he built (Geneva, NKJV) he builded (KJV)
Gen. 12:8 called on (Geneva, NKJV) called upon (KJV)
Gen. 12:11 to Sarai (Geneva, NKJV) unto Sarai (KJV)
Gen. 12:13 my life may be preserved by thee (Geneva) my soul shall live because of thee (KJV) I may live because of you (NKJV)
Gen. 12:15 unto Pharaoh (Geneva) before Pharaoh (KJV) to Pharaoh (NKJV)
Gen. 12:17 But the (Geneva, NKJV) And the (KJV)
Gen. 13:1 Then Abram (Geneva, NKJV) And Abram (KJV)
Gen. 13:1 from Egypt (Geneva, NKJV) out of Egypt (KJV)
Gen. 13:3 journey (Geneva, NKJV) journeys (KJV)
Gen. 13:3 to the place (Geneva, NKJV) unto the place (KJV)
Gen. 13:5 who went (Geneva, NKJV) which went (KJV)
Gen. 13:7 the Canaanites and the Perizzites (Geneva, NKJV) the Canaanite and the Perizzite (KJV)
Gen. 13:10 goest (Geneva) comest (KJV) go (NKJV)
Gen. 13:11 chose unto him (Geneva) chose him (KJV) chose for himself (NKJV)
Gen. 13:12 even to Sodom (Geneva) toward Sodom (KJV) even as far as Sodom (NKJV)
Gen. 13:13 against the Lord (Geneva) before the LORD (KJV) against the LORD (NKJV)
Gen. 14:9 four kings against five (Geneva, NKJV) four kings with five (KJV)
Gen. 14:10 Now the (Geneva, NKJV) And the (KJV)
Gen. 14:11 Then they (Geneva, NKJV) And they (KJV)
Gen. 14:12 They took Lot also (Geneva) And they took Lot (KJV) They also took Lot (NKJV)
Gen. 14:13 Then (Geneva, NKJV) And (KJV)
Gen. 14:19 of God most high (Geneva) of the most high God (KJV) of God Most High (NKJV)
Gen. 14:20 tithe of all (Geneva) tithes of all (KJV) a tithe of all (NKJV)
Gen. 14:21 to Abram (Geneva, NKJV) unto Abram (KJV)
Gen. 15:13 Then (Geneva, NKJV) And (KJV)
Gen. 15:13 to Abram (Geneva, NKJV) unto Abram (KJV)
Gen. 16:3 Then Sarai (Geneva, NKJV) And Sarai (KJV)
Gen. 16:5 Then Sarai (Geneva, NKJV) And Sarai (KJV)
Gen. 16:5 to Abram (Geneva, NKJV) unto Abram (KJV)
Gen. 16:6 to Sarai (Geneva, NKJV) unto Sarai (KJV)

Gen. 16:6 roughly (Geneva) hardly (KJV) harshly (NKJV)
Gen. 16:13 Then she called (Geneva, NKJV) And she called (KJV)
Gen. 17:1 When Abram (Geneva, NKJV) And when Abram (KJV)
Gen. 17:3 Then Abram fell (Geneva, NKJV) And Abram fell (KJV)
Gen. 17:7 to be God (Geneva, NKJV) to be a God (KJV)
Gen. 17:11 between (Geneva, NKJV) betwixt (KJV)
Gen. 17:14 that person (Geneva, NKJV) that soul (KJV)
Gen. 17:19 Then God (Geneva, NKJV) And God (KJV)
Gen. 18:2 to the ground (Geneva, NKJV) toward the ground (KJV)
Gen. 18:4 be bought (Geneva, NKJV) be fetched (KJV)
Gen. 18:5 And I will bring (Geneva, NKJV) And I will fetch (KJV)
Gen. 18:7 ran to (Geneva, NKJV) ran unto (KJV)
Gen. 18:7 took a tender and good calf (Geneva, NKJV) fetcht a calf tender and good (KJV)
Gen. 18:8 which he had prepared (Geneva, NKJV) which he had dressed (KJV)
Gen. 18:15 But Sarah (Geneva, NKJV) Then Sarah (KJV)
Gen. 18:19 do righteousness (Geneva, NKJV) do justice (KJV)
Gen. 18:29 to him (Geneva, NKJV) unto him (KJV)
Gen. 18:32 Then he said (Geneva, NKJV) And he said (KJV)
Gen. 19:1 in the evening (Geneva, NKJV) at even (KJV)
Gen. 19:1 Lot saw *them* (Geneva, NKJV) Lot seeing *them* (KJV)
Gen. 19:5 said to him (Geneva, NKJV) said unto him (KJV)
Gen. 19:9 So they pressed (Geneva, NKJV) And they pressed (KJV)
Gen. 19:12 Then the men (Geneva, NKJV) And the men (KJV)
Gen. 19:15 punishment of the city (Geneva, NKJV) iniquity of the city (KJV)
Gen. 19:20 See now (Geneva, NKJV) Behold now (KJV)
Gen. 19:30 Then Lot (Geneva, NKJV) And Lot (KJV)
Gen. 19:33 So they (Geneva, NKJV) And they (KJV)
Gen. 20:14 Then Abimelech (Geneva, NKJV) And Abimelech (KJV)
Gen. 21:4 Then Abraham (Geneva, NKJV) And Abraham (KJV)
Gen. 21:4 when he was (Geneva, NKJV) being (KJV)
Gen. 21:7 to Abraham (Geneva, NKJV) unto Abraham (KJV)
Gen. 21:12 But God (Geneva, NKJV) And God (KJV)
Gen. 21:14 So Abraham (Geneva, NKJV) And Abraham (KJV)
Gen. 21:16 of about (Geneva, NKJV) as it were (KJV)
Gen. 21:25 rebuked (Geneva, NKJV) reproved (KJV)
Gen. 21:26 know (Geneva, NKJV) wot (KJV)
Gen. 21:29 Then Abimelech (Geneva, NKJV) And Abimelech (KJV)
Gen. 22:1 God did prove (Geneva) God did tempt (KJV) God tested (NKJV)
Gen. 22:3 went to (Geneva, NKJV) went unto (KJV)
Gen. 22:11 But the Angel (Geneva, NKJV) And the angel (KJV)
Gen. 22:11 from heaven (Geneva, NKJV) out of heaven (KJV)
Gen. 22:16 because (Geneva, NKJV) for because (KJV)
Gen. 23:1 twenty and seven (Geneva) seven and twenty (KJV) twenty-seven (NKJV)
Gen. 23:3 Then Abraham (Geneva, NKJV) And Abraham (KJV)
Gen. 23:4 among you, give (Geneva) with you: give (KJV) among you. Give (NKJV)
Gen. 23:7 Then Abraham (Geneva, NKJV) And Abraham (KJV)
Gen. 23:9 among you (Geneva, NKJV) amongst you (KJV)
Gen. 23:11 No (Geneva, NKJV) Nay (KJV)
Gen. 23:12 Then Abraham (Geneva, NKJV) And Abraham (KJV)
Gen. 23:15 between (Geneva, NKJV) betwixt (KJV)
Gen. 23:17 So the (Geneva, NKJV) And the (KJV)
Gen. 24:1 Now Abraham (Geneva, NKJV) And Abraham (KJV)
Gen. 24:5 to him (Geneva, NKJV) unto him (KJV)
Gen. 24:7 who took (Geneva, NKJV) which took (KJV)
Gen. 24:9 this matter (Geneva, NKJV) that matter (KJV)
Gen. 24:10 to the city (Geneva, NKJV) unto the city (KJV)

Gen. 24:24 to him (Geneva, NKJV) unto him (KJV)
Gen. 24:25 Moreover she said (Geneva, NKJV) She said moreover (KJV)
Gen. 24:29 Now Rebekah (Geneva, NKJV) And Rebekah (KJV)
Gen. 24:30 he went (Geneva, NKJV) he came (KJV)
Gen. 24:32 Then the (Geneva, NKJV) And the (KJV)
Gen. 24:37 Now (Geneva, NKJV) And (KJV)
Gen. 24:42 to the well (Geneva, NKJV) unto the well (KJV)
Gen. 24:47 Then I (Geneva, NKJV) And I (KJV)
Gen. 24:53 Then the (Geneva, NKJV) And the (KJV)
Gen. 24:59 So they (Geneva, NKJV) And they (KJV)
Gen. 24:61 Then Rebekah (Geneva, NKJV) And Rebekah (KJV)
Gen. 24:62 Now (Geneva, NKJV) And (KJV)
Gen. 24:62 Beer-lahai-roi (Geneva) well Lahari-roi (KJV) Beer Lahai Roi (NKJV)
Gen. 24:65 to the servant (Geneva, NKJV) unto the servant (KJV)
Gen. 25:7 seventy and five (Geneva) threescore and fifteen (KJV) seventy-five (NKJV)
Gen. 25:11 Beer-lahai-roi (Geneva) well Lahai-roi (KJV) Beer Lahai Roi (NKJV)
Gen. 25:22 But the (Geneva, NKJV) And the (KJV)
Gen. 25:23 to her (Geneva, NKJV) unto her (KJV)
Gen. 25:26 And afterward (Geneva) And after that (KJV) Afterward (NKJV)
Gen. 25:29 Now (Geneva, NKJV) And (KJV)
Gen. 25:29 weary (Geneva, NKJV) faint (KJV)
Gen. 25:33 to him (Geneva, NKJV) unto him (KJV)
Gen. 26:1 besides (Geneva, NKJV) beside (KJV)
Gen. 26:1 to Abimelech (Geneva, NKJV) unto Abimelech (KJV)
Gen. 26:3 Dwell (Geneva, NKJV) Sojourn (KJV)
Gen. 26:6 So (Geneva, NKJV) And (KJV)
Gen. 26:9 Then Abimelech (Geneva, NKJV) And Abimelech (KJV)
Gen. 26:20 But the (Geneva, NKJV) And the (KJV)
Gen. 26:28 between us (Geneva, NKJV) betwixt us (KJV)
Gen. 26:33 So he (Geneva, NKJV) And he (KJV)
Gen. 26:35 And they were (Geneva, NKJV) Which were (KJV)
Gen. 27:2 Then he (Geneva, NKJV) And he (KJV)
Gen. 27:10 Then (Geneva, NKJV) And (KJV)
Gen. 27:13 But his (Geneva, NKJV) And his (KJV)
Gen. 27:15 clothes (Geneva, NKJV) raiment (KJV)
Gen. 27:15 elder son (Geneva, NKJV) eldest son (KJV)
Gen. 27:18 to his father (Geneva, NKJV) unto his father (KJV)
Gen. 27:19 to his father (Geneva, NKJV) unto his father (KJV)
Gen. 27:22 near to (Geneva, NKJV) near unto (KJV)
Gen. 27:28 wheat (Geneva) corn (KJV) grain (NKJV)
Gen. 27:33 Then (Geneva, NKJV) And (KJV)
Gen. 27:37 Then (Geneva, NKJV) And (KJV)
Gen. 28:1 Then (Geneva, NKJV) And (KJV)
Gen. 28:7 had obeyed (Geneva, NKJV) obeyed (KJV)
Gen. 28:9 to Ishmael (Geneva, NKJV) unto Ishmael (KJV)
Gen. 28:10 Now (Geneva, NKJV) And (KJV)
Gen. 28:11 And he came (Geneva, NKJV) And he lighted (KJV)
Gen. 28:12 Then he (Geneva, NKJV) And he (KJV)
Gen. 28:16 Then (Geneva, NKJV) And (KJV)
Gen. 28:16 awoke (Geneva, NKJV) awaked (KJV)
Gen. 28:18 Then (Geneva, NKJV) And (KJV)
Gen. 28:20 Then (Geneva, NKJV) And (KJV)
Gen. 28:20 clothes (Geneva) raiment (KJV) clothing (NKJV)
Gen. 29:5 Then he (Geneva, NKJV) And he (KJV)
Gen. 29:7 Then he said (Geneva, NKJV) And he said (KJV)
Gen. 29:8 But they (Geneva, NKJV) And they (KJV)

Gen. 29:16 Now Laban (Geneva, NKJV) And Laban (KJV)
Gen. 29:21 Then (Geneva, NKJV) And (KJV)
Gen. 29:21 to Laban (Geneva, NKJV) unto Laban (KJV)
Gen. 29:28 Then (Geneva, NKJV) And (KJV)
Gen. 30:3 to her (Geneva, NKJV) unto her (KJV)
Gen. 30:4 Then she (Geneva, NKJV) And she (KJV)
Gen. 30:4 to her (Geneva, NKJV) unto her (KJV)
Gen. 30:6 Then (Geneva, NKJV) And (KJV)
Gen. 30:8 Then (Geneva, NKJV) And (KJV)
Gen. 30:25 to Laban (Geneva, NKJV) unto Laban (KJV)
Gen. 30:36 between (Geneva, NKJV) betwixt (KJV)
Gen. 31:6 all my might (Geneva, NKJV) all my power (KJV)
Gen. 31:11 to me (Geneva, NKJV) unto me (KJV)
Gen. 31:14 Then (Geneva, NKJV) And (KJV)
Gen. 31:19 idols (Geneva) images (KJV) household idols (NKJV)
Gen. 31:23 Then he (Geneva, NKJV) And he (KJV)
Gen. 31:31 Then (Geneva, NKJV) And (KJV)
Gen. 31:34 maids (Geneva) maidservants' (KJV) maids' (NKJV)
Gen. 31:36 Then (Geneva, NKJV) And (KJV)
Gen. 31:37 between (Geneva, NKJV) betwixt (KJV)
Gen. 31:49 because he said (Geneva, NKJV) for he said (KJV)
Gen. 31:51 between (Geneva, NKJV) betwixt (KJV)
Gen. 31:53 between (Geneva, NKJV) betwixt (KJV)
Gen. 32:3 Then (Geneva, NKJV) And (KJV)
Gen. 32:4 to my lord (Geneva, NKJV) unto my lord (KJV)
Gen. 32:16 between (Geneva, NKJV) betwixt (KJV)
Gen. 32:29 Then (Geneva, NKJV) And (KJV)
Gen. 33:8 Then (Geneva, NKJV) And (KJV)
Gen. 33:18 came safe to (Geneva) came to Shalem (KJV) came safely to (NKJV)
Gen. 33:19 pitched his tent (Geneva, NKJV) spread his tent (KJV)
Gen. 34:4 to his father (Geneva, NKJV) unto his father (KJV)
Gen. 34:6 Then (Geneva, NKJV) And (KJV)
Gen. 34:7 very angry (Geneva, NKJV) very wroth (KJV)
Gen. 34:29 in the houses (Geneva, NKJV) in the house (KJV)
Gen. 34:30 Then (Geneva, NKJV) And (KJV)
Gen. 35:1 Then God said to (Geneva, NKJV) And God said unto (KJV)
Gen. 35:4 in their hands (Geneva, NKJV) in their hand (KJV)
Gen. 35:27 Then (Geneva, NKJV) And (KJV)
Gen. 36:6 had gotten (Geneva) had got (KJV) had gained (NKJV)
Gen. 36:7 so great (Geneva) more than (KJV) too great (NKJV)
Gen. 36:7 flocks (Geneva) cattle (KJV) livestock (NKJV)
Gen. 36:22 And the sons (Geneva, NKJV) And the children (KJV)
Gen. 36:23 sons (Geneva, NKJV) children (KJV)
Gen. 36:24 sons (Geneva, NKJV) children (KJV)
Gen. 36:26 the sons (Geneva, NKJV) the children (KJV)
Gen. 36:27 sons (Geneva, NKJV) children (KJV)
Gen. 36:28 sons (Geneva, NKJV) children (KJV)
Gen. 36:36 When Hadad (Geneva, NKJV) And Hadad (KJV)
Gen. 37:12 Then (Geneva, NKJV) And (KJV)
Gen. 37:21 But (Geneva, NKJV) And (KJV)
Gen. 37:22 might deliver (Geneva, NKJV) might rid (KJV)
Gen. 37:30 returned to (Geneva, NKJV) returned unto (KJV)
Gen. 38:3 So she (Geneva, NKJV) And she (KJV)
Gen. 38:6 Then Judah (Geneva, NKJV) And Judah (KJV)
Gen. 38:8 to Onan (Geneva, NKJV) unto Onan (KJV)
Gen. 38:18 Then he (Geneva, NKJV) And he (KJV)

Gen. 38:23 Then Judah (Geneva, NKJV) And Judah (KJV)
Gen. 39:1 Now Joseph (Geneva, NKJV) And Joseph (KJV)
Gen. 39:4 So Joseph (Geneva, NKJV) And Joseph (KJV)
Gen. 39:4 favour (Geneva) grace (KJV) favor (NKJV)
Gen. 39:8 said to (Geneva, NKJV) said unto (KJV)
Gen. 39:8 knoweth not (Geneva) wotteth not (KJV) does not know (NKJV)
Gen. 39:10 with her (Geneva, NKJV) by her (KJV)
Gen. 39:12 but he left (Geneva, NKJV) and he left (KJV)
Gen. 39:17 Then she (Geneva, NKJV) And she (KJV)
Gen. 39:19 his anger (Geneva, NKJV) his wrath (KJV)
Gen. 40:1 offended (Geneva, NKJV) had offended (KJV)
Gen. 40:2 angry (Geneva, NKJV) wroth (KJV)
Gen. 40:2 chief butler (Geneva, NKJV) chief of the butlers (KJV)
Gen. 40:2 chief baker (Geneva, NKJV) chief of the bakers (KJV)
Gen. 40:23 Yet the chief butler did not remember (Geneva, NKJV)
           Yet did not the chief butler remember (KJV)
Gen. 41:10 angry (Geneva, NKJV) wroth (KJV)
Gen. 41:14 came to Pharaoh (Geneva, NKJV) came in unto Pharaoh (KJV)
Gen. 41:15 to Joseph (Geneva, NKJV) unto Joseph (KJV)
Gen. 41:18 in the meadow (Geneva, NKJV) in a meadow (KJV)
Gen. 41:23 sprang (Geneva, NKJV) sprung (KJV)
Gen. 41:25 Then Joseph (Geneva, NKJV) And Joseph (KJV)
Gen. 41:28 to Pharaoh (Geneva, NKJV) unto Pharaoh (KJV)
Gen. 41:39 to Joseph (Geneva, NKJV) unto Joseph (KJV)
Gen. 41:41 to Joseph (Geneva, NKJV) unto Joseph (KJV)
Gen. 41:42 garments (Geneva, NKJV) vestures (KJV)
Gen. 41:53 plenty (Geneva, NKJV) plenteousness (KJV)
Gen. 41:54 famine (Geneva, NKJV) dearth (KJV)
Gen. 41:55 Go to Joseph (Geneva, NKJV) Go unto Joseph (KJV)
Gen. 42:6 Now Joseph (Geneva, NKJV) And Joseph (KJV)
Gen. 42:12 But he (Geneva, NKJV) And he (KJV)
Gen. 42:18 Then Joseph (Geneva, NKJV) And Joseph (KJV)
Gen. 42:36 to them (Geneva, NKJV) unto them (KJV)
Gen. 42:37 Then Reuben (Geneva, NKJV) And Reuben (KJV)
Gen. 42:38 But he (Geneva, NKJV) And he (KJV)
Gen. 43:8 Then (Geneva, NKJV) And (KJV)
Gen. 43:8 to Israel (Geneva, NKJV) unto Israel (KJV)
Gen. 43:13 to the man (Geneva, NKJV) unto the man (KJV)
Gen. 43:16 to the steward (Geneva, NKJV) to the ruler (KJV)
Gen. 43:16 and kill meat (Geneva) and slay (KJV) and slaughter an animal (NKJV)
Gen. 43:23 to them (Geneva, NKJV) unto them (KJV)
Gen. 43:24 So the (Geneva, NKJV) And the (KJV)
Gen. 43:30 affection (Geneva) bowels (KJV) heart (NKJV)
Gen. 44:4 to his steward (Geneva, NKJV) unto his steward (KJV)
Gen. 44:7 do such a thing (Geneva, NKJV) do according to this thing (KJV)
Gen. 44:14 So Judah (Geneva, NKJV) And Judah (KJV)
Gen. 44:15 Know ye not (Geneva) Wot ye not (KJV) Did you not know (NKJV)
Gen. 44:27 Then (Geneva, NKJV) And (KJV)
Gen. 44:29 death (Geneva) mischief (KJV) calamity (NKJV)
Gen. 44:32 to my father (Geneva, NKJV) unto my father (KJV)
Gen. 45:3 Then Joseph (Geneva, NKJV) And Joseph (KJV)
Gen. 46:5 Then (Geneva, NKJV) And (KJV)
Gen. 46:27 seventy (Geneva, NKJV) threescore and ten (KJV)
Gen. 46:28 Then he (Geneva, NKJV) And he (KJV)
Gen. 46:29 to Goshen to meet Israel his father (Geneva, NKJV)
           to meet Israel his father to Goshen (KJV)

Gen. 46:31 Then Joseph (Geneva, NKJV) And Joseph (KJV)
Gen. 46:31 said to his (Geneva, NKJV) said unto his (KJV)
Gen. 47:3 Then Pharaoh (Geneva, NKJV) And Pharaoh (KJV)
Gen. 47:5 to Joseph (Geneva, NKJV) unto Joseph (KJV)
Gen. 47:13 Now (Geneva, NKJV) And (KJV)
Gen. 47:15 So when (Geneva, NKJV) And when (KJV)
Gen. 47:17 So they (Geneva, NKJV) And they (KJV)
Gen. 47:19 Why shall (Geneva, NKJV) Wherefore shall (KJV)
Gen 47:29 near (Geneva, NKJV) nigh (KJV)
Gen. 47:31 Then he (Geneva, NKJV) And he (KJV)
Gen. 48:3 Then (Geneva, NKJV) And (KJV)
Gen. 48:20 So he (Geneva, NKJV) And he (KJV)
Gen. 50:1 Then Joseph (Geneva, NKJV) And Joseph (KJV)
Gen. 50:3 seventy (Geneva, NKJV) threescore and ten (KJV)
Gen. 50:13 For his sons (Geneva, NKJV) And his sons (KJV)
Gen. 50:22 So Joseph (Geneva, NKJV) And Joseph (KJV)
Exod. 1:1 to Egypt (Geneva, NKJV) into Egypt (KJV)
Exod. 1:8 who (Geneva, NKJV) which (KJV)
Exod. 1:10 Come (Geneva, NKJV) Come on (KJV)
Exod. 2:3 But when (Geneva, NKJV) And when (KJV)
Exod. 2:5 Then the (Geneva, NKJV) And the (KJV)
Exod. 2:15 this matter (Geneva, NKJV) this thing (KJV)
Exod. 2:17 Then the (Geneva, NKJV) And the (KJV)
Exod. 3:5 Then (Geneva, NKJV) And (KJV)
Exod. 3:11 But Moses (Geneva, NKJV) And Moses (KJV)
Exod. 3:13 Then Moses (Geneva, NKJV) And Moses (KJV)
Exod. 3:22 shall ask (Geneva, NKJV) shall borrow (KJV)
Exod. 4:1 Then Moses (Geneva, NKJV) And Moses (KJV)
Exod. 4:13 But he (Geneva, NKJV) And he (KJV)
Exod. 4:20 Then Moses (Geneva, NKJV) And Moses (KJV)
Exod. 4:22 to Pharaoh (Geneva, NKJV) unto Pharaoh (KJV)
Exod. 5:19 diminish (Geneva, NKJV) minish (KJV)
Exod. 6:7 be your God (Geneva, NKJV) be to you a God (KJV)
Exod. 7:1 to Moses (Geneva, NKJV) unto Moses (KJV)
Exod. 7:15 Go unto (Geneva) Get thee unto (KJV) Go to (NKJV)
Exod. 7:15 meet him (Geneva) against he come (KJV) to meet him (NKJV)
Exod. 7:19 to Moses (Geneva, NKJV) unto Moses (KJV)
Exod. 7:19 over the waters (Geneva, NKJV) upon the waters (KJV)
Exod. 7:19 over their streams (Geneva, NKJV) upon their streams (KJV)
Exod. 7:19 over their rivers (Geneva, NKJV) upon their rivers (KJV)
Exod. 7:19 over their ponds (Geneva, NKJV) upon their ponds (KJV)
Exod. 7:19 over their pools (Geneva, NKJV) upon their pools (KJV)
Exod. 8:12 Then Moses (Geneva, NKJV) And Moses (KJV)
Exod. 8:12 concerning the frogs (Geneva, NKJV) because of the frogs (KJV)
Exod. 8:20 to Moses (Geneva, NKJV) unto Moses (KJV)
Exod. 8:25 Then Pharaoh (Geneva, NKJV) And Pharaoh (KJV)
Exod. 8:30 So Moses (Geneva, NKJV) And Moses (KJV)
Exod. 9:7 Then Pharaoh (Geneva, NKJV) And Pharaoh (KJV)
Exod. 9:8 to Moses (Geneva, NKJV) unto Moses (KJV)
Exod. 9:9 blisters (Geneva) blains (KJV) sores (NKJV)
Exod. 9:10 Then they (Geneva, NKJV) And they (KJV)
Exod. 9:10 blisters (Geneva) blains (KJV) sores (NKJV)
Exod. 9:22 to Moses (Geneva, NKJV) unto Moses (KJV)
Exod. 9:31 flax and the barley were (Geneva, NKJV) flax and the barley was (KJV)
Exod. 9:33 hands to the (Geneva, NKJV) hands unto the (KJV)
Exod. 9:34 thunder (Geneva, NKJV) thunders (KJV)

Exod. 9:35 So the heart (Geneva, NKJV) And the heart (KJV)
Exod. 10:2 know that I (Geneva, NKJV) know how that I (KJV)
Exod. 10:4 tomorrow (Geneva, NKJV) to morrow (KJV)
Exod. 10:8 So Moses (Geneva, NKJV) And Moses (KJV)
Exod. 10:8 to them (Geneva, NKJV) unto them (KJV)
Exod. 10:15 throughout all (Geneva, NKJV) through all (KJV)
Exod. 10:24 Then Pharaoh (Geneva, NKJV) And Pharaoh (KJV)
Exod. 10:24 Go (Geneva, NKJV) Go ye (KJV)
Exod. 11:6 Then there (Geneva, NKJV) And there (KJV)
Exod. 11:7 against none of the children of Israel shall (Geneva, NKJV)
          against any of the children of Israel shall not (KJV)
Exod. 11:10 So Moses (Geneva, NKJV) And Moses (KJV)
Exod. 12:1 to Moses (Geneva, NKJV) unto Moses (KJV)
Exod. 12:3 the tenth (Geneva, NKJV) the tenth *day* (KJV)
Exod. 12:35 asked (Geneva, NKJV) borrowed (KJV)
Exod. 12:37 Then the (Geneva, NKJV) And the (KJV)
Exod. 13:12 womb (Geneva, NKJV) matrix (KJV)
Exod. 13:13 among thy sons (Geneva) among thy children (KJV) among your sons (NKJV)
Exod. 13:15 womb (Geneva, NKJV) matrix (KJV)
Exod. 13:15 the firstborn of my sons (Geneva, NKJV) the firstborn of my children (KJV)
Exod. 13:20 So they (Geneva, NKJV) And they (KJV)
Exod. 13:20 camped (Geneva, NKJV) encamped (KJV)
Exod. 14:2 Speak to (Geneva, NKJV) Speak unto (KJV)
Exod. 14:2 camp (Geneva, NKJV) encamp (KJV)
Exod. 14:9 camping (Geneva, NKJV) encamping (KJV)
Exod. 14:13 to the people (Geneva, NKJV) unto the people (KJV)
Exod. 14:18 Then the (Geneva, NKJV) And the (KJV)
Exod. 14:24 Now (Geneva, NKJV) And (KJV)
Exod. 14:25 For he took (Geneva) And took (KJV) And He took (NKJV)
Exod. 14:26 Then the (Geneva, NKJV) And the (KJV)
Exod. 14:26 to Moses (Geneva, NKJV) unto Moses (KJV)
Exod. 15:27 seventy (Geneva, NKJV) threescore and ten (KJV)
Exod. 15:27 camped (Geneva, NKJV) encamped (KJV)
Exod. 16:1 came to (Geneva, NKJV) came unto (KJV)
Exod. 16:3 to them (Geneva, NKJV) unto them (KJV)
Exod. 16:3 brought us out into (Geneva, NKJV) brought us forth into (KJV)
Exod. 16:6 Then Moses (Geneva, NKJV) And Moses (KJV)
Exod. 16:16 in his tent (Geneva, NKJV) in his tents (KJV)
Exod. 16:18 did measure (Geneva) did mete (KJV) measured (NKJV)
Exod. 16:19 morning (Geneva, NKJV) the morning (KJV)
Exod. 16:20 morning (Geneva, NKJV) the morning (KJV)
Exod. 16:25 Then Moses (Geneva, NKJV) And Moses (KJV)
Exod. 16:32 hath commanded (Geneva) commandeth (KJV) has commanded (NKJV)
Exod. 16:33 to Aaron (Geneva, NKJV) unto Aaron (KJV)
Exod. 17:1 camped (Geneva, NKJV) pitched (KJV)
Exod. 17:2 contended (Geneva, NKJV) did chide (KJV)
Exod. 17:4 cried to (Geneva, NKJV) cried unto (KJV)
Exod. 17:7 contention (Geneva, NKJV) chiding (KJV)
Exod. 17:9 to Joshua (Geneva, NKJV) unto Joshua (KJV)
Exod. 17:14 to Moses (Geneva, NKJV) unto Moses (KJV)
Exod. 17:14 in the book (Geneva, NKJV) in a book (KJV)
Exod. 18:6 to Moses (Geneva, NKJV) unto Moses (KJV)
Exod. 18:12 Then Jethro (Geneva, NKJV) And Jethro (KJV)
Exod. 19:2 camped (Geneva, NKJV) had pitched (KJV)
Exod. 19:10 Go to (Geneva, NKJV) Go unto (KJV)
Exod. 19:16 the sound (Geneva, NKJV) the voice (KJV)

Exod. 19:17 brought the people (Geneva, NKJV) brought forth the people (KJV)
Exod. 20:11 and the earth (Geneva, NKJV) and earth (KJV)
Exod. 20:21 So the (Geneva, NKJV) And the (KJV)
Exod. 21:2 he shall serve six years (Geneva, NKJV) six years he shall serve (KJV)
Exod. 21:5 But if (Geneva, NKJV) And if (KJV)
Exod. 21:9 if he hath (Geneva) if he have (KJV) if he has (NKJV)
Exod. 21:9 the custom (Geneva, NKJV) the manner (KJV)
Exod. 21:11 paying no money (Geneva) without money (KJV) without *paying* money (NKJV)
Exod. 21:32 gore (Geneva) push (KJV) gores (NKJV)
Exod. 22:26 before the sun go down (Geneva) by that the sun goeth down (KJV) before the sun goes down (NKJV)
Exod. 22:27 garment (Geneva, NKJV) raiment (KJV)
Exod. 23:29 the beasts (Geneva, NKJV) the beast (KJV)
Exod. 24:1 Come up to (Geneva, NKJV) Come up unto (KJV)
Exod. 24:2 not come near (Geneva, NKJV) not come nigh (KJV)
Exod. 24:4 mountain (Geneva, NKJV) hill (KJV)
Exod. 24:12 mountain (Geneva, NKJV) mount (KJV)
Exod. 24:13 mountain (Geneva, NKJV) mount (KJV)
Exod. 24:15 Then Moses (Geneva, NKJV) And Moses (KJV)
Exod. 24:15 covered the mountain (Geneva, NKJV) countered the mount (KJV)
Exod. 24:17 mountain (Geneva, NKJV) mount (KJV)
Exod. 24:18 mountain (Geneva, NKJV) mount (KJV)
Exod. 25:1 Then the (Geneva, NKJV) And the (KJV)
Exod. 25:19 at the one end (Geneva, NKJV) on the one end (KJV)
Exod. 25:19 at the other end (Geneva, NKJV) on the other end (KJV)
Exod. 25:21 will give (Geneva, NKJV) shall give (KJV)
Exod. 26:25 So (Geneva, NKJV) And (KJV)
Exod. 26:28 through the (Geneva, NKJV) in the (KJV)
Exod. 28:8 And the embroidered (Geneva) And the curious (KJV) And the intricately woven (NKJV)
Exod. 28:29 So Aaron (Geneva, NKJV) And Aaron (KJV)
Exod. 28:38 So it (Geneva, NKJV) And it (KJV)
Exod. 29:16 kill the ram (Geneva, NKJV) slay the ram (KJV)
Exod. 29:30 That son (Geneva, NKJV) *And* that son (KJV)
Exod. 30:20 lest they die (Geneva, NKJV) that they die not (KJV)
Exod. 31:3 Spirit of God (Geneva, NKJV) spirit of God (KJV)
Exod. 31:10 garments of the ministration (Geneva) cloths of service (KJV) garments of Ministry (NKJV)
Exod. 32:1 know (Geneva, NKJV) wot (KJV)
Exod. 32:15 mountain (Geneva, NKJV) mount (KJV)
Exod. 32:18 victory (Geneva, NKJV) mastery (KJV)
Exod. 32:19 came near (Geneva, NKJV) came nigh (KJV)
Exod. 32:24 to them (Geneva, NKJV) unto them (KJV)
Exod. 32:33 to Moses (Geneva, NKJV) unto Moses (KJV)
Exod. 32:35 So the (Geneva, NKJV) And the (KJV)
Exod. 33:5 to Moses (Geneva, NKJV) unto Moses (KJV)
Exod. 33:6 So the (Geneva, NKJV) And the (KJV)
Exod. 33:12 Then Moses (Geneva, NKJV) And Moses (KJV)
Exod. 33:15 Then he (Geneva, NKJV) And he (KJV)
Exod. 33:21 the rock (Geneva, NKJV) a rock (KJV)
Exod. 33:22 cleft (Geneva, NKJV) clift (KJV)
Exod. 34:19 womb (Geneva, NKJV) matrix (KJV)
Exod. 34:28 So he (Geneva, NKJV) And he (KJV)
Exod. 34:30 come near him (Geneva, NKJV) come nigh him (KJV)
Exod. 34:32 came near (Geneva, NKJV) came nigh (KJV)
Exod. 35:1 Then Moses (Geneva, NKJV) And Moses (KJV)

Exod. 35:5 Take from (Geneva, NKJV) Take ye from (KJV)
Exod. 35:9 in the ephod (Geneva, NKJV) for the ephod (KJV)
Exod. 35:29 hearts (Geneva, NKJV) heart (KJV)
Exod. 36:6 a commandment (Geneva, NKJV) commandment (KJV)
Exod. 36:30 So there (Geneva, NKJV) And there (KJV)
Exod. 37:9 toward the mercyseat (Geneva, NKJV) to the mercy seatward (KJV)
Exod. 38:25 seventy and five (Geneva) threescore and fifteen (KJV) seventy-five (NKJV)
Exod. 39:1 garments (Geneva, NKJV) cloths (KJV)
Exod. 39:5 And the broidered (Geneva) And the curious (KJV) And the intricately woven (NKJV)
Exod. 39:7 had commanded (Geneva, NKJV) commanded (KJV)
Exod. 40:1 Then (Geneva, NKJV) And (KJV)
Exod. 40:34 the cloud (Geneva, NKJV) a cloud (KJV)
Lev. 1:1 Now (Geneva, NKJV) And (KJV)
Lev. 1:8 Then (Geneva, NKJV) And (KJV)
Lev. 1:9 he shall wash (Geneva, NKJV) shall he wash (KJV)
Lev. 2:2 burn it for a memorial (Geneva) burn the memorial of it (KJV)
          burn it *as* a memorial (NKJV)
Lev. 2:5 But if (Geneva, NKJV) And if (KJV)
Lev. 2:8 to the altar (Geneva, NKJV) unto the altar (KJV)
Lev. 3:1 male (Geneva, NKJV) a male (KJV)
Lev. 3:14 Then he (Geneva, NKJV) And he (KJV)
Lev. 4:3 offer (Geneva, NKJV) bring (KJV)
Lev. 4:17 in the blood (Geneva, NKJV) *in some* of the blood (KJV)
Lev. 4:26 for him concerning his sin (Geneva, NKJV) for him as concerning his sin (KJV)
Lev. 4:30 Then the priest (Geneva, NKJV) And the priest (KJV)
Lev. 6:2 that which was put to him of trust (Geneva) in fellowship (KJV) about a pledge (NKJV)
Lev. 6:2 robbery (Geneva, NKJV) thing taken away by violence (KJV)
Lev. 6:8 Then the (Geneva, NKJV) And the (KJV)
Lev. 6:30 But no (Geneva, NKJV) And no (KJV)
Lev. 8:15 and Moses (Geneva, NKJV) And he (KJV)
Lev. 8:16 Then he (Geneva, NKJV) And he (KJV)
Lev. 8:19 Moses killed it (Geneva, NKJV) he killed it (KJV)
Lev. 8:27 in Aaron's hands (Geneva, NKJV) upon Aaron's hands (KJV)
Lev. 9:8 killed the calf (Geneva, NKJV) slew the calf (KJV)
Lev. 10:3 come near (Geneva, NKJV) come nigh (KJV)
Lev. 10:14 they are (Geneva, NKJV) they be (KJV)
Lev. 10:30 So when Moses (Geneva, NKJV) And when Moses (KJV)
Lev. 11:16 ostrich (Geneva, NKJV) owl (KJV)
Lev. 11:16 the seameaw (Geneva) the cuckow (KJV) the seagull (NKJV)
Lev. 11:24 evening (Geneva, NKJV) even (KJV)
Lev. 12:6 to the priest (Geneva, NKJV) unto the priest (KJV)
Lev. 13:2 a swelling (Geneva, NKJV) a rising (KJV)
Lev. 13:3 on the sore (Geneva, NKJV) on the plague (KJV)
Lev. 13:4 But if the (Geneva, NKJV) If the (KJV)
Lev. 13:6 the sore (Geneva, NKJV) the plague (KJV)
Lev. 13:10 the swelling (Geneva, NKJV) the rising (KJV)
Lev. 13:16 to the priest (Geneva, NKJV) unto the priest (KJV)
Lev. 14:13 kill the lamb (Geneva, NKJV) slay the lamb (KJV)
Lev. 14:56 a swelling (Geneva, NKJV) a rising (KJV)
Lev. 17:2 to his sons (Geneva, NKJV) unto his sons (KJV)
Lev. 17:2 to all the children (Geneva, NKJV) unto all the children (KJV)
Lev. 18:22 with the male (Geneva) with mankind (KJV) with a male (NKJV)
Lev. 18:22 with a woman (Geneva, NKJV) with womankind (KJV)
Lev. 18:23 abomination (Geneva) confusion (KJV) perversion (NKJV)
Lev. 18:29 the persons (Geneva, NKJV) the souls (KJV)
Lev. 19:8 from his people (Geneva, NKJV) from among his people (KJV)

Lev. 19:9 ye shal (Geneva) thou shalt (KJV) you shall (NKJV)
Lev. 20:6 that person (Geneva, NKJV) that soul (KJV)
Lev. 20:13 male (Geneva, NKJV) mankind (KJV)
Lev. 21:3 is near (Geneva, NKJV) is nigh (KJV)
Lev. 21:7 divorced (Geneva, NKJV) put away (KJV)
Lev. 21:21 come near (Geneva, NKJV) come nigh (KJV)
Lev. 21:24 to all (Geneva, NKJV) unto all (KJV)
Lev. 22:3 that person (Geneva, NKJV) that soul (KJV)
Lev. 22:6 person (Geneva, NKJV) soul (KJV)
Lev. 22:12 holy offerings (Geneva, NKJV) holy things (KJV)
Lev. 22:18 to all (Geneva, NKJV) unto all (KJV)
Lev. 23:29 person (Geneva, NKJV) soul (KJV)
Lev. 23:30 person (Geneva, NKJV) soul (KJV)
Lev. 23:40 fruit (Geneva, NKJV) boughs (KJV)
Lev. 23:44 So Moses (Geneva, NKJV) And Moses (KJV)
Lev. 25:10 to all (Geneva, NKJV) unto all (KJV)
Lev. 25:42 brought out (Geneva, NKJV) brought forth out (KJV)
Lev. 26:14 obey me (Geneva) hearken unto me (KJV) obey Me (NKJV)
Lev. 26:18 obey me (Geneva) hearken unto me (KJV) obey Me (NKJV)
Lev. 26:27 obey me (Geneva) hearken unto me (KJV) obey Me (NKJV)
Lev. 27:13 valuation (Geneva, NKJV) estimation (KJV)
Lev. 27:14 shall dedicate (Geneva) shall sanctify (KJV) dedicates (NKJV)
Lev. 27:17 dedicate (Geneva) sanctify (KJV) dedicates (NKJV)
Lev. 27:18 dedicate (Geneva) sanctify (KJV) dedicates (NKJV)
Lev. 27:22 dedicate (Geneva) sanctify (KJV) dedicates (NKJV)
Lev. 27:25 valuation (Geneva) estimations (KJV) valuations (NKJV)
Lev. 27:26 firstborn (Geneva, NKJV) firstling (KJV)
Num. 1:3 and above (Geneva, NKJV) and upward (KJV)
Num. 1:50 of the Testimony (Geneva, NKJV) of testimony (KJV)
Num. 1:51 near (Geneva, NKJV) nigh (KJV)
Num. 1:52 armies (Geneva, NKJV) hosts (KJV)
Num. 1:53 of the Testimony (Geneva, NKJV) of testimony (KJV)
Num. 2:2 shall camp (Geneva, NKJV) shall pitch (KJV)
Num. 2:3 according to their armies (Geneva, NKJV) throughout their armies (KJV)
Num. 2:4 seventy and four (Geneva) threescore and fourteen (KJV) seventy-four (NKJV)
Num. 3:6 may serve him (Geneva, NKJV) may minister unto him (KJV)
Num. 3:10 near (Geneva, NKJV) nigh (KJV)
Num. 3:38 near (Geneva, NKJV) nigh (KJV)
Num. 3:41 firstborn of the cattle (Geneva) firstlings among the cattle (KJV) firstborn among the livestock (NKJV)
Num. 3:43 seventy and three (Geneva) threescore and thirteen (KJV) seventy-three (NKJV)
Num. 4:5 Aaron and his sons shall come (Geneva, NKJV) Aaron shall come, and his sons (KJV)
Num. 5:15 to the priest (Geneva, NKJV) unto the priest (KJV)
Num. 5:31 be free (Geneva, NKJV) be guiltless (KJV)
Num. 6:3 fresh grapes (Geneva, NKJV) moist grapes (KJV)
Num. 6:8 holy to (Geneva, NKJV) holy unto (KJV)
Num. 6:9 if any die (Geneva) is any man die (KJV) if anyone dies (NKJV)
Num. 6:27 So they (Geneva, NKJV) And they (KJV)
Num. 7:1 finished the setting up (Geneva) fully set up (KJV) finished setting up (NKJV)
Num. 7:2 Then the (Geneva, NKJV) That the (KJV)
Num. 7:6 So Moses (Geneva, NKJV) And Moses (KJV)
Num. 7:9 But to (Geneva, NKJV) But unto (KJV)
Num. 7:89 Moses went (Geneva, NKJV) Moses was gone (KJV)
Num. 8:7 water of purification (Geneva, NKJV) water of purifying (KJV)
Num. 8:11 a shake offering (Geneva) an offering (KJV) a wave offering (NKJV)
Num. 8:13 a shake offering (Geneva) an offering (KJV) a wave offering (NKJV)

Num. 8:13 to the (Geneva, NKJV) unto the (KJV)
Num. 8:19 come near (Geneva, NKJV) come nigh (KJV)
Num. 8:21 a shake offering (Geneva) an offering (KJV) a wave offering (NKJV)
Num. 9:10 a corpse (Geneva, NKJV) a dead body (KJV)
Num. 10:25 according to their armies (Geneva, NKJV) throughout their hosts (KJV)
Num. 10:29 Reuel (Geneva, NKJV) Raguel (KJV)
Num. 10:33 So they (Geneva, NKJV) And they (KJV)
Num. 11:2 Then the people (Geneva, NKJV) And the people (KJV)
Num. 11:24 So Moses (Geneva, NKJV) And Moses (KJV)
Num. 11:25 Then the (Geneva, NKJV) And the (KJV)
Num. 12:4 said (Geneva, NKJV) spake (KJV)
Num. 12:5 Then the (Geneva, NKJV) And the (KJV)
Num. 12:8 words (Geneva) speeches (KJV) sayings (NKJV)
Num. 12:15 So Miriam (Geneva, NKJV) And Miriam (KJV)
Num. 13:23 Then thy came (Geneva, NKJV) And they came (KJV)
Num. 13:30 Then Caleb (Geneva, NKJV) And Caleb (KJV)
Num. 13:33 like grasshoppers (Geneva, NKJV) as grasshoppers (KJV)
Num. 14:39 Then Moses (Geneva, NKJV) And Moses (KJV)
Num. 15:30 But the person (Geneva, NKJV) But the soul (KJV)
Num. 15:35 Then the (Geneva, NKJV) And the (KJV)
Num. 16:5 to Korah (Geneva, NKJV) unto Korah (KJV)
Num. 16:15 Then Moses (Geneva, NKJV) And Moses (KJV)
Num. 16:15 very angry (Geneva, NKJV) very wroth (KJV)
Num. 16:18 So (Geneva, NKJV) And (KJV)
Num. 16:25 Then Moses (Geneva, NKJV) And Moses (KJV)
Num. 16:33 So they (Geneva, NKJV) They (KJV)
Num. 16:43 Then Moses and Aaron (Geneva, NKJV) And Moses and Aaron (KJV)
Num. 16:47 Then Aaron (Geneva, NKJV) And Aaron (KJV)
Num. 17:9 Then Moses (Geneva, NKJV) And Moses (KJV)
Num. 18:3 near (Geneva, NKJV) nigh (KJV)
Num. 18:4 near (Geneva, NKJV) nigh (KJV)
Num. 18:7 near (Geneva, NKJV) nigh (KJV)
Num. 18:15 firstborn of unclean (Geneva, NKJV) firstling of unclean (KJV)
Num. 18:17 firstborn of a cow (Geneva, NKJV) firstling of a cow (KJV)
Num. 18:17 firstborn of a sheep (Geneva, NKJV) firstling of a sheep (KJV)
Num. 18:17 firstborn of a goat (Geneva, NKJV) firstling of a goat (KJV)
Num. 18:22 come near (Geneva, NKJV) come nigh (KJV)
Num. 18:24 For the tithes (Geneva, NKJV) But the tithes (KJV)
Num. 18:24 for an inheritance (Geneva) to inherit (KJV) as an inheritance (NKJV)
Num. 20:4 Why (Geneva, NKJV) And why (KJV)
Num. 20:10 bring (Geneva, NKJV) fetch (KJV)
Num. 21:9 So Moses (Geneva, NKJV) And Moses (KJV)
Num. 21:21 Then Israel (Geneva, NKJV) And Israel (KJV)
Num. 21:23 But Sihon (Geneva, NKJV) And Sihon (KJV)
Num. 21:34 Then the (Geneva, NKJV) And the (KJV)
Num. 22:6 know (Geneva, NKJV) wot (KJV)
Num. 22:9 Then God (Geneva, NKJV) And God (KJV)
Num. 22:21 So Balaam (Geneva, NKJV) And Balaam (KJV)
Num. 22:26 Then the (Geneva, NKJV) And the (KJV)
Num. 22:28 Then the (Geneva, NKJV) And the (KJV)
Num. 22:37 Then Balak (Geneva, NKJV) And Balak (KJV)
Num. 22:39 So Balaam (Geneva, NKJV) And Balaam (KJV)
Num. 22:40 Then Balak (Geneva, NKJV) And Balak (KJV)
Num. 23:1 bullocks (Geneva) oxen (KJV) bulls (NKJV)
Num. 23:3 Then Balaam (Geneva, NKJV) And Balaam (KJV)
Num. 23:6 So (Geneva, NKJV) And (KJV)

Num. 23:11 Then Balak (Geneva, NKJV) And Balak (KJV)
Num. 23:23 sorcery (Geneva, NKJV) enchantment (KJV)
Num. 23:25 Then Balak (Geneva, NKJV) And Balak (KJV)
Num. 23:28 So Balak (Geneva, NKJV) And Balak (KJV)
Num. 23:29 Then Balaam (Geneva, NKJV) And Balaam (KJV)
Num. 24:8 him out (Geneva, NKJV) him forth out (KJV)
Num. 24:10 Then (Geneva, NKJV) And (KJV)
Num. 24:17 near (Geneva, NKJV) nigh (KJV)
Num. 24:17 all the sons (Geneva, NKJV) all the children (KJV)
Num. 24:21 the rock (Geneva, NKJV) a rock (KJV)
Num. 25:1 Now (Geneva, NKJV) And (KJV)
Num. 25:2 people ate (Geneva, NKJV) people did eat (KJV)
Num. 25:10 Then (Geneva, NKJV) And (KJV)
Num. 26:3 So Moses (Geneva, NKJV) And Moses (KJV)
Num. 26:5 firstborn (Geneva, NKJV) eldest son (KJV)
Num. 26:18 sons of Gad (Geneva, NKJV) children of Gad (KJV)
Num. 26:22 seventy and six (Geneva) threescore and sixteen (KJV) seventy-six (NKJV)
Num. 26:26 The sons of Zebulun (Geneva, NKJV) *Of* the sons of Zebulun (KJV)
Num. 26:29 The sons of Manasseh (Geneva, NKJV) Of the sons of Manasseh (KJV)
Num. 26:31 Of Asriel (Geneva) And *of* Asriel (KJV) *of* Asriel (NKJV)
Num. 26:32 Of Shemida (Geneva) And *of* Shemida (KJV) *of* Shemida (NKJV)
Num. 26:44 sons of Asher (Geneva, NKJV) children of Asher (KJV)
Num. 27:15 Then Moses (Geneva, NKJV) And Moses (KJV)
Num. 27:17 Who may (Geneva, NKJV) Which may (KJV)
Num. 27:22 So Moses (Geneva, NKJV) And Moses (KJV)
Num. 28:12 of fine flour (Geneva, NKJV) of flour (KJV)
Num. 28:13 of fine flour (Geneva, NKJV) of flour (KJV)
Num. 29:15 each of the fourteen lambs (Geneva, NKJV)
          each lamb of the fourteen lambs (KJV)
Num. 31:3 to the people (Geneva, NKJV) unto the people (KJV)
Num. 31:14 angry (Geneva, NKJV) wroth (KJV)
Num. 31:20 garment (Geneva, NKJV) raiment (KJV)
Num. 31:33 seventy and two (Geneva) threescore and twelve (KJV) seventy-two (NKJV)
Num. 31:37 seventy and five (Geneva) threescore and fifteen (KJV) seventy-five (NKJV)
Num. 32:12 Except (Geneva) Save (KJV) except (NKJV)
Num. 32:33 So Moses (Geneva, NKJV) And Moses (KJV)
Num. 33:9 seventy (Geneva, NKJV) threescore and ten (KJV)
Deut. 1:4 Ashtaroth (Geneva, NKJV) Astaroth (KJV)
Deut. 1:7 in the mountain (Geneva) in the hills (KJV) in the mountains (NKJV)
Deut. 1:12 can I alone bear (Geneva, NKJV) can I myself alone bear (KJV)
Deut. 1:28 hearts (Geneva, NKJV) heart (KJV)
Deut. 1:30 God, who (Geneva, NKJV) God which (KJV)
Deut. 1:32 Yet for all this (Geneva) Yet in this thing (KJV) Yet, for all that (NKJV)
Deut. 2:9 Then the (Geneva, NKJV) And the (KJV)
Deut. 2:11 They also were (Geneva) Which also were (KJV) They were also (NKJV)
Deut. 2:19 near (Geneva, NKJV) nigh (KJV)
Deut. 2:24 Rise (Geneva, NKJV) Rise ye (KJV)
Deut. 3:26 angry (Geneva, NKJV) wroth (KJV)
Deut. 4:1 to do (Geneva) for to do (KJV) to observe (NKJV)
Deut. 4:7 near (Geneva, NKJV) nigh (KJV)
Deut. 4:11 Then (Geneva, NKJV) And (KJV)
Deut. 4:11 you (Geneva, NKJV) ye (KJV)
Deut. 4:15 Take (Geneva, NKJV) Take ye (KJV)
Deut. 4:41 separated (Geneva) severed (KJV) set apart (NKJV)
Deut. 5:5 to declare (Geneva, NKJV) to shew (KJV)
Deut. 5:23 to me (Geneva, NKJV) unto me (KJV)

Deut. 7:25 covet (Geneva, NKJV) desire (KJV)
Deut. 8:5 know (Geneva, NKJV) consider (KJV)
Deut. 8:9 scarcity (Geneva, NKJV) scarceness (KJV)
Deut. 9:10 Then the (Geneva, NKJV) And the (KJV)
Deut. 10:22 seventy (Geneva, NKJV) threescore and ten (KJV)
Deut. 11:3 signs (Geneva, NKJV) miracles (KJV)
Deut. 11:25 No man shall (Geneva, NKJV) There shall no man (KJV)
Deut. 11:30 the plain (Geneva, NKJV) the champaign (KJV)
Deut. 12:6 firstborn (Geneva, NKJV) firstlings (KJV)
Deut. 12:15 heart desireth (Geneva) soul lusteth after (KJV) heart desires (NKJV)
Deut. 12:17 firstborn (Geneva, NKJV) firstlings (KJV)
Deut. 12:20 heart desireth (Geneva) soul lusteth after (KJV) heart desires (NKJV)
Deut. 12:21 heart desireth (Geneva) soul lusteth after (KJV) heart desires (NKJV)
Deut. 13:5 But that prophet (Geneva, NKJV) And that prophet (KJV)
Deut. 13:7 near (Geneva, NKJV) nigh (KJV)
Deut. 13:13 wicked men (Geneva) *Certain* men, the children of Belial (KJV) Corrupt men (NKJV)
Deut. 14:15 ostrich (Geneva, NKJV) owl (KJV)
Deut. 14:15 seameaw (Geneva) cuckow (KJV) sea gull (NKJV)
Deut. 14:23 firstborn (Geneva, NKJV) firstlings (KJV)
Deut. 14:26 heart desireth (Geneva) soul lusteth after (KJV) heart desires (NKJV)
Deut. 14:26 or sheep (Geneva, NKJV) or for sheep (KJV)
Deut. 14:26 heart desireth (Geneva) soul desireth (KJV) heart desires (NKJV)
Deut. 15:9 wicked thought in thine heart (Geneva) thought in thy wicked heart (KJV) wicked thought in your heart (NKJV)
Deut. 15:19 firstborn males (Geneva, NKJV) firstling males (KJV)
Deut. 15:19 shear the firstborn (Geneva, NKJV) shear the firstling (KJV)
Deut. 16:22 piller (Geneva) image (KJV) sacred pillar (NKJV)
Deut. 19:3 manslayer (Geneva, NKJV) slayer (KJV)
Deut. 19:4 manslayer (Geneva, NKJV) slayer (KJV)
Deut. 19:5 striketh (Geneva) fetcheth a stroke (KJV) swings a stroke (NKJV)
Deut. 19:6 manslayer (Geneva, NKJV) slayer (KJV)
Deut. 19:9 besides (Geneva, NKJV) beside (KJV)
Deut. 20:8 like his heart (Geneva, NKJV) as his heart (KJV)
Deut. 20:10 near (Geneva, NKJV) nigh (KJV)
Deut. 20:19 smiting an axe (Geneva) forcing an axe (KJV) wielding an ax (NKJV)
Deut. 21:1 is not (Geneva, NKJV) be not (KJV)
Deut. 21:3 put to labour (Geneva) wrought with (KJV) worked (NKJV)
Deut. 21:22 is put (Geneva, NKJV) be to be put (KJV)
Deut. 22:2 near (Geneva, NKJV) nigh (KJV)
Deut. 22:9 divers kinds of (Geneva) divers (KJV) different kinds of (NKJV)
Deut. 22:18 Then (Geneva, NKJV) And (KJV)
Deut. 22:30 uncover (Geneva, NKJV) discover (KJV)
Deut. 23:22 abstainest (Geneva) shall forbear (KJV) abstain (NKJV)
Deut. 25:17 out of Egypt (Geneva, NKJV) forth out of Egypt (KJV)
Deut. 26:1 come into (Geneva, NKJV) come in unto (KJV)
Deut. 26:4 Then (Geneva, NKJV) And (KJV)
Deut. 26:5 answer and say (Geneva, NKJV) speak and say (KJV)
Deut. 26:8 us out of Egypt (Geneva, NKJV) us forth out of Egypt (KJV)
Deut. 26:18 precious (Geneva) peculiar (KJV) special (NKJV)
Deut. 27:15 carved (Geneva, NKJV) graven (KJV)
Deut. 28:1 obey (Geneva, NKJV) hearken (KJV)
Deut. 28:2 obey (Geneva, NKJV) hearken (KJV)
Deut. 28:10 Then (Geneva, NKJV) And (KJV)
Deut. 28:15 obey (Geneva, NKJV) hearken (KJV)
Deut. 28:40 olives shall fall (Geneva) olive shall cast *his fruit* (KJV) olives shall drop off (NKJV)
Deut. 28:45 obeyedst not (Geneva) hearkenedst not (KJV) did not obey (NKJV)

Deut. 28:48 in need of all things (Geneva, NKJV) in want of all things (KJV)
Deut. 28:56 venture (Geneva, NKJV) adventure (KJV)
Deut. 28:67 were evening (Geneva, NKJV) were even (KJV)
Deut. 28:67 at evening (Geneva, NKJV) at even (KJV)
Deut. 28:68 I said (Geneva, NKJV) I spake (KJV)
Deut. 29:7 Sihon king (Geneva, NKJV) Sihon the king (KJV)
Deut. 29:7 Og king (Geneva, NKJV) Og the king (KJV)
Deut. 29:25 out of the land (Geneva, NKJV) forth out of the land (KJV)
Deut. 30:14 very near (Geneva, NKJV) very nigh (KJV)
Deut. 30:15 life and good, death and evil (Geneva, NKJV) life and good, and death and evil (KJV)
Deut. 30:18 pronounce (Geneva) denounce (KJV) announce (NKJV)
Deut. 31:1 Then Moses (Geneva, NKJV) And Moses (KJV)
Deut. 31:7 called Joshua (Geneva, NKJV) called unto Joshua (KJV)
Deut. 31:13 known it (Geneva, NKJV) know *any thing* (KJV)
Deut. 31:14 Then (Geneva, NKJV) And (KJV)
Deut. 31:14 So Moses (Geneva, NKJV) And Moses (KJV)
Deut. 32:19 provocation (Geneva, NKJV) provoking (KJV)
Josh. 2:10 you came (Geneva, NKJV) ye came (KJV)
Josh. 2:10 you did (Geneva, NKJV) ye did (KJV)
Josh. 2:21 cord (Geneva, NKJV) line (KJV)
Josh. 2:22 departed (Geneva, NKJV) went (KJV)
Josh. 3:1 Then Joshua (Geneva, NKJV) And Joshua (KJV)
Josh. 3:5 tomorrow (Geneva, NKJV) to morrow (KJV)
Josh. 3:15 brink (Geneva) brim (KJV) edge (NKJV)
Josh. 4:3 where you (Geneva, NKJV) where ye (KJV)
Josh. 4:10 So the (Geneva, NKJV) For the (KJV)
Josh. 5:3 circumcised the sons of Israel (Geneva, NKJV) circumcised the children of Israel (KJV)
Josh. 5:5 For all (Geneva, NKJV) Now all (KJV)
Josh. 5:7 their sons (Geneva, NKJV) their children (KJV)
Josh. 6:6 Then Joshua (Geneva, NKJV) And Joshua (KJV)
Josh. 6:10 Now Joshua (Geneva, NKJV) And Joshua (KJV)
Josh. 7:6 Then Joshua (Geneva, NKJV) And Joshua (KJV)
Josh. 8:7 Then you (Geneva, NKJV) Then ye (KJV)
Josh. 8:11 near (Geneva, NKJV) nigh (KJV)
Josh. 8:18 Then (Geneva, NKJV) And (KJV)
Josh. 8:29 evening (Geneva, NKJV) eventide (KJV)
Josh. 8:31 had commanded (Geneva, NKJV) commanded (KJV)
Josh. 8:35 had commanded (Geneva, NKJV) commanded (KJV)
Josh. 9:3 But (Geneva, NKJV) And (KJV)
Josh. 9:4 craftily (Geneva, NKJV) wilily (KJV)
Josh. 9:7 Then the men (Geneva, NKJV) And the men (KJV)
Josh. 9:9 his fame (Geneva) the fame of him (KJV) His fame (NKJV)
Josh. 9:15 So Joshua (Geneva, NKJV) And Joshua (KJV)
Josh. 9:19 Then all (Geneva, NKJV) But all (KJV)
Josh. 9:24 for our lives (Geneva, NKJV) of our lives (KJV)
Josh. 10:5 *and* the king of Eglon (Geneva, NKJV) the king of Eglon (KJV)
Josh. 10:23 brought out (Geneva, NKJV) brought forth (KJV)
Josh. 11:4 many people (Geneva, NKJV) much people (KJV)
Josh. 11:11 all the persons (Geneva) all the souls (KJV) all the people (NKJV)
Josh. 11:12 So all (Geneva, NKJV) And all (KJV)
Josh. 11:12 had commanded (Geneva, NKJV) commanded (KJV)
Josh. 11:15 had commanded Moses (Geneva, NKJV) commanded Moses (KJV)
Josh. 11:16 low country (Geneva) valley (KJV) lowland (NKJV)
Josh. 11:20 had commanded Moses (Geneva, NKJV) commanded Moses (KJV)
Josh. 12:8 in the hillsides (Geneva) in the springs (KJV) in the slopes (NKJV)
Josh. 13:2 regions (Geneva) borders (KJV) territory (NKJV)

Josh. 13:5 to Hamath (Geneva, NKJV) into Hamath (KJV)
Josh. 13:6 mountains (Geneva, NKJV) hill country (KJV)
Josh. 13:23 according to their families (Geneva, NKJV) after their families (KJV)
Josh. 13:24 Also Moses (Geneva) And Moses (KJV) Moses also (NKJV)
Josh. 13:29 Also Moses (Geneva) And Moses (KJV) Moses also (NKJV)
Josh. 13:29 according to (Geneva, NKJV) by (KJV)
Josh. 14:5 had commanded (Geneva, NKJV) commanded (KJV)
Josh. 15:10 Then (Geneva, NKJV) And (KJV)
Josh. 15:13 Kiriath-arba (Geneva) the city of Arba (KJV) Kiriath Arba (NKJV)
Josh. 15:57 Kain (Geneva, NKJV) Cain (KJV)
Josh. 17:9 border (Geneva, NKJV) coast (KJV)
Josh. 17:9 border of Manasseh (Geneva, NKJV) coast of Manasseh (KJV)
Josh. 17:14 Then the (Geneva, NKJV) And the (KJV)
Josh. 17:16 mountain (Geneva) hill (KJV) mountain country (NKJV)
Josh. 18:8 Then the men (Geneva, NKJV) And the men (KJV)
Josh. 18:9 So the men (Geneva, NKJV) And the men (KJV)
Josh. 18:10 Then Joshua (Geneva, NKJV) And Joshua (KJV)
Josh. 19:1 came out (Geneva, NKJV) came forth (KJV)
Josh. 19:17 The fourth (Geneva, NKJV) *And* the fourth (KJV)
Josh. 19:28 Ebron (Geneva, NKJV) Hebron (KJV)
Josh. 19:29 border turneth (Geneva) coast turneth (KJV) border turned (NKJV)
Josh. 19:40 The seventh (Geneva, NKJV) *And* the seventh (KJV)
Josh. 21:3 So the (Geneva, NKJV) And the (KJV)
Josh. 21:7 according to their (Geneva, NKJV) by their (KJV)
Josh. 21:8 had commanded (Geneva, NKJV) commanded (KJV)
Josh. 21:11 Kiriath-arba (Geneva) the city of Arba (KJV) Kiriath Arba (NKJV)
Josh. 21:11 mountain (Geneva) hill *country* (KJV) mountains (NKJV)
Josh. 21:3 So the children (Geneva, NKJV) And the children (KJV)
Josh. 21:43 So the (Geneva, NKJV) And the (KJV)
Josh. 21:43 had sworn (Geneva, NKJV) sware (KJV)
Josh. 22:9 So the (Geneva, NKJV) And the (KJV)
Josh. 22:13 Then the (Geneva, NKJV) And the (KJV)
Josh. 23:1 Joshua was old (Geneva, NKJV) Joshua waxed old (KJV)
Josh. 23:13 for certain (Geneva, NKJV) for a certainty (KJV)
Jud. 1:4 Then Judah (Geneva, NKJV) And Judah (KJV)
Jud. 1:7 Seventy (Geneva, NKJV) Threescore and ten (KJV)
Jud. 1:9 the low country (Geneva) the valley (KJV) the lowland (NKJV)
Jud. 1:20 Moses had said (Geneva, NKJV) Moses said (KJV)
Jud. 1:21 But the (Geneva, NKJV) And the (KJV)
Jud. 2:2 covenant (Geneva, NKJV) league (KJV)
Jud. 2:11 Then the (Geneva, NKJV) And the (KJV)
Jud. 2:23 immediately (Geneva, NKJV) hastily (KJV)
Jud. 3:4 obey (Geneva, NKJV) hearken (KJV)
Jud. 3:5 the Hittites (Geneva, NKJV) Hittites (KJV)
Jud. 3:7 So the (Geneva, NKJV) And the (KJV)
Jud. 3:11 So the land (Geneva, NKJV) And the land (KJV)
Jud. 3:25 the key (Geneva, NKJV) a key (KJV)
Jud. 4:6 Then she (Geneva, NKJV) And she (KJV)
Jud. 4:14 Then Deborah (Geneva, NKJV) And Deborah (KJV)
Jud. 5:5 before (Geneva, NKJV) from before (KJV)
Jud. 5:12 sing a song (Geneva, NKJV) utter a song (KJV)
Jud. 5:21 hast marched (Geneva) hast trodden down (KJV) march on (NKJV)
Jud. 6:10 you have not (Geneva, NKJV) ye have not (KJV)
Jud. 6:20 bread (Geneva, NKJV) cakes (KJV)
Jud. 7:7 Then the (Geneva, NKJV) And the (KJV)
Jud. 8:14 seventy and seven (Geneva) threescore and seventeen (KJV)

seventy-seven (NKJV)
Jud. 8:29 Then Jerubbaal (Geneva, NKJV) And Jerubbaal (KJV)
Jud. 8:30 seventy (Geneva, NKJV) threescore and ten (KJV)
Jud. 9:1 Then Abimelech (Geneva, NKJV) And Abimelech (KJV)
Jud. 9:2 in the audience (Geneva) in the ears (KJV) in the hearing (NKJV)
Jud. 9:2 seventy (Geneva, NKJV) threescore and ten (KJV)
Jud. 9:3 in the audience (Geneva) in the ears (KJV) in the hearing (NKJV)
Jud. 9:4 seventy (Geneva, NKJV) threescore and ten (KJV)
Jud. 9:5 seventy (Geneva, NKJV) threescore and ten (KJV)
Jud. 9:7 you men (Geneva, NKJV) ye men (KJV)
Jud. 9:8 forth to anoint (Geneva, NKJV) forth *on a time* to anoint (KJV)
Jud. 9:10 Then the trees (Geneva, NKJV) And the trees (KJV)
Jud. 9:13 But the vine (Geneva, NKJV) And the vine (KJV)
Jud. 9:18 seventy (Geneva, NKJV) threescore and ten (KJV)
Jud. 9:24 seventy (Geneva, NKJV) threescore and ten (KJV)
Jud. 9:34 So Abimelech (Geneva, NKJV) And Abimelech (KJV)
Jud. 9:36 tops of the mountains (Geneva, NKJV) top of the mountains (KJV)
Jud. 9:53 But a certain (Geneva, NKJV) And a certain (KJV)
Jud. 10:1 After Abimelech (Geneva, NKJV) And after Abimelech (KJV)
Jud. 11:10 said to (Geneva, NKJV) said unto (KJV)
Jud. 11:19 our place (Geneva, NKJV) my place (KJV)
Jud. 11:25 far better (Geneva) any thing better (KJV) any better (NKJV)
Jud. 12:3 So when (Geneva) And when (KJV)
Jud. 12:10 Then Ibzan died (Geneva, NKJV) Then died Ibzan (KJV)
Jud. 12:14 seventy (Geneva, NKJV) threescore and ten (KJV)
Jud. 13:8 prayed to (Geneva, NKJV) intreated (KJV)
Jud. 14:1 Now Samson (Geneva, NKJV) And Samson (KJV)
Jud. 14:12 Then Samson (Geneva, NKJV) And Samson (KJV)
Jud. 15:8 So he (Geneva, NKJV) And he (KJV)
Jud. 15:14 to Lehi (Geneva, NKJV) unto Lehi (KJV)
Jud. 15:14 from his hands (Geneva, NKJV) from off his hands (KJV)
Jud. 15:16 Then Samson (Geneva, NKJV) And Samson (KJV)
Jud. 16:7 cords (Geneva) withs (KJV) bowstrings (NKJV)
Jud. 16:13 to Samson (Geneva, NKJV) unto Samson (KJV)
Jud. 16:14 he awoke (Geneva, NKJV) he awaked (KJV)
Jud. 16:26 Then Samson (Geneva, NKJV) And Samson (KJV)
Jud. 16:28 Then Samson (Geneva, NKJV) And Samson (KJV)
Jud. 16:31 sepulchre (Geneva) buryingplace (KJV) tomb (NKJV)
Jud. 18:10 lack nothing (Geneva) no want (KJV) no lack (NKJV)
Jud. 19:4 young woman's father (Geneva, NKJV) damsel's father (KJV)
Jud. 19:5 young woman's father (Geneva, NKJV) damsel's father (KJV)
Jud. 19:6 young woman's father (Geneva, NKJV) damsel's father (KJV)
Jud. 19:9 young woman's father (Geneva, NKJV) damsel's father (KJV)
Jud. 19:21 fodder (Geneva, NKJV) provender (KJV)
Jud. 19:22 wicked men (Geneva) sons of Belial (KJV) perverted men (NKJV)
Jud. 19:24 virgin (Geneva, NKJV) maiden (KJV)
Jud. 19:30 consult (Geneva) take advice (KJV) take counsel (NKJV)
Jud. 20:13 wicked men (Geneva) men, the children of Belial (KJV) perverted men (NKJV)
Jud. 20:21 came out (Geneva, NKJV) came forth out (KJV)
Jud. 20:23 evening (Geneva, NKJV) even (KJV)
Jud. 20:26 evening (Geneva, NKJV) even (KJV)
Jud. 21:6 were sorry (Geneva) repented (KJV) grieved (NKJV)
Jud. 21:10 most valiant (Geneva, NKJV) valiantest (KJV)
Jud. 21:13 Then the (Geneva, NKJV) And the (KJV)
Jud. 21:24 So the (Geneva, NKJV) And the (KJV)
Ruth 1:3 Then Elimelech (Geneva, NKJV) And Elimelech (KJV)

Ruth 1:6 Moab that the (Geneva, NKJV) Moab how that the (KJV)
Ruth 1:9 you may (Geneva, NKJV) ye may (KJV)
Ruth 1:11 But Naomi (Geneva, NKJV) And Naomi (KJV)
Ruth 1:14 Then they (Geneva, NKJV) And they (KJV)
Ruth 2:2 find favour (Geneva) find grace (KJV) find favor (NKJV)
Ruth 2:3 family (Geneva, NKJV) kindred (KJV)
Ruth 2:10 favour (Geneva) grace (KJV) favor (NKJV)
Ruth 2:17 evening (Geneva, NKJV) even (KJV)
Ruth 3:6 So she (Geneva, NKJV) And she (KJV)
Ruth 3:10 Then (Geneva, NKJV) And (KJV)
Ruth 3:13 the duty (Geneva, NKJV) the part (KJV)
Ruth 3:18 the matter this day (Geneva, NKJV) the thing this day (KJV)
1 Sam. 1:16 a wicked woman (Geneva, NKJV) a daughter of Belial (KJV)
1 Sam. 1:19 Then they (Geneva, NKJV) And they (KJV)
1 Sam. 1:20 Hannah conceived (Geneva, NKJV) Hannah had conceived (KJV)
1 Sam. 1:23 best (Geneva, NKJV) good (KJV)
1 Sam. 2:2 besides (Geneva, NKJV) beside (KJV)
1 Sam. 2:12 wicked men (Geneva) sons of Belial (KJV) corrupt (NKJV)
1 Sam. 2:13 was seething (Geneva) was in seething (KJV) was boiling (NKJV)
1 Sam. 3:1 Now (Geneva, NKJV) And (KJV)
1 Sam. 3:8 Then Eli perceived (Geneva, NKJV) And Eli perceived (KJV)
1 Sam. 3:11 Then the (Geneva, NKJV) And the (KJV)
1 Sam. 3:20 from Dan to (Geneva, NKJV) from Dan even to (KJV)
1 Sam. 4:11 died (Geneva, NKJV) were slain (KJV)
1 Sam. 5:1 Then the (Geneva, NKJV) And the (KJV)
1 Sam. 6:3 If you send (Geneva, NKJV) If ye send (KJV)
1 Sam. 6:8 Then take (Geneva, NKJV) And take (KJV)
1 Sam. 6:11 they set the ark (Geneva, NKJV) they laid the ark (KJV)
1 Sam. 6:21 take it up (Geneva, NKJV) fetch it up (KJV)
1 Sam. 7:1 Then the men (Geneva, NKJV) And the men (KJV)
1 Sam. 7:1 took (Geneva, NKJV) fetched (KJV)
1 Sam. 7:3 Then Samuel (Geneva, NKJV) And Samuel (KJV)
1 Sam. 7:14 to Gath (Geneva, NKJV) unto Gath (KJV)
1 Sam. 8:20 So Samuel (Geneva, NKJV) And Samuel (KJV)
1 Sam. 9:4 So he (Geneva, NKJV) And he (KJV)
1 Sam. 9:5 When they (Geneva, NKJV) *And* when they (KJV)
1 Sam. 10:6 Then the Spirit (Geneva, NKJV) And the Spirit (KJV)
1 Sam. 10:23 brought him (Geneva, NKJV) fetched him (KJV)
1 Sam. 10:27 wicked men (Geneva) children of Belial (KJV) rebels (NKJV)
1 Sam. 11:12 Then the people (Geneva, NKJV) And the people (KJV)
1 Sam. 11:15 So all (Geneva, NKJV) And all (KJV)
1 Sam. 13:20 mattock (Geneva, NKJV) coulter (KJV)
1 Sam. 13:21 shares (Geneva) mattocks (KJV) plowshares (NKJV)
1 Sam. 13:21 mattocks (Geneva, NKJV) coulters (KJV)
1 Sam. 14:8 shew (Geneva) discover (KJV) show (NKJV)
1 Sam. 14:11 shewed themselves (Geneva) discovered themselves (KJV) showed themselves (NKJV)
1 Sam. 15:27 lap of his coat (Geneva) skirt of his mantle (KJV) edge of his robe (NKJV)
1 Sam. 17:2 in battle array (Geneva, NKJV) the battle in array (KJV)
1 Sam. 17:48 near (Geneva, NKJV) nigh (KJV)
1 Sam. 17:55 When Saul (Geneva, NKJV) And when Saul (KJV)
1 Sam. 17:56 young man (Geneva, NKJV) stripling (KJV)
1 Sam. 18:10 a spear (Geneva, NKJV) a javelin (KJV)
1 Sam. 18:11 the spear (Geneva, NKJV) the javelin (KJV)
1 Sam. 19:10 spear (Geneva, NKJV) javelin (KJV)
1 Sam. 19:13 head (Geneva, NKJV) bolster (KJV)

1 Sam. 19:16 head (Geneva, NKJV) bolster (KJV)
1 Sam. 20:3 again (Geneva, NKJV) moreover (KJV)
1 Sam. 20:7 angry (Geneva, NKJV) wroth (KJV)
1 Sam. 20:11 to David (Geneva, NKJV) unto David (KJV)
1 Sam. 20:12 Then Jonathan (Geneva, NKJV) And Jonathan (KJV)
1 Sam. 20:12 to David (Geneva, NKJV) unto David (KJV)
1 Sam. 20:33 spear (Geneva, NKJV) javelin (KJV)
1 Sam. 20:37 place where the arrow was (Geneva, NKJV) place of the arrow (KJV)
1 Sam. 20:40 Then Jonathan (Geneva, NKJV) And Jonathan (KJV)
1 Sam. 20:40 bows and arrows (Geneva) artillery (KJV) weapons (NKJV)
1 Sam. 20:41 As soon (Geneva, NKJV) *And* as soon (KJV)
1 Sam. 21:2 to Ahimelech (Geneva, NKJV) unto Ahimelech (KJV)
1 Sam. 21:5 David then (Geneva) And David (KJV) Then David (NKJV)
1 Sam. 22:8 a covenant (Geneva, NKJV) a league (KJV)
1 Sam. 22:13 Then Saul (Geneva, NKJV) And Saul (KJV)
1 Sam. 22:16 Then the (Geneva, NKJV) And the (KJV)
1 Sam. 22:19 Also Nob (Geneva, NKJV) And Nob (KJV)
1 Sam. 22:22 I am the cause (Geneva) I have occasioned (KJV) I have caused (NKJV)
1 Sam. 23:8 Then Saul (Geneva, NKJV) And Saul (KJV)
1 Sam. 23:18 So (Geneva, NKJV) And (KJV)
1 Sam. 23:22 is subtile and crafty (Geneva) dealeth very subtilly (KJV) is very crafty (NKJV)
1 Sam. 23:26 on the other side (Geneva, NKJV) on that side (KJV)
1 Sam. 23:27 to Saul (Geneva, NKJV) unto Saul (KJV)
1 Sam. 24:3 inward parts (Geneva) sides (KJV) recesses (NKJV)
1 Sam. 24:22 So David (Geneva, NKJV) And David (KJV)
1 Sam. 24:22 went up (Geneva, NKJV) gat them up (KJV)
1 Sam. 25:1 Then Samuel (Geneva, NKJV) And Samuel (KJV)
1 Sam. 25:10 Then Nabal (Geneva, NKJV) And Nabal (KJV)
1 Sam. 25:13 And about four hundred men went up after David (Geneva)
        and there went up after David about four hundred men (KJV)
        And about four hundred men went up with David (NKJV)
1 Sam. 25:14 Now one (Geneva, NKJV) But one (KJV)
1 Sam. 25:29 man hath risen (Geneva) man is risen (KJV) man has risen (NKJV)
1 Sam. 25:32 Then David (Geneva, NKJV) And David (KJV)
1 Sam. 25:42 maids (Geneva) damsels (KJV) maidens (NKJV)
1 Sam. 26:7 his head (Geneva, NKJV) his bolster (KJV)
1 Sam. 26:11 his head (Geneva, NKJV) his bolster (KJV)
1 Sam. 26:12 Saul's head (Geneva, NKJV) Saul's bolster (KJV)
1 Sam. 26:16 his head (Geneva, NKJV) his bolster (KJV)
1 Sam. 27:10 roving (Geneva) road (KJV) raid (NKJV)
1 Sam. 28:1 to David (Geneva, NKJV) unto David (KJV)
1 Sam. 28:4 Then the (Geneva, NKJV) And the (KJV)
1 Sam. 28:24 Now the (Geneva, NKJV) And the (KJV)
1 Sam. 28:24 baked (Geneva, NKJV) did bake (KJV)
1 Sam. 29:4 But the princes (Geneva, NKJV) And the princes (KJV)
1 Sam. 30:13 ago (Geneva, NKJV) agone (KJV)
1 Sam. 31:9 temple (Geneva, NKJV) house (KJV)
2 Sam. 1:6 Then the young (Geneva, NKJV) And the young (KJV)
2 Sam. 1:14 put forth (Geneva, NKJV) stretch forth (KJV)
2 Sam. 1:15 Then David (Geneva, NKJV) And David (KJV)
2 Sam. 1:17 Then David (Geneva, NKJV) And David (KJV)
2 Sam. 2:3 And David brought up the men that were with him (Geneva)
        And his men that were with him did David bring up (KJV)
        And David brought up the men who were with him (NKJV)
2 Sam. 2:4 Then the men (Geneva, NKJV) And the men (KJV)
2 Sam. 2:14 Then Abner (Geneva, NKJV) And Abner (KJV)

2 Sam. 3:12 Then Abner (Geneva, NKJV) And Abner (KJV)
2 Sam. 3:12 covenant (Geneva, NKJV) league (KJV)
2 Sam. 3:13 covenant (Geneva, NKJV) league (KJV)
2 Sam. 3:21 Then Abner (Geneva, NKJV) And Abner (KJV)
2 Sam. 4:1 all Israel (Geneva, NKJV) all the Israelites (KJV)
2 Sam. 4:3 because (Geneva, NKJV) And (KJV)
2 Sam. 5:3 covenant (Geneva, NKJV) league (KJV)
2 Sam. 5:6 who spake (Geneva) which spake (KJV) who spoke (NKJV)
2 Sam. 5:8 Now David (Geneva, NKJV) And David (KJV)
2 Sam. 5:12 knew (Geneva, NKJV) perceived (KJV)
2 Sam. 5:13 more sons and daughters were born (Geneva, NKJV)
              were yet sons and daughters born (KJV)
2 Sam. 5:23 turn about behind them (Geneva) fetch a compass behind
              them (KJV) circle around behind them (NKJV)
2 Sam. 6:22 low (Geneva) base (KJV) humble (NKJV)
2 Sam. 7:12 thy body (Geneva) thy bowels (KJV) your body (NKJV)
2 Sam. 7:18 Then King David went in (Geneva, NKJV) Then went king David in (KJV)
2 Sam. 7:22 besides (Geneva, NKJV) beside (KJV)
2 Sam. 8:12 the son (Geneva, NKJV) son (KJV)
2 Sam. 9:3 Then the king (Geneva, NKJV) And the king (KJV)
2 Sam. 11:1 remained (Geneva, NKJV) tarried still (KJV)
2 Sam. 11:8 a present (Geneva) a mess *of meat* (KJV) a gift *of food* (NKJV)
2 Sam. 11:12 Then David (Geneva, NKJV) And David (KJV)
2 Sam. 12:1 Then (Geneva, NKJV) And (KJV)
2 Sam. 12:1 came to him (Geneva, NKJV) came unto him (KJV)
2 Sam. 12:7 Then Nathan (Geneva, NKJV) And Nathan (KJV)
2 Sam. 12:13 Then David (Geneva, NKJV) And David (KJV)
2 Sam. 12:29 So David (Geneva, NKJV) And David (KJV)
2 Sam. 12:30 from his head (Geneva, NKJV) from off his head (KJV)
2 Sam. 13:10 Then Amnon (Geneva, NKJV) And Amnon (KJV)
2 Sam. 13:39 And King David (Geneva, NKJV) And *the soul of* king David (KJV)
2 Sam. 14:13 bring (Geneva, NKJV) fetch (KJV)
2 Sam. 15:3 Then Absalom (Geneva, NKJV) And Absalom (KJV)
2 Sam. 15:5 near (Geneva, NKJV) nigh (KJV)
2 Sam. 16:8 brought (Geneva, NKJV) returned (KJV)
2 Sam. 16:10 But the king (Geneva, NKJV) And the king (KJV)
2 Sam. 17:23 went home (Geneva, NKJV) gat him home (KJV)
2 Sam. 18:19 that (Geneva, NKJV) how that (KJV)
2 Sam. 19:5 Then Joab (Geneva, NKJV) And Joab (KJV)
2 Sam. 19:24 returned in peace (Geneva, NKJV) came again in peace (KJV)
2 Sam. 19:32 man of very great substance (Geneva) very great man (KJV) very rich man (NKJV)
2 Sam. 19:34 to Jerusalem (Geneva, NKJV) unto Jerusalem (KJV)
2 Sam. 20:15 on the ramper (Geneva) in the trench (KJV) by the rampart (NKJV)
2 Sam. 22:3 my strength (Geneva, NKJV) my rock (KJV)
2 Sam. 22:8 angry (Geneva, NKJV) wroth (KJV)
2 Sam. 22:31 shield (Geneva, NKJV) buckler (KJV)
2 Sam. 22:35 bow of brass (Geneva) bow of steel (KJV) bow of bronze (NKJV)
2 Sam. 22:48 subdue (Geneva) bringeth down (KJV) subdues (NKJV)
2 Sam. 22:51 to David (Geneva, NKJV) unto David (KJV)
2 Sam. 23:6 wicked (Geneva) *sons* of Belial (KJV) *sons* of rebellion (NKJV)
2 Sam. 24:5 valley of Gad (Geneva) river of Gad (KJV) ravine of Gad (NKJV)
1 Kings 1:9 sacrificed (Geneva, NKJV) slew (KJV)
1 Kings 1:19 offered (Geneva) slain (KJV) sacrificed (NKJV)
1 Kings 1:29 who hath (Geneva) that hath (KJV) who has (NKJV)
1 Kings 1:30 in my place (Geneva, NKJV) in my stead (KJV)
1 Kings 2:1 near (Geneva, NKJV) nigh (KJV)

1 Kings 2:15 Then he (Geneva, NKJV) And he (KJV)

1 Kings 2:30 Come out (Geneva, NKJV) Come forth (KJV)

1 Kings 2:31 and smite him (Geneva) and fall upon him (KJV) and strike him down (NKJV)

1 Kings 2:34 and smote him (Geneva) and fell upon him (KJV) and struck (NKJV)

1 Kings 2:38 So Shimei (Geneva, NKJV) And Shimei (KJV)

1 Kings 2:46 smote him (Geneva) fell upon him (KJV) struck him down (NKJV)

1 Kings 3:2 the high places (Geneva, NKJV) high places (KJV)

1 Kings 3:19 woman's son (Geneva, NKJV) woman's child (KJV)

1 Kings 3:20 from my side (Geneva, NKJV) from beside me (KJV)

1 Kings 3:20 laid him (Geneva, NKJV) laid it (KJV)

1 Kings 3:21 give my son suck (Geneva) give my child suck (KJV) nurse my son (NKJV)

1 Kings 3:24 Then (Geneva, NKJV) And (KJV)

1 Kings 3:27 him (Geneva, NKJV) it (KJV)

1 Kings 3:28 justice. (Geneva, NKJV) judgment. (KJV)

1 Kings 4:24 on every side (Geneva, NKJV) on all sides (KJV)

1 Kings 4:30 of the East (Geneva, NKJV) of the east country (KJV)

1 Kings 5:1 loved David (Geneva, NKJV) a lover of David (KJV)

1 Kings 5:9 to the sea (Geneva, NKJV) unto the sea (KJV)

1 Kings 5:9 in rafts (Geneva, NKJV) in floats (KJV)

1 Kings 5:11 beaten oil (Geneva) pure oil (KJV) pressed oil (NKJV)

1 Kings 5:15 seventy (Geneva, NKJV) threescore and ten (KJV)

1 Kings 8:12 in the dark cloud (Geneva, NKJV) in the thick darkness (KJV)

1 Kings 8:30 hear (Geneva, NKJV) hearken (KJV)

1 Kings 8:59 near (Geneva, NKJV) nigh (KJV)

1 Kings 9:15 to build (Geneva, NKJV) for to build (KJV)

1 Kings 10:9 righteousness (Geneva, NKJV) justice (KJV)

1 Kings 10:15 besides (Geneva, NKJV) Beside (KJV)

1 Kings 11:2 hearts (Geneva, NKJV) heart (KJV)

1 Kings 11:8 outlandish wives (Geneva) strange wives (KJV) foreign wives (NKJV)

1 Kings 11:10 had commanded (Geneva, NKJV) commanded (KJV)

1 Kings 11:25 besides (Geneva, NKJV) beside (KJV)

1 Kings 11:25 evil (Geneva) mischief (KJV) trouble (NKJV)

1 Kings 11:26 a widow (Geneva, NKJV) a widow woman (KJV)

1 Kings 11:30 Then Ahijah (Geneva, NKJV) And Ahijah (KJV)

1 Kings 11:37 heart (Geneva, NKJV) soul (KJV)

1 Kings 12:10 Then the (Geneva, NKJV) And the (KJV)

1 Kings 12:11 scourges (Geneva, NKJV) scorpions (KJV)

1 Kings 12:14 scourges (Geneva, NKJV) scorpions (KJV)

1 Kings 12:15 had spoken (Geneva, NKJV) spake (KJV)

1 Kings 12:24 obeyed (Geneva, NKJV) hearkened (KJV)

1 Kings 13:2 sacrifice (Geneva, NKJV) offer (KJV)

1 Kings 13:6 Then (Geneva, NKJV) And (KJV)

1 Kings 13:7 Then (Geneva, NKJV) And (KJV)

1 Kings 13:8 But (Geneva, NKJV) And (KJV)

1 Kings 13:21 Because (Geneva, NKJV) Forasmuch (KJV)

1 Kings 14:2 go to Shiloh (Geneva, NKJV) get thee to Shiloh (KJV)

1 Kings 16:17 Then Omri (Geneva, NKJV) And Omri (KJV)

1 Kings 17:10 bring me (Geneva, NKJV) Fetch me (KJV)

1 Kings 18:2 great (Geneva) sore (KJV) severe (NKJV)

1 Kings 18:25 prepare (Geneva, NKJV) dress (KJV)

1 Kings 18:26 prepared it (Geneva, NKJV) dressed it (KJV)

1 Kings 20:23 Then the (Geneva, NKJV) And the (KJV)

1 Kings 21:7 Then Jezebel (Geneva, NKJV) And Jezebel (KJV)

1 Kings 21:18 to take possession (Geneva, NKJV) to possess (KJV)

1 Kings 22:17 Then he said (Geneva, NKJV) And he said (KJV)

2 Kings 1:2 fell through the lattice (Geneva, NKJV) fell down through a lattice (KJV)

2 Kings 1:3 no God in Israel (Geneva, NKJV) not a God in Israel (KJV)

2 Kings 1:4 the bed (Geneva, NKJV) that bed (KJV)

2 Kings 1:4 So Elijah departed (Geneva, NKJV) And Elijah departed (KJV)

2 Kings 1:5 returned (Geneva, NKJV) turned back (KJV)

2 Kings 1:6 return (Geneva, NKJV) turn again (KJV)

2 Kings 1:6 no God in Israel (Geneva, NKJV) not a God in Israel (KJV)

2 Kings 1:16 Because (Geneva, NKJV) Forasmuch as (KJV)

2 Kings 2:2 Then Elijah (Geneva, NKJV) And Elijah (KJV)

2 Kings 2:2 to Elisha (Geneva, NKJV) unto Elisha (KJV)

2 Kings 2:2 But Elisha said (Geneva, NKJV) And Elisha said *unto him* (KJV)

2 Kings 2:3 came out (Geneva, NKJV) came forth (KJV)

2 Kings 2:22 word of Elisha (Geneva, NKJV) saying of Elisha (KJV)

2 Kings 2:25 out of the forest (Geneva) out of the wood (KJV) out of the woods (NKJV)

2 Kings 3:8 Then (Geneva, NKJV) And (KJV)

2 Kings 3:18 small thing (Geneva) light thing (KJV) simple matter (NKJV)

2 Kings 3:25 destroyed (Geneva, NKJV) beat down (KJV)

2 Kings 4:14 no son (Geneva, NKJV) no child (KJV)

2 Kings 4:38 Elisha returned (Geneva, NKJV) Elisha came again (KJV)

2 Kings 4:38 famine (Geneva, NKJV) dearth (KJV)

2 Kings 4:42 Then (Geneva, NKJV) And (KJV)

2 Kings 4:43 servant (Geneva, NKJV) servitor (KJV)

2 Kings 4:43 Give it unto the people (Geneva) Give the people (KJV) Give *it* to the people (NKJV)

2 Kings 4:44 left over (Geneva, NKJV) left *thereof* (KJV)

2 Kings 5:1 in the sight of his lord (Geneva) with his master (KJV) in the eyes of his master (NKJV)

2 Kings 5:1 *but* a leper (Geneva, NKJV) *but he was* a leper (KJV)

2 Kings 5:9 Then Naaman (Geneva, NKJV) So Naaman (KJV)

2 Kings 5:12 Abanah (Geneva, NKJV) Abana (KJV)

2 Kings 5:17 load of this earth (Geneva) burden of earth (KJV) loads of earth (NKJV)

2 Kings 6:1 too little (Geneva) too strait (KJV) too small (NKJV)

2 Kings 6:2 Go (Geneva, NKJV) Go ye (KJV)

2 Kings 7:3 Now there were (Geneva, NKJV) And there were (KJV)

2 Kings 7:6 had caused (Geneva, NKJV) had made (KJV)

2 Kings 7:6 great army (Geneva, NKJV) great host (KJV)

2 Kings 7:7 their lives (Geneva, NKJV) their life (KJV)

2 Kings 8:7 Then Elisha (Geneva, NKJV) And Elisha (KJV)

2 Kings 8:10 to him (Geneva, NKJV) unto him (KJV)

2 Kings 8:16 Now in (Geneva, NKJV) And in (KJV)

2 Kings 8:19 for ever (Geneva) alway (KJV) forever (NKJV)

2 Kings 8:21 went to Zair (Geneva, NKJV) went over to Zair (KJV)

2 Kings 8:27 like the house (Geneva, NKJV) as *did* the house (KJV)

2 Kings 9:5 army (Geneva, NKJV) host (KJV)

2 Kings 9:5 a message (Geneva, NKJV) an errand (KJV)

2 Kings 9:21 Then Joram (Geneva, NKJV) And Joram (KJV)

2 Kings 9:23 Then Joram (Geneva, NKJV) And Joram (KJV)

2 Kings 9:27 pursued (Geneva, NKJV) followed (KJV)

2 Kings 10:4 could not stand (Geneva, NKJV) stood not (KJV)

2 Kings 10:17 the word (Geneva, NKJV) the saying (KJV)

2 Kings 10:18 Then Jehu (Geneva, NKJV) And Jehu (KJV)

2 Kings 11:11 right side (Geneva, NKJV) right corner (KJV)

2 Kings 11:19 took the captains (Geneva, NKJV) took the rulers (KJV)

2 Kings 12:7 the temple (Geneva, NKJV) the house (KJV)

2 Kings 12:11 paid it out (Geneva, NKJV) laid it out (KJV)

2 Kings 13:2 did evil (Geneva, NKJV) did *that which was* evil (KJV)

2 Kings 13:5 a deliverer (Geneva, NKJV) a saviour (KJV)

2 Kings 13:15 Take a bow (Geneva, NKJV) Take bow (KJV)

2 Kings 13:19 angry (Geneva, NKJV) wroth (KJV)
2 Kings 14:24 did evil (Geneva, NKJV) did *that which was* evil (KJV)
2 Kings 15:5 in an house apart (Geneva) in a several house (KJV) in an isolated house (NKJV)
2 Kings 15:10 killed him (Geneva, NKJV) slew him (KJV)
2 Kings 15:18 did evil (Geneva, NKJV) did *that which was* evil (KJV)
2 Kings 15:25 in his stead (Geneva) in his room (KJV) in his place (NKJV)
2 Kings 17:10 upon every (Geneva) in every (KJV) on every (NKJV)
2 Kings 17:13 Turn from your evil ways (Geneva, NKJV) Turn ye from your evil ways (KJV)
2 Kings 17:14 Nevertheless (Geneva, NKJV) Notwithstanding (KJV)
2 Kings 17:17 witchcraft (Geneva, NKJV) divination (KJV)
2 Kings 17:40 obeyed not (Geneva) did not hearken (KJV) did not obey (NKJV)
2 Kings 18:8 watchtower (Geneva, NKJV) tower of the watchmen (KJV)
2 Kings 18:23 give (Geneva, NKJV) deliver (KJV)
2 Kings 19:27 dwelling (Geneva) abode (KJV) dwelling place (NKJV)
2 Kings 19:37 the temple (Geneva, NKJV) the house (KJV)
2 Kings 19:37 land of Ararat (Geneva, NKJV) land of Armenia (KJV)
2 Kings 21:2 did evil (Geneva, NKJV) did *that which was* evil (KJV)
2 Kings 21:7 all the tribes (Geneva, NKJV) all tribes (KJV)
2 Kings 21:20 did evil (Geneva, NKJV) did *that which was* evil (KJV)
2 Kings 22:2 all the ways (Geneva, NKJV) all the way (KJV)
2 Kings 22:7 they deal (Geneva, NKJV) they dealt (KJV)
2 Kings 22:9 So Shaphan (Geneva, NKJV) And Shaphan (KJV)
2 Kings 22:13 obeyed (Geneva, NKJV) hearkened unto (KJV)
2 Kings 22:16 and on (Geneva, NKJV) and upon (KJV)
2 Kings 22:18 who sent (Geneva, NKJV) which sent (KJV)
2 Kings 22:20 thee to (Geneva) thee unto (KJV) you to (NKJV)
2 Kings 23:21 Then the king (Geneva, NKJV) And the king (KJV)
2 Kings 23:32 did evil (Geneva, NKJV) did *that which was* evil (KJV)
2 Kings 23:37 did evil (Geneva, NKJV) did *that which was* evil (KJV)
2 Kings 24:9 did evil (Geneva, NKJV) did *that which was* evil (KJV)
2 Kings 25:8 to Jerusalem (Geneva, NKJV) unto Jerusalem (KJV)
2 Kings 25:15 basins (Geneva, NKJV) bowls (KJV)
1 Chron. 1:5 The sons of Japeth *were* Gomer (Geneva, NKJV) The sons of Japheth; Gomer (KJV)
1 Chron. 1:7 Tarshishah (Geneva, NKJV) Tarshish (KJV)
1 Chron. 1:8 The sons of Ham *were* Cush (Geneva, NKJV) The sons of Ham; Cush (KJV)
1 Chron. 1:11 Lehabim (Geneva, NKJV) and Lehabim (KJV)
1 Chron. 1:17 The sons of Shem *were* Elam (Geneva, NKJV) The sons of Shem; Elam (KJV)
1 Chron. 1:28 The sons of Abraham *were* Izhak (Geneva) The sons of Abraham; Isaac (KJV) The sons of Abraham *were* Isaac (NKJV)
1 Chron. 1:29 *was* Nabaioth (Geneva, NKJV) Nebaioth (KJV)
1 Chron. 1:33 *were* Ephah (Geneva, NKJV) Ephah (KJV)
1 Chron. 1:41 The son of Anah (Geneva, NKJV) The sons of Anah (KJV)
1 Chron. 1:41 *was* Dishon (Geneva, NKJV) Dishon (KJV)
1 Chron. 1:42 Zaavan (Geneva, NKJV) Zavan (KJV)
1 Chron. 1:43 these were (Geneva) these *are* (KJV) these *were* (NKJV)
1 Chron. 1:43 before a king (Geneva, NKJV) before *any* king (KJV)
1 Chron. 1:44 Bela died (Geneva, NKJV) Bela was dead (KJV)
1 Chron. 1:54 these were (Geneva) These *are* (KJV) These *were* (NKJV)
1 Chron. 2:1 were the sons (Geneva) *are* the sons (KJV) *were* the sons (NKJV)
1 Chron. 2:3 to him (Geneva, NKJV) unto him (KJV)
1 Chron. 2:7 son (Geneva, NKJV) sons (KJV)
1 Chron. 2:8 The son also (Geneva) And the sons (KJV) The son (NKJV)
1 Chron. 2:15 *and* David (Geneva, NKJV) David (KJV)
1 Chron. 2:31 *was* Ishi (Geneva, NKJV) Ishi (KJV)
1 Chron. 2:32 *were* Jether (Geneva, NKJV) Jether (KJV)

1 Chron. 2:33 *were* Peleth (Geneva, NKJV) Peleth (KJV)
1 Chron. 2:55 Hammath (Geneva, NKJV) Hemath (KJV)
1 Chron. 3:22 Shemaiah *were* (Geneva, NKJV) Shemaiah; (KJV)
1 Chron. 3:23 Neariah *were* (Geneva, NKJV) Neariah; (KJV)
1 Chron. 4:7 Jezohar (Geneva) Jezoar (KJV) Zohar (NKJV)
1 Chron. 4:9 him in (Geneva) him with (KJV) *him* in (NKJV)
1 Chron. 4:13 Kenaz *were* (Geneva, NKJV) Kenaz; (KJV)
1 Chron. 4:19 sons of the wife of Hodiah (Geneva) sons of *his* wife Hodiah (KJV) sons of Hodiah's wife (NKJV)
1 Chron. 5:5 Reaiah (Geneva, NKJV) Reaia (KJV)
1 Chron. 5:13 Eber (Geneva, NKJV) Heber (KJV)
1 Chron. 5:18 shield (Geneva, NKJV) buckler (KJV)
1 Chron. 5:19 Naphish (Geneva, NKJV) Nephish (KJV)
1 Chron. 5:25 God had destroyed (Geneva, NKJV) God destroyed (KJV)
1 Chron. 6:3 And the sons of Aaron (Geneva, NKJV) The sons also of Aaron (KJV)
1 Chron. 6:10 it was he (Geneva, NKJV) he *it is* (KJV)
1 Chron. 6:48 And their brethren (Geneva, NKJV) Their brethren also (KJV)
1 Chron. 6:54 their towns (Geneva) their castles (KJV) their settlements (NKJV)
1 Chron. 7:17 son of Ulam (Geneva, NKJV) sons of Ulam (KJV)
1 Chron. 7:23 because affliction was (Geneva) because it went evil (KJV) because tragedy had come (NKJV)
1 Chron. 7:39 Rizia (Geneva, NKJV) Rezia (KJV)
1 Chron. 8:13 and Beriah (Geneva, NKJV) Beriah also (KJV)
1 Chron. 8:22 Eber (Geneva, NKJV) Heber (KJV)
1 Chron. 9:2 And the (Geneva, NKJV) Now the (KJV)
1 Chron. 9:36 son *was* Abdon (Geneva, NKJV) son Abdon (KJV)
1 Chron. 11:11 son of Hachmoni (Geneva) an Hachmonite (KJV) son of a Hachmonite (NKJV)
1 Chron. 11:14 the field (Geneva) *that* parcel (KJV) *that* field (NKJV)
1 Chron. 11:15 the army (Geneva, NKJV) the host (KJV)
1 Chron. 11:44 Otham (Geneva) Hothan (KJV) Hotham (NKJV)
1 Chron. 12:8 spear and shield (Geneva) shield and buckler (KJV) shield and spear (NKJV)
1 Chron. 12:40 near (Geneva, NKJV) nigh (KJV)
1 Chron. 13:2 said to all (Geneva, NKJV) said unto all (KJV)
1 Chron. 13:5 Hamath (Geneva, NKJV) Hemath (KJV)
1 Chron. 13:11 was angry (Geneva) was displeased (KJV) became angry (NKJV)
1 Chron. 14:1 cedar trees (Geneva, NKJV) timber of cedar (KJV)
1 Chron. 14:14 said to him (Geneva, NKJV) said unto him (KJV)
1 Chron. 14:16 So David did (Geneva, NKJV) David therefore did (KJV)
1 Chron. 15:12 And he said (Geneva) And said (KJV) He said (NKJV)
1 Chron. 16:1 tabernacle (Geneva, NKJV) tent (KJV)
1 Chron. 16:10 hearts (Geneva, NKJV) heart (KJV)
1 Chron. 16:13 O seed (Geneva, NKJV) O ye seed (KJV)
1 Chron. 16:15 Remember (Geneva, NKJV) Be ye mindful (KJV)
1 Chron. 16:19 few in number (Geneva, NKJV) few (KJV)
1 Chron. 16:24 among the nations (Geneva, NKJV) among the heathen (KJV)
1 Chron. 16:30 Tremble (Geneva, NKJV) Fear (KJV)
1 Chron. 17:2 to David (Geneva, NKJV) unto David (KJV)
1 Chron. 17:9 appoint (Geneva, NKJV) ordain (KJV)
1 Chron. 17:11 fulfilled (Geneva, NKJV) expired (KJV)
1 Chron. 17:14 establish (Geneva, NKJV) settle (KJV)
1 Chron. 17:14 for ever (Geneva) for evermore (KJV) forever (NKJV)
1 Chron. 17:20 besides (Geneva, NKJV) beside (KJV)
1 Chron. 17:25 revealed (Geneva, NKJV) told (KJV)
1 Chron. 18:11 the silver and gold (Geneva, NKJV) the silver and the gold (KJV)
1 Chron. 19:3 And the princes (Geneva, NKJV) But the princes (KJV)
1 Chron. 19:3 to search (Geneva, NKJV) for to search (KJV)

1 Chron. 19:14 near (Geneva, NKJV) nigh (KJV)
1 Chron. 20:2 Then David (Geneva, NKJV) And David (KJV)
1 Chron. 21:5 seventy (Geneva, NKJV) threescore and ten (KJV)
1 Chron. 22:16 Of gold (Geneva, NKJV) Of the gold (KJV)
1 Chron. 24:15 Happizzer (Geneva) Aphses (KJV) Happizzez (NKJV)
1 Chron. 26:6 to Shemaiah (Geneva, NKJV) unto Shemaiah (KJV)
1 Chron. 26:26 the army (Geneva, NKJV) the host (KJV)
1 Chron. 27:32 Jehonathan (Geneva, NKJV) Jonathan (KJV)
1 Chron. 28:1 Now David (Geneva, NKJV) And David (KJV)
1 Chron. 28:1 served the king (Geneva, NKJV) ministered to the king (KJV)
1 Chron. 28:2 King David (Geneva, NKJV) David the king (KJV)
1 Chron. 29:10 Therefore (Geneva, NKJV) Wherefore (KJV)
1 Chron. 29:11 in heaven (Geneva, NKJV) in the heaven (KJV)
1 Chron. 29:11 in earth (Geneva, NKJV) in the earth (KJV)
1 Chron. 29:11 head over all (Geneva, NKJV) head above all (KJV)
1 Chron. 29:16 all this abundance (Geneva, NKJV) all this store (KJV)
1 Chron. 29:18 and Israel (Geneva, NKJV) and of Israel (KJV)
2 Chron. 1:17 to all the kings (Geneva, NKJV) for all the kings (KJV)
2 Chron. 2:1 Then (Geneva, NKJV) And (KJV)
2 Chron. 2:2 seventy (Geneva, NKJV) threescore and ten (KJV)
2 Chron. 2:9 great and wonderful (Geneva, NKJV) wonderful great (KJV)
2 Chron. 2:16 in rafts (Geneva, NKJV) in flotes (KJV)
2 Chron. 2:18 seventy (Geneva, NKJV) threescore and ten (KJV)
2 Chron. 2:18 people to work (Geneva) people a work (KJV) people work (NKJV)
2 Chron. 4:5 contained (Geneva, NKJV) received and held (KJV)
2 Chron. 5:1 So (Geneva, NKJV) Thus (KJV)
2 Chron. 5:3 at the feast (Geneva, NKJV) in the feast (KJV)
2 Chron. 5:12 And the Levites (Geneva) Also the Levites (KJV) and the Levites (NKJV)
2 Chron. 5:14 because of the cloud (Geneva, NKJV) by reason of the cloud (KJV)
2 Chron. 6:1 in the dark cloud (Geneva, NKJV) in the thick darkness (KJV)
2 Chron. 6:14 in heaven (Geneva, NKJV) in the heaven (KJV)
2 Chron. 6:14 in earth (Geneva) in the earth (KJV) on earth (NKJV)
2 Chron. 6:14 and mercy (Geneva, NKJV) and *shewest* mercy (KJV)
2 Chron. 6:17 And now (Geneva, NKJV) Now then (KJV)
2 Chron. 6:20 toward this (Geneva, NKJV) upon this (KJV)
2 Chron. 6:20 toward the place (Geneva, NKJV) upon the place (KJV)
2 Chron. 6:23 to bring his way (Geneva) by recompensing his way (KJV) by bringing
his way (NKJV)
2 Chron. 6:25 heaven (Geneva, NKJV) the heavens (KJV)
2 Chron. 6:27 in heaven (Geneva) from heaven (KJV) *in* heaven (NKJV)
2 Chron. 6:28 famine (Geneva, NKJV) dearth (KJV)
2 Chron. 6:28 plague or (Geneva, NKJV) sore or (KJV)
2 Chron. 6:30 and give (Geneva, NKJV) and render (KJV)
2 Chron. 6:34 When (Geneva, NKJV) If (KJV)
2 Chron. 6:34 to battle (Geneva, NKJV) to war (KJV)
2 Chron. 6:35 heaven (Geneva, NKJV) the heavens (KJV)
2 Chron. 6:39 heaven (Geneva, NKJV) the heavens (KJV)
2 Chron. 7:1 fire came (Geneva, NKJV) the fire came (KJV)
2 Chron. 7:5 bullocks (Geneva) oxen (KJV) bulls (NKJV)
2 Chron. 7:10 for David (Geneva, NKJV) unto David (KJV)
2 Chron. 7:12 for myself (Geneva) to myself (KJV) for Myself (NKJV)
2 Chron. 7:20 among all people (Geneva) among all nations (KJV) among all peoples (NKJV)
2 Chron. 7:21 to this land (Geneva, NKJV) unto this land (KJV)
2 Chron. 7:22 And they shall answer (Geneva) And it shall be answered (KJV) Then they will
answer (NKJV)
2 Chron. 8:1 when Solomon (Geneva, NKJV) wherein Solomon (KJV)

2 Chron. 8:2 gave to (Geneva) had restored to (KJV) had given to (NKJV)

2 Chron. 8:6 also Baalath (Geneva, NKJV) And Baalath (KJV)

2 Chron. 9:1 she came (Geneva, NKJV) she was come (KJV)

2 Chron. 9:4 waiters (Geneva, NKJV) ministers (KJV)

2 Chron. 9:5 thy sayings (Geneva) thine acts (KJV) your words (NKJV)

2 Chron. 9:10 wood (Geneva, NKJV) trees (KJV)

2 Chron. 9:11 wood (Geneva, NKJV) trees (KJV)

2 Chron. 9:24 armour (Geneva) harness (KJV) armor (NKJV)

2 Chron. 10:16 departed to their tents (Geneva, NKJV) went to their tents (KJV)

2 Chron. 11:14 ministering (Geneva) executing (KJV) serving (NKJV)

2 Chron. 11:16 And after the *Levites* (Geneva, NKJV) And after them (KJV)

2 Chron. 11:23 his sons (Geneva, NKJV) his children (KJV)

2 Chron. 13:1 In the eighteenth year (Geneva, NKJV) Now in the eighteenth year (KJV)

2 Chron. 13:5 you (Geneva, NKJV) ye (KJV)

2 Chron. 14:7 to Judah (Geneva, NKJV) unto Judah (KJV)

2 Chron. 14:8 army (Geneva, NKJV) army *of men* (KJV)

2 Chron. 14:8 shields and spears (Geneva, NKJV) targets and spears (KJV)

2 Chron. 15:6 troubled (Geneva, NKJV) did vex (KJV)

2 Chron. 15:11 bullocks (Geneva) oxen (KJV) bulls (NKJV)

2 Chron. 16:10 prison (Geneva, NKJV) prison house (KJV)

2 Chron. 16:13 So Asa (Geneva, NKJV) And Asa (KJV)

2 Chron. 17:19 besides (Geneva, NKJV) beside (KJV)

2 Chron. 18:9 threshing floor (Geneva, NKJV) void place (KJV)

2 Chron. 18:19 persuade (Geneva, NKJV) entice (KJV)

2 Chron. 18:20 persuade (Geneva, NKJV) entice (KJV)

2 Chron. 18:21 persuade (Geneva, NKJV) entice (KJV)

2 Chron. 19:4 So Jehosphaphat (Geneva, NKJV) And Jehoshaphat (KJV)

2 Chron. 21:8 a king over them (Geneva) themselves a king (KJV) a king over themselves (NKJV)

2 Chron. 21:17 not a son (Geneva, NKJV) never a son (KJV)

2 Chron. 22:12 whiles (Geneva) and (KJV) while (NKJV)

2 Chron. 23:9 And Jehoiada (Geneva, NKJV) Moreover Jehoiada (KJV)

2 Chron. 23:13 by his pillar (Geneva, NKJV) at his pillar (KJV)

2 Chron. 23:17 And all (Geneva, NKJV) Then all (KJV)

2 Chron. 24:13 restored the house (Geneva, NKJV) set the house (KJV)

2 Chron. 24:24 a very great army (Geneva, NKJV) a very great host (KJV)

2 Chron. 25:7 a man of God came (Geneva, NKJV) came a man of God (KJV)

2 Chron. 25:10 So Amaziah (Geneva, NKJV) Then Amaziah (KJV)

2 Chron. 25:11 Then Amaziah (Geneva, NKJV) And Amaziah (KJV)

2 Chron. 25:16 prophet ceased (Geneva, NKJV) prophet forbare (KJV)

2 Chron. 25:20 sought the gods (Geneva, NKJV) sought after the gods (KJV)

2 Chron. 26:15 corners (Geneva, NKJV) bulwarks (KJV)

2 Chron. 29:6 done evil (Geneva, NKJV) done *that which was* evil (KJV)

2 Chron. 29:7 They have also (Geneva, NKJV) Also they have (KJV)

2 Chron. 29:23 Then they (Geneva, NKJV) And they (KJV)

2 Chron. 29:32 seventy (Geneva, NKJV) threescore and ten (KJV)

2 Chron. 29:36 Then Hezekiah (Geneva, NKJV) And Hezekiah (KJV)

2 Chron. 30:9 return (Geneva, NKJV) turn again (KJV)

2 Chron. 32:1 things faithfully *described* (Geneva) things and the establishment thereof (KJV) deeds of faithfulness (NKJV)

2 Chron. 33:2 did evil (Geneva, NKJV) did *that which was* evil (KJV)

2 Chron. 33:33 So Hezekiah (Geneva, NKJV) And Hezekiah (KJV)

2 Chron. 33:6 sons (Geneva, NKJV) children (KJV)

2 Chron. 34:5 Also he (Geneva) And he (KJV) He also (NKJV)

2 Chron. 35:14 prepared (Geneva, NKJV) made ready (KJV)

2 Chron. 35:21 messengers (Geneva, NKJV) ambassadors (KJV)

2 Chron. 36:5 did evil (Geneva, NKJV) did *that which was* evil (KJV)
2 Chron. 36:9 did evil (Geneva, NKJV) did *that which was* evil (KJV)
2 Chron. 36:12 did evil (Geneva, NKJV) did *that which was* evil (KJV)
2 Chron. 36:15 early (Geneva, NKJV) betimes (KJV)
2 Chron. 36:17 virgin (Geneva, NKJV) maiden (KJV)
2 Chron. 36:19 precious (Geneva, NKJV) goodly (KJV)
2 Chron. 36:21 seventy (Geneva, NKJV) threescore and ten (KJV)
2 Chron. 36:23 commanded (Geneva, NKJV) charged (KJV)
Ezra 1:2 commanded (Geneva, NKJV) charged (KJV)
Ezra 1:6 besides all (Geneva, NKJV) beside all (KJV)
Ezra 2:1 to Jerusalem (Geneva, NKJV) unto Jerusalem (KJV)
Ezra 2:42 The sons (Geneva, NKJV) The children (KJV)
Ezra 2:43 sons of Ziha (Geneva, NKJV) children of Ziha (KJV)
Ezra 2:44 sons of Keros (Geneva, NKJV) children of Keros (KJV)
Ezra 2:46 sons of Hagab (Geneva, NKJV) children of Hagab (KJV)
Ezra 2:61 sons of the priests (Geneva, NKJV) children of the priests (KJV)
Ezra 4:2 we have sacrificed (Geneva, NKJV) we do sacrifice (KJV)
Ezra 4:13 built (Geneva, NKJV) builded (KJV)
Ezra 4:21 built (Geneva, NKJV) builded (KJV)
Ezra 7:6 Ezra came up (Geneva, NKJV) Ezra went up (KJV)
Ezra 7:24 upon any (Geneva) touching any (KJV) on any (NKJV)
Ezra 8:17 I gave them commandment (Geneva) I sent them with commandment (KJV) I gave them a command (NKJV)
Ezra 8:30 received (Geneva, NKJV) took (KJV)
Ezra 8:36 beyond the River (Geneva, NKJV) on this side the river (KJV)
Neh. 3:1 built (Geneva, NKJV) builded (KJV)
Neh. 3:20 other portion (Geneva) other piece (KJV) other section (NKJV)
Neh. 3:27 another portion (Geneva) another piece (KJV) another section (NKJV)
Neh. 4:2 finish it in a day (Geneva) make an end in a day (KJV) complete it in a day (NKJV)
Neh. 4:3 was beside him (Geneva, NKJV) was by him (KJV)
Neh. 4:6 So we built (Geneva, NKJV) So built we (KJV)
Neh. 4:10 is weakened (Geneva) is decayed (KJV) is failing (NKJV)
Neh. 5:3 famine (Geneva, NKJV) dearth (KJV)
Neh. 5:8 according to (Geneva, NKJV) after (KJV)
Neh. 5:19 Remember me (Geneva, NKJV) Think upon me (KJV)
Neh. 6:14 remember (Geneva, NKJV) think (KJV)
Neh. 7:8 sons of Parosh (Geneva, NKJV) children of Parosh (KJV)
Neh. 7:10 sons of Arah (Geneva, NKJV) children of Arah (KJV)
Neh. 7:16 sons of Bebai (Geneva, NKJV) children of Bebai (KJV)
Neh. 7:59 sons of Amon (Geneva, NKJV) children of Amon (KJV)
Neh. 8:15 bring olive branches (Geneva, NKJV) fetch olive branches (KJV)
Neh. 9:12 with a pillar of fire (Geneva, NKJV) by a pillar of fire (KJV)
Neh. 9:20 Spirit (Geneva, NKJV) spirit (KJV)
Esther 1:10 seven eunuchs (Geneva, NKJV) seven chamberlains (KJV)
Esther 1:12 eunuchs (Geneva, NKJV) chamberlains (KJV)
Esther 1:15 eunuchs (Geneva, NKJV) chamberlains (KJV)
Esther 1:19 royal decree (Geneva, NKJV) royal commandment (KJV)
Esther 2:2 beautiful young (Geneva, NKJV) fair young (KJV)
Esther 2:3 beautiful young (Geneva, NKJV) fair young (KJV)
Esther 2:9 favour (Geneva) kindness (KJV) favor (NKJV)
Esther 2:14 eunuch (Geneva, NKJV) chamberlain (KJV)
Esther 2:15 eunuch (Geneva, NKJV) chamberlain (KJV)
Esther 2:21 eunuchs (Geneva, NKJV) chamberlains (KJV)
Esther 4:4 eunuchs (Geneva, NKJV) chamberlains (KJV)
Esther 4:10 Then Esther (Geneva, NKJV) Again Esther (KJV)
Esther 6:2 eunuchs (Geneva, NKJV) chamberlains (KJV)

Esther 6:2 lay hands (Geneva, NKJV) lay hand (KJV)

Esther 6:14 eunuchs (Geneva, NKJV) chamberlains (KJV)

Esther 7:1 Queen Esther (Geneva, NKJV) Esther the queen (KJV)

Esther 7:9 eunuchs (Geneva, NKJV) chamberlains (KJV)

Esther 8:3 wickedness (Geneva) mischief (KJV) evil (NKJV)

Esther 9:20 near and far (Geneva, NKJV) nigh and far (KJV)

Esther 9:29 Queen Esther (Geneva, NKJV) Esther the queen (KJV)

Esther 10:3 second (Geneva, NKJV) next (KJV)

Job 1:5 every day (Geneva) continually (KJV) regularly (NKJV)

Job 1:11 stretch out (Geneva, NKJV) put forth (KJV)

Job 1:17 have taken them (Geneva) have carried them away (KJV) took them away (NKJV)

Job 1:20 garment (Geneva) mantle (KJV) robe (NKJV)

Job 2:5 stretch (Geneva, NKJV) put (KJV)

Job 3:11 why died I not (Geneva) *why* did I not give up the ghost (KJV) *Why* did I not perish (NKJV)

Job 3:11 womb (Geneva, NKJV) belly (KJV)

Job 3:21 search (Geneva, NKJV) dig (KJV)

Job 3:24 water (Geneva, NKJV) waters (KJV)

Job 7:8 I shall be no longer (Geneva) I am not (KJV) I shall no longer be (NKJV)

Job 8:4 sons (Geneva, NKJV) children (KJV)

Job 8:14 confidence (Geneva, NKJV) hope (KJV)

Job 9:5 He removeth (Geneva) Which removeth (KJV) He removes (NKJV)

Job 9:5 when he overturneth (Geneva) which overturneth (KJV) When He overturns (NKJV)

Job 9:6 He (Geneva, NKJV) Which (KJV)

Job 9:7 He (Geneva, NKJV) Which (KJV)

Job 9:8 He (Geneva, NKJV) Which (KJV)

Job 9:9 He (Geneva, NKJV) Which (KJV)

Job 9:10 He (Geneva, NKJV) Which (KJV)

Job 9:13 God will not (Geneva, NKJV) *If* God will not (KJV)

Job 9:31 in the pit (Geneva, NKJV) in the ditch (KJV)

Job 9:33 umpire (Geneva) daysman (KJV) mediator (NKJV)

Job 10:6 out my sin (Geneva, NKJV) after my sin (KJV)

Job 10:9 pray (Geneva, NKJV) beseech (KJV)

Job 11:15 Then truly (Geneva) For then (KJV) Then surely (NKJV)

Job 12:1 Then Job (Geneva, NKJV) And Job (KJV)

Job 12:22 the shadow of death to light (Geneva, NKJV) to light the shadow of death (KJV)

Job 13:3 But I (Geneva, NKJV) Surely I (KJV)

Job 15:10 older (Geneva, NKJV) elder (KJV)

Job 15:26 shield (Geneva, NKJV) bucklers (KJV)

Job 16:3 words of wind (Geneva, NKJV) vain words (KJV)

Job 16:5 comfort of my lips (Geneva, NKJV) moving of my lips (KJV)

Job 17:1 grave (Geneva, NKJV) graves (KJV)

Job 19:3 ye are impudent toward me (Geneva) ye make yourselves strange to me (KJV) you have wronged me (NKJV)

Job 19:4 with me (Geneva, NKJV) with myself (KJV)

Job 19:13 removed (Geneva, NKJV) put (KJV)

Job 19:25 on the earth (Geneva, NKJV) upon the earth (KJV)

Job 20:3 correction (Geneva) check (KJV) rebuke (NKJV)

Job 20:25 cometh upon (Geneva) *are* upon (KJV) *come* upon (NKJV)

Job 21:15 Who is (Geneva, NKJV) What is (KJV)

Job 21:29 their signs (Geneva, NKJV) their tokens (KJV)

Job 22:2 to himself (Geneva, NKJV) unto himself (KJV)

Job 22:14 circle of heaven (Geneva, NKJV) circuit of heaven (KJV)

Job 22:16 before the time (Geneva) out of time (KJV) before their time (NKJV)

Job 23:7 reason (Geneva, NKJV) dispute (KJV)

Job 26:8 broken (Geneva, NKJV) rent (KJV)

Job 26:13 Spirit (Geneva, NKJV) spirit (KJV)
Job 29:10 The voice of princes (Geneva) The nobles (KJV) The voice of nobles (NKJV)
Job 30:1 mock me (Geneva) have me in derision (KJV) mock at me (NKJV)
Job 30:8 children of villains (Geneva) children of base men (KJV) sons of vile men (NKJV)
Job 30:29 ostriches (Geneva, NKJV) owls (KJV)
Job 31:11 wickedness (Geneva, NKJV) heinous crime (KJV)
Job 32:14 your words (Geneva, NKJV) your speeches (KJV)
Job 32:18 compelleth (Geneva) constraineth (KJV) compels (NKJV)
Job 34:11 to his way (Geneva, NKJV) to his ways (KJV)
Job 34:15 return (Geneva, NKJV) turn again (KJV)
Job 36:6 afflicted (Geneva) poor (KJV) oppressed (NKJV)
Job 39:10 will he plow (Geneva, NKJV) will he harrow (KJV)
Job 39:14 in the dust (Geneva, NKJV) in dust (KJV)
Job 41:20 boiling pot (Geneva, NKJV) seething pot (KJV)
Ps. 1:3 whose leaf (Geneva, NKJV) his leaf (KJV)
Ps. 4:2 lies (Geneva) leasing (KJV) falsehood (NKJV)
Ps. 4:7 wheat (Geneva) corn (KJV) grain (NKJV)
Ps. 5:6 lies (Geneva) leasing (KJV) falsehood (NKJV)
Ps. 6:3 troubled (Geneva, NKJV) vexed (KJV)
Ps. 6:10 turn back (Geneva, NKJV) return (KJV)
Ps. 9:6 O enemy (Geneva, NKJV) O thou enemy (KJV)
Ps. 10:5 always prosper (Geneva) always grievous (KJV) always prospering (NKJV)
Ps. 13:6 sing to the (Geneva, NKJV) sing unto the (KJV)
Ps. 18:2 shield (Geneva, NKJV) buckler (KJV)
Ps. 18:4 wickedness (Geneva) ungodly men (KJV) ungodliness (NKJV)
Ps. 18:7 angry (Geneva, NKJV) wroth (KJV)
Ps. 18:24 sight (Geneva, NKJV) eyesight (KJV)
Ps. 18:30 shield (Geneva, NKJV) buckler (KJV)
Ps. 18:34 bow of brass (Geneva) bow of steel (KJV) bow of bronze (NKJV)
Ps. 20:4 purpose (Geneva, NKJV) counsel (KJV)
Ps. 21:12 their faces (Geneva, NKJV) face of them (KJV)
Ps. 22:8 trusted in (Geneva, NKJV) trusted on (KJV)
Ps. 22:13 They gape (Geneva, NKJV) They gaped (KJV)
Ps. 22:26 The poor (Geneva, NKJV) The meek (KJV)
Ps. 22:27 turn to (Geneva, NKJV) turn unto (KJV)
Ps. 22:28 he ruleth (Geneva) he is the governor (KJV) He rules (NKJV)
Ps. 25:20 Keep my soul (Geneva, NKJV) O keep my soul (KJV)
Ps. 26:5 the assembly (Geneva, NKJV) the congregation (KJV)
Ps. 27:12 adversaries (Geneva, NKJV) enemies (KJV)
Ps. 28:3 malice (Geneva) mischief (KJV) evil (NKJV)
Ps. 28:4 their reward (Geneva) their desert (KJV) what they deserve (NKJV)
Ps. 32:6 flood (Geneva, NKJV) floods (KJV)
Ps. 32:6 near him (Geneva, NKJV) nigh unto him (KJV)
Ps. 33:14 his dwelling (Geneva) his habitation (KJV) His dwelling (NKJV)
Ps. 33:16 great strength (Geneva, NKJV) much strength (KJV)
Ps. 33:17 A horse (Geneva, NKJV) An horse (KJV)
Ps. 34:18 near (Geneva, NKJV) nigh (KJV)
Ps. 38:11 my plague (Geneva, NKJV) my sore (KJV)
Ps. 38:12 wicked things (Geneva) mischievous things (KJV) destruction (NKJV)
Ps. 39:2 more stirred (Geneva) stirred (KJV) stirred up (NKJV)
Ps. 39:6 in a shadow (Geneva) in a vain shew (KJV) like a shadow (NKJV)
Ps. 39:10 plague (Geneva, NKJV) stroke (KJV)
Ps. 40:7 roll (Geneva) volume (KJV) scroll (NKJV)
Ps. 40:9 declared (Geneva) preached (KJV) proclaimed (NKJV)
Ps. 42:11 help (Geneva, NKJV) health (KJV)
Ps. 43:5 help (Geneva, NKJV) health (KJV)

Ps. 44:2 planted (Geneva, NKJV) plantedst (KJV)
Ps. 45:6 scepter of righteousness (Geneva, NKJV) right sceptre (KJV)
Ps. 51:11 holy Spirit (Geneva) holy spirit (KJV) Holy Spirit (NKJV)
Ps. 51:12 Restore to me (Geneva, NKJV) Restore unto me (KJV)
Ps. 52:1 wickedness (Geneva) mischief (KJV) evil (NKJV)
Ps. 53:3 corrupt (Geneva, NKJV) filthy (KJV)
Ps. 60:6 measure (Geneva, NKJV) mete (KJV)
Ps. 66:5 sons of men (Geneva, NKJV) children of men (KJV)
Ps. 66:6 river (Geneva, NKJV) flood (KJV)
Ps. 68:10 dwelled (Geneva) hath dwelt (KJV) dwelt (NKJV)
Ps. 68:14 Zalmon (Geneva, NKJV) Salmon (KJV)
Ps. 68:15 mountain of God (Geneva, NKJV) hill of God (KJV)
Ps. 68:15 mountain of Bashan (Geneva, NKJV) hill of Bashan (KJV)
Ps. 68:16 mountain (Geneva, NKJV) hill (KJV)
Ps. 68:21 will wound (Geneva, NKJV) shall wound (KJV)
Ps. 68:23 in blood (Geneva, NKJV) in the blood (KJV)
Ps. 68:25 maids (Geneva) damsels (KJV) maidens (NKJV)
Ps. 68:34 Ascribe (Geneva, NKJV) Ascribe ye (KJV)
Ps. 68:34 to God (Geneva, NKJV) unto God (KJV)
Ps. 69:3 is dry (Geneva, NKJV) is dried (KJV)
Ps. 69:18 Draw near (Geneva, NKJV) Draw nigh (KJV)
Ps. 69:34 in them (Geneva, NKJV) therein (KJV)
Ps. 70:1 be ashamed (Geneva) be put to confusion (KJV) be put to shame (NKJV)
Ps. 72:2 equity (Geneva) judgment (KJV) justice (NKJV)
Ps. 73:1 pure in heart (Geneva, NKJV) a clean heart (KJV)
Ps. 74:4 banners (Geneva, NKJV) ensigns (KJV)
Ps. 74:15 brakest up (Geneva) didst cleave (KJV) broke open (NKJV)
Ps. 75:8 full mixt (Geneva) full of mixture (KJV) fully mixed (NKJV)
Ps. 77:18 round about (Geneva) in the heaven (KJV) in the whirlwind (NKJV)
Ps. 78:19 prepare (Geneva, NKJV) furnish (KJV)
Ps. 78:45 swarm of flies (Geneva) divers sorts of flies (KJV) swarms of flies (NKJV)
Ps. 78:62 to the sword (Geneva, NKJV) unto the sword (KJV)
Ps. 79:12 to our neighbours (Geneva) unto our neighbours (KJV) to our neighbors (NKJV)
Ps. 80:5 hast fed (Geneva) feedest (KJV) have fed (NKJV)
Ps. 80:5 given (Geneva, NKJV) givest (KJV)
Ps. 80:6 hast made (Geneva) makest (KJV) have made (NKJV)
Ps. 81:2 song (Geneva, NKJV) psalm (KJV)
Ps. 81:3 Blow the trumpet (Geneva, NKJV) Blow up the trumpet (KJV)
Ps. 81:4 this is (Geneva) this *was* (KJV) this *is* (NKJV)
Ps. 83:9 Kishon (Geneva, NKJV) Kison (KJV)
Ps. 83:11 like Zebah (Geneva, NKJV) as Zebah (KJV)
Ps. 83:14 forest (Geneva) wood (KJV) woods (NKJV)
Ps. 84:7 appear before God in Zion (Geneva) in Zion appeareth before God (KJV) appears before God in Zion (NKJV)
Ps. 85:9 is near (Geneva, NKJV) is nigh (KJV)
Ps. 87:5 the most High (Geneva, NKJV) the highest (KJV)
Ps. 88:3 near to the grave (Geneva, NKJV) nigh unto the grave (KJV)
Ps. 88:13 come before (Geneva) prevent (KJV) comes before (NKJV)
Ps. 89:3 sworn to (Geneva, NKJV) sworn unto (KJV)
Ps. 89:10 mighty arm (Geneva, NKJV) strong arm (KJV)
Ps. 89:14 Righteousness (Geneva, NKJV) Justice (KJV)
Ps. 89:18 our shield (Geneva, NKJV) our defence (KJV)
Ps. 89:19 in a vision (Geneva, NKJV) in vision (KJV)
Ps. 91:7 come near (Geneva, NKJV) come nigh (KJV)
Ps. 91:10 come near (Geneva, NKJV) come nigh (KJV)
Ps. 92:2 To declare (Geneva, NKJV) To shew forth (KJV)

Ps. 92:12 like a palm tree (Geneva, NKJV) like the palm tree (KJV)
Ps. 92:15 To declare (Geneva, NKJV) To shew (KJV)
Ps. 93:1 established (Geneva, NKJV) stablished (KJV)
Ps. 94:10 the nations (Geneva, NKJV) the heathen (KJV)
Ps. 94:13 pit is (Geneva, NKJV) pit be (KJV)
Ps. 95:4 heights (Geneva, NKJV) strength (KJV)
Ps. 96:5 the people (Geneva) the nations (KJV) the peoples (NKJV)
Ps. 96:7 families (Geneva, NKJV) kindreds (KJV)
Ps. 96:9 tremble (Geneva, NKJV) fear (KJV)
Ps. 96:10 the nations (Geneva, NKJV) the heathen (KJV)
Ps. 97:2 foundation (Geneva, NKJV) habitation (KJV)
Ps. 97:5 The mountains (Geneva, NKJV) The hills (KJV)
Ps. 97:9 most high (Geneva, NKJV) high (KJV)
Ps. 98:1 his right hand, and holy arm have (Geneva) his right hand, and his holy arm, hath (KJV)
        His right hand and His holy arm have (NKJV)
Ps. 98:2 revealed (Geneva, NKJV) openly shewed (KJV)
Ps. 98:2 sight of the nations (Geneva, NKJV) sight of the heathen (KJV)
Ps. 98:4 sing praises (Geneva, NKJV) sing praise (KJV)
Ps. 98:5 to the (Geneva, NKJV) unto the (KJV)
Ps. 98:9 is come (Geneva) cometh (KJV) is coming (NKJV)
Ps. 99:5 Exalt (Geneva, NKJV) Exalt ye (KJV)
Ps. 101:4 evil (Geneva) wicked *person* (KJV) wickedness (NKJV)
Ps. 101:5 destroy (Geneva, NKJV) cut off (KJV)
Ps. 102:3 like an hearth (Geneva) as an hearth (KJV) like a hearth (NKJV)
Ps. 102:13 wilt arise (Geneva) shalt arise (KJV) will arise (NKJV)
Ps. 103:13 As a father (Geneva, NKJV) Like as a father (KJV)
Ps. 103:19 in heaven (Geneva, NKJV) in the heavens (KJV)
Ps. 104:8 to the place (Geneva, NKJV) unto the place (KJV)
Ps. 104:20 creep forth (Geneva) do creep *forth* (KJV) creep about (NKJV)
Ps. 104:23 to his work (Geneva, NKJV) unto his work (KJV)
Ps. 104:29 hide (Geneva, NKJV) hidest (KJV)
Ps. 104:30 send (Geneva, NKJV) sendest (KJV)
Ps. 105:17 a slave (Geneva, NKJV) a servant (KJV)
Ps. 105:22 ancients (Geneva) senators (KJV) elders (NKJV)
Ps. 105:25 craftily (Geneva, NKJV) subtilly (KJV)
Ps. 105:31 swarms of flies (Geneva, NKJV) divers sorts of flies (KJV)
Ps. 105:36 beginning (Geneva) chief (KJV) first (NKJV)
Ps. 105:38 had fallen (Geneva, NKJV) fell (KJV)
Ps. 106:7 rebelled (Geneva, NKJV) provoked (KJV)
Ps. 106:34 people (Geneva) nations (KJV) peoples (NKJV)
Ps. 107:11 despised (Geneva, NKJV) contemned (KJV)
Ps. 107:24 They see (Geneva, NKJV) These see (KJV)
Ps. 107:35 pools of water (Geneva, NKJV) standing water (KJV)
Ps. 107:39 diminished (Geneva, NKJV) minished (KJV)
Ps. 108:7 measure (Geneva, NKJV) mete (KJV)
Ps. 109:4 to prayer (Geneva) *unto* prayer (KJV) *to* prayer (NKJV)
Ps. 109:6 adversary (Geneva) Satan (KJV) accuser (NKJV)
Ps. 109:23 shaken off (Geneva, NKJV) tossed up and down (KJV)
Ps. 114:8 water pools (Geneva) standing water (KJV) pool of water (NKJV)
Ps. 116:6 he saved me (Geneva, NKJV) he helped me (KJV)
Ps. 118:12 were quenched (Geneva, NKJV) are quenched (KJV)
Ps. 119:25 to the dust (Geneva, NKJV) unto the dust (KJV)
Ps. 119:31 to thy (Geneva) unto thy (KJV) to Your (NKJV)
Ps. 119:38 to (Geneva, NKJV) unto (KJV)
Ps. 119:71 may learn (Geneva, NKJV) might learn (KJV)
Ps. 119:78 *and* falsely (Geneva) without a cause (KJV) with falsehood (NKJV)

Ps. 119:86 help me (Geneva, NKJV) help thou me (KJV)

Ps. 119:107 to (Geneva, NKJV) unto (KJV)

Ps. 119:130 to the simple (Geneva, NKJV) unto the simple (KJV)

Ps. 119:132 Look upon me (Geneva, NKJV) Look thou upon me (KJV)

Ps. 119:133 Direct my steps (Geneva, NKJV) Order my steps (KJV)

Ps. 119:146 I will keep (Geneva, NKJV) I shall keep (KJV)

Ps. 119:150 draw near (Geneva, NKJV) draw nigh (KJV)

Ps. 119:157 swerve (Geneva) decline (KJV) turn from (NKJV)

Ps. 119:160 is truth (Geneva, NKJV) is true (KJV)

Ps. 122:1 said to me (Geneva, NKJV) said unto me (KJV)

Ps. 124:5 swelling waters (Geneva) proud waters (KJV) swollen waters (NKJV)

Ps. 126:1 brought again (Geneva) turned again (KJV) brought back (NKJV)

Ps. 126:4 bring again (Geneva) Turn again (KJV) Bring back (NKJV)

Ps. 129:5 ashamed (Geneva) confounded (KJV) put to shame (NKJV)

Ps. 132:6 in Ephrathah (Geneva, NKJV) at Ephrathah (KJV)

Ps. 132:6 the forest (Geneva) the wood (KJV) the woods (NKJV)

Ps. 132:12 sons (Geneva, NKJV) children (KJV)

Ps. 133:2 border (Geneva) skirts (KJV) edge (NKJV)

Ps. 135:1 Praise the name (Geneva, NKJV) Praise ye the name (KJV)

Ps. 135:21 in Jerusalem (Geneva, NKJV) at Jerusalem (KJV)

Ps. 136:24 rescued (Geneva, NKJV) redeemed (KJV)

Ps. 138:5 sing of the ways (Geneva, NKJV) sing in the ways (KJV)

Ps. 139:7 Spirit (Geneva, NKJV) spirit (KJV)

Ps. 139:16 without form (Geneva) unperfect (KJV) unformed (NKJV)

Ps. 140:2 evil things (Geneva, NKJV) mischiefs (KJV)

Ps. 140:4 my steps (Geneva, NKJV) my goings (KJV)

Ps. 143:2 none (Geneva) no man (KJV) no one (NKJV)

Ps. 143:9 I hid me with thee (Geneva) I flee unto thee to hide me (KJV) In you I take shelter (NKJV)

Ps. 144:4 like (Geneva, NKJV) as (KJV)

Ps. 144:7 deliver me (Geneva) rid me (KJV) rescue me (NKJV)

Ps. 144:11 Rescue me (Geneva, NKJV) Rid me (KJV)

Ps. 144:15 *are* the people (Geneva, NKJV) *is that* people (KJV)

Ps. 145:5 I will mediate (Geneva, NKJV) I will speak (KJV)

Ps. 145:18 near (Geneva, NKJV) nigh (KJV)

Ps. 146:4 departeth (Geneva) goeth forth (KJV) departs (NKJV)

Ps. 146:7 justice (Geneva, NKJV) judgment (KJV)

Ps. 147:4 counteth (Geneva) telleth (KJV) counts (NKJV)

Ps. 148:6 established (Geneva, NKJV) stablished (KJV)

Ps. 148:7 depths (Geneva, NKJV) deeps (KJV)

Prov. 1:5 and increase (Geneva, NKJV) and will increase (KJV)

Prov. 1:25 despised (Geneva) set at nought (KJV) disdained (NKJV)

Prov. 1:27 like a whirlwind (Geneva, NKJV) as a whirlwind (KJV)

Prov. 2:1 within (Geneva, NKJV) with (KJV)

Prov. 2:7 shield (Geneva, NKJV) buckler (KJV)

Prov. 2:14 in doing evil (Geneva, NKJV) to do evil (KJV)

Prov. 2:18 to death (Geneva, NKJV) unto death (KJV)

Prov. 3:34 humble (Geneva, NKJV) lowly (KJV)

Prov. 4:8 embrace her (Geneva, NKJV) doest embrace her (KJV)

Prov. 4:16 evil (Geneva, NKJV) mischief (KJV)

Prov. 5:8 near (Geneva, NKJV) nigh (KJV)

Prov. 6:4 Give no sleep (Geneva, NKJV) Give not sleep (KJV)

Prov. 6:14 evil (Geneva, NKJV) mischief (KJV)

Prov. 6:21 enticed (Geneva) forced (KJV) seduced (NKJV)

Prov. 7:19 husband (Geneva, NKJV) goodman (KJV)

Prov. 8:3 entry of the doors (Geneva) coming in at the doors (KJV) entrance of the doors (NKJV)

Prov. 8:12 counsels (Geneva) witty inventions (KJV) discretion (NKJV)
Prov. 9:1 built (Geneva, NKJV) builded (KJV)
Prov. 9:4 is destitute of wisdom (Geneva) wanteth understanding (KJV) lacks understanding (NKJV)
Prov. 9:15 that pass by (Geneva) passengers (KJV) who pass by (NKJV)
Prov. 10:6 righteous (Geneva, NKJV) just (KJV)
Prov. 10:17 correction (Geneva, NKJV) reproof (KJV)
Prov. 10:23 do wickedly (Geneva) do mischief (KJV) do evil (NKJV)
Prov. 11:5 upright (Geneva) perfect (KJV) blameless (NKJV)
Prov. 11:10 joy (Geneva) shouting (KJV) jubilation (NKJV)
Prov. 11:27 evil (Geneva, NKJV) mischief (KJV)
Prov. 11:28 leaf (Geneva) branch (KJV) foliage (NKJV)
Prov. 12:1 correction (Geneva, NKJV) reproof (KJV)
Prov. 12:5 deceitful (Geneva, NKJV) deceit (KJV)
Prov. 12:21 evil (Geneva, NKJV) mischief (KJV)
Prov. 12:22 an abomination (Geneva, NKJV) abomination (KJV)
Prov. 13:4 have plenty (Geneva) be made fat (KJV) be made rich (NKJV)
Prov. 13:14 to turn away (Geneva) to depart (KJV) to turn *one* away (NKJV)
Prov. 13:17 evil (Geneva) mischief (KJV) trouble (NKJV)
Prov. 13:19 A desire (Geneva, NKJV) The desire (KJV)
Prov. 14:15 will consider (Geneva) looketh well (KJV) considers (NKJV)
Prov. 14:15 steps (Geneva, NKJV) going (KJV)
Prov. 14:19 evil shall bow (Geneva) evil bow (KJV) evil will bow (NKJV)
Prov. 15:5 correction (Geneva, NKJV) reproof (KJV)
Prov. 15:10 correction (Geneva, NKJV) reproof (KJV)
Prov. 15:11 sons of men (Geneva, NKJV) children of men (KJV)
Prov. 16:26 The person (Geneva, NKJV) He (KJV)
Prov. 17:5 He that (Geneva) Whoso (KJV) He who (NKJV)
Prov. 17:20 evil (Geneva, NKJV) mischief (KJV)
Prov. 19:15 person (Geneva, NKJV) soul (KJV)
Prov. 19:23 *leadeth* (Geneva) *tendeth* (KJV) *leads* (NKJV)
Prov. 20:2 like the roaring (Geneva, NKJV) as the roaring (KJV)
Prov. 20:4 because of winter (Geneva, NKJV) by reason of the cold (KJV)
Prov. 20:6 who can find a faithful man (Geneva, NKJV) a faithful man who can find (KJV)
Prov. 20:11 pure and right (Geneva, NKJV) pure, and whether it be right (KJV)
Prov. 20:17 afterward (Geneva, NKJV) afterwards (KJV)
Prov. 20:18 by counsel (Geneva) with good advice (KJV) by wise counsel (NKJV)
Prov. 20:24 steps (Geneva, NKJV) goings (KJV)
Prov. 21:4 A haughty look (Geneva, NKJV) An high look (KJV)
Prov. 21:5 to poverty (Geneva, NKJV) to want (KJV)
Prov. 21:8 perverted (Geneva) forward (KJV) perverse (NKJV)
Prov. 21:9 contentious woman (Geneva, NKJV) brawling woman (KJV)
Prov. 22:16 poverty (Geneva, NKJV) want (KJV)
Prov. 22:17 Incline (Geneva, NKJV) Bow down (KJV)
Prov. 23:11 against thee (Geneva) with thee (KJV) against you (NKJV)
Prov. 23:18 hope (Geneva, NKJV) expectation (KJV)
Prov. 23:20 gluttons (Geneva) riotous eaters of flesh (KJV) gluttonous eaters of meat (NKJV)
Prov. 24:13 eat honey (Geneva, NKJV) eat thou honey (KJV)
Prov. 24:14 hope (Geneva, NKJV) expectation (KJV)
Prov. 24:24 to the wicked (Geneva, NKJV) unto the wicked (KJV)
Prov. 25:3 heavens (Geneva, NKJV) heaven (KJV)
Prov. 25:24 contentious (Geneva, NKJV) brawling (KJV)
Prov. 26:2 sparrow (Geneva, NKJV) bird (KJV)
Prov. 27:4 raging (Geneva) outrageous (KJV) a torrent (NKJV)
Prov. 27:23 Be diligent (Geneva, NKJV) Be thou diligent (KJV)
Prov. 28:1 none (Geneva) no man (KJV) no one (NKJV)

Prov. 28:3 raging rain (Geneva) sweeping rain (KJV) driving rain (NKJV)
Prov. 28:7 gluttons (Geneva, NKJV) riotous *men* (KJV)
Prov. 28:14 evil (Geneva) mischief (KJV) calamity (NKJV)
Prov. 28:22 A man (Geneva, NKJV) He (KJV)
Prov. 29:3 wasteth (Geneva) spendeth (KJV) wastes (NKJV)
Prov. 29:24 declareth (Geneva) bewrayeth (KJV) reveals (NKJV)
Prov. 30:23 hateful woman (Geneva, NKJV) odious woman (KJV)
Prov. 31:22 fine linen (Geneva, NKJV) silk (KJV)
Eccl. 2:4 my great works (Geneva) me great works (KJV) my works great (NKJV)
Eccl. 2:4 I have built (Geneva) I builded (KJV) I built (NKJV)
Eccl. 2:8 have gathered unto me (Geneva) gathered me (KJV) gathered for myself (NKJV)
Eccl. 2:8 have provided (Geneva) gat (KJV) acquired (NKJV)
Eccl. 3:20 to one place (Geneva, NKJV) unto one place (NKJV)
Eccl. 4:8 neither son (Geneva, NKJV) neither child (KJV)
Eccl. 6:7 soul (Geneva, NKJV) appetite (KJV)
Eccl. 6:8 knoweth how to walk (Geneva) knoweth to walk (KJV) knows *how* to walk (NKJV)
Eccl. 7:6 For like (Geneva, NKJV) For as (KJV)
Eccl. 8:5 He that (Geneva) Whoso (KJV) He who (NKJV)
Eccl. 10:7 on horses (Geneva, NKJV) upon horses (KJV)
Eccl. 10:7 on the ground (Geneva, NKJV) upon the earth (KJV)
Eccl. 10:10 and one (Geneva) and he (KJV) And one (NKJV)
Eccl. 10:14 multiplieth words (Geneva) is full of words (KJV) multiplies words (NKJV)
Eccl. 12:14 will bring (Geneva, NKJV) shall bring (KJV)
Song of Solomon 1:6 sons (Geneva, NKJV) children (KJV)
Song of Solomon 1:13 between (Geneva, NKJV) betwixt (KJV)
Song of Solomon 2:2 Like a lily (Geneva, NKJV) As the lily (KJV)
Song of Solomon 2:3 Like (Geneva, NKJV) As (KJV)
Song of Solomon 2:3 the forest (Geneva) the wood (KJV) the woods (NKJV)
Song of Solomon 2:7 O daughters (Geneva, NKJV) (ye daughters (KJV)
Song of Solomon 3:5 O daughters (Geneva, NKJV) O ye daughters (KJV)
Song of Solomon 4:1 hair is like (Geneva, NKJV) hair is as (KJV)
Song of Solomon 4:4 built (Geneva, NKJV) builded (KJV)
Song of Solomon 4:6 I will go (Geneva, NKJV) I will get (KJV)
Song of Solomon 4:16 to his garden (Geneva, NKJV) into his garden (KJV)
Song of Solomon 5:4 heart (Geneva, NKJV) bowels (KJV)
Song of Solomon 5:12 His eyes are like doves (Geneva, NKJV)
    His eyes are as *the eyes* of doves (KJV)
Song of Solomon 6:5 like a flock (Geneva, NKJV) as a flock (KJV)
Song of Solomon 6:6 like a flock (Geneva, NKJV) as a flock (KJV)
Song of Solomon 6:12 chariots of my noble people (Geneva, NKJV)
        chariots of Ammi-nadib (KJV)
Song of Solomon 6:13 you see (Geneva, NKJV) ye see (KJV)
Song of Solomon 7:4 neck *is* like (Geneva, NKJV) neck *is* as (KJV)
Song of Solomon 7:7 like a palm tree (Geneva, NKJV) like to a palm tree (KJV)
Song of Solomon 7:12 my love (Geneva, NKJV) my loves (KJV)
Song of Solomon 8:10 peace (Geneva, NKJV) favour (KJV)
Isa. 1:4 to anger (Geneva, NKJV) unto anger (KJV)
Isa. 1:13 I cannot suffer (Geneva) I cannot away with (KJV) I cannot endure (NKJV)
Isa. 2:3 Come and let us (Geneva, NKJV) Come ye and let us (KJV)
Isa. 2:4 and rebuke (Geneva, NKJV) and shall rebuke (KJV)
Isa. 2:6 are full (Geneva) be replenished (KJV) are filled (NKJV)
Isa. 3:5 The people (Geneva, NKJV) And the people (KJV)
Isa. 3:11 to the wicked (Geneva, NKJV) unto the wicked (KJV)
Isa. 5:2 stones of it (Geneva) stones thereof (KJV) its stones (NKJV)
Isa. 5:3 between (Geneva, NKJV) betwixt (KJV)
Isa. 5:7 are his pleasant (Geneva) his pleasant (KJV) are His pleasant (NKJV)

Isa. 5:14 itself (Geneva, NKJV) herself (KJV)
Isa. 5:19 near (Geneva, NKJV) nigh (KJV)
Isa. 6:3 to another (Geneva, NKJV) unto another (KJV)
Isa. 6:5 I said (Geneva, NKJV) said I (KJV)
Isa. 6:7 And he touched (Geneva, NKJV) And he laid (KJV)
Isa. 7:2 the forest (Geneva) the wood (KJV) the woods (NKJV)
Isa. 7:13 Then he said (Geneva, NKJV) And he said (KJV)
Isa. 7:14 the virgin (Geneva, NKJV) a virgin (KJV)
Isa. 7:25 sheep (Geneva, NKJV) lesser cattle (KJV)
Isa. 8:15 shall fall (Geneva, NKJV) fall (KJV)
Isa. 8:19 whisper (Geneva, NKJV) peep (KJV)
Isa. 8:21 afflicted (Geneva) hardly bestead (KJV) hard pressed (NKJV)
Isa. 8:22 to the earth (Geneva, NKJV) unto the earth (KJV)
Isa. 9:1 the Gentiles (Geneva, NKJV) the nations (KJV)
Isa. 10:9 like Arpad (Geneva, NKJV) as Arphad (KJV)
Isa. 10:11 to Samaria (Geneva, NKJV) unto Samaria (KJV)
Isa. 10:15 saw exalt itself (Geneva, NKJV) saw magnify itself (KJV)
Isa. 10:28 his armour (Geneva) his carriages (KJV) his equipment (NKJV)
Isa. 12:2 and song (Geneva, NKJV) and *my* song (KJV)
Isa. 12:6 O inhabitant (Geneva, NKJV) thou inhabitant (KJV)
Isa. 13:2 Lift up (Geneva, NKJV) Lift ye up (KJV)
Isa. 13:21 ostriches (Geneva, NKJV) owls (KJV)
Isa. 14:11 sound (Geneva, NKJV) noise (KJV)
Isa. 14:18 sleep in glory (Geneva, NKJV) lie in glory (KJV)
Isa. 15:2 to the temple (Geneva, NKJV) to Bajith (KJV)
Isa. 15:6 grass (Geneva, NKJV) hay (KJV)
Isa. 16:9 upon thy summer fruits (Geneva) for thy summer fruits (KJV) over your summer fruits (NKJV)
Isa. 18:2 vessels of reeds (Geneva) vessels of bulrushes (KJV) vessels of reed (NKJV)
Isa. 18:7 a present (Geneva, NKJV) the present (KJV)
Isa. 19:3 their counsel (Geneva, NKJV) the counsel thereof (KJV)
Isa. 19:8 into the river (Geneva) into the brooks (KJV) into the River (NKJV)
Isa. 19:10 heavy in heart (Geneva) ponds for fish (KJV) troubled of soul (NKJV)
Isa. 20:1 to Ashdod (Geneva, NKJV) unto Ashdod (KJV)
Isa. 21:9 two horsemen (Geneva) couple of horsemen (KJV) pair of horsemen (NKJV)
Isa. 21:13 against Arabia (Geneva, NKJV) upon Arabia (KJV)
Isa. 21:14 O inhabitants (Geneva, NKJV) The inhabitants (KJV)
Isa. 22:2 full of noise (Geneva, NKJV) full of stirs (KJV)
Isa. 22:15 to Shebna (Geneva, NKJV) unto Shebna (KJV)
Isa. 23:4 Be ashamed (Geneva, NKJV) Be thou ashamed (KJV)
Isa. 23:17 at the end (Geneva, NKJV) after the end (KJV)
Isa. 24:7 wine faileth (Geneva) wine mourneth (KJV) wine fails (NKJV)
Isa. 25:5 the song (Geneva, NKJV) the branch (KJV)
Isa. 25:8 death forever (Geneva, NKJV) death in victory (KJV)
Isa. 26:4 Trust (Geneva, NKJV) Trust ye (KJV)
Isa. 26:10 mercy (Geneva) favour (KJV) grace (NKJV)
Isa. 26:20 pass over (Geneva) be overpast (KJV) is past (NKJV)
Isa. 27:9 broken in pieces (Geneva) beaten in sunder (KJV) are beaten to dust (NKJV)
Isa. 28:2 like a tempest of hail (Geneva, NKJV) as a tempest of hail (KJV)
Isa. 28:8 no place *is clean* (Geneva, NKJV) *that there is* no place *clean* (KJV)
Isa. 28:22 bonds (Geneva, NKJV) bands (KJV)
Isa. 29:3 ramparts (Geneva) forts (KJV) siege works (NKJV)
Isa. 29:7 strong holds (Geneva) munition (KJV) fortress (NKJV)
Isa. 29:8 soul longeth (Geneva) soul hath appetite (KJV) soul still craves (NKJV)
Isa. 29:9 they are blind and make you blind (Geneva) Cry ye out and cry (KJV) Blind yourselves and be blind (NKJV)

Isa. 29:12 that cannot read (Geneva) that is not learned (KJV) who is illiterate (NKJV)
Isa. 29:12 can not read (Geneva) am not learned (KJV) am not literate (NKJV)
Isa. 29:13 honour me with their lips (Geneva) with their lips do honour me (KJV) honor Me with their lips (NKJV)
Isa. 29:14 I will again do (Geneva, NKJV) I will proceed to do (KJV)
Isa. 29:16 the thing formed (Geneva, NKJV) the thing framed (KJV)
Isa. 29:16 fashioned it (Geneva) framed it (KJV) formed it (NKJV)
Isa. 30:12 Therefore (Geneva, NKJV) Wherefore (KJV)
Isa. 30:12 Because you (Geneva, NKJV) Because ye (KJV)
Isa. 30:17 ship mast (Geneva) beacon (KJV) pole (NKJV)
Isa. 30:22 images of silver (Geneva, NKJV) graven images of silver (KJV)
Isa. 30:24 till (Geneva) ear (KJV) work (NKJV)
Isa. 30:28 up to the neck (Geneva, NKJV) to the midst of the neck (KJV)
Isa. 30:31 the rod (Geneva, NKJV) a rod (KJV)
Isa. 31:4 As (Geneva, NKJV) Like as (KJV)
Isa. 31:8 by the sword (Geneva) with the sword (KJV) by a sword (NKJV)
Isa. 32:2 refuge (Geneva) covert (KJV) cover (NKJV)
Isa. 32:3 The eyes (Geneva, NKJV) And the eyes (KJV)
Isa. 32:6 do wickedly (Geneva) to practise hypocrisy (KJV) to practice ungodliness (NKJV)
Isa. 32:7 counsels (Geneva) devices (KJV) plans (NKJV)
Isa. 32:12 Men (Geneva) They (KJV) People (NKJV)
Isa. 32:15 the Spirit (Geneva, NKJV) the spirit (KJV)
Isa. 34:4 from the vine (Geneva, NKJV) off from the vine (KJV)
Isa. 34:5 Edom (Geneva, NKJV) Idumea (KJV)
Isa. 34:6 Edom (Geneva, NKJV) Idumea (KJV)
Isa. 34:11 pelican (Geneva, NKJV) cormorant (KJV)
Isa. 34:11 hedgehog (Geneva) bittern (KJV) porcupine (NKJV)
Isa. 34:13 ostriches (Geneva, NKJV) owls (KJV)
Isa. 34:17 in it (Geneva, NKJV) therein (KJV)
Isa. 35:3 Strengthen (Geneva, NKJV) Strengthen ye (KJV)
Isa. 36:3 the son of Hilkiah (Geneva, NKJV) Hilkiah's son (KJV)
Isa. 36:3 the son of Asaph (Geneva, NKJV) Asaph's son (KJV)
Isa. 36:11 to thy servants (Geneva) unto thy servants (KJV) to your servants (NKJV)
Isa. 36:12 on the wall (Geneva, NKJV) upon the wall (KJV)
Isa. 36:13 Hear (Geneva, NKJV) Hear ye (KJV)
Isa. 36:15 be given (Geneva, NKJV) be delivered (KJV)
Isa. 37:3 no strength (Geneva, NKJV) not strength (KJV)
Isa. 37:9 come out (Geneva, NKJV) come forth (KJV)
Isa. 37:34 forest of his fruitful places (Geneva) forest of his Carmel (KJV)
its fruitful forest (NKJV)
Isa. 37:26 made it (Geneva, NKJV) done it (KJV)
Isa. 37:28 dwelling (Geneva) abode (KJV) dwelling place (NKJV)
Isa. 37:38 land of Ararat (Geneva, NKJV) land of Armenia (KJV)
Isa. 38:11 among the inhabitants (Geneva, NKJV) with the inhabitants (KJV)
Isa. 38:13 like a lion (Geneva, NKJV) as a lion (KJV)
Isa. 38:15 he hath done it (Geneva) himself hath done it (KJV) He Himself has done it (NKJV)
Isa. 38:13 praise thee (Geneva) celebrate thee (KJV) praise You (NKJV)
Isa. 39:2 treasures (Geneva, NKJV) precious things (KJV)
Isa. 40:2 Speak (Geneva, NKJV) Speak ye (NKJV)
Isa. 40:12 counted (Geneva) meted out (KJV) measured (NKJV)
Isa. 40:19 an image (Geneva, NKJV) a graven image (KJV)
Isa. 41:23 that you (Geneva, NKJV) that ye (KJV)
Isa. 41:26 Surely (Geneva, NKJV) yea (KJV)
Isa. 42:1 Spirit (Geneva, NKJV) spirit (KJV)
Isa. 43:10 You (Geneva, NKJV) Ye (KJV)
Isa. 43:12 therefore you (Geneva) therefore ye (KJV) Therefore you (NKJV)

Isa. 43:14 fugitives (Geneva, NKJV) nobles (KJV)
Isa. 43:19 shal you (Geneva) shall ye (KJV) Shall you (NKJV)
Isa. 43:20 ostriches (Geneva, NKJV) owls (KJV)
Isa. 43:23 sheep (Geneva, NKJV) small cattle (KJV)
Isa. 44:3 Spirit (Geneva, NKJV) spirit (KJV)
Isa. 44:5 name (Geneva, NKJV) surname (KJV)
Isa. 44:9 an image (Geneva, NKJV) a graven image (NKJV)
Isa. 44:16 burneth the half (Geneva) burneth part (KJV) burns half (NKJV)
Isa. 44:19 half of it (Geneva, NKJV) part of it (KJV)
Isa. 44:22 like a (Geneva, NKJV) as a (KJV)
Isa. 45:1 doors (Geneva) two leaved gates (KJV) double doors (NKJV)
Isa. 45:5 besides me (Geneva) beside me (KJV) besides Me (NKJV)
Isa. 45:6 besides me (Geneva) beside me (KJV) besides Me (NKJV)
Isa. 45:6 none other (Geneva, NKJV) none else (KJV)
Isa. 45:10 to *his* father (Geneva, NKJV) unto *his* father (KJV)
Isa. 45:11 you (Geneva, NKJV) ye (KJV)
Isa. 45:14 other (Geneva, NKJV) else (KJV)
Isa. 45:22 none other (Geneva, NKJV) none else (KJV)
Isa. 45:22 he shall say (Geneva, NKJV) shall *one* say (KJV)
Isa. 46:3 womb (Geneva, NKJV) belly (KJV)
Isa. 46:7 bear it (Geneva, NKJV) bear him (KJV)
Isa. 46:9 other (Geneva, NKJV) else (KJV)
Isa. 46:12 stubborn hearted (Geneva) stouthearted (KJV) stubborn-hearted (NKJV)
Isa. 47:2 pass through (Geneva, NKJV) pass over (KJV)
Isa. 47:11 destruction (Geneva) mischief (KJV) trouble (NKJV)
Isa. 48:5 carved image (Geneva, NKJV) graven image (KJV)
Isa. 48:10 as silver (Geneva, NKJV) with silver (KJV)
Isa. 48:15 his way shall prosper (Geneva) he shall make his way prosperous (KJV) his way will prosper (NKJV)
Isa. 48:16 Come near (Geneva, NKJV) Come ye near (KJV)
Isa. 49:6 small (Geneva, NKJV) light (KJV)
Isa. 49:23 faces (Geneva, NKJV) face (KJV)
Isa. 50:11 all you (Geneva, NKJV) all ye (KJV)
Isa. 52:11 Depart (Geneva, NKJV) Depart ye (KJV)
Isa. 54:3 increase (Geneva) break forth (KJV) expand (NKJV)
Isa. 55:1 come (Geneva, NKJV) come ye (KJV)
Isa. 56:1 Keep (Geneva, NKJV) Keep ye (KJV)
Isa. 56:12 Come (Geneva, NKJV) Come ye (KJV)
Isa. 56:12 will bring wine (Geneva, NKJV) will fetch wine (KJV)
Isa. 57:17 and was angry (Geneva, NKJV) and was wroth (KJV)
Isa. 59:9 darkness (Geneva, NKJV) obscurity (KJV)
Isa. 59:10 twilight (Geneva, NKJV) night (KJV)
Isa. 60:5 riches (Geneva) forces (KJV) wealth (NKJV)
Isa. 60:8 like a cloud (Geneva, NKJV) as a cloud (KJV)
Isa. 61:1 poor (Geneva, NKJV) meek (KJV)
Isa. 63:2 winepress (Geneva, NKJV) winefat (KJV)
Isa. 63:5 sustained me (Geneva) upheld me (KJV) sustained Me (NKJV)
Isa. 64:12 above measure (Geneva) very sore (KJV) very severely (NKJV)
Isa. 66:16 judge (Geneva, NKJV) plead (KJV)
Jer. 1:5 in the womb (Geneva, NKJV) in the belly (KJV)
Jer. 2:27 a tree (Geneva, NKJV) a stock (KJV)
Jer. 4:4 hearts (Geneva, NKJV) heart (KJV)
Jer. 4:5 Declare (Geneva, NKJV) Declare ye (KJV)
Jer. 4:5 Blow (Geneva, NKJV) Blow ye (KJV)
Jer. 5:1 Run to (Geneva, NKJV) Run ye to (KJV)
Jer. 5:6 wilderness (Geneva) evenings (KJV) deserts (NKJV)

Jer. 5:6 destroy (Geneva, NKJV) spoil (KJV)
Jer. 6:4 Prepare war (Geneva, NKJV) Prepare ye war (KJV)
Jer. 6:16 Stand in the ways (Geneva, NKJV) Stand ye in the ways (KJV)
Jer. 7:8 you trust (Geneva, NKJV) ye trust (KJV)
Jer. 7:9 Will you (Geneva, NKJV) Will ye (KJV)
Jer. 7:11 den of thieves (Geneva, NKJV) den of robbers (KJV)
Jer. 7:24 would not obey (Geneva) hearkened not (KJV) did not obey (NKJV)
Jer. 8:21 I am heavy (Geneva) I am black (KJV) I am mourning (NKJV)
Jer. 9:11 heap (Geneva, NKJV) heaps (KJV)
Jer. 9:17 skillful (Geneva, NKJV) cunning (KJV)
Jer. 9:18 water (Geneva, NKJV) waters (KJV)
Jer. 10:16 maker (Geneva) former (KJV) Maker (NKJV)
Jer. 12:13 reaped (Geneva, NKJV) shall reap (KJV)
Jer. 13:15 Hear and give (Geneva, NKJV) Hear ye and give (KJV)
Jer. 15:12 brass (Geneva) steel (KJV) bronze (NKJV)
Jer. 17:20 Hear (Geneva, NKJV) Hear ye (KJV)
Jer. 18:8 to bring (Geneva, NKJV) to do (KJV)
Jer. 19:14 where (Geneva, NKJV) whither (KJV)
Jer. 20:3 brought Jeremiah (Geneva, NKJV) brought forth Jeremiah (KJV)
Jer. 22:10 Weep not (Geneva, NKJV) Weep ye not (KJV)
Jer. 22:30 Write this man (Geneva, NKJV) Write ye this man (KJV)
Jer. 23:8 where I (Geneva, NKJV) whither I (KJV)
Jer. 23:9 his holy words (Geneva) the words of his holiness (KJV) His holy words (NKJV)
Jer. 23:29 like a fire (Geneva, NKJV) like as a fire (KJV)
Jer. 23:38 if you say (Geneva) since ye say (KJV) since you say (NKJV)
Jer. 25:27 Drink (Geneva, NKJV) Drink ye (KJV)
Jer. 29:16 Therefore thus (Geneva, NKJV) *Know* that thus (KJV)
Jer. 29:28 build houses (Geneva, NKJV) build ye houses (KJV)
Jer. 30:11 by judgement (Geneva) in measure (KJV) in justice (NKJV)
Jer. 33:13 the plain (Geneva) the vale (KJV) the lowland (NKJV)
Jer. 34:17 obeyed (Geneva, NKJV) hearkened (KJV)
Jer. 35:5 Drink wine (Geneva, NKJV) Drink ye wine (KJV)
Jer. 35:13 obey (Geneva, NKJV) hearken to (KJV)
Jer. 35:16 obeyed (Geneva, NKJV) hearkened unto (KJV
Jer. 36:15 that we may hear (Geneva) in our ears (KJV) in our hearing (NKJV)
Jer. 39:4 between (Geneva, NKJV) betwixt (KJV)
Jer. 44:14 to dwell there (Geneva, NKJV) to sojourn (KJV)
Jer. 46:14 proclaim in Noph (Geneva, NKJV) publish in Noph (KJV)
Jer. 49:19 dwelling place (Geneva, NKJV) habitation (KJV)
Jer. 50:2 Declare (Geneva, NKJV) Declare ye (KJV)
Jer. 50:36 soothsayers (Geneva, NKJV) liars (KJV)
Jer. 51:19 maker (Geneva) former (KJV) Maker (NKJV)
Jer. 52:2 did evil (Geneva, NKJV) did *that which was* evil (KJV)
Jer. 52:12 King Nebuchadnezzar king (Geneva, NKJV) Nebuchadrezzar king (KJV)
Jer. 52:18 pots (Geneva, NKJV) caldrons (KJV)
Lam. 1:13 and turned me back (Geneva, NKJV) he hath turned me back (KJV)
Lam. 1:21 pronounced (Geneva) called (KJV) announced (NKJV)
Lam. 2:13 liken to them (Geneva) equal to them (KJV) compare with you (NKJV)
Lam. 2:14 false prophecies (Geneva, NKJV) false burdens (KJV)
Lam. 2:17 purposed (Geneva, NKJV) devised (KJV)
Lam. 3:41 hearts (Geneva, NKJV) heart (KJV)
Lam. 3:62 their whispering (Geneva, NKJV) their device (KJV)
Lam. 4:15 dwell (Geneva, NKJV) sojourn (KJV)
Lam. 4:16 scattered (Geneva, NKJV) divided (KJV)
Ezek. 1:12 every one (Geneva) they (KJV) each one (NKJV)
Ezek. 1:13 went lightning (Geneva, NKJV) went forth lightning (KJV)

Ezek. 1:22 wonderful (Geneva) terrible (KJV) awesome (NKJV)
Ezek. 2:2 the Spirit (Geneva, NKJV) the spirit (KJV)
Ezek. 2:7 rebellious (Geneva, NKJV) most rebellious (KJV)
Ezek. 3:5 unknown (Geneva) strange (KJV) unfamiliar (NKJV)
Ezek. 3:12 the Spirit (Geneva, NKJV) the spirit (KJV)
Ezek. 3:14 the Spirit (Geneva, NKJV) the spirit (KJV)
Ezek. 3:24 the Spirit (Geneva, NKJV) the spirit (KJV)
Ezek. 7:26 Calamity (Geneva) Mischief (KJV) Diasaster (NKJV)
Ezek. 8:3 stretched out (Geneva, NKJV) put forth (KJV)
Ezek. 8:3 the Spirit (Geneva, NKJV) the spirit (KJV)
Ezek. 10:17 the *cherubims* stood (Geneva) they stood (KJV) the *cherubim* stood (NKJV)
Ezek. 11:1 the Spirit (Geneva, NKJV) the spirit (KJV)
Ezek. 11:24 the Spirit (Geneva, NKJV) the spirit (KJV)
Ezek. 12:3 captivity (Geneva, NKJV) removing (KJV)
Ezek. 13:13 a stormy wind to break forth (Geneva, NKJV) rend it with a stormy wind (KJV)
Ezek. 13:18 vails (Geneva) kerchiefs (KJV) veils (NKJV)
Ezek. 13:21 vails (Geneva) kerchiefs (KJV) veils (NKJV)
Ezek. 16:28 insatiable (Geneva, NKJV) unsatiable (KJV)
Ezek. 16:55 former state (Geneva, NKJV) former estate (KJV)
Ezek. 16:63 be ashamed (Geneva, NKJV) be confounded (KJV)
Ezek. 20:38 where they dwell (Geneva, NKJV) where they sojourn (KJV)
Ezek. 20:39 obey me (Geneva) hearken unto me (KJV) obey Me (NKJV)
Ezek. 25:4 men of the East (Geneva) men of the east (KJV)
Ezek. 25:10 men of the East (Geneva, NKJV) men of the east (KJV)
Ezek. 27:19 merchandise (Geneva, NKJV) market (KJV)
Ezek. 27:31 They (Geneva, NKJV) And they (KJV)
Ezek. 28:2 I am a god (Geneva) I *am* a God (KJV) I *am* a god (NKJV)
Ezek. 28:9 I am a god (Geneva) I *am* God (KJV) I *am* a god (NKJV)
Ezek. 29:7 with their hand (Geneva) by thy hand (KJV) with the hand (NKJV)
Ezek. 32:9 also trouble (Geneva, NKJV) also vex (KJV)
Ezek. 34:4 The weak (Geneva, NKJV) The diseased KJV)
Ezek. 36:29 deliver (Geneva, NKJV) save (KJV)
Ezek. 37:1 the Spirit (Geneva, NKJV) the spirit (KJV)
Ezek. 37:14 Spirit (Geneva, NKJV) spirit (KJV)
Ezek. 38:7 Prepare thyself (Geneva) Be thou prepared (KJV) Prepare yourself (NKJV)
Ezek. 39:6 dwell safely (Geneva) dwell carelessly (KJV) live in security (NKJV)
Ezek. 39:11 a place there for burial in Israel (Geneva) a place there of graves in Israel (KJV) a
burial place there in Israel (NKJV)
Ezek. 41:2 the entry (Geneva) the door (KJV) the entryway (NKJV)
Ezek. 46:3 entry (Geneva) door (KJV) entrance (NKJV)
Ezek. 46:3 on the Sabbaths (Geneva, NKJV) in the sabbaths (KJV)
Ezek. 46:4 on the Sabbath day (Geneva, NKJV) in the sabbath day (KJV)
Ezek. 46:13 daily make (Geneva, NKJV) daily prepare (KJV)
Ezek. 46:18 shall not take of the people's inheritance (Geneva)
              shall not take of the people's inheritance by oppression (KJV)
              shall not take any of the people's inheritance (NKJV)
Ezek. 46:24 the kitchen (Geneva) the places of them that boil (KJV) the kitchens (NKJV)
Ezek. 47:22 you shall divide (Geneva) ye shall divide (KJV) you will divide (NKJV)
Dan. 1:9 chief of the eunuchs (Geneva, NKJV) prince of the eunuchs (KJV)
Dan. 1:11 chief (Geneva, NKJV) prince (KJV)
Dan. 1:18 chief (Geneva, NKJV) prince (KJV)
Dan. 4:9 chief (Geneva, NKJV) master (KJV)
Dan. 5:5 appeared (Geneva, NKJV) came forth (KJV)
Dan. 5:7 purple (Geneva, NKJV) scarlet (KJV)
Dan. 5:16 purple (Geneva, NKJV) scarlet (KJV)
Dan. 5:29 purple (Geneva, NKJV) scarlet (KJV)

Dan. 6:2 rulers (Geneva) presidents (KJV) governors (NKJV)
Dan. 6:7 any god (Geneva, NKJV) any God (KJV)
Dan. 6:12 any god (Geneva, NKJV) any God (KJV)
Dan. 7:5 like a bear (Geneva, NKJV) like to a bear (KJV)
Dan. 7:9 thrones were set up (Geneva) thrones were cast down (KJV) thrones were put in place (NKJV)
Dan. 7:11 presumptuous words (Geneva) great words (KJV) pompous words (NKJV)
Dan. 8:10 it grew up (Geneva, NKJV) it waxed great (KJV)
Dan. 8:26 seal (Geneva, NKJV) shut (KJV)
Dan. 9:7 open shame (Geneva) confusion of faces (KJV) shame of face (NKJV)
Dan. 10:7 great fear (Geneva) great quaking (KJV) great terror (NKJV)
Dan. 10:12 humble thyself (Geneva) chasten thyself (KJV) humble yourself (NKJV)
Dan. 11:12 he shall not *still* prevail (Geneva) he shall not be strengthened by it (KJV) he will not prevail (NKJV)
Dan. 11:17 to destroy (Geneva, NKJV) corrupting (KJV)
Hos. 1:7 Yet I (Geneva, NKJV) But I (KJV)
Hos. 2:1 Say unto (Geneva) Say ye unto (KJV) Say to (NKJV)
Hos. 3:1 to me (Geneva, NKJV) unto me (KJV)
Hos. 3:3 abide with me (Geneva, NKJV) abide for me (KJV)
Hos. 4:9 their deeds (Geneva, NKJV) their doings (KJV)
Hos. 4:16 unruly (Geneva) backsliding (KJV) stubborn (NKJV)
Hos. 6:1 return to (Geneva, NKJV) return unto (KJV)
Hos. 9:17 obey (Geneva, NKJV) hearken (KJV)
Hos. 10:5 calf (Geneva, NKJV) calves (KJV)
Hos. 10:13 you have plowed (Geneva, NKJV) ye have plowed (KJV)
Hos. 12:1 the wind (Geneva, NKJV) wind (KJV)
Hos. 12:7 He is Canaan (Geneva) He is a merchant (KJV) A cunning Canaanite (NKJV)
Hos. 12:11 field (Geneva, NKJV) fields (KJV)
Hos. 13:4 no God (Geneva, NKJV) no god (KJV)
Joel 1:2 elders (Geneva, NKJV) old men (KJV)
Joel 2:1 Blow the trumpet (Geneva, NKJV) Blow ye the trumpet (KJV)
Joel 2:1 it is at hand (Geneva, NKJV) it is nigh at hand (KJV)
Joel 2:28 my Spirit (Geneva) my spirit (KJV) My Spirit (NKJV)
Joel 3:13 Put in (Geneva, NKJV) Put ye in (KJV)
Amos 1:5 Beth-Eden (Geneva, NKJV) house of Eden (KJV)
Amos 2:2 Kerioth (Geneva, NKJV) Kirioth (KJV)
Amos 2:7 pervert (Geneva, NKJV) turn aside (KJV)
Amos 2:15 shall not escape (Geneva, NKJV) shall not deliver *himself* (KJV)
Amos 3:9 Proclaim (Geneva, NKJV) Publish (KJV)
Amos 3:13 Hear (Geneva, NKJV) Hear ye (KJV)
Amos 5:8 Pleiades and Orion (Geneva, NKJV) the seven stars and Orion (KJV)
Amos 5:8 dark as night (Geneva, NKJV) dark with night (KJV)
Amos 5:14 you have spoken (Geneva, NKJV) ye have spoken (KJV)
Amos 5:26 Siccuth your king (Geneva) tabernacle of your Moloch (KJV) Sikkuth your king (NKJV)
Amos 6:2 Go you (Geneva) Pass ye (KJV) Go over (NKJV)
Amos 6:5 sing (Geneva, NKJV) chant (KJV)
Amos 6:12 wormwood (Geneva, NKJV) hemlock (KJV)
Obad. 1:6 treasures searched (Geneva) hidden things sought up (KJV) hidden treasures shall be sought after (NKJV)
Jonah 1:5 lay down (Geneva) lay (KJV) had lain down (NKJV)
Jonah 2:6 from the pit (Geneva, NKJV) from corruption (KJV)
Jonah 3:3 to Nineveh (Geneva, NKJV) unto Nineveh (KJV)
Micah 1:8 ostriches (Geneva, NKJV) owls (KJV)
Micah 2:7 the Spirit (Geneva, NKJV) the spirit (KJV)
Micah 2:10 Arise (Geneva, NKJV) Arise ye (KJV)
Micah 6:5 devised (Geneva) consulted (KJV) counseled (NKJV)

Micah 6:15 but not reap (Geneva, NKJV) but thou shalt not reap (KJV)
Nahum 2:7 smiting (Geneva) tabering (KJV) beating (NKJV)
Nahum 2:12 dens with spoil (Geneva) dens with ravin (KJV) dens with flesh (NKJV)
Hab. 1:14 fish (Geneva, NKJV) fishes (KJV)
Hab. 2:7 prey (Geneva) booties (KJV) booty (NKJV)
Zeph. 1:3 fish (Geneva, NKJV) fishes (KJV)
Zeph. 1:12 lights (Geneva) candles (KJV) lamps (NKJV)
Zeph. 1:15 destruction (Geneva) wasteness (KJV) devastation (NKJV)
Zeph. 2:8 borders (Geneva, NKJV) border (KJV)
Zeph. 2:14 pelican (Geneva, NKJV) cormorant (KJV)
Zeph. 2:15 besides me (Geneva, NKJV) beside me (KJV)
Hag. 1:1 King Darius (Geneva, NKJV) Darius the king (KJV)
Hag. 1:12 Jehozadak (Geneva, NKJV) Josedech (KJV)
Hag. 1:14 Jehozadak (Geneva, NKJV) Josedech (KJV)
Hag. 2:2 Jehozadak (Geneva, NKJV) Josedech (KJV)
Hag. 2:4 Jehozadak (Geneva, NKJV) Josedech (KJV)
Hag. 2:16 wine press (Geneva) pressfat (KJV) wine vat (NKJV)
Zech. 1:6 determined to do (Geneva, NKJV) thought to do (KJV)
Zech. 1:14 zeal (Geneva, NKJV) jealousy (KJV)
Zech. 1:15 a little angry (Geneva, NKJV) a little displeased (KJV)
Zech. 6:11 Jehozadak (Geneva, NKJV) Josedech (KJV)
Zech. 7:9 compassion (Geneva, NKJV) compassions (KJV)
Zech. 7:12 Spirit (Geneva, NKJV) spirit (KJV)
Zech. 8:3 I will return (Geneva, NKJV) I am returned (KJV)
Zech. 8:15 determined (Geneva, NKJV) thought (KJV)
Zech. 9:8 will camp (Geneva, NKJV) will encamp (KJV)
Zech. 11:12 wages (Geneva, NKJV) price (KJV)
Zech. 12:3 heavy stone (Geneva, NKJV) burdensome stone (KJV)
Zech. 12:10 Spirit (Geneva, NKJV) spirit (KJV)
Zech. 13:2 depart (Geneva, NKJV) pass (KJV)
Mal. 1:10 in vain (Geneva) for nought (KJV)
Mal. 3:15 blessed (Geneva, NKJV) happy (KJV)
Mal. 3:16 spake (Geneva) spake often (KJV) spoke (NKJV)
Mal. 4:4 Remember the Law (Geneva, NKJV) Remember ye the law (KJV)

Matt. 1:18 betrothed (Geneva, NKJV) espoused (KJV)
Matt. 1:19 secretly (Geneva, NKJV) privily (KJV)
Matt. 1:20 the son of David (Geneva) thou son of David (KJV) son of David (NKJV)
Matt. 2:3 heard *this* (Geneva, NKJV) heard *these things* (KJV)
Matt. 2:4 asked (Geneva) demanded (KJV) inquired (NKJV)
Matt. 2:6 feed (Geneva) rule (KJV) shepherd (NKJV)
Matt. 2:9 they had seen (Geneva, NKJV) they saw (KJV)
Matt. 2:16 all the male children (Geneva, NKJV) all the children (KJV)
Matt. 3:2 Repent (Geneva, NKJV) Repent ye (KJV)
Matt. 3:13 came (Geneva, NKJV) cometh (KJV)
Matt. 4:2 hungry (Geneva, NKJV) an hungred (KJV)
Matt. 4:6 and said (Geneva, NKJV) And saith (KJV)
Matt. 4:6 over (Geneva, NKJV) concerning (KJV)
Matt. 4:8 devil took (Geneva, NKJV) devil taketh (KJV)
Matt. 4:8 and shewed (Geneva) and sheweth (KJV) and showed (NKJV)
Matt. 4:9 said (Geneva, NKJV) saith (KJV)
Matt. 4:10 said (Geneva, NKJV) saith (KJV)
Matt. 4:19 said (Geneva, NKJV) saith (KJV)
Matt. 5:21 said unto (Geneva) said by (KJV) said to (NKJV)
Matt. 5:27 said to (Geneva, NKJV) said by (KJV)
Matt. 5:29 cause thee to offend (Geneva) offend thee (KJV) causes you to sin (NKJV)

Matt. 5:30 make thee to offend (Geneva) offend thee (KJV) causes you to sin (NKJV)
Matt. 5:33 said to (Geneva, NKJV) said by (KJV)
Matt. 5:33 to the Lord (Geneva, NKJV) unto the Lord (KJV)
Matt. 6:8 like them (Geneva, NKJV) like unto them (KJV)
Matt. 6:25 be not careful (Geneva) take no thought (KJV) do not worry (NKJV)
Matt. 7:5 Hypocrite (Geneva, NKJV) Thou hypocrite (KJV)
Matt. 8:4 Jesus said (Geneva, NKJV) Jesus saith (KJV)
Matt. 8:7 Jesus said (Geneva, NKJV) Jesus saith (KJV)
Matt. 8:13 Then Jesus (Geneva, NKJV) And Jesus (KJV)
Matt. 8:17 He took (Geneva) Himself took (KJV) He Himself took (NKJV)
Matt. 8:18 And when (Geneva, NKJV) Now when (KJV)
Matt. 8:19 Then (Geneva, NKJV) And (KJV)
Matt. 8:25 Then (Geneva, NKJV) And (KJV)
Matt. 8:26 said (Geneva, NKJV) saith (KJV)
Matt. 8:33 Then (Geneva, NKJV) And (KJV)
Matt. 9:2 sins are forgiven (Geneva, NKJV) sins be forgiven (KJV)
Matt. 9:5 sins are forgiven (Geneva, NKJV) sins be forgiven (KJV)
Matt. 9:6 go to (Geneva, NKJV) go unto (KJV)
Matt. 9:8 to men (Geneva, NKJV) unto men (KJV)
Matt. 9:9 said to (Geneva, NKJV) saith unto (KJV)
Matt. 9:11 said to (Geneva, NKJV) said unto (KJV)
Matt. 9:17 do they (Geneva, NKJV) do men (KJV)
Matt. 9:28 Jesus said (Geneva, NKJV) Jesus saith (KJV)
Matt. 9:31 But when they were departed, they (Geneva, NKJV) But they, when they were departed (KJV)
Matt. 9:37 said he to (Geneva) saith he unto (KJV) He said to (NKJV)
Matt. 10:18 to them (Geneva, NKJV) against them (KJV)
Matt. 10:27 on (Geneva, NKJV) upon (KJV)
Matt. 10:36 enemies (Geneva, NKJV) foes (KJV)
Matt. 11:8 to see (Geneva, NKJV) for to see (KJV)
Matt. 11:9 to see (Geneva, NKJV) for to see (KJV)
Matt. 11:14 to come (Geneva, NKJV) for to come (KJV)
Matt. 11:22 say to you (Geneva, NKJV) say unto you (KJV)
Matt. 11:27 to whom (Geneva, NKJV) to whomsoever (KJV)
Matt. 12:2 And when (Geneva, NKJV) But when (KJV)
Matt. 12:2 Sabbath (Geneva, NKJV) sabbath day (KJV)
Matt. 12:8 of the Sabbath (Geneva, NKJV) of the Sabbath day (KJV)
Matt. 12:25 But Jesus (Geneva, NKJV) And Jesus (KJV)
Matt. 12:31 every sin (Geneva, NKJV) All manner of sin (KJV)
Matt. 12:34 how can you (Geneva, NKJV) how can ye (KJV)
Matt. 12:39 said to them (Geneva, NKJV) said unto them (KJV)
Matt. 13:3 Then he (Geneva) And he (KJV) Then He (NKJV)
Matt. 13:3 to them (Geneva, NKJV) unto them (KJV)
Matt. 13:4 And as he sowed (Geneva, NKJV) And when he sowed (KJV)
Matt. 13:5 no depth (Geneva, NKJV) no deepness (KJV)
Matt. 13:10 said to (Geneva, NKJV) said unto (KJV)
Matt. 13:10 to them (Geneva, NKJV) unto them (KJV)
Matt. 13:13 do not see (Geneva, NKJV) see not (KJV)
Matt. 13:28 to them (Geneva, NKJV) unto them (KJV)
Matt. 13:33 to them (Geneva, NKJV) unto them (KJV)
Matt. 13:34 to them (Geneva, NKJV) unto them (KJV)
Matt. 13:37 to them (Geneva, NKJV) unto them (KJV)
Matt. 13:51 Jesus said (Geneva, NKJV) Jesus saith (KJV)
Matt. 13:57 to them (Geneva, NKJV) unto them (KJV)
Matt. 14:8 platter (Geneva, NKJV) charger (KJV)
Matt. 14:9 because of (Geneva, NKJV) for (KJV)

Matt. 14:11 platter (Geneva, NKJV) charger (KJV)
Matt. 14:16 to them (Geneva, NKJV) unto them (KJV)
Matt. 14:16 to go away (Geneva, NKJV) depart (KJV)
Matt. 14:31 said to him (Geneva, NKJV) said unto him (KJV)
Matt. 14:35 were sick (Geneva, NKJV) were diseased (KJV)
Matt. 15:6 of no (Geneva, NKJV) of none (KJV)
Matt. 15:8 near (Geneva, NKJV) nigh (KJV)
Matt. 15:10 said to them (Geneva, NKJV) said unto them (KJV)
Matt. 15:15 to him (Geneva) unto him (KJV) to Him (NKJV)
Matt. 15:25 she came (Geneva, NKJV) came she (KJV)
Matt. 15:26 good (Geneva, NKJV) meet (KJV)
Matt. 15:26 whelps (Geneva) dogs (KJV) little dogs (NKJV)
Matt. 15:27 whelps (Geneva) dogs (KJV) little dogs (NKJV)
Matt. 15:37 fragments (Geneva, NKJV) broken *meat* (KJV)
Matt. 16:3 O hypocrites (Geneva) O ye hypocrites (KJV) Hypocrites (NKJV)
Matt. 16:6 and Sadducees (Geneva) and of the Sadducees (KJV) and the Sadducees (NKJV)
Matt. 16:12 of the Pharisees and Sadducees (Geneva, NKJV) of the Pharisees and of the Sadducees (KJV)
Matt. 16:15 He said (Geneva, NKJV) He saith (KJV)
Matt. 16:17 said to him (Geneva, NKJV) said unto him (KJV)
Matt. 16:22 took him aside (Geneva) took him (KJV) took Him aside (NKJV)
Matt. 16:23 but the things (Geneva, NKJV) but those (KJV)
Matt. 17:1 Jesus took (Geneva, NKJV) Jesus taketh (KJV)
Matt. 17:2 clothes (Geneva, NKJV) raiment (KJV)
Matt. 17:4 said to Jesus (Geneva, NKJV) said unto Jesus (KJV)
Matt. 17:25 He said (Geneva, NKJV) He saith (KJV)
Matt. 17:27 Nevertheless (Geneva, NKJV) Notwithstanding (KJV)
Matt. 18:1 the disciples came (Geneva, NKJV) came the disciples (KJV)
Matt. 18:12 go (Geneva, NKJV) goeth (KJV)
Matt. 18:12 seek (Geneva, NKJV) seeketh (KJV)
Matt. 18:16 by the mouth (Geneva, NKJV) in the mouth (KJV)
Matt. 18:17 refuse (Geneva) neglect (KJV) refuses (NKJV)
Matt. 18:22 Jesus said (Geneva, NKJV) Jesus saith (KJV)
Matt. 18:25 his master (Geneva, NKJV) his lord (KJV)
Matt. 18:26 Master (Geneva, NKJV) Lord (KJV)
Matt. 18:32 Then his master (Geneva, NKJV) Then his lord (KJV)
Matt. 19:18 He said (Geneva, NKJV) He saith (KJV)
Matt. 19:27 said to him (Geneva) said unto him (KJV) said to Him (NKJV)
Matt. 20:16 many are called (Geneva, NKJV) many be called (KJV)
Matt. 20:26 your servant (Geneva, NKJV) your minister (KJV)
Matt. 20:28 to be served, but to serve (Geneva, NKJV) to be ministered unto, but to minister
Matt. 20:30 O Lord, the son of David (Geneva) O Lord, *thou* son of David (KJV) O Lord, Son of David (NKJV)
Matt. 20:31 the son of David (Geneva) *thou* son of David (KJV) Son of David (NKJV)
Matt. 20:33 said to him (Geneva) say unto him (KJV) said to Him (NKJV)
Matt. 21:1 near (Geneva, NKJV) nigh (KJV)
Matt. 21:2 to them (Geneva, NKJV) unto them (KJV)
Matt. 21:6 So the disciples (Geneva, NKJV) And the disciples (KJV)
Matt. 21:7 and set (Geneva, NKJV) and they set (KJV)
Matt. 21:13 to them (Geneva, NKJV) unto them (KJV)
Matt. 21:14 Then (Geneva, NKJV) And (KJV)
Matt. 21:15 But when (Geneva, NKJV) And when (KJV)
Matt. 21:18 was hungry (Geneva, NKJV) hungered (KJV)
Matt. 21:19 And seeing (Geneva, NKJV) And when he saw (KJV)
Matt. 21:19 said to it (Geneva, NKJV) said unto it (KJV)
Matt. 21:31 They said (Geneva, NKJV) They say (KJV)

Matt. 21:31 Jesus said (Geneva, NKJV) Jesus saith (KJV)
Matt. 21:41 They said (Geneva, NKJV) They say (KJV)
Matt. 21:42 Jesus said (Geneva, NKJV) Jesus saith (KJV)
Matt. 22:8 said (Geneva, NKJV) saith (KJV)
Matt. 22:12 said (Geneva, NKJV) saith (KJV)
Matt. 22:20 said (Geneva, NKJV) saith (KJV)
Matt. 22:21 They said (Geneva, NKJV) They say (KJV)
Matt. 22:21 to Caesar (Geneva, NKJV) unto Caesar (KJV)
Matt. 22:31 concerning (Geneva, NKJV) touching (KJV)
Matt. 22:37 to him (Geneva, NKJV) unto him (KJV)
Matt. 22:42 They said (Geneva, NKJV) They say (KJV)
Matt. 23:16 blind guides (Geneva, NKJV) ye blind guides (KJV)
Matt. 23:24 strain out (Geneva, NKJV) strain at (KJV)
Matt. 23:27 tombs (Geneva, NKJV) sepulchres (KJV)
Matt. 24:1 to shew (Geneva) for to shew (KJV) to show (NKJV)
Matt. 24:32 is near (Geneva, NKJV) is nigh (KJV)
Matt. 24:46 master (Geneva, NKJV) lord (KJV)
Matt. 24:48 But if (Geneva, NKJV) But and if (KJV)
Matt. 24:48 master (Geneva, NKJV) lord (KJV)
Matt. 25:8 to the wise (Geneva, NKJV) unto the wise (KJV)
Matt. 25:10 wedding (Geneva, NKJV) marriage (KJV)
Matt. 26:26 And his (Geneva) His (KJV) But his (NKJV)
Matt. 26:2 is the Passover (Geneva, NKJV) is *the feast* of the passover (KJV)
Matt. 26:7 very costly (Geneva, NKJV) very precious (KJV)
Matt. 26:7 *at the table* (Geneva, NKJV) *at meat* (KJV)
Matt. 26:15 And said (Geneva) And said *unto them* (KJV) and said (NKJV)
Matt. 26:31 said (Geneva, NKJV) saith (KJV)
Matt. 26:38 said (Geneva, NKJV) saith (KJV)
Matt. 26:40 came (Geneva, NKJV) cometh (KJV)
Matt. 26:44 So he (Geneva) And he (KJV) So He (NKJV)
Matt. 26:45 came (Geneva, NKJV) cometh (KJV)
Matt. 26:48 had given (Geneva, NKJV) gave (KJV)
Matt. 26:55 to take (Geneva, NKJV) for to take (KJV)
Matt. 26:66 worthy to die (Geneva) guilty of death (KJV) deserving of death (NKJV)
Matt. 27:14 But he (Geneva) And he (KJV) But He (NKJV)
Matt. 27:19 sent to him (Geneva, NKJV) sent unto him (KJV)
Matt. 27:22 Pilate said (Geneva, NKJV) Pilate saith (KJV)
Matt. 27:22 They all said to him (Geneva, NKJV) They all say unto him (KJV)
Matt. 27:56 Among whom (Geneva, NKJV) Among which (KJV)
Matt. 27:56 sons (Geneva, NKJV) children (KJV)
Matt. 28:5 But the angel (Geneva, NKJV) And the angel (KJV)
Matt. 28:5 said to (Geneva, NKJV) said unto (KJV)
Matt. 28:8 So they (Geneva, NKJV) And they (KJV)
Matt. 28:19 Go therefore (Geneva, NKJV) Go ye therefore (KJV)
Mark 1:3 Prepare the way (Geneva, NKJV) Prepare ye the way (KJV)
Mark 1:6 Now John (Geneva, NKJV) And John (KJV)
Mark 1:15 repent and (Geneva, NKJV) repent ye and (KJV)
Mark 2:4 near (Geneva, NKJV) nigh (KJV)
Mark 3:10 to touch him (Geneva) for to touch him (KJV) to touch Him (NKJV)
Mark 4:12 they should turn (Geneva, NKJV) they should be converted (KJV)
Mark 4:36 left (Geneva) had sent away (KJV) had left (NKJV)
Mark 4:38 in the stern (Geneva, NKJV) in the hinder part of the ship (KJV)
Mark 4:38 awoke (Geneva, NKJV) awake (KJV)
Mark 4:38 and said (Geneva, NKJV) and say (KJV)
Mark 5:13 were drowned (Geneva) were choked (KJV) drowned (NKJV)
Mark 5:15 they came (Geneva, NKJV) they come (KJV)

Mark 5:15 and saw (Geneva, NKJV) and see (KJV)
Mark 6:1 disciples followed (Geneva, NKJV) disciples follow (KJV)
Mark 6:2 the Sabbath (Geneva, NKJV) the sabbath day (KJV)
Mark 6:26 refuse her (Geneva, NKJV) reject her (KJV)
Mark 6:30 to Jesus (Geneva, NKJV) unto Jesus (KJV)
Mark 6:32 So they (Geneva, NKJV) And they (KJV)
Mark 6:33 But the (Geneva, NKJV) And the (KJV)
Mark 6:34 saw a great multitude (Geneva, NKJV) saw much people (KJV)
Mark 6:37 But he (Geneva) He (KJV) But He (NKJV)
Mark 6:42 So they (Geneva, NKJV) And they (KJV)
Mark 6:51 Then he went (Geneva, NKJV) And he went (KJV)
Mark 6:52 because their (Geneva, NKJV) for their (KJV)
Mark 7:12 do anything (Geneva, NKJV) do ought (KJV)
Mark 7:14 multitude (Geneva, NKJV) people (KJV)
Mark 7:16 any (Geneva) any man (KJV) anyone (NKJV)
Mark 7:23 defile a man (Geneva, NKJV) defile the man (KJV)
Mark 7:27 good (Geneva, NKJV) meet (KJV)
Mark 7:29 Then he (Geneva) And he (KJV) Then He (NKJV)
Mark 7:30 lying on (Geneva, NKJV) laid upon (KJV)
Mark 7:32 they brought (Geneva, NKJV) they bring (KJV)
Mark 7:36 commanded (Geneva, NKJV) charged (KJV)
Mark 8:2 continued with (Geneva, NKJV) been with (KJV)
Mark 8:3 for some of them (Geneva, NKJV) for divers of them (KJV)
Mark 8:11 to dispute (Geneva, NKJV) to question (KJV)
Mark 8:22 came (Geneva, NKJV) cometh (KJV)
Mark 9:5 Then Peter (Geneva, NKJV) And Peter (KJV)
Mark 9:6 knew not (Geneva) wist not (KJV) did not know (NKJV)
Mark 9:10 So they (Geneva, NKJV) And they (KJV)
Mark 9:14 disputing (Geneva, NKJV) questioning (KJV)
Mark 9:22 the water (Geneva, NKJV) the waters (KJV)
Mark 9:24 help my unbelief (Geneva, NKJV) help thou mine unbelief (KJV)
Mark 9:25 unclean spirit (Geneva, NKJV) foul spirit (KJV)
Mark 9:35 said to them (Geneva, NKJV) said unto them (KJV)
Mark 9:36 a little child (Geneva, NKJV) a child (KJV)
Mark 9:43 cause thee to offend (Geneva) offend thee (KJV) causes you to sin (NKJV)
Mark 9:45 cause thee to offend (Geneva) offend thee (KJV) causes you to sin (NKJV)
Mark 9:47 cause thee to offend (Geneva) offend thee (KJV) causes you to sin (NKJV)
Mark 10:2 came and asked him (Geneva) came to him, and asked him (KJV) came and asked Him (NKJV)
Mark 10:9 Therefore what God (Geneva, NKJV) What God therefore (KJV)
Mark 10:9 let not man separate (Geneva, NKJV) let not man put asunder (KJV)
Mark 10:11 he said (Geneva) he saith (KJV) He said (NKJV)
Mark 10:13 Then they (Geneva, NKJV) And they (KJV)
Mark 10:13 little children (Geneva, NKJV) young children (KJV)
Mark 10:14 said to them (Geneva, NKJV) said unto them (KJV)
Mark 10:18 to him (Geneva, NKJV) unto him (KJV)
Mark 10:20 to him (Geneva) unto him (KJV) to Him (NKJV)
Mark 10:22 But he was (Geneva, NKJV) And he was (KJV)
Mark 10:27 But Jesus looked (Geneva, NKJV) And Jesus looking (KJV)
Mark 10:33 to the scribes (Geneva, NKJV) unto the scribes (KJV)
Mark 10:35 Then James (Geneva, NKJV) And James (KJV)
Mark 10:37 said to him (Geneva) said unto him (KJV) said to Him (NKJV)
Mark 10:42 said to them (Geneva, NKJV) saith unto them (KJV)
Mark 10:42 authority over them (Geneva, NKJV) authority upon them (KJV)
Mark 10:43 your servant (Geneva, NKJV) your minister (KJV)
Mark 10:44 chief (Geneva) chiefest (KJV) first (NKJV)

Mark 10:45 but to serve (Geneva, NKJV) but to minister (KJV)
Mark 10:46 a great multitude (Geneva, NKJV) a great number of people (KJV)
Mark 10:47 the Son of David (Geneva) *thou* son of David (KJV) Son of David (NKJV)
Mark 10:48 O Son of David (Geneva) *Thou* son of David (KJV) Son of David (NKJV)
Mark 10:49 they called the (Geneva, NKJV) they call the (KJV)
Mark 10:51 may receive (Geneva, NKJV) might receive (KJV)
Mark 10:52 Then Jesus (Geneva, NKJV) And Jesus (KJV)
Mark 11:1 near (Geneva, NKJV) nigh (KJV)
Mark 11:1 to Bethphage (Geneva, NKJV) unto Bethphage (KJV)
Mark 11:1 he sent (Geneva) he sendeth (KJV) He sent (NKJV)
Mark 11:2 said to them (Geneva, NKJV) saith unto them (KJV)
Mark 11:6 So they let (Geneva, NKJV) and they let (KJV)
Mark 11:14 said to it (Geneva, NKJV) said unto it (KJV)
Mark 11:15 they came (Geneva, NKJV) they come (KJV)
Mark 11:22 answered and said (Geneva, NKJV) answering saith (KJV)
Mark 11:27 Then they came (Geneva, NKJV) And they come (KJV)
Mark 11:28 said (Geneva, NKJV) say (KJV)
Mark 11:33 Jesus answered and said (Geneva, NKJV) Jesus answering saith (KJV)
Mark 12:1 in parables (Geneva, NKJV) by parables (KJV)
Mark 12:3 they took him (Geneva, NKJV) they caught him (KJV)
Mark 12:8 So they took (Geneva, NKJV) And they took (KJV)
Mark 12:10 Have ye (Geneva) And have ye (KJV) Have you (NKJV)
Mark 12:16 So they (Geneva, NKJV) And they (KJV)
Mark 12:17 answered and said (Geneva, NKJV) answering said (KJV)
Mark 12:19 leave *his* wife (Geneva) leave *his* wife *behind him* (KJV) leaves *his* wife behind (NKJV)
Mark 12:22 So (Geneva, NKJV) And (KJV)
Mark 12:24 answered and said (Geneva, NKJV) answering said (KJV)
Mark 12:28 Then (Geneva, NKJV) And (KJV)
Mark 12:29 Jesus answered (Geneva, NKJV) And Jesus answered (KJV)
Mark 12:38 long robes (Geneva, NKJV) long clothing (KJV)
Mark 12:44 poverty (Geneva, NKJV) want (KJV)
Mark 13:2 answered and said (Geneva, NKJV) answering said (KJV)
Mark 13:19 tribulation (Geneva, NKJV) affliction (KJV)
Mark 13:21 Then if (Geneva, NKJV) And then if (KJV)
Mark 13:22 deceive (Geneva, NKJV) seduce (KJV)
Mark 13:33 Take heed (Geneva, NKJV) Take ye heed (KJV)
Mark 13:35 Watch therefore (Geneva, NKJV) Watch ye therefore (KJV)
Mark 14:3 at table (Geneva) at meat (KJV) at the table (NKJV)
Mark 14:6 But Jesus said (Geneva, NKJV) And Jesus said (KJV)
Mark 14:10 Then (Geneva, NKJV) And (KJV)
Mark 14:13 and said (Geneva, NKJV) and saith (KJV)
Mark 14:16 So his (Geneva) And his (KJV) So His (NKJV)
Mark 14:17 came (Geneva, NKJV) cometh (KJV)
Mark 14:26 to the (Geneva, NKJV) into the (KJV)
Mark 14:27 Then Jesus (Geneva, NKJV) And Jesus (KJV)
Mark 14:31 I will not deny thee (Geneva) I will not deny thee in any wise (KJV) I will not deny You (NKJV)
Mark 14:33 And he took (Geneva) And he taketh (KJV) And He took (NKJV)
Mark 14:37 Then he came (Geneva) And he cometh (KJV) Then He came (NKJV)
Mark 14:38 The spirit indeed (Geneva, NKJV) The spirit truly (KJV)
Mark 14:41 came (Geneva, NKJV) cometh (KJV)
Mark 14:46 Then they (Geneva, NKJV) And they (KJV)
Mark 14:50 Then they (Geneva, NKJV) And they (KJV)
Mark 14:55 but found none (Geneva, NKJV) and found none (KJV)
Mark 14:57 Then (Geneva, NKJV) And (KJV)

Mark 14:70 But he (Geneva, NKJV) And he (KJV)
Mark 15:1 led (Geneva, NKJV) carried (KJV)
Mark 15:2 Then Pilate (Geneva, NKJV) And Pilate (KJV)
Mark 15:15 So Pilate (Geneva, NKJV) And *so* Pilate (KJV)
Mark 15:19 and spat (Geneva, NKJV) and did spit (KJV)
Mark 15:21 they brought (Geneva, NKJV) they bring (KJV)
Mark 15:36 Let him alone (Geneva) Let alone (KJV) Let Him alone (NKJV)
Mark 15:43 asked the body (Geneva) craved the body (KJV) asked for the body (NKJV)
Mark 15:46 in a tomb (Geneva, NKJV) in a sepulchre (KJV)
Mark 16:5 long white robe (Geneva, NKJV) long white garment (KJV)
Luke 1:29 thought (Geneva) cast in her mind (KJV) considered (NKJV)
Luke 1:38 Then (Geneva, NKJV) And (KJV)
Luke 1:65 Then fear (Geneva, NKJV) And fear (KJV)
Luke 2:10 Then the (Geneva, NKJV) And the (KJV)
Luke 2:12 to you (Geneva, NKJV) unto you (KJV)
Luke 2:43 finished the days (Geneva, NKJV) fulfilled the days (KJV)
Luke 2:48 So when they (Geneva, NKJV) And when they (KJV)
Luke 3:14 The soldiers likewise (Geneva) And the soldiers likewise (KJV) Likewise the soldiers (NKJV)
Luke 3:24 *The son* of Matthat (Geneva) Which was *the son* of Mattat (KJV) *the son* of Matthat (NKJV)
Luke 3:24 *the son* of Levi (Geneva, NKJV) which was *the son* of Levi (KJV)
Luke 3:24 *the son* of Melchi (Geneva, NKJV) which was *the son* of Melchi (KJV)
Luke 3:24 *the son* of Joseph (Geneva, NKJV) which was *the son* of Joseph (KJV)
Luke 3:25 *the son* of Amos (Geneva, NKJV) which was *the son* of Amos (KJV)
Luke 3:25 *the son* of Naum (Geneva, NKJV) which was *the son* of Naum (KJV)
Luke 3:25 *the son* of Esli (Geneva, NKJV) which was *the son* of Esli (KJV)
Luke 3:26 *The son* of Maath (Geneva, NKJV) Which was *the son* of Maath (KJV)
Luke 3:26 *the son* of Semei (Geneva, NKJV) which was *the son* of Semei (KJV)
Luke 3:26 *the son* of Joseph (Geneva, NKJV) which was *the son* of Joseph (KJV)
Luke 3:27 *the son* of Rhesa (Geneva, NKJV) which was *the son* of Rhesa (KJV)
Luke 3:27 *the son* of Zorobabel (Geneva, NKJV) which was *the son* of Zorobabel (KJV)
Luke 3:27 *the son* of Neri (Geneva, NKJV) which was *the son* of Neri (KJV)
Luke 3:28 *the son* of Addi (Geneva, NKJV) which was *the son* of Addi (KJV)
Luke 3:28 *the son* of Cosam (Geneva, NKJV) which was *the son* of Cosam (KJV)
Luke 3:28 *the son* of Er (Geneva, NKJV) which was *the son* of Er (KJV)
Luke 3:29 *the son* of Eliezer (Geneva, NKJV) which was *the son* of Eliezer (KJV)
Luke 3:29 *the son* of Matthat (Geneva, NKJV) which was *the son* of Matthat (KJV)
Luke 3:29 *the son* of Levi (Geneva, NKJV) which was *the son* of Levi (KJV)
Luke 3:30 *the son* of Joseph (Geneva, NKJV) which was *the son* of Joseph (KJV)
Luke 3:30 *the son* of Jonan (Geneva, NKJV) which was *the son* of Jonan (KJV)
Luke 3:31 *the son* of Nathan (Geneva, NKJV) which was *the son* of Nathan (KJV)
Luke 3:31 *the son* of David (Geneva, NKJV) which was *the son* of David (KJV)
Luke 3:32 *The son* of Jesse (Geneva) which was *the son* of Jesse (KJV) *the son* of Jesse (NKJV)
Luke 3:32 *the son* of Obed (Geneva, NKJV) which was *the son* of Obed (KJV)
Luke 3:32 *the son* of Booz (Geneva) which was *the son* of Booz (KJV) *the son* of Boaz (NKJV)
Luke 3:32 *the son* of Salmon (Geneva, NKJV) which was *the son* of Salmon (KJV)
Luke 3:34 *the son* of Isaac (Geneva, NKJV) which was *the son* of Isaac (KJV)
Luke 3:34 *the son* of Abraham (Geneva, NKJV) which was *the son* of Abraham (KJV)
Luke 3:35 *the son* of Eber (Geneva, NKJV) which was *the son* of Heber (KJV)
Luke 3:36 *the son* of Lamech (Geneva, NKJV) which was *the son* of Lamech (KJV)
Luke 3:37 *the son* of Enoch (Geneva, NKJV) which was *the son* of Enoch (KJV)
Luke 3:37 *the son* of Jared (Geneva, NKJV) which was *the son* of Jared (KJV)
Luke 3:37 *the son* of Cainan (Geneva, NKJV) which was *the son* of Cainan (KJV)
Luke 3:38 *the son* of Seth (Geneva, NKJV) which was *the son* of Seth (KJV)
Luke 3:38 *the son* of Adam (Geneva, NKJV) which was *the son* of Adam (KJV)

Luke 3:38 *the son* of God (Geneva, NKJV) which was *the son* of God (KJV)
Luke 4:2 was hungry (Geneva, NKJV) hungered (KJV)
Luke 4:4 But Jesus (Geneva, NKJV) And Jesus (KJV)
Luke 4:5 Then the devil (Geneva, NKJV) And the devil (KJV)
Luke 4:5 shewed him (Geneva) shewed unto him (KJV) showed Him (NKJV)
Luke 4:9 Then he brought (Geneva, NKJV) And he brought (KJV)
Luke 4:12 answered and said (Geneva, NKJV) answering said (KJV)
Luke 4:16 to read (Geneva, NKJV) for to read (KJV)
Luke 4:20 and gave (Geneva, NKJV) and he gave (KJV)
Luke 4:32 with authority (Geneva, NKJV) with power (KJV)
Luke 4:41 the Christ (Geneva, NKJV) Christ (KJV)
Luke 4:41 him to be the Christ (Geneva) he was Christ (KJV) He was
the Christ (NKJV)
Luke 4:43 But he (Geneva) And he (KJV) but he (NKJV)
Luke 5:5 answered and said (Geneva, NKJV) answering said (KJV)
Luke 5:5 all night (Geneva, NKJV) all the night (KJV)
Luke 5:7 to their partners (Geneva) unto *their* partners (KJV) to *their* partners (NKJV)
Luke 5:12 saw Jesus (Geneva, NKJV) seeing Jesus (KJV)
Luke 5:18 Then (Geneva, NKJV) And (KJV)
Luke 5:19 bed (Geneva, NKJV) couch (KJV)
Luke 5:22 answered and said (Geneva, NKJV) answering said (KJV)
Luke 5:23 sins are (Geneva, NKJV) sins be (KJV)
Luke 5:24 bed (Geneva, NKJV) couch (KJV)
Luke 5:29 Then Levi (Geneva, NKJV) And Levi (KJV)
Luke 5:31 answered and said (Geneva, NKJV) answering said (KJV)
Luke 5:33 Then they said (Geneva, NKJV) And they said (KJV)
Luke 6:4 took and ate (Geneva, NKJV) did take and eat (KJV)
Luke 6:10 as whole as the other (Geneva, NKJV) whole as the other (KJV)
Luke 6:22 men hate (Geneva, NKJV) men shall hate (KJV)
Luke 6:22 you, and revile *you* (Geneva, NKJV) you *from their company,* and shall reproach *you* (KJV)
Luke 6:24 to you (Geneva, NKJV) unto you (KJV)
Luke 6:25 to you (Geneva, NKJV) unto you (KJV)
Luke 6:26 to you (Geneva, NKJV) unto you (KJV)
Luke 6:27 to you (Geneva, NKJV) unto you (KJV)
Luke 6:36 of the Most High (Geneva, NKJV) of the Highest (KJV)
Luke 6:42 Hypocrite (Geneva, NKJV) Thou hypocrite (KJV)
Luke 6:45 good (Geneva, NKJV) that which is good (KJV)
Luke 6:46 But why (Geneva, NKJV) And why (KJV)
Luke 7:7 say the word (Geneva, NKJV) say in a word (KJV)
Luke 7:12 near (Geneva, NKJV) nigh (KJV)
Luke 7:14 coffin (Geneva) bier (KJV) open coffin (NKJV)
Luke 7:16 Then (Geneva, NKJV) And (KJV)
Luke 7:22 answered and said (Geneva, NKJV) answering said (KJV)
Luke 7:37 sat at table (Geneva) sat at meat (KJV) sat at the table (NKJV)
Luke 7:40 answered and said (Geneva, NKJV) answering said (KJV)
Luke 7:44 Then (Geneva, NKJV) And (KJV)
Luke 7:49 at table (Geneva) at meat (KJV) at the table (NKJV)
Luke 8:9 Then his (Geneva, NKJV) And his (KJV)
Luke 8:13 But they (Geneva) They (KJV) But the ones (NKJV)
Luke 8:17 come to light (Geneva, NKJV) come abroad (KJV)
Luke 8:21 But he (Geneva) And he (KJV) But he (NKJV)
Luke 8:26 they sailed (Geneva, NKJV) they arrived (KJV)
Luke 8:39 what great things (Geneva, NKJV) how great things (KJV)
Luke 9:3 to them (Geneva, NKJV) unto them (KJV)
Luke 9:14 Then he said (Geneva) And he said (KJV) Then He said (NKJV)

Luke 9:17 So they did (Geneva, NKJV) And they did (KJV)
Luke 9:19 answered and said (Geneva, NKJV) answering said (KJV)
Luke 9:20 Peter answered and said (Geneva, NKJV) Peter answering said (KJV)
Luke 9:30 two men talked with him (Geneva) there talked with him two men (KJV)
          two men talked with Him (NKJV)
Luke 9:41 Then Jesus answered (Geneva, NKJV) And Jesus answering (KJV)
Luke 9:61 at mine house (Geneva) at home at my house (KJV) at my house (NKJV)
Luke 10:9 near (Geneva, NKJV) nigh (KJV)
Luke 10:12 to you (Geneva, NKJV) unto you (KJV)
Luke 10:17 to us (Geneva, NKJV) unto us (KJV)
Luke 10:23 to his (Geneva) unto *his* (KJV) to *His* (NKJV)
Luke 10:27 answered and said (Geneva, NKJV) answering said (KJV)
Luke 10:30 answered and said (Geneva, NKJV) answering said (KJV)
Luke 11:30 sign to (Geneva, NKJV) sign unto (KJV)
Luke 11:39 to him (Geneva, NKJV) unto him (KJV)
Luke 11:41 clean to you (Geneva, NKJV) clean unto you (KJV)
Luke 11:42 to you (Geneva, NKJV) unto you (KJV)
Luke 11:47 to you (Geneva, NKJV) unto you (KJV)
Luke 11:52 to you (Geneva, NKJV) unto you (KJV)
Luke 12:17 lay up (Geneva) bestow (KJV) store (NKJV)
Luke 12:36 master (Geneva, NKJV) lord (KJV)
Luke 12:42 master (Geneva, NKJV) lord (KJV)
Luke 12:43 master (Geneva, NKJV) lord (KJV)
Luke 12:45 master (Geneva, NKJV) lord (KJV)
Luke 12:47 master's (Geneva, NKJV) lord's (KJV)
Luke 13:2 answered and said (Geneva, NKJV) answering said (KJV)
Luke 13:15 Hypocrite (Geneva, NKJV) *Thou* hypocrite (KJV)
Luke 13:18 What is the kingdom (Geneva, NKJV) Unto what is the kingdom (KJV)
Luke 13:18 compare it (Geneva, NKJV) resemble it (KJV)
Luke 13:19 made nests (Geneva) lodged (KJV) nested (NKJV)
Luke 14:8 place (Geneva, NKJV) room (KJV)
Luke 14:10 sit at table (Geneva) sit at meat (KJV) sit at the table (NKJV)
Luke 14:15 Now when (Geneva, NKJV) And when (KJV)
Luke 14:15 at table (Geneva) at meat (KJV) at the table (NKJV)
Luke 14:16 to him (Geneva, NKJV) unto him (KJV)
Luke 14:18 But they all (Geneva, NKJV) And they all (KJV)
Luke 14:21 his master (Geneva, NKJV) his lord (KJV)
Luke 14:23 Then the master (Geneva, NKJV) And the lord (KJV)
Luke 15:1 to hear (Geneva, NKJV) for to hear (KJV)
Luke 15:3 to them (Geneva, NKJV) unto them (KJV)
Luke 15:12 So he divided (Geneva, NKJV) And he divided (KJV)
Luke 15:15 Then he went (Geneva, NKJV) And he went (KJV)
Luke 15:16 swine ate (Geneva, NKJV) swine did eat (KJV)
Luke 15:23 And bring the (Geneva, NKJV) And bring hither the (KJV)
Luke 15:25 near (Geneva, NKJV) nigh (KJV)
Luke 15:29 answered and said (Geneva, NKJV) answering said (KJV)
Luke 16:3 my master (Geneva, NKJV) my lord (KJV)
Luke 16:5 his master's (Geneva, NKJV) his lord's (KJV)
Luke 16:5 my master (Geneva, NKJV) my lord (KJV)
Luke 16:6 to him (Geneva, NKJV) unto him (KJV)
Luke 16:23 saw Abraham (Geneva, NKJV) seeth Abraham (KJV)
Luke 16:24 Then he cried (Geneva, NKJV) And he cried (KJV)
Luke 16:29 Abraham said (Geneva, NKJV) Abraham saith (KJV)
Luke 17:1 to the disciples (Geneva, NKJV) unto the disciples (KJV)
Luke 17:6 mulberry tree (Geneva, NKJV) sycamine tree (KJV)
Luke 17:6 by the roots (Geneva, NKJV) by the root (KJV)

Luke 17:17 answered and said (Geneva, NKJV) answering said (KJV)
Luke 17:27 They ate (Geneva, NKJV) They did eat (KJV)
Luke 17:28 they built (Geneva, NKJV) they builded (KJV)
Luke 18:2 in a certain city (Geneva, NKJV) in a city (KJV)
Luke 18:13 to heaven (Geneva, NKJV) unto heaven (KJV)
Luke 18:35 near (Geneva, NKJV) nigh (KJV)
Luke 18:38 the Son of David (Geneva) *thou* son of David (KJV) Son of David (NKJV)
Luke 18:39 O Son of David (Geneva) *Thou* son of David (KJV) Son of David (NKJV)
Luke 19:2 chief receiver of the tribute (Geneva) chief among the publicans (KJV) chief tax collector (NKJV)
Luke 19:9 to him (Geneva, NKJV) unto him (KJV)
Luke 19:11 near to (Geneva) nigh to (KJV) near (NKJV)
Luke 19:17 good servant (Geneva, NKJV) thou good servant (KJV)
Luke 19:22 said (Geneva, NKJV) saith (KJV)
Luke 19:24 said to (Geneva, NKJV) said unto (KJV)
Luke 19:32 So (Geneva, NKJV) And (KJV)
Luke 19:37 near (Geneva, NKJV) nigh (KJV)
Luke 19:40 But he (Geneva) And he (KJV) But He (NKJV)
Luke 20:6 But if we (Geneva, NKJV) But and if we (KJV)
Luke 20:16 He will come (Geneva, NKJV) He shall come (KJV)
Luke 20:29 Now there were (Geneva, NKJV) There were therefore (KJV)
Luke 20:31 Then the third (Geneva, NKJV) And the third (KJV)
Luke 20:34 answered and said (Geneva, NKJV) answering said (KJV)
Luke 20:35 counted (Geneva, NKJV) accounted (KJV)
Luke 20:36 the Sons of God (Geneva) the children of God (KJV) sons of God (NKJV)
Luke 20:38 the God (Geneva, NKJV) a God (KJV)
Luke 20:39 answered and said (Geneva, NKJV) answering said (KJV)
Luke 22:47 these (Geneva) the same (KJV) These (NKJV)
Luke 21:19 By your patience (Geneva, NKJV) In your patience (KJV)
Luke 21:36 Watch therefore (Geneva, NKJV) Watch ye therefore (KJV)
Luke 21:38 to hear (Geneva, NKJV) for to hear (KJV)
Luke 22:1 near (Geneva, NKJV) nigh (KJV)
Luke 22:5 agreed (Geneva, NKJV) covenanted (KJV)
Luke 22:9 to him (Geneva) unto him (KJV) to Him (NKJV)
Luke 22:12 Then (Geneva, NKJV) And (KJV)
Luke 22:13 So they (Geneva, NKJV) And they (KJV)
Luke 22:15 Then (Geneva, NKJV) And (KJV)
Luke 22:23 Then they (Geneva, NKJV) And they (KJV)
Luke 22:27 For who is greater (Geneva, NKJV) For whether is greater (KJV)
Luke 22:27 at table (Geneva) at meat (KJV) at the table (NKJV)
Luke 22:28 And ye (Geneva) Ye (KJV) But you (NKJV)
Luke 22:40 came to the place (Geneva, NKJV) was at the place (KJV)
Luke 22:57 But he denied (Geneva, NKJV) And he denied (KJV)
Luke 22:58 But Peter said (Geneva, NKJV) And Peter said (KJV)
Luke 22:70 to them (Geneva, NKJV) unto them (KJV)
Luke 23:1 Then the whole (Geneva, NKJV) And the whole (KJV)
Luke 23:2 to pay (Geneva, NKJV) to give (KJV)
Luke 23:5 But they (Geneva, NKJV) And they (KJV)
Luke 23:5 Judea (Geneva, NKJV) Jewry (KJV)
Luke 23:8 exceedingly glad (Geneva, NKJV) exceeding glad (KJV)
Luke 23:13 Then Pilate (Geneva, NKJV) And Pilate (KJV)
Luke 23:18 to us (Geneva, NKJV) unto us (KJV)
Luke 23:19 insurrection (Geneva, NKJV) sedition (KJV)
Luke 23:23 But they (Geneva, NKJV) And they (KJV)
Luke 23:24 So Pilate (Geneva, NKJV) And Pilate (KJV)
Luke 23:25 insurrection (Geneva, NKJV) sedition (KJV)

Luke 23:27 a great multitude (Geneva, NKJV) a great company (KJV)
Luke 23:32 two others (Geneva, NKJV) two other (KJV)
Luke 23:35 the Christ (Geneva, NKJV) Christ (KJV)
Luke 23:36 The soldiers also (Geneva, NKJV) And the soldiers also (KJV)
Luke 23:39 the Christ (Geneva, NKJV) Christ (KJV)
Luke 23:53 tomb (Geneva, NKJV) sepulchure (KJV)
Luke 24:5 said to them (Geneva, NKJV) said unto them (KJV)
Luke 24:28 near (Geneva, NKJV) nigh (KJV)
Luke 24:30 at table (Geneva) at meat (KJV) at the table (NKJV)
Luke 24:31 Then their (Geneva, NKJV) And their (KJV)
John 1:5 in the darkness (Geneva, NKJV) in darkness (KJV)
John 1:12 he gave (Geneva) gave he (KJV) He gave (NKJV)
John 1:21 the Prophet (Geneva, NKJV) that prophet (KJV)
John 1:25 the Christ (Geneva, NKJV) that Christ (KJV)
John 1:39 He said (Geneva, NKJV) He saith (KJV)
John 1:41 found (Geneva, NKJV) findeth (KJV)
John 1:41 said unto him (Geneva) saith unto him (KJV) said to him (NKJV)
John 1:45 found (Geneva, NKJV) findeth (KJV)
John 1:45 and said (Geneva, NKJV) and saith (KJV)
John 1:46 Philip said (Geneva, NKJV) Philip saith (KJV)
John 1:48 Nathanael said (Geneva, NKJV) Nathanael saith (KJV)
John 2:3 the wine failed (Geneva) they wanted wine (KJV) they ran out of wine (NKJV)
John 2:4 Jesus said (Geneva, NKJV) Jesus saith (KJV)
John 2:5 His mother said (Geneva, NKJV) His mother saith (KJV)
John 2:7 Jesus said (Geneva, NKJV) Jesus saith (KJV)
John 2:14 And he found (Geneva) And found (KJV) And He found (NKJV)
John 2:15 with the sheep (Geneva, NKJV) and the sheep (KJV)
John 2:25 and had no need (Geneva, NKJV) And needed not (KJV)
John 3:4 Nicodemus said (Geneva, NKJV) Nicodemus saith (KJV)
John 3:7 said to (Geneva, NKJV) said unto (KJV)
John 3:10 teacher (Geneva, NKJV) master (KJV)
John 3:18 in him (Geneva) on him (KJV) in Him (NKJV)
John 3:34 by measure (Geneva, NKJV) by measure *unto him* (KJV)
John 3:36 in the Son (Geneva, NKJV) on the Son (KJV)
John 4:5 came (Geneva, NKJV) cometh (KJV)
John 4:7 Jesus said (Geneva, NKJV) Jesus saith (KJV)
John 4:16 Jesus said (Geneva, NKJV) Jesus saith (KJV)
John 4:23 in spirit and truth (Geneva, NKJV) in spirit and in truth (KJV)
John 4:26 Jesus said (Geneva, NKJV) Jesus saith (KJV)
John 4:27 with a woman (Geneva, NKJV) with the woman (KJV)
John 4:28 and said (Geneva, NKJV) and saith (KJV)
John 4:34 Jesus said (Geneva, NKJV) Jesus saith (KJV)
John 4:35 I say to you (Geneva, NKJV) I say unto you (KJV)
John 4:37 For (Geneva, NKJV) And (KJV)
John 4:37 the saying (Geneva, NKJV) that saying (KJV)
John 4:39 in him (Geneva) on him (KJV) in Him (NKJV)
John 4:42 they said (Geneva, NKJV) said (KJV)
John 4:49 before (Geneva, NKJV) ere (KJV)
John 4:50 Jesus said (Geneva, NKJV) Jesus saith (KJV)
John 5:2 in Hebrew (Geneva, NKJV) in the Hebrew tongue (KJV)
John 5:3 sick folk (Geneva) impotent folk (KJV) sick people (NKJV)
John 5:7 The sick man (Geneva, NKJV) The impotent man (KJV)
John 5:8 Jesus said (Geneva, NKJV) Jesus saith (KJV)
John 5:10 to him (Geneva, NKJV) unto him (KJV)
John 5:13 knew not (Geneva) wist not (KJV) did not know (NKJV)
John 5:14 Jesus found (Geneva, NKJV) Jesus findeth (KJV)

John 5:24 in him (Geneva) on him (KJV) in Him (NKJV)
John 5:29 condemnation (Geneva, NKJV) damnation (KJV)
John 6:4 near (Geneva, NKJV) nigh (KJV)
John 6:5 great multitude (Geneva, NKJV) great company (KJV)
John 6:19 they saw (Geneva, NKJV) they see (KJV)
John 6:19 near (Geneva, NKJV) nigh (KJV)
John 6:20 he said (Geneva) he saith (KJV) He said (NKJV)
John 6:26 ate (Geneva, NKJV) did eat (KJV)
John 6:29 in him (Geneva) on him (KJV) in Him (NKJV)
John 6:34 Then they said (Geneva, NKJV) Then said they (KJV)
John 6:35 in him (Geneva) on him (KJV) in Him (NKJV)
John 6:40 in him (Geneva) on him (KJV) in Him (NKJV)
John 6:48 the bread (Geneva, NKJV) that bread (KJV)
John 6:58 the bread (Geneva, NKJV) that bread (KJV)
John 6:62 *What* then if (Geneva, NKJV) *What* and if (KJV)
John 6:63 the Spirit (Geneva, NKJV) the spirit (KJV)
John 6:67 to the twelve (Geneva, NKJV) unto the twelve (KJV)
John 6:69 and know (Geneva, NKJV) and are sure (KJV)
John 6:69 the Christ (Geneva, NKJV) that Christ (KJV)
John 7:1 Judea (Geneva, NKJV) Jewry (KJV)
John 7:21 to them (Geneva, NKJV) unto them (KJV)
John 7:26 to him (Geneva) unto him (KJV) to Him (NKJV)
John 7:27 the Christ (Geneva, NKJV) Christ (KJV)
John 7:31 in him (Geneva) on him (KJV) in Him (NKJV)
John 7:31 When the Christ (Geneva, NKJV) When Christ (KJV)
John 7:35 Grecians (Geneva) Gentiles (KJV) Greeks (NKJV)
John 7:38 in me (Geneva) on me (KJV) in Me (NKJV)
John 7:39 in him (Geneva) on him (KJV) in Him (NKJV)
John 7:42 that the Christ (Geneva, NKJV) That Christ (KJV)
John 7:51 a man (Geneva, NKJV) *any* man (KJV)
John 8:1 And Jesus (Geneva) Jesus (KJV) But Jesus (NKJV)
John 8:3 Then the scribes (Geneva, NKJV) And the scribes (KJV)
John 8:25 Jesus said (Geneva, NKJV) Jesus saith (KJV)
John 8:30 in him (Geneva) on him (KJV) in Him (NKJV)
John 8:41 We are (Geneva) We be (KJV) We were (NKJV)
John 8:52 to him (Geneva) unto him (KJV) to Him (NKJV)
John 8:55 keep his word (Geneva) keep his saying (KJV) keep His word (NKJV)
John 9:24 glory (Geneva, NKJV) praise (KJV)
John 9:35 in the Son (Geneva, NKJV) on the Son (KJV)
John 9:38 Then he said (Geneva, NKJV) And he said (KJV)
John 10:42 in him (Geneva) on him (KJV) in Him (NKJV)
John 11:8 The disciples (Geneva) *His* disciples (KJV) *The* disciples (NKJV)
John 11:8 said (Geneva, NKJV) say (KJV)
John 11:8 lately (Geneva, NKJV) of late (KJV)
John 11:18 near (Geneva, NKJV) nigh (KJV)
John 11:23 Jesus said (Geneva, NKJV) Jesus saith (KJV)
John 11:24 Martha said (Geneva, NKJV) Martha saith (KJV)
John 11:38 came (Geneva NKJV) cometh (KJV)
John 11:40 Jesus said (Geneva, NKJV) Jesus saith (KJV)
John 12:4 said (Geneva, NKJV) saith (KJV)
John 12:10 to death also (Geneva, NKJV) also to death (KJV)
John 12:11 in Jesus (Geneva, NKJV) on Jesus (KJV)
John 12:12 a great multitude (Geneva, NKJV) much people (KJV)
John 12:17 witness (Geneva, NKJV) record (KJV)
John 12:21 And they came (Geneva) The same came therefore (KJV) Then they came (NKJV)
John 12:22 Philip came and told (Geneva, NKJV) Philip cometh and telleth (KJV)

John 12:34 that the Christ (Geneva, NKJV) that Christ (KJV)
John 12:44 And Jesus cried (Geneva) Jesus cried (KJV) Then Jesus cried (NKJV)
John 12:46 in me (Geneva) on me (KJV) in Me (NKJV)
John 13:6 came (Geneva, NKJV) cometh (KJV)
John 13:8 Peter said (Geneva, NKJV) Peter saith (KJV)
John 13:9 Simon Peter said (Geneva, NKJV) Simon Peter saith (KJV)
John 13:10 Jesus said (Geneva, NKJV) Jesus saith (KJV)
John 13:16 master (Geneva, NKJV) lord (KJV)
John 13:17 blessed (Geneva, NKJV) happy (KJV)
John 13:21 had said these things (Geneva, NKJV) had thus said (KJV)
John 13:25 said (Geneva, NKJV) saith (KJV)
John 13:37 can I not (Geneva, NKJV) cannot I (KJV)
John 14:5 Thomas said (Geneva, NKJV) Thomas saith (KJV)
John 14:6 Jesus said (Geneva, NKJV) Jesus saith (KJV)
John 14:8 Philip said (Geneva, NKJV) Philip saith (KJV)
John 14:9 Jesus said (Geneva, NKJV) Jesus saith (KJV)
John 14:12 in me (Geneva) on me (KJV) in Me (NKJV)
John 14:22 said (Geneva, NKJV) saith (KJV)
John 15:15 master (Geneva, NKJV) lord (KJV)
John 15:20 master (Geneva, NKJV) lord (KJV)
John 16:9 in me (Geneva) on me (KJV) in Me (NKJV)
John 16:18 know not (Geneva) cannot tell (KJV) do not know (NKJV)
John 16:31 you (Geneva, NKJV) ye (KJV)
John 17:20 in me (Geneva) on me (KJV) in Me (NKJV)
John 18:3 came (Geneva, NKJV) cometh (KJV)
John 18:5 Jesus said (Geneva, NKJV) Jesus saith (KJV)
John 18:16 to her (Geneva, NKJV) unto her (KJV)
John 18:21 what I said (Geneva, NKJV) what I have said (KJV)
John 18:39 But you (Geneva, NKJV) But ye (KJV)
John 19:13 in Hebrew (Geneva, NKJV) in the Hebrew (KJV)
John 19:15 Pilate said (Geneva, NKJV) Pilate saith (KJV)
John 19:17 in Hebrew (Geneva, NKJV) in the Hebrew (KJV)
John 19:20 near (Geneva, NKJV) nigh (KJV)
John 19:24 garments (Geneva, NKJV) raiment (KJV)
John 19:42 was near (Geneva) was nigh at hand (KJV) was nearby (NKJV)
John 20:1 and saw (Geneva, NKJV) and seeth (KJV)
John 20:1 from the tomb (Geneva, NKJV) from the sepulchre (KJV)
John 20:2 she ran and came (Geneva, NKJV) she runneth and cometh (KJV)
John 20:6 came (Geneva, NKJV) cometh (KJV)
John 20:6 saw (Geneva, NKJV) seeth (KJV)
John 20:7 kerchief (Geneva) napkin (KJV) handkerchief (NKJV)
John 20:12 saw (Geneva, NKJV) seeth (KJV)
John 20:22 Receive the (Geneva, NKJV) Receive ye the (KJV)
John 20:29 Jesus said (Geneva, NKJV) Jesus saith (KJV)
John 21:3 Simon Peter said (Geneva, NKJV) Simon Peter saith (KJV)
John 21:10 Jesus said (Geneva, NKJV) Jesus saith (KJV)
John 21:13 came and took (Geneva, NKJV) cometh and taketh (KJV)
John 21:13 gave (Geneva, NKJV) giveth (KJV)
John 21:15 Jesus said (Geneva, NKJV) Jesus saith (KJV)
John 21:15 He said (Geneva, NKJV) He saith (KJV)
John 21:16 He said (Geneva, NKJV) He saith (KJV)
John 21:17 He said (Geneva, NKJV) He saith (KJV)
John 21:17 to him the third time (Geneva, NKJV) unto him the third time (KJV)
John 21:17 Jesus said (Geneva, NKJV) Jesus saith (KJV)
John 21:19 he said to him (Geneva) he saith unto him (KJV) He said to him (NKJV)
John 21:20 saw (Geneva, NKJV) seeth (KJV)

John 21:21 said to Jesus (Geneva, NKJV) saith to Jesus (KJV)
John 21:22 Jesus said (Geneva, NKJV) Jesus saith (KJV)
John 21:23 to him (Geneva, NKJV) unto him (KJV)
Acts 1:3 presented (Geneva, NKJV) shewed (KJV)
Acts 1:3 that he had suffered (Geneva) his passion (KJV) His suffering (NKJV)
Acts 1:4 he commanded (Geneva) commanded (KJV) He commanded (NKJV)
Acts 1:4 but to wait (Geneva, NKJV) but wait (KJV)
Acts 1:19 their own language (Geneva, NKJV) their proper tongue (KJV)
Acts 1:20 charge (Geneva) bishopric (KJV) office (NKJV)
Acts 1:22 be made (Geneva) be ordained (KJV) become (NKJV)
Acts 1:23 presented (Geneva) appointed (KJV) proposed (NKJV)
Acts 1:28 on Matthias (Geneva, NKJV) upon Matthias (KJV)
Acts 2:8 language (Geneva, NKJV) tongue (KJV)
Acts 2:13 They are full (Geneva, NKJV) These men are full (KJV)
Acts 2:15 since it is (Geneva, NKJV) seeing it is (KJV)
Acts 2:25 David saith (Geneva) David speaketh (KJV) David says (NKJV)
Acts 2:34 sit at (Geneva, NKJV) sit thou on (KJV)
Acts 3:12 So when Peter (Geneva, NKJV) And when Peter (KJV)
Acts 3:12 or godliness (Geneva, NKJV) or holiness (KJV)
Acts 3:17 I know (Geneva, NKJV) I wot (KJV)
Acts 3:18 thus fulfilled (Geneva, NKJV) so fulfilled (KJV)
Acts 3:23 shall be (Geneva, NKJV) shall come to pass (KJV)
Acts 3:25 to Abraham (Geneva, NKJV) unto Abraham (KJV)
Acts 3:26 your iniquities (Geneva, NKJV) his iniquities (KJV)
Acts 4:2 in Jesus *Name* (Geneva) through Jesus (KJV) in Jesus (NKJV)
Acts 4:18 So they (Geneva, NKJV) And they (KJV)
Acts 4:28 to do (Geneva, NKJV) For to do (KJV)
Acts 5:16 were all healed (Geneva, NKJV) were healed every one (KJV)
Acts 5:21 all the elders (Geneva, NKJV) all the senate (KJV)
Acts 5:35 Men of Israel (Geneva, NKJV) Ye men of Israel (KJV)
Acts 5:41 So they (Geneva, NKJV) And they (KJV)
Acts 6:11 against Moses and God (Geneva, NKJV) against Moses and *against* God (KJV)
Acts 7:6 But God (Geneva, NKJV) And God (KJV)
Acts 7:11 famine (Geneva, NKJV) dearth (KJV)
Acts 7:17 near (Geneva, NKJV) nigh (KJV)
Acts 7:20 acceptable unto God (Geneva) exceeding fair (KJV) well pleasing to God (NKJV)
Acts 7:25 that God (Geneva, NKJV) how that God (KJV)
Acts 7:38 congregation (Geneva, NKJV) church (KJV)
Acts 7:40 know not (Geneva) wot not (KJV) do not know (NKJV)
Acts 8:1 to his death (Geneva, NKJV) unto his death (KJV)
Acts 8:7 with a loud (Geneva, NKJV) with loud (KJV)
Acts 8:23 For I see (Geneva, NKJV) For I perceive (KJV)
Acts 8:27 to worship (Geneva, NKJV) for to worship (KJV)
Acts 9:8 from the ground (Geneva, NKJV) from the earth (KJV)
Acts 9:9 ate nor drank (Geneva, NKJV) did eat nor drink (KJV)
Acts 9:16 how many things (Geneva, NKJV) how great things (KJV)
Acts 9:22 the Christ (Geneva, NKJV) very Christ (KJV)
Acts 9:25 through the wall (Geneva, NKJV) by the wall (KJV)
Acts 9:38 near (Geneva, NKJV) nigh (KJV)
Acts 10:2 household (Geneva, NKJV) house (KJV)
Acts 10:9 near (Geneva, NKJV) nigh (KJV)
Acts 11:1 Now the (Geneva, NKJV) And the (KJV)
Acts 11:25 to seek (Geneva, NKJV) for to seek (KJV)
Acts 11:26 first called Christians (Geneva, NKJV) called Christians first (KJV)
Acts 11:28 famine (Geneva, NKJV) dearth (KJV)
Acts 12:4 the passover (Geneva, NKJV) Easter (KJV)

Acts 12:9 knew not (Geneva) wist not (KJV) did not know (KJV)
Acts 13:10 straight ways (Geneva, NKJV) right ways (KJV)
Acts 13:16 hearken (Geneva) give audience (KJV) listen (KJV)
Acts 13:20 about four (Geneva, NKJV) about the space of four (KJV)
Acts 13:22 will do (Geneva, NKJV) shall fulfill (KJV)
Acts 13:35 wilt not (Geneva) shalt no (KJV) will not (NKJV)
Acts 13:36 with his fathers (Geneva, NKJV) unto his fathers (KJV)
Acts 14:8 had never walked (Geneva, NKJV) never had walked (KJV)
Acts 14:14 But when (Geneva, NKJV) *Which* when (KJV)
Acts 14:15 O men (Geneva) Sirs (KJV) Men (NKJV)
Acts 14:23 in whom (Geneva, NKJV) on whom (KJV)
Acts 14:25 to Attalia (Geneva, NKJV) into Attalia (KJV)
Acts 14:26 commended (Geneva, NKJV) recommended (KJV)
Acts 15:3 sent (Geneva, NKJV) brought (KJV)
Acts 15:7 know that (Geneva, NKJV) know how that (KJV)
Acts 15:23 and the brethren (Geneva, NKJV) and brethren (KJV)
Acts 15:25 to us (Geneva, NKJV) unto us (KJV)
Acts 15:29 from things (Geneva, NKJV) from meats (KJV)
Acts 15:40 commended (Geneva, NKJV) recommended (KJV)
Acts 16:4 to keep (Geneva, NKJV) for to keep (KJV)
Acts 16:10 to preach (Geneva, NKJV) for to preach (KJV)
Acts 16:14 things which Paul spake (Geneva) things which were spoken of Paul (KJV)
things spoken by Paul (NKJV)
Acts 16:22 *them* to be beaten with rods (Geneva, NKJV) to beat *them* (KJV)
Acts 16:31 household (Geneva, NKJV) house (KJV)
Acts 16:34 household (Geneva, NKJV) house (KJV)
Acts 17:4 joined in company (Geneva) consorted (KJV) joined (NKJV)
Acts 17:6 But when they (Geneva, NKJV) And when they (KJV)
Acts 17:26 to dwell (Geneva, NKJV) for to dwell (KJV)
Acts 17:34 among whom (Geneva) among the which (KJV) among them (NKJV)
Acts 18:5 the Christ (Geneva, NKJV) Christ (KJV)
Acts 18:28 the Christ (Geneva, NKJV) Christ (KJV)
Acts 19:28 Now when they (Geneva, NKJV) And when they (KJV)
Acts 19:33 to the people (Geneva, NKJV) unto the people (KJV)
Acts 20:1 to go (Geneva, NKJV) for to go (KJV)
Acts 20:9 overcome with sleep (Geneva) sunk down with sleep (KJV) overcome by sleep (NKJV)
Acts 20:10 But Paul (Geneva, NKJV) And Paul (KJV)
Acts 20:13 Then we (Geneva, NKJV) And we (KJV)
Acts 20:28 whereof (Geneva) over the which (KJV) among which (NKJV)
Acts 21:38 the Egyptian (Geneva, NKJV) that Egyptian (KJV)
Acts 22:2 he said (Geneva, NKJV) he saith (KJV)
Acts 22:6 as I journeyed (Geneva, NKJV) as I made my journey (KJV)
Acts 22:6 near (Geneva, NKJV) nigh (KJV)
Acts 22:8 to me (Geneva, NKJV) unto me (KJV)
Acts 22:17 Syrtes (Geneva) quicksands (KJV) Syrtis *Sands* (NKJV)
Acts 22:20 clothes (Geneva, NKJV) raiment (KJV)
Acts 22:21 Then he (Geneva) And he (KJV) Then He (NKJV)
Acts 22:27 to him (Geneva, NKJV) unto him (KJV)
Acts 22:30 On the next day (Geneva) On the morrow (KJV) The next day (NKJV)
Acts 23:3 to him (Geneva, NKJV) unto him (KJV)
Acts 23:9 Then there (Geneva, NKJV) And there (KJV)
Acts 23:14 oath (Geneva, NKJV) curse (KJV)
Acts 23:32 And the next day (Geneva) On the morrow (KJV) The next day (NKJV)
Acts 23:34 read *it* (Geneva, NKJV) read *the letter* (KJV)
Acts 24:1 came down (Geneva, NKJV) descended (KJV)
Acts 24:4 courtesy (Geneva, NKJV) clemency (KJV)

Acts 24:11 to worship (Geneva, NKJV) for to worship (KJV)
Acts 25:30 commanded his accusers (Geneva, NKJV) gave commandment to his accusers (KJV)
Acts 25:34 had read it (Geneva) had read *the letter* (KJV) had read *it* (NKJV)
Acts 26:1 So Paul (Geneva, NKJV) Then Paul (KJV)
Acts 26:4 from the beginning (Geneva, NKJV) at the first (KJV)
Acts 26:18 eyes, that (Geneva) eyes, *and* (KJV) eyes *in order* (NKJV)
Acts 26:28 to become (Geneva, NKJV) to be (KJV)
Acts 28:21 Then they (Geneva, NKJV) And they (KJV)
Acts 28:21 any evil (Geneva, NKJV) any harm (KJV)
Acts 28:24 some were persuaded (Geneva, NKJV) some believed (KJV)
Acts 28:27 should return (Geneva) should be converted (KJV) turn (NKJV)
Rom. 1:4 the Spirit (Geneva, NKJV) the spirit (KJV)
Rom. 1:17 For by it (Geneva) For therein (KJV) For in it (NKJV)
Rom. 1:23 incorruptible (Geneva, NKJV) uncorruptible (KJV)
Rom. 2:2 But we know (Geneva, NKJV) But we are sure (KJV)
Rom. 2:9 Grecian (Geneva) Gentile (KJV) Greek (NKJV)
Rom. 2:23 in the law (Geneva, NKJV) of the law (KJV)
Rom. 3:4 words (Geneva, NKJV) sayings (KJV)
Rom. 4:4 wages (Geneva, NKJV) reward (KJV)
Rom. 4:20 strengthened (Geneva, NKJV) strong (KJV)
Rom. 5:11 rejoice in God (Geneva, NKJV) joy in God (KJV)
Rom. 5:20 abounded much more (Geneva, NKJV) did much more abound (KJV)
Rom. 6:10 to God (Geneva, NKJV) unto God (KJV)
Rom. 6:11 to God (Geneva, NKJV) unto God (KJV)
Rom. 6:16 give (Geneva) yield (KJV) present (NKJV)
Rom. 8:19 revealed (Geneva) manifestation (KJV) revealing (NKJV)
Rom. 8:23 but we also (Geneva, NKJV) but ourselves also (KJV)
Rom. 9:5 Of whom are (Geneva, NKJV) Whose are (KJV)
Rom. 9:18 he hath mercy (Geneva) hath he mercy (KJV) He has mercy (NKJV)
Rom. 9:22 prepared (Geneva, NKJV) fitted (KJV)
Rom. 10:3 to the righteousness (Geneva, NKJV) unto the righteousness (KJV)
Rom. 10:8 near (Geneva, NKJV) nigh (KJV)
Rom. 11:2 Know ye not (Geneva) Wot ye not (KJV) do you not know (NKJV)
Rom. 11:4 to him (Geneva, NKJV) unto him (KJV)
Rom. 11:4 to Baal (Geneva, NKJV) to *the image of* Baal (KJV)
Rom. 11:10 always (Geneva, NKJV) alway (KJV)
Rom. 12:3 to everyone (Geneva, NKJV) to every man (KJV)
Rom. 13:2 judgment (Geneva, NKJV) damnation (KJV)
Rom. 13:10 doeth (Geneva) worketh (KJV) does (NKJV)
Rom. 14:6 observeth the day (Geneva) regardeth the day (KJV) observes the day (NKJV)
Rom. 14:6 observeth it (Geneva) regardeth it (KJV) observes it (NKJV)
Rom. 14:6 to the Lord; and (Geneva, NKJV) unto the Lord; and (KJV)
Rom. 14:6 observeth not the day (Geneva) regardeth not the day (KJV) does not observe the day (NKJV)
Rom. 14:23 condemned (Geneva, NKJV) damned (KJV)
Rom. 15:25 to Jerusalem (Geneva, NKJV) unto Jerusalem (KJV)
Rom. 16:9 Urbanus (Geneva, NKJV) Urbane (KJV)
Rom. 16:14 Greet (Geneva, NKJV) Salute (KJV)
Rom. 16:25 establish (Geneva, NKJV) stablish (KJV)
1 Cor. 1:26 you see (Geneva, NKJV) ye see (KJV)
1 Cor. 2:5 should not be (Geneva, NKJV) should not stand (KJV)
1 Cor. 2:12 but the Spirit (Geneva, NKJV) but the spirit (KJV)
1 Cor. 3:4 For when one (Geneva, NKJV) For while one (KJV)
1 Cor. 3:10 to me (Geneva, NKJV) unto me (KJV)
1 Cor. 3:10 upon it (Geneva) thereupon (KJV) on it (KJV)
1 Cor. 3:19 catcheth (Geneva) taketh (KJV) catches (NKJV)

1 Cor. 4:6 Now these things (Geneva, NKJV) And these things (KJV)
1 Cor. 4:9 as men (Geneva, NKJV) as it were (KJV)
1 Cor. 4:14 beloved children (Geneva, NKJV) beloved sons (KJV)
1 Cor. 6:8 ye yourselves (Geneva) ye (KJV) you yourselves (NKJV)
1 Cor. 7:5 one another (Geneva, NKJV) one the other (KJV)
1 Cor. 7:32 without care (Geneva, NKJV) without carefulness (KJV)
1 Cor. 8:1 love (Geneva, NKJV) charity (KJV)
1 Cor. 8:5 many lords (Geneva, NKJV) lords many (KJV)
1 Cor. 9:3 My defense (Geneva, NKJV) Mine answer (KJV)
1 Cor. 9:18 authority (Geneva, NKJV) power (KJV)
1 Cor. 9:20 I may win (Geneva) I might gain (KJV) I might win (NKJV)
1 Cor. 9:22 I may win (Geneva) I might gain (KJV) I might win (NKJV)
1 Cor. 10:14 my beloved (Geneva, NKJV) my dearly beloved (KJV)
1 Cor. 10:32 Grecians (Geneva) Gentiles (KJV) Greeks (NKJV)
1 Cor. 11:30 sick (Geneva, NKJV) sickly (KJV)
1 Cor. 12:13 Grecians (Geneva) Gentiles (KJV) Greeks (NKJV)
1 Cor. 13:1 love (Geneva, NKJV) charity (KJV)
1 Cor. 13:2 love (Geneva, NKJV) charity (KJV)
1 Cor. 13:3 love (Geneva, NKJV) charity (KJV)
1 Cor. 13:4 Love (Geneva, NKJV) Charity (KJV)
1 Cor. 13:4 love envieth (Geneva) charity envieth (KJV) love does not envy (NKJV)
1 Cor. 13:8 Love (Geneva, NKJV) Charity (KJV)
1 Cor. 13:13 hope, love (Geneva, NKJV) hope, charity (KJV)
1 Cor. 13:13 *is* love (Geneva, NKJV) *is* charity (KJV)
1 Cor. 14:1 love (Geneva, NKJV) charity (KJV)
1 Cor. 14:20 be of a ripe age (Geneva) be men (KJV) be mature (NKJV)
1 Cor. 15:42 *The body* is sown (Geneva, NKJV) It is sown (KJV)
1 Cor. 15:52 last trumpet (Geneva, NKJV) last trump (KJV)
1 Cor. 16:12 howbeit (Geneva) but (KJV) however (NKJV)
1 Cor. 16:14 love (Geneva, NKJV) charity (KJV)
1 Cor. 16:15 given (Geneva) addicted (KJV) devoted (NKJV)
2 Cor. 1:1 to the church (Geneva, NKJV) unto the church (KJV)
2 Cor. 1:5 through Christ (Geneva, NKJV) by Christ (KJV)
2 Cor. 1:11 in prayer (Geneva, NKJV) by prayer (KJV)
2 Cor. 1:18 God is faithful (Geneva, NKJV) God is true (KJV)
2 Cor. 2:17 make merchandise (Geneva) corrupt (KJV) peddling (NKJV)
2 Cor. 3:12 boldness (Geneva, NKJV) plainness (KJV)
2 Cor. 3:18 mirror (Geneva, NKJV) glass (KJV)
2 Cor. 4:2 of shame (Geneva, NKJV) of dishonesty (KJV)
2 Cor. 4:16 Therefore we (Geneva, NKJV) For which cause we (KJV)
2 Cor. 5:1 destroyed (Geneva, NKJV) dissolved (KJV)
2 Cor. 5:9 to him (Geneva) of him (KJV) to Him (NKJV)
2 Cor. 6:3 We give (Geneva, NKJV) Giving (KJV)
2 Cor. 6:6 purity (Geneva, NKJV) pureness (KJV)
2 Cor. 6:11 O Corinthians (Geneva, NKJV) O ye Corinthians (KJV)
2 Cor. 6:15 believer (Geneva, NKJV) he that believeth (KJV)
2 Cor. 7:3 live together (Geneva, NKJV) live with you (KJV)
2 Cor. 7:14 true (Geneva, NKJV) a truth (KJV)
2 Cor. 8:8 diligence of others (Geneva, NKJV) forwardness of others (KJV)
2 Cor. 8:14 their lack (Geneva, NKJV) their want (KJV)
2 Cor. 9:4 Lest if (Geneva, NKJV) Lest haply if (KJV)
2 Cor. 9:11 all liberality (Geneva, NKJV) all bountifulness (KJV)
2 Cor. 9:12 necessities (Geneva) want (KJV) needs (NKJV)
2 Cor. 10:7 in himself (Geneva, NKJV) to himself (KJV)
2 Cor. 11:5 not inferior (Geneva) not a whit behind (KJV) not at all inferior (NKJV)
2 Cor. 11:9 and had need (Geneva) and wanted (KJV) and in need (NKJV)

2 Cor. 12:2 I know (Geneva, NKJV) I knew (KJV)

2 Cor. 12:3 And I know (Geneva, NKJV) And I knew (KJV)

2 Cor. 13:3 toward you (Geneva, NKJV) to youward (KJV)

2 Cor. 13:5 are in the faith (Geneva, NKJV) be in the faith (KJV)

Gal. 1:16 Gentiles (Geneva, NKJV) heathen (KJV)

Gal. 1:17 to Damascus (Geneva, NKJV) unto Damascus (KJV)

Gal. 1:21 I went (Geneva, NKJV) I came (KJV)

Gal. 2:9 the Gentiles (Geneva, NKJV) the heathen (KJV)

Gal. 2:11 to his face (Geneva, NKJV) to the face (KJV)

Gal. 2:16 no flesh shall be justified (Geneva, NKJV)
           shall no flesh be justified (KJV)

Gal. 2:21 Christ died (Geneva, NKJV) Christ is dead (KJV)

Gal. 3:8 the Gentiles (Geneva, NKJV) the heathen (KJV)

Gal. 3:26 sons of God (Geneva, NKJV) children of God (KJV)

Gal. 4:8 are not gods (Geneva, NKJV) are no gods (KJV)

Gal. 4:14 trial (Geneva, NKJV) temptation (KJV)

Gal. 5:18 led by the Spirit (Geneva, NKJV) led of the Spirit (KJV)

Eph. 1:19 toward us (Geneva, NKJV) to usward (KJV)

Eph. 2:13 once were (Geneva, NKJV) sometimes were (KJV)

Eph. 2:13 made near (Geneva, NKJV) made nigh (KJV)

Eph. 2:17 near (Geneva, NKJV) nigh (KJV)

Eph. 3:12 in him (Geneva) of him (KJV) in Him (NKJV)

Eph. 3:19 may be filled (Geneva, NKJV) might be filled (KJV)

Eph. 3:21 all generations (Geneva, NKJV) all ages (KJV)

Eph. 4:16 knit (Geneva, NKJV) compacted (KJV)

Eph. 4:26 Be angry (Geneva, NKJV) Be ye angry (KJV)

Eph. 4:32 forgave you (Geneva, NKJV) hath forgiven you (KJV)

Eph. 5:8 were once darkness (Geneva, NKJV) were sometimes darkness (KJV)

Eph. 5:10 to the Lord (Geneva, NKJV) unto the Lord (KJV)

Eph. 5:17 but understand (Geneva, NKJV) but understanding (KJV)

Eph. 5:29 Lord *doeth* (Geneva) Lord (KJV) Lord *does* (NKJV)

Eph. 6:12 in the (Geneva, NKJV) in (KJV)

Phil. 1:8 very heart (Geneva) bowels (KJV) affection (NKJV)

Phil. 1:12 turned (Geneva, NKJV) fallen (KJV)

Phil. 2:1 compassion (Geneva) bowels (KJV) affection (NKJV)

Phil. 2:3 than himself (Geneva, NKJV) than themselves (KJV)

Phil. 2:30 which was lacking (Geneva) your lack (KJV) what was lacking (NKJV)

Phil. 4:15 concerning (Geneva, NKJV) as concerning (KJV)

Phil. 4:17 Not that I (Geneva, NKJV) Not because I (KJV)

Phil. 4:19 And my God (Geneva, NKJV) But my God (KJV)

Col. 1:4 and of your love (Geneva, NKJV) and of the love *which ye have* (KJV)

Col. 1:17 and in him (Geneva) and by him (KJV) and in Him (NKJV)

Col. 3:7 walked once (Geneva) walked some time (KJV) once walked (NKJV)

Col. 3:12 tender mercy (Geneva) bowels of mercies (KJV) tender mercies (NKJV)

Col. 3:14 love (Geneva, NKJV) charity (KJV)

1 Thess. 1:4 beloved brethren (Geneva, NKJV) brethren beloved (KJV)

1 Thess. 1:8 toward God (Geneva, NKJV) to Godward (KJV)

1 Thess. 3:3 ye yourselves know (Geneva) yourselves know (KJV) you yourselves know (NKJV)

1 Thess. 3:6 love (Geneva, NKJV) charity (KJV)

1 Thess. 4:16 the trumpet (Geneva, NKJV) the trump (KJV)

1 Thess. 5:2 ye yourselves know (Geneva) yourselves know (KJV) you yourselves know (NKJV)

1 Thess. 5:13 Be at peace (Geneva, NKJV) *And* be at peace (KJV)

2 Thess. 1:3 love (Geneva, NKJV) charity (KJV)

2 Thess. 2:4 doeth sit as God (Geneva) as God sitteth (KJV) sits as God (NKJV)

2 Thess. 2:7 now withholdeth (Geneva) now letteth (KJV) now restrains (NKJV)

2 Thess. 2:10 among them (Geneva) in them (KJV) among those (NKJV)

2 Thess. 3:7 ye yourselves know (Geneva) yourselves know (KJV) you yourselves know (NKJV)
2 Thess. 3:9 authority (Geneva, NKJV) power (KJV)
1 Tim. 1:1 our hope (Geneva, NKJV) *which is* our hope (KJV)
1 Tim. 1:3 in Ephesus (Geneva, NKJV) at Ephesus (KJV)
1 Tim. 1:5 love (Geneva, NKJV) charity (KJV)
1 Tim. 1:19 having faith (Geneva, NKJV) holding faith (KJV)
1 Tim. 2:12 permit (Geneva, NKJV) suffer (KJV)
1 Tim. 2:15 love (Geneva, NKJV) charity (KJV)
1 Tim. 3:3 gentle (Geneva, NKJV) patient (KJV)
1 Tim. 3:11 Likewise (Geneva, NKJV) Even so (KJV)
1 Tim. 3:16 manifested (Geneva, NKJV) manifest (KJV)
1 Tim. 3:16 in glory (Geneva, NKJV) into glory (KJV)
1 Tim. 4:12 love (Geneva, NKJV) charity (KJV)
1 Tim. 4:14 eldership (Geneva, NKJV) presbytery (KJV)
1 Tim. 5:1 exhort (Geneva, NKJV) intreat (KJV)
1 Tim. 5:18 wages (Geneva, NKJV) reward (KJV)
1 Tim. 5:10 that the rest (Geneva, NKJV) that others (KJV)
2 Tim. 2:22 love (Geneva, NKJV) charity (KJV)
2 Tim. 3:10 love (Geneva, NKJV) charity (KJV)
2 Tim. 4:7 the crown (Geneva, NKJV) a crown (KJV)
2 Tim. 4:16 all forsook (Geneva, NKJV) all *men* forsook (KJV)
Titus 1:8 one that loveth goodness (Geneva) lover of good men (KJV) lover of what is good (NKJV)
Titus 1:12 always (Geneva, NKJV) alway (KJV)
Titus 2:2 love (Geneva, NKJV) charity (KJV)
Titus 3:3 in times past (Geneva) sometimes (KJV) once (NKJV)
Titus 3:13 lack nothing (Geneva, NKJV) nothing be wanting (KJV)
Philemon 1:7 hearts (Geneva, NKJV) bowels (KJV)
Heb. 3:1 Therefore (Geneva, NKJV) Wherefore (KJV)
Heb. 3:6 whose house we are (Geneva, NKJV) whose house are we (KJV)
Heb. 3:9 Where (Geneva, NKJV) When (KJV)
Heb. 3:18 obeyed not (Geneva) believed not (KJV) did not obey (NKJV)
Heb. 4:2 word that they heard (Geneva) word preached (KJV) word which they heard (NKJV)
Heb. 4:7 appointed (Geneva) limiteth (KJV) designates (NKJV)
Heb. 4:11 disobedience (Geneva, NKJV) unbelief (KJV)
Heb. 4:12 lively (Geneva) quick (KJV) living (NKJV)
Heb. 4:13 open (Geneva, NKJV) opened (KJV)
Heb. 6:6 If they fall (Geneva, NKJV) If they shall fall (KJV)
Heb. 6:6 crucify again (Geneva, NKJV) crucify … afresh (KJV)
Heb. 6:8 near (Geneva, NKJV) nigh (KJV)
Heb. 7:19 near (Geneva, NKJV) nigh (KJV)
Heb. 8:1 sitteth (Geneva) is set (KJV) is seated (NKJV)
Heb. 8:4 seeing there are priests (Geneva) seeing that there are priests (KJV) since there are priests (NKJV)
Heb. 8:10 be their God (Geneva, NKJV) be to them a God (KJV)
Heb. 9:6 the service (Geneva) the service *of God* (KJV) the services (NKJV)
Heb. 10:4 of bulls and goats (Geneva, NKJV) of bulls and of goats (KJV)
Heb. 10:7 Then I said (Geneva, NKJV) Then said I (KJV)
Heb. 10:13 tarrieth (Geneva) expecting (KJV) waiting (NKJV)
Heb. 10:23 hope (Geneva, NKJV) faith (KJV)
Heb. 10:33 Partly while you (Geneva, NKJV) Partly whilst ye (KJV)
Heb. 11:5 taken away (Geneva, NKJV) translated (KJV)
Heb. 11:7 household (Geneva, NKJV) house (KJV)
Heb. 11:9 tents (Geneva, NKJV) tabernacles (KJV)
Heb. 12:28 shaken (Geneva, NKJV) moved (KJV)
Heb. 13:4 among all (Geneva, NKJV) in all (KJV)

Heb. 13:16 distribute (Geneva) communicate (KJV) share (NKJV)
Heb. 13:24 Know that (Geneva, NKJV) Know *this*, that (KJV)
James 1:3 Knowing that (Geneva, NKJV) Knowing *this*, that (KJV)
James 1:4 lacking nothing (Geneva, NKJV) wanting nothing (KJV)
James 1:5 reproached no man (Geneva) upbraideth not (KJV) without reproach (NKJV)
James 2:6 the rich oppress (Geneva, NKJV) rich men oppress (KJV)
James 3:4 rudder (Geneva, NKJV) helm (KJV)
James 3:12 olives (Geneva, NKJV) olive berries (KJV)
James 4:4 maketh himself the enemy (Geneva) is the enemy (KJV) makes himself an enemy (NKJV)
James 4:6 to the humble (Geneva, NKJV) unto the humble (KJV)
James 4:8 near (Geneva, NKJV) nigh (KJV)
James 4:10 will lift (Geneva, NKJV) shall lift (KJV)
James 5:11 count them blessed (Geneva, NKJV) count them happy (KJV)
James 5:11 and merciful (Geneva, NKJV) and of tender mercy (KJV)
1 Peter 1:13 on the grace (Geneva) for the grace (KJV) upon the grace (NKJV)
1 Peter 1:22 love one another (Geneva, NKJV) *see that ye* love one another (KJV)
1 Peter 2:6 be ashamed (Geneva) be confounded (KJV) be put to shame (NKJV)
1 Peter 3:6 any terror (Geneva, NKJV) any amazement (KJV)
1 Peter 3:14 blessed (Geneva, NKJV) happy (KJV)
1 Peter 4:3 drunkenness (Geneva, NKJV) excess of wine (KJV)
1 Peter 4:3 drinkings (Geneva) banquetings (KJV) drinking parties (NKJV)
1 Peter 4:8 fervent love (Geneva, NKJV) fervent charity (KJV)
1 Peter 4:8 for love (Geneva, NKJV) for charity (KJV)
1 Peter 4:14 blessed (Geneva, NKJV) happy (KJV)
1 Peter 4:14 the Spirit of glory (Geneva, NKJV) the spirit of glory (KJV)
1 Peter 5:14 of love (Geneva, NKJV) of charity (KJV)
2 Peter 1:1 of our God and Saviour Jesus Christ (Geneva) of God and our Saviour Jesus Christ (KJV) of our God and Savior Jesus Christ (NKJV)
2 Peter 1:7 love (Geneva, NKJV) charity (KJV)
2 Peter 2:10 and (Geneva, NKJV) But (KJV)
2 Peter 2:13 wages (Geneva, NKJV) reward (KJV)
2 Peter 2:16 he was rebuked (Geneva, NKJV) was rebuked (KJV)
2 Peter 2:17 the black darkness (Geneva) the mist of darkness (KJV) the blackness of darkness (NKJV)
2 Peter 3:9 toward us (Geneva, NKJV) to us-ward (KJV)
2 Peter 3:15 to you (Geneva, NKJV) unto you (KJV)
1 John 2:20 anointment (Geneva) unction (KJV) anointing (NKJV)
1 John 2:26 deceive (Geneva, NKJV) seduce (KJV)
1 John 2:27 is true (Geneva, NKJV) is truth (KJV)
1 John 3:16 love (Geneva, NKJV) love *of God* (KJV)
Jude 1:8 these dreamers (Geneva, NKJV) these *filthy* dreamers (KJV)
Jude 1:19 These are (Geneva, NKJV) These be (KJV)
Jude 1:25 and for ever (Geneva) and ever (KJV) and forever (NKJV)
Rev. 1:12 Then I (Geneva, NKJV) And I (KJV)
Rev. 1:13 to the feet (Geneva, NKJV) to the foot (KJV)
Rev. 2:10 the crown of life (Geneva, NKJV) a crown of life (KJV)
Rev. 2:13 Satan's throne (Geneva, NKJV) Satan's seat (KJV)
Rev. 2:19 love (Geneva, NKJV) charity (KJV)
Rev. 2:29 to the churches (Geneva, NKJV) unto the churches (KJV)
Rev. 3:1 but thou (Geneva) and (KJV) but you (NKJV)
Rev. 3:4 wilt not watch (Geneva) shalt not watch (KJV) will not watch (NKJV)
Rev. 3:21 sit (Geneva) am set down (KJV) sat down (NKJV)
Rev. 4:11 will (Geneva, NKJV) pleasure (KJV)
Rev. 5:6 Lamb as though it (Geneva, NKJV) Lamb as it (KJV)
Rev. 5:11 Then I (Geneva, NKJV) And I (KJV)

Rev. 7:9 After these things (Geneva, NKJV) After this (KJV)
Rev. 8:1 about half an hour (Geneva, NKJV) about the space of half an hour (KJV)
Rev. 8:3 Then another (Geneva, NKJV) And another (KJV)
Rev. 8:10 Then the third (Geneva, NKJV) And the third (KJV)
Rev. 9:13 Then the sixth (Geneva, NKJV) And the sixth (KJV)
Rev. 9:15 to (Geneva, NKJV) for to (KJV)
Rev. 10:9 So I went (Geneva, NKJV) And I went (KJV)
Rev. 10:9 said to him (Geneva, NKJV) said unto him (KJV)
Rev. 10:10 Then I took (Geneva, NKJV) And I took (KJV)
Rev. 11:19 Then the temple (Geneva, NKJV) And the temple (KJV)
Rev. 11:19 covenant (Geneva, NKJV) testament (KJV)
Rev. 12:4 to devour (Geneva, NKJV) for to devour (KJV)
Rev. 12:14 the presence (Geneva, NKJV) the face (KJV)
Rev. 12:16 But the earth (Geneva, NKJV) And the earth (KJV)
Rev. 13:3 wondered and followed (Geneva) wondered after (KJV) marveled and followed (NKJV)
Rev. 13:7 over every (Geneva, NKJV) over all (KJV)
Rev. 13:7 nation (Geneva, NKJV) nations (KJV)
Rev. 13:14 signs (Geneva, NKJV) miracles (KJV)
Rev. 14:1 Then I looked (Geneva, NKJV) And I looked (KJV)
Rev. 14:6 Then I saw (Geneva, NKJV) And I saw (KJV)
Rev. 14:17 Then another (Geneva, NKJV) And another (KJV)
Rev. 15:10 throne (Geneva, NKJV) seat (KJV)
Rev. 15:16 in Hebrew (Geneva, NKJV) in the Hebrew tongue (KJV)
Rev. 17:13 power and authority (Geneva, NKJV) power and strength (KJV)
Rev. 17:9 Here is (Geneva, NKJV) And here is (KJV)
Rev. 18:2 loud voice (Geneva, NKJV) strong voice (KJV)
Rev. 18:21 Then a mighty (Geneva, NKJV) And a mighty (KJV)
Rev. 19:1 of a great multitude (Geneva, NKJV) of much people (KJV)
Rev. 19:1 to the Lord (Geneva, NKJV) unto the Lord (KJV)
Rev. 19:5 Then a voice (Geneva, NKJV) And a voice (KJV)
Rev. 21:9 Come (Geneva, NKJV) Come hither (KJV)

Do these facts from the Geneva Bible, the KJV, and the NKJV show the KJV-only use of inconsistent, unjust measures or standards in their positive assertions concerning the Geneva compared to their extreme, negative allegations concerning the NKJV? In addition, these many pages of differences between the 1560 Geneva Bible, the KJV, and the NKJV should indicate a great deal of the range of differences that can be found in Bible translations from the same basic underlying original language texts of Scripture. Many of these differences could be considered minor, but some could be considered significant, important, and major. These actual differences show the possibility that differences that KJV-only advocates claim or assume have to be textual in the NKJV could fail into the range of what could be merely translational. It is not always easy to determine whether a difference between translations is a matter of text or a matter of translation. One translation may render an original language word with one word while another translation may render the same word with several words or even with a phrase or clause. In some cases, the difference in rendering could fall into the range of all the different meanings that an original language could have. In other cases, a rendering that appears to be a possible textual difference could instead be a translation difference involving a non-literal, dynamic-equivalent rendering versus a literal rendering. In another possible example of what may appear to be a textual difference when it could involve a difference in translation, the makers of one translation may choose not to have an English rendering for an original language word for which the makers of another translation give one. In some cases, these type examples may overlap with dynamic equivalent type.

KJV-only claims concerning word-for-word translating considered

Many KJV defenders typically will make assertions that would suggest that they believe in word preservation or verbal ["every word"] preservation of the Scriptures. Their advocating of verbal preservation may be what leads them to advocate word-for-word translating. Do KJV defenders advocate use of just measures that are applied consistently and justly to all Bible translations as to what would actually constitute word-for-word translating? Many KJV defenders will claim or suggest that one English translation [the KJV] can be asserted to be the preserved word of God. Is perfect verbal preservation being directly claimed for the KJV? Would biblical preservation in effect have to be redefined to attempt to apply it accurately to the KJV?

KJV defenders evidently do not apply consistently and justly their seeming measure that would in effect attempt to require a translation to have an accurate or word-for-word English rendering for each and every original language word in a verse. H. D. Williams gave the following definition of **word-for-word translating**: "rendering a word or words in a receptor language the same as in a source-language" (*Word-for-Word Translating*, p. xx). H. D. Williams asserted: "Literal word-for-word translating is translating words in the source language for words in the receptor language so far as the syntax of the receptor-language will allow" (p. 4). Bob Steward declared: "Translation work is designed to bring the exact equivalent from the sender language to the receptor language" (*Why Not the NKJV*, p. 6). Troy Clark contended: "The entire King James Bible has been translated from the original books **the whole way** by formal (verbal) equivalency. That is, each word being translated into the new language must be the same, literal word being translated from. Word equals Word" (*Perfect Bible*, p. 39). Troy Clark claimed: "God wants **every word** equally preserved" (p. 45). Doug Stauffer asserted: "In order for a translation to be authoritative, strict adherence to the words of the Holy Spirit must be used. Therefore, a strict adherence to a word-for-word translation must be followed" (*One Book Stands Alone*, p. 253). James Rasbeary claimed that all seven English Bibles "translated word for word, which is called formal equivalency" (*What's Wrong with the Old Black Book*, p. 91). James Rasbeary maintained that "the King James Bible is a **word-for-word** translation" (p. 183). Dennis Anderson asserted: "When the King James Bible was translated, forty-seven scholarly men took that which had been given by inspiration and translated it into English. That is **Preservation**" (*The Flaming Torch*, Summer, 1995, p. 6). Concerning the KJV, William Grady referred to "its word-for-word translation" (*Given by Inspiration*, p. 106). Thomas Strouse maintained that "the KJV is a word for word, 'Static Equivalent' translation" (*Lord God Hath Spoken*, p. 22). Dennis Corle contended that "somewhere there must be an every word and every jot and tittle Bible," which he suggested is the KJV (*God's Inspired Book*, p. 11). R. B. Ouellette claimed that the KJV "is a literal translation of the correct and pure Greek and Hebrew texts" (*A More Sure Word*, p. 8). Gail Riplinger maintained that the KJV is a "word-for-word translation of the Hebrew and Greek Bibles" (*In Awe of Thy Word*, p. 270). Gail Riplinger also contended that the KJV has "literal, word-for-word renderings of the Greek text" and claimed that it shows "all words, even if they seem repetitive" (p. 288). Riplinger claimed that "the KJV is the only English formal equivalency translation of the pure Greek and Hebrew Bible" (p. 90). Ed DeVries declared: "Formal Equivalence demands that if it is a verb in the Greek or Hebrew, it must be a verb in the English. If it is a noun in the Greek or Hebrew it must be a noun in the English and so forth" (*Divinely Inspired*, p. 43). David H. Sorenson asserted: "The Traditional Text and the King James Version reflect the purified verbal transmission of God's very words to this hour. Though the King James Version *as a translation* is not inspired, verbal preservation has carried the *results* of inspiration through to this hour in the King James Version. Those results are inerrancy and infallibility" (*God's Perfect Book*, p. 211). David Cloud claimed that the KJV "was an accurate formal equivalency translation" and that it "gave weight to every word in the original language text" (*Examining the King James Only*, p. 7). David Cloud maintained that "the translator's job is to faithfully transmit the words and message from the original into the receptor language as literally as possible" (*Bible Version Question/Answer*, p. 12). David Cloud commented: "But if we are not careful about every word of the underlying Hebrew and Greek texts, the foundation of Scripture will be weakened and the resulting translations will be corrupted" (p. 32). Jack Hyles claimed: "Every single word of God has been preserved in the King James Bible, the only Bible" (*Need for an Every-Word Bible*, p. 97). D. A. Waite maintained that the KJV "preserves all of the Hebrew, Aramaic, and Greek Words of the Bible by means of an accurate English translation of those **Words**" (*Fundamental Deception of Bible Preservation*, p. 75). Waite asserted: "In our King James Bible, we have God's **Words** kept intact in English because of its accurate translation of the verbal plenary preserved Hebrew, Aramaic, and Greek **Words** that underlie it" (p. 130). Waite claimed that "the King James accurately translates every Hebrew and Greek Word into the English language" (*Foes of the KJB Refuted*, p. 39). Waite declared: "I believe that the King James Bible 'preserves' (with a small 'p') by means of an accurate translation into the English language, every word of the Hebrew and Greek texts that underlie it" (p. 98). Waite maintained that "the King James translators adopted a method of **verbal equivalence**; and **formal equivalence**, that is, the words from the Greek or Hebrew were rendered as closely as possible into the English. The same is true for the forms of those words" (*Defending the KJB*, p. 90). By the technique of dynamic equivalence, D. A. Waite claimed that a translator "can choose to eliminate what God has explicitly and definitely stated, word for word, in the Hebrew or in the Greek" and that "this word, or that word, or several words if he wants to, he need not bother to translate, or put into the language" (p. 122). Waite asserted: "If you ADD to the Word of God what you think is implicit in the words, that is disobedience" (p. 124).

A consistent, just application of these claims made by KJV defenders themselves could raise a number of interesting, thought-provoking questions. Does the 1611 KJV actually give a completely accurate or inerrant English rendering for each and every original language word in every verse as some KJV defenders seem to assume or directly suggest in their own statements? How is every individual preserved original-language word of Scripture actually kept intact and unchanged in the KJV when the 1611 KJV changed them to different words and even gave no English word for some of them as the KJV translators themselves clearly acknowledged in some of their marginal notes? How would giving no English word for a Hebrew word found in a verse or a Greek word found in a verse be taking every inspired word and giving an accurate translation of that word and be preserving that word in English? Would Waite and other KJV defenders in effect suggest that the KJV subtracts from God's words or adopted "the diabolical principle of subtraction" (*Defending the KJB*, p. 91) when it does not give an English translation for a noun in the KJV's underlying Hebrew Old Testament text or for a noun in the Greek New Testament text as they would do concerning the NKJV? If the KJV translators did not give an English word for some preserved original language words of Scripture found in their underlying texts, would that suggest that the English-speaking believer has no assurance that he can read every word of God in the KJV? Would KJV defenders suggest that the KJV is not authoritative in any places where it does not strictly adhere to word-for-word translating, where it does not give an English word for an original language word, where it gives what could be considered a dynamic equivalent rendering and not the exact equivalent, and where it added to the word of God the words the transalators thought were implicit in the original-language words? Would KJV defenders suggest that the KJV translators did not translate what God explicitly said in those cases where they did not translate word-for-word, did not show all words, did not give an English word for an original language word, did not preserve the same word order, or added words in English for which there were no original-language words of Scripture? How could the KJV preserve every original language word of Scripture when it is a fact that it provides no English word for some of them? Is the foundation of Scripture weakened by the fact that the KJV translators did not translate word-for-word literally or changed the form of words in many places? Would a consistent, just application of KJV-only allegations against the NKJV in effect maintain that the KJV cannot properly be called a word-for-word translation and an every-word Bible? Do KJV defenders in effect paint themselves into a corner if they refuse to apply their own stated principles or measures consistently and justly? If KJV defenders will not apply their own set of criteria or own measures concerning word-for-word translating consistently and justly to the KJV, does that indicate use of the fallacy of special pleading for the KJV? Will KJV defenders think soundly and seriously about their own assertions and claims and then answer valid questions based on a consistent application of them?

Different translators, including the KJV translators, may differ in whether they think it is necessary in English to give a rendering for an original language word or whether they may think that their total English rendering of a phrase or verse includes the meaning of the word for which they do not give an individual rendering. Dave Brunn asserted: "There are places in every English version where the translators chose to omit a particular Hebrew or Greek word rather than to reflect it literally in their translation" (*One Bible, Many Versions*, p. 107). Dave Brunn claimed that "there is no such thing as a consistently word-for-word translation in English" (p. 129). Donald Brake asserted: "It must be remembered that no translation is really a word-for-word equivalence" (*New Interpreter's Dictionary of the Bible*, Vol. 5, p. 749). Alan O-Reilly claimed: "No translation from one language into another can be verbatim, or word-for-word" (*O Biblios*, p. 29). Peter Ruckman asserted: "No translation of Any Greek text would be a *good* translation if it were 'word for word'" (*Alexandrian Cult*, Part Eight, p. 17). Alan Macgregor maintained that "no formal equivalence translation since Wycliffe's relies completely on the use of direct word for word translation" (*400 Years On*, p. 184). William D. Mounce claimed: "The very reason that people want a word-for-word translation is that they believe there's not going to be any interpretation, and that's simply not true. All translation involves interpretation" (*Greek for the Rest of Us*, p. 24). William Mounce asserted: "One of the problems of going word for word is that it's interpretive, the very thing that it tries not to be" (p. 26).

If the KJV translators are given the interpretive latitude of not having to give an English word for each and every original language word found in a verse, why are other Bible translators not given the same latitude? When the KJV translators are sometimes allowed to interpret what God meant instead of translating literally and word-for-word what God said, why should other Bible translators not be given the same latitude? If the KJV translators are permitted to omit providing a rendering for one original-language word based on their understanding of the literal meaning of the entire sentence instead of the literal meaning of each individual word, will other Bible translators be given the same discretion? When consistent, just measures and standards are used and applied, can the NKJV properly be asserted to be just as faithful overall to the Received Text as the Geneva Bible and the KJV are? When consistent, just standards are used or are applied, can the NKJV be asserted overall to be as much a word-for-word translation or formal equivalent translation as the Geneva Bible or the KJV are? The Scriptures support the use of just measures.

In the following examples, some possible places of where the KJV may not have an individual, literal, form-equivalent, accurate English rendering for each and every original language word in verses in its underlying texts are given. Sometimes in their own marginal notes the KJV translators themselves clearly acknowledged and pointed out that they did not provide in their English text a literal word-for-word rendering of each and every original language word in every verse. Their marginal notes reveal that it was possible in some of these cases for the KJV translators to give a literal, word-for-word rendering as they themselves did in their own marginal notes. Therefore, it can be soundly and justly concluded that the KJV translators themselves clearly refuted any suggestion that they strictly provided every time it was possible a word-for-word English rendering for each and every preserved original-language word of Scripture. In some cases, the KJV translators may give in their English text a non-literal, non-formal-equivalent, or dynamic-equivalent rendering while in others it is clear from the direct first-hand evidence given by the translators in their marginal notes that they choose to give no English word for an original-language word. In cases involving a conjunction, the KJV translators may not give a marginal note that indicates and acknowledges that they omitted an original language word. In order to point out more clearly these examples to English readers, some English translations made from the same basic original language texts as used in the making of the KJV are quoted in the comparisons. Along with sometimes citing the Matthew's Bible, the Geneva Bible, the Bishops' Bible, or the NKJV, one of the other translations cited is *Young's Literal Translation*. In his 1862 preface to the first edition, Robert Young wrote: "It has been no part of the Translator's plan to attempt to form a New Hebrew or Greek Text—he has therefore somewhat rigidly adhered to the received ones." Another source checked for these examples would be the original language texts and English renderings in Jay Green's 1986 *The Interlinear Bible*. Will KJV defenders apply justly and strictly their own stated demand or measure for strict word-for-word translating to these examples?

Possible examples of non-word-for-word or non-formal-equivalent renderings in the KJV

Genesis 1:20 [1611 margin—"Heb. face of the firmament of heaven"]
in the open firmament of heaven [1611 KJV]
on the face of the expanse of the heavens [Young's Literal Translation—YLT]
across the face of the firmament of the heavens [NKJV]
on the face of the expanse of the heavens [Literal Translation in *Interlinear Bible*]

Genesis 5:20 [Hebrew has two conjunctions in this number]
nine hundred sixty and two years [1611 KJV]
nine hundred and sixty and two years [YLT]
nine hundred and sixty-two years [NKJV]

Genesis 7:22 [1611 margin—"Hebr. The breath of the spirit of life"]
Every thing in whose nostrils the spirit of life did breathe [1560 Geneva Bible]
All in whose nostrils *was* the breath of life [1611 KJV]
All in whose nostrils *is* breath of a living spirit [YLT]
All in whose nostrils *was* the breath of the spirit of life [NKJV]

Genesis 12:4
Abram *was* seventy and five years old [1611 KJV]
Abram *is* a son of five and seventy years [YLT]

Genesis 13:8
we *be* brethren [1611 KJV] [1611 margin—"Hebr. men brethren"]
we *are* men—brethren [YLT]
we *are* men, brothers [Literal Translation in *Interlinear Bible*]

Genesis 17:8 [1611 margin—"Heb. of thy sojournings"]
the land wherein thou art a stranger [1611 KJV]
the land of thy sojournings [YLT]
the land of your sojourning [Literal Translation in *Interlinear Bible*]

Genesis 17:12 [1611 margin--"Hebr. a son of eight days"]
And every man child of eight days old [1560 Geneva Bible]
And every manchild of eight days old [1602 Bishops' Bible]
And he that is eight days old [1611 KJV]
And a son of eight days [YLT] [Literal Translation in *Interlinear Bible*]

Genesis 23:6
a prince of God [1537 Matthew's Bible; 1560 Geneva Bible; 1602 Bishops' Bible]
a mighty prince [1611 KJV] [1611 margin—"Hebr. a Prince of God"]
a prince of God [YLT]

Genesis 30:8
With godly wrestlings [1602 Bishops' Bible]
With great wrestlings [1611 KJV] [1611 margin—"Heb. wrestlings of God"]
With wrestlings of God [YLT]
with struggles of God [Literal Translation in *Interlinear Bible*]

Genesis 30:39 [Hebrew has word for "flocks" twice in verse]
and brought forth [1611 KJV]
and the flock beareth [YLT]
and the flocks brought forth [NKJV]

Genesis 31:2

as in times past [1560 Geneva Bible]
as it was wont to be [1602 Bishops' Bible]
as before [1611 KJV] [1611 margin—"Hebr. as yesterday and the day before"]
as the day before yesterday [Literal Translation in *Interlinear Bible*]

Genesis 37:1 [1611 margin—"Heb. of his fathers sojournings"]
wherein his father was a stranger [1611 KJV]
of his father's sojournings [YLT]
of his father's travels [Literal Translation in *Interlinear Bible*]

Genesis 43:16
and kill meat [1560 Geneva Bible]
and slay [1611 KJV] [1611 margin—"Heb. kill a killing"]
and slaughter an animal [YLT] [NKJV]

Genesis 44:7 [the word for God is not in Hebrew]
God forbid [1611 KJV]
far be it [YLT]
Far be it [NKJV] [Literal Translation in *Interlinear Bible*]

Genesis 47:8
How old art thou [1611 KJV] [1611 margin—"how many are the days of the years of thy life"]
How many *are* the days of the years of thy life [YLT]
How many are the days of the years of your life [Literal Translation in *Interlinear Bible*]

Exodus 10:25
give us [1611 KJV] [1611 margin—"Heb. into our hands"]
give in our hand [YLT]
give into our hands [Literal Translation in *Interlinear Bible*]

Exodus 18:16
between every man and his neighbour [1537 Matthew's Bible; 1602 Bishops' Bible]
between one and another [1611 KJV] [1611 margin—"Hebr. a man and his fellow"]
between a man and his neighbor [YLT] [Literal Translation in *Interlinear Bible*]

Exodus 32:11
the LORD his God [1611 KJV] [1611 margin—"Hebr. the face of the Lord"]
the face of Jehovah his God [YLT] [Literal Translation in *Interlinear Bible*]

Exodus 38:28 [Hebrew has two conjunctions in this number]
seven hundred and seventy & five [1560 Geneva Bible]
seven hundred seventy and five [1611 KJV]
seven hundred and five and seventy [YLT]
seven hundred and seventy-five [NKJV]

Exodus 40:2
In the *first* day of the first month in the *very* first of *the same* month [1560 Geneva Bible]
On the first day of the first month [1611 KJV]
On the first day of the month, in the first month [YLT]
On the first day of the month, on the first of the month [Literal Translation in *Interlinear Bible*]

Leviticus 2:1 [Hebrew has the word usually translated soul]
If any soul will offer [1530 Tyndale's, 1537 Matthew's Bible]
And when any will offer [1611 KJV]
And when a person bringeth [YLT]
And when a person brings [Literal Translation in *Interlinear Bible*]

Leviticus 6:12
shall burn wood on it every morning [1611 KJV]
hath burned on it wood morning by morning [YLT]
shall burn wood on it morning by morning [Literal Translation in *Interlinear Bible*]

Leviticus 14:7
into the broad field [1560 Geneva Bible]
into the field [1602 Bishops' Bible]
Into the open field [1611 KJV] [1611 margin—"Hebr. upon the face of the field"]
on the face of the field [YLT]

Leviticus 14:10
ewe lamb of the first year [1611 KJV] [1611 margin—"Hebr. the daughter of her year"]
ewe-lamb, daughter of a year [YLT]
ewe lamb, daughter of a year [Literal Translation in *Interlinear Bible*]

Numbers 10:11
And in the second year, in the second month, *and* in the twentieth *day* of the month [1560 Geneva]
And it came to pass on the twentieth *day* of the second month, in the second year [1611 KJV]
In the second year in the second month, in the twentieth of the month [YLT]

Numbers 17:10
the rebellious children [1560 Geneva Bible; 1602 Bishops' Bible]
the rebels [1611 KJV] [1611 margin—"Hebr. children of rebellion"]
the sons of rebellion [YLT] [Literal Translation in *Interlinear Bible*]

Deuteronomy 3:18
men of war [1560 Geneva Bible]
meet for the war [1611 KJV] [1611 margin—"Heb. sons of power"]
the sons of might [YLT]
the warriors [Literal Translation in *Interlinear Bible*]

Deuteronomy 5:7 [Hebrew word translated "face" 328 times; "presence" 70 times]
before my face [1560 Geneva Bible]
before me [1611 KJV]
in My presence [YLT]

Joshua 9:11
Take victuals with you [1611 KJV] [1611 margin—"Hebr. In your hand"]
Take in your hand provision [YLT]
Take provisions in your hand [Literal Translation in *Interlinear Bible*]

Joshua 22:29
God forbid [1611 KJV]
Far be it [YLT] [NKJV] [Literal Translation in *Interlinear Bible*]

Joshua 24:15
unto you [1611 KJV]
in your eyes [YLT] [Literal Translation in *Interlinear Bible*]

Judges 6:8
a Prophet [1611 KJV] [1611 margin—"Heb. a man, a Prophet"]
a man, a prophet [YLT] [Literal Translation in *Interlinear Bible*]

Judges 11:3
fled from his brethren [1611 KJV] [1611 margin—"Heb from the face"]
fleeth from the face of his brethren [YLT]
fled from the face of his brothers [Literal Translation in *Interlinear Bible*]

Judges 16:1
an harlot [1611 KJV] [1611 margin—"Heb. a woman an harlot"]
a woman, a harlot [YLT]
a harlot, a woman [Literal Translation in *Interlinear Bible*]

Judges 19:1 [1611 margin—"Heb. a woman a concubine, or a wife a concubine"]
took to wife a concubine [1560 Geneva Bible]
took to him a concubine [1611 KJV]
taketh to him a wife, a concubine [YLT]
took a wife to himself, a concubine [Literal Translation in *Interlinear Bible*]

Judges 19:9
to thy tent [1560 Geneva Bible; 1602 Bishops' Bible]
home [1611 KJV] [1611 margin—"Heb. to thy tent"]
to thy tent [YLT]
to your tent [Literal Translation in *Interlinear Bible*]

1 Samuel 14:15
with fear by God [1560 Geneva Bible]
the fear that was sent of God [1602 Bishops' Bible]
a very great trembling [1611 KJV] [1611 margin—"Hebr. a trembling of God"]
a trembling of God [YLT] [Literal Translation in *Interlinear Bible*]

1 Samuel 14:25
honey upon the ground [1611 KJV]
honey on the face of the field [YLT]

1 Samuel 28:15
by prophets [1611 KJV] [1611 margin—"Hebr. by the hand of prophets"]
by the hand of the prophets [YLT] [Literal Translation in *Interlinear Bible*]

1 Samuel 28:17
spake by mine hand [1560 Geneva Bible]
spake by me [1611 KJV] [1611 margin—"Hebr. mine hand"]
hath spoken by my hand [YLT]
spoke by my hand [Literal Translation in *Interlinear Bible*]

2 Samuel 16:16
God save the king [1611 KJV] [1611 margin—"Heb. let the king live"]
Let the king live [YLT] [Literal Translation in *Interlinear Bible*]
Long live the king [NKJV]

2 Samuel 22:45
Strange children [1602 Bishops' Bible]
Strangers [1611 KJV] [1611 margin—"Heb. sons of the stranger"]
Sons of a stranger [YLT]
The sons of strangers [Literal Translation in *Interlinear Bible*]

1 Kings 1:25
God save king Adonijah [1611 KJV] [1611 margin—"Hebr. Let king Adonijah live"]
Let king Adonijah love [YLT] [Literal Translation in *Interlinear Bible*]

Long live king Adonijah [NKJV]

1 Kings 13:6
besought the LORD [1611 KJV] [1611 margin—"Hebr. the face of the LORD"]
appeaseth the face of Jehovah [YLT]
entreated the face of Jehovah [Literal Translation in *Interlinear Bible*]

1 Kings 16:12
by the hand of Jehu the Prophet [1560 Geneva Bible; 1602 Bishops' Bible]
by Jehu the prophet [1611 KJV] [1611 margin—"Heb. by the hand of"]
by the hand of Jehu the prophet [YLT] [Literal Translation in *Interlinear Bible*]

1 Kings 17:16
by the hand of Eliah [1560 Geneva Bible]
by the hand of Elias [1602 Bishops' Bible]
by Elijah [1611 KJV] [1611 margin—"Heb. by the hand of"]
by the hand of Elijah [YLT] [Literal Translation in *Interlinear Bible*]

2 Kings 8:9
in his hand [1560 Geneva Bible]
with him [1611 KJV] [1611 margin—"Heb. in his hand"]
in his hand [YLT] [Literal Translation in *Interlinear Bible*]

2 Kings 9:36
by the hand of his servant [1602 Bishops' Bible]
by his servant [1611 KJV] [1611 margin—"Heb. by the hand of"]
by the hand of his servant [YLT] [Literal Translation in *Interlinear Bible*]

2 Kings 10:10
by the hand of his servant Elias [1602 Bishops' Bible]
by his servant Elijah [1611 KJV] [1611 margin—"Heb. by the hand of"]
by the hand of His servant Elijah [YLT] [Literal Translation in *Interlinear Bible*]

2 Kings 13:25
returned, and took [1560 Geneva Bible]
went again, and took [1602 Bishops' Bible]
took again [1611 KJV] [1611 margin—"Heb. returned and took"]
turneth and taketh [YLT]
returned and took [Literal Translation in *Interlinear Bible*]

2 Kings 17:13
by all the prophets [1611 KJV] [1611 margin—"Heb. by the hand of all"]
by the hand of every prophet [YLT]
by the hand of all His prophets [Literal Translation in *Interlinear Bible*]

2 Kings 19:23
By the hand of thy messengers [1602 Bishops' Bible]
By thy messengers [1611 KJV] [1611 margin—"Heb. by the hand of"]
By the hand of thy messengers [YLT]
By the hand of your messengers [Literal Translation in *Interlinear Bible*]

2 Kings 21:16
from corner to corner [1560 Geneva Bible; 1602 Bishops' Bible]
from one end to another [1611 KJV] [1611 margin—"Heb. from mouth to mouth"]
mouth to mouth [YLT]
from mouth to mouth [Literal Translation in *Interlinear Bible*]

2 Kings 24:2
by his servants the prophets [1611 KJV] [1611 margin—"Heb. by the hand of"]
by the hand of His servants the prophets [YLT] [Literal Translation in *Interlinear Bible*]

1 Chronicles 11:3
by the hand of Samuel [1537 Matthew's; 1560 Geneva Bible; 1602 Bishops' Bible]
by Samuel [1611 KJV] [1611 margin—"Heb. by the hand of"]
by the hand of Samuel [YLT] {Literal Translation in *Interlinear Bible*]

2 Chronicles 2:17
the strangers [1611 KJV] [1611 margin—"Hebr. the men the strangers"]
the men, the sojourners [YLT]
the men, the strangers [Literal Translation in *Interlinear Bible*]

2 Chronicles 19:6
in the cause *and* judgment [1560 Geneva Bible]
in the judgment [1611 KJV] [1611 margin—"Hebr. in the matter of judgment"]
in the matter of judgment [YLT] [Literal Translation in *Interlinear Bible*]

2 Chronicles 23:18
by the appointment of David [1560 Geneva Bible]
by David [1611 KJV] [1611 margin—"Hebr. by the hands of David"]
by the hands of David [YLT] [Literal Translation in *Interlinear Bible*]

2 Chronicles 29:25
by the hand of his Prophets [1560 Geneva Bible]
through the hand of the Prophets [1602 Bishops' Bible]
by his prophets [1611 KJV] [1611 margin—"Heb. by the hand of"]
by the hand of His prophets [YLT] [Literal Translation in *Interlinear Bible*]

Ezra 9:11
from corner to corner [1560 Geneva Bible]
from one end to another [1611 KJV] [1611 margin—"Heb. from mouth to mouth"]
from mouth unto mouth [YLT]
from one mouth to mouth [Literal Translation in *Interlinear Bible*]

Nehemiah 9:30
by the hand of thy Prophets [1560 Geneva Bible; 1602 Bishops' Bible]
in thy Prophets [1611 KJV] [1611 margin—"Heb. in the hand of thy Prophets"]
by the hand of Thy prophets [YLT]

Job 1:19 [note in NKJV states that "LXX omits across"]
came a great wind from beyond the wilderness [1560 Geneva Bible]
came a mighty great wind from beyond the wilderness [1602 Bishops' Bible]
came a great wind from the wilderness [1611 KJV]
a great wind hath come from over the wilderness [YLT]
a great wind came from across the wilderness [NKJV]

Job 21:28
where is the tabernacle of the wicked's dwelling [1560 Geneva Bible]
where *are* the dwelling places of the wicked [1611 KJV]
where the tent—the tabernacles of the wicked [YLT]
where *is* the tent, the dwelling place of the wicked [NKJV]

Job 36:14

Their soul dieth in youth [1560 Geneva Bible]
Thus shall their soul perish in foolishness [1602 Bishops' Bible]
They die in youth [1611 KJV] [1611 margin—"Hebr. their soul dieth"]
Their soul dieth in youth [YLT]
Their soul dies in youth [Literal Translation in *Interlinear Bible*]

Job 42:9
the person of Job [1537 Matthew's Bible; 1602 Bishops' Bible]
Job [1611 KJV] [1611 margin—"Heb. the face of Job"]
the face of Job [YLT] [Literal Translation in *Interlinear Bible*]

Psalm 18:44
the strangers [1611 KJV] [1611 margin—"Heb. the sons of the stranger"]
Sons of a stranger [YLT]
the sons of foreigners [Literal Translation in *Interlinear Bible*]

Psalm 29:1
ye sons of the mighty [1560 Geneva Bible]
O ye mighty [1611 KJV] [1611 margin—"Hebr. ye sons of the mighty"]
ye sons of the mighty [YLT]
sons of mighty ones [Literal Translation in *Interlinear Bible*]

Psalm 36:6
the great mountains [1611 KJV] [1611 margin—"Hebr. the mountains of God"]
mountains of God [YLT]
the hills of God [Literal Translation in *Interlinear Bible*]

Psalm 49:11
from generation to generation [1560 Geneva Bible]
from one generation to another [1602 Bishops' Bible]
to all generations [1611 KJV] [1611 margin—"Heb. to generation and generation"]

Psalm 66:1
all ye *inhabitants* of the earth [1560 Geneva Bible]
all ye lands [1611 KJV] [1611 margin—"Heb. all the earth"]
all the earth [YLT] [NKJV] [Literal Translation in *Interlinear Bible*]

Psalm 131:2
myself [1611 KJV] [1611 margin—"Heb. my soul"]
my soul [YLT] [NKJV] [Literal Translation in *Interlinear Bible*]

Psalm 132:3
nor come upon my palet *or* bed [1560 Geneva Bible]
nor go up into my bed [1611 KJV]
if I go up on the couch of my bed [YLT] [Literal Translation in *Interlinear Bible*]

Proverbs 7:20
with him [1611 KJV] [1611 margin—"Heb. in his hand"]
in his hand [YLT] [Literal Translation in *Interlinear Bible*]

Proverbs 21:9
a contentious woman [1560 Geneva Bible]
a chiding and an angry woman [1602 Bishops' Bible]
a brawling woman [1611 KJV] [1611 margin—"Heb. a woman of contentions"]
a woman of contentions [YLT]
a contentious woman [NKJV] [Literal Translation in *Interlinear Bible*]

Song of Solomon 4:5
two young roes that are twins [1611 KJV]
two fawns, Twins of a roe [YLT]
two fawns, Twins of a gazelle [NKJV]
two fawns, twins of a gazelle [Literal Translation in *Interlinear Bible*]

Isaiah 5:24
as the flame of fire [1560 Geneva Bible]
as the fire [1611 KJV] [1611 margin—"Hebr. the tongue of fire"]
as a tongue of fire [YLT]
as the tongue of fire [Literal Translation in *Interlinear Bible*]

Isaiah 19:8
nets upon the waters [1611 KJV]
nets on the face of the waters [YLT]
nets on the surface of the waters [Literal Translation in *Interlinear Bible*]

Isaiah 20:2
by the hand of Isaiah [1560 Geneva Bible]
by the hand of Esay [1602 Bishops' Bible]
by Isaiah [1611 KJV] [1611 margin—"Heb. by the hand of Isaiah"]
by the hand of Isaiah [YLT]

Isaiah 21:15
from the drawn sword [1611 KJV] [1611 margin—"Heb. from the face"]
From the face of the stretched-out sword [YLT]

Isaiah 37:24
By thy servants [1611 KJV] [1611 margin—"Heb. By the hand of thy servants"]
By the hand of thy servants [YLT]

Isaiah 40:2
Comfort Hierusalem at the heart [1602 Bishops' Bible]
Speak ye comfortably to Jerusalem [1611 KJV] [1611 margin—"Heb. to the heart"]
Speak to the heart of Jerusalem [YLT]
Speak lovingly to the heart of Jerusalem [Literal Translation in *Interlinear Bible*]

Isaiah 46:2
their soul [1560 Geneva Bible]
themselves [1611 KJV] [1611 margin—"Hebr. their soul"]
their soul [Literal Translation in *Interlinear Bible*]

Jeremiah 14:1
concerning the dearth [1611 KJV] [1611 margin—"Heb. the words of the dearths or restraints"]
concerning the matter of the dearths [YLT]
concerning the matter of droughts [Literal Translation in *Interlinear Bible*]

Jeremiah 18:4
he returned and made it [1560 Geneva Bible]
he began anew, and made [1602 Bishops' Bible]
he made it again [1611 KJV] [1611 margin—"Hebr. returned and made"]
he hath turned and he maketh it [YLT]
returning, he made it [Literal Translation in *Interlinear Bible*]

Jeremiah 50:1

by the ministry of Jeremiah [1560 Geneva Bible]
by Jeremiah [1611 KJV] [1611 margin—"Hebr. by the hand of Jeremiah"]
by the hand of Jeremiah [YLT]

Ezekiel 37:17
join them one to another into one stick [1611 KJV]
bring them near one to another, to thee, for one stick [YLT]
join them one to another for yourself into one stick [NKJV]

Ezekiel 44:7
strangers [1611 KJV] [1611 margin—"Heb. children of a stranger"]
sons of a stranger [YLT]
the sons of aliens [Literal Translation in *Interlinear Bible*]

Hosea 10:7
upon the water [1611 KJV] [1611 margin—"Heb the face of the water"]
on the face of the waters [YLT]
on the face of the water [Literal Translation in *Interlinear Bible*]

Joel 3:6
the Grecians [1611 KJV] [1611 margin—"Heb. the sons of the Grecians"]
the sons of Javan [YLT]
the sons of the Greeks [Literal Translation in *Interlinear Bible*]

Jonah 4:10
which came up in a night [1611 KJV] [1611 margin—"Heb. was the son of the night"]
which a son of a night was [YLT]
which was the son of a night [Literal Translation in *Interlinear Bible*]

Micah 7:3
the corruption of his soul [1560 Geneva Bible; 1602 Bishops' Bible]
his mischievous desire [1611 KJV] [1611 margin—"Heb. the mischiefs of the soul"]
the mischief of his soul [YLT]
the lust of his soul [Literal Translation in *Interlinear Bible*]

Zephaniah 1:2
from off the land [1611 KJV] [1611 margin—"Heb. the face of the land"]
from the face of the ground [YLT] [Literal Translation in *Interlinear Bible*]
From the face of the land [NKJV]

Haggai 1:1
by the ministry of the Prophet Haggai [1560 Geneva Bible]
by the ministry of the prophet Aggeus [1602 Bishops' Bible]
by Haggai [1611 KJV] [1611 margin—"Heb. by the hand of Haggai"]
by the hand of Haggai [YLT]

Haggai 2:1
by the ministry of the prophet Haggai [1560 Geneva Bible]
by the ministry of the prophet Aggeus [1602 Bishops' Bible]
by the prophet Haggai [1611 KJV] [1611 margin--"Heb. by the hand of"]
by the hand of Haggai the prophet [YLT]

Zechariah 7:2
to pray before the LORD [1611 KJV] [1611 margin—"Heb. to intreat the face of the Lord"]
to appease the face of Jehovah [YLT]
to seek the favor of the face of Jehovah [Literal Translation in *Interlinear Bible*]

Zechariah 7:7
by the ministry of the former prophets [1560 Geneva Bible]
by the former prophets [1611 KJV] [1611 margin—"Hebr. by the hand of"]
by the hand of the former prophets [YLT]

Zechariah 7:12
by the ministry of the former prophets [1560 Geneva Bible]
by the former prophets [1611 KJV] [1611 margin—"Hebr. by the hand of"]
by the hand of the former prophets {YLT]

Malachi 1:1
by the ministry of Malachi [1560 Geneva Bible; 1602 Bishops' Bible]
by Malachi [1611 KJV] [1611 margin—"Heb. by the hand of Malachi"]
by the hand of Malachi [YLT] [Literal Translation in *Interlinear Bible*]

John 10:24 [Greek has the word translated soul]
How long dost thou make us to doubt [1611 KJV]
Till when our soul dost thou hold in suspense [YLT]
How long do you lift up our soul [Literal Translation in *Interlinear Bible*]

Acts 7:20
a proper child in the sight of God [1537 Matthew's Bible]
acceptable unto God [1560 Geneva Bible; 1602 Bishops' Bible]
exceeding fair [1611 KJV] [1611 margin—"Or, fair to God"]
fair to God [YLT]
well pleasing to God [NKJV]
beautiful to God [Literal Translation in *Interlinear Bible*]

Acts 15:23
And wrote letters by them [1611 KJV]
having written through their hand [YLT]
writing by their hand [Literal Translation in *Interlinear Bible*]

Romans 3:4 [word for God not in the Greek]
God forbid [1611 KJV]
let it not be! [YLT]
Certainly not! [NKJV]
Let it not be! [Literal Translation in *Interlinear Bible*]

Romans 5:19
so by [1611 KJV]
so also through [YLT]
so also by [NKJV] [Literal Translation in *Interlinear Bible*]

2 Corinthians 5:12
in the face [1560 Geneva Bible; 1602 Bishops' Bible]
in appearance [1611 KJV] [1611 margin—"Gr. in the face"]
in face [YLT]

2 Corinthians 12:15
will be bestowed for your souls [1560 Geneva Bible]
will be spent for your souls [1602 Bishops' Bible]
be spent for you [1611 KJV] [1611 margin—"Gr. your souls"]
be entirely spent for your souls [YLT]
be spent for your souls [Literal Translation in *Interlinear Bible*] [NKJV]

Hebrews 4:2
the word that they heard [1560 Geneva Bible]
the word preached [1611 KJV] [1611 margin—"Gr. the word of hearing"]
the word heard [YLT]
the word which they heard [NKJV]

James 2:17
in itself [1560 Geneva Bible; 1602 Bishops' Bible]
being alone [1611 KJV] [1611 margin—"Gr. by it self"]
by itself [YLT] [NKJV] [Literal Translation in *Interlinear Bible*]

3 John 14
mouth to mouth [1560 Geneva Bible; 1602 Bishops' Bible]
face to face [1611 KJV] [1611 margin—"Gr. mouth to mouth"]
mouth to mouth [YLT] [Literal Translation in *Interlinear Bible*]

The marginal notes in the 1611 KJV provide sound, convincing evidence concerning several of the preceding examples. Concerning Genesis 7:22, KJV defender Charles Surrett acknowledged that "the Heb[rew] has 2 words, so Heb[rew] supports NKJV" (*Certainty of the Words*, p. 88). At Genesis 43:16, Green's *The Interlinear Bible* has two Hebrew words in its text [Strong's Concordance numbers 2873 and 2874] (p. 40). At Proverbs 9:2 in the KJV, these same two Hebrew words were translated "hath killed her beasts." Concerning Genesis 43:16, Charles Surrett asserted that the Hebrew "supports NKJV" (p. 107). At Job 21:28, James D. Price suggested that the KJV with the support of the Latin Vulgate omitted translating a Hebrew word meaning "tent" (*King James Onlyism*, p. 581). James D. Price maintained that the Bomberg text at Psalm 132:3 has the Hebrew for "couch of my bed" (p. 575). At Ezekiel 37:17, Price indicated that in agreement with the Latin Vulgate that the KJV omitted translating Hebrew, which would be rendered "for yourself" (p. 582). Concerning Genesis 5:17; 5:20; 5:25, and Exodus 38:28, Alan Macgregor acknowledged that "the AV omits the conjunction 'and' where its use in Hebrew was superfluous in Elizabethan English" (*400 Years On*, p. 276). E. W. Bullinger maintained that when the Greek, *kai*, is used to mean *also* that "in 60 places (in the A.V.) it is not translated at all" (*Figures of Speech*, p. 90). At Romans 5:19, Surrett asserted that "'also' is omitted in KJV, but in NKJV and Greek" (*Certainty of the Words*, p. 117). Kirk DiVietro claimed: "The conjunction does not always need to be translated into English. This is a matter of translator's discretion and not textual reading" (*Where the KJB Leaves the Greek Text*, p. 13). Kirk DiVietro also asserted: "The article does not always need to be translated into English. This is a matter of translator's discretion and not textual reading" (p. 15). Gail RIplinger claimed: "Greek has only the definite article (the); it has no indefinite articles (a, an). To compound matters, Greek and English do not use articles in an identically parallel manner" (*Hazardous Materials*, p. 455). In another example of where the KJV may not translate every original language word, E. W. Bullinger suggested: "In Acts 15:23, the A. V. omits 'by the hands of them,' and substitutes the word '*letters*' in italics" (*Figures of Speech*, p. 411). Will KJV defenders be consistent and just in giving the Geneva Bible translators and the NKJV translators the same amount of wide latitude or discretion in revising and translating that they are evidently willing to give to the KJV translators?

Marginal notes in Bible translations considered

The Church of England translators of the KJV did not make any claims or demands that their translation should never be altered, revised, corrected, or improved. These translators did not claim that their translation was perfect. In fact, these KJV translators even argued that it was good to amend our translations, which would include their own. In their 1611 preface as a response to those who criticized the amending of translations, they wrote: "For to whomever was it imputed for a fault (by such as were wise) to go over that which he had done, and to amend it where he saw cause?" In addition, KJV defender Edward Hills noted: "As the marginal notes indicate, the King James translators did not regard their work as perfect or inspired" (*The KJV Defended*, p. 216). Referring to the marginal notes, Thomas Abbot commented: "The English Bible carries with it, in every page, the profession of its own imperfection" (*English Bible*, p. 10). In their preface, the KJV translators declared: "Does not a margin do well to admonish the reader to seek further, and not to conclude or dogmatize upon this or that peremptorily [absolutely]?" In contrast to the facts, Ian Paisley incorrectly claimed that the KJV "has nothing in the margin demonstrating that the text could or should be corrected or has an alternative to be considered" (*My Plea*, p. 78). In an appendix in Waite's *Defined KJB*, S. H. Tow condemned the NKJV's preface for encouraging "further inquiry by readers" (p. 1682), but he does not condemn the KJV's preface for doing the same thing.

In the marginal notes in the 1611 KJV, its translators sometimes gave the more literal meaning of the original Hebrew or Greek, sometimes gave alternative translations, and sometimes even gave variant readings. Laurence Vance cited the report to the Synod of Dort about the translating of the KJV as stating: "where a Hebrew or Greek word admits two meanings of a suitable kind, the one was to be expressed in the text, the other in the margin. The same to be done where a different reading was found in good copies" (*King James, His Bible*, p. 47). F. H. A. Scrivener noted that 4,111 of the 6,637 marginal notes in the Old Testament of the 1611 "express the more literal meaning of the original Hebrew or Chaldee" and "2156 give alternative renderings (indicated by the word 'Or' prefixed to them) which in the opinion of the Translators are not very less probable than those in the text" (*Authorized Edition*, p. 41). Scrivener also pointed out that 67 marginal notes in the 1611 O. T. "refer to various readings of the original, in 31 of which the marginal variation (technically called *Keri*) of the Masoretic revisers of the Hebrew is set in competition with the reading in the text" (Ibid.). Scrivener maintained that in the N. T. of the 1611 that 37 marginal notes relate to various readings (p. 56). He also listed those 37 notes (pp. 58-59) [Matt. 1:11, Matt. 7:14, Matt. 9:26, Matt. 24:31, Matt. 26:26, Mark 9:16, Luke 2:38, Luke 10:22, Luke 17:36, John 18:13, Acts 13:18, Acts 25:6, Rom 5:17, Rom. 7:6, Rom. 8:11, 1 Cor. 15:31, 2 Cor. 13:4, Gal. 4:15, Gal. 4:17, Eph. 6:9, 1 Tim. 4:15, Heb. 4:2, Heb. 9:2, Heb. 11:4, James 2:18, 1 Pet. 1:4, 1 Pet. 2:21, 2 Pet. 2:2, 2 Pet. 2:11, 2 Pet. 2:18, 2 John 8, Rev. 3:14, Rev. 6:8, Rev. 13:1, Rev. 13:5, Rev. 14:13, Rev. 17:5]. The 1762 Cambridge edition added 15 more textual marginal notes (p. 59). The 1769 Oxford edition is said to have added at least one more. KJV defender Edward F. Hills also confirmed that 37 of the KJV's N. T. marginal notes give variant readings (*KJV Defended*, p. 216). Hills acknowledged that 16 more textual N. T. marginal notes were added in the 1700's (*Believing Bible Study*, p. 206). John Eadie also affirmed that the KJV's N. T. has "thirty-five such textual notes," and he listed them (*English Bible*, II, p. 212-213). In addition, John Eadie referred to "at least sixty-seven notes referring to various readings of the Hebrew" (p. 210). Jack Lewis maintained that the 1611 edition of the KJV has 31 notes that "gave the Masoretic difference between *Qere* and *Ketib*" (Burke, *Translation*, p. 88).

On the other hand, KJV-only author D. A. Waite claimed that in the 1611 that there are only "eleven verses where Greek variants are mentioned" or that "there are just eleven marginal notes in the New Testament that speak of Greek variants or different Greek readings" (*Fundamentalist Distortions*, pp. 18, 35). In one book, David Cloud favorably cited Waite's count and claimed that the count of 37 variant textual readings in the 1611 KJV's N. T. is "inflated" (*Examining*, p. 81). However in another book, David Cloud acknowledged that 104 marginal notes ("37 in the New Testament) offered a variant textual reading" (*Bible Version Question/Answer*, p. 157). The variant readings or textual variants indicated in the KJV were not always introduced with a consistent term or formula. Furthermore, KJV-only advocates seem to ignore the fact of the additional textual marginal notes in the standard 1762 Cambridge and 1769 Oxford KJV editions. In addition, they seem to be unaware of the fact of the 1869 edition of the KJV's N. T. that had hundreds of textual marginal notes from Codex Sinaiticus, Codex Vaticanus, and Codex Alexandrinus.

The KJV translators themselves considered their marginal notes to be an important part of their work.   In the General Preface to his commentary, Adam Clarke observed:

> Our conscientious translators, not being able in
> several cases to determine which of two meanings
> borne by a word, or which of two words is found in
> different copies, should be admitted into the text,
> adopted the measure of receiving *both*, placing one
> in the *margin* and the other in the *text*, thus leaving the
> reader at liberty to adopt either, both of which in their
> apprehension stood nearly in the same authority.   On
> this very account the marginal readings are essential
> to our version, and I have found, on collating many of
> them with the originals, that those in the *margin* are to
> be preferred to those in the *text* in the proportion of at
> least eight to ten (I, p. 21).

Adam Clarke indicated that those editions of the KJV that omitted the marginal notes of the KJV translators were leaving out an essential part of their work.   Glenn Conjurske also pointed out that the marginal notes "formed an integral part of the King James Version of 1611" (*Olde Paths*, Oct., 1992, p. 227).   T. S. Bell asserted: "In the view of these translators, under one of the imperative rules by which they worked, these marginal readings were as much a part of the translation as any part of the text" (*British Millennial Harbinger*, Vol. XI, p. 481).   Bell contended: "No edition of King James' Version can, by any possibility, be called the work of the revisers of that version, that is devoid of the marginal readings" (Ibid.).

At Hebrews 6:1, Backus maintained that the 1611 KJV has in the margin "a literal translation of the Vulgate 'the word of the beginning of Christ'" (*Reformed Roots*, p. 147).   At Matthew 4:12, Backus asserted that the 1611 KJV put "the Vulgate reading 'delivered up' in the margin" (p. 48).   Scrivener suggested that the 1611 marginal note at 2 John 8 came from the Vulgate (*Authorized Edition*, p. 59).   In its marginal note at Mark 7:3, the 1611 KJV has an alternative translation, the literal meaning of the Greek, and the translation of a church father: "Or, diligently, in the Original, with the fist; Theophilact, up to the elbow."   The KJV translators put the following marginal note in the 1611 for "mercies" at Acts 13:34:   "Greek, [*hosios*] *holy*, or *just things*; which word in the Septuagint, both in the place of Isaiah 55:3, and in many others, use for that which is in the Hebrew *mercies*."   At Acts 13:18, the 1611 KJV has another marginal note that refers to the Septuagint and that refers to a church father--Chrysostom.

At Luke 10:22, the textual marginal note in the 1611 stated: "Many ancient copies add these words, 'And turning to his disciples, he said.'"   The 1560 edition of the Geneva Bible has in its text at the beginning of Luke 10:22 the following: "Then he turned to his disciples."   Scrivener suggested that the words in the 1611 margin at Luke 10:22 "are from the Complutensian edition and Stephen's of 1550" (*Authorized Edition*, p. 58).   At Luke 17:36, the textual marginal note in the 1611 stated: "This 36 verse is wanting in most of the Greek copies." At 2 Peter 2:2, the textual marginal note in the 1611 noted: "Or, lascivious wages, as some copies read."   At Acts 25:6, the textual marginal note in the 1611 was the following: "as some copies read, no more then eight or ten days."

Other marginal notes that gave variant readings in the 1611 KJV can be found at Judges 19:2, Ezra 10:40, Psalm 102:3, Matthew 1:11, Matthew 26:26, Acts 13:18, 1 Corinthians 15:31, Ephesians 6:9, James 2:18, 1 Peter 2:21, 2 Peter 2:11, and 18.   The 1611 marginal note beginning with "or" at Hebrews 5:2 could be properly considered a textual note since it basically agrees with Beza and the Geneva translation ["which is able sufficiently to have compassion"] while the makers of the KJV may follow the Latin Vulgate reading "who can have compassion" in their text.   At Hebrews 5:7, the 1611 marginal note beginning with "or" could be considered a textual note since it indicates the reading of Erasmus ["pro sus reverential"] as followed by Tyndale's and the Great Bible.   In addition, the 1611 marginal note beginning with "or" at Romans 8:11 ["because of his spirit] could also be considered a textual note since Edward F. Hills presented this as a textual difference or variation in editions of the Textus Receptus with Beza having "by his Spirit" and Erasmus and Stephanus having "because of his Spirit" (*KJV Defended*, p. 222).   Scrivener listed Romans 8:11 as one of thirty-seven NT textual marginal notes in the 1611 (*Authorized Edition*, p. 58).   Scrivener indicated that the 1611 marginal note beginning with "or" at Revelation 6:8 "to him" is with "Complutensian, Vulgate, [and] Bishops' Bible" (p. 59). Backus noted that "at Matthew 7:14 the 'how' reading occurs in AV margin (after the Vulgate)" (*Reformed Roots*, p. 70), and Scrivener listed it as a textual note (*Authorized Edition*, p. 58).   At Mark 1:34, Backus indicated that the KJV followed the Bishops'/Tyndale/Vulgate reading "because they knew him" while "keeping the Beza/Geneva reading ['to say that they knew him"] as marginal alternative" (*Reformed Roots*, p. 66).   In the 1611 at Mark 14:72, Backus asserted that "the Vulgate reading 'he began to weep' is suggested as a marginal alternative along with 'he wept abundantly' after Erasmus" (p. 75).   At Galatians 4:15, Backus maintained that the KJV "adopts the Vulgate text more explicitly than Bois, reading 'Where is then,' but inserting the TR reading in the margin" (pp. 135-136).   In its marginal note at Luke 8:18, the 1611 KJV evidently has the Latin Vulgate reading "thinking that he hath" (p. 84).   At Luke 7:30, the 1611 KJV is said to put the Latin Vulgate reading "frustrated" in its marginal note (p. 83).   Concerning Luke 8:18, Backus suggested that "the Vulgate reading 'thinking that he hath'" is "retained in the margin" (p. 84).   At Luke 17:20, Backus indicated that Whittingham, Geneva, Bishops, and KJV all read "with observation" in the text after the Vulgate while the 1611 marginal note "with outward show" is after Beza (p. 87).   Backus asserted that the KJV follows the Latin Vulgate and reads "within you" at Luke 17:21 and "inserts the Bezan reading 'among you' as marginal alternative" (p. 87). At Romans 1:28 in the 1611 edition, Backus maintained that the "Revisers suggest the Bois/Beza reading as a marginal alternative" (p. 114).   Backus asserted that at Romans 5:12 the KJV "inserts the Bezan reading 'in whom' in the margin" (p. 159).   At Romans 8:22, Backus maintained that the KJV "adopts the Bezan reading in the text and the Vulgate/Erasmus reading in the margin" (p. 118).   Concerning 1 Corinthians 10:30, Backus observed: "The Vulgate/Erasmus alternative 'or by thanksgiving' as suggested by [KJV translator Andrew] Downes is inserted in the AV margin" (p. 131).   As seen in some of the above examples (Matt. 4:12, Mark 1:34, Mark 14:72, Luke 7:30, Luke 8:18, Luke 17:20, Luke 17:21, Rom. 1:28, Rom. 5:12, Rom. 8:22, 1 Cor. 10:30, Heb. 5:2, Heb. 5:7, Heb. 6:1), Backus identified another ten or more 1611 NT marginal notes as being textual that Scrivener may not have noticed as beng such and that he did not include in his count or list of thirty-seven.   Thus, Scrivener's count of textual notes in the 1611 is evidently incomplete and is not inflated.

John R. Kohlenberger III pointed out a textual variant in the marginal note in the 1611 edition at Deuteronomy 28:22.   John R. Kohlenberger asserted: "This variant is caused by the change of a single vowel point in Hebrew (*horch* versus the Masoretic *herch*) and likely reflects the Vulgate *et aestu*" (Burke, *Translation*, p. 50).   Kohlenberger noted: "An example of an alternative reading that is not clearly stated is found at Luke 2:38: 'that looked for redemption in Hierusalem'; note: 'Or, Israel.'   This reading is not found in printed texts, but it is in Rheims" (p. 52).   There may be some other marginal notes in the 1611 that present differences between the Geneva Bible as compared to the KJV that could possibly be considered textual notes.

A 1672 edition of the KJV [with the notes of the Geneva Bible] has a textual marginal note at Matthew 27:9 ["Seeing this prophesy is read in Zech. 11:12, it cannot be denied but Jeremy's name crept into the text either through the printers fault, or by some others ignorance: it may be also that it came out of the margin, by reason of the abbreviation of the letters"].   This same 1672 edition of the KJV has this marginal note at Matthew 1:23 ["There is in the Hebrew and Greek text, an article added, to point out the woman, and set her forth plainly; as you would say, That virgin, or a certain virgin"].   At Matthew 22:37, this 1672 KJV edition has this note ["The

Hebrew text readeth, Deut. 6:5, with thine heart, soul, and strength: and in Mark 12:30 and Luke 10:27 we read with soul, heart, strength, and thought"].

One of the additional textual marginal notes added in 1762 is the one at Revelation 22:19 as found in the 2005 *New Cambridge Paragraph Bible*: "Or, from the tree of life" (p. 1868). Oxford KJV editions printed in 1810, 1821, 1835, 1857, 1865, 1868, and 1885, and Cambridge KJV editions printed in 1769, 1872, and 1887 have this same marginal note. Another example is found at Hebrews 10:17 ["Some copies have, Then he said, And their"]. At 2 John 12, a marginal note was added in 1762 [Gr. mouth to mouth]. At Revelation 15:3, Scrivener maintained that the marginal note added in 1762 gave two alternative readings: one from the Complutensian, "which is much the best supported," and the other from the Clementive Vulgate ["or, nations, or ages"] (*Authorized Edition,* p. 59).

Some of these actual notes in KJV editions are the same-type textual marginal notes or footnotes that KJV-only advocates have claimed are harmful to the faith. S. H. Tow claimed that the "NKJV translators undermine God's word with deadly 'footnotes,'" and he contended that such textual notes "cast doubt on the Scriptural text" (Waite, *Defined KJB,* p. 1682). David Cloud contended that the footnotes in the NKJV tempt "the readers to discount the authority of the passages questioned in footnotes" (*Bible Version Question/Answer*, p. 377). David Cloud referred to what he alleged were "doubt-producing readings in the margin" (Ibid.). Malcolm Watts claimed: "By their very existence these variant readings cast doubt on the very words of Holy Scripture and upon the doctrine of Divine Inspiration and Preservation" (*The NKJV*, pp. 5-6). The presence of one such textual note in the 1611 KJV or in any other editions of the KJV would in effect condemn the KJV-only view for its evident inconsistency, hypocrisy, or unjust measures when it strongly blasts the NKJV and other translations for the same-type notes. There was an edition of the NKJV available without the textual notes so that the NKJV could be read without them.

As noted and firmly documented earlier, KJV-only authors themselves have maintained that the New Testaments of the Geneva Bible and the KJV are both translated from the Received Text or from the same basic Greek texts. On the other hand, KJV-only advocates attempt to suggest that the New Testaments of the KJV and the NKJV are not translated from the same Greek texts. Are consistent, just measures being used in KJV-only assertions concerning the underlying New Testament text of both the Geneva Bible and of the NKJV? Are some KJV-only advocates ignoring the actual amount of textual variation in the twenty to thirty differing printed editions of the Textus Receptus? William Grady acknowledged that the KJV "was *not* a direct translation of any *one* edition of the *Textus Receptus*, but rather embodied an *eclectic* text (i.e., constructed from several sources)" (*Given by Inspiration*, p. 292). If the Geneva Bible could have any textual differences and still be asserted by KJV-only authors to be translated from the same Greek NT text as the KJV, why could the same not be true concerning the NKJV? It is fair, reasonable, and scriptural to ask that the same just measures be applied consistently. In their own assertions concerning the Geneva Bible, would KJV-only advocates overlook or ignore actual textual differences, including some that are significant, between the Geneva Bible and the KJV? The marginal notes in the 1611 edition of the KJV pointed out some of these textual differences so those should not be too hard to find. Other examples can be found by comparing the Geneva Bible and the KJV in places where the varying Textus Receptus editions are pointed out to have differed. Surely, any actual textual differences between the Geneva Bible and the KJV would be relevant facts to be considered.

Possible and Actual Textual Differences between the 1560 Geneva Bible and the 1611 KJV

Matthew 1:11 "Jacim. And Jacim begat" [these words in 1560 Geneva Bible are not in the 1611 KJV] [see also 1611 edition's marginal note]

Matthew 1:20

Joseph the son of David, [1560 Geneva Bible]
Joseph, thou son of David, [1611 KJV] ["thou"--possible Luther's German Bible influence]

David Norton asserted: "The most obvious sign of Luther is 'thou son of David', which has no warrant in the Greek" (*KJB: A Short History*, p. 36).   Norton claimed: "The retention of Coverdale's (and Luther's) 'thou son of David' might be carelessness.   It is untrue to the Greek" (p. 39).

Matthew 2:11
found [1560 Geneva Bible] [Stephanus, Beza] (see Backus, pp. 45-46)
saw [1611 KJV] [Complutensian]

Matthew 4:10
Avoid Satan [1560 Geneva Bible] [Latin Vulgate]
Get thee hence, Satan [1611 KJV] [Beza]

Matthew 4:12
John was delivered up [1560 Geneva Bible] [Vulgate] (see Backus, p. 48)
John was cast into prison [1611 KJV] [Beza]

Matthew 5:21
said unto them [1560 Geneva Bible]
said by them [1611 KJV] [Beza] [see 1611 marginal note]

Matthew 5:21
shall be culpable of judgment [1560 Geneva Bible] [early Beza]
shall be in danger of the judgment [1611 KJV] [later Beza]

Matthew 5:27
said to them [1560 Geneva Bible]
said by them [1611 KJV]

Matthew 5:29
right eye cause thee to offend [1560 Geneva Bible] [Beza] (see Backus, p. 51)
right eye offend thee [1611 KJV] [possible Vulgate] [see 1611 marginal note]

Matthew 5:30
right hand make thee to offend [1560 Geneva Bible]
right hand offend thee [1611 KJV]

Matthew 5:33
said to them [1560 Geneva Bible]
said by them [1611 KJV]

Matthew 5:47
what singular thing do ye [1560 Geneva Bible] (see Backus, p. 52)
what do ye more *than others* [1611 KJV] [Beza]

Matthew 6:34
for the morrow shall care for itself [1560 Geneva Bible] [Vulgate] (Backus, p. 54)
for the morrow shall take thought for the things of itself [1611 KJV] [Beza]

Matthew 8:18
to go over *the water* [1560 Geneva Bible]
to depart unto the other side [1611 KJV]

Matthew 8:23
into the ship [1560 Geneva Bible] [Stephanus]
into a ship [1611 KJV]

Matthew 9:4
But when Jesus saw their thoughts [1560 Geneva Bible]
And Jesus knowing their thoughts [1611 KJV]

Matthew 9:26
And this [1560 Geneva Bible]
And the [1611 KJV] [see 1611 marginal note]

Matthew 10:9
Possess not gold [1560 Geneva Bible] [Latin Vulgate] (see Backus, p. 58)
Provide neither gold [1611 KJV] [Beza]

Matthew 10:18
in witness to them [1560 Geneva Bible]
for a testimony against them [1611 KJV] [Beza]

Matthew 11:28
I will ease you [1560 Geneva Bible] [Latin Vulgate]
I will give you rest [1611 KJV] [Beza]

Matthew 14:2
great works are wrought by him [1560 Geneva Bible] (see Backus, pp. 59-60)
mighty works do shew forth themselves in him [1611 KJV] [see 1611 margin]

Matthew 18:19
Again, verily, I say unto you [1560 Geneva Bible] (see Backus, p. 61)
Again I say unto you [1611 KJV]

Matthew 18:26
and besought him [1560 Geneva Bible] (see Backus, p. 62)
and worshipped him [1611 KJV] [Beza] [see 1611 marginal note]

Matthew 21:32
were not moved with repentance afterward [1560 Geneva Bible]
repented not afterward [1611 KJV]

Matthew 26:15
And said [1560 Geneva Bible]
And said unto them [1611 KJV] [Latin Vulgate] ["unto them" in italics in later KJV's]

Matthew 26:26
and when he had given thanks [1560 Geneva Bible] (see Backus, pp. 64-65)
and blessed it [1611 KJV] [see 1611 marginal note]

Mark 1:34
to say that they knew him [1560 Geneva Bible] [Beza] (see Backus, p. 66)
because they knew him [1611 KJV] [Tyndale/Vulgate] [see 1611 marginal note]

Mark 2:14
And as Jesus passed by [1560 Geneva Bible]
And as he passed by [1611 KJV]

Mark 6:10
til ye depart from thence [1560 Geneva Bible]
til ye depart from that place [1611 KJV] [Beza]

Mark 7:2
common [1560 Geneva Bible] [Erasmus, Vulgate]
defiled [1611 KJV] [Beza] [see 1611 marginal note]

Mark 8:14
And they had forgotten [1560 Geneva Bible]
Now the disciples had forgotten [1611 KJV] [the 1769 KJV edition would put "the disciples" in
italics by comparison to the 1550 Stephanus TR edition, but this textual difference is found in an
edition of Beza likely followed by the KJV translators]

Mark 8:24
I see men for I see them walking like trees [1560 Geneva Bible] [Erasmus] (see Backus, p. 72)
I see men as trees, walking [1611 KJV] [Beza]

Mark 9:16
among yourselves [1560 Geneva Bible] [Beza, Latin Vulgate] (see Backus, p. 72)
with them [1611 KJV] [see 1611 marginal note]

Mark 10:2
Pharisees came and asked him [1560 Geneva Bible]
Pharisees came to him and asked him [1611 KJV]

Mark 10:42
they which delight to bear rule [1560 Geneva Bible] [early Beza]
they which are accounted to rule [1611 KJV] [later Beza] [see 1611 marginal note]

Mark 12:20
There [1560 Geneva Bible] [Stephanus]
Now there [1611 KJV] [Beza]

Mark 13:37
And those things that I say unto you [1560 Geneva Bible] [Stephanus]
And what I say unto you [1611 KJV]

Mark 15:3 "but he answered not" [these words in KJV are not in 1560 Geneva Bible and other
pre-1611 English Bibles] [Complutensian reading introduced in Bishops' Bible]

Luke 1:28
thou *that art* freely beloved [1560 Geneva Bible] [Beza] (see Backus, pp. 79, 91)
thou that art highly favoured [1611 KJV] [Erasmus]

Luke 6:16
Judas [1560 Geneva Bible] [Stephanus]
And Judas [1611 KJV]

Luke 7:28
then John [1560 Geneva Bible]
than John the Baptist [1611 KJV]

Luke 8:14
bring forth no fruit [1560 Geneva Bible] [Erasmus] (see Backus, pp. 83-84)
bring no fruit to perfection [1611 KJV] [Beza]

Luke 8:29
was carried [1560 Geneva Bible] [Erasmus & Latin Vulgate] (see Backus, p. 84)
was driven [1611 KJV] [Beza]

Luke 9:22
and the third day rise again [1560 Geneva Bible] [Vulgate]
and be raised the third day [1611 KJV] [Beza]

Luke 10:19
nothing shall hurt you [1560 Geneva Bible]
nothing shall by any means hurt you [1611 KJV]

Luke 10:22 "Then he turned to his disciples" [these words in 1560 Geneva Bible from an edition of Stephanus are not in 1611 KJV's text] [see 1611 marginal note] (see also Backus, pp. 85-86)

Did the makers of the KJV remove words from the text of a pre-1611 English Bible and put them in a marginal note?

Luke 11:3
for the day [1560 Geneva Bible] [Beza] (see Backus, p. 86)
day by day [1611 KJV] [Erasmus] [see 1611 marginal note]

Luke 12:56
the face of the earth, and of the sky [1560 Geneva Bible] [Stephanus]
the face of the sky and of the earth [1611 KJV] [Complutensian]

Luke 15:13
So not long after [1560 Geneva Bible]
And not many days after [1611 KJV] [Latin—*non post multos dies*]
[Daniell maintained that the "KJV followed the Latin" (*Bible in English*, p. 363)]

Luke 15:26
one of his servants [1560 Geneva Bible] [Stephanus]
one of the servants [1611 KJV] [Beza]

Luke 17:36 [this verse in the KJV is not in the 1560 Geneva Bible and some other pre-1611 English Bibles]
The 1560 Geneva Bible has a verse 36 but it is what is verse 37 in the KJV. [see 1611 marginal note] (see also Backus, p. 88)

Luke 20:32
And last of all, the woman died also [1560 Geneva Bible]
Last of all the woman died also [1611 KJV]

John 4:31
the disciples [1560 Geneva Bible]
his disciples [1611 KJV]

John 7:3
see thy works [1560 Geneva Bible]
see the works [1611 KJV]

John 8:6 "as though he heard them not" [these words in KJV are not in 1560 Geneva Bible and some other pre-1611 English Bibles]

John 8:59 "going through the midst of them, and so passed by" [these words in KJV are not in 1560 Geneva Bible and some other pre-1611 English Bibles]

John 12:26
and if any man serve me [1560 Geneva Bible] [Stephanus]
if any man serve me [1611 KJV] [possible Latin Vulgate influence]

John 13:31
When he was gone out [1560 Geneva Bible]
Therefore, when he was gone out [1611 KJV]

John 14:1 "And he said to his disciples" [1560 Geneva Bible] [Erasmus] [these words found in several of the pre-1611 English Bibles are not in KJV]

John 14:6
and the Truth [1560 Geneva Bible] [Textus Receptus]
the truth [1611 KJV] [many KJV editions from 1638 Cambridge, including the 1769 Oxford, and until 1800 and even till the 1844 Cambridge had "and the truth"]

John 14:23
keep my word [1560 Geneva Bible] [Stephanus]
keep my words [1611 KJV]

John 16:2
They shall excommunicate you [1560 Geneva Bible]
They shall put you out of the synagogues [1611 KJV]

Acts 1:26
and he was by a common consent counted [1560 Geneva Bible]
and he was numbered [1611 KJV]

Acts 3:3
desired to receive an alms [1560 Geneva Bible]
asked an alms [1611 KJV]

Acts 8:10
To whom they gave heed [1560 Geneva Bible]
To whom they all gave heed [1611 KJV]

Acts 8:13
the signs and great miracles [1560 Geneva Bible]
the miracles and signs [1611 KJV]

Acts 8:37
And Philip said unto him [1560 Geneva Bible]
And Philip said [1611 KJV]

Acts 14:23
And when they had ordained them elders by election [1560 Geneva Bible] [TR with possible influence from Latin NT of Erasmus or of Beza]
And when they had ordained them elders [1611 KJV] [TR with possible textual influence from Latin Vulgate perhaps by means of 1582 Rheims]

Acts 25:6
no more than ten days [1560 Geneva Bible]
more than ten days [1611 KJV] [see 1611 marginal note]

Acts 27:29
lest they should have fallen [1560 Geneva Bible]
lest we should have fallen [1611 KJV]

Romans 5:17
by the offence of one [1560 Geneva Bible]
by one man's offence [1611 KJV] [see 1611 marginal note]

Romans 8:11
because that his Spirit [1560 Geneva Bible]
by his Spirit [1611 KJV]
[see 1611 marginal note, and see Edward F. Hills' book *KJV Defended*, p. 222 where he presented this as a textual difference between the TR editions by Beza and those by Erasmus and Stephanus]

Romans 8:22
that every creature [1560 Geneva Bible] [Erasmus] (see Backus, p. 118)
that the whole creation [1611 KJV] [Beza] [see 1611 marginal note]

Romans 8:31
If God be on our side [1560 Geneva Bible]
If God be for us [1611 KJV] [possible Latin Vulgate influence]

Romans 9:6
Notwithstanding it cannot be that [1560 Geneva] [early Beza] (see Backus, p. 119)
Not as though [1611 KJV] [1598 Beza]

Romans 14:2
One believeth that he may eat [1560 Geneva Bible]
For one believeth that he may eat [1611 KJV]

Romans 16:4
their own neck [1560 Geneva Bible] [TR Greek word for neck is singular in number]
their own necks [1611 KJV] [Latin Vulgate word for neck is plural]

Romans 16:20
with you. [1560 Geneva Bible]
with you. Amen. [1611 KJV] [Beza]

1 Corinthians 5:7
for Christ our Passover [1560 Geneva Bible]
For even Christ our passover [1611 KJV]

1 Corinthians 7:26
present necessity [1560 Geneva Bible]
present distress [1611 KJV] [see 1611 marginal note]

1 Corinthians 7:29
because the time is short [1560 Geneva Bible]
the time is short [1611 KJV] [Erasmus]

1 Corinthians 15:31
our rejoicing [1560 Geneva Bible]
your rejoicing [1611 KJV] [see 1611 marginal note]

2 Corinthians 10:10
saith he [1560 Geneva Bible]
say they [1611 KJV]

Galatians 2:4
For all the false brethren [1560 Geneva Bible] [Erasmus]
And that because of false brethren [1611 KJV]

Galatians 3:1
to whom Jesus Christ was described in your sight [1560 Geneva Bible] [Vulgate]
before whose eyes Jesus Christ hath been evidently set forth [1611 KJV] [Beza]

Galatians 4:15
What was [1560 Geneva Bible] (see Backus, pp. 135-136)
Where is [1611 KJV] [Latin Vulgate influence] [see 1611 margin]

Ephesians 6:7
serving the Lord [1560 Geneva Bible] [Stephanus]
doing service, as to the Lord [1611 KJV]

Philippians 3:20
But our conversation [1560 Geneva Bible]
For our conversation [1611 KJV]

Colossians 1:4
and of *your* love toward all saints [1560 Geneva Bible]
and of the love which ye have to all the saints [1611 KJV] [Latin Vulgate]
[Later KJV editions put "which ye have" in italics]

Colossians 1:24
Now rejoice I in my sufferings [1560 Geneva Bible]
Who now rejoice in my sufferings [1611 KJV] [possible Latin Vulgate influence]

1 Timothy 1:2
Christ Jesus our Lord [1560 Geneva Bible]
Jesus Christ our Lord [1611 KJV]

1 Timothy 3:10
let them minister [1560 Geneva Bible]
let them use the office of a deacon [1611 KJV]

Hebrews 10:26
willingly [1560 Geneva Bible] [Erasmus]
wilfully [1611 KJV]

James 2:18
out of thy works [1560 Geneva Bible]
without thy works [1611 KJV] [see 1611 marginal note]

James 4:2
ye envy, and have indignation [1560 Geneva Bible] [Erasmus]
ye kill, and desire to have [1611 KJV]

1 Peter 2:12
And have your conversation honest [1560 Geneva Bible]
Having your conversation honest [1611 KJV]

1 Peter 3:18
quickened in the spirit [1560 Geneva Bible] [Erasmus]
quickened by the Spirit [1611 KJV] [Beza]

1 Peter 3:19
the spirits that were in prison [1560 Geneva Bible]
the spirits in prison [1611 KJV]

2 Peter 2:9
out of temptation [1560 Geneva Bible]
out of temptations [1611 KJV]

1 John 2:23b
[*but*] *he that acknowledgeth the Son hath the Father also* [1611 KJV]
[this second half of this verse in KJV is not in 1560 Geneva Bible and some other pre-1611
English Bibles because not found in early TR editions]

1 John 3:1
Knoweth you not [1560 Geneva Bible]
Knoweth us not [1611 KJV]

1 John 3:16
love [1560 Geneva Bible]
love of God [1611 KJV] [the 1769 KJV would later put the words "of God" in italics based on the
1550 Stephanus] [Greek words for "of God" in Complutensian Greek perhaps from Vulgate]

1 John 3:23
as he gave commandment [1560 Geneva Bible]
as he gave us commandment [1611 KJV]

Revelation 2:24
I say, the rest [1560 Geneva Bible]
I say, and unto the rest [1611 KJV] [According to this author's research, one or more of Beza's
TR editions have an "and" not in earlier TR editions]

Revelation 5:11
elders, & there were thousand thousands [1560 Geneva Bible] [Stephanus]
elders, and the number of them was ten thousand times ten thousand and thousands of
thousands [1611 KJV] [Beza]

Revelation 10:7
even the mystery [1560 Geneva Bible]
the mystery [1611 KJV]

Revelation 11:17
hast received thy great might [1560 Geneva Bible]
hast taken to thee thy great might [1611 KJV]

Revelation 13:10
If any lead into captivity [1560 Geneva Bible]
He that leadeth into captivity [1611 KJV]

Revelation 16:5
and Holy [1560 Geneva Bible] [Erasmus, Stephanus]
and shalt be [1611 KJV] [KJV followed conjecture introduced by Beza in his Greek text]

Revelation 16:11
and for their sores [1560 Geneva Bible] [Stephanus]
and their sores [1611 KJV]

Revelation 17:5
mother of whoredoms [1560 Geneva Bible]
mother of harlots [1611 KJV] [see 1611 marginal note]

Revelation 17:9
Here [1560 Geneva Bible] [Stephanus, Beza]
And here [1611 KJV] [possible direct or indirect Latin Vulgate influence]

Revelation 20:12
both great and small [1560 Geneva Bible]
small and great [1611 KJV]

Several of these possible or actual textual differences between the Geneva Bible and the KJV may be minor, but some of them are significant or major. Can an absolutely pure text have this many textual variations or even any? Can any KJV defender present a list of claimed textual differences between the KJV and the NKJV that are greater in number and greater in significance than these possible examples between the 1560 Geneva Bible and the KJV [two English Bibles that KJV-only advocates have asserted are "basically the same Bibles" or are "practically identical"]? Do these actual differences between the Geneva Bible and the KJV also suggest that possible textual differences involving one word or a phrase can sometimes fall into the range of what could be considered translation differences? D. A. Waite claimed to "have found at least three places" where the NKJV translators did not use the same Greek text as the KJV translators (*Critical Answer to Michael Sproul's*, p. 37). Those three places could possibly fall into the range of differences that involve matters of translation. Even if these three were really textual, they would still not involve nearly as much textual variation as between the Geneva Bible and the KJV, and KJV defenders including Waite still assert that the Geneva Bible's NT was based on the Received Text. The fact that KJV-only advocates assert that the pre-1611 English Bibles with some significant textual variations (including whole verses) are based on the same Greek New Testament as the KJV while alleging that the NKJV supposedly is not would indicate KJV-only inconsistency, hypocrisy and use of unjust measures.

Arthur Farstad, executive editor of the NKJV, asserted: "The text of the New King James Version itself is the traditional one used by Luther and Calvin, as well as by such Catholic scholars as Erasmus, who produced it. Later (1633) it was called the *Textus Receptus*, or 'TR'" (*NKJV in the Great Tradition,* p. 111). In note 9, Arthur Farstad commented that "deeper reflection led us to adhere to the traditional King James text" (p. 116). Farstad quoted the following from the guidelines for the making of the NKJV: "the Traditional texts of the Greek and Hebrew will be used" (p. 34). Concerning the NKJV, James D. Price observed: "Constant reference was made to the printed edition of the Hebrew Bible used by the translators of 1611, the second Bomberg edition edited by Jacob ben Chayyim. In those few places where the Bomberg text differed from the Stuttgart edition, the Bomberg reading was followed" (*King James Onlyism,* p. 307). Price listed "nine differences that affect translation" and demonstrated that the NKJV followed the Bomberg edition in those nine places (pp. 222-223). The preface to the NKJV clearly pointed out concerning its Hebrew Old Testament text the fact of "frequent comparisons being made with the Bomberg edition of 1524-25" (p. xxiii). While the NKJV translators made use of a different printed edition of the Hebrew Masoretic text, they actually followed the same Hebrew text as was used in the making of the KJV. In the very small number of places (only eight or nine have been identified) where their printed edition of the Hebrew Masoretic text differed from the Bomberg edition of Chayyim, the NKJV translators followed the same Hebrew text that underlies the KJV. Therefore, KJV defenders jump to a wrong conclusion when they claim a different Hebrew text was used for the NKJV's Old Testament. R.

B. Ouellette's claim that "a completely different Old Testament text was used" in the making of the NKJV is not true (*A More Sure Word*, p. 57).

KJV defender David Norris acknowledged that the NKJV can "be classed largely as a revision rather than a retranslation" (*Big Picture,* p. 367). KJV defender David Sorenson admitted that the NKJV's N. T. "is translated from the Textus Receptus" (*Touch Not,* p. 240). David Sorenson also listed the NKJV as being "based upon the Received Text" (p. 10). Laurence Vance acknowledged that the NKJV's "New Testament was based on the Received Text" (*Brief History*, p. 92). Joe Gresham claimed that the NKJV "follows the same ancient manuscripts as the KJV" (*Dealing with Devil's Deception*, p. 149). KJV-only author Samuel Gipp acknowledged that the NKJV "is based on the correct Antiochian manuscripts" (*Answer Book,* p. 104). Wilbur Pickering maintained that "the King James Version (AV) and the New King James Version (NKJV) reflect a form of the text based upon the many later MSS" (*Identity of the NT Text II*, p. 1; *Identity of the NT Text IV*, p. 2). Pickering indicated that the Majority Text edition by Zane Hodges and Arthur Farstad would "differ somewhat from the Textus Receptus upon which the KJV and NKJV are based" (*Identity of the NT Text IV*, p. 317, footnote 3). KJV-only author Jack McElroy admitted that the "NKJV is translated from the same Greek New Testament and virtually the same Hebrew Old Testament as the 1611 King James Bible" (*Which Bible Would Jesus Use*, p. 135). Charles Surrett, who is biased toward the KJV, indicated that at least "72 times" the KJV's underlying Greek New Testament text supported the NKJV's renderings in the book of Romans over the KJV's renderings (*Certainty of the Words*, p. 123).

In his list of formal equivalent translations, William Einwechter included the NKJV along with the KJV, and he noted that the NKJV is "based on the TR" (*English Bible Translations,* pp. 17, 29). Kerby Fannin listed the NKJV and MKJV as being "based on the Received Text" (*While Men Slept,* pp. 469-470). Michael Sproul referred to "the fact that the NKJV is translated from the same Greek text as the original KJV" (*God's Word Preserved*, p. 39, footnote 51). J. G. Vos as revised by M. L. Strauss noted: "The primary distinction of the NKJV is its textual basis, utilizing the Textus Receptus, the edition of the Greek NT behind the KJV" (*Zondervan Encyclopedia of the Bible*, Vol. 5, p. 1007). Gary Zeolla affirmed that the NKJV is "based on the same Greek text as the KJV, the TR" (*Differences between Bible Versions,* pp. 20, 66). Gary Zeolla suggested that "the KJV and NKJV attempt to translate the original text as word for word as possible" (p. 61). Zeolla asserted that "the NKJV is highly readable and is extremely accurate" (p. 68). Gary Zeolla maintained that the NKJV "is every bit as faithful to the original text as the KJV, even more so at times" (p. 242). Gregory Tyree listed the NKJV and the KJV as literal translations of the Majority text family (*Does It Really Matter*, p. 77). In the introduction to the *Eastern/Greek Oxthodox Bible*, Laurent Cleenewerck maintained that the NKJV is "based on the Textus Receptus and follows the formal-equivalency approach and general style of the KJV" (p. 17). Norman Geisler and William Nix observed: "The diligent efforts by the revisers of *The New King James Version* to produce an English Bible that retains as much of the classic King James Version as possible while at the same time bringing its English up-to-date has been achieved to a great degree" (*General Introduction to the Bible,* p. 599). Alec Gilmore described the NKJV as "little more than a language update" (*Dictionary*, p. 119). William Paul claimed that "the NKJV is virtually the King James Version, only without the 17th century archaic word forms" (*English Language Bible,* p. 80). William D. Mounce described the NKJV as the "American revision" of the KJV (*Greek for the Rest of Us*, p. 264). Jim Taylor listed the NKJV as a revision of the KJV (*In Defense of the TR*, p. 101). In the editor's preface of John Maxwell's commentary on Deuteronomy in *The Communicator's Commentary*, Lloyd J. Ogilvie maintained that the NKJV "combines with integrity the beauty of language, underlying Hebrew and Greek textual basis, and thought-flow of the 1611 King James Version, while replacing obsolete verb forms and other archaisms with everyday contemporary counterparts for greater readability" (p. 10). In *The Inspirational Study Bible* [NKJV edition], Max Lucado asserted: "The New King James Version preserves the precise scholarship of the original King James Version while updating the literary form of the text" (p. v). Max Lucado added: "The NKJV is a dependable version of the classic text in language that makes sense for today's readers" (Ibid.). Ron Rhodes wrote: "The New King James Version (NKJV) is a revision of the King James Version (KJV) in modern English"

(*Complete Guide*, p. 113). Ron Rhodes added: "The NKJV significantly updates the KJV, making it a much more accurate translation" (p. 114). Estus Pirkle wrote: "In my opinion, the New King James Version is the greatest English translation that is available today to English readers. It is based on the same Hebrew and Greek texts (Textus Receptus) used by the 1611 KJV translators" (*The 1611 KJB*, p. 177). Wilbur Pickering asserted: "Until such a time as a good translation of the Majority Text becomes available, the best current English version of the NT is the NKJV—an excellent translation of a good Greek text" (*Identity of NT Text II*, p. 183). The special committee on Bible Versions for the Baptist Missionary Association Theological Seminary reported that the NKJV "seems to be as faithful to the Hebrew and Greek texts as the earlier versions" (bmats.edu/about-us/bible-versions). Jack Lewis claimed that "the NKJV is a deliberate effort to turn the processes of scholarship back to the state of textual knowledge prior to the influence of Westcott-Hort" (*English Bible*, p. 333).

More KJV-only allegations concerning the NKJV considered

After the presentation of many facts from and concerning the Geneva Bible, the KJV, and the NKJV, it should now be very clear that the generalized, broad-sweeping KJV-only accusations against the NKJV are inconsistent, misleading, and incorrect when considered in the light of all the relevant evidence as evaluated by consistent, just measures or standards. Based on these facts, it is very clear that a different measure has been used by KJV-only advocates for the Geneva Bible than the one used for the NKJV. The evidence indicates that KJV defenders do not apply the same exact measures consistently and justly to the translating in the KJV that they attempt to apply to the translating in the Geneva Bible or in the NKJV. This need for the use of consistent, just measures in order to seek to make righteous judgments will be applied to some of the specific accusations that KJV-only advocates have made concerning certain renderings in the NKJV.

D. A. Waite's book contended that when the NKJV "changes pronoun to noun" at 1 Samuel 20:2, it is a supposed example of "not faithfulness in translation" or "not accuracy in translation" (*NKJV compared to KJV*, pp. 27, xiii). The 1537 Matthew's Bible, one of the pre-1611 English Bibles of which the KJV was a revision, has "Jonathan" instead of "he" at this verse just as the NKJV does. Waite claimed: "There is little reason for a translator who is faithful in his translating to change a pronoun and make it into a noun. That is interpretation. That is not translation" (*Defending the KJB*, p. 127). Are KJV defenders or KJV-only advocates willing to apply their own stated claims, measures, and principles consistently and justly? Would they complain about or condemn the KJV for adding a noun in English where there was not a noun in the Hebrew or Greek? Would they actually claim that it would be wrong or sin for the KJV translators to change a part of speech in the Hebrew or Greek to another part of speech in English?

For example, the KJV changed "him" at 1 Samuel 20:18 in the 1535 Coverdale's Bible and Geneva Bible to "David." The KJV inserted this noun that was not in the Hebrew, and it did not put this addition in italics. According to a consistent application of Waite's very own assertion, were the KJV translators guilty of interpretation and not translation? Would Waite ask why the KJV translators did not leave it the way the Holy Spirit wrote it as he asked about the NKJV translators (see p. 129 in *Defending the KJB*)? Was a double standard used since the same standard is not applied to the KJV? The English translation of the 1637 Dutch authorized version has "him" at 1 Samuel 20:18. Where the 1560 Geneva Bible has the pronoun "he" at 1 Kings 20:12, the KJV substituted the noun "Ben-hadad" in italics. The English translation of the Dutch Bible has "he" at 1 Kings 20:12. In verse 24 of 1 Kings 9, the Geneva Bible and the KJV replaced "he" in Coverdale's with "Solomon" in italics. The Dutch Bible translated into English has "he" at this verse with the annotation: ["Solomon"]. Coverdale's rendering "his heart" (Gen. 45:26) became "Jacob's heart" in the Geneva, Bishops', and KJV. The Geneva Bible placed this inserted word "Jacob's" in italics, but the KJV does not. Waite claimed: "Wherever the King

James translators added words, they put those words in *italics* to show that the word does not appear in the Hebrew or the Greek but was added to convey the meaning for the English reader" (*Foes,* p. 96).   At 2 Kings 9:25, the KJV put "Jehu" in italics where the Matthew's Bible has "he." The KJV inserted "said Ahab" in italics at 1 Kings 20:34 when this addition was not in Coverdale's, Matthew's, and Bishops'.   "Moses" was added in italics at Numbers 15:23 in the KJV when it was not in the Hebrew and was not in Tyndale's, Matthew's, and Coverdale's. Other examples where the KJV inserted a noun in italics include the following: "Abraham" (Gen. 21:33), "Samuel" (1 Sam. 9:24, 25), "Ish-bosheth" (2 Sam. 3:7), "Joram" (2 Sam. 8:10), "David" (2 Sam. 13:37, 1 Chron. 15:1, 1 Chron. 23:5, 1 Chron. 28:19), and "Beh-hadad" (1 Kings 20:34). At Acts 7:8, Tyndale's, Coverdale's, Matthew's, and Great Bibles have "he" where the KJV substituted "Abraham" in italics.   The Geneva and Bishops' have "Moses" in italics (Exod. 10:18) where the KJV has "he."   At Numbers 23:4, Tyndale's, Geneva, and Bishops' have "Balaam said" where the KJV has "he said."   At James 4:6, the Geneva and Bishops' have "the Scripture" while the KJV has "he."

Does a consistent application of claims and accusations in books defending the KJV in effect suggest that the KJV also has examples of unfaithfulness or inaccuracy in translation?   If these same kind of changes made by the KJV translators in their revision of the earlier English Bibles are not to be considered dynamic equivalencies, then it would show that Waite's claims about these same kind of changes made by the NKJV translators in their revision of the KJV would also be invalid.   That also suggests that Waite's claim to have found 2,000 dynamic equivalencies in the NKJV based on these same kind of changes may be inaccurate and incorrect unless Waite in effect wants to suggest that the KJV may have many dynamic equivalencies.   Was the KJV a revision of earlier English Bibles that had many dynamic equivalencies according to a consistent application of KJV-only reasoning?   Too often claims and accusations concerning dynamic equivalencies in KJV-only books have been taken to such an inconsistent extreme that these claims seem to have become invalid or practically useless. Do KJV-only advocates actually reject consistently and absolutely all dynamic equivalency if examples of it can be pointed out in the pre-1611 English Bibles of which the KJV was a revision and even in the KJV itself?   Do KJV defenders consider any examples of dynamic equivalent renderings in the KJV to be inaccuracy and unfaithfulness in translation or to be translation errors?

At Amos 6:12, the Wycliffe's Bible, Coverdale's Bible, Matthew's Bible, Great Bible, Geneva Bible, and Bishops' Bible all translate one Hebrew word as "wormwood."   On the other hand, the 1611 KJV changed this rendering in the pre-1611 English Bible to "hemlock."   What truth of the original demanded that this change be introduced into the English Bible?   Would this change of noun in the 1611 KJV be considered a dynamic equivalency?   Was this change an improvement or was this change merely for the sake of variety?   If the pre-1611 English Bibles were not wrong in their rendering at Amos 6:12, why make the change at all?   What sound reasons required that the same Hebrew word translated at Amos 5:7 as "wormwood" by the KJV translators be translated by a different English word at Amos 6:12?   Is the KJV's rendering "wormwood" at Amos 5:7 an accurate, faithful translation of the Hebrew word?   Is the NKJV's rendering "wormwood" at Amos 6:12 an accurate, faithful translation of the Hebrew word?

H. B. Tristram affirmed that "*La'anah* is always translated 'wormwood,' excepting in Amos 6:12, where it is rendered 'hemlock'" (*Natural History of the Bible,* p. 493).   *The Companion Bible* [a KJV edition] has a note for the word "hemlock" at this verse indicating that this is a reference to the Pentateuch "(Deut. 29:18, same word as 'wormwood')" (p. 1240).   At Amos 5:7, this same source again has a note that points out this same reference (p. 1237).   *Young's Analytical Concordance* defined this Hebrew word as "wormwood" (p. 475).   *Gesenius' Hebrew-Chaldee Lexicon* has the definition "wormwood" (p. 440) as does Green's *Concise Lexicon* (p. 121).   A *Reader's Hebrew Bible* has the note "wormwood" for this Hebrew word (p. 1033).   *Wilson's O. T. Word Studies* defined this Hebrew word as "wormwood" (p. 490).   William Newcome (1729-1800) translated it "wormwood" in his version of the Minor Prophets (p. 44).   William Groser maintained that the word "hemlock" at Amos 6:12 "should be 'wormwood' as in other places" (*Trees and Plants,* p. 195). *Unger's Bible Dictionary* maintained that "hemlock [was] an unfortunate translation of the Hebrew ... *laanah* (Amos 6:12), which should be, as in R. V., 'wormwood'" (p. 1138). The Jewish author of *Bible Flowers and Flower Lore* wrote: "The wormwood was known to the ancient Jews by the designation 'La'anah,' and the Authorized Version, in every place where the word is found, saving one, correctly renders it by its rightful botanic equivalent. This exception is in the sixth chapter of Amos. And in this passage the translators of the Anglican Bible have, probably for variety's sake, used the word 'hemlock' instead of 'wormwood.' Why, it is impossible to conjecture; for the Hebrew word in this instance is the same as that correctly rendered in all other passages where it occurs by the English term wormwood" (pp. 47-48).

In an example of a specific KJV-only accusation concerning the NKJV, Raymond Blanton protested that "mansions" at John 14:2 was replaced with "dwelling places" in the NKJV (*Perilous Times,* October, 1994, p. 5). James Son claimed: "For the most part, the modern translations substitute the word 'rooms' and the words 'dwelling places' for the word 'mansions'" (*New Athenians,* p. 215). Kent Rabe claimed that the Spanish Reina-Valera differs from the Greek Received Text at John 14:2 by changing "mansions" to "dwelling places" (*Double Exposure,* p. 35).

Three early pre-1611 English Bibles from the Greek Received Text have this same rendering "dwelling places" as an edition of the NKJV is claimed to have had while the 1535 Coverdale's Bible and 1538 Coverdale's Duoglott have "dwellings." The 1543 Spanish Enzinas also has "moradas" [dwelling] at John 14:2. Luther's German Bible has "Wonungn" [dwellings] at John 14:2. Concerning this verse, Martin Luther wrote: "First of all, they should know of the many abodes for them with the Father" (*Luther's Works,* Vol. 24, p. 26). Wycliffe's Bible has "dwellings" at John 14:2. At this verse, the 1657 English edition of *The Dutch Annotations* has "In my Father's house [That is, in heaven] are many dwellings [or abidings, or abiding places]." The KJV translators themselves rendered this same Greek word as "abode" at John 14:23. Would the KJV's own rendering at John 14:23 provide support for use of the same rendering at John 14:2? Would Gail Riplinger claim that "abode" was the KJV's perfect built-in definition for its rendering mansion?

Ken Barker noted: "The word 'mansions' in King James's day had the idea of 'manse,' which was a dwelling" (*Accuracy Defined & Illustrated,* p. 91). In 1604, Robert Cawdrey defined mansion as "an abiding place" (*Table Alphabetical*). In his 1828 Dictionary, Noah Webster gave the first definition of mansion as "any place of residence; a house; a habitation." He then listed the usage of "mansion" at John 14:2 as an example of this definition. Waite's *Defined KJB* gave the following definition for mansion: "resting, abiding, or dwelling places" (p. 1418). David Cloud's *Concise KJB Dictionary* has this meaning: "an abode" (p. 58). *The Liberty Annotated Study Bible* gave the following note for *mansions*: "Lit. dwellings" (p. 1639). Green's *Concise Lexicon* defined the Greek word used at John 14:2 and 23 as "an abode, dwelling" (p. 85). A Bible Word List in the back of the Cambridge Standard Text Edition of the KJV defined *mansions* as "resting places, abiding places." The rendering "mansions" likely came from the Latin Vulgate rendering in this verse: *mansiones*. Perhaps unaware of the likely source of this word and its meaning in the 1600's, James Son claimed that "*Mansions* is the exact word that the Lord wants us to have" (*New Athenians,* p. 216). Do many present-day readers of the KJV understand the meaning of the word "mansions" as it was used in the 1500's and 1611 or do they read another meaning into this word?

On her cassette entitled "Detailed Update," Gail Riplinger had claimed the following concerning the NKJV: "Every time they change from the King James to something different they follow the New World Translation of Jehovah Witnesses." In her book, she suggested that the rendering "disobedience" at Romans 15:31 and Hebrews 4:11 and the rendering "obey" at John

3:36 are doctrinal errors from the Jehovah Witness Bible (*New Age Bible Versions*, p. 255). The 1560 Geneva Bible has "disobedience" at Hebrews 4:11 and "disobedient" at Romans 15:31, and the KJV translators even listed it in the margin of the 1611 as an acceptable translation. Were the KJV translators recommending a Jehovah Witnesses' reading as an acceptable alternative translation according to a consistent application of Riplinger's allegation? The 1557 Whittingham's New Testament also has "disobedient" at Romans 15:31 but has "stubbornness" at Hebrews 4:11. At John 3:36, Whittingham's and Geneva Bible have "obeyeth not" where the KJV has "believeth not." Barry Burton claimed that the NASB rendering "does not obey the Son" at John 3:36 teaches "salvation is by obedience" (*Let's Weigh the Evidence,* p. 30). Robert Baker implied that translations which have "disobedient" or similar words at Romans 11:30-32 and Hebrews 3:18 "change justification by faith to salvation through works" (*Another Bible,* p. 9). At Romans 11:30-31, the margin of the 1611 KJV has "Or, obeyed" as an acceptable alternative translation for "believed." At Hebrews 3:18, the Great and Bishops' Bibles have "that were not obedient" while Whittingham's and the Geneva Bible have "that obeyed not."

On the other hand, Tyndale's, Coverdale's, Matthew's, Coverdale's Duoglott, Great, and Bishops' Bibles have "believeth not" at Romans 10:21 while the Geneva and KJV have "disobedient." In addition, Tyndale's, Coverdale's, Matthew's, and Coverdale's Duoglott have "children of unbelief" at Colossians 3:6c while the KJV has "children of disobedience." "Children of unbelief" was also the rendering at Ephesians 2:2 in Tyndale's, Coverdale's, Matthew's and Great and the rendering at Ephesians 5:6 in Tyndale's, Coverdale's, and Matthew's. The KJV has "children of disobedience" at both verses. Wycliffe's Bible had "sons of unbelief" (Eph. 2:2, 5:6). Romans 15:31 and Romans 10:21 have the same Greek word while Hebrews 4:11, Ephesians 2:2, Ephesians 5:6, Colossians 3:6 have the same Greek word with both of these words coming from the same Greek word. At Acts 5:37, Tyndale's, Matthew's, and Great Bibles have "believed" where the KJV has "obeyed." "Believe" is the rendering of Tyndale's, Coverdale's, Matthew's, Great, and Whittingham's at Galatians 3:1. "Obey" is the KJV's rendering for this verse. Tyndale's, Coverdale's, Matthew's, Great, and Bishops' Bibles have "believe not" at 1 Peter 2:7 while the KJV has "be disobedient." At 1 Peter 3:1, Tyndale's, Coverdale's, and Matthew's have "believe not" while the KJV has "obey not."

Concerning 1 Peter 2:7-8 in his commentary on Peter, Gordon Clark noted:

> While the participle here is etymologically *unbelievers,*
> the King James Version is not incorrect in saying
> the *disobedient.* The verb has both meanings, for the
> very good reason that unbelief or distrust is an idea
> not far removed from disobedience. The man who
> distrusts Christ will not obey him, and the man
> who disobeys does not believe (p. 83).

George Campbell asserted: "The terms rendered sometimes *believing* and sometimes *obeying,* are commonly of so extensive signification as to include both senses, and are therefore used interchangeably" (*Lectures on Ecclesiastical History*, p. 50). Would the claim of Riplinger consistently applied suggest that the KJV changed the good renderings of the good earlier Bibles to Jehovah Witnesses' renderings at Romans 10:21, Ephesians 2:2, Colossians 3:6, 1 Peter 2:7, and other verses? Would KJV-only advocates claim that the KJV teaches salvation by obedience in these verses? It seems fair and just to suggest that KJV-only advocates should check their information more carefully before they jump to their hasty and inconsistent accusations.

Gail Riplinger claimed: "All new versions, in their attempt to present a 'works' based salvation mistranslate *pistis* as 'faithfulness'" in Galatians 5:22 (*New Age Bible Versions,* p. 257). Riplinger suggested or implied that the NKJV supported "works salvation" because of its rendering "faithfulness" at Galatians 5:22 (*Language of KJB,* p. 149). Tyndale's, Coverdale's, Matthew's, and Great Bibles in the KJV-only view's line of good Bibles all had "faithfulness" at Galatians 5:22. Is Riplinger suggesting that William Tyndale, in effect the primary translator of the KJV, and Miles Coverdale were attempting to present a works-based salvation? Was the KJV a revision of earlier Bibles that supported "works salvation?" KJV-only advocates fail to consider how a consistent application of their own claims would apply to the English foundation that underlies the KJV.

In her tract attacking and misrepresenting the NKJV, Gail Riplinger claimed that the "NKJV copies Jehovah Witness Version" at Acts 7:45 and Hebrews 4:8 by having the rendering "Joshua" instead of having the rendering "Jesus" as the KJV does. Part of this tract was also published in the *Church Bus News* (April-June, 1996, p. 26). Riplinger had earlier claimed that the "new versions use dynamic equivalencies frequently, such as translating 'Jesus' as "Joshua' in Acts 7:45 and Hebrews 4:8" (*New Age Bible Versions,* p. 127). Gail Riplinger and Wally Beebe asserted that "the NKJV even turns 'Jesus' into "Joshua' in Acts 7:45 and Hebrews 4:8" (*Church Bus News,* July-Sept., 2002, p. 17). Peter Ruckman claimed that Acts 7:45 "has been purposely mistranslated in the ASV and New ASV as 'Joshua'" (*Problem Texts,* p. 338). Were the KJV translators following a Jehovah Witnesses' reading when they stated in the margin of the 1611 concerning their reading "Jesus" at Hebrews 4:8 the following: "That is Joshua"? A mark by "Jesus" at Hebrews 4:8 in the Geneva Bible referred to this marginal note: "He speaketh of Joshua the son of Nun." Waite's *Defined KJB* gave the following note for "Jesus" at Hebrews 4:8: "i.e. Joshua (*Heb* equivalent of Jesus)" (p. 1589). At this verse in his multi-volume commentary, KJV-only author David Sorenson wrote: "The New Testament name *Jesus* is also a translation of the Old Testament name *Joshua.* Clearly, it is Joshua at the end of the exodus which is so referred to here" (p. 32).

Gail Riplinger, who claimed to have collated the pre-1611 English Bibles, did not share with her readers the fact that several of the early good English Bibles have this same rendering as the NKJV. At Hebrews 4:8, Tyndale's, Coverdale's, Matthew's, Coverdale's Duoglott, Great, Taverner's, and Whittingham's have "Joshua." At Acts 7:45, Tyndale's, Coverdale's, Matthew's, and Great Bibles have "Joshua." Were the majority of the earlier 1500's English Bibles which have "Joshua" at Acts 7:45 and Hebrews 4:8 copying the 1950's Jehovah Witnesses' Version? Did the old Peshitta Syriac follow a Jehovah Witnesses' reading in these verses? The Peshitta even adds "the son of Nun" to make sure that it is clear that Joshua is referred to in Hebrews 4:8. Did John Wesley in 1754 copy a Jehovah Witnesses' reading in these verses? All the editions of Luther's German Bible published during Luther's lifetime have "Josua" (Joshua) at Acts 7:45 and Hebrews 4:8. Would Ruckman claim that William Tyndale and Martin Luther purposely mistranslated Acts 7:45? Would Ruckman claim that Tyndale's and Luther's Bible were "inferior" translations produced by critics?

The 1808 translation by Charles Thomson, signer of the Declaration of Independence and secretary of the Continental Congress, has "Joshua" at Acts 7:45 as did the 1842 revision of the KJV by Baptists. The 1866 American Bible Union New Testament has "Joshua" in both these verses. The 1833 Webster's Bible has the center column note "or, Joshua" at Acts 7:45 and "That is, Joshua" at Hebrews 4:8. The 1917 Scofield Reference Bible has the center column note "Joshua" at Acts 7:45 and Hebrews 4:8. The 1657 *Dutch Annotations* has at Jesus at Acts 7:45 the following: "That is Joshua, the son of Nun, whereby we see that the names Joshua and Jesus are all one name." Concerning Acts 7:45 in his commentary, David Sorenson asserted: "The *Jesus* mentioned in verse 45 is a reference to Joshua" (p. 365).

The fact should be obvious that a 1950's Jehovah Witnesses' Version did not even exist when the old Syriac, Luther's German Bible, and several of the early English Bibles had the reading "Joshua" in these verses. It is also interesting to note that Wally Beebe's 1975 Bus Worker's Edition of the KJV has "Joshua" in the text at Acts 7:45 and that it has a note listing

"Joshua" as an alternative translation at the end of Hebrews 4:8. Would Riplinger claim that the edition of the KJV in Beebe's Bus Worker's Bible copied from the Jehovah Witnesses? *The Liberty Annotated Study Bible* [KJV], *the Criswell Study Bible* [KJV], and *the Rice Reference Bible* [KJV] also have "Joshua" in the text at Acts 7:45.

The evidence should be clear and overwhelming that it was wrong and false to claim that the NKJV copies the Jehovah Witnesses' Version at Acts 7:45 and Hebrews 4:8. For **Jesus** at Acts 7:45, *The Rock of Ages Study Bible* has this note: "Not our Lord, but Joshua, who succeeded Moses. Joshua is a shorter form of the Hebrew name Jehoshua. Jesus is the Greek name for Joshua, just as Henry is the English spelling of the German name Heinrich" (p. 1535). In his commentary on the Gospel of Luke, G. Campbell Morgan observed that "Jesus is merely the Anglicising of the Greek name; and the Greek name rendered Jesus is the Greek form of a very well-known and common Hebrew name, Joshua; and Joshua is really an abbreviation of the name Jehoshua" (p. 40). In his commentary on Acts, J. Vernon McGee noted about 7:45: "Jesus in this passage refers to Joshua. Joshua is the Hebrew name, and Jesus is the Greek" (p. 83). In his 1857 commentary on Acts, J. A. Alexander stated: "*Jesus,* the Septuagint form of *Joshua,* occurs also in Heb. 4:8, and in both cases creates some confusion in the minds of English readers" (p. 294). Bullinger maintained that "Jesus=Joshua, the son of Nun" at Acts 7:45 and Hebrews 4:8 (*Lexicon,* pp. 422-423). In his commentary on Acts, H. A. Ironside wrote: "The word 'Jesus' here of course is really Joshua. It is the same name, but we somehow think of 'Jesus' as applying only to our blessed Saviour" (p. 173). Concerning this verse in the 1839 Baptist edition of the *Comprehensive Commentary* edited by William Jenks and Joseph Warne, this is stated: "The tabernacle was brought in by those who came *with Jesus,* that is, *Joshua,* as, for distinction-sake, and to prevent mistakes, it ought to be read, both here and Hebrews 4:8" (p. 38). The ABS's Committee on Versions commented: "Thus in Acts 7:45 and Hebrews 4:8, we find the name *Jesus,* which the common reader will naturally refer only to the Saviour; while in reality it is simply the Greek form for *Joshua,* and should properly have been so written" (*Statements,* p. 7). It could also be noted that the New Testament used the name "Jesus" to refer to a man also called "Justus" (Col. 4:11).

Gail Riplinger's false claim, which seems to attempt to condemn the NKJV by associating it with a cult, is based on the ad hominem (poisoning the well) fallacy. Did Riplinger intend or desire to injure the good name and reputation of the NKJV translators by making these false, and perhaps even slanderous, or libelous statements concerning the NKJV? Does not Riplinger's claim "bear false witness" against the NKJV and its translators (Exod. 20:16, Prov. 6:19, 14:5, Rom. 13:9)? Riplinger wrote: "Anything based on a false premise will eventually have to resort to lies to defend itself" (*Blind Guides,* p. 58). Did Riplinger possibly assume or start with a false premise that the NKJV copied the Jehovah Witnesses' Version? Defending Riplinger, Waite wrote: "If she has made an error of fact or quotation, she is willing to admit it and correct it" (*Foes,* p. 55). Have these errors been corrected or are these false claims still being published in her tract? In her new book, Riplinger seemed to tone down her claim to "how the NKJV matches Jehovah Witness Version" (*Language of the KJB,* p. 148). Has the false claim actually been corrected or has a synonym been substituted for "copy?" Is her new claim still misleading? By using her faulty reasoning, a comparison could be made entitled "how the KJV matches the Jehovah Witness Version" or "how the KJV matches the Latin Vulgate."

To make Hebrews 4:8 refer to Jesus Christ would present problems for KJV-only advocates. The KJV translators avoided these problems by clearly stating in the margin that this referred to Joshua. No temporary earthly rest in Canaan while Satan is still the god of this world can be the promised rest of God. In his commentary on Hebrews, Oliver B. Greene noted the following about this verse: "The truth set forth here is this: If the Canaan rest that the Israelites received under Joshua had been the rest of God for His people, then God would not have spoken through David of another day, when His people would enter into rest" (p. 141). In order to distinguish between the Canaan rest and the promised rest of God, the writer of Hebrews used a different Greek word for "rest" in verse 9--*sabbatismos.*

In this same tract, Gail Riplinger also implied that the "NKJV copies Jehovah Witness Version" and "demotes Jesus Christ" at Acts 4:27 and 30 with its rendering "holy Servant Jesus" while the KJV has "holy child Jesus." Riplinger claimed: "In the NKJV, as well as in all new versions, with a swift kick from a lexicon, Jesus slips down from God's 'Son' and 'child' to a 'servant' like Phoebe (e. g. see Acts 3:13, 3:26, 4:27, 4:30)" (*Hazardous Materials,* p. 115). In his KJV-only tract entitled "Which Bible," David Hoffman listed Acts 4:27 and 30 as verses to check for "major doctrinal changes." Doug Stauffer asked: ""Does your version reduce Jesus to God's servant rather than His Son in Acts 3:13, 3:26, 4:27, or 4:30" (*One Book Stands,* p. 297)? In his tract "A Careful Look at the NKJV," M. H. Reynolds claimed that the NKJV translators at Acts 4:27 "inserted erroneous words and meanings from corrupted modern Bible versions into the NKJV text." Lloyd Streeter maintained that the NKJV "weakens the deity of Christ, for example, in Acts 3:13, 26; Acts 4:27, 30" (*75 Problems,* p. 42). Gary Miller claimed that "the New King James version demotes Jesus from being the *exalted* Son of God to a *lowly* servant, like any sinful human" (*Why the KJB,* p. 42). In his tract "A Critique of the NKJV," Peter Ruckman cited the NKJV rendering at Acts 4:27 as "another attack on Christ's Deity, which omitted 'child.'" Ruckman also wrote: "If the Greek text has made the mistake of writing a word in Acts 4:27 which could be translated 'Servant' or 'Child,' the Holy Spirit will resolve the ambiguity with 'thy holy child Jesus,' giving Him the preeminent place as God's Son; not 'servant'" (*Handbook of Manuscript Evidence,* p. 136). Al Lacy claimed: "The NKJV translators have slapped Jesus in the face by lowering Him from God's CHILD to God's SERVANT" (*Can I Trust My Bible,* p. 262). Lloyd Streeter contended that "'servant' weakens the incarnation and deity of Christ" (*75 Problems,* p. 193).

This same Greek word found at Acts 4:27 and 30 was also used of Jesus at Matthew 12:18a where it was translated "servant" in the KJV. However, it was translated "child" in Wycliffe's, 1534 Tyndale's, Matthew's, Great, and Bishops' Bibles and as "son" in 1526 Tyndale's. Why is this difference important in Acts 4:27 and 30 but unimportant in Matthew 12:18? Does the KJV's rendering at Matthew 12:18 demonstrate that the NKJV translators used one of renderings which the Greek NT text would allow? Concerning Acts 4:27 but not concerning Matthew 12:18, Morton asked: "Which exalts the Lord Jesus Christ the most, being called God's servant or God's child?" (*Which Translation Should You Trust,* p. 43). Would Ruckman claim that the KJV rendering at Matthew 12:18 was "another attack on Christ's Deity?" Riplinger claimed that the NKJV translators took the "Sonship away from the Lord Jesus Christ" and made him merely a "servant" (*Which Bible is God's Word,* p. 42). Would Morton, Riplinger, Stauffer, and Ruckman claim that the KJV translators took away the Sonship of the Lord Jesus Christ at Matthew 12:18 and made him merely a "servant?" The prophet Isaiah had referred to Christ as the servant of the Lord (Isa. 42:1-4, Isa. 52:13). Did the 1885 translation by John Nelson Darby, 1897 *Interlinear Greek-English New Testament* by George Ricker Berry, or the 1901 ASV copy the 1950's Jehovah Witness Version with their rendering "holy servant Jesus" at Acts 4:27 and 30?

The Companion Bible has this note for "child" at Acts 4:27: "child=servant, Greek *pais,* as in v. 25" (p. 1585). The 1657 English edition of *The Dutch Annotations* has the following note for "thy holy child Jesus" at Acts 4:27: "or servant, minister, See Acts 3:13, 26, see also Matthew 8:6 compared with Luke 7:2 and here verse 25." Concerning Acts 3:13, A. T. Robertson noted: "This phrase occurs in Isaiah 42:1; 52:13 about the Messiah except the name 'Jesus' which Peter adds" (*Word Pictures,* III, p. 43). Concerning Acts 3:13 in his 1851 commentary as edited by Alvah Hovey in the American Baptist Publication Society's *American Commentary on the N. T.,* Horatio Hackett (1808-1875) wrote: "*pais,* not son=*huios,* but servant=Heb. *ebhedh,* which was one of the prophetic appellations of the Messiah, especially in the second part of Isaiah. (See Matt. 12:18, as compared with Isa. 42:1). The term occurs again in this sense in v. 26; 4:27, 30" (pp. 59-60). Concerning Acts 4:27, John Gill noted: "Unless the word should rather be rendered *servant,* as it is in verse 25 and which is a character that belongs to Christ, and is often given him as Mediator, who, as such, is God's righteous servant" (*Exposition,* VIII, p. 176).

To accuse the NKJV of copying the Jehovah Witnesses' Version when the NKJV translators did not copy it or even consult it is slanderous.   To accuse the NKJV translators of taking away the Sonship of the Lord Jesus Christ is ridiculous.   The Greek word *pais* in these verses was used for both *child* or *servant* with the meaning determined by the context.   Greek has a different word for "son"--*huios.*   The KJV translated this word *pais* as "servant" 10 times, "child" 7 times, and "son" 3 times.   James D. Price explained that the real reason for this choice of rendering in the book of Acts in the NKJV is that the translators thought that in this context Peter was alluding to Isaiah 52:13, which identifies Christ as the Servant of the LORD (*False Witness,* p. 25).   This first-hand statement from a NKJV translator would refute Riplinger's speculation and accusation that the reason for the NKJV's rendering was a lexicon.   Does professed love for the KJV justify such false and seemingly malicious attacks on other translations such as the NKJV?

Gail Riplinger also claimed that "the NKJV demotes Jesus Christ" at Matthew 18:26 with its rendering "Master" (*Church Bus News,* April-June, 1996, p. 26).   How can the NKJV be demoting Jesus Christ at this verse when the word in this text was not addressed to Jesus?   The word was being addressed to a certain king.   Would Riplinger claim that the 1560 Geneva Bible somehow demotes Jesus Christ at this verse with this same rendering "Master?"   Several of the other early English Bibles such as Tyndale's, Coverdale's, Matthew's, Great, and Whittingham's have the rendering "Sir" at Matthew 18:26.   The 1389 Wycliffe's Bible and Coverdale's Duoglott have no rendering for this Greek word.   Did these early English Bibles demote Jesus Christ?   Of course not!   The KJV translators rendered this same Greek word as "master" in a few verses, and eleven times they rendered this same word as "Sir."   Riplinger later claimed that it was an error when the Geneva Bible used the term "master" instead of "Lord" for this Greek word (*Which Bible is God's Word,* p. 52).   Would Riplinger claim that it was an error when the KJV translated this same Greek word as "master?"

In addition, it is also ridiculous to claim that "the NKJV demotes Jesus Christ" at Luke 13:8 with its translation of this same Greek word as "Sir" (Ibid.).   In the context of Luke 13:6-9, it is clear that the caretaker or dresser of the vineyard is addressing the owner of the vineyard as "Sir."   Would Riplinger condemn the KJV translators for translating this same Greek word as "Sir" when addressed to Jesus at John 4:11, 15, 19, 49?   Would Riplinger claim that Murdock's New Testament and the Lamsa Bible honor Jesus more with their rendering "My lord" at John 4:11, 15, 19, 49?   Haak's 1657 English Bible has "Lord" at John 4:49 instead of "Sir."   At Revelation 7:14, the earlier English Bibles had "Lord" while the KJV revised it to "Sir."

As examples to support his broad-sweeping allegations against the NKJV, KJV-only author William Grady had cited from the Song of Solomon what he claimed were "pronounced examples of NKJV affinity with the RSV and NASV" (*Final Authority,* pp. 305-310).   Grady's assumption or accusation that the NKJV supposedly copied the RSV or has a direct relationship or affinity to the RSV instead of translating accurately the original languages will be demonstrated to be incorrect by sound evidence.

The 1560 Geneva Bible agreed with the NKJV translation of the Hebrew word *shalom* as "peace" at Song of Solomon 8:10.   Clearly KJV-only advocates fail to apply the same measures to the Geneva Bible that they attempt to apply to the NKJV.   The KJV translators themselves usually translated this Hebrew word as "peace" and placed in the margin of the 1611 at this verse the following note: "Heb. peace."   Would Grady in effect condemn the KJV translators for saying that this Hebrew word means "peace" in their marginal note?   Estus Pirkle noted that the 1534 German Bible, 1526 French Bible, and 1569 Spanish Bible have "peace" at Song of Solomon 8:10 (*The 1611 KJB,* p. 533).

It is interesting that Grady did not condemn the NKJV for having "turtledove" at Song of Solomon 2:12 in agreement with the Hebrew and even the RSV instead of the KJV's "turtle." Perhaps, Grady knew that this was the same Hebrew word translated "turtledove" other places in the KJV. Coverdale's Bible, Matthew's Bible, and Great Bible have "turtledove" in this verse. At Song of Solomon 5:12, the Geneva Bible has the same translation as the NKJV: "his eyes are like doves." The KJV added in italics an extra "the eyes." D. A. Waite had asserted: "By implicit addition to that text, they say that these words can be implied by the context and you can go ahead and add them in your translation-which to me is not a translation but a perversion of Scripture" (*Defending the KJB,* p. 121). He also alleged: "If you ADD to the Word of God what you think is implicit in the words, that is disobedience" (p. 124). While Waite was actually stating his claims about a different verse in a modern translation instead of about this verse in the KJV, his statements would seem to apply here and to some other verses in the KJV if his statements are to be regarded as based on consistent, valid, sound, and just measures.

The 1560 Geneva Bible and 1853 Leeser's Old Testament also agreed with the NKJV reading at Song of Solomon 6:12: "chariots of my noble people" while the 1535 Coverdale's Bible and 1537 Matthew's Bible have "the chariots of the prince of my people." *The Companion Bible* noted that the KJV followed the Septuagint, Arabic, Ethiopic, and Latin Vulgate by treating this phrase as a proper name "Ammi-nadib" while the Hebrew is "the chariots of my people, the noble," or "of my noble people" (p. 927). The *Dutch Annotations* has this note: "Some render it, *upon the chariots of Amminadib,* making of two words one." The *Rice Reference Bible* has this note for this verse: "Or, set me on the chariots of my willing people" (p. 719). The Geneva Bible has "sons of my mother" at 1:6. Would Grady suggest that the 1560 Geneva Bible copied the 1952 RSV at this verse?

Another NKJV rendering that William Grady uses as an example is "cakes of raisins" at 2:5 instead of the KJV's "flagons." Waite's *Defined KJB* gave the following note for "flagons:" "*Heb* raisin-cakes" (p. 913). Green's *Concise Lexicon* defined the Hebrew word used in this verse as "raisin-cake" (p. 26). The 1842 revision of the KJV and the 1885 translation by John Nelson Darby have "raisin-cakes" at 2:5. The 1535 Coverdale's and 1537 Matthew's have "grapes" at 2:5. *The Companion Bible* has this note for 2:5: "flagons=grape-cakes" (p. 923). *Baker Encyclopedia of Bible Plants* noted that "compressed cakes of raisins are very sustaining (Song of Solomon 2:5)" (p. 100). At his entry "flagon," Laurence Vance acknowledged: "Since the Bible mentions 'dried grapes,' it is possible that it is grapes that is being referred to" (*Archaic Words,* p. 144). Jack Moorman identified "flagons" at this verse as "raisin cakes" (*Conies,* p. 30). At its entry "flagon," David Cloud's *Way of Life Encyclopedia* has two definitions: "a cake of grapes" and "a container for wine" (p. 150). Concerning Song of Solomon 2:5, Ronald Bridges and Luther Weigle noted that "the word represented by 'flagon' is *ashishah,* which means a pressed 'cake of raisins'" (*KJB Word Book,* p. 135).

Another of Grady's examples of where the KJV supposedly has a RSV reading is "sixty" at Song of Solomon 6:8. Did the 1833 Webster's Bible and 1853 Leeser's Old Testament supposedly copy the RSV with their rendering "sixty" instead of "threescore" at Song of Solomon 6:8? Waite's *Defined KJB* defined "threescore" as "sixty." Was Grady implying that "sixty" in the NKJV is an inaccurate or unclear rendering of God's preserved Word in the Hebrew at this verse? An additional example cited by Grady was "who veils herself" in the NKJV at 1:7. The 1862 Young's Literal Translation and the 1885 translation by John Nelson Darby has the rendering "as one veiled" (1:7). At this same verse, Leeser's Old Testament has "like a veiled mourner" while the 1917 translation by Jews has "that veileth herself." Evidently, Grady is unaware of the rendering in the margin of the 1611 KJV at this verse: ("'Or, as one that is veiled"). Haak's 1657 translation from the authorized Dutch Bible ["that covereth herself"] at this verse also shows Grady's claim to be incorrect. In the seventh verse of chapter six, Leeser's has "behind thy veil" while Grady suggested that the rendering "behind your veil" came from the RSV.

William Grady also condemned the NKJV rendering of 2 Corinthians 2:17 ("peddling the word of God") which agrees with the Geneva Bible rendering ("make merchandise of the word of God"). Without comparing the NKJV to the Hebrew and Greek or even to the earlier pre-1611 English Bibles, Grady incorrectly contended that the NKJV is "nothing more than a resuscitated African Bible from the hand of Origen" (*Final Authority,* p. 310). This misleading and even false claim by Grady does not provide sound evidence for a KJV-only view. The English translation of the Byzantine Greek Patriarchal Text of 1904 translated 2 Corinthians 2:17 as "peddle the word of God."

William Grady also complained that the word "appearance" at 1 Thessalonians 5:22 was supposedly missing in the NKJV (*Final Authority,* p. 310). In his tract concerning the NKJV, M. H. Reynolds, Jr. claimed that the NKJV inserted an erroneous word from corrupted modern Bible versions into their text when it changed "appearance" to "form" at 1 Thessalonians 5:22. Would Grady, Reynolds, and other KJV-only advocates complain about the fact that the word "appearance" was not in several of the earlier English Bibles at this verse? The 1557 Whittingham's New Testament translated 1 Thessalonians 5:22 as follows: "Abstain from all kind of evil." Blackford Condit suggested that Whittingham's rendering at this verse was superior to the KJV's rendering (*History,* pp. 239-240). The Spanish Valera Bible as printed by the International Bible Association has the rendering "especie de mal" [species or kind of evil]. The 1543 Enzinas Spanish N. T. as reprinted by the Broken Arrow Baptist Church has the rendering "genero de mal" [kind or class of evil].

In his commentary on Thessalonians, Gordon Clark noted that the Greek noun [*eidos*] in this verse in theology "almost always means kind or species" (p. 69). Spiros Zodhiates wrote that this Greek noun in this verse referred to "the form of evil" (*Complete Word Study Dictionary,* p. 507). Concerning 1 Thessalonians 5:22, A. T. Robertson pointed out that "the papyri give several examples of *eidos* in the sense of class or kind and that idea suits best here" (*Word Pictures,* IV, p. 38). In his commentary on Thessalonians, William Hendriksen indicated that this verse means: "From every *form* (or *kind*, not *appearance* here) of evil *hold off*" (p. 140). Concerning "appearance," Marvin Vincent wrote: "As commonly explained, abstain from everything that even looks like evil. But the word signifies *form* or *kind*. Compare Luke 3:22; John 5:37. . . . It never has the sense of *semblance*. Moreover, it is impossible to abstain from everything that looks like evil" (*Word Studies,* IV, p. 51).

Concerning 1 Chronicles 6:28 in the NKJV, Malcolm Watts claimed: "(*Vashni*), the name of Samuel's firstborn son, is changed to Joel after the Septuagint, Syriac, and Arabic. He appears to be called both names (see verse 33 and 1 Samuel 8:2), but there is no textual justification for the other name being included here" (*NKJV: A Critique,* p. 2). D. A. Waite listed this rendering in the NKJV as a dynamic equivalency and claimed that it came from a non-Masoretic text (*NKJV compared to KJV,* p. 36). Concerning this verse, E. W. Bullinger asserted: "Here there is an Ellipsis of the name of the firstborn: while the [Hebrew] word, *Vashn*i, when otherwise pointed means 'and the second' so that the verse reads, 'And the sons of Samuel; the firstborn [*Joel*] and the second Abiah. This agrees with the Syriac Version'" (*Figures of Speech,* p. 5). Bullinger added: "'Joel' is supplied from verse 33 (see also 1 Sam. 8:2, and the note in Ginsburg's edition of the Hebrew Bible)" (Ibid.). Bullinger maintained that "Vashni is not a proper name, but means 'the second'" (p. 104 note). *The International Standard Bible Encyclopaedia* also noted: "The explanation of this is that in 1 Chronicles 6:28 the word taken as a proper name is really 'and second'" (Vol. 5, p. 3046). Is there actually no sound justification to supply words in italics when there is a use of a Hebrew figure of speech such as an Ellipsis that omits a word or words since the KJV translators do the same thing in several other verses? One example would be at 2 Kings 25:3 where the makers of the KJV added two words in italics to supply words omitted in an Ellipsis ["And on the ninth *day* of the fourth *month*"]. Bullinger noted: "The Hebrew reads, 'and on the ninth month.' But the *Ellipsis* is correctly supplied from

Jeremiah 52:6" (*Figures of Speech*, p. 20). Would D. A. Waite consider the places where the KJV supplies words omitted in an Ellipsis dynamic equivalent renderings?

Do KJV defenders also ignore the evidence that there are places where the KJV translators may have amended the traditional Hebrew Masoretic text using other textual sources and readings in other verses in the same manner that they allege concerning the NKJV? At 1 Chronicles 9:41, the KJV translators amended the Masoretic Text by adding "and Ahaz" in italics perhaps because these words are found in the Latin Vulgate, Syriac Version, and 1 Chronicles 8:35. Robert Girdlestone maintained that the A. V. "does not hesitate to use these" ["conjectural emendations based on the analogy of similar cases existing in the 'repeated passages'"], and he gave as one case when the A. V. "inserts the words '*and Ahaz*' into the text of 1 Chronicles 9:41 on the strength of chapter 8:35" (*Foundation,* p. 190). The word "garrisons" in italics at 1 Chronicles 18:6 may be supplied from 2 Samuel 8:6. Again the KJV translators in effect altered the Masoretic Text by adding "the first" in italics at 1 Chronicles 24:23 perhaps influenced by the example of the Latin Vulgate and 1 Chronicles 23:19 when these words were not in the Masoretic text. At 2 Chronicles 35:11 in the KJV, the Masoretic Text reading "sprinkled" is amended to "sprinkled the blood" in agreement with the LXX, Latin Vulgate, and Syriac Versions. The KJV put the Keri marginal reading ["into the middle court"] in the text at 2 Kings 20:4 and put the Masoretic textual reading in its 1611 marginal note: "or, city." At 2 Samuel 5:8, the clause "he shall be chief and captain" is added from 1 Chronicles 11:6. The words "his hand" at 2 Samuel 6:6 may be borrowed from 1 Chronicles 13:9. At 2 Samuel 8:3, the KJV "follows the *Keri*" [the marginal reading] instead of the textual reading of the Masoretic Text by inserting "Euphrates" (Ginsburg, *Introduction,* p. 310). Ginsburg maintained that the KJV followed the example of the Latin Vulgate by inserting "mine eye" at 1 Samuel 24:10 (p. 291). At 2 Samuel 8:4, the word "chariots" in "a thousand *chariots*" is likely added from 1 Chronicles 18:4. The added words in italics ["he lift up his spear"] at 2 Samuel 23:8 may come from 1 Chronicles 11:11. At Numbers 20:26, the words in italics ["unto his people"] may be added from Numbers 20:24. "Thorns" in italics at Judges 2:8 may be taken from Joshua 23:13. Does this example of 1 Chronicles 6:28 demonstrate clearly that KJV defenders do not give the same latitude to the NKJV translators that they in effect give to the translators of the Geneva Bible and the KJV?

At 2 Samuel 5:21, it is claimed that the NKJV "changes verb" (Waite, *NKJV Compared to KJV,* p. 32), and this type change is alleged by Waite to be "not faithfulness in translation," "not accuracy in translation," "not reliability in translation," and "diabolical dynamic equivalency" (p. xi). The 1535 Coverdale's Bible on the KJV-only view's line of good Bibles has the same rendering as the NKJV at 2 Samuel 5:21 ["David and his men carried them away"]. Is this rendering "carried away" actually unfaithful and inaccurate when compared to the Massoretic Text? This NKJV rendering is a literal translation of the Hebrew and is not a dynamic equivalency. The KJV itself literally translated this same Hebrew word used at 2 Samuel 5:21 as "carried away" at 2 Chronicles 14:13 and 16:16. Does this demonstrate that the NKJV translators used a rendering which the Hebrew text allows according to the KJV's own rendering at 2 Chronicles 14:13? It would be the KJV that does not have a strictly literal rendering of what the Hebrew says at 2 Samuel 5:21. James D. Price maintained: "The KJV followed the Targum, emending the MT to harmonize with a parallel passage [1 Chron. 14:12] unnecessarily" (*Textual Emendations,* pp. 16, 61; see also *King James Onlyism,* p. 291). The 1560 Geneva Bible also had made this rendering and had as a note its reason for it--"1 Chronicles 14:12." In his Jewish commentary on Samuel, S. Goldman claimed: "The Chronicler supplies the gloss (adopted by the Targum and Kimchi) *and they were burned with fire*" (p. 218). Doug Stauffer implied that the NIV's rendering ["carried them off"] at 2 Samuel 5:21 "elevates idol worship" (*One Book Stands,* pp. 209-210). Does this example clearly and soundly demonstrate that KJV defenders are not just and fair in their allegations against the NKJV since they do not make the same allegations when the KJV translated the same original-langauge words the same way?

The 1611 edition of the KJV had the following note that gave the literal meaning of the

Hebrew as an acceptable alternative rendering: "Or, took them away." The 1537 Matthew's Bible, the 1540 Great Bible, and the 1657 English translation of the authorized Dutch Bible have this rendering: "David and his men took them up." In agreement with Matthew's Bible, the 1842 revision of the KJV had the 1611's marginal note in the text "took them away." Thomas Newberry (1811-1901) in his KJV Study Bible has this note for this verse: "took them up" (p. 388). Does the evidence show that KJV-only advocates apply the same exact measures, standards, and principles to the KJV as they do to other translations or do they use unrighteous divers measures and make unrighteous judgments in their claims concerning the NKJV? Would KJV-only advocates suggest that the KJV translators elevated idol worship in their marginal note at this verse? Would Stauffer claim that for the KJV to be authoritative at this verse "a strict adherence to a word-for-word translation must be followed" (*One Book Stands,* p. 253)? Does the KJV actually have the most literal translation of the Hebrew word at 2 Samuel 5:21?

James D. Price asserted: "Although justification can be found for a number of emendations made to the Masoretic text by the King James translators, many more of their emendations cannot be justified" (*King James Onlyism*, p. 287), and he listed 82 claimed cases of justifiable emendations and 146 claimed cases of unjustifiable emendations (pp. 561-590). Concerning his lists in an appendix, James D. Price noted: "Emendations in the Old Testament are regarded as departures from the Bomberg second edition edited by Jacob ben Chayyim, the Old Testament *Textus Receptus*" (p. 280). Price acknowledged that "some of the emendations currently in the King James Version were made by English translators prior to 1611" (p. 282). Alan Macgregor maintained that in a number of instances "the NKJV restores the reading of the Masoretic Text where the AV had chosen a different textual authority" (*400 Years On*, p. 249). Would KJV defenders apply the same exact measures to any claimed examples of emendations in the KJV that they do to their own claimed examples in the NKJV? If examples of claimed textual emendation are passed over or excused as possible alternative renderings in the KJV, would the same latitude be given to those in the NKJV?

James D. Price claimed that at Isaiah 19:10 all Hebrew manuscripts have a word which means "soul" while the KJV reads "fish" following the Latin Vulgate (*Textual Emendations,* pp. 16, 58; see also *King James Onlyism*, pp. 291, 409, 581). Arthur Farstad also maintained that the KJV followed the Latin Vulgate with its rendering "fish" at Isaiah 19:10 (*NKJV: In the Great Tradition,* p. 50). While the 1610 Catholic Douay version from the Latin Vulgate has "fishes" in this verse, the 1853 English translation of the Hebrew by Isaac Leeser, the 1864 *Jewish School and Family Bible* by Abraham Benisch, the 1916 English Version of the Scriptures according to the Masoretic Text by Alexander Harkavy, and the 1917 English translation of the Masoretic Text by Jews have "soul" as does *The Interlinear Bible*.

The influence of the Latin Vulgate could have been indirect, direct, or both indirect and direct. Miles Coverdale had used the rendering "fish" in his 1540 Great Bible, and it may have been his translation of the Latin Vulgate's rendering. The Bishops' Bible kept "fish" from the Great Bible, and the Bishops' Bible may have been the direct English source of the KJV's rendering. James D. Price clearly acknowledged: "Some of the emendations currently in the King James Version were made by English translators prior to 1611. It may be assumed that the King James translators approved some of the emendations made by their predecessors and allowed them to remain uncorrected" (*King James Onlyism*, p. 282). On the other hand, the Geneva Bible translators rendered the Hebrew word in this verse as "heart." In many instances as may be the case here, the Geneva Bible translators are said to have restored "the literal meaning of the Hebrew text which had been obscured, through ignorance or through following secondary sources, in all the earlier English versions" (Daiches, *KJV of the English Bible*, p. 179). The KJV translators usually translated this same Hebrew word in other passages as "soul" (475 times), "life" (117 times), "person" (29 times), "mind" (15 times), or "heart" (15 times). The 1611 KJV had a marginal note for "fish:" "Heb. of living things." *The Companion Bible's* note at Isaiah 19:10 stated: "or, work for wages shall be grieved in soul. Fish=souls. Heb. *nephesh*"

(p. 954).   KJV defender Edward Hills acknowledged: "Sometimes also the influence of the Septuagint and the Latin Vulgate is discernible in the King James Old Testament" (*KJV Defended*, p. 223).   Is Isaiah 19:10 a possible or even a likely example of a direct or indirect influence of the Latin Vulgate on the KJV translators?   Does the NKJV accurately translate this Hebrew word with its rendering "soul" at Isaiah 19:10?   Will KJV defenders give the same latitude to the NKJV translators that they evidently give to the KJV translators?   If the KJV had the rendering "soul" at Isaiah 19:10 and if the NKJV had the rendering "fish," would Waite claim that this change of noun was a dynamic equivalency?

Another example of where it is sometimes claimed that the Latin Vulgate influenced the KJV is at Lamentations 2:20.   For example, in a marginal note at this verse, the *KJV-NKJV Parallel Reference Bible* suggested that the source of the KJV's rendering "a span long" was the Vulgate (p. 1019).   R. Payne Smith maintained that "children of a span long" is "the rendering of the Vulgate and Aquila, but it has little to recommend it" (Cook, *Bible Commentary,* V, p. 591).   James D. Price indicated that the reading "children a span long" was an unjustifiable emendation supported only by the Latin Vulgate (*King James Onlyism,* p. 582).   These assertions would relate to the KJV as a translation and not as a revision of the pre-1611 English Bibles.   If these claims are accurate, the influence of the Vulgate here may be indirect since the KJV kept the rendering of some of the earlier English Bibles such as Bishops', Geneva, Great, and Coverdale's.   Wycliffe's Bible from the Latin has the following rendering: "little children at the measure of an hand."

The KJV translators themselves gave in their marginal note for this phrase the following acceptable, alternative translation of the Hebrew: "swaddled with their hands."   This rendering in their marginal note is similar to the one that some sources maintain is the accurate translation of the Hebrew.   The *Liberty Annotated Study Bible* asserted that the meaning of the Masoretic Text here was "they have cuddled" (p. 1188).   Benjamin Blayney translated it as "little ones dandled on their hands" in his translation of Jeremiah and Lamentations (p. 207).   The 1917 English translation of the Masoretic text by Jews translated the same phrase as "children that are dandled in the hands."   The *Theological Wordbook of the O. T.* has the following definition for *tippuhim*:   "dandling" (p. 352).   Isaac Leeser's 1853 translation of the Hebrew was "babies they have tenderly nursed."   Abraham Benisch's 1864 translation was "children of tender nursing."   Green's *Concise Lexicon* defined it as "tender care" and indicated the connection of this Hebrew word with the Hebrew word translated "swaddled" at Lamentations 2:22.   The *Ryrie Study Bible* has the following note for this phrase: "who had been tenderly cared for" (p. 1177).   Haak's 1657 English translation of the Dutch Bible translated the phrase as follows: "little children that are carried upon the hands."

Gail Riplinger claimed in her tract that the "NKJV omits the word 'God' 51 times" (*Church Bus News,* April-June, 1996, p. 26).   This inaccurate claim seems to be based on a simple comparison of the NKJV to the KJV and not on a comparison to the preserved Scriptures in the original languages.   This count likely does not even take into consideration the places where the KJV has the word "God" added in italics.   In response to this misleading charge, James D. Price noted:

> The truth is that the KJV added the word "God" in
> fifty one or more places where the Hebrew or Greek
> text did not contain it--and that without using italics
> in most cases.   This was because the KJV used
> dynamic equivalence paraphrases such as "God
> forbid," "God save the king," or "God speed"
> instead of a more literal expression in good English.
> In all these places the NKJV made the KJV more
> literal and more faithful to the Hebrew and Greek

texts without undermining the place of God in
the Bible (*False Witness,* p. 4).

Price then discussed these times and demonstrated the faithfulness of the NKJV to the Hebrew and Greek texts underlying the KJV.

Jack Lewis maintained that "the phrases 'God forbid' (1 Sam. 14:45; etc.) and 'would God' (Num. 11:29) add the word 'God' to the text" (*English Bible,* p. 44).   Harold Rawlings claimed that "the KJV is replete with dynamic idioms like 'God forbid' and 'God save the king' that have no exact verbal equivalent in the original" (*Trial by Fire,* p. 192).   In the introduction to his 1833 revision of the KJV, Noah Webster noted that the phrase *God forbid* was used several times in the KJV "without any authority from the original languages for the name of God" (p. ix).   The KJV has "God forbid" eight times in the Old Testament and fifteen times in the New Testament. Michael Sproul maintained that "'God forbid' is a dynamic equivalent of a Greek idiom in the English language" (*God's Word Preserved,* p. 346).   D. A. Waite acknowledged that the Greek for the KJV's "God forbid" would be literally translated as "may it not be" (*Foes,* p. 96).   KJV-only author David Cloud described this example as "'a little something like' that which is called dynamic equivalency today" (*Bible Version Question/Answer,* p. 157).   KJV-only author William Grady asserted that "occasionally" the KJV translators "even had the 'audacity' to insert an English idiom, with no manuscript authority whatsoever, such as the phrase 'God forbid'" (*Given by Inspiration,* p. 44).   David Daniell indicated that Luther's German Bible has "*das sey ferne* (be that far away)" instead of "God forbid" (*William Tyndale,* p. 142).   Concerning "God forbid" at 1 Corinthians 6:15, A. T. Robertson noted: "The word "God' is not here" (*Word Pictures,* IV, p. 106).

At Acts 10:14, Tyndale's and Matthew's Bibles have "God forbid" while the KJV has "Not so."   At Acts 11:8, Tyndale's, Matthew's, Whittingham's, and Geneva Bibles have "God forbid" while the KJV again has "Not so."   At 2 Samuel 20:20, the Geneva and Bishops' Bibles have "God forbid" twice while the KJV has "Far be it" twice.   This verse has the same Hebrew word twice that the KJV rendered "God forbid" several other times.   At 1 Samuel 20:9, the 1560 Geneva's rendering ["God keep it from thee"] and the Bishops' rendering ["God keep that from thee"] were revised in the KJV ["Far be it from thee"].   Would Riplinger and other KJV-only advocates claim that the KJV omitted the name of God from the English Bible at these verses as they inconsistently allege against the NKJV concerning other verses?

Were the KJV translators always completely faithful to their underlying original-language texts and always consistent in following the renderings of the earlier English Bibles?   Instead of keeping the rendering of the earlier English Bibles, the KJV translators corrected the addition of the word "God" in several of them at 1 Kings 1:31.   At Nehemiah 2:3, Coverdale's and Matthew's Bibles have a rendering with the name of God ["God save the king's life for ever"] and the Geneva and Bishops' Bibles have a similar rendering ["God save the king for ever"].   The KJV does not add the name of God at this verse ["let the king live for ever"].   At Daniel 2:4, Coverdale's, Matthew's, and Bishops' Bibles have the name of "God" ["O king, God save thy life for ever"] where the Geneva and KJV does not.   Coverdale's and Matthew's also have a similar rendering at the following verses (Dan. 3:9, 5:10, 6:6, 6:21).

In their marginal notes in the 1611 KJV, the KJV translators acknowledged that the literal meaning of the Hebrew at 1 Samuel 10:24, 2 Samuel 16:16, 2 Kings 11:12, and 2 Chronicles 23:11 was "let the king live" and at 1 Kings 1:25 "let king Adonijah live."   Perhaps because of their note at verse 25, the KJV translators did not include this marginal note at 1 Kings 1:34 and 39 where it reads "God save King Solomon."   The Geneva Bible translators also had marginal notes giving the literal meaning of the Hebrew at 1 Samuel 10:24, 2 Samuel 16:16, and 1 Kings 1:25.   Concerning 2 Samuel 16:16, James Edmunds and T. S. Bell claimed: "The [KJV] translators affixed to the exclamation the term 'God,' for the purpose, doubtless, of making it more emphatic, and to convey the idea of the special protection of the Almighty as extended over kings, that inasmuch as they ruled by Divine right, so they were the special objects of Divine protection" (*Discussion on Revision*, p. 145). Edmunds and Bell also maintained that "in order to assist the tyrant James in riveting a yoke upon the necks of the people" that the makers of the KJV "did not hesitate to make holy writ utterly repeatedly, God save the king—a phrase not only never written by the Holy Spirit, but at war with all of God's revelation on kingly governments" (p. 113). Concerning 2 Chronicles 23:11, KJV-only author Jack McElroy acknowledged: "The Hebrew text literally says 'Let the king live,' whereas the translators presented the text idiomatically as 'God save the king'" (*Which Bible Would Jesus Use*, p. 173). God's Word in the Hebrew does not contain the word "God" nor the word "save" in these verses. The KJV translators themselves translated the same Hebrew word used here as "live" many times. Why didn't the KJV translators put the literal meaning of the Hebrew in the text rather than in the margin? Why did they inconsistently revise or correct the same rendering in the earlier English Bibles at other verses while keeping them at some? The 1853 Leeser's, 1917 Holy Scriptures According to the Masoretic Text, and 1985 TANAKH all have "Long live the king" as the translation of the Hebrew at 1 Samuel 10:24, 2 Samuel 16:16, 2 Kings 11:12, and 2 Chronicles 23:11. It would clearly be incorrect to claim that modern translations such as the NKJV are omitting the word "God" in these verses.

Not applying his own question, measure, and reasoning consistently to the KJV, D. A. Waite asked: "Is it 'needed' to add the Name of God when the Name of Deity is not in the Hebrew or Greek texts? I do not believe that it is" (*Foes of the KJB*, p. 19). Waite also wrote: "They are adding God's name when God's name is not in the Hebrew. Is that dynamic equivalence 'needed?' Is that necessary or needful to add God's name when God is not there? No, this is an error" (Ibid.). Waite would condemn the NKJV for adding "noun for deity" (*NKJV compared to KJV*, p. 2), but he does not apply the same measure and say it would be error when the KJV translators did the same thing. According to a consistent application of Waite's own stated assertions and measures, is he suggesting that it is an error when the KJV added the name of God when it was not in the original language texts? Not applying his own assertion to the KJV, H. D. Williams also claimed concerning a different translation: "God is not in the source-language-text" (*Word-for-Word*, p. 233). Kirk DiVietro claimed: "The King James/TR defenders do not ask the new bibles to enter anything into their translations that is not in the original texts" (*Anything But the KJB*, p. 58). However, the evidence clearly indicates that many KJV defenders in effect do sometimes ask or demand that translators put words into their translations that are not in the preserved Scriptures in the original languages. Do KJV-only advocates in effect demand that God alter His Word in Heaven to match some edition of the KJV?

At Matthew 28:9, Tyndale's 1526 New Testament and 1535 Coverdale's Bible have "God speed you." The KJV translators did not keep this addition of the word "God" although they kept it at 2 John 10 and 11. In his introduction to his translation of the Bible, Noah Webster suggested that *God speed* may be a mistake for *good speed* (p. ix). Webster noted that the adjective *good* in Saxon was spelled *god*. He continued: "In the phrase used in scripture, which seems to have been formerly proverbial, the Saxon *god* for *good* has continued to be written with a single vowel, and the word being mistaken for the name of the Supreme Being, it came to be written with a capital initial, *God*" (Ibid.). Webster declared: "*God speed*, as now used, is as improper as *God welfare, God success,* or *God happiness*" (p. x). At the entry for *God speed*, David Cloud noted that it is "an old English phrase for greeting" and that "the same Greek word is translated "hail" (Matt. 26:49), "rejoice" (2 John 4), "greeting" (Acts 15:23, James 1:1), and "farewell" (2 Cor. 13:11)" (*Way of Life Encyclopedia*, p. 166; *Concise KJB Dictionary*, p. 40). William Wright maintained that it was "a salutation, signifying literally, good speed or success" (*Bible Word-Book*, p. 290).

The KJV corrected the addition of the phrase "to God" at Galatians 5:12 in the earlier English Bibles ["I would to God"]. On the other hand, the KJV retained this same addition from the earlier English Bibles at 1 Corinthians 4:8. In his introduction, Noah Webster noted: "These phrases ["*Would God, would to God*"] occur in several passages in which they are not authorized by the original languages, in which the name of the Supreme Being is not used; but the insertion of them in the version, has given countenance to the practice of introducing them into discourses and public speeches, with a levity that is incompatible with a due veneration for the name of God" (p. ix). In his 1833 Bible, Webster corrected the addition of the name of God at 1 Corinthians 4:8 just as the KJV translators had at Galatians 5:12. At its entry *would to God*, William Swinton as edited by T. J. Conant maintained "this exclamation is purely English, and is not found in the Hebrew or Greek Scriptures" (*Bible Word-Book*, p. 106). In the O. T., the KJV has these renderings [would God, would to God] at several verses where a Hebrew name for God is not found (Exod. 16:3, Num. 11:29, 14:2, 20:3, Deut. 28:67, Josh. 7:7, Jud. 9:29, 2 Sam. 18:33, 2 Kings 5:3). At Deuteronomy 28:67, the 1535 Coverdale's Bible had not added the name of God in its rendering ["Who shall give me evening"] as the KJV had ["Would God it were even"]. Webster also corrected this addition of the name of God at this verse with his rendering ["O that it were evening"]. At eight other verses, one or more of the earlier English Bibles have the rendering "would God" or "would to God" where the KJV does not have the name "God" (Gen. 30:34, 2 Sam. 23:15, Est. 7:4, Job 13:5, Job 16:4, Job 19:24, Job 23:3, Jer. 9:2).

When one of the early English Bibles has the name of God where the KJV does not, do they honor the name of God more than the KJV in those places? Would a consistent application of the stated assertions of KJV-only advocates in effect condemn the KJV for omitting the name "God" at places where one of the early Bibles has it? A few examples include Genesis 23:6 where Tyndale's, Coverdale's, Matthew's, Great, Geneva, and Bishops' Bibles have "a prince of God" while the KJV has "mighty prince." A marginal note in the 1611 KJV stated: "Hebr. a Prince of God." Some other translations such as Haak's translation of the Dutch Bible, Leeser's Old Testament, Young's Literal Translation, Rotherham's Emphasized Bible, and the Lamsa Bible also have "prince of God" at this verse. At Genesis 30:8 and Exodus 9:28, some of the early English Bibles have the name "God" where the KJV does not. Tyndale's and Matthew's Bibles have "a fear sent of God" (1 Sam. 14:15) while the KJV has "a very great trembling" with the marginal note "Hebr. a trembling of God." At this verse, the Geneva Bible has "with fear by God." The 1657 Haak's has "a trembling of God." Coverdale's Bible has "wrath of the LORD" and Bishops' Bible has "wrath of God" where the KJV has only "wrath" (2 Chron. 24:18). At Mark 14:62, Wycliffe's Bible has "virtue of God" and the Geneva and Bishops' Bibles have "power of God" while the KJV only has "power." At 1 Peter 5:2, Coverdale's Duoglott and the Douay-Rheims have "according to God" while the Great Bible has "after a godly sort." At 1 Samuel 12:6, the Peshitta as translated in the Lamsa Bible has "The LORD is the only God" while the KJV has "It is the LORD." The Lamsa Bible has "the LORD" at 1 Samuel 7:14 where the KJV does not. According to a consistent application of KJV-only reasoning, do the early Bibles honor God more in any of these verses than does the KJV?

D. A. Waite claimed that the NKJV rendering "Rock" at Habakkuk 1:12 "changes noun," "omits noun for Deity," and "omits adjective" (*NKJV compared to KJV*, pp. 15, 68). In his introductory remarks, Waite asserted that the examples he cited from the NKJV are "not faithfulness in translation," "not accuracy in translation," "not reliability in translation," and "diabolical dynamic equivalency" (pp. xi-xv). This is another inconsistent, inaccurate, and unfair attack on the NKJV based on use of unjust measures. In the margin of the 1611, the KJV translators themselves gave the literal meaning of the Hebrew word as follows: "Heb. rock." Kirk DiVietro asserted: "One does not pervert the word of God when he translates what he finds in the text accurately" (*Anything but the KJV*, p. 58). The NKJV has a literal, accurate rendering of the Hebrew, not a dynamic equivalency as Waite alleged. In other references, the KJV translators themselves rendered this same Hebrew word as "rock," including references where this word was used of God. At Deuteronomy 32:4, the same Hebrew word was translated "mighty God" in the Geneva Bible and "most mighty God" in the Bishops' Bible while it was revised to "Rock" in the KJV. Would Waite claim that the KJV omits adjective and omits noun for

Deity at Deuteronomy 32:4 when compared to the Geneva Bible or to the Bishops' Bible? Would Waite suggest that this change made in the KJV to the pre-1611 English Bible at Deuteronomy 32:4 was not faithfulness and accuracy in translation? At Deuteronomy 32:15 and 32:30, the Geneva Bible translated the same Hebrew word as "strong God" which the KJV translated it "Rock" in both verses. It is again clear that KJV-only advocates fail to apply their own reasoning and claims consistently and justly. Over and over, it is evident that KJV-only advocates will attack other translations such as the NKJV for being more consistent, faithful, or accurate to the same Hebrew and Greek texts used by the KJV translators.

In another example, D. A. Waite contended that the NKJV rendering "strength" at 2 Samuel 22:3 "changes noun" (*NKJV Compared to KJV*, p. 11). Waite had asserted that these renderings from the NKJV that he listed in his booklet were "not faithfulness in translation," "not accuracy in translation," "not reliability in translation," and "diabolical dynamic equivalency" (pp xi-xv). Would Waite also claim that the five places in the KJV where the same Hebrew word is translated as strength (Ps. 18:2, Ps. 19:14, Ps. 73:26, Ps. 144:1, Isa. 26:4) were examples of inaccurate dynamic equivalencies? Waite claimed that "the King James Bible translators did not use dynamic equivalency" (*Foes of the KJB Refuted*, p. 62). According to a consistent application of Waite's own measures and examples for claiming use of dynamic equivalency in the NKJV, the KJV translators did also use it. Either Waite's allegation against the NKJV would be incorrect or else his claim that the KJV translators did not use dynamic equivalency would be incorrect. Malcolm Watts claimed that the "the God of my rock" at 2 Samuel 22:3 "is wrongly rendered 'the God of my strength'" in the NKJV (*NKJV: A Critique*, p. 3). Would Watts assert that the KJV translators wrongly rendered this Hebrew word as "strength" five times? The 1560 Geneva Bible, part of the English foundation underlying the KJV, translated this Hebrew word as "strength" at 2 Samuel 22:3. At Isaiah 26:4 where the KJV translators rendered this Hebrew word along with another Hebrew word as "everlasting strength," they put the following as a marginal note: "Heb. the rock of ages."

KJV-only advocates claim that the KJV teaches the deity of Christ more clearly than all other translations including the NKJV. Timothy Morton claimed: "The King James Version is the only English Bible still published that contains every true biblical reference to the deity of Christ" (*Which Translation Should You Trust*, p. 52). Morton also contended: "While the new 'Bibles' demean Christ in many key passages, the King James exalts Him at every opportunity" (Ibid., p. 62). Gail Riplinger incorrectly asserted: "The deity of Christ has disappeared in a number of places in the New King James" (*Which Bible Is God's Word*, p. 41). Gail Riplinger claimed: "The new versions always demote the Lord" (*Hazardous Materials*, p. 453). After demonstrating verse by verse that Riplinger's claim in her tract that the NKJV demotes Christ is false, James D. Price maintained that "the NKJV is stronger on the deity of Christ than the KJV" (*False Witness*, p. 22). Concerning this KJV-only allegation, Kirk DiVietro, a KJV-only advocate, acknowledged: "Perhaps some of us state the case a little strongly" (*Anything But the KJB*, p. 63).

Did the KJV clearly exalt Christ as God at its opportunity to follow the good rendering of many of the pre-1611 English Bibles at 2 Peter 1:1? The NKJV in agreement with several pre-1611 English Bibles and many post-1611 English Bibles clearly, precisely, and accurately identifies Jesus Christ as "our God and Saviour" at 2 Peter 1:1. A modern spelling edition of the 1388 Wycliffe's Bible rendered the last part of this verse as "righteousness of our God and Saviour Jesus Christ." William Tyndale in 1534, Miles Coverdale in 1535, and John Rogers in 1537 translated the last part of 2 Peter 1:1 as "righteousness that cometh of our God and Saviour Jesus Christ." In his 1538 Latin-English New Testament, Miles Coverdale rendered it "righteousness of our God and Saviour Jesus Christ." The 1539 Great Bible, 1557 Whittingham's New Testament, 1560 Geneva Bible, 1568 Bishops' Bible, 1576 Tomson's New Testament, 1657 Haak's English translation of the Dutch Bible, 1755 Wesley's New Testament, 1842 Baptist or Bernard's, 1862 Young's Literal Translation, 1866 American Bible Union Version,

1982 NKJV, 1994 Majority Text Interlinear, and a number of other English translations translate it "righteousness of our God and Saviour [or Savior] Jesus Christ."   Thomas Goodwin maintained that "[Theodore] Beza reads it, 'our God and our Saviour Jesus Christ,'" and that "it clearly meant one person, viz. Christ" (*Works*, VIII, p. 283).

At 2 Peter 1:1, the 2005 Cambridge edition of the KJV has this note taken from the standard 1762 Cambridge edition: "Gr. of our God and Saviour."   KJV editions printed at Oxford in 1810, 1821, 1835, 1857, 1865, 1868, and 1885, and at Cambridge in 1769, 1844, 1872, and 1887 also have this same note indicating the accurate translation and meaning of the Greek.   An earlier KJV edition printed in London in 1711 had the same note and a cross reference to Titus 2:13.   Granville Sharp observed: "In the margin of our present version the proper reading is '*of our God and Saviour*,' manifestly referring both titles to one person" (*Remarks*, p. 22).   Concerning 2 Peter 1:1 in the Westminster Annotations printed in 1645, this note was also given: "Gr. Of our God and Saviour Jesus Christ."   Thus, the Bible scholars at the Westminster Assembly agreed with the pre-1611 English Bible translators and the editors of some standard KJV editions.   Concerning 2 Peter 1:1 in a sermon printed in 1722, Edmund Calamy maintained that "the very construction of the words seems plainly to intimate that Jesus Christ is *our God*, as well as *our Saviour*" (*Thirteen Sermons*, p. 41).

James White maintained that "our God and Savior Jesus Christ" is the proper translation of the Greek according to the Granville Sharp's rule (*King James Only Controversy*, p. 268).   Granville Sharp (1735-1813) cited 2 Peter 1:1 as his first example "of sentences which fall under the first rule, and are improperly rendered in the English version [KJV]" (*Remarks*, p. 20).   James D. Price noted that "the Greek grammatical construction here identifies Jesus Christ as God and Savior" (*King James Onlyism*, p. 323).   Concerning this verse in his multi-volume commentary, David Sorenson wrote: "Though it is not quite as evident in English, in the Received Text, the phrase literally reads, 'the righteousness of our God and Savior Jesus Christ'" (p. 228).   Kenneth Wuest asserted: "The expression, 'God and our Saviour' is in a construction in the Greek text which demands that we translate, 'our God and Saviour, Jesus Christ" (*In These Last Days*, p. 17).   John Ankerberg and John Weldon maintained that "Greek scholars Dana and Mantley, in their *A Manual Grammar of the Greek New Testament*, confirm the truth of Sharp's rule, and then explain: 'Second Peter 1:1 … means that Jesus is our God and Savior" (*Facts On Jehovah's Witnesses*, p. 24).

John L. Dagg (1794-1884) indicated that the rendering in our common English version at 2 Peter 1:1 should be emended to "the righteousness of our God and Saviour, Jesus Christ" (*Manual of Theology*, pp. 183-184).   Concerning 2 Peter 1:1, Matthew Henry (1662-1714) commented: "This Jesus Christ, is God, yea, *our God*, as it is in the original" (*Exposition*, Vol. 2, p. 544).   Timothy Dwight (1752-1817) proclaimed: "According to the original, of our God and Saviour, Jesus Christ" (*Theology Explained*, Vol. I, p. 525; Vol. II, p. 69).   Timothy Dwight suggested that "the common translation is a violation of the Greek" (Ibid.).   Thomas Goodwin (1600-1680) contended that "as by God and the Father is meant God the Father so by God and our Saviour is meant Jesus Christ" (*Works*, VIII, p. 283).   In his commentary on 1 and 2 Peter, Gordon Clark translated the phrase as "of our God and Savior, Jesus Christ" (*New Heavens, New Earth*, p. 170).   Gordon Clark concluded: "Other references to 'our Lord and Savior Jesus Christ' do not diminish the deity asserted here in 1:1" (p. 171).   At 2 Peter 1:1 in his edition of the KJV with commentary, Adam Clarke (1760?-1832) maintained that the KJV's rendering "is not a proper translation of the original, which is literally, *of our God and Saviour Jesus Christ*; and this reading, which is indicated in the margin, should have been received in the text; and it is absolute proof that St. Peter calls Jesus Christ God."   At his verse, the *MacArthur Study Bible* stated concerning "our God and Savior Jesus Christ:" The Greek construction has only one article before this phrase, making the entire phrase refer to the same person" (p. 1952).   At this phrase at this verse, *The Henry Morris Study Bible* stated: "This expression could better be rendered as 'our God and Saviour Jesus Christ'" (p. 1947).   In his commentary on 2 Peter & Jude, John

MacArthur noted: "The Greek construction places just one article before the phrase **God and Savior**, which makes both terms refer to the same person. Thus Peter identifies Jesus, not just as Savior, but as God (cf. 1:11; 2:20, 3:2, 18; Isa. 43:3, 11:45, 21; 60:16; Rom. 9:5; Col. 2:9; Titus 2:13; Heb. 1:8), the author and agent of salvation. The apostle made the same relation clear in his Pentecost sermon, in which he took the Old Testament truth of God and applied it to Jesus (Acts 2:21-36; cf. Matt. 1:21; Acts 4:12; 5:31)" (p. 23). John Gill (1697-1771) commented that "precious faith is obtained through the righteousness of our God and Saviour Jesus Christ, 2 Peter 1:1" (*Body of Doctrinal and Practical Divinity*, p. 145).

Surprisingly, the 1611 edition of the KJV has a comma after God at 2 Peter 1:1 [God, and our Saviour Jesus Christ], and that comma seems to have remained in most KJV editions printed up to the 1769 Oxford edition. The 1743 Cambridge and 1760 Cambridge editions had actually removed it before the 1769. Even the first KJV edition printed in America in 1782 and KJV editions printed at Oxford in 1788 and in 1795 still have a comma after God at 2 Peter 1:1. How does this comma in most KJV editions up to the 1769 Oxford affect the understanding and interpretation of this verse? Concerning this verse in his 1633 commentary on 2 Peter, Thomas Adams observed: "Some read these words by disjoining them; of God, and of our Saviour," which would seem to refer to the rendering in the 1611. In his commentary on several books of the Bible including 2 Peter, Thomas Holland attempted to defend the rendering in the KJV as he asserted: "While the phrase *our God and Savior Jesus Christ* is a clear testimony to Christ's deity, the phrase *God and our Savior Jesus Christ* likewise has reference to God and Savior being the same person, namely Jesus Christ" (p. 289).

At its note for 2 Peter 1:1, *the Reformation Heritage KJV Study Bible* noted: "Literally, 'our God and Savior, Jesus Christ,' describing one divine person--the same Greek phrase appears in v. 11, but with 'Lord" in place of 'God.' Christ is Lord and God (John 1:1; 20:28; Rom. 9:5)" (p. 1829). James Scholefield maintained that this verse has "the same construction as in verse 11" where it was rendered in the KJV as "of our Lord and Saviour Jesus Christ" (*Hints*, p. 157). A. T. Robertson wrote: "In 2 Peter 1:11 and 3:18, the pronoun 'our' comes after 'Lord,' but that makes no difference in the idiom. It is 'our Lord and Saviour,' and it is so translated in the English versions. But we have precisely the same idiom in 2 Peter 1:1, 'our God and Saviour Jesus Christ'" (*The Minister*, p. 63). Robertson asserted: "The idiom compels the translation, 'our God and Saviour Jesus Christ" (p. 64). Concerning 2 Peter 1:1, Ralph Wardlaw noted in 1815: "An instance of construction, in every respect the same, occurs at the eleventh verse of this same chapter" (*Discourses*, p. 75). Wardlaw asserted: "It is just as improper to render the words in the first verse, 'through the righteousness of God and our Saviour Jesus Christ,' (unless the appellations 'God and our Saviour' be understood as both connecting with 'Jesus Christ') as it would be to render those in this verse [1:11] 'in the kingdom of the Lord and our Saviour Jesus Christ'" (p. 76). Do KJV-only advocates oppose the same measures and principles being applied to 2 Peter 1:1 as would be applied to 2 Peter 1:11?

Likewise, at Titus 2:13, the NKJV, the MKJV, and several other English translations read "our great God and Savior Jesus Christ," more clearly presenting the deity of Christ than the KJV does. John Wesley translated it as "the great God, even our Saviour Jesus Christ." Joseph Benson observed that Theodore Beza maintained "that one person only is spoken of, namely, Jesus Christ" (*New Testament*, II, p. 472). Granville Sharp noted that Beza "insists, however, that these two titles do not refer to two distinct persons, because the article is omitted before the second" (*Remarks*, p. 22). In the 1599 edition of the Geneva Bible, this note is given for Titus 2:13: "Christ is here most plainly called that mighty God." Francis Turretin (1623-1687) as translated by George Giger wrote: "He is called 'the great God' (Tit. 2:13)--certainly not the Father, but the Son because only one article is prefixed to the words God and Saviour (which would not be the case if they were two persons)" (*Institutes*, I, p. 284). In his 1657 English translation of the 1637 Dutch Annotations at this verse, Theodore Haak noted: "That is, of Jesus Christ, our great God and Saviour; for both these titles are here ascribed to Jesus Christ."

Concerning Titus 2:13 in the Westminster Annotations printed in 1645, this is stated: "To the confutation and confusion of all that deny the Deity of Christ, the Apostle here calleth him not only God, but the great God." In a sermon printed in 1722, Edmund Calamy stated: "There being no article prefixed to *Saviour*, it follows, that the *Great God*, and the *Saviour* spoken of, must be the very same, even *Jesus Christ*, who is mentioned" (*Thirteen Sermons*, pp. 37-38).

A. T. Robertson asserted that our great God and Saviour Jesus Christ "is the necessary meaning of the one article with *theou* and *soteros* just as in 2 Peter 1:1 (*Word Pictures*, IV, p. 604). Concerning Titus 2:13, Granville Sharp stated: "This testimony, therefore, of the sacred text, in favour of our Lord's divine nature, ought not to be withheld from the mere English reader" (*Remarks*, p. 51). William Hendriksen wrote: "No valid reason has ever been found which would show that the (Granville Sharp) rule does not apply in the present case [Titus 2:13]" (*Timothy and Titus*, p. 375). Prince Hoare cited or reported that "the only sense in which the Greek Fathers understand that important passage, for instance, Titus 2:13, is that which is ascribed to it by Mr. Sharp" (*Memoirs of Granville Sharp*, I, p. 501). Thomas Burgess (1756-1837) wrote: "That Jesus Christ is 'our great God and Saviour,' we know from the testimony of St. Paul (Titus 2:13), interpreted by the unanimous judgment of the Greek Fathers, and of all the Latin Fathers but one, concurring with an invariable idiom of the Greek language" (*Tracts on the Divinity of Christ*, p. 134). Albert Barnes observed: "The ancients, in general, interpreted it as meaning, 'The glorious appearing of our great God and Saviour Jesus Christ.' This sense has been vindicated by the labours of Beza, Whitby, Bull, Matthaei, and Middleton (on the Greek article), and is the common interpretation of those who claim to be orthodox" (*Notes on the Epistles of Paul*, p. 316).

Concerning Titus 2:13, Warren Wiersbe wrote: "This verse boldly affirms that Jesus Christ is God, for there is only one article in the Greek" (*Be Faithful*, p. 110). R. A. Torrey asserted that "in the correct translation of Titus 2:13 … our Lord Jesus is spoken of as, 'our great God and Saviour Jesus Christ" (*Fundamental Doctrines*, p. 78). Concerning the rendering "of our great God and Saviour Jesus Christ," James Boise asserted: "This is the simplest and most natural construction grammatically; one article with both genitives, and the pronoun limiting both" (*Notes on the Greek Text*, p. 570). Concerning Titus 2:13, R. L. Dabney asserted: "It should be 'of our great God and Saviour, Jesus Christ" (*Systematic Theology*, p. 190). In answer to the question "do the Scriptures teach that Christ is the true God," William Weeks cited: "Titus 2:13—Greek, 'our great God and Saviour Jesus Christ'" (*Catechism of Scripture Doctrine*, p. 8).

The 1611 edition of the KJV had a comma after God at Titus 2:13 [the great God, and our Saviour Jesus Christ]. The first KJV edition printed in America in 1782 and KJV editions printed at Oxford in 1788 and 1795 still have a comma after God at Titus 2:13. Scrivener observed: "In regard to weightier matters, the comma put by 1611 after "God" in Titus 2:13 is fitly removed by 1769 modern, that 'the great God and our Saviour' may be seen to be joint predicates of the same Divine person" (*Authorized Edition*, p. 87). The 1743 and 1760 Cambridge editions edited by F. S. Parris had removed the comma at Titus 2:13 before the 1769 Oxford followed them. Concerning Titus 2:13, J. H. Murray maintained that the KJV "makes it as if two persons were spoken of, the Father and the Son; where the Son only, in the original Greek, is mentioned" (*Help*, p. 64). Concerning the KJV's rendering at this verse, Gordon Clark observed: "This allows the objector to separate the great God from our Lord Jesus Christ" (*Trinity*, p. 16). James D. Price asserted: "Some versions, like the KJV and ASV, do not render this verse as referring to Christ as God" (*King James Onlyism*, p. 323). In 1829, Edward Burton contended: "In our authorized version, the words certainly do not necessarily imply that *our Saviour Jesus Christ* is *the great God*; but if we were to translate them, as we are equally authorized in doing, '*the glorious appearing of our great God and Saviour Jesus Christ*,' it would be obvious to every reader, that the expression *great God* referred to Jesus Christ" (*Testimonies*, p. 113).

John Dick (1764-1833) included Titus 2:13 as an example of verses "in which the name of God is given to our Saviour, but the evidence does not appear to common readers, in consequence of the manner in which they have been translated" (*Lectures on Theology*, I, p. 316). John Dick gave "our Great God and Saviour Jesus Christ" as "a translation more conformable to the original" (p. 317). I. M. Halderman wrote: "Under the inspiration of the Holy Spirit the Apostle Paul speaks of Him as 'our **great God** and Saviour Jesus Christ' (correct reading) (Titus 2:13)" (*Bible Expositions,* I, p. 456). Augustus Strong regarded Titus 2:13 to be "a direct, definite, and even studied declaration of Christ's divinity" (*Systematic Theology,* p. 307). William Evans listed Titus 2:13 as a place where Jesus Christ is called God (*Great Doctrines of the Bible,* p. 58). Likewise, Michael Bere cited Titus 2:13 as a place where Jesus is called God (*Bible Doctrines for Today,* Book I, p. 170). In its note for this verse, *the Holman KJV Study Bible* noted: "The reference to Jesus as God and Saviour is a strong affirmation of His deity" (p. 2045). In his commentary on the Pastoral Epistles, John Philips stated: "Both phrases refer to the same individual. Here we have a clear affirmation of the deity of Christ. He who is 'the Great God' is also 'our Saviour Jesus Christ'" (p. 288). E. W. Bullinger quoted from Titus 2:13 once as follows: "of our great God and Saviour" (*Figures,* p. 505), and he maintained that the latter clause of this verse is a "*hendiadys*: One person being meant, not two" (p. 669). J. L. Dagg advocated that the rendering at Titus 2:13 be amended to "our great God and Saviour, Jesus Christ" (*Manual of Theology,* pp. 183-184). Edward Bickersteth presented or rendered it as "our Great God and Saviour Jesus Christ" (*Rock of Ages,* p. 44). Concerning Titus 2:13, Ralph Wardlaw wrote: "To avoid all ambiguity, and to express the precise sense of the original, they ought to be rendered, 'the glorious appearing of our great God and Saviour Jesus Christ'" (*Discourses,* p. 76). Timothy Dwight asserted concerning Titus 2:13: "In the Greek it is *the Great God even our Saviour Jesus Christ*, or our Great God and Saviour Jesus Christ" (*Theology Explained,* I, p. 526).

The context of Titus 2:13 concerning the appearing clearly indicates that there is a reference to one person--our God and Saviour Jesus Christ. John Ankerberg and John Weldon maintained that "even the context of Titus 2:13 shows that one Person, not two, was in Paul's mind, for Paul wrote of the 'glorious appearing' of that Person" (*Facts on Jehovah's Witnesses,* p. 24). Gordon Clark noted: "The subject matter is the glorious return of our Lord. One person returns; not the Father, but the Son. Hence the great God and Jesus is the same person" (*The Trinity,* p. 17). Clark added: "It is difficult in Greek to separate 'of us' (our) from 'the great God'" (Ibid.). In his commentary on the Pastoral Epistles, Gordon Clark observed: "A more doctrinal argument is that only Christ *appears*--the second coming is not a coming of the Father; therefore the great God who appears must be Christ" (p. 224). In his commentary on Titus, John MacArthur asserted: "Our great God and Savior is one of the many plain declarations in Scripture of the deity of Jesus Christ." MacArthur also noted that "both of the singular pronouns in the following verse [14] ('who,' *hos,* and 'Himself,' *heauton*) refer back to a single person" (p. 120). MacArthur added: "Perhaps most importantly, the New Testament nowhere speaks of the appearing or Second Coming of God the Father but only of the Son" (p. 121). John Gill wrote: "He is called 'the great God,' whose glorious appearing, and not the Father's, saints are directed to look for; besides, this great God, is explained of Jesus Christ our Saviour in the next clause, Titus 2:13" (*Complete Body,* pp. 240-241). Reformer Francis Turretin noted: "*Epiphaneia* is never attributed to the Father, but always to Christ. He, whose advent we look for, is said to have given himself for us (Tit. 2:14), which applies to Christ alone" (*Institutes,* I, p. 284). Consider also 2 Timothy 1:10--"appearing of our Saviour Jesus Christ." James Buswell noted: "It is clear from the entire New Testament that it is Christ whose glorious appearing is expected: Christ Jesus is our great God and Saviour" (*Systematic Theology,* p. 104). Concerning this verse in his *Commentary on the Pastoral Epistles,* H. Harvey noted: "The following context, in the relative clause (verse 14), 'who gave himself for us,' plainly relates only to Christ, but naturally requires us to take the whole preceding expression, 'our Great God and Saviour, Jesus Christ,' as its antecedent" (pp. 139-140). Concerning this verse in his commentary, Robert Horton asserted: "The qualifying description of verse 14, which refer to Jesus Christ, completely overbalances the sentence if Christ is to be separated from 'the great God'" (p. 186).

At Romans 9:5, some pre-1611 English Bibles and some post-1611 English translations translate the verse clearly to indicate that Christ is "God." For example, the 1560 Geneva Bible translated the end of this verse as follows: "Christ *came*, who is God over all blessed for ever, Amen." A note in the Geneva Bible stated concerning Romans 9:5: "A most manifest testimony of the Godhead and divinity of Christ." James D. Price identified the NKJV as one of the versions that translate Romans 9:5 "in an unambiguous way, making it clear that the Greek text refers to Christ as God" (*King James Onlyism*, p. 322). Concerning Romans 9:5 in a sermon printed in 1722, Edmund Calamy asserted: "He is declared to be *God over all, blessed for ever*" (*Thirteen Sermons*, p. 38). In comments about Romans 9:5, John Dagg observed: "Christ is here called God; not in some subordinate sense, but over all, and blessed for ever" (*Manual of Theology*, p. 182). Concerning this verse in the American Baptist Publication Society's *American Commentary on the New Testament*, Albert Arnold wrote: "We adhere to the simplest and most natural punctuation and explanation of the verse, therefore, and regard it as a direct affirmation of the Godhead of Christ, parallel with John 1:1 and 20:28" (p. 220). John Brown pointed out: "He [Christ] is not only 'over all,' but 'God over all'--God in no Inferior or secondary sense, but, as the prophet says, 'the mighty God' [Isa. 9:6]; as Paul elsewhere says, 'the great God our Saviour' [Tit. 2:13]; and as John says, 'the true God and eternal life' [1 John 5:20]" (*Analytical Exposition of Romans*, p. 306). Charles Hodge wrote: "Paul evidently declares that Christ, who, he had just said, was, as to his human nature, or as a man, descended from the Israelites, is, in another respect, the supreme God, or God over all, and blessed for ever" (*Romans*, p. 300). Concerning Romans 9:5, Gordon Clark stated: "The meaning clearly is, 'Christ ... who being God over all is blessed forever'" (*Trinity*, p. 16). James Buswell asserted that "Paul referred to Christ with the words, 'He being God over all, blessed for evermore' (Rom. 9:5)" (*Systematic Theology*, p. 104). Concerning "God blessed for ever" at Romans 9:5, Francis Turretin asserted: "This cannot be referred by a doxological apostrophe to the Father because neither the thing demands, nor will the series of words admit it. The article with the participle is relative; not beginning a new sentence, but continuing one already begun. Nor can it be referred to the Father, but to Christ, the immediately preceding antecedent" (*Institutes*, I, p. 284). Francis Bassett maintained that this verse (Rom. 9:5) shows "how seriously the teaching conveyed in a group of words may be affected by mere varieties of punctuation" (*Examination*, p. 64).

At John 8:58, some English translations, such as Wesley's New Testament, the 1961 Wuest's Expanded Translation, 1971 KJII, 1982 NKJV, 1985 Literal Translation in *The Interlinear Bible*, 1990 MKJV, 2010 English Majority Text Version, 2014 Modern English Version, and Wilbur Pickering's 2016 English translation, capitalize "I AM" to make sure the reader knows that Christ was claiming here to be God. Does the NKJV along with these other English translations more clearly indicate a connection between this verse and Exodus 3:14 than does the KJV? Oliver B. Greene wrote that "in John 8:58 He [Christ] told the Jews, 'Before Abraham was, I AM'" (*Bible Truth*, p. 105). In this same book, Oliver B. Greene noted that Jesus "had plainly told the Pharisees, 'Before Abraham was, I AM' (John 8:58), and they took up stones to stone Him because He applied Jehovah's name to Himself" (p. 87). I. M. Halderman asserted: "The 'I AM' of John 8:58, is the 'I AM' of Exodus 3:14" (*Bible Expositions*, I, p. 519). Peter Ruckman referred to "the tremendous 'I AM' (John 8:58)" (*Bible Babel*, p. 40). Jay Green maintained that "those [translations] who do not capitalize 'I AM' fail to reveal to the reader why the Jews picked up stones to stone Christ. It was because by saying I AM, our Lord was telling them that He was God" (*Gnostics, the New Versions*, p. 34). At John 8:58, the 1560 Geneva Bible has this marginal note for "I am": "Not only God, but the Mediator between God and man, appointed from before all eternity." In his commentary on John, Elmer Towns observed: "The Jews of Christ's time knew that when He said, 'I am,' He was claiming, 'I am Jehovah of the Old Testament.'" Towns added: "Christ is implying, 'I am ... I am,' the self-existent One. He is claiming to be their God" (p. xiv).

In additions to the allegations against a number of renderings in the NKJV, some KJV defenders have also attacked it for a symbol put on its title page by its publisher Thomas Nelson. In a section heading, Ben Pierce alleged that the NKJV's cover has a "Satanic triquetra symbol" (*Valiant for the Truth*, p. 202).   James Rasbeary contended that "it is an ancient pagan symbol still used today by Satanists, pagans, witches, and New Agers" (*What's Wrong with the Old Black Book*, p. 200).   Gail Riplinger claimed that "the number 666 in the forum of a Mobius symbol appears on the cover of the *New King James Version*" (*New Age Bible Versions*, p. 101).   James Melton contended that the NKJV logo "is a '666' symbol of the pagan trinity which was used in the ancient Egyptian mysteries" (*Fighting Back*, p. 24).   Charles Barrier alleged that the symbol "is actually a witchcraft symbol used to represent the *Pagan Trinity* or *Unholy Trinity*, and is a number symbol representing an intertwined 666" (*Looking for the Lamp*, p. 12).

Just because a symbol may have been used by others with a different meaning is not actually proof that is its meaning as used by the NKJV's publisher Thomas Nelson.   Can knowledge of the publisher's own actual meaning for its symbol be gained?   In its 1991 KJV-NKJV Parallel Bible, Thomas Nelson identified its logo on the NKJV's title page as "an ancient symbol for the Trinity."   The publisher maintained that its triquetra "comprises three interwoven arcs, distinct yet equal and inseparable, symbolizing that the Father, Son, and Holy Spirit are three distinct yet equal Persons and indivisibly one God."   Therefore, this publisher has clearly stated and identified its authentic meaning determined for its use of this symbol.   Gary Zeolla maintained that "the triquetra is not an 'image' of God that people create to worship" and that "it is a symbol used to illustrate a very difficult theological concept" (*Differences Between Bible Versions*, p. 192).   Dean Moe wrote: "The triquetra is a three-pointed trinangular figure portraying the 'three-in-one' of the Trinity" (*Christian Symbols Handbook*, p. 32).   In KJV-only seeming attempts to smear the NKJV by use of a guilt-by-association argument, do KJV-only advocates ignore the possibility that the same symbol can be used with different meanings just as the same word can be used with different meanings?   How does this symbol have any bearing on the accuracy or inaccuracy of the translating in the NKJV?   For example, should the symbol or token of a rainbow (Gen. 9:13) be considered to have the same meaning for believers as it may have for many unbelievers or pagans?

Would KJV defenders use the same measures and condemn the KJV if a publisher included any symbol or symbols for God?   Did the first 1611 edition of the KJV have any symbols or images to depict God the Father, the Lord Jesus Christ, the Holy Spirit, or the Trinity?   Laurence Vance acknowledged that "the engraved title page depicts the Trinity in the upper panel in the form of the Divine Name, a dove, and a lamb" (*King James, His Bible,* p. 55).   Gordon Campbell maintained that "the godhead is represented by symbols rather than pictorial representation" (*Bible*, p. 100).   Concerning the engraved 1611 title page, Alister McGrath maintained that "the upper panel depicts the Trinity in a conventional style" (*In the Beginning*, p. 207).   McGrath noted that "the 'lamb and flag' is generally interpreted as a symbol of the resurrection of the crucified Christ" (p. 209).   Benson Bobrick affirmed that the 1611 title page depicted "the Holy Spirit in the form of a dove" (*Wide as the Waters*, p. 252).   At the bottom of the title page of the 1611 KJV, Geddes MacGregor observed that it has "a traditional symbol of the redeeming work of Christ, especially in the Eucharist--a pelican 'vulning' herself, that is, wounding herself with her beak to feed her young with her own blood" (*Literary History,* p. 205).   Concerning the 1611 title page, Derek Wilson asserted that "an interesting feature is the inclusion of Catholic imagery" (*People's Bible*, p. 123).   Gordon Campbell claimed: "The figure of Peter is strikingly Catholic: not only is he the sole possessor of the keys (whereas on the Coverdale cover all apostles have been issued with keys), but he is paired with Paul on either side of the godhead, which is the normal arrangement in Catholic altarpieces" (*Bible*, pp. 100-101).   Derek Wilson noted: "The apostles are shown with the traditional symbols of their martyrdom and, at the foot of the page, there is a drawing of a pelican in her piety (a heraldic device depicting a pelican feeding her young with her own blood), which Catholic convention employed to represent the sacrifice of Christ in the mass" (*People's Bible*, p. 123).   Steve Halla wrote: "Boel's choice of iconography reflects King James's desire for Christian unity by combining both traditional 'Catholic' iconography, such as Peter and Paul and the Pelican feeding its young, with iconography distinctly reflective of Protestant iconoclastic sensibilities" (Neste, *KJV400*, p. 119). Alister McGrath observed: "There is a curious irony to this symbol. In the Middle Ages, the image of a pelican came to be linked with the Lord's Supper or Mass, especially with the medieval ecclesiastical feast of Corpus Christi" (*In the Beginning*, p. 210). Benson Bobrick maintained that the 1611 title page has "a pelican (symbol of Christ) shown feeding her young with blood from her own breast" (*Wide as the Waters*, p. 252). In an example of another KJV edition, a Family and Library Reference Edition published by Good News Publishers (with a 1968 copyright date by Royal Publishers) has a page of historic Christian symbols that are also used on its border designs and other special pages. These symbols include a symbol for the Trinity. Did the publisher of the 1982 NKJV possibly or likely get the idea of using a symbol for the Trinity from an earlier edition of the KJV?

Would KJV-only advocates use the same measures and condemn the 1611 KJV if its publisher used any pagan symbols or images in it? At Psalm 141 and 1 Peter 3, the 1611 edition of the KJV has an initial letter with a figure of the Greek god Pan. In the initial letter for Matthew 1 and Revelation 1, the 1611 KJV has an illustration with the Roman god Neptune with sea horses. At Romans 1, the 1611 edition of the KJV has an initial letter with a naked, sprouting nymph Daphne. It may be that some of the initial letters in the original 1611 KJV edition with mythological scenes may be from the same source as those used in an edition of the Bishops' Bible. T. H. Darlow and H. F. Moule suggested that some of the ornamental initials in the 1611 resemble "those used in folio editions of the Bishops' Bible" (*Historical Catalogue,* I, p. 135). In introductory articles in Hendrickson's reprint of the 1611 KJV, Alfred Pollard pointed out: "In the New Testament two of the mythological ten-line set, the use of which in the Bishops' Bible had justly been censured, reappear at the beginning of Matthew and Romans" (p. 45, footnote 2). John Eadie affirmed that the printers of the 1611 used some of "the same head pieces, woodcuts, and other embellishments, which had appeared in the Bishops'" (*English Bible,* II, p. 291). Eadie pointed out that "the figure of Neptune with his trident and horses, which appears so often in the Bishops', stands at the beginning of Matthew" (p. 291). H. W. Hoare noted that the figure "of Neptune with his trident and horses was borrowed from the Bishops' Bible" (*Evolution,* pp. 274-275). William Loftie affirmed that "the figure of Neptune, which in the largests of the Bishops' was made frequently available, now headed the gospel of St. Matthew" [in the 1611] (*Century of Bibles,* p. 6). The initial letters can be seen in the large 1611 digital reproduction by Greyden Press, in the 2010 reprint of the 1611 by Oxford University Press, and in the 2011 reprint by Zondervan, but the 1611 reprints in Roman type published by Thomas Nelson or Hendrickson Publishers do not have them. David Norton has a page of illustrations that included three initials from the 1611 in his book, and he asserted that it is unlikely that the KJV translators approved of their use (*Textual History*, pp. 51-52). Gordon Campbell wrote: "The initials portraying Daphne and Neptune had been used in the Bishops' Bible, and had attracted censure from some quarters, so their reuse must have been deliberate. In any case, there was no reason for the translators to disapprove" (*Bible*, p. 101). Donald Brake commented: "Many consider it a mystery why the King James translators, all ministers of the gospel, allowed pagan images to illustrate the initial letters of God's Word. While readers today might consider depictions of mythological images contrary to the biblical message, the translators likely did not view them as a threat to Christian belief" (*Visual History of the KJB*, pp. 179-180). Donald Brake asserted that the 1611's initial letter at Hebrews 1 is a "demonic face with bat wings" (p. 178). Brake maintained that the 1611's initial letter at 2 Corinthians 1, Galatians 1, Philippians 1, 2 Thessalonians 1, Philemon 1, and 1 Peter 1 is "two demons depicted with horns and pitchforks" (p. 179). In addition, the 1611 KJV edition referred to the signs of the Zodiac in its calendar: "Sol in Aquario" (p. xvii), "Sol in Piscibus" (p. xviii), "Sol in Aries" (p. xix), "Sol in Tauro" (p. xx), "Sol in Gemini" (p. xxi), etc.

Some publishers have printed editions of the KJV with lodge or masonic symbols on the cover, title page, or presentation pages. Some examples of these would be a 1928 edition printed by Oxford University Press, a 1940 edition printed by A. J. Holman, a 1941 edition printed by A. J. Holman, a 1946 edtion by the National Bible Press, a 1949 edition by John A. Hertel, an undated edition by World Publishing Company, and an undated edition printed by the Oxford University Press with lessons of the Order of the Eastern Star. The 1928 Oxford KJV edition has a masonic symbol [a square & compass with a G in the middle] on its cover and on presentation pages. The 1940 A. J. Holman KJV edition also has this same masonic symbol on its front cover and on presentation pages. This 1940 edition also has copyright dates of 1924, 1925, 1929, 1930, 1932, 1933, 1935, and 1939, indicating that this masonic edition may have been printed other years. Three of the above mentioned KJV editions have a star on the cover for the Order of the Eastern Star.

How does a publisher's use of a symbol have any direct bearing on the accuracy or inaccuracy of the translating in a Bible translation? Would allegations concerning a symbol on the cover or title page possibly be an example of use of a red herring fallacy? It also seems to be an improper effort to associate the NKJV translators with unbelievers that had no part in its making [fallacy of guilt by association]. Furthermore, sound evidence clearly demonstrated that KJV-only advocates have not applied their own allegations about symbols to those that have been printed in or on editions of the KJV. Would that suggest that their allegations concerning this symbol on editions of the NKJV involved use of double standards or unjust measures?

In a taped interview with Texe Marrs, Gail Riplinger asserted that "the KJV always has easier words than the NKJV." Gail Riplinger asked: "Why does the NKJV use harder words than the KJV?" (*Language of the KJB*, p. 152). KJV defender R. B. Ouellette claimed that it would be a false statement to say that the KJV "is harder to read and understand than modern Bibles" (*A More Sure Word*, p. 150). As support for his claim, R. B. Ouellette asserted that the KJV "has a significantly lower average syllable count" (Ibid.). Jim Taylor claimed that "the NKJV is slightly more difficult to read than the King James Version" (*In Defense of the TR*, p. 103). Gail Riplinger maintained that "the KJV averages less syllables per word" (*Language*, p. 159). Gail Riplinger claimed that the KJV's average was 1.310 syllables per word and that the NKJV's average was 1.313 syllables per word (p. 160). Would three one-thousandths [.003] be a significant difference?

Furthermore, there may be some sound reasons that explain why the KJV may have a lower average syllable count that would have no direct bearing on whether or not it is actually easier to read and especially on whether or not it is easier to understand. For example, in most editions of the KJV there are several commonly used words that are divided into two or more words where the exact same word united as one word in another English translation may count as a longer, multi-syllable word. Some examples include "to day," "to morrow," "for ever," "for evermore," "son in law," "father in law," "mother in law," "daughter in law," "strong holds," "way side," "high way," "good will," "any more," "any thing," "mean while," "mean time," "some time," "sea side," "sea shore," "mad man," "free man," and "cart wheel." There may also be other such words. While later KJV editors changed or corrected a few of the uses of "lift" in the 1611 edition for the past tense "lifted," there are other times where a present KJV has "lift" while the NKJV may have "lifted." Sometimes the NKJV may have an adverb spelling which may add a syllable while the KJV has an adjective spelling used as an adverb [for example, "more frequently" in the NKJV for "more frequent" in the KJV]. The KJV may present numbers with more words with fewer syllables [for example "forty and three" in the KJV where the NKJV has "forty-three"]. A few words may be united in the KJV that are divided into two words in another translation. Overall, because several of those words divided in the KJV are much more commonly used words, they would contribute to giving the KJV a lower average syllable count. Those divided words do not actually make the KJV easier to read and easier to understand. By the way, some present KJV editions would unite some of those words such as "to day" to either "to-day" or "today" so that those KJV editions would have a different average syllable count. Many times the 1611 KJV edition had "shall be" united as one, longer word "shalbe," and it would likely have a different average syllable count than a present KJV edition.   The KJV could perhaps have as many as several thousand uses of the one-syllable word "and" where the NKJV does not, which would also lower the KJV's syllable count.   More importantly, the KJV has a number of archaic words or words used with archaic meanings that may be shorter or have fewer syllables than their present English equivalents.   Some examples could include the following: "turtle" for "turtledove," "vale" for "valley," "dearth" for "famine," "trump" for "trumpet," "tongue" for "language," "coasts" for "borders," "host" for "army," "wood" for "woods" or "forest," "table" for "tablet," "even" for "evening," "let" for "hinder," "anon" for "immediately," "oft" for "often," "sod" for "boiled," "awaked" for "awakened," "jeoparded" for "jeopardized," "mete" for "measure," "dure" for "endure," "ware" for "aware," "quick" for "living" or "alive," "mean" for "common," "still" for "continually," "attent" for "attentive," "by and by" for "immediately," "ere" for "before," "minish" for "diminish," "fine" for "refine," "grave" or "engrave," "astonied" for "astonished," "strange" for "foreign," and "rid" for "deliver."   While such words may help reduce the KJV's average syllable count, they do not actually make it easier to read and understand.   Do KJV-only advocates prove that average syllable counts would clearly demonstrate which English translation is actually easier for readers to understand?   Sound reasons or factors have indicated why KJV-only claims concerning "average syllable count" may be misleading and misused.   Mark Ward observed that reading-level "tools measure a word's complexity by syllable count, but that's not a reliable way of judging whether a word can be understood" (*Authorized*, p. 54).   Mark Ward also asserted: "Reading-level analyses run by computers do not yield reliable or useful results when applied to archaic English" (p. 59).   KJV defenders or KJV-only authors do not actually prove the broad-sweeping assertion that the KJV is easier to read and easier to understand than the NKJV to be true.

R. B. Ouellette alleged that "the New King James [is] more than 19,000 words shorter than the King James Bible" (*A More Sure Word*, p. 147), but he does not provide documentation or any evidence for his claim.   Do KJV defenders check to see if the KJV may have more words than the number found in its own original-language texts?   Do KJV defenders check the evidence and see whether there may be valid or sound reasons for a difference in number of words in Bible translations?   One English word alone could account for a majority of these claimed fewer words in the NKJV.   According to concordances, the KJV has the word "and" 51,713 times while the NKJV has "and" 38,260 times.   As the Geneva Bible sometimes does, the NKJV may have another coordinating conjunction instead of "and" in many places.   Nevertheless, the NKJV does likely omit use of a conjunction "and" in thousands of places where the KJV has it.   Hebrew and Greek may frequently repeat the coordinating conjunction "and" where it is considered unnecessary or even incorrect in present-day standard English.   Places where it sometimes considered unnecessary to include "and" in presenting the meaning of the original-language words include at the beginning of sentences, in series of nouns or other words, and in the presentation of numbers.   The KJV itself does not have this word "and" every time the Hebrew or Greek may have an equivalent coordinating conjunction.   KJV defender Kirk DiVietro claimed: "The conjunction does not always need to be translated into English.   This is a matter of translator's discretion and not textual reading" (*Where the KJB Leaves the Greek Text*, p. 8). The previous paragraph about syllable counts would explain one reason why the NKJV may be supposedly hundreds of words shorter than the KJV.   In this case, the NKJV may have the exact same words as the KJV, but it may present as one word many times what the KJV presents as two words or three words.   In several and perhaps many cases, the NKJV may accurately present the same basic meaning with fewer words than in the KJV.   For example, the NKJV may accurately use two words (its foot) where it takes the KJV four words to present the same meaning (the foot of it).   Sometimes the KJV may use several English words or a phrase to translate one original-language word while the NKJV may translate it by using one English word. In places, the NKJV may translate without adding any or as many words in italics.   One example would be where the NKJV has "did evil" several times while the KJV has "did *that which was* evil." It may also be possible that updating Elizabethan English to present-day standard English could sometimes result in the use of fewer words.   There may be other valid or good reasons for why the NKJV may have fewer words in some places than the KJV has.   Would the same measure be used to suggest that the KJV should have the same exact number of words in every verse that was in the pre-1611 English Bibles? The makers of the KJV omitted many words, phrases, or clauses found in the Bishops' Bible of which the KJV was officially a revision, and believers did not object to it having fewer words. Facts from the Geneva Bible also demonstrated that there were many differences in number of words in many cases between translating in it and translating in the KJV.

Concluding observations concerning three English Bibles and a KJV-only view

In example after example, it should have become very clear that KJV defenders or KJV-only advocates have not applied their own stated principles, standards, criteria, or measures for Bible translations consistently, soundly, and justly. In their writings, many KJV-only authors have not clearly and precisely defined all their terms that would relate to the subject of Bible translations. Furthermore, they have not demonstrated that their definitions and understanding of their terms are correct. They also have not shown that they would apply the terms consistently and justly. Would they attempt to impose their inconsistent or imperfect definitions and understandings on other believers? The same exact measures or criteria applied to the Geneva Bible or to the KJV have not been applied consistently and justly to the NKJV. Likewise, the same exact measures applied to the NKJV have not been applied consistently and justly to the Geneva Bible and the KJV. KJV defenders themselves have in effect become witnesses against themselves when their own claims concerning the Geneva Bible are compared to their claims against the NKJV. Actual facts from the Geneva Bible, the KJV, and the NKJV make clear and convincing the case for observing or concluding that unjust measures or double standards have been used by KJV defenders in their inconsistent and extreme allegations against the NKJV. This evident use of inconsistent, unjust measures or standards is wrong and contrary to scriptural truth. Righteous judgments cannot be made using unscriptural, unjust measures. All the sound evidence and relevant facts have not been consistently and carefully considered by KJV defenders in their writings. Instead, many important, relevant, significant facts have been overlooked, ignored, or avoided by KJV defenders. KJV-only advocates have evidently jumped to hasty generalizations concerning the NKJV based on too little evidence, on biased evidence, or on use of unjust measures. Important facts from the 1560 Geneva Bible have soundly countered or refuted several misleading or inaccurate KJV-only allegations against the NKJV. The KJV-only reasoning evident in their very own allegations against the NKJV cannot be applied consistently and justly without harming the KJV itself.

KJV-only allegations against the NKJV clearly demonstrate that many KJV-only advocates do not approach the NKJV with the same attitude with which they would approach the Geneva Bible or the KJV. They seem to approach the NKJV as a Bible critic instead as a serious, seeking reader of a Bible translation. Evidently, KJV-only advocates come to inspect a mirror [the NKJV] (perhaps using a magnifying glass) instead of coming to see themselves in this mirror of the Scriptures translated into present-day English in the NKJV. Do they only look inconsistently and critically **at** this mirror and refuse to look **in** it? Would they read the NKJV as the word of God translated into English and with a willingness to obey and apply the scriptural truths in its verses to their own lives? Because they may come to the NKJV solely as a critic or because they may read against it, they may be unable to see that it would belong in the same family of Bible translations as the Geneva Bible and the KJV. They do not respect, accept, or believe the NKJV as a good Bible translation which can communicate to them the words of God in English. Could KJV-only advocates suppose that they see errors in the NKJV because they had already assumed that they are there or because they have been told that they were there? Perhaps their own KJV-only bias could prevent them from being able to see the places where the Geneva Bible and the NKJV more accurately translates the same underlying original-language texts of Scripture than the KJV does. Could rejection of consistent truth and actual facts keep them from being able to see that the NKJV would be clearly a better overall English translation than the Geneva Bible which KJV-only advocates have praised? KJV-only advocates will inconsistently accuse others of being critics while they themselves may act as subjective, intemperate, extreme critics of Bible translations such as the NKJV.

In KJV-only writings, no positive, clear, consistent, wholesome, sound, just, true, scriptural case has been made for a modern KJV-only view. KJV-only authors have not actually demonstrated that the KJV-only view is the most consistent position with what the Bible says about itself since some important KJV-only claims and aspects of KJV-only reasoning conflict with a just application of scriptural truths. KJV-only advocates have not clearly proven that their human KJV-only reasoning is consistent, sound, just, true, and scriptural. KJV-only authors have not resolved and settled the Bible translation issue. KJV-only advocates have made conflicting and even contradictory claims that fail to lead soundly to their unproven KJV-only conclusions. The fallacies (false arguments) often evident in stated KJV-only reasoning are obviously not true. A modern KJV-only view or doctrine has not been demonstrated to be determined and advocated solely from the Scriptures themselves. KJV-only opinions and inconsistent human KJV-only reasoning with use of unjust measures and use of fallacies have led and will lead to errors in concept concerning translation, Scripture, inspiration, and preservation. It has been demonstrated by sound evidence, actual facts, and scriptural truths that human KJV-only reasoning/teaching has led to actual errors in KJV-only assertions concerning the Geneva Bible, in KJV-only claims for the KJV, and in KJV-only allegations against the NKJV. According to scriptural truths, God would have a controversy with the use of unjust measures evident in KJV-only writings. A KJV-only view in which its own stated principles, measures, or standards are not applied consistently, soundly, and justly to all Bible translations that should be on its good line/stream is hardly a view worth holding and advocating. Evidently based on their own writings, KJV defenders or KJV-only advocates will accept selectively any data or evidence assumed to support their view while they will reject all the data, facts, and evidence to the contrary regardless of its quality and quantity. How would KJV defenders disobeying scriptural instructions or scriptural commands by making some false accusations or false reports against the NKJV and its translators be honoring God and the Scriptures? A proper, sound defense of the KJV as what it actually is will be hindered and even harmed by the use of unjust measures or double standards and by the use of fallacies that are evident in KJV-only claims and allegations. If pro-KJV advocates are followers of that which is only good in the advocating of their only claims for the KJV or of their KJV-only view, how could examining carefully, consistently, and justly those claims harm (1 Peter 3:13)?

D. A. Waite claimed: "The New King James is not a revision of The King James Bible, but a completely different translation" (*Central Seminary Refuted*, p. 24). When all the relevant evidence is justly acknowledged and evaluated, the NKJV can properly and accurately be considered a revision of the KJV in the same sense (univocally) or after the same fashion that the KJV was a revision of the pre-1611 English Bibles such as the Geneva Bible or the Bishops' Bible. Just as the KJV is considered a revision of Tyndale, the NKJV could also be. Many actual verifiable facts have clearly demonstrated that the KJV translators made the same-type changes or revisions to the pre-1611 English Bibles that NKJV translators made to the KJV. All the many changes that the KJV translators made to the pre-1611 English Bibles are not entirely different than the changes that the NKJV translators made to the KJV. The KJV was not merely a slight or minor revision of the pre-1611 English Bibles as verifiable facts from those Bibles would demonstrate and have demonstrated. The KJV translators even made some textual changes or revisions to the pre-1611 English Bibles of which the KJV is a revision. The KJV could be considered as much an extensive revision of the trusted Geneva Bible and of the Bishops' Bible as the NKJV is of the KJV. Hundreds and even thousands of differences could be noted between the Geneva Bible and the KJV, and yet KJV-only authors have claimed that they are "basically the same" Bibles. The makers of the KJV were Bible revisers of the pre-1611 English Bible just as the makers of the NKJV were Bible revisers of the 1611 KJV. The KJV and the NKJV can soundly and justly be considered to be as much "basically the same" Bibles as the Geneva Bible and the KJV are considered to be. If the Geneva Bible and the KJV can properly be considered "practically identical," the KJV and the NKJV could also be considered the same. The NKJV can soundly and accurately be regarded as a genuine revision of the KJV in the same sense as the KJV is a genuine revision of the Geneva Bible or the Bishops' Bible.

The NKJV can soundly or justly be considered part of the same family of Bibles, from the same original-language manuscript trail, on the same tree of Bibles, or in the same stream of Bibles as the Geneva Bible and as the KJV. According to a consistent application of the KJV-only view's good-tree-of-Bibles or pure-stream-of-Bibles argument, the NKJV should be placed on the same tree/stream/line with the Geneva Bible, the KJV, and its other included Bibles. The NKJV would reflect the heritage of the Received Text as well as the Geneva Bible or the KJV do. Along with being a revision of earlier English Bibles, the NKJV is also a translation of the preserved Scriptures in the original languages in the same sense (univocally) that the Geneva Bible and the KJV are. In addition, the NKJV can as soundly or justly be classified as being overall a literal or formal-equivalent translation in the same sense as the Geneva Bible or the KJV can be. The NKJV is the word of God translated into English in the same sense (univocally) or in the same way that the Geneva Bible or the KJV is the word of God translated into English. As a Bible translation, the NKJV is profitable for doctrine in the same way and in the same sense that the Geneva Bible and the KJV are profitable for doctrine. Scriptural truths and many facts from the Geneva Bible, the KJV, and the NKJV have provided sound support for these observations or conclusions. Will KJV-only advocates deal objectively and justly with all the facts provided for their consideration? KJV defenders have failed to make a sound, convincing case for their allegations against the NKJV.

An accurate translation of God's Word may be properly used as a reliable authority for that language. A good Bible translation has sufficient derived authority without any need to try to claim that it is something that it is not. Saying an accurate translation can be **a** proper standard or authority is very different from claiming that it is **the** final authority [beyond which there is no other]. According to scriptural truths, any errors introduced into a Bible translation by imperfect men can be and should be corrected. It was sound and scriptural for actual errors in the 1611 edition of the KJV to be corrected and for actual errors in later KJV editions to be corrected. On earth, the final or highest authority for settling or trying differences between Bible translations should be the preserved Scriptures in the original languages. Any accurate translation must remain connected with the preserved Scriptures in the original languages as a branch to the true vine. To separate purposefully a translation from its underlying original-language texts would be to undermine or destroy that translation's actual foundation, and it could act as invitation to doctrinal error in one's doctrine of the Bible. What is built on a foundation cannot be helped by advocating a view that in effect harms or diminishes that foundation. According to a proper and true meaning of the terms and in agreement with scriptural truths, it is not right to promote a translation as the final authority or the ultimate absolute standard above its own sources or foundations--the preserved Word of God in the original languages. The final authority for the Scriptures clearly existed before 1611, and the Scriptures do not teach that the final authority for the Scriptures changed in 1611. Suggesting that one English translation in 1611 is the final authority would in effect be an attempt to bind the word of God to that single translation. The word of God is not bound (2 Tim. 2:9).

Believers should not listen to human teaching that causes them to err from the words of knowledge and truth (Prov. 19:27). A view based on some truth and some false claims or fallacies will only create a new false position. The way to discern error is with the truth. The way to dispel error is with the truth. It would be unsound and wrong to teach the commandments, opinions, assumptions, or traditions of men as being a doctrine of God (Mark 7:7-9, 13). Would a KJV-only view leave English-speaking believers dependent upon one exclusive group of Church of England critics/scholars in 1611? The fear of the LORD is the beginning of wisdom (Prov. 1:7, Prov. 1:29). Divers weights and divers measures, both of them *are* alike abominations to the LORD (Prov. 20:10). Would the demonstrated KJV-only use of unscriptural, unjust measures in many of the misleading, extreme allegations against the NKJV indicate the fear of the LORD? Would the abomination of the use of unjust measures honor God? Is the fear of the LORD soundly understood (Prov. 2:5) if it is thought that use of unjust measures would be in agreement with it? Would the use of unscriptural, unjust measures and fallacies be a hindrance and stumbling-block or a help and stepping-stone in the pursuit or advocating of truth? Truth cannot be defended nor advocated by the use of unscriptural, unjust measures and by use of fallacies. Fallacies would not be sound or powerful arguments for a KJV-only view. Human KJV-only reasoning and tradition may hinder any effort to accept and obey scriptural truths consistently and justly. Actual KJV-only claims have been taken seriously and applied consistently and justly. Is the making of righteous judgments (John 7:24) evident in the documented inconsistent and extreme KJV-only allegations against the NKJV? Will the instruction provided in many facts from the Geneva Bible, the KJV, and the NKJV and in the presentation of scriptural truths be accepted or despised? While this writer acknowledges his own bias in favor of the KJV, he has attempted to apply the wisdom from the Scriptures without partiality and without hypocrisy (James 3:17). This writer has attempted to avoid showing partiality or respect of persons to any one group of Bible translators over another group. To have respect of persons towards the KJV translators or any other group of Bible translators would be to commit sin (James 2:9). KJV-only requirements of doctrinal soundness and biblical holiness for Bible translators have not been consistently and justly applied to the Church of England translators of the KJV.

The view of Bible translations presented in this book is based on a sound acceptance of scriptural truths, and it is in agreement with the views of the early English Bible translators including the KJV translators. A consistent, sound, scriptural view of Bible translation should apply universally to Bible translations in all languages which believers speak, not just concerning translation into English. The same exact standards, measures, and principles that would apply justly and soundly to the translating of the Scriptures into languages other than English would also apply justly to its translating into English. A modern KJV-only view has not been soundly demonstrated to be an actual improvement over the view of Bible translation held by the early English translators including the KJV translators and the view of Bible translation held by translators of the Scriptures into languages other than English. A consistent, scriptural view of Bible translation would be true both before and after 1611 while a modern KJV-only view has not been demonstrated to be true before 1611. A KJV-only view has not been clearly shown to be based on wholesome words of scriptural truths applied consistently, soundly, and justly. Serious problems are evident in human KJV-only reasoning. KJV-only advocates have not proven soundly and justly that a KJV-only view is taught in or commanded by the Scriptures; therefore, all believers are at liberty to disagree with it.

Believers are at liberty in Christ to esteem which Bible translation that they may prefer, but these personal preferences or opinions of men would not be actual Bible doctrine. Mere personal, individual, or subjective preferences should not be permitted to become possibly a stumbling-block for other believers (Rom. 14:13). Over a period of time, the personal preferences of a group of believers could also become a tradition of men, which may be incorrectly taught as being a doctrine or commandment of God (Mark 7:7-9, Col. 2:8). Do KJV-only advocates put a human doctrine of tradition over scriptural truths? Each faithful believer must search, examine, judge, and decide for himself concerning the issue of Bible translation as he must every other doctrine (John 5:39, 1 Thess. 5:21, Acts 17:11, John 7:24, 1 John 2:27, Rom. 14:5). Thomas Henderson Pritchard stated: "If the Bible is our supreme and exclusive rule of duty, and if each individual is personally accountable for the discharge of that duty, then it follows, as a logical necessity, that every man has a right to read and interpret the Bible for himself" (Jenkens, *Baptist Doctrines,* p. 314). Each believer will personally give account of themselves to God (Rom. 14:12). Believers should walk in truth and in love (3 John 3-4, 2 John 4, Eph. 5:2, Eph. 4:15, 21, John 8:32). Believers are encouraged to prove all things, to prove what is acceptable to the Lord, and to hold fast that which is good (1 Thess. 5:21; Rom. 12:9,

Eph. 5:10).   They should judge righteous judgment (John 7:24) and apply sound, just measures/standards justly.   They should be willing to give scripturally-based answers concerning their views concerning Bible translations.

Bibliography

ABC's of the Bible. Pleasantville, NY: Reader's Digest Association, 1991.

Allen, David. *The Jewel in the King's Crown: The Story of the King James Bible.* Stoke-on-Trent: Berith Publications, 2010.

Allen, Ward. *Translating the N. T. Epistles 1604-1611.* Ann Arbor: University Microfilms, 1977.

Allen, Ward S. and Edward C. Jacobs. *The Coming of the King James Gospels: A Collation of the Translators' Work-in-progress.* Fayetteville: University of Arkansas Press, 1995.

Anderson, Christopher. *Annals of the English Bible.* London, 1845.

Andrewes, Lancelot. *A Pattern of Catechistical Doctrine.* Library of Anglo-Catholic Theology. Vol. VI. Oxford: John Henry, 1846.

Backus, Irena Doruta. *The Reformed Roots of the English New Testament: The Influence of Theodore Beza on the English New Testament.* Pittsburgh: Pickwick Press, 1980.

Bahnsen, Greg L. *Always Ready.* Edited by Robert Booth. Atlanta: American Vision, 1996.

Barker, Kenneth. *Accuracy Defined & Illustrated.* Colorado Springs: International Bible Society, 1995.

Barnett, Robert J. *The Word of God on Trial.* Calvary Baptist Church, 1981.

Barrier, Charles. *Looking for the Lamp.* Lansing: Calvary Publishing, 2010.

Bates, Michael. *Inspiration, Preservation and the KJV.* Ft. Pierce, FL: Faith Baptist Church Publications, 2008.

Beza, Theodore. *The Christian Faith.* Translated by James Clark. East Sussex, England: Focus Christian Ministries Trust, 1992.

Beza, Theodore. *A Little Book of Christian Questions and Responses.* Translated by Kirk Summers. Allison Park, PA: Pickwick Publications, 1986.

The Bible: Geneva Edition: 1st Printing, 1st edition: 1560. Litchfield Park, AZ: The Bible Museum, 2006.

Bloom, Harold. *The Shadow of a Great Rock.* New Haven: Yale University Press, 2011.

Bobrick, Benson. *Wide as the Waters: The Story of the English Bible and the Revolution It Inspired.* New York: Simon & Schuster, 2001.

Borders, Bruce A. *The Only Bible: The King James Version.* Borders Publishing, 2011.

Boyes, J. *The Englishman's Bible.* London: Wesleyan Conference Office, [1879].

Braemer, Marty. *This Little Light.* Claysburg, PA: Revival Fires, 1997.

Bradley, William. *To All Generations.* Claysburg, PA, 1996.

Bradley, William. *Purified Seven Times.* Claysburg, PA: Revival Fires Publishing, 1998.

Bragg, Melvyn. *The Book of Books: The Radical Impact of the King James Bible 1611-2011.* Berkeley: Counterpoint, 2011.

Brake, Donald L. *A Visual History of the English Bible.* Grand Rapids: Baker Books, 2008.

Brake, Donald L. with Shelly Beach. *A Visual History of the King James Bible.* Grand Rapids: Baker Books, 2011.

Brakel, Wilhelmus. *The Christian's Reasonable Service.* Grand Rapids: Reformation Heritage Books, 1992.

Branson, Roy. *KJV 1611: Perfect!* Bristol: Landmark Publications, 1996.

Brook, Benjamin. *Lives of the Puritans.* London: James Black, 1813.

Brown, David L. *The Indestructible Book.* Cleveland, GA: Old Path Publications, 2015.

Brown, John. *The History of the English Bible.* Cambridge: University Press, 1912.

Bruce, F. F. *History of the Bible in English.* Third Edition. New York: Oxford University Press, 1978.

Brunn, Dave. *One Bible, Many Versions.* Downers Grove, IL: Inter-Varsity Press, 2013.

Bullinger, E. W. *Figures of Speech Used in the Bible.* Grand Rapids: Baker Book House, 1968.

Burke, David G., John F. Kutsko, and Philip H. Towner (eds.). *The King James Version at 400: Assessing its Genius as Bible Translation and Its Literary Influence.* Atlanta: Society of Biblical Literature, 2013.

Burke, David (ed.). *Translation That Openeth the Window: Reflections on the History And Legacy of the King James Bible.* Atlanta: Society of Biblical Literature, 2009.

Butterworth, Charles. *The Literary Lineage of the King James Bible.* New York: Octagon Books, 1941.

Byers, William. *The History of the KJB and the People Called Baptist.* 1987.

Calamy, Edmund. *Thirteen Sermons Concerning the Doctrine of the Trinity.* London: John Clark, 1722.

Campbell, Gordon. *Bible: The Story of the King James Version 1611-2011.* Oxford: Oxford University Press, 2010.

Carleton, James G. *The Part of the Rheims in the Making of the English Bible.* Oxford: At the Clarendon Press, 1902.

Carnell, Edward John. *An Introduction to Christian Apologetics.* Grand Rapids: William B. Eerdmans Publishing Company, 1948.

Carson, D. A. *The King James Version Debate.* Grand Rapids: Baker Book House, 1979.

Carter, Mickey. *Things That Are Different Are Not the Same.* Haines City, FL: Landmark Baptist Press, 1993.

Cimino, Dick. *The Book.* Harlingen, TX: Wonderful Word Publishers, 1974.

Clark, Gordon. *God's Hammer.* Jefferson, MD: The Trinity Foundation, 1982.

Clark, Gordon. *Lord God of Truth.* Hobbs, NM: The Trinity Foundation, 1994.

Clark, Troy G. *The Perfect Bible.* Copyright 2008. [Third Edition, 2012]

Clarke, Adam (ed.). *The Holy Bible with a Commentary and Critical Notes.* London: Thomas Tagg, 1839.

Cleenewerck, Laurent (ed.). *The Eastern/Greek Oxthodox Bible: New Testament.* 2013.

Cloud, David. *Answering the Myths on the Bible Version Debate.* Port Huron, MI: Way of Life Literature, 2006. Corrected in 2009.

Cloud, David. *The Bible Version Question/Answer Database.* Port Huron, MI: Way of Life Literature, 2005.

Cloud, David. *Examining "The King James Only Controversy."* Second Edition. Port Huron, MI: Way of Life Literature, 1998.

Cloud, David. *Faith vs. the Modern Bible Versions.* Port Huron, MI: Way of Life, 2005.

Cloud, David. *For Love of the Bible.* Oak Harbor, WA: Way of Life Literature, 1995.

Cloud, David. *The Glorious History of the KJB.* Port Huron, MI: Way of Life, 2006.

Cloud, David. *Rome and the Bible.* Oak Harbor, WA: Way of Life, 1996.

Cloud, David (ed.). *Way of Life Encyclopedia of the Bible & Christianity.* Oak Harbor, WA: Way of Life Literature, 1993.

Coats, Daryl R. *NKJV Nonsense.* Natchitoches, LA: Blessed Hope Baptist Church, 1992.

Comfort, Ray. *The Evidence Bible.* Gainesville, FL: Bridge-Logos Publishers, 2003.

The Companion Bible. London: Samuel Bagster, 1969.

Conant, H. C. *The English Bible: History of the Translation of the Holy Scriptures into the English Tongue.* New York: Sheldon & Company, 1859.

Condit, Blackford. *The History of the English Bible.* New York: A. S. Barnes, 1882.

Cone, Spencer and William Wyckoff (eds.). *The Commonly Received Version of the New Testament with several hundred emendations.* New York, 1850 and 1851.

Connolly, W. Ken. *The Indestructible Book.* Grand Rapids: Baker Books, 1996.

Cooper, W. R. (ed.). *The Wycliffe New Testament 1388.* London: The British Library, 2002.

Corle, Dennis. *God's Inspired Book—the Bible.* Claysburg, PA: Revival Fires Publishing, 2009.

Countryman, Jack. *The Treasure of God's Word. Celebrating 400 Years of the KJB.* Nashville: Thomas Nelson, 2010.

Coverdale, Miles. *The Coverdale Bible 1535* (facsimile with introduction by S. L. Greenslade). Kent: William Dawson & Sons, 1975.

Coverdale, Miles. *The New Testament both in Latin and English.* Paris: Fraunces Regnault, 1538.

Crystal, David. *The Cambridge Encyclopedia of the English Language.* Cambridge: Cambridge University Press, 1995.

Crystal, David. *Begat: The King James Bible and the English Language.* Oxford: Oxford University Press, 2010.

Curtis, Thomas. *The Existing Monopoly: an Inadequate Protection of the Authorised Version of Scripture.* London, 1833.

Dabney, Robert L. *Lectures in Systematic Theology.* Grand Rapids: Zondervan Pub., 1972.

Dagg, John L. *A Manual of Theology*. Harrisonburg, VA: Gano Books, 1990.

Daiches, David. *The King James Version of the English Bible*. Archon Books, 1941.

Daniell, David. *The Bible in English: Its History and Influence*. New Haven: Yale University Press, 2003.

Daniell, David (ed.). *Tyndale's New Testament*. (1534 edition, modern-spelling). New Haven: Yale University Press 1989.

Daniell, David (ed.). *Tyndale's Old Testament*. (Pentateuch of 1530, Joshua to 2 Chronicles of 1537, And Jonah). New Haven: Yale University Press, 1992.

Daniell, David. *William Tyndale: A Biography*. New Haven: Yale University Press, 1994.

Daniels, David W. *Answers to your Bible Version Questions*. Ontario, CA: Chick Publications, 2003.

Daniels, David W. and Jack McElroy. *Can You Trust Just One Bible?* Ontario, CA: Chick, 2015.

Darlow, T. H. and H. F. Moule. *Historical Catalogue of the Printed Editions of Holy Scriptures*. London: The Bible House, 1903.

Davies, T. Lewis. *Bible English: Chapters on Old and Disused Expression in the Authorized Version*. London: George Bell and Sons, 1875.

Dearden, Robert R., Jr. *The Guiding Light on the Great Highway*. Philadelphia: John C. Winston Company, 1929.

Decker, Rodney J. *The English Bible*. Kansas City: Calvary Baptist College, 1993.

DeVries, Ed. *Divinely Inspired, Inerrantly Preserved*. Lake Charles, LA: School of Biblical & Theological Studies, 1998.

Dick, John. *Lectures on Theology*. Philadelphia, 1841.

DiVietro, Kirk D. *Anything But the King James Bible*. Collingswood, NJ: Bible for Today, 1995.

DiVietro, Kirk D. *Where the KJB Leaves the Greek Text of Theodore Beza 1598*. Collingswood, NJ: The Bible for Today, 1996.

Dore, J. R. *Old Bibles*. Second Edition. London: Eyre and Spottiswoode, 1888.

Dwight, Timothy. *Theology Explained and Defended*. London: William Bagnes, 1819.

Eadie, John. *The English Bible*. London: Macmillan and Co., 1876.

Edgar, Andrew. *The Bibles of England*. London: Alexander Gardner, 1889.

Einwechter, William O. *English Bible Translations: By What Standard?* Mill Hall, PA: Preston/Speed Publications, 1996.

The English Hexapla Exhibiting the Six Important English Translations of the New Testament Scriptures. London: Samuel Bagster and Sons, 1841.

Eoyang, Eugene Chen. *Borrowed Plumage: Polemical Essays on Translation*. New York, 2003.

Evans, William. *The Great Doctrines of the Bible*. Chicago: Moody Press, 1912.

Farnham, Jeff. *God's Forever Word*. Murfreesboro: Sword of the Lord Publishers, 2013.

Farstad, Arthur. *The New King James Version: In the Great Tradition*. Nashville: Thomas Nelson Publishers, 1989.

Faust, Joey. *The Word: God Will Keep It*. Venus, TX: Fundamental Books, 2011.

Fellure, Tim. *Neither jot nor tittle*. Milton, FL: Victory Baptist Press, 2005.

Ferrari, Andrea. *John Diodati's Doctrine of Holy Scripture*. Grand Rapids: Reformation Heritage Books, 2006.

Ferrell, Lori. *The Bible and the People*. London: Yale University Press, 2008.

Fisk, Samuel. *Calvinistic Paths Retraced*. Murfreesboro: Biblical Evangelism Press, 1985.

Frame, John M. *Apologetics to the Glory of God*. Phillipsburg, NJ: Presbyterian and Reformed Publishing Company, 1994.

Freeman, J. M. *A Short History of the English Bible*. New York, 1891.

Fulke, William. *Confutation of the Rhemish Testament*. New York: Leavitt, Lord, and Co., 1834.

Fulke, William. *A Defence of the Sincere and True Translations of the Holy Scriptures into the English Tongue*. Edited by Charles Hartshore. Cambridge: The University Press, 1843.

Fuller, David Otis (ed.). *True or False?* Grand Rapids: Grand Rapids International, 1973.

Fuller, David Otis (ed.). *Which Bible?* Second Edition. Grand Rapids: Grand Rapids International Publications, 1971.

Geisler, Norman and Ronald Brooks. *Come, Let Us Reason*. Grand Rapids: Baker Books, 1990.

Geisler, Norman and William Nix. *A General Introduction to the Bible*. Chicago: Moody Press, 1986.

Gell, Robert. *An Essay toward the Amendment of the Last English Translation of the Bible.* London: R. Norton, 1659.

The Geneva Bible. A Facsimile of the 1560 Edition. Peabody, MA: Hendrickson Publishers, 2007.

The 1599 Geneva Bible. White Hall, WV: Tolle Lege Press, 2006. [Modern spelling edition]

Gill, John. *A Body of Doctrinal and Practical Divinity.* London: Whittingham and Rowland, 1815.

Gill, John. *Exposition of the Whole Old Testament.* Vol. III. London: printed for George Keith, 1780.

Gilmore, Alec. *A Dictionary of the English Bible and its Origins.* Sheffield: Sheffield Academic Press, 2000.

Ginsburg, Christian D. *The Massoreth Ha-Massoreth of Elias Levita.* 1867. Kessinger Publishing's Rare Reprint.

Gipp, Samuel. *The Answer Book.* Bible & Literature Foundation, 1989.

Gipp, Samuel. *Is Our English Bible Inspired?* Miamitown, OH: DayStar Publishing, 2004.

Girdlestone, Robert B. *How to Study the English Bible.* London: Religious Tract Society, 1894.

Grady, William P. *Final Authority.* Schererville, IN: Grady Publications, 1993.

Grady, William P. *Given By Inspiration.* Swartz Creek, MI: Grady Publications, 2010.

Grainger, James Moses. *Studies in the Syntax of the King James Version.* Chapel Hill: The University Press, 1907.

reen, Jay. *Gnostics, the New Versions.* Lafayette: Sovereign Grace Publishers, 1994.

Green, Jay P. (ed.). *The Interlinear Bible.* Peabody, MA: Hendrickson Publishers, 1986.

Green, Steve and Todd Hillard. *The Bible in America.* Second Edition. Oklahoma City, OK: Dust Jacket Press, 2013.

Greider, John C. *The English Bible Translations and History.* Xlibris Corporation, 2005.

Gresham, Joe W. *Dealing with the Devil's Deception.* Fort Worth: Fourth Angel's Publishing, 2001.

Groser, William. *Trees and Plants Mentioned in the Bible.* Second Edition. Religious Tract Society, 1895.

Gutjahr, Paul C. *An American Bible: A History of the Good Book in the United States.* Stanford: Stanford University Press, 1999.

Hallihan, C. P. *The Authorised Version: A Wonderful and Unfinished History.* London: Trinitarian Bible Society, 2010.

Hamlin, Hannibal. *The Bible in Shakespeare.* Oxford: Oxford University Press, 2013.

Hamlin, Hannibal and Norman W. Jones (eds.). *The King James Bible after 400 Years.* Cambridge: Cambridge University Press, 2010.

Hammond, Gerald. *The Making of the English Bible.* New York: Philosophical Library, 1983.

Harris, Jason. *The Doctrine of Scripture.* Australia: InFocus, 2013.

Henry, Matthew. *An Exposition of the New Testament.* Edinburgh: E. and J. Robertsons, 1759.

Hills, Edward F. *Believing Bible Study.* Des Moines: Christian Research Press 1977.

Hills, Edward F. *The King James Version Defended.* Des Moines: Christian Research Press, 1984.

Holland, Thomas. *Crowned with Glory: The Bible from Ancient Texts to Authorized Version.* Lincoln: Writers Club Press, 2000.

Hollner, Michael. *The King James Only Debate.* Winter Springs, FL: Write the Vision Ministry, 2018.

The Holy Bible, an Exact Reprint Page for Page of the Authorized Version Published In the Year 1611. Oxford: At the University Press, 1833.

The Holy Bible; being the English Version of the Old and New Testaments made by order of King James I, carefully revised and amended by several Biblical Scholars. Philadelphia: J. B. Lippincott, 1842. Published for David Bernard.

The Holy Bible. Cambridge: Thomas Buck and Roger Daniel, 1638.

The Holy Bible 1611. Columbus, Ohio: Greyden Press, 2000.

The Holy Bible 1611 Edition. (King James Version). Nashville: Thomas Nelson Publishers, 1990.

The Holy Bible 1611 Edition. (King James Version). Peabody, MA: Hendrickson Publishers, 2003.

The Holy Bible: The Great Light in Masonry. Masonic Edition. Philadelphia: A. J. Holman, 1940.

Hopkins, Norman. *The Right Bible.* Toast, NC: Patriot Publications, 1998.

Hyles, Jack. *The Need for an Every-Word Bible.* Hammond, IN: Hyles Publications, 2003.

Jassin, Lloyd J. and Steven C. Schechter. *The Copyright Permission and Libel Handbook.* New York: John Wiley & Sons, Inc., 1998.

Jenkens, Charles. *Baptist Doctrines*. Baptist Heritage Press, 1890.

Jensen, Irving L. *Jensen's Survey of the Old Testament*. Chicago: Moody Publishers, 1978.

Johnson, Anthony. *An Historical Account of the Several English Translations*. London, 1730.

Jones, Floyd. *Which Version is the Bible?* The Bible for Today, 1998.

Kahler, James C. *A Charted History of the Bible*. Miamitown: Daystar Publishing, 2007.

Kerr, John Stevens. *Ancient Texts Alive Today: The Story of the English Bible*. Edited by Charles Houser. New York: American Bible Society, 1999.

King James Easy-Reading Study Bible. Goodyear, AZ: G. E. M. Publishing, 2002.

King James Easy-Reading Study Bible. Humbolt, TN: Kings Word Press, 2010.

KJV-NKJV Parallel Reference Bible. Nashville: Nelson Bibles, 1991.

Know the Word Study Bible [KJV]. Nashville: Thomas Nelson, 2017.

Krans, Jan. *Beyond What Is Written: Erasmus and Beza as Conjectural Critics of the New Testament*. Boston: Brill, 2006.

Kriessman, Charles. *Modern Version Failures*. Collingswood, NJ: Bible for Today, 2014.

Lacy, Al. *Can I Trust My Bible?* Littleton, CO: Al Lacy Publications, 1991.

Latourette, Kenneth. *A History of Christianity*. New York: HarperCollins Publishers, 1975.

Letis, Theodore. *The Revival of the Ecclesiastical Text and the Claims of the Anabaptists*. Ft. Wayne: Institute for Reformation Biblical Studies, 1992.

Levinson, Bernard M. and Joshua A. Berman. *The King James Bible at 400*. 2010.

Levy, Ian Christopher. *John Wyclif: On the Truth of Holy Scripture*. Kalamazoo, MI: Medieval Institute Publications, 2001.

Lewis, Jack P. *The English Bible from KJV to NIV*. Second Edition. Grand Rapids: Baker Book House, n. d.

Lewis, John. *A Complete History of the Several Translation of the Holy Bible and New Testament Into English*. (Second Edition). London: H. Woodfall, 1739.

Lightfoot, Neil. *How We Got Our Bible*. Grand Rapids: Baker Book House, 1988.

Loftie, William. *A Century of Bibles*. 1872.

Lovett, Richard. *The Printed English Bible 1525-1885*. New York: Fleming H. Revell Co., n. d.

Lowndes, William. *British Librarian, or Book-Collector's Guide*. London: Whittaker and Co., 1839.

Lucado, Max (ed.). *The Inspirational Study Bible*. NKJV. Dallas: Word Bibles, 1995.

Luchan, T. S. *From the Mind of God to the Heart of Men*. Hunker, PA: Hilltop Publications, 2015.

MacArthur, John (ed.). *The MacArthur Study Bible*. NKJV. Nashville: Word Bibles, 1997.

Macgregor, Alan J. *400 Years On: How does the Authorised Version Stand Up in the 21st Century?* Visionsolutions, 2010.

MacGregor, Geddes. *The Bible in the Making*. Philadelphia: J. B. Lippincott, 1959.

MacGregor, Geddes. *A Literary History of the Bible*. Nashville: Abingdon Press, 1968.

MacLean, W. *The Providential Preservation of the Greek Text of the New Testament*. Third Edition. Westminster Standard Publication, 1977.

Madden, D. K. *Remarks on the NKJV and Revised Authorised Version*. Tasmainia, Australia, 1989.

Mangalwadi, Vishal. *The Book That Made Your World*. Nashville: Thomas Nelson, 2011.

May, Herbert. *Our English Bible in the Making*. Philadelphia: The Westminster Press, 1965.

McAfee, Cleland Boyd. *Greatest English Classic: A Study of the KJV*. New York, 1912.

McArdle, Jeff. *The Bible Believer's Guide to Elephant Hunting*. Pensacola, FL: Valera Bible Society, 2003.

McBerry, Ray. *A Clash of Swords: The Baptist Origins of our English Bible*. 1999.

McElroy, Jack. *Which Bible Would Jesus Use? The Bible Version Controversy Explained and Resolved*. Shirley, MA: McElroy Publishing, 2003.

McGrath, Alister. *In the Beginning: The Story of the KJB*. New York: Doubleday, 2001.

Melton, James L. *The Bible Believers Helpful Little Handbook*. Sharon, TN: Bible Baptist Church, 1995.

Melton, James L. *Fighting Back*. Sharon, TN: Bible Baptist Church, 1997.

Miller, Gary. *Why the KJB is the Perfect Word of God*. Ontario, CA: Chick Publications, 2006.

Moe, Dean. *Christian Symbols Handbook*. Minneapolis: Augsbury Publishing House, 1985.

Mombert, Jacob I. *A Hand-book of the English Versions of the Bible*. New York: Anson Randolph, 1883.

Moore, Ed. *The Final Authority on the Final Authority*. Newalla, OK: Country Cathedrals, 2004.

Moore, Helen and Julian Reid (eds). *Manifold Greatness: The Making of the King James Bible*. Oxford: Bodleian Library, 2011.

Moorman, Jack. *Forever Settled: A Survey of the Documents and History of the Bible*. Collingswood: The Bible for Today, n. d.

Moorman, J. A. *When the KJV Departs from the "Majority Text."* Collingswood: Dean Burgon Society, 2010.

Morton, Timothy. *From the Original Texts to the English Bible*. Sutton, WV: Morton

Publications, 2006.

Morton, Timothy. *Which Translation Should You Trust?*   Sutton, WV: Morton
Publications, 1993.

Moulton, W. F. *The History of the English Bible.*   London: Cassell, 1878.

Mounce, William D.   Greek for the Rest of Us.   Grand Rapids: Zondervan, 2003.

Murray, Chester. *The Authorized King James Bible Defended.*   Ozark Books, 1983.

Neste, Ray Van (ed.). *KJV400:   The Legacy & Impact of the KJV.*   Memphis: BorderStone
Press, 2012.

Nicolson, Adam. *God's Secretaries: The Making of the King James Bible.*   New York:
HarperCollins, 2003.

Nordstrom, John Anthony. *Stained with Blood: A One-Hundred Year History of the English Bible.*
Bloomington, IN: WestBow Press, 2014.

Norris, David W. *The Big Picture.*   England: Authentic Word, 2004.

Norris, Rick. *Facts from 400 Years of KJV Editions: Do We Use a 1769 KJV?*   Eleventh Edition.
Statesville, NC: Unbound Scriptures Publications, 2010, 2017.

Norris, Rick. *Today's KJV and 1611 Compared and More.*   Fourth Edition.   Statesville, NC:
Unbound Scriptures Publications, 2006, 2013.

Norris, Rick. *The Unbound Scriptures.*   Fayetteville, NC: Unbound Scriptures Publications, 2003.

Norton, David (ed.). *The Bible: King James Version.*   Penguin Classics Edition.
London: Penguin Books, 2006.

Norton, David. *A History of the English Bible as Literature.*   Cambridge: Cambridge University
Press, 2000.

Norton, David. *The King James Bible: A Short History from Tyndale to Today.*
Cambridge: Cambridge University Press, 2011.

Norton, David (ed.). *The New Cambridge Paragraph Bible.* Cambridge:
Cambridge University Press, 2005.

Norton, David (ed.). *The New Cambridge Paragraph Bible.*   Revised Edition.   Cambridge:
Cambridge University Press, 2011.

Norton, David. *A Textual History of the King James Bible.*   Cambridge: Cambridge
University Press, 2005.

O'Neal, Michael D. *Do We Have the Word of God?*   Albany, Georgia, 1995.

Opfell, Olga. *The King James Bible Translators.*   Jefferson, NC: McFarland, 1992.

O'Reilly, Alan. *"O Biblios" The Book.*   Durham, UK: Covenant Publishing, n. d.

O'Sullivan, Orlaith (ed.). *The Bible as Book—The Reformation.*   London: The British
Library & Oak Knoll Press, 2000.

Paine, Gustavus. *The Men Behind the KJV.*   Grand Rapids: Baker Book House, 1959.

Paisley, Ian. *My Plea for the Old Sword.*   Belfast, IR: Ambassador Productions, 1997.

Pastoor, Charles and Galen Johnson. *A to Z of the Puritans.*   Lanham: The Scarecrow Press, 2009.

Paterson, James. *The Liberty of the Press, Speech, and Public Worship.*   London: MacMillan, 1880.

Paul, William E. *English Language Bible Translators.*   Jefferson, NC: McFarland & Company, 2003.

Penniman, Josiah H. *A Book about the English Bible.*   New York: MacMillan Company, 1919.

Perry, Lloyd & Robert Culver. *How to Search the Scriptures.*   Grand Rapids: Baker Book House, 1967.

Pickering, Wilbur N. *God Has Preserved His Text: The Divine Preservation of the New Testament.*
Columbus, SC: Creative Commons, 2017.

Pickering, Wilbur N. *The Identity of the New Testament Text II.*   Third Edition.   Eugene, OR:
Wipf and Stock Publishers, 2003.

Pickering, Wilbur N. *The Identity of the New Testament Text IV.*   Columbus, SC, 2014.

Pickering, Wilbur N. *The Sovereign Creator Has Spoken.*   New Testament Translation with
Commentary.   Columbus, SC: Creative Commons, 2016.

Pierce, Ben C. *Valiant for the Truth.*   2011.

Pirkle, Estus. *The 1611 KJV Bible: A Study.*   Southhaven, MS: The King's Press, 1994.

Price, Ira Maurice. *Ancestry of our English Bible.*   Philadelphia: Sunday School Times, 1907.

Price, James D. *The False Witness of G. A. Riplinger's Death Certificate for the NKJV.*
Unpublished paper, 1996.

Price, James D. *King James Onlyism: a New Sect.*   Singapore: Saik Wah Press, 2006.

Rabe, Kent. *Double Exposure.*   Pearce, AR: Broken Arrow Baptist Church, 1994.

Raidabaugh, P. W. *History of the English Bible.*   Cleveland, 1885.

Rasbeary, James M. *What's Wrong with the Old Black Book?*   2007.

Rasbeary, James. *What's Wrong with the RSV, NIV, & NKJV?*   Wylie, TX: Lighthouse
Baptist Publications, 2009.

Rawlings, Harold. *Trial by Fire.*   Wellington, FL: The Rawlings Foundation, 2004.

Ray, Jasper James. *God Wrote Only One Bible.*   The Eye Opener Publishers, 1955, 1983.

Reagan, David F. *The King James Version of 1611: The Myth of "Early Revisions."* Knoxville, TN: Trinity Baptist Temple, 1986.

Rhodes, Neil with Gordon Kendal and Louise Wilson (eds.). *English Renaissance Translation Theory.* London: Modern Humanities Research Association, 2013.

Rhodes, Ron. *The Challenge of the Cults and New Religions.* Grand Rapids: Zondervan, 2001.

Rhodes, Ron. *The Complete Guide to Bible Translations.* Eugene, OR: Harvest House Publishers, 2009.

Rice, Edwin W. *Our Sixty-six Sacred Books.* Philadelphia: American Sunday-School Union, 1893.

Rice, John R. (ed.). *The Rice Reference Bible.* Nashville: Thomas Nelson, 1981.

Riplinger, Gail. *Blind Guides.* Ararat, VA: A. V. Publications, 1995.

Riplinger, Gail. *Hazardous Materials: Greek & Hebrew Study Dangers, The Voice of Strangers, the Men Behind the Smokescreen.* Ararat, VA: A.V. Publications, 2008.

Riplinger, Gail. *The Hidden History of the English Scriptures.* Ararat, VA: A. V. Publications, 2010.

Riplinger, Gail. *In Awe of Thy Word.* Ararat, VA: A. V. Publications, 2003.

Riplinger, Gail. *The Language of the King James Bible.* Ararat, VA: A. V. Publications, 1998.

Riplinger, G. A. *New Age Versions.* Shelbyville, TN: Bible & Literature Missionary Foundation, 1993.

Riplinger, Gail. *Which Bible is God's Word?* Hearthstone Publishing, 1994.

Robinson, H. Wheeler (ed.). *The Bible in its Ancient and English Versions.* Westport: Greenwood Press, 1940.

Rockwell, Jerry (general ed.). *The Rock of Ages Study Bible.* Fourth Edition. Cleveland, TN: Rock of Ages Press, 2012.

Ruckman, Peter. *The Alexandrian Cult.* Bible Baptist Bookstore, 1980. Eight booklets.

Ruckman, Peter. *The Bible Babel.* Bible Baptist Bookstore, 1964.

Ruckman, Peter. *Biblical Scholarship.* Pensacola: Bible Baptist Bookstore, 1988.

Ruckman, Peter. *The Christian's Handbook of Manuscript Evidence.* Pensacola, FL: Pensacola Bible Press, 1970.

Ruckman, Peter. *Differences in the King James Version Editions.* Pensacola, FL: Bible Believers Press, 1983.

Ruckman, Peter. *How to Teach the "Original" Greek.* Pensacola: Bible Believers, 1992.

Ruckman, Peter. *King James Onlyism versus Scholarship Onlyism.* Bible Believers Press, 1992.

Ruckman, Peter. *The Monarch of the Books.* 1980.

Ruckman, Peter. *The Ruckman Reference Bible.* Pensacola: BB Bookstore, 2009.

Ruckman, Peter. *The Scholarship Only Controversy.* Bible Believers Press, 1996.

Ruckman, Peter. *Theological Studies.* Book Fifteen. 1988.

Ruckman, Peter. *Why I Believe the KJV is the Word of God.* 1988.

Ryrie, Charles. *Ryrie Study Bible.* KJV. Expanded Edition. Chicago: Moody Press, 1994.

Ryken, Leland. *Worldly Saints—The Puritans as They Really Were.* Grand Rapids: Academic Books, 1986.

Sargent, Robert. *English Bible: Manuscript Evidence.* Oak Harbor, WA: Bible Baptist Church Publications, n. d.

Sawyer, John W. *The Legacy of Our English Bible.* 1990.

Scofield, C. I. (ed.). *The Scofield Reference Bible: KJV.* New York: Oxford University Press, 1909, 1917, 1945.

Scrivener, F. H. A. *The Authorized Edition of the English Bible (1611).* Cambridge: At the University Press, 1884.

Scrivener, F. H. A. (ed.). *The Cambridge Paragraph Bible of the Authorized English Version.* Cambridge: At the University Press, 1873.

The Self-Interpreting Bible. Explanatory Notes by John Brown. A New Edition. Edinburgh: Thomas Ireland, 1831.

The Self-Pronouncing Sunday-School Teachers' Bible. Philadelphia: National Publishing Company, 1895.

Settlemoir, J. C. *Landmarkism Under Fire: A Handbook of Baptist Polity on Church Constitution.* Lizton, IN: New Testament Baptist Church, 2017.

Sightler, Harold, Ben Carter, and Jack Manly. *The Bible and How It Came to Us.* Greenville, SC: Bright Spot Hour, 2010.

Sightler, James H. *A Testimony Founded For Ever: The KJB Defended in Faith and History.* Greenville: Sightler Publications, 1999.

Smyth, J. Paterson. *How We Got Our Bible.* New York: James Pott & Co., 1928.

Son, James H. *The New Athenians.* Lubbock: Praise Publishing, 1992.

Sorenson, David. *Neither Oldest Nor Best.* Duluth, MN: Northstar Ministries, 2017.

Sorenson, David. *God's Perfect Book.* Duluth, MN: Northstar Ministries, 2009.

Sorenson, David. *Touch Not the Unclean Thing.* Duluth, MN: Northstar, 2000.

Sproul, Michael D. *God's Word Preserved*. Tempe, AZ: Whetstone Precepts Press, 2005.

Stauffer, Douglas D. *One Book One Authority*. Millbrook: McCowen Mills Publishers, 2012.

Stauffer, Douglas D. *One Book Stands Alone*. Millbrook: McCowen Mills Publishers, 2001.

Steward, Bob. *God's Invisible Hand on the KJV*. Harrison, Michigan, 1989.

Steward, Bob. *Why Not the New King James Version of the Bible*? 1996.

Stim, Richard. *Patent, Copyright & Trademark*. Ninth Edition. Berkeley, CA: Nolo, 2007.

Stone, Larry. *The Story of the Bible*. Nashville: Thomas Nelson, 2010.

Strand, Brad (ed.). *The Strand Study Bible*. Minneapolis: Rood Scholar Press, 2009.

Streeter, Lloyd. *Seventy-five Problems with Central Baptist Seminary's Book The Bible Version Debate*.
    LaSalle: First Baptist Church, 2001.

Strong, Augustus. Systematic Theology. Old Tappan: Fleming Revell, 1907.

Strouse, Thomas M. *The Lord God Hath Spoken: A Guide to Bibliology*. Tabernacle Baptist
    Theological Press, 1982.

Strype, John. *The Life and Acts of Matthew Parker*. Oxford: Clarendon Press, 1821.

Surrett, Charles L. *Certainty of the Words*. Kings Mountain, NC: Surrett Family Publications, 2013.

Surrett, Charles L. *Which Greek Text*? Kings Mountain, NC: Surrett Family Publications, 1999.

Tabb, M. H. *The Inspiration and Preservation of Scripture*. Fort Walton Beach, FL:
    Foundation Ministries, 2010.

Taliaferro, Bradford B. *Bible Version Encyclopedia*. Bradford Taliaferro, 2007.

Taliaferro, Bradford B. *Encyclopedia of English Language Bible Versions*. Jefferson, NC:
    McFarland & Company, 2013.

Taylor, Jim. *In Defense of the Textus Receptus: God's Preserved Word to Every Generation*.
    Cleveland, OH: Old Paths Publications, 2016.

Tebbel, John. *A History of Book Publishing in the United States*. New York: R. R. Bowker, 1972.

Tenney, Merrill (ed.). *The Zondervan Encyclopedia of the Bible*. Revised, full-color Edition. Grand
    Rapids: Zondervan, 2009.

Timpson, Thomas. *Bible Triumphs*. London, 1853.

Tristram, H. B. *The Natural History of the Bible*. Third Edition. London: Society for Promoting
    Christian Knowledge, 1873.

Turretin, Francis. *Institutes of Elenctic Theology*. Translated by George Giger. Phillipsburg, NJ:
    P & R Publishing, 1992.

Turton, Thomas. *The Text of the English Bible*. 1833.

Tyndale, William. *Doctrinal Treatises*. Cambridge: The University Press, 1848.

Tyree, Gregory. *Does It Really Matter Which Bible I Use*? Madison Heights, VA, 2013.

Vance, Laurence. *Archaic Words & the Authorized Version*. Vance Publications, 1996.

Vance, Laurence M. *A Brief History of English Bible Translations*. Pensacola, FL: Vance
    Publications, 1993.

Vance, Laurence M. *King James, His Bible, and Its Translators*. Pensacola, FL: Vance
    Publications, 2006.

Vance, Laurence M. *The Making of the King James Bible: The New Testament*. Orlando, FL:
    Vance Publications, 2015.

Vanhoozer, Kevin J. *Is There a Meaning in This Text*? Grand Rapids: Zondervan, 1998.

Virkler, Henry A. *A Christian's Guide to Critical Thinking*. Nashville: Thomas Nelson, 1993.

Waite, D. A. *The Authorized Version 1611 Compared to Today's King James Version*.
    Collingswood, NJ: The Bible for Today, 1985.

Waite, D. A. *Bob Jones University's Errors on Bible Preservation*. The Bible for Today, 2006.

Waite, D. A. *Central Seminary Refuted on Bible Versions*. The Bible for Today, 1999.

Waite, D. A. *A Critical Answer to James Price's King James Onlyism*. Collingswood, NJ:
    The Bible for Today Press, 2009.

Waite, D. A. *A Critical Answer to Michael Sproul's God's Word Preserved*. Collingswood, NJ:
    The Bible for Today Press, 2008.

Waite, D. A. *Defects in the New King James Version*. The Bible for Today, 1987.

Waite, D. A. *Defending the King James Bible*. Collingswood, NJ: The Bible for Today Press, 1992.

Waite, D. A. (ed.). *The Defined King James Bible*. Collingswood, NJ:
    The Bible for Today, 1998.

Waite, D. A. *Foes of the KJB Refuted*. Collingswood, NJ: The Bible for Today, 1997.

Waite, D. A. *Fundamentalist Deception on Bible Preservation*. The Bible for Today Press, 2005.

Waite, D. A. *Fundamentalist Distortions on Bible Versions*. The Bible for Today Press, 1999.

Waite, D. A. *Fundamentalist Mis-Information on Bible Versions*. The Bible for Today Press, 2000.

Waite, D. A. *Fuzzy Facts from Fundamentalists on Bible Versions*. The Bible for Today, 2002.

Waite, D. A. *The NKJV Compared to the KJV*. The Bible for Today, 1990.

Waite, D. A. *A Warning on Gail Riplinger's KJB & Multiple Inspiration Heresy*. The Bible for Today, 2010.

Walker, Williston. *A History of the Christian Church*. Third Edition. New York: Charles Scribner's Sons, 1970.

Ward, Mark. Authorized: *The Use & Misuse of the KJB*. Bellingham, WA: Lexham Press, 2018.

Watts, Malcolm H. *The New King James Version: A Critique*. Trinitarian Bible Society, 2008.

Webster, Noah. *The Webster Bible*. Grand Rapids: Baker Book House, 1987.

Weeks, William R. *A Catechism of Scripture Doctrine*. Second Edition. Albany: E. and E. Hosford, 1818.

West, Nathaniel. *A Complete Analysis of the Holy Bible*. New York: Charles Scribner, 1853.

Westcott, Stephen P. (ed.). *Wickliffe's New Testament*. Fellsmere, FL: Reformation Media, 2005.

Weigle, Luther A. (ed.). *The New Testament Octapla*. New York: Thomas Nelson, 1962.

Whitaker, William. *A Disputation on Holy Scripture against the Papists*. Cambridge University Press, 1849.

White, Steven J. White's Dictionary of the King James Language. Volume One A-E. 2004.

White, Steven J. *White's Dictionary of the King James Language*. Volume Two F-H. Lexington, KY: Steven White, 2010.

Whitten, E. W. *The Truth According to Scripture*. Coral Springs, FL: Alpha-Stellar Books, 2003.

Williams, H. D. *The Miracle of Biblical Inspiration*. Cleveland, GA: Old Paths Publications, 2009.

Williams, H. D. *The Pure Words of God*. Cleveland, GA: Old Paths Publications, 2008.

Williams, H. D. *Word-For-Word Translating of the Received Texts*. Collingswood, NJ: The Bible for Today Press, 2007.

Williams, H. Wayne. *Does God Have a Controversy with the KJB?* The Ol' Lighthouse Publication, 1997.

Williams, James B. and Randolph Shaylor (eds.). *From the Mind of God to the Mind of Man*. Greenville: Ambassador-Emerald, 1999.

Wilson, Derek. *The People's Bible: The Remarkable History of the KJV*. Oxford: Lion Hudson, 2010.

Winter, Mickey. *The Bible—The King James Version on Trial*. Bible for Today, n. d.

Wood, J. G. *Story of the Bible Animals*. Philadelphia: Charles Foster, 1888.

Wrede, W. H. T. *A Short History of the Privilege of Bible & Prayer Book Printing at the University Press Cambridge*. Toronto: MacMillian Company, 1948.

Wright, John. *Early Bibles of America*. New York: Thomas Whittaker, 1892.

Wright, William Aldis. *Bible Word-Book*. Second Edition. London: MacMillan, 1889.

Young, Edward. *Thy Word is Truth*. Grand Rapids: William B. Eerdmans, 1957.

Young, Robert. *Young's Literal Translation of the Holy Bible*. Revised Edition. Grand Rapids: Baker Book House, 1898.

Zeolla, Gary F. *Differences between Bible Versions*. 1st Books Library, 1994, 2001.

Zodhiates, Spiros (ed.). *The Hebrew-Greek Key Study Bible*. Grand Rapids: Baker Book House, 1984.

Zodhiates, Spiros (ed.). *Hebrew-Greek Key Word Study Bible*. Revised Edition. Chattanooga, TN: AMG Publishers, 1991.

Zodhiates, Spiros and Warren Baker (eds.). *Hebrew-Greek Key Word Study Bible*. Second Revised Edition. Chattanooga, TN: AMG Publishers, 2008.

For more information about the KJV-only view, see this author's book entitled *The Unbound Scriptures*. This book has a bibliography of over 1,000 sources, including over 100 books and pamphlets by KJV-only authors. It can be used as a sourcebook to examine many claims of the KJV-only view. Some articles on this issue are also found at the following web site: www.unboundscriptures.com

<u>Comments about book *The Unbound Scriptures*</u>

"This long-awaited volume should immediately find a spot on every pastor's bookshelf and be carefully read by every teacher and Christian who wishes to be informed on the Bible translation issue. ... We are glad to recommend it."
--Dr. Robert Sumner, editor of *The Biblical Evangelist* and author of several books
[review in January-February, 2004, issue, p. 2]

"This book should be read by every pastor and student of the Bible who has been troubled by this new dogma and by those who have been pressured into accepting this view without valid proof."
--James D. Price, Ph.D., executive editor of NKJV's O. T. and author of *King James Onlyism*

"*Unbound Scriptures* is an outstanding study of the various KJV arguments."
--Fred Butler, former KJV-only advocate, www.fredsbibletalk.com/theunboundscriptures.html

"The book is extensively documented, well-researched, easy to read, and refutes much of the lies and misinformation that is being spread today."
--Rod Mattoon, pastor and author of several commentaries. This quote is found in his book *Treasures from Romans*, p. 514.

"Rick's book is highly recommended for any reader struggling with the KJV-only view."
--Gary Zeolla, editor of *Darkness to Light* newsletter and author of *Differences Between Bible Versions* and *Analytical-Literal Translation of the N. T.*

"Regardless of where one stands on the King James Version-only controversy, *The Unbound Scriptures* will be of prime interest on the subject. One cannot help but admire the labor that has gone into this volume; it is filled with readable information."
--review in the *Baptist Bulletin*, July, 2004, p. 40.

"Rick has just published a 'magnum opus' on the KJO issue called, *The Unbound Scriptures*."
--Charles R. Wood, *A Pastoral Epistle*, November, 2003 issue [Vol. 17, No. 183].

"Norris has examined with great care and thoroughness--and patience that might make Job envious--an immense quantity of KJV-only literature. From it, he has compiled the general and specific claims of KJVOism and has shown by fully documented evidence that a very large percentage of what is confidently affirmed regarding the KJV is based on ignorance of the facts, denial of documented facts, and misrepresentation of the facts."
--Doug Kutilek, M. A., Th.M.; author, Bible teacher in Biblical languages and Bible exposition

"Norris's position is not new--it is the time old historic position of Spurgeon, Moody, Torrey, Warfield, John R. Rice, Clearwaters, Bob Jones, and scores more."
--Ed Reese, editor of *Reese Chronological Bible*

Beginning January 1, 2019, the first edition (2003) of my book *The Unbound Scriptures* is no longer available for sale by its author.   Perhaps an expanded, revised second edition will later be available from an on-demand publisher.

Contact the author at the following email address: rick1560@juno.com or by mail at the following address.

Rick Norris, 508 Westminster Drive, Statesville, NC   28677

Other publications are available from the following publisher: www.lulu.com

In a 600+ page book entitled *Facts from 400 Years of KJV Editions: Do We Use a 1769 KJV*, data and many facts from a partial examination of over 500 editions of the KJV are presented. This book demonstrates that today's varying KJV editions are not identical to the 1769 Oxford edition.   It lists over 2,500 variations and differences that can be found in the many varying editions of the KJV from 1611 until this day.   Misleading or inaccurate KJV-only claims about varying KJV editions are answered by facts.

A booklet entitled *Today's KJV and 1611 Compared and More* compares the text of the 1611 edition of the KJV to the text of a post-1900 or present Oxford KJV edition in the Scofield Reference Bible, listing over 2,000 differences.   It demonstrates that typical KJV-only counts of the number of differences between the 1611 edition and today's KJV and count of the number of "substantial" differences are inaccurate.   It answers and refutes some inaccurate claims concerning KJV editions.

In another booklet entitled *Could the 1611 KJV Have Been Better*, this author presents evidence that indicates that many of the renderings in the 1611 edition that later editors corrected or changed were the responsibility of the KJV translators themselves and not the fault of the 1611 printers.   This booklet also has other interesting information, including some about 14 changes said to have been introduced by prelates into the text of the 1611 and some about the influence of the 1582 Rheims New Testament on the KJV.

Another booklet entitled *KJV-only Myths about Archaic Words* is an expanded and revised edition of over 100 pages of information covered in a chapter of around 20 pages in my earlier book *The Unbound Scriptures*.   It provides several pages of examples where the KJV updated or revised archaic-type words or language in the Bishops' Bible while keeping similar words in other cases.

+